Kentucky Illustrated

Kentucky Illustrated

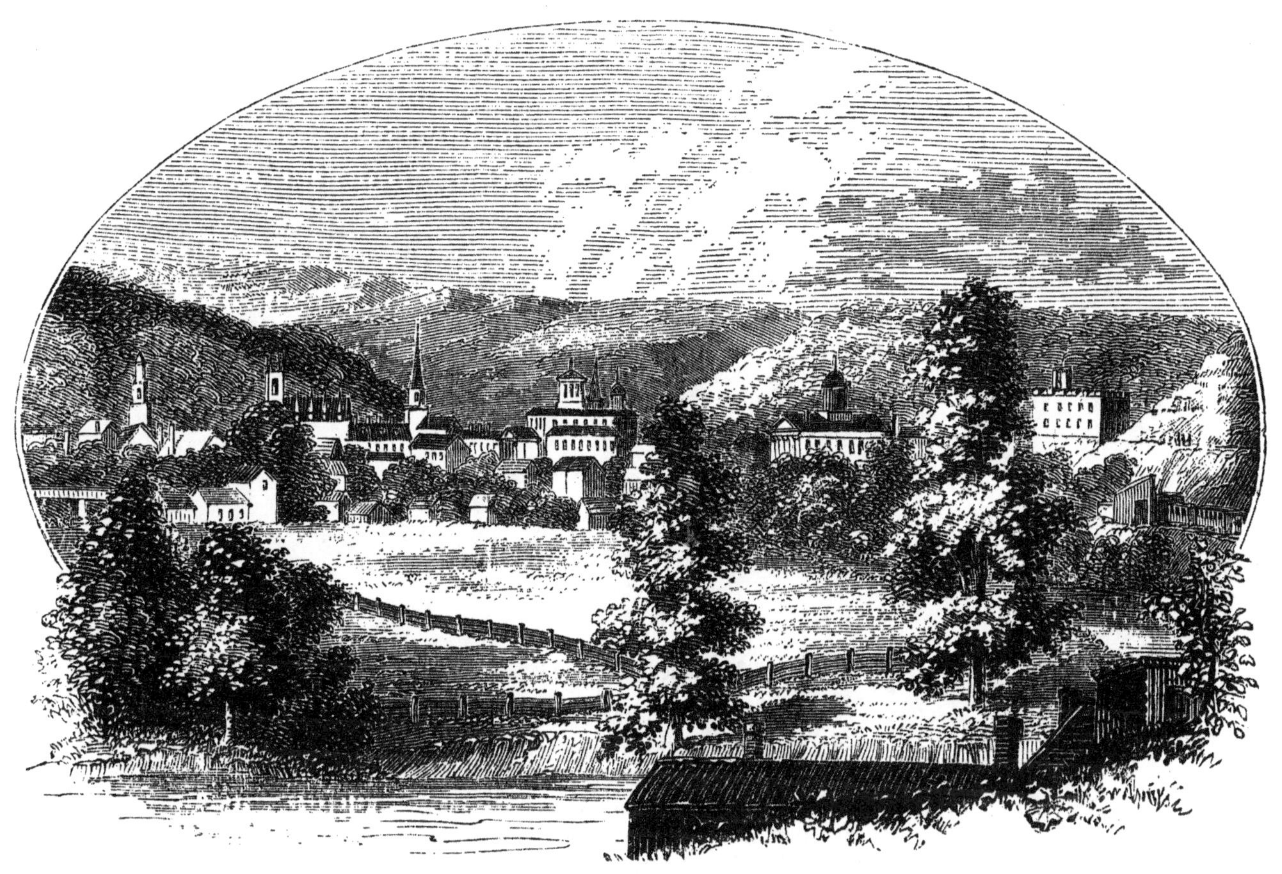

The First Hundred Years

Martin F. Schmidt

With Introductions by James C. Klotter

THE UNIVERSITY PRESS OF KENTUCKY

Frontispiece: A southeastern view of Frankfort, with the Capitol and other public buildings in the center and the Kentucky River in the foreground.

Wood engraving from Howe's *Our Whole Country*, 1861.

Scholarly publisher for the Commonwealth,
serving Bellarmine College, Berea College, Centre
College of Kentucky, Eastern Kentucky University,
The Filson Club, Georgetown College, Kentucky
Historical Society, Kentucky State University,
Morehead State University, Murray State University,
Northern Kentucky University, Transylvania University,
University of Kentucky, University of Louisville,
and Western Kentucky University.

Editorial and Sales Offices: Lexington, Kentucky 40508-4008

Kentucky illustrated / [compiled by] Martin F. Schmidt ; with
introductions by James C. Klotter.
p. cm.
Includes bibliographical references.
ISBN: 978-0-8131-5589-0
1. Kentucky—History—Pictorial works. 2. Wood-engraving—19th
century—Kentucky. 3. Wood-engraving, American—Kentucky.
I. Schmidt, Martin F., 1918-
F452.K395 1992
976.9—dc20 92-5724

∞

Contents

Preface

This volume of early views of Kentucky results from my personal interest in Kentucky history, which has extended over nearly fifty years. This interest has been partially satisfied by collecting the views as I found them individually in the prints market or by locating them in the various periodicals and books where they first appeared.

Each of the views included in this volume was originally created by skilled artisans who worked in tandem to produce it for publication. The original publication of these prints was accomplished from relief engravings on wood blocks, from intaglio engravings on copper or steel plates, or from drawings on lithographic stones.

Pictographs representing houses in Louisville appeared on the 1784 John Filson map of Kentucky, and similar symbols were used on the "Plan of the Rapids of the Ohio," published in 1793 in Gilbert Imlay's *American Geography.* Accurate contemporary illustration of local scenes in Kentucky began in 1795 when a view of the statehouse at Frankfort was published in the *New York Magazine.*

For many years after this beginning, authentic views appeared infrequently. The creation and reproduction of Kentucky scenes and portraits lagged far behind those of the Atlantic states. Kentucky's energies were concentrated on development and the need to change its frontier condition by clearing land and creating simple towns and villages. This focus allowed a minimum of sophistication. There was little to stir a publisher's interest in the commonwealth's localities, and its scenic beauty and natural attractions had yet to be appreciated.

A primitive and sketchy inset entitled "View of Louisville from near Clarkesville" appeared in a plan of the falls area made in 1806 by Jared Brooks. A fanciful engraving of the rustic convent school of the Sisters of Loretto in Nelson County was published in Belgium about 1816. In 1821 the first three well-delineated Kentucky views appeared in Adlard Welby's *A Visit to North America.* A transfer-printed Staffordshire bowl of about 1825 bears a view of the waterfront at Louisville, and in 1826 a view of the falls and Louisville was published in Paris from a drawing made thirty years earlier by a French army officer and explorer.

In the mid-1820s trained draftsmen and graphic artists began to arrive in the region. In 1828 Enoch Gridley of Cincinnati engraved Matthew Jouett's view of Transylvania University for Charles Caldwell's book on Horace Holley. The same year Samuel M. Lee, also of Cincinnati, drew views of Frankfort, Covington, and Newport for James Hall's *Western Souvenir* of 1828. An etching of "Shipping-Port on the Ohio," a picture of the Louisville hospital, and the Transylvania view noted above all appeared from about 1828 to 1830 on Staffordshire bowls, plates, and pitchers.

The *Family Magazine,* which commenced publication in Cincinnati in 1836, was the first periodical in the early West to use numerous illustrations. In March 1836 it published a wood engraving of Daniel Boone that was copied in that year to produce the earliest separate print of a figure or scene known to have been made in Kentucky—an advertising handbill lithographed by Colin Milne in Louisville. The following year Milne also printed a leaflet for the Richmond Female Academy that included a view of the school, and he produced a set of animal pictures from drawings and paintings by Edward Troye.

The year 1837 brought a view of Mammoth Cave published in Paris and a view of the cave's entrance drawn by Robert M. Bird and published to accompany his article in *American Monthly Magazine.* The use of Kentucky scenes in books and magazines continued to increase as illustrators and publishers became more attracted to the state's towns, institutions, scenery, and important events. The Civil War increased these activities in the west in an important way, as the weekly illustrated periodicals of the day, especially *Harper's Weekly* and *Frank Leslie's Illustrated Newspaper,* employed artists to follow the armies and produce sketches for prompt publication.

From the 1870s through the mid-1890s—when photoengraving and photolithography became the most popular reproduction processes—a proliferation of Kentucky scenes appeared in newspapers, popular magazines, county atlases, regional handbooks and guidebooks, railroad promotional material, commercial and industrial directories, and those publications designed to fill the vanity needs of farmers, home owners, storekeepers, industrialists large and small, and regional proponents. A comprehensive republication of all the views made during Kentucky's first century would produce a volume of unmanageable size. A representative group of views published through 1895 has been selected for this volume.

The views were made to show the actual or approximate appearance of the scenes at about the time of publication. Unless otherwise noted, engravers and those who drew pictures on lithographic stones worked from sketches provided to them for this purpose or from drawings or paintings created originally for purposes other than reproduction. Photographs began to enter this process in the 1860s, and as they became available to engravers and lithographers they eventually led to substantial replacement of the skilled work of individual illustrators.

Following their first appearance, a number of the views were reproduced later where they complemented particular texts or periodical articles. Some have appeared in recent works such as *Views of Louisville Since 1766,* compiled by Dr. Samuel W. Thomas for the *Courier-Journal* and *Louisville Times,* and *Louisville Panorama,* compiled by Ray C. Riebel for Liberty National Bank and Trust Company. Some of these views—along with others not included in this volume—have been chosen to accompany the text of recent histories of Kentucky counties. This type of reuse of the illustrations commenced relatively soon after the first views made their appearance. The illustrations that appeared in the *Family Magazine,* published in Cincinnati in the 1830s and 1840s, were seen again, sometimes slightly altered, in later publications. The publishers of the Civil War illustrated newspapers used their own illustrations frequently as they found markets for historical texts, compilations of battles and leaders, and related works.

The selection of views for this volume was made from a large number of potential choices on the basis of their perceived interest for the largest number of viewers. Not included here are many views in state and local directories that show us—when they can be found—individual business houses and small factories. In a few instances the same engraving served for several locations, for only a few readers would recognize the duplication. Promotional brochures, booklets, or essays prepared to publicize or describe the state, a region, or a locality often reprinted illustrations from various available sources.

Kentucky's centennial year and the commercial development of photoengraving arrived at about the same time. As soon as there were chemical means for making the pictures and for transferring the pictures to the printing surface—that is, photography and photoengraving—the use of illustration burst from the previous limitations set by artists and artisans. All of the views included in this selection felt the touch of the artist, architect, etcher, painter, engraver, or lithographer before they were seen in publication.

The deficiency of this volume is immediately apparent: its coverage of the state is limited. This is caused partly by space restrictions but primarily by the uneven work of the publishers and their illustrators; they gave their attention most especially to the largest and most populous places and to those where some institution was noteworthy. We could wish for a comprehensive pictorial survey, county by county, such as we might attempt in our own era, but it is not available in the early views.

For their help in providing information related to several of the illustrations, I wish to thank Charles King of the Kenton County Library, Nancy Baird of the Kentucky Library at Western Kentucky State University, and reference staff librarians at Louisville Free Public Library, the Filson Club, and the Bell County Library. I am also grateful to Dr. Samuel W. Thomas for encouragement and advice during the course of this project.

—Martin F. Schmidt

Introduction

Kentucky. The name itself meant different things to diverse people at various times. To those on the Euro-American frontier, waiting, wanting to cross the mountain barrier, Kentucky was not just the land of tomorrow; it was the place for the present. For those pioneers, Kentucky meant that their once-dreary futures might be brighter, that their children's lives could be better. The land offered hope, and they embraced that vision with unbridled fervor. An exodus to a promised land began.

Yet throughout the commonwealth's history, a duality in its character has existed. That supposed Eden-like land held many dangers. Settlers who came with high desires for freedom and for the future also brought with them slaves. This place of democracy and an open society also featured classes and its own brand of aristocracy. Enlightened people, some of whom formed a community known as "the Athens of the West," at the same time did not develop a long-term support for public education.

As time passed, those contrasting parts of the Kentucky character did not fade away. These hospitable people, devoted to family, found themselves fighting bitterly against one another, against home, in a civil war, a Brothers' War, that left deep wounds that were remembered for generations. Physical scars of another kind marked the landscape of the state as the natural beauty and unspoiled environment of Kentucky warred constantly with the forces of change. A traditional place in many ways, the commonwealth struggled with modernization, sometimes seeking it, at other moments rejecting it. In short, Kentucky, from its beginning to the present, has been, as Thomas D. Clark so aptly termed it, "a land of contrast."

The elements forming the state's character emerged from a diversity of forces. The first West, Kentucky merged as a borderland between sections, East and West, North and South. It sent sons and daughters to all regions, often losing some of its brightest minds as a result. Even within the commonwealth, different forces tugged at any unifying agent; the eastern coal fields sometimes seemed another world to those living in the distant Jackson Purchase just as urban dwellers appeared an alien people to agrarian Kentuckians. Political divisions, whether between Whigs and Democrats, or Republicans and Democrats, or, often, just between Democrats themselves, caused further splits. Labor differences, class divisions, family feuds—all could create further turmoil. A seemingly limitless number of counties added to an atmosphere where vision extended only to county borders, or perhaps only next door.

Yet, if standing divided, Kentucky did not fall. Other elements operated at the same time to create not division but unity. Despite differences, the people of this artificially bounded region called Kentucky still thought of themselves as Kentuckians. Increasingly a homogeneous people, insulated from many forces shaping modern America, such as later waves of immigration, the commonwealth's citizens identified with a common heritage based on shared cultural values. Being Kentuckians remained important to a large portion of those living in the state. "My Old Kentucky Home" still meant something.

But to those residing outside the state, the meaning of Kentucky and its national image grew out of another set of factors. Whether in print or in illustrations, Kentucky appeared sometimes alien to those living in the commonwealth. It stressed aspects of the state, such as thoroughbred racing, in which only a select few had involvement, or it emphasized heroes, such as Daniel Boone, who may have seemed to have little bearing on present-day lives.

Illustrations played an important role in shaping the Kentucky image, both internal and external. Even the illiterate—and there were many in pre-twentieth-century America—could look at pictures and construct a mental view of what Kentucky was like. Based on extant illustrations, that world was, of course, varied, but it featured several constants. Kentucky, in the developing image, was where Daniel Boone fought off hostile Indians and opened up the western frontier. The people emerging from that violent world were rough but recognized the beauty around them. In time, another group matured and the new state featured a pleasing elite who sampled spas and springs, built fine mansions and public buildings, and lived on attractive farms and plantations. There might appear interesting aberrations, such as the Shakers, but life, in the main, remained traditional. Forces of change intruded, of course, as pictures of cities, riverboats, railroads, and industries showed. But still Kentucky remained—according to illustrators—a fairly pleasant locale except for occasional disasters, natural and otherwise, and a rather unpleasant and uncivil war.

Obviously, great changes were taking place in the late eighteenth century and throughout the nineteenth, and Kentucky was affected by them. A sense of that emerges in part in the illustrations, as rough cabins give way to finely designed buildings and as dirt roads surrender supremacy to steel rails. But so many of the important transformations taking place remained almost out of sight. The uncertain revolution that came with slavery's end—and the extreme violence of that era—never happened in the illustrators' Kentucky. Quiet advances—sometimes too quiet, such as the increasing number of children in school—attracted little interest. A growing industrial working class in cities found few to depict their lives. The slow movement toward women's rights remained virtually unportrayed. Illustrators were much more successful in representing surface modifications, as in the transition from roads to steamboats to rail, than they were in picturing those things that could suggest the vast social changes going on all around them.

All that, of course, was not unique to Kentucky. The growing interest in illustrated magazines such as *Leslie's* and *Harper's* (sparked by the Civil War), the proliferation of "ladies" magazines and of major literary periodicals, the spread of a popular "yellow journalism" later in the century—these things touched Kentucky just as they did other places. Charges of selectivity, of unfairness, of biased presentations came from across America. On the other hand, some excellent illustrators turned their talents to a faithful reproduction of the era around them and left fine visual records of times long gone. If much was ignored, or if some was selective, there was also much that was of high quality. The resulting images of Kentucky may not always have been fair representations of the essence of the state, yet at the same time they did show what were still valid images of at least a part of that Kentucky.

In short, these illustrations should be viewed as representing the values, the biases, the cultural norms of their time, and should be examined as to how those factors influenced the development of the state's image. But they should be seen in a simpler way as well. They should be enjoyed in their own right, without deep analysis or study. At one level, they enlighten us; at another, they entertain. For those often nameless illustrators who spent long hours recording in visual form the world around them, that would have been reward enough.

—*James C. Klotter*

The Techniques of Printed Illustration

Despite the long history of printing—which originated in the East by at least the eighth century and spread to Europe by the early fifteenth—there are really only three fundamental types of prints: relief printing, made from raised areas of the printing surface; intaglio, from recessed areas; and planographic, from the surface itself.

Relief

Relief printing is the earliest type by some six centuries. In this method the areas that are to receive ink stand in relief—that is, they are raised—on the block or plate. The rubber-stamp pictures that children impress are simple examples of this type of printing. The raised areas of the stamp touch the stamp pad and then the paper, creating the image.

The earliest form of relief printing on paper is the woodcut—a print made from a planed block of seasoned cherry or other suitable wood. Gouges and chisels are used to remove the unwanted areas. Gray tones can be simulated by hatching (cutting a series of close lines) and similar techniques. The completed block is then inked and, typically, printed on an ordinary press.

Toward the end of the eighteenth century there came into use a new method of cutting wood blocks. The end grain of very hard wood was preferred, and the design was cut with an engraver's tool, resulting in fine detail and typified by white lines scooped from solid black areas. The new process became known as "wood engraving"—something of a misnomer because the overall process remained a relief one, in contrast to true engraving, which is an intaglio process.

Intaglio

Unlike relief printing, the second main category of printmaking techniques has the lines that are to be printed formed *below* the surface of the plate. Such processes are called intaglio (in-TAHL-yo)—meaning "incised"—and include etching and engraving.

In engraving, the earliest dated example being from 1446, the desired design is cut into a metal plate with a tool called a burin. This tool has a sharp V-shaped end that scoops a thin sliver from the surface of the plate. Greater pressure produces a wider groove, and a variable or "sculpted" line is typical. Tones are produced by thickening of line, hatching, and cross-hatching.

The surface of the metal plate is inked, then wiped so as to leave ink in the grooves. When a sheet of dampened paper is placed on the plate, covered with padding, and subjected to sufficient pressure—much more than that required for relief printing—the paper is pressed into the grooves and lifts out the ink to produce a print.

The other main type of intaglio print is the etching, which uses acid rather than the burin to produce the recessed lines. The plate is coated with a protective substance, and a needle is used to draw the design. This scratches away the coating and exposes the metal. Bathing the plate with acid etches the lines traced by the needle into the plate. After cleaning, the plate is inked and printed much like an engraved one.

Planographic

In planographic printing the ink lies *on* the printing surface, not on raised or in recessed areas. The most important planographic printmaking process is lithography, invented in Germany in 1798. Put simply, this process is based on the natural antipathy of grease and water.

The drawing is done on a lithographic stone—or a comparable surface such as a roughened plate—using greasy crayon or a similar substance in liquid form that is applied by pen or brush. Following some minor preparatory processes, the drawing is ready for printing. The stone is moistened; because the greasy drawing repels water, only the nondrawing areas become damp. A greasy ink is then rolled over the stone. The damp areas now repel the substance and the ink coats only the greasy lines of the drawing. A sheet of dampened paper is laid on the stone, covered, and subjected to pressure from a roller. The process is repeated for successive prints.

Additional Techniques and Refinements

Color was added to prints first by hand coloring, then by incorporating color into the printing process. Some of the processes are complicated, but with woodcuts additional blocks were commonly used to carefully superimpose one color imprint over another. A similar approach was used in lithography. At first separate flat tints were applied by multiple blocks in what is called tinted lithography. Later, the inks from different blocks were overprinted to create special color effects and produce true color lithographs. Still later, when such prints were commercially produced, they became known as chromolithographs.

Another advance was the use of photography, which began to be applied to printmaking in the 1860s. In much the same way that a tintype was produced, photographic images were developed on wood blocks and carved to produce very realistic wood engravings called photoxylographs. Eventually advancements made possible the conversion of the photographic image to a printing plate without the intervention of the artist's hand and tool.

Though other processes are employed in printmaking, the basic methods—relief, intaglio, and planographic—gave rise to the advancements. They bridged the gap between the time when one-of-a-kind works of art were accessible to only a few and our own era of mass production in which we find ourselves surrounded by an almost bewildering array of printed images.

—*Joe Nickell*

ONE

The Frontier Years

Those who lived in the East heard conflicting stories and eventually viewed varying images concerning Kentucky and its people. Was this territory beyond the mountains a rich land, blessed by nature, where idyllic settlers could clear the forests and prosper? Or was it a place of death and danger, where hostile natives lurked, waiting to ensnare innocent and unwitting families? Was Kentucky the "land of tomorrow," the "dark and bloody ground," or both—or neither?

Those conflicting images of this first West met in the person of Daniel Boone. Only one of many skilled frontier leaders, he alone garnered early publicity, in the form of his supposed "autobiography" in John Filson's 1784 *Discovery, Settlement, and Present State of Kentucke.* In the numerous adaptations of that basic story, Boone came to represent not only the mythical Kentuckian but the archetypal frontiersman as well. Later illustrations of frontier Kentucky usually ignored the other explorers and focused almost solely on Boone.

The images presented two men: Boone, the philosophical man of nature, at home in the woods; or, conversely, Boone, the daring fighter of Indians, ridding the land of ferocious savages. In truth, "Old Dan'l" fit neither stereotype perfectly, for he was not only explorer and military leader, but also legislator and landholder. He was a complex man continually trying to adapt to new and changing situations.

But each of the Boone images tended to show only one side of the man. One group portrayed the fighting Boone, attacking dangerous animals, rescuing captive girls, conquering threatening Indians. The other image—often realistically portraying Boone in the more correct non-coonskin cap—presented instead the natural man, exploring new worlds, seeking peace, searching out unknown wilds. But even fidelity to a simple stereotype did not ensure historical accuracy. In one illustration, for example, Boone is shown standing before his supposed frontier home in the wilds of Kentucky, yet the home is built of what appear to be finely sawed planks, worthy of a good sawmill.

Of course, frontier Kentucky was much more than Daniel Boone. Indian mounds, built by people no longer inhabiting the state, intrigued early illustrators; and, in much the same way Boone was, Native Americans were represented by two conflicting views—the noble savage, or simply the bloodthirsty one. Other images focused on the early forts and the grand plans for real or even nonexistent towns.

But the images also ignored much. Early Kentuckians such as James Harrod, founder of Harrodsburg, and Benjamin Logan, leader at St. Asaph's (Stanford) seem to have been almost forgotten. Women and slaves literally remained out of the pictures. Those who led military actions or who guided the new state—people like George Rogers Clark and Isaac Shelby—did not attract the attention of the illustrators either. Yet from the first settlement at Harrodsburg in 1774 until statehood in 1792, such people had been building a commonwealth. Despite defeats, such as the Battle of Blue Licks in 1782, and despite extreme difficulties, such as the hard winter of 1779–1780, these settlers persevered; and by 1790, over seventy thousand had made their way to this land called Kentucky. Those men and women helped form what soon became the first western state for frontier America, a commonwealth that would, in the next half-century, take its place as one of the most important states in the nation. The famous—and the nameless—founded Kentucky.

—J.C.K.

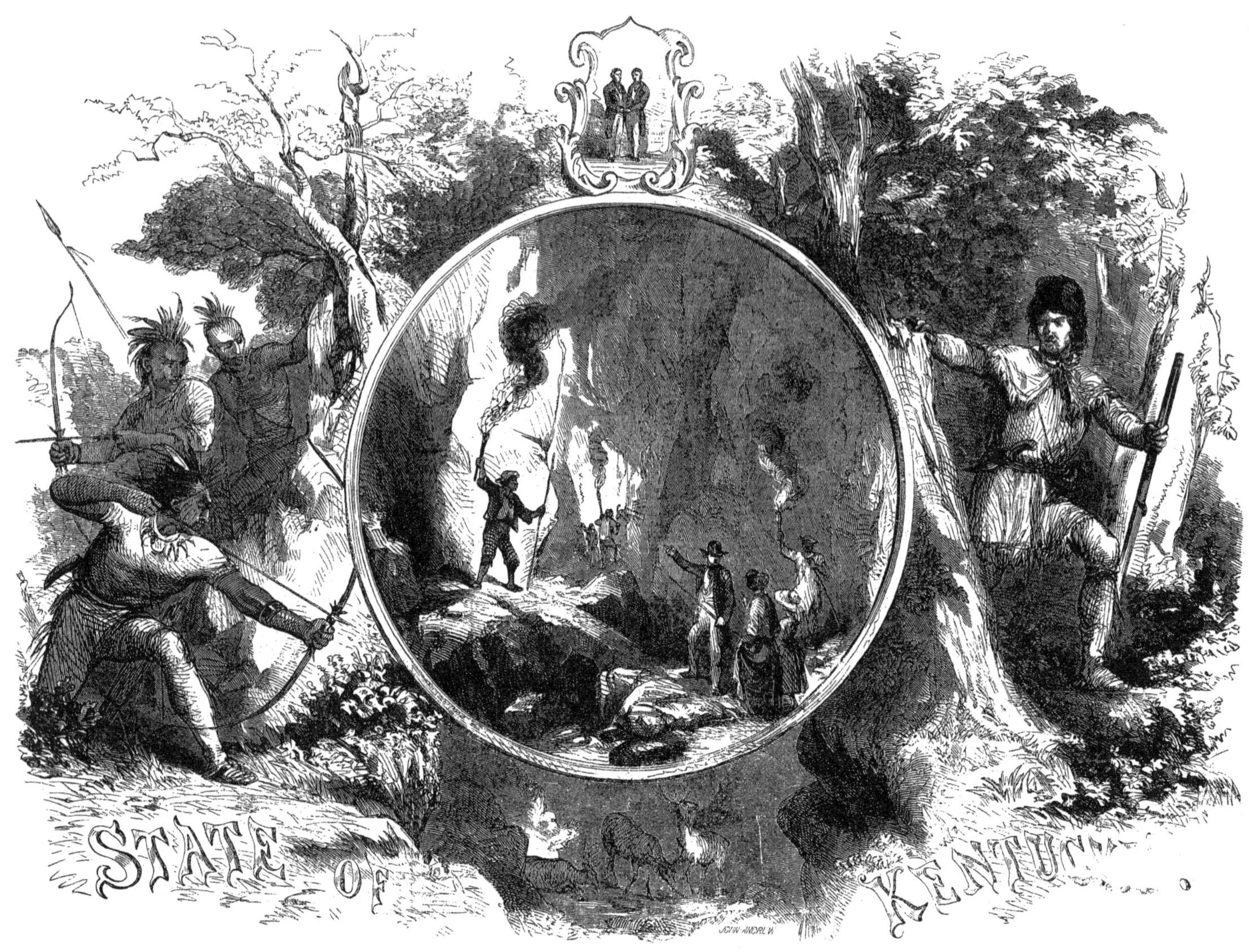

Kentucky has been represented as a land of natural wonders and as a land of danger. Both images are depicted in this composite view showing Mammoth Cave in an inset, surrounded by a scene of a woodsman confronted by hostile Indians. When originally published, the accompanying article described this illustration as a party of Indians on the warpath and "one of the world-renowned Hunters of Kentucky in his forest garb."

Wood engraving from *Ballou's Pictorial Drawing-Room Companion*, November 1856. Engraved by John Andrew from a drawing by Billings, possibly Hammett Billings, Boston, or E.T. Billings, a portrait painter.

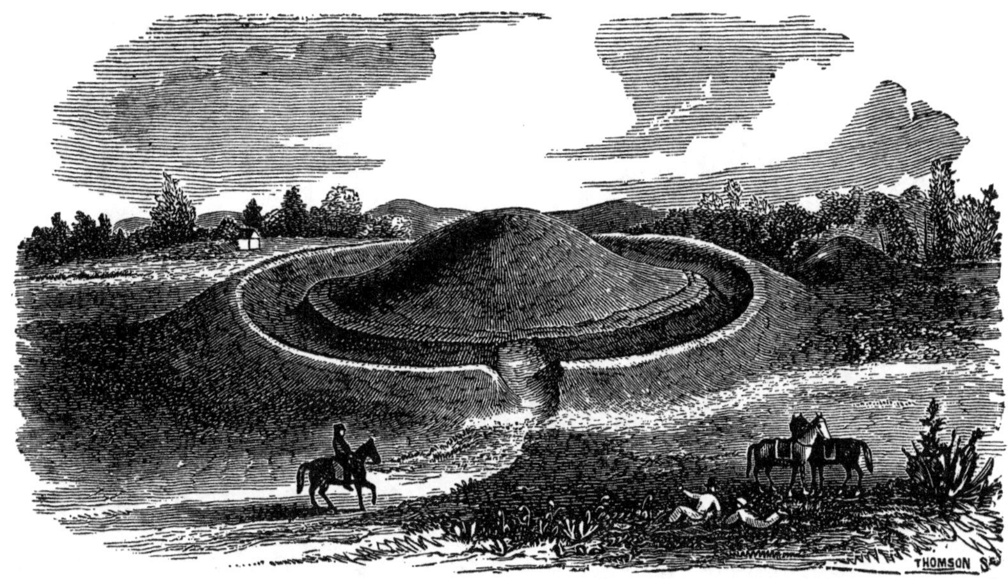

Early illustrators were fascinated by the ancient people who inhabited Kentucky long before the settlers established their communities. The symmetrical earthwork shown here was located in Greenup County about one mile west of the interconnected ancient works that stood on both sides of the Ohio River at the mouth of the Scioto. The central mound was approached by a narrow gateway through the parapet and by a causeway over the ditch.

Wood engraving from Lewis Collins's *Historical Sketches of Kentucky,* 1847. Engraved by Charles W. Thomson, Cincinnati, from the survey and notes of James McBride.

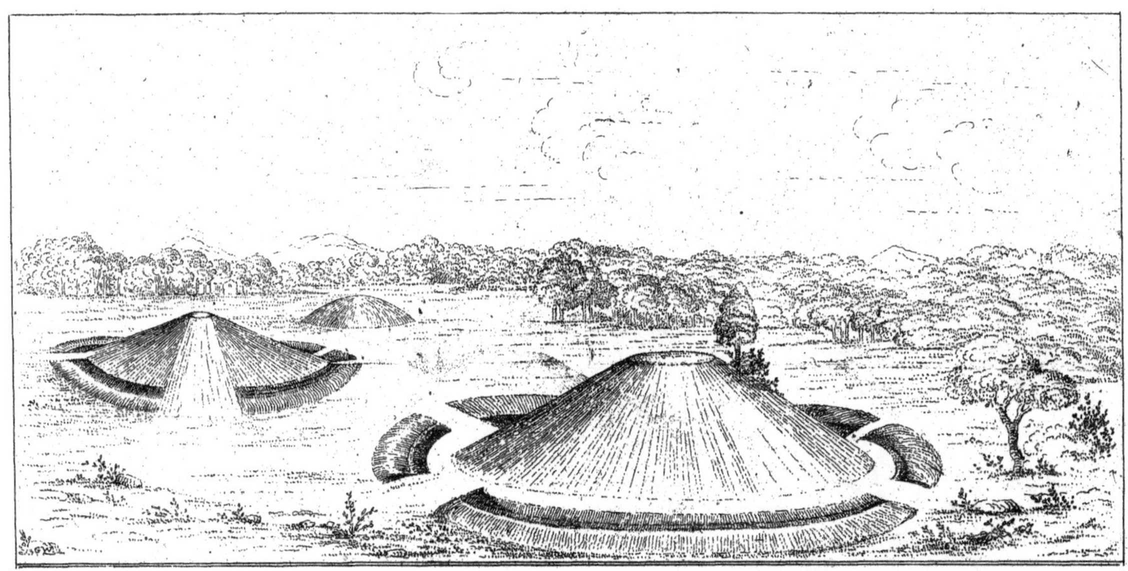

A group of tumuli, or burial mounds, stood near the banks of Somerset Creek. The group of works consisted of the larger mound, which was twenty-five feet high, three smaller mounds, and a nearby circular earthwork about 350 feet in diameter. The site, west of Mt. Sterling in Montgomery County, was investigated by Constantine S. Rafinesque in 1820. When he published his study in 1824, Rafinesque claimed to have identified 148 sites, the greater part of which he surveyed himself, in his search for evidence of the people called the Mound Builders.

Lithograph from an unknown publication. Printing or lithography by Anastatic Press.

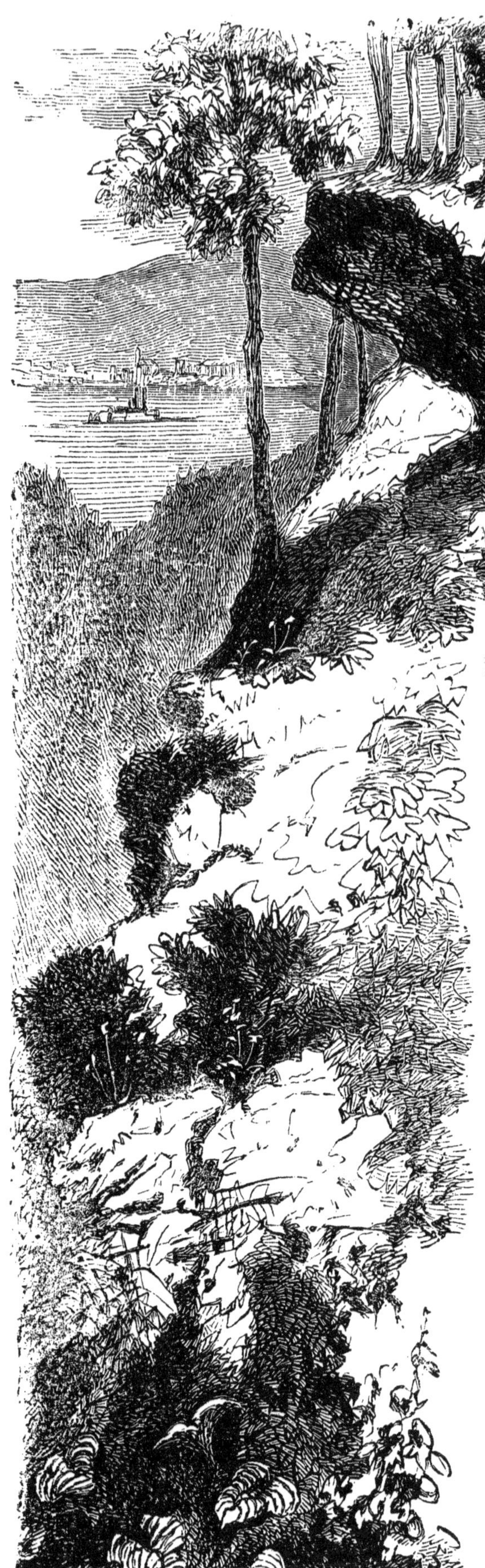

Ele Bowen described this "high and bold precipice" called Indian Fort "nearly opposite" Madison, Indiana. It overhung the banks of the Ohio River and afforded a ten-mile view of the river. The ancient fortification was situated two and a half miles above Carrollton. According to Richard H. Collins's history of 1874, the fort was originally an area of three or four acres enclosed by rough stone walls. When Collins saw it in 1872, it was covered by large timber trees but the remains of the fort were "still to be seen."

Wood engraving from Bowen's *Rambles in the Path of the Steam-Horse,* 1855, from a drawing by Emile F. Beaulieu.

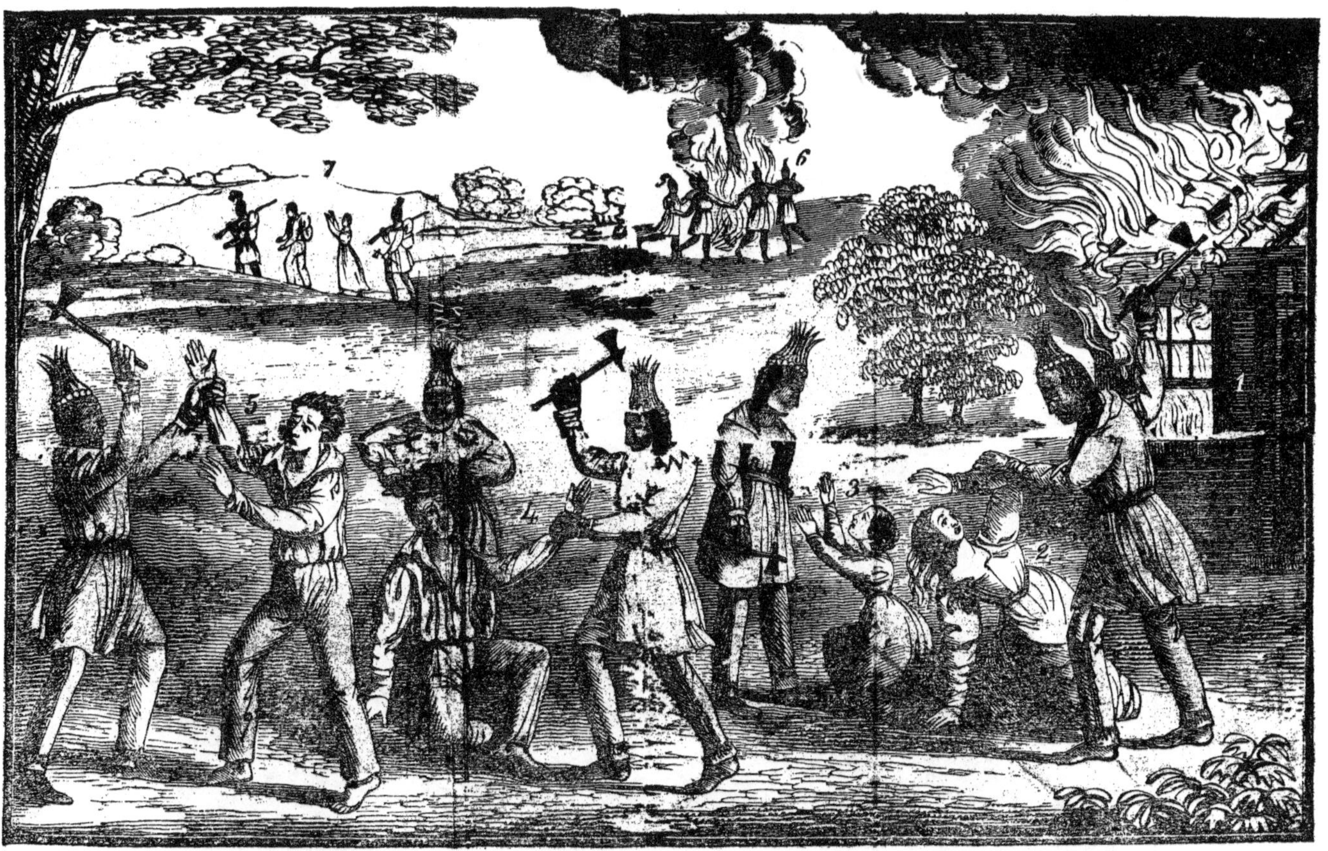

From the early 1770s through the mid-1790s, conflict between Indians and settlers resulted in numerous deaths and slowed the flow of newcomers into Kentucky. This view, the earliest depiction of such a subject, shows the massacre of the family of Thomas Baldwin, who lost his wife and three children in the attack. While Baldwin's narrative is uncorroborated and was recounted to an unidentified writer when Baldwin was eighty-five years old, it is likely to be a true story. The description of events seems to place his residence at the time of the massacre about two days' walk from Boonesborough on the Kentucky River, around 1783 or 1784. According to the narrative, his experiences had a profound effect on Baldwin, who, "since the melancholy period of the destruction of his unfortunate family, has dwelt entirely alone, in a hut of his own construction, secluded from human society, in the extreme western part of the State of Kentucky."

Wood engraving from an unknown author's booklet, *Narrative of the Massacre by the Savages of the Wife and Children of Thomas Baldwin*, 1835.

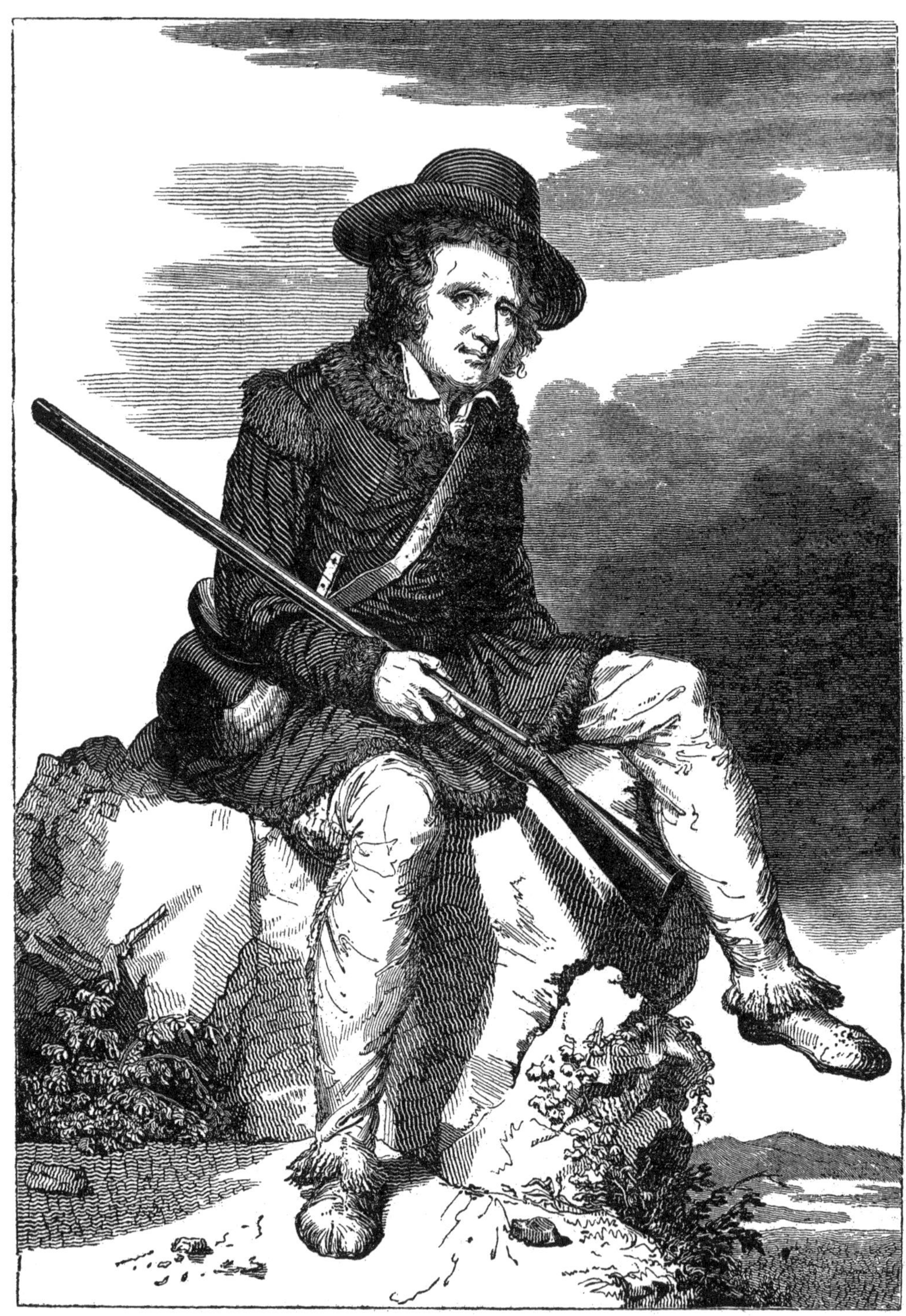

This engraving of Daniel Boone depicts him in the costume of a western hunter, without the mythic coonskin cap. This portrait was used in 1836 in the first edition of the *Family Magazine* and was copied in 1837 for an early advertisement of Colin Milne of Louisville, the first lithographer west of the Alleghenies. It also appeared in Lewis Collins's *Historical Sketches of Kentucky* in 1847.

Wood engraving from the *Family Magazine,* 1836. Engraved by William D. Redfield, New York, from a portrait by John G. Chapman.

A slightly later portrait shows Boone in the cap, moccasins, and leather that became so associated with him.

Wood engraving from Bogart's *Daniel Boone and the Hunters of Kentucky,* 1859. Engraved by Charles F. Damoreau, New York.

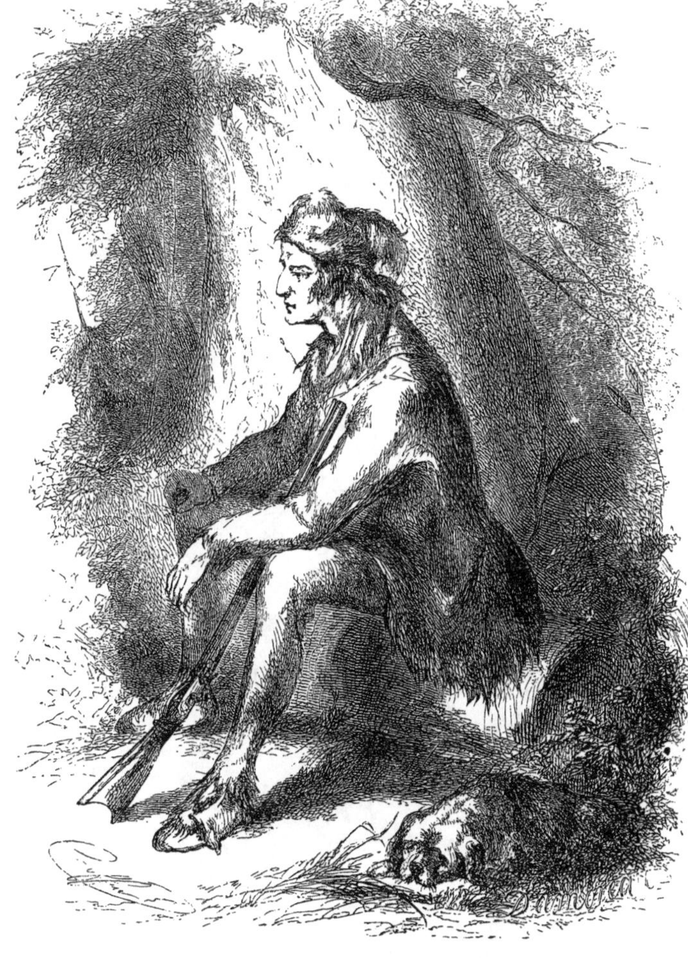

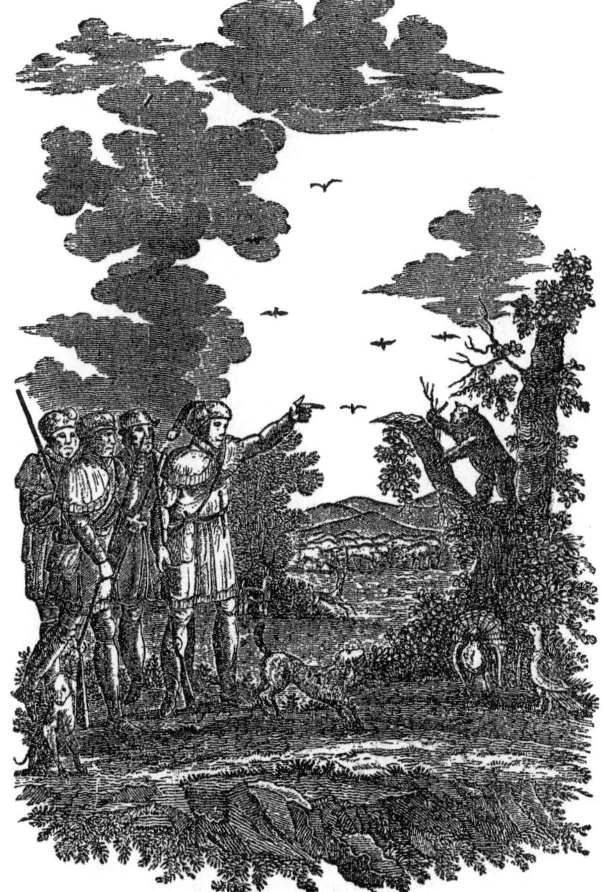

Another aspect of Daniel Boone's personality—the "natural man"—was presented less often in the published materials of the time. Yet this rough illustration clearly shows that part of his image. It depicts the occasion in early June 1769 when Boone and five companions reached the Red River in Kentucky and stood at the summit of the mountains admiring the forested hills, valleys, and winding river courses of Kentucky. Timothy Flint touched on this part of Boone's character, writing that "He loved nature in all her aspects of beauty and grandeur with the intensest admiration. He never wearied of admiring the charming natural landscapes spread before him; and, to his latest days, his spirit in old age seemed to revive in the season of spring."

Wood engraving from Flint's *First White Man of the West,* 1849. Probably engraved by Curtis Doolittle or Samuel Munson, Cincinnati.

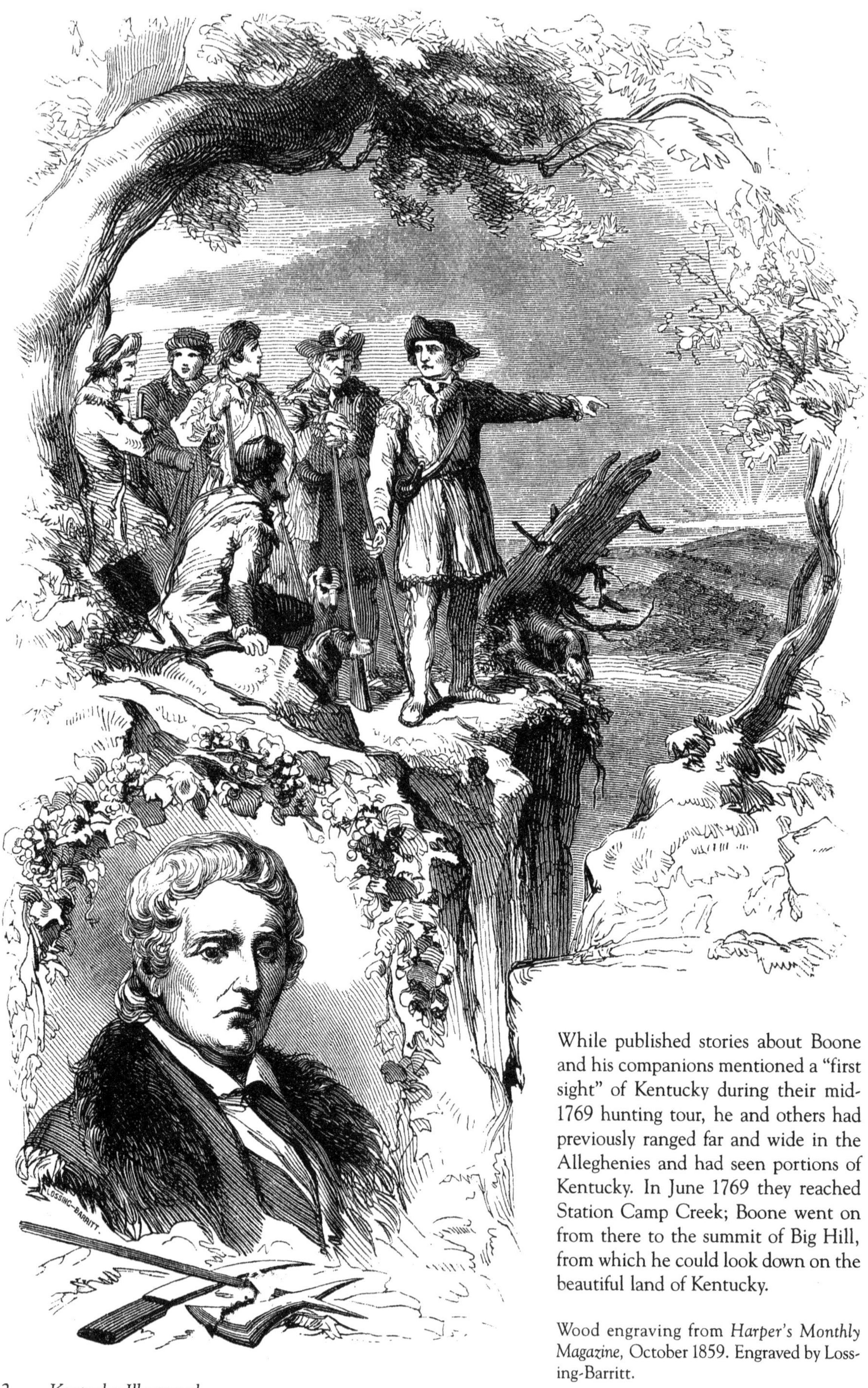

While published stories about Boone and his companions mentioned a "first sight" of Kentucky during their mid-1769 hunting tour, he and others had previously ranged far and wide in the Alleghenies and had seen portions of Kentucky. In June 1769 they reached Station Camp Creek; Boone went on from there to the summit of Big Hill, from which he could look down on the beautiful land of Kentucky.

Wood engraving from *Harper's Monthly Magazine*, October 1859. Engraved by Lossing-Barritt.

The heroic image of Daniel Boone appeared in various forms. While exploring Kentucky alone in 1770, he supposedly encountered a bear and wounded it with his rifle, which "only served to render the animal mad with rage and pain." When he saw that he would have no time to reload, he used his rifle as a shield and waited with knife in hand for the bear's attack. According to Timothy Flint, "within a foot of him, it reared itself erect to grasp him with its huge paws. In this position it pressed upon the knife until the whole blade was buried in its body." Boone undoubtedly killed many bears over the years and is said to have left his initials carved on trees after several of these incidents. By the time this illustration appeared, such a story would have been a logical inclusion in any Boone biography.

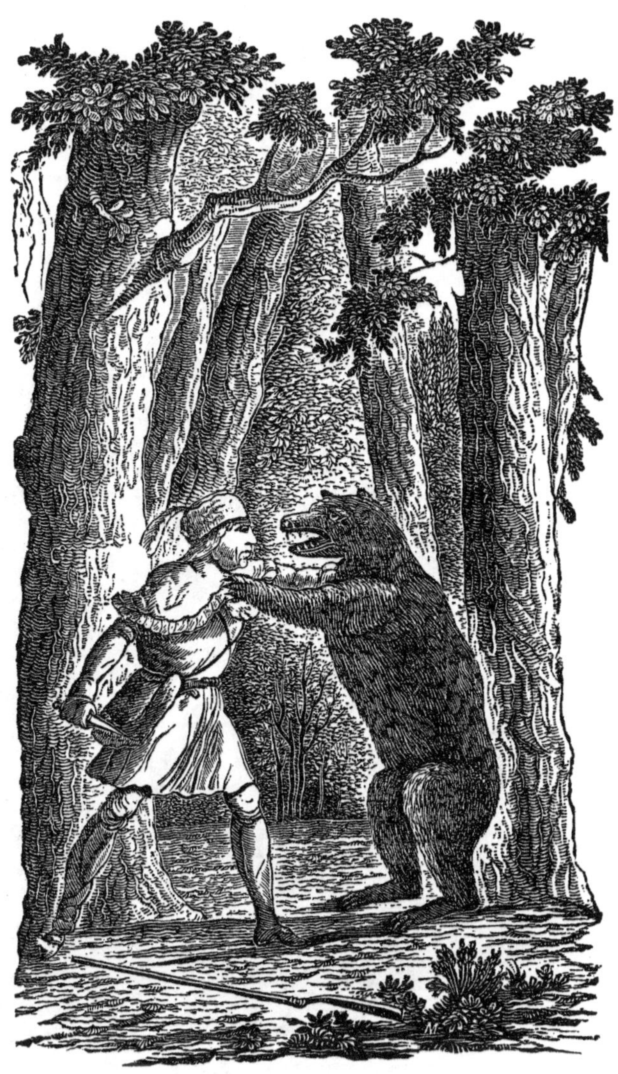

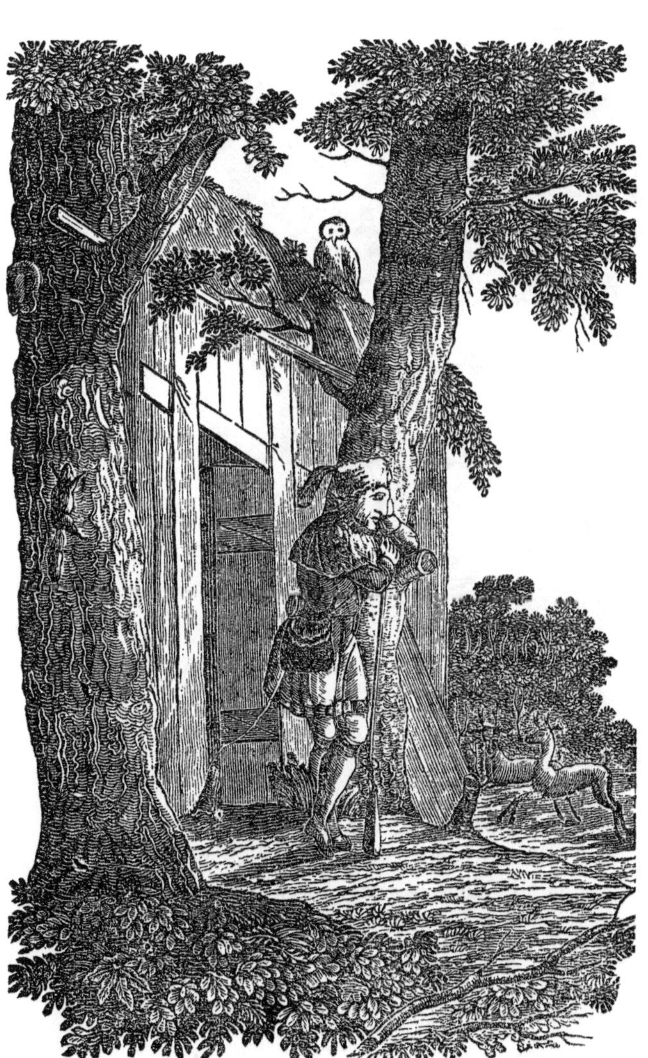

Timothy Flint's text, published sixty years after the events recorded, describes Boone contemplating his fortunes near his cabin in the forest. Flint writes that during the time he spent alone in the wilderness waiting for his brother to return from North Carolina with supplies, Boone used his cabin as headquarters but did not sleep there. "Often made aware on his return to the cabin that the Indians had discovered it, and visited it during his absence," Boone preferred to sleep in canebrakes and caves, frequently changing his position. The artist or engraver has supplied the explorer with a shelter constructed of neatly sawed planks.

Wood engravings from Flint's *First White Man of the West,* 1849. Probably engraved by Curtis Doolittle or Samuel Munson, Cincinnati.

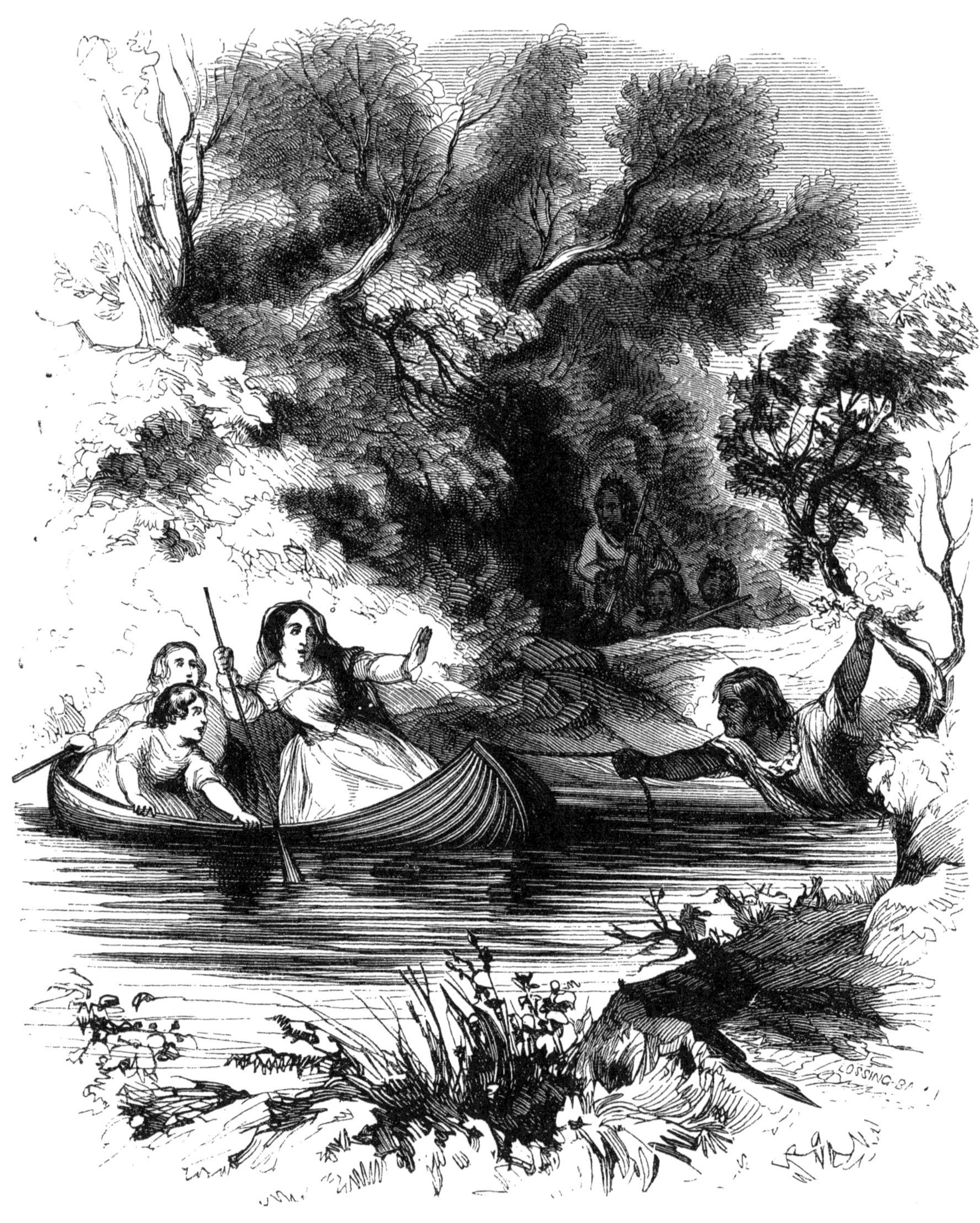

One of the most widely known incidents in the life of Daniel Boone occurred near Boonesborough on July 7, 1776. Boone's daughter Jemima and Richard Callaway's daughters Betsey and Fanny were captured on the Kentucky River when their canoe drifted close to a group of Indians hidden on the river bank. The girls were carried away by the Indians but were rescued uninjured two days later by Boone and Callaway and a party of frontiersmen. An episode based on this adventure appears in James Fenimore Cooper's *The Last of the Mohicans.*

Wood engraving from *Harper's Monthly Magazine,* October 1859. Engraved by Lossing-Barritt.

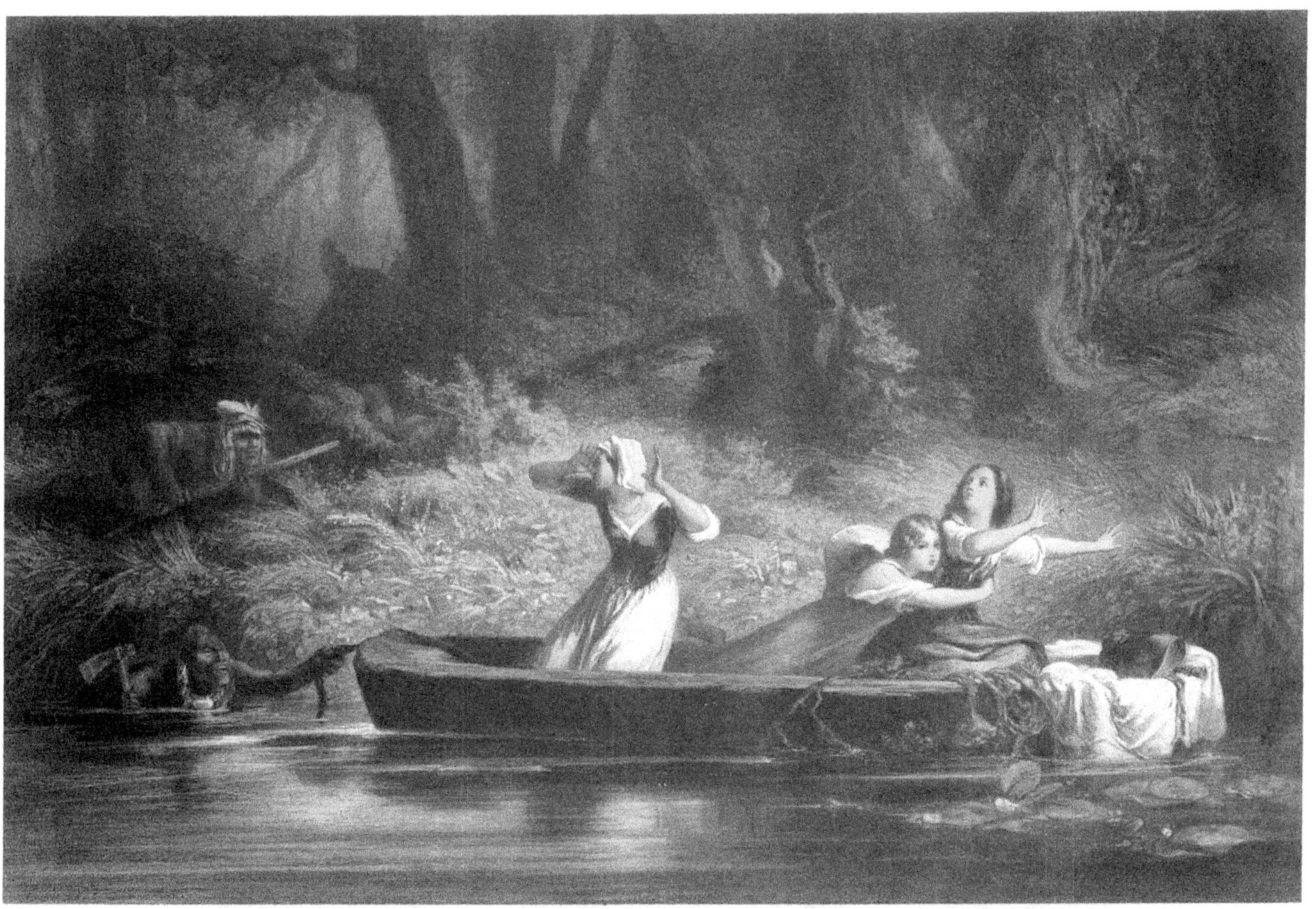

This print and a companion print from original paintings by Jean-François Millet were early chromolithographs published for decorative and display purposes. This one shows the capture of Boone's and Callaway's daughters. Timothy Flint, in *First White Man of the West,* says the girls were captured while wandering in the woods near Boonesborough, and a party of men from the garrison pursued the girls' captors for fifteen days. While attempting a rescue, Boone and Callaway were captured themselves and were about to be killed when other frontiersmen attacked the Indians and rescued both men and their daughters. Thus was built the legend of Daniel Boone.

Chromolithograph published by Goupil, Paris, 1852. Composed and drawn on stone by Charles Bodmer from a painting by Jean-François Millet. Printed by Lemercier of Paris.

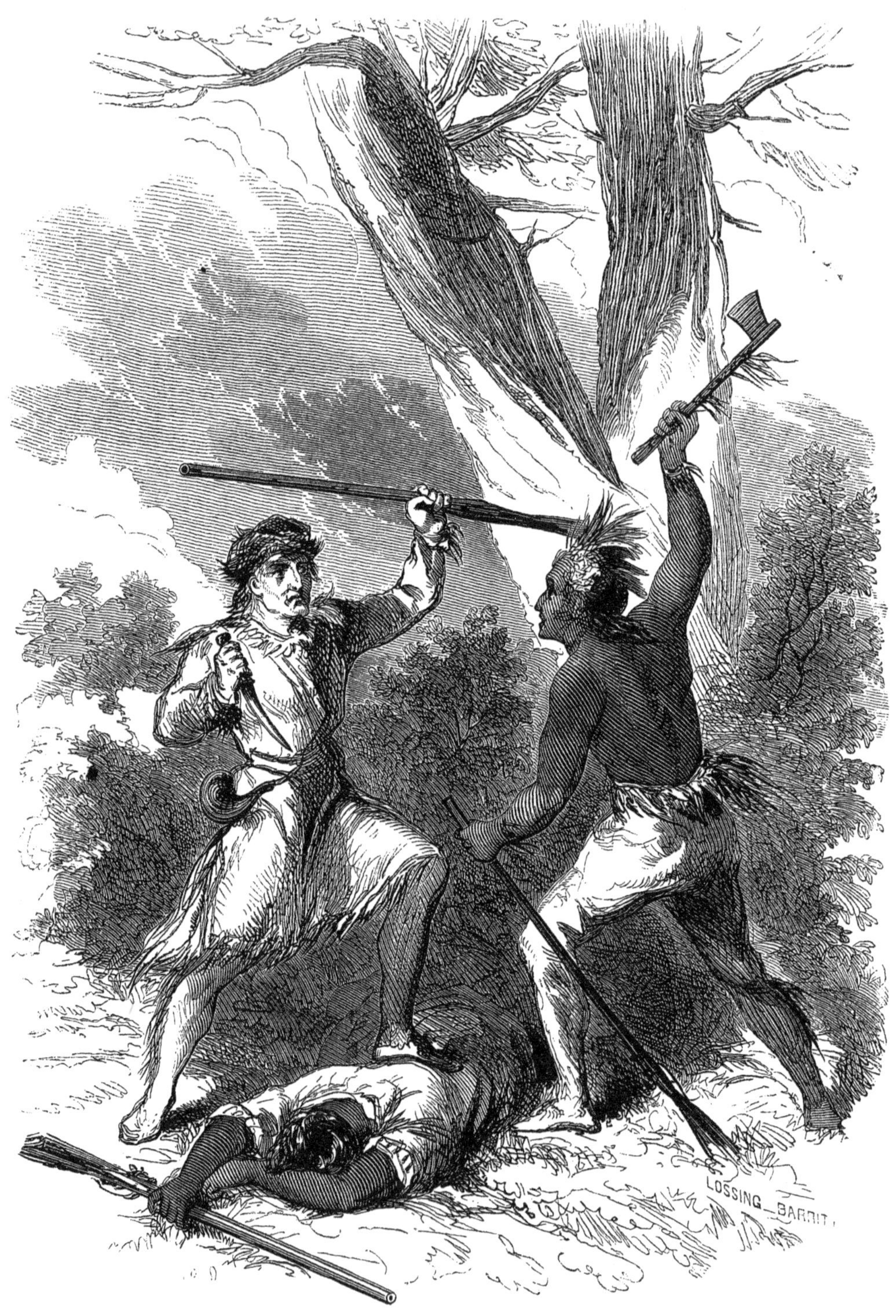

A writer for *Harper's Monthly* recounts the story depicted in this view from "one of the earliest biographers." In January 1778 Boone led a party of men to the Blue Licks to make salt. While hunting in the area Boone was attacked by several Indians. While in this version Boone shot one and—with his foot upon the body of the fallen Indian—plunged his knife into the body of the second, in reality he was seized and spent several months in captivity.

Wood engraving from *Harper's Monthly Magazine,* October 1859. Engraved by Lossing-Barritt.

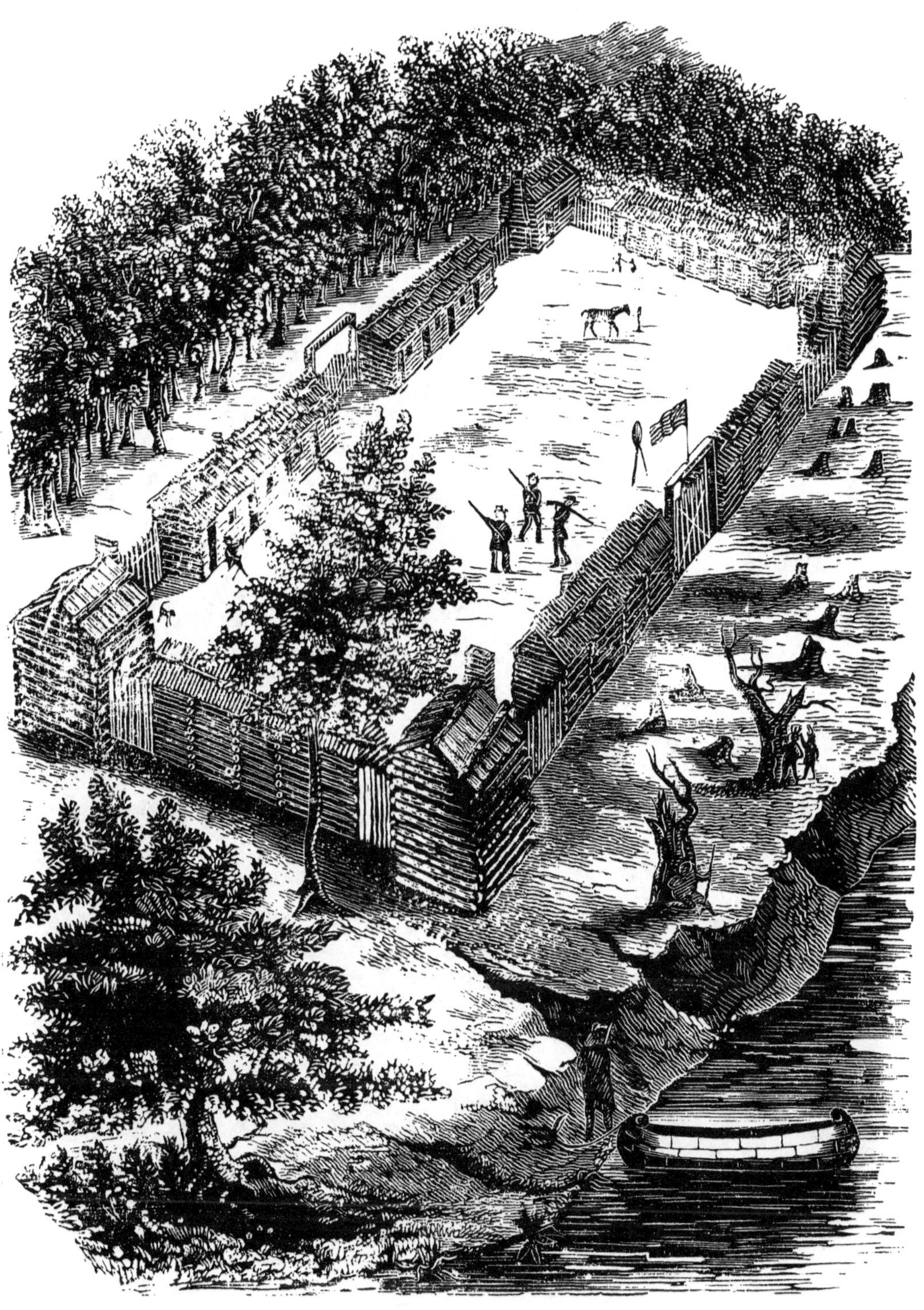

For the fort at Boonesborough, Daniel Boone selected a site close to the junction of Otter Creek and the Kentucky River. Two cabins with connecting palisades were built in April 1775. Soon after that, Col. Richard Henderson, who suggested the name for the site, laid out plans for more extensive works of defense, and these additions were completed in June. The size of the fort was reported to have been about 260 feet long by 150 feet wide.

Wood engraving from Lewis Collins's *Historical Sketches of Kentucky,* 1847. Engraved by Charles W. Thomson, Cincinnati, from a design by Collins.

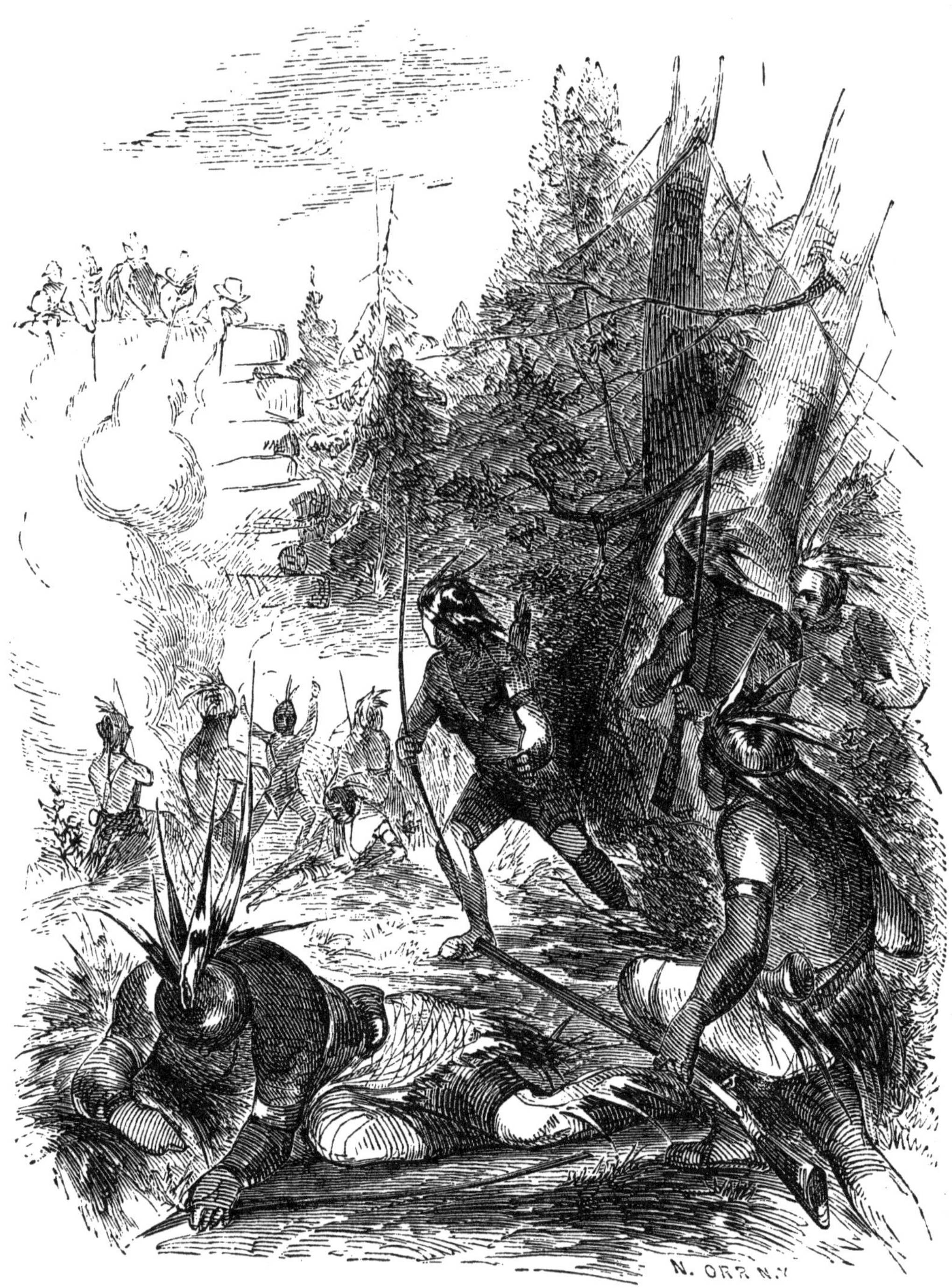

According to W.H. Bogart's account, in August 1778, a force of more than four hundred Indians and a small number of Canadians led by Chief Blackfish and Captain Du Quesne demanded the surrender of Fort Boonesborough. The pioneers, under the leadership of Daniel Boone, attempted to negotiate a treaty and thus gained time to prepare themselves and bring in provisions before the fighting began. They fought off attacks for nine days before the siege was lifted and the Indians dispersed.

Wood engraving from Bogart's *Daniel Boone and the Hunters of Kentucky*, 1859. Engraved by N. Orr, New York.

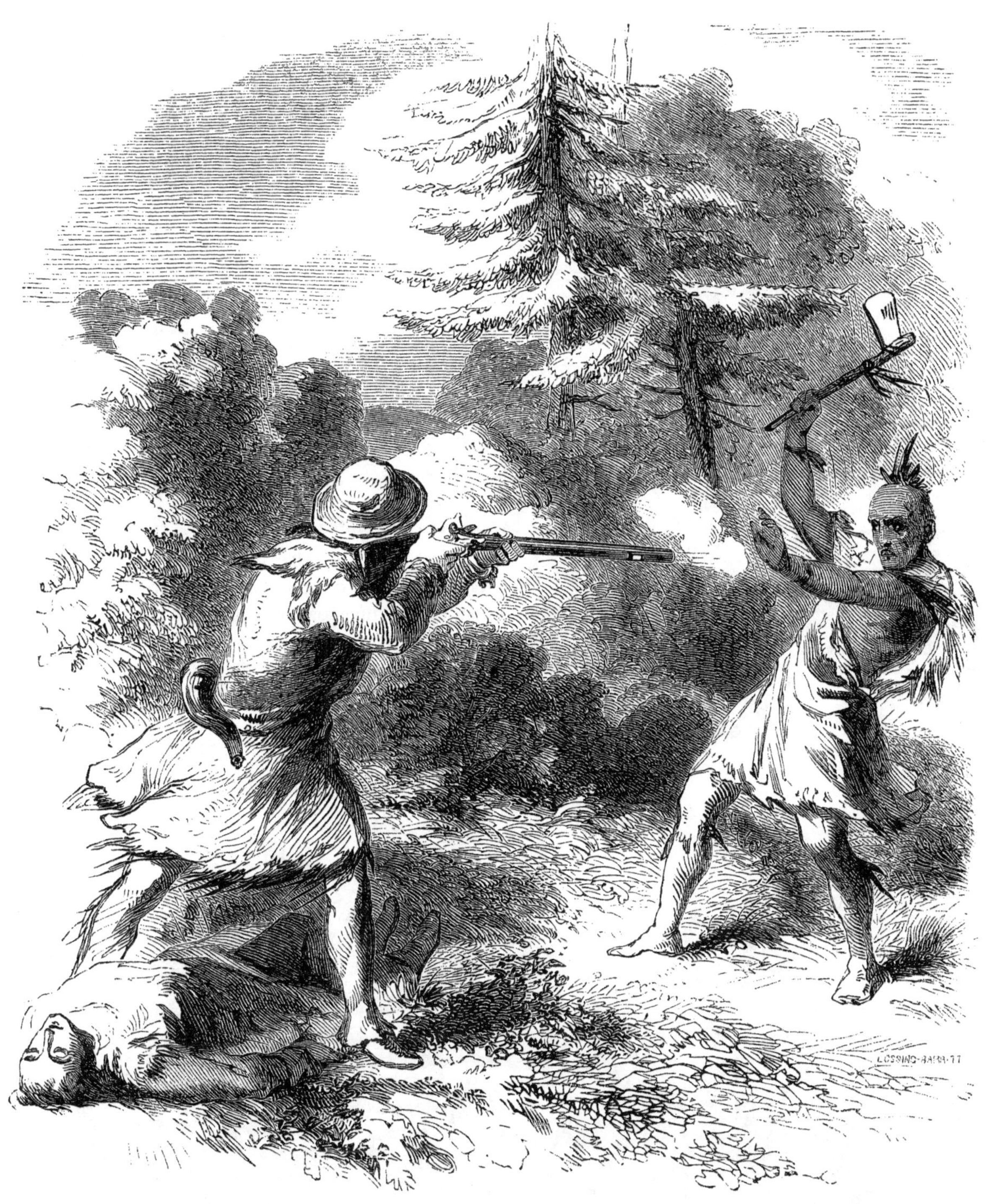

The Battle of Blue Licks was a frontier tragedy in which settlers, including Daniel Boone, pursued Indians into an ambush in August 1782. During the battle Boone's advice on tactics was ignored, and his son Israel was killed. Boone is said to have fought off Indians so that he could carry away the boy's body instead of leaving it on the battlefield as was the fate of many of the men who were killed that day.

Wood engraving from *Harper's Monthly Magazine,* October 1859. Engraved by Lossing-Barritt.

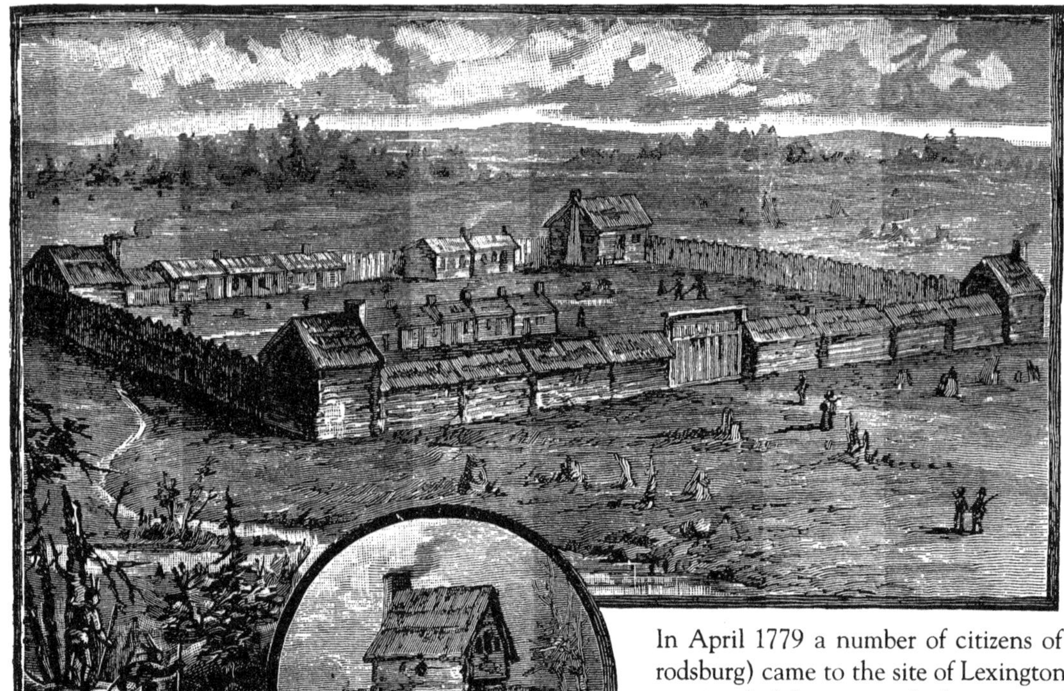

In April 1779 a number of citizens of Harrodstown (Harrodsburg) came to the site of Lexington to settle. The town consisted of three rows of cabins, two of which constituted a portion of the walls of the stockade surrounding the square. A blockhouse commanded the public spring. The stockade of the fort enclosed a part of what is now Main Street between Mill and Broadway. A town plan was adopted and lots distributed in December 1781.

Wood engraving from Z.F. Smith's *History of Kentucky,* 1886.

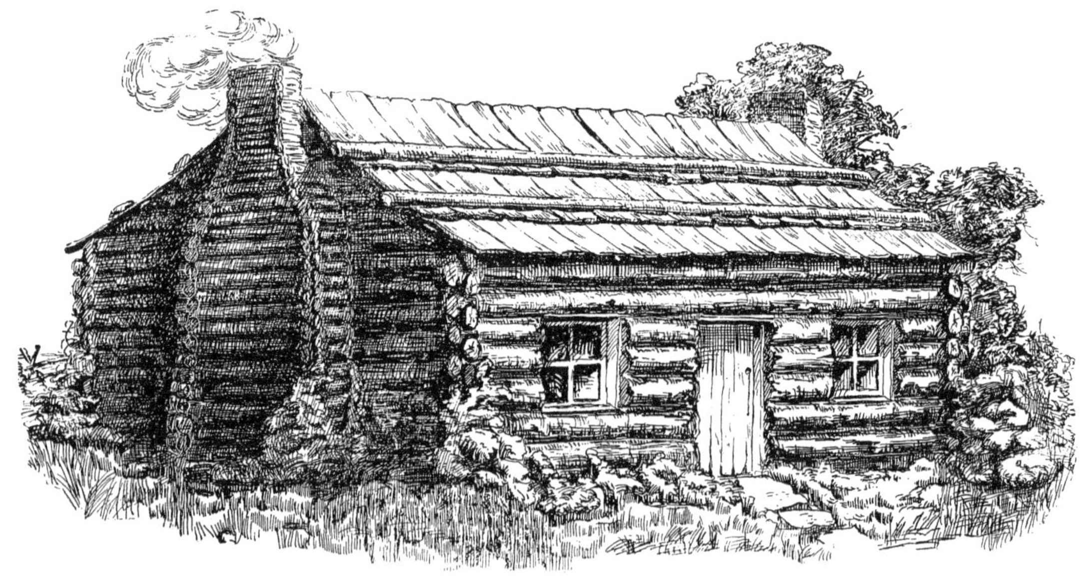

In the summer of 1783, the first courthouse in Kentucky and a jail of hewed and sawed logs were erected where Danville is now located. It was in this building that Kentucky's 1792 constitution was written. The town was laid off in 1785. In 1828 the log courthouse building was acquired by the Masonic order; later it was bought by the Methodist church. Today a log replica stands in Constitution Square Park.

Wood engraving from Elliott's *Illustrated Centennial Record of the State of Kentucky,* 1892.

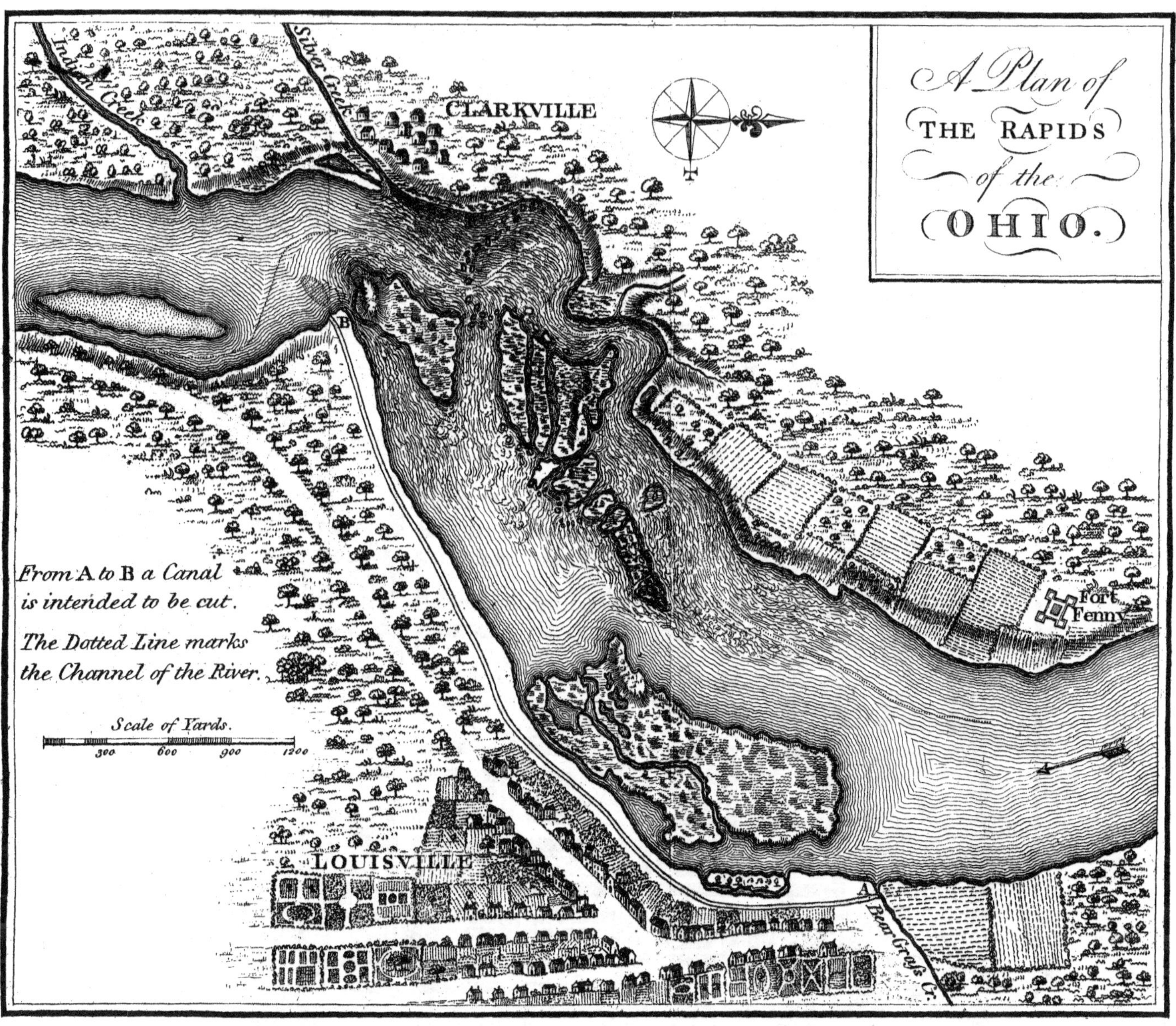

Of the many early plans for an urban presence, some, such as Louisville, were realized, and some remained plans forever. This illustration shows Gilbert Imlay's plan of the rapids of the Ohio, which evolved into a sort of bird's-eye view when he added trees and houses in "Clarksville" and along three streets in Louisville. The federal census of 1790 enumerated only two hundred people in Louisville, so Imlay's houses may have come close to an accurate representation of the village.

Copper engraving from Imlay's *Topographical Description of the Western Territory of North America*, 1793. Engraved by Thomas Conder.

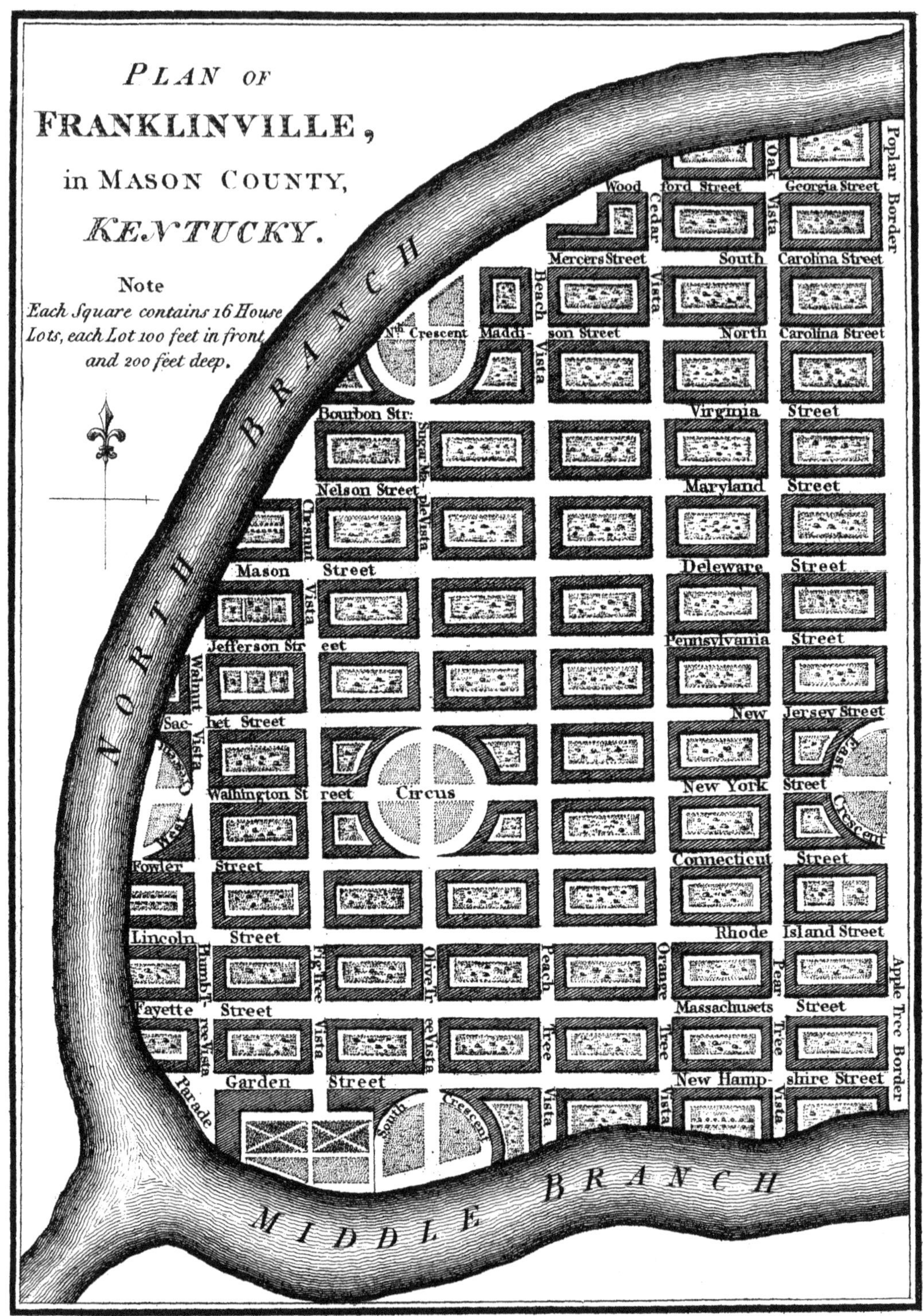

This new town was proposed for a location on the north fork of the Kentucky River at its junction with the middle fork in what finally became Lee County. It appears on several maps of the late eighteenth century. The township was to have 115,000 acres and was promoted as the seat of a soon-to-be-formed county. Investors who came to America to examine their property found nothing but unchanged wilderness. It is not known whether Franklinville was a speculator's sham or a legitimate effort that failed.

Copper engraving from Winterbotham's *Historical, Geographical, Commercial and Philosophical View of the American United States,* 1795. Engraved by John Russell of London.

TWO

The Natural World

No existing accounts record the reactions of the first humans who viewed the land now known as Kentucky. Countless and nameless Native Americans discovered the region's water system and network of caves; they explored the rich forests and noted the unique landmarks. Nor did the first Europeans to enter Kentucky—likely some French explorer or trapper or some forgotten English colonist—leave any detailed description of the attitude. Not until the mid-eighteenth century, when Thomas Walker and Christopher Gist made separate forays into Kentucky, are such full, written chronicles preserved.

But the feelings of wonderment and awe those and other eighteenth-century figures experienced when they viewed Kentucky probably only mirrored the outlook of the thousands before them, as it certainly did thousands after them. The very entrance into the region, through Cumberland Gap, caused people to pause, to think, and to write about that feature and its history. Novelist James Lane Allen and his companion, for instance, rode tired horses to the top of the Gap in 1885. "As we stood in the passway," he wrote, "amid the deepening shadows of twilight, and the solemn repose of the mighty landscape, the Gap seemed to be crowded with two invisible and countless pageants of human life, the one passing in, the other passing out; and the air grew thick with ghostly utterances—primeval sounds, undistinguishable and strange, of creatures nameless and never seen by man; the wild rush of whoops of retreating and pursuing tribes; the slow steps of watchful pioneers; the wail of dying children and the songs of homeless women; the muffled tread of routed and broken armies—all the sounds of surprise and delight, victory and defeat, hunger and pain and weariness and despair, that the human heart can utter." The natural world of Kentucky caused the imagination to soar, and illustrators tried to capture that majesty in their visual presentations so that all Americans could know Kentucky's wonders.

Rock formations, chimney rocks, natural bridges, various falls—all these fascinated engravers. But by far the most popular attraction was Mammoth Cave. Tourists viewed the cavern with amazement, consumptives with hope, and manufacturers with profit motives. Visitors from foreign lands made it a particular stop on their American trip, while citizens of the United States joined them in enjoying a tour of the Gothic Chapel (Stalagmite Hall) or of the subterranean river system. The vastness of it all delighted illustrators, who periodically told the cave's story in their engravings. Such publicity, when coupled with published guidebooks and word-of-mouth accounts, made the dark land beneath Kentucky's soil a national treasure.

The state's resources were many, and not all were static, unchanging geologic features. Kentucky is said to have the most miles of navigable waterways of any state in the contiguous United States. Very early the people sought to harness that water for personal use through wells and water systems and through mineral spring "watering places."

The various "springs"—at Harrodsburg, Crab Orchard, and elsewhere—offered healing waters as their stated drawing card. But in actuality, the springs took second place to social gathering as a stimulant for visiting. Large and elegant ballrooms attracted visitors from across the South and all over Kentucky. Men and women in elegant attire joined others of their age and class in those fashionable resorts; marriages often resulted from such attendance at "The Springs." Others, however, eschewed the frivolity and simply "took the waters" as they sought cures for ailments or just a brief solace from the cares they bore.

But nature was not always a positive force in Kentucky life. The healing waters, the natural beauty, the physical wonders—all these would be forgotten when a vengeful nature struck out in fury. Almost from the earliest period of settlement, the rich and lush land that settlers had described to friends back beyond the mountains turned its other face in fury. The terrible winter of 1779-1780, for example, kept snow on the ground for months, froze the rivers, and left a trail of dying animals, as well as shivering and starving people. No engraver recorded that suffering, nor the unbelievably destructive earthquake of 1811. But in the late nineteenth century, illustrators did portray the havoc of an 1883 Ohio River flood and the wreckage of the 1890 tornado in Louisville. Those disasters reminded Kentuckians that the contradiction of beauty and death present in frontier Kentucky's history would be a part, as well, of the natural world they inhabited, long after the frontier had passed.

—*J.C.K.*

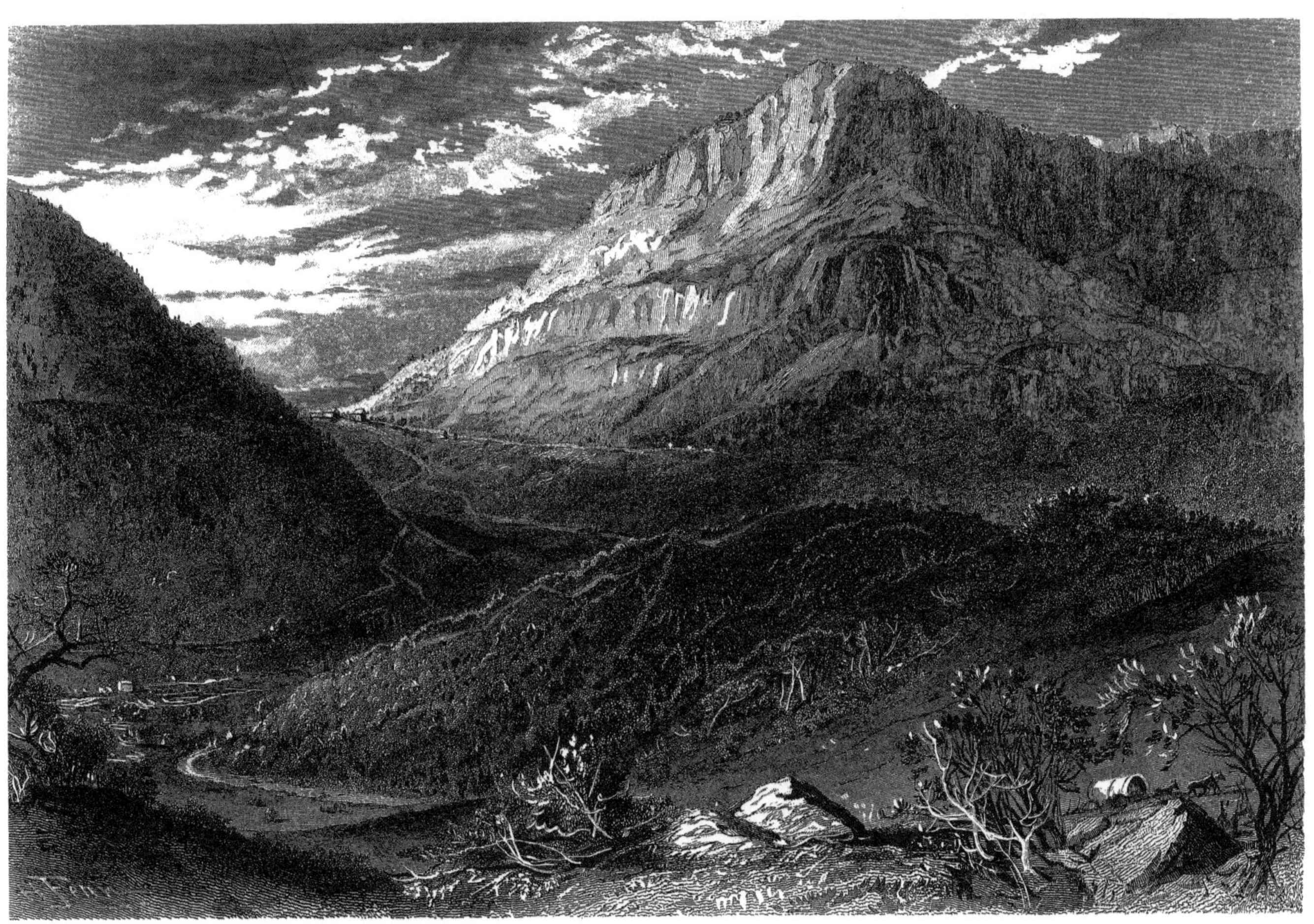

In 1750 Dr. Thomas Walker, one of the earliest explorers of eastern Kentucky, entered the state through what was then called Cave Gap. Walker renamed the Gap in honor of the Duke of Cumberland. Between 1775 and 1796, an estimated two hundred thousand pioneering men and women passed through what had been a path for Indians and buffalo before becoming part of the Wilderness Road. The Gap became strategically important and trenches and gun positions were placed there during the Civil War. In 1953, ten thousand acres in Kentucky and the same number in Virginia and Tennessee became Cumberland Gap National Historical Park, the third national park—after Mammoth Cave and the Lincoln homesite—to be established in Kentucky.

Copper engraving by H. Fenn, published by D. Appleton & Co., New York, 1872.

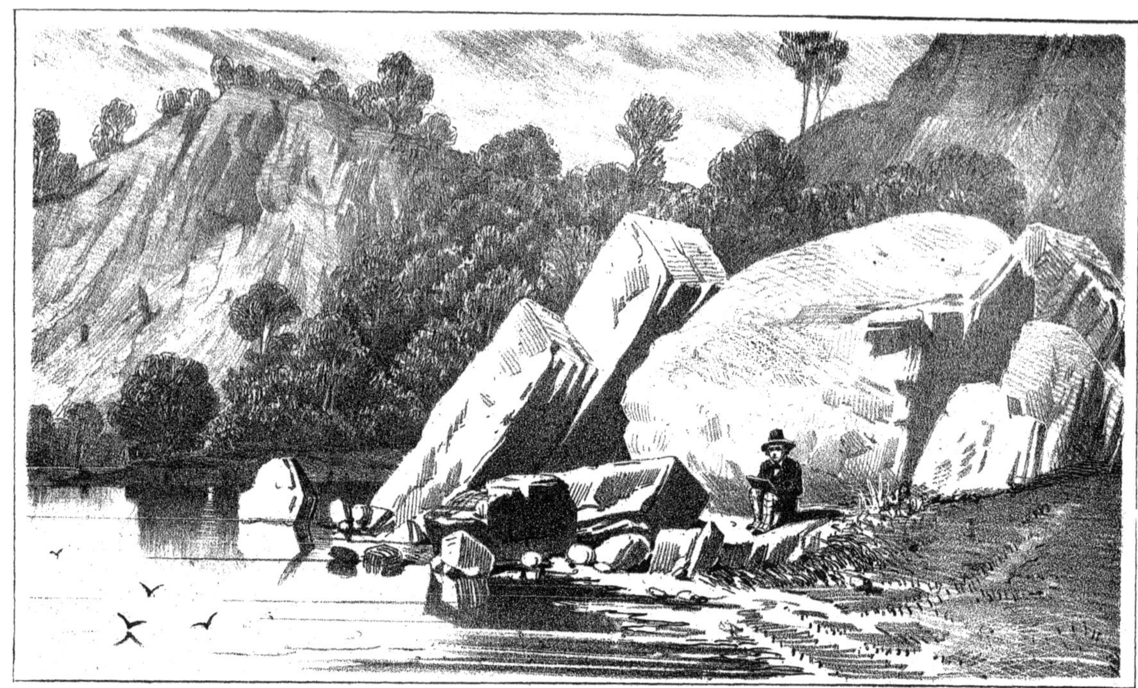

Early French explorers who observed iron conglomerate lying along the great rust-colored banks of the Mississippi River on the Kentucky side just south of the Ohio's confluence called them "Iron Banks." The term appears on maps of the late eighteenth century. The artist has placed himself in this view of a detached mass of soft quaternary sandstone fallen from a cliff along the Iron Banks in Hickman County. Only the first volume of the geological survey's published reports was embellished with these interesting drawings.

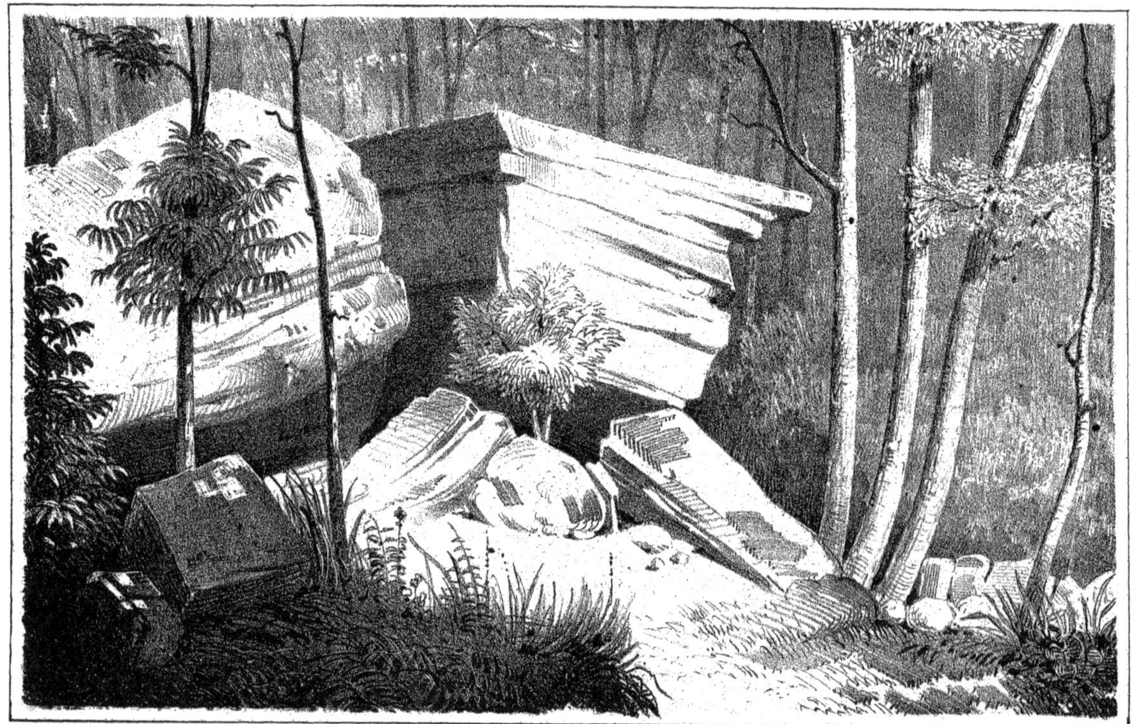

Anvil Rock in Union County derives its name from the shape of this mass of sandstone.

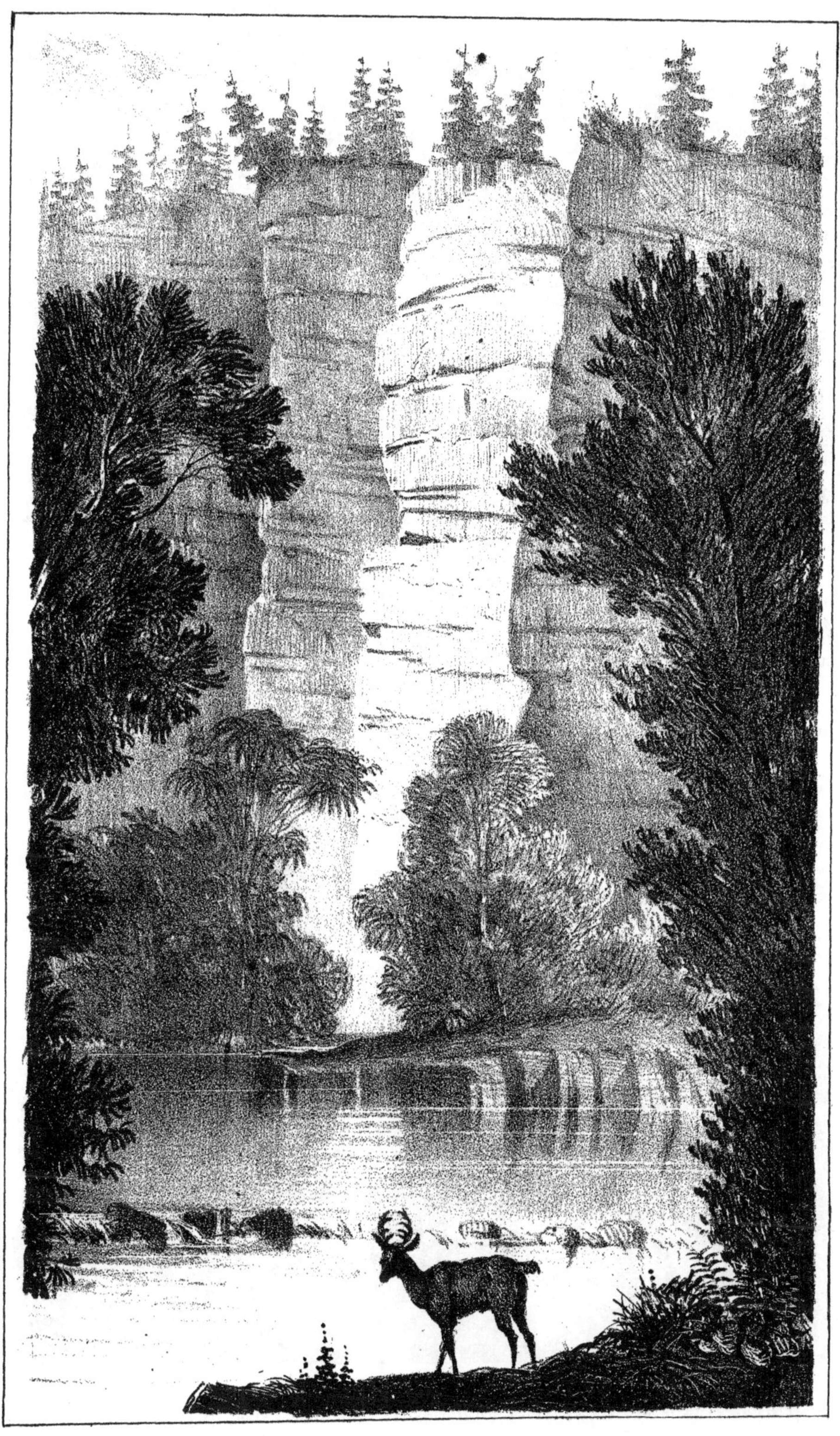

Cliffs of conglomerate based on Archimedes limestone are 190 feet high at the mouth of Dismal Creek in Edmondson and Grayson Counties.

All three lithographs from Owen's *Report of the Geological Survey in Kentucky,* 1856. Lithographed by Robyn & Co., Louisville, from a drawing by David Dale Owen.

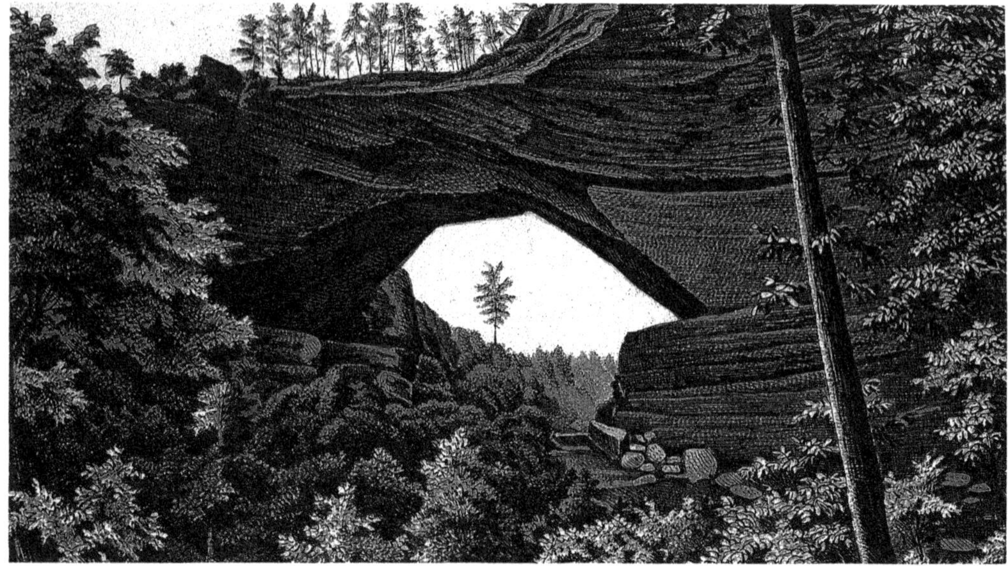

Natural Bridge near Beaver Gap was not mentioned in the state geological survey reports of the 1850s nor in Richard Collins's history of 1874. This one is located near the former route of the Cincinnati Southern Railway in what is now McCreary County, on or near the Cumberland River between Parker's Lake and Flat Rock.

Lithograph from *Views on the Cincinnati Southern Railway* souvenir view booklet, 1880. Photographed and published by James Mullen, Lexington.

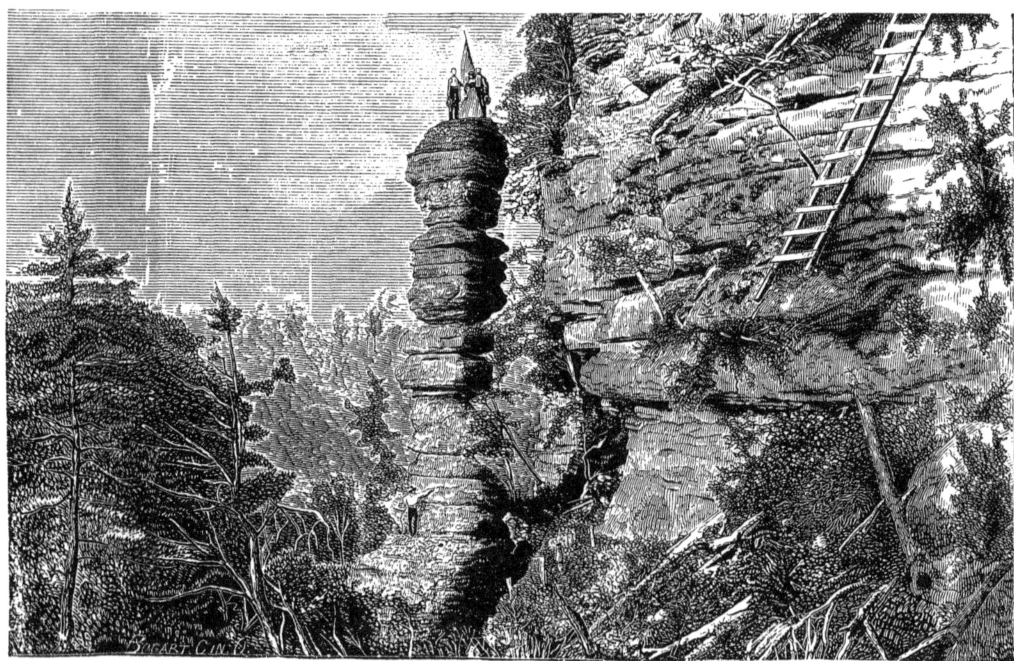

The palisades of the Kentucky River gorge have been called awesome by some travelers and enchanting by others. This immense freestanding column is located upriver from Shakertown in the area of Camp Nelson. In Richard H. Collins's history the formation is called Chimney Rock, but the view was located in that volume adjacent to a lengthy description of a similar rock formation that Collins called the Devil's Pulpit; both names may have been used for this site. It is likely that this is the same column currently marked on Kentucky River navigation charts as Candle Stick Rock.

Wood engraving from Collins's *History of Kentucky,* 1874. Engraved by John H. Bogart, Cincinnati.

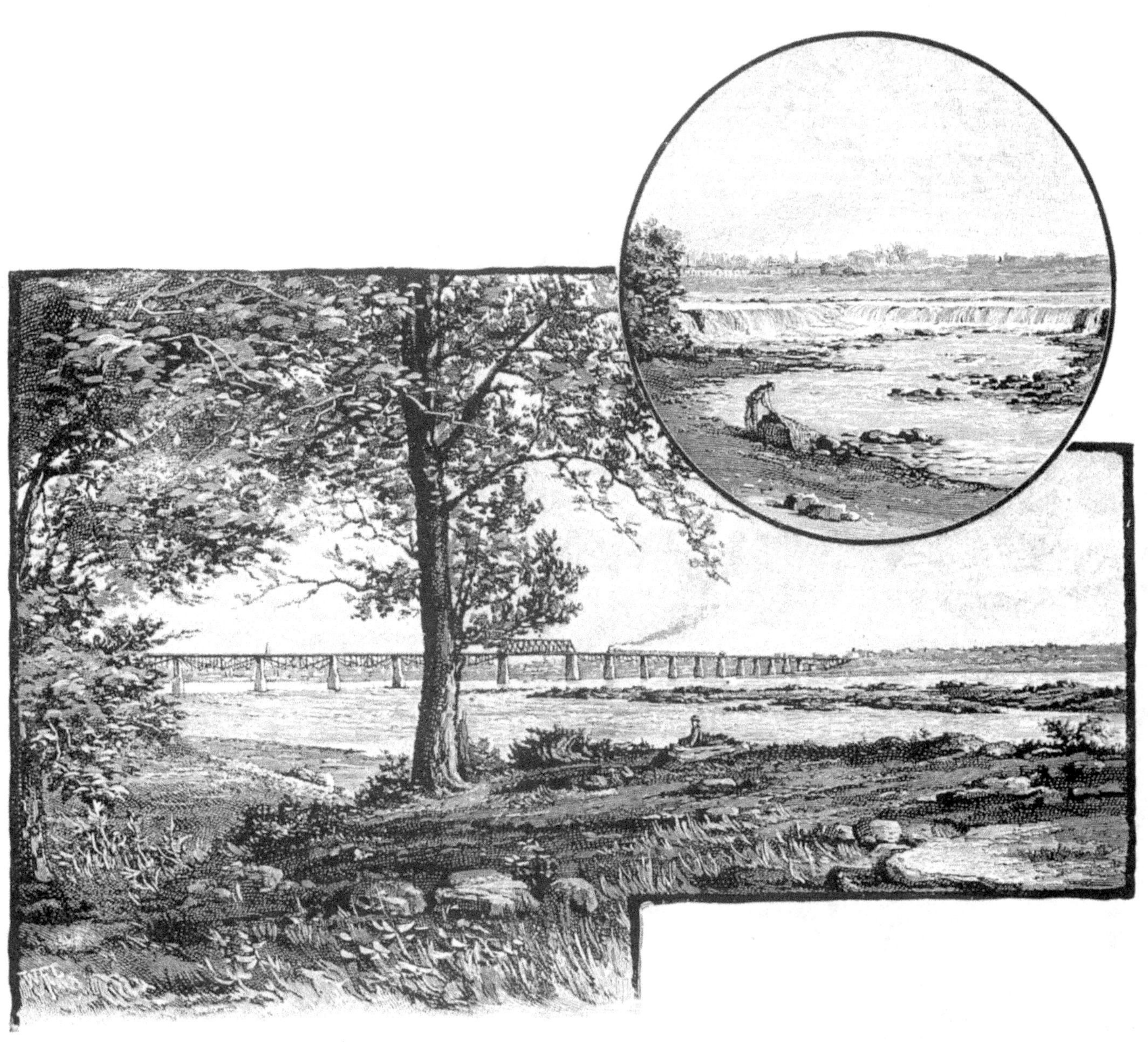

The falls or rapids of the Ohio are one of the reasons that Louisville was settled at that location, and they have figured prominently in its social and economic history ever since. The point at which the river makes its greatest fall is said to be shifting eastward at an extremely slow pace and is now at the place commonly known as "the falls," where a portion of the area consists of an ancient coral reef.

Wood engraving from the Louisville Board of Trade's *The City of Louisville and a Glimpse of Kentucky,* 1887.

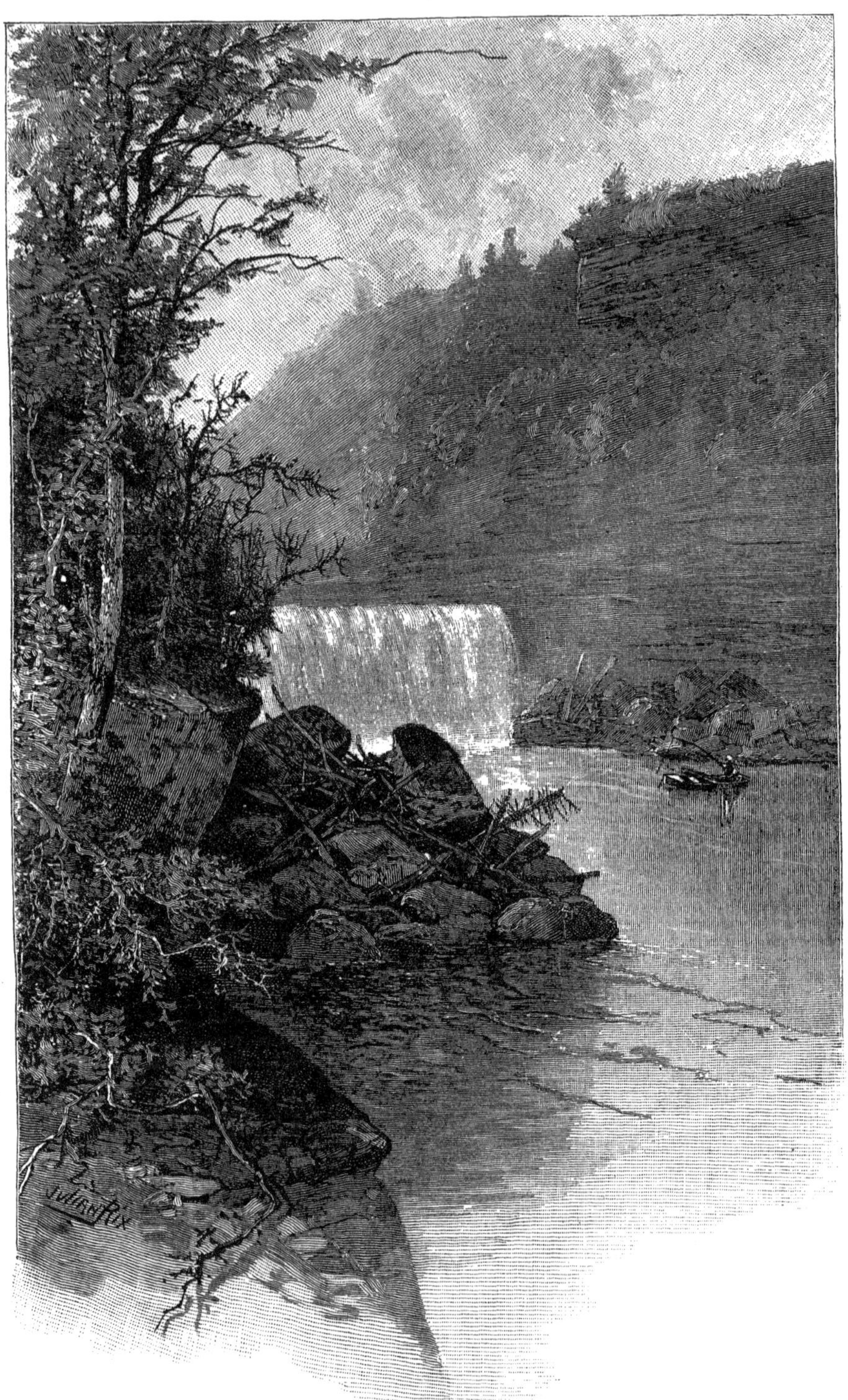

The falls of the Cumberland were the "head of navigation" for that river, according to Jedediah Morse's *American Gazetteer* published in 1804. From the falls, Morse tells us, five hundred miles of navigable water extend to its confluence with the Ohio. Lewis Collins noted simply that the falls were "among the most remarkable objects in the state." About 1850 rumors that a rich constituent of silver had been found in the stratum of ore at the foot of the falls created a wave of excitement. Shares were sold in a company to undertake its extraction, but no silver was found. James Lane Allen traveled to the falls in the summer of 1885 and described "the bow-crowned mist that floated upward in shapes of ethereal lightness." That spectrum formed in the mist when the moon is full is the only moonbow on the continent.

Wood engraving from Allen's *The Blue-Grass Region of Kentucky*, 1892, from a drawing by Julian Rix, New York.

Mammoth Cave (*right*) had been known to local people and a few visitors from about 1800, but this is the first illustration to call attention to its wonders. Because of its nitrous earth, the cave was the location of important saltpeter production during the years 1808–1814. The availability of cheaper imported saltpeter brought an end to production at the cave, and thereafter its attraction was its natural wonders.

Wood engraving from Rochelle's *États-Unis d'Amerique*, Paris, 1837, from a drawing by Danvin.

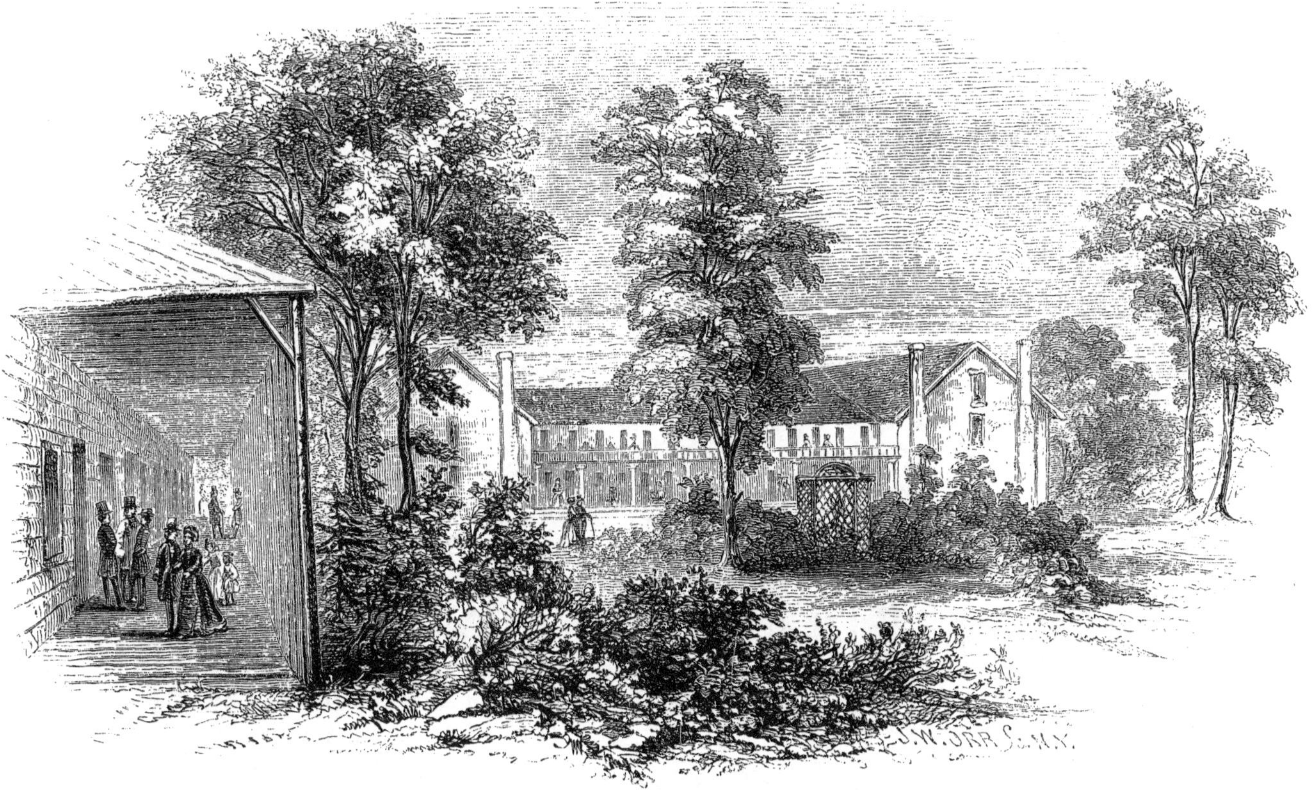

An earnest effort to attract tourists to Mammoth Cave began after Dr. John Croghan bought the property in 1840. Within a year more than one thousand people had visited. Croghan built a hotel containing a ballroom and a ten-pin alley, with pavilions between a quarter mile and a half mile inside the cave for those who preferred to view it from that location. The complex lasted until destroyed by fire in 1916.

Wood engraving from Martin's *Pictorial Guide to the Mammoth Cave,* 1851. Engraved by J. W. Orr.

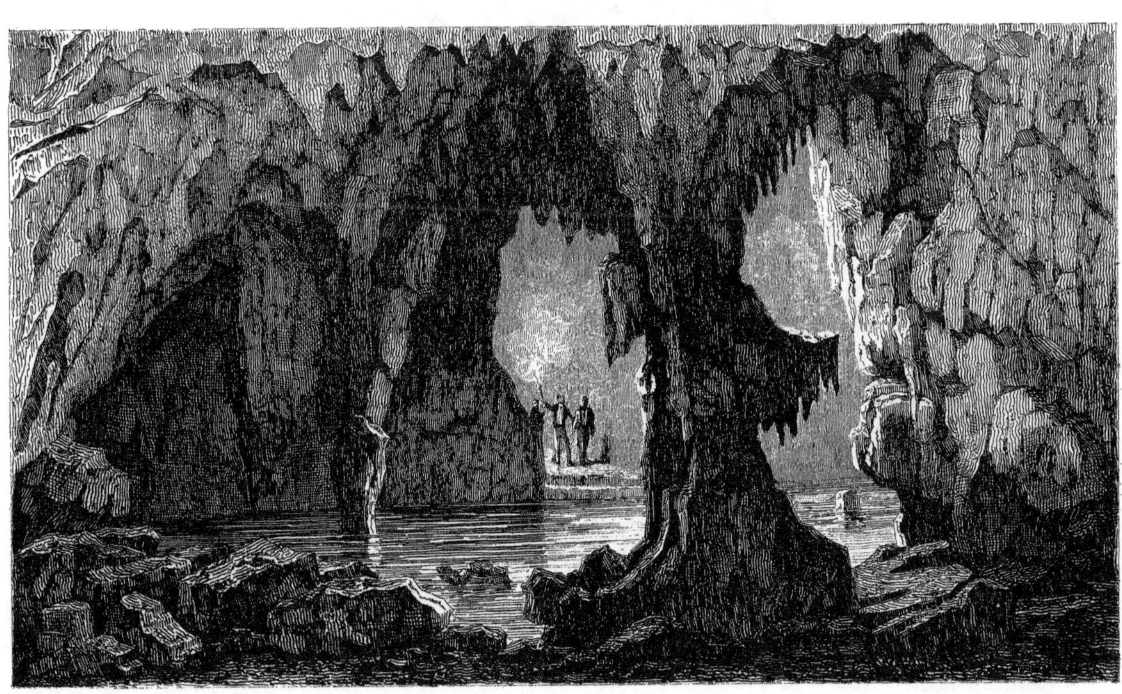

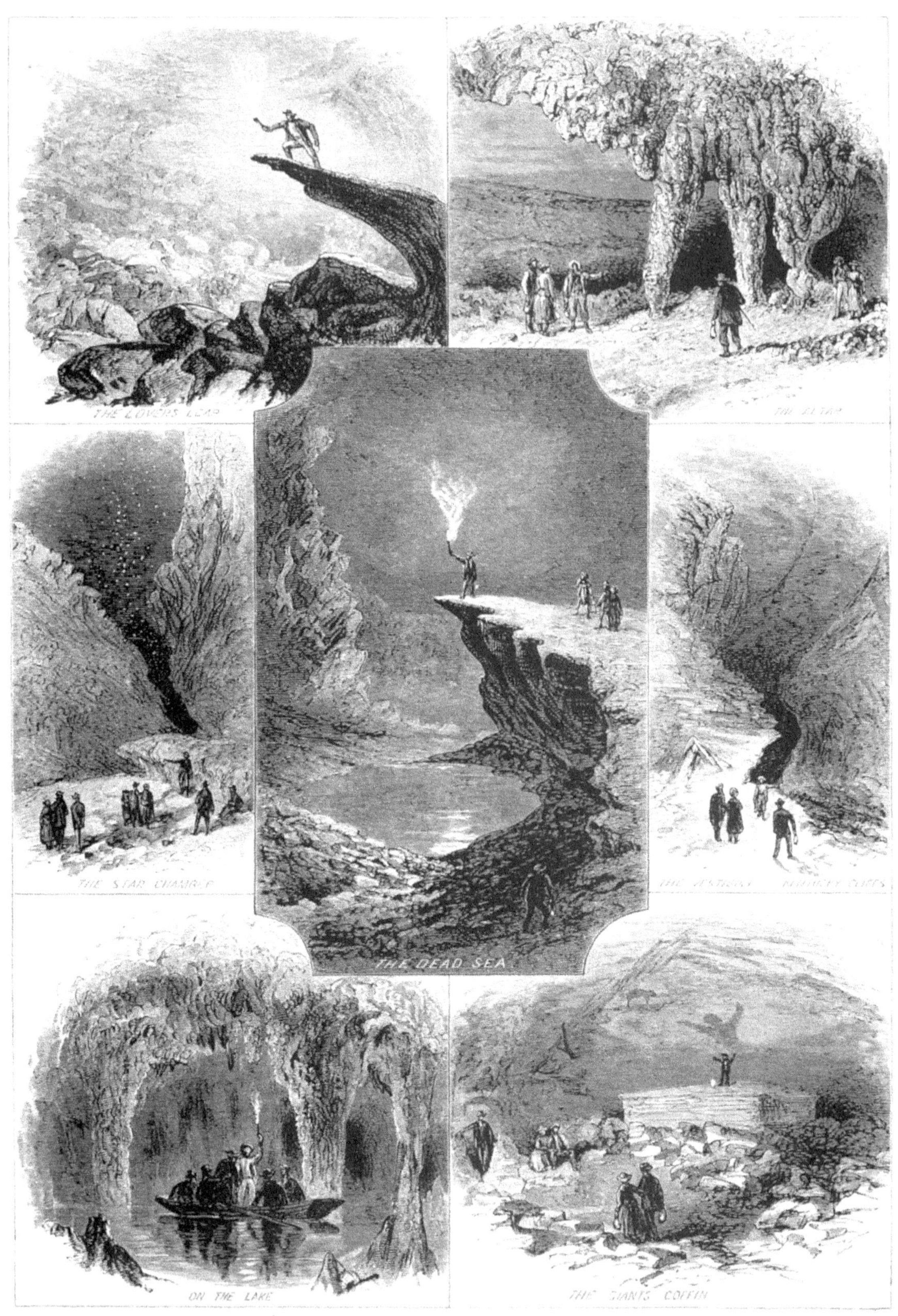

The article that accompanied these views related what tourists who visited Mammoth Cave could expect to see. The author was impressed with the massive stalactites that "take fifty years to grow to the thickness of a sheet of paper." He also described the number of bats, writing "thousands of the little creatures are found snarling and curling their delicate lips at all intruders."

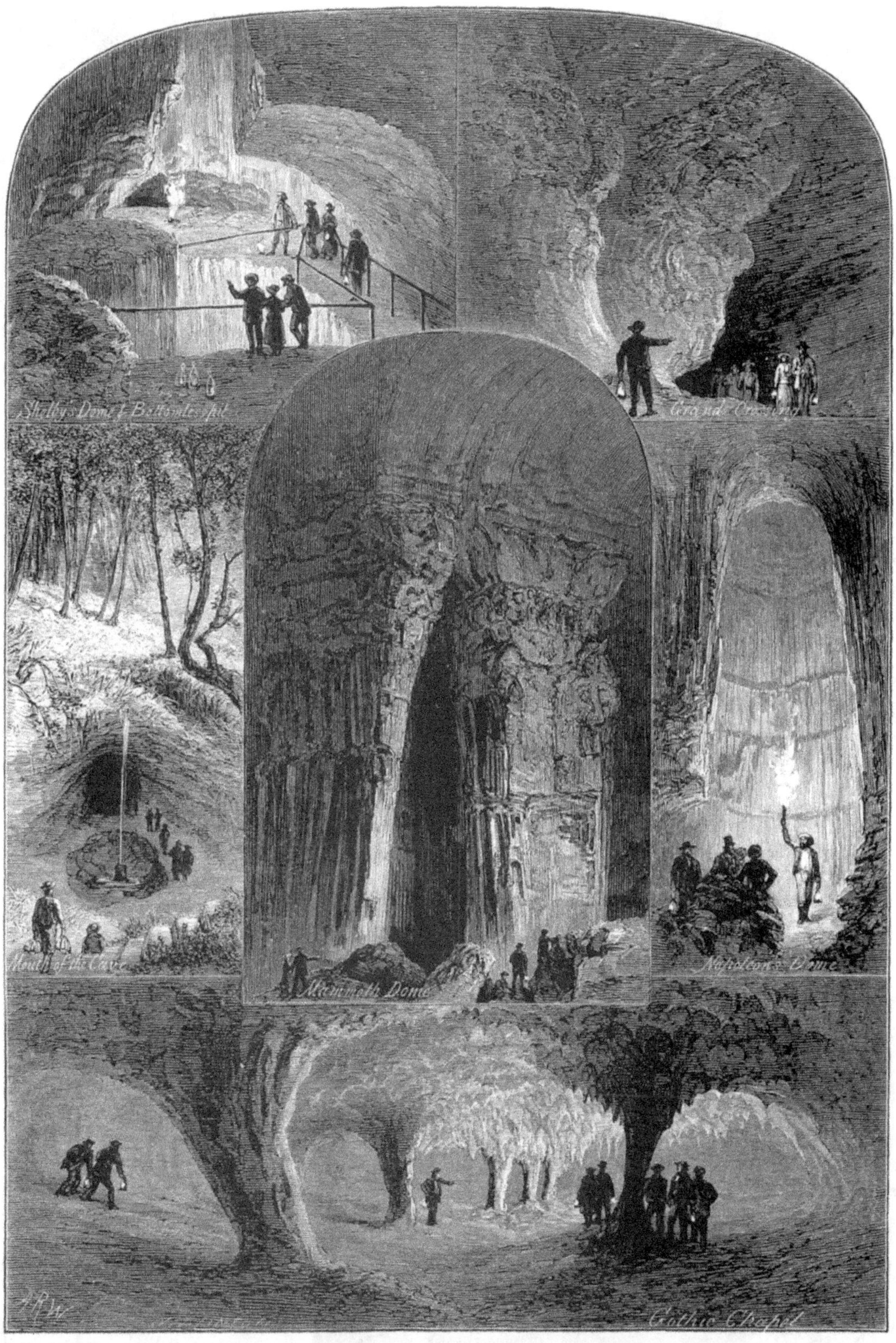

The views on these two pages show the engravers' habit of making small engravings with borders that would then be fitted together into full-page illustrations.

Wood engravings from Bryant's *Picturesque America,* published by D. Appleton & Co, New York, 1874. Engraved by V.V. Linton from drawings by Alfred R. Waud.

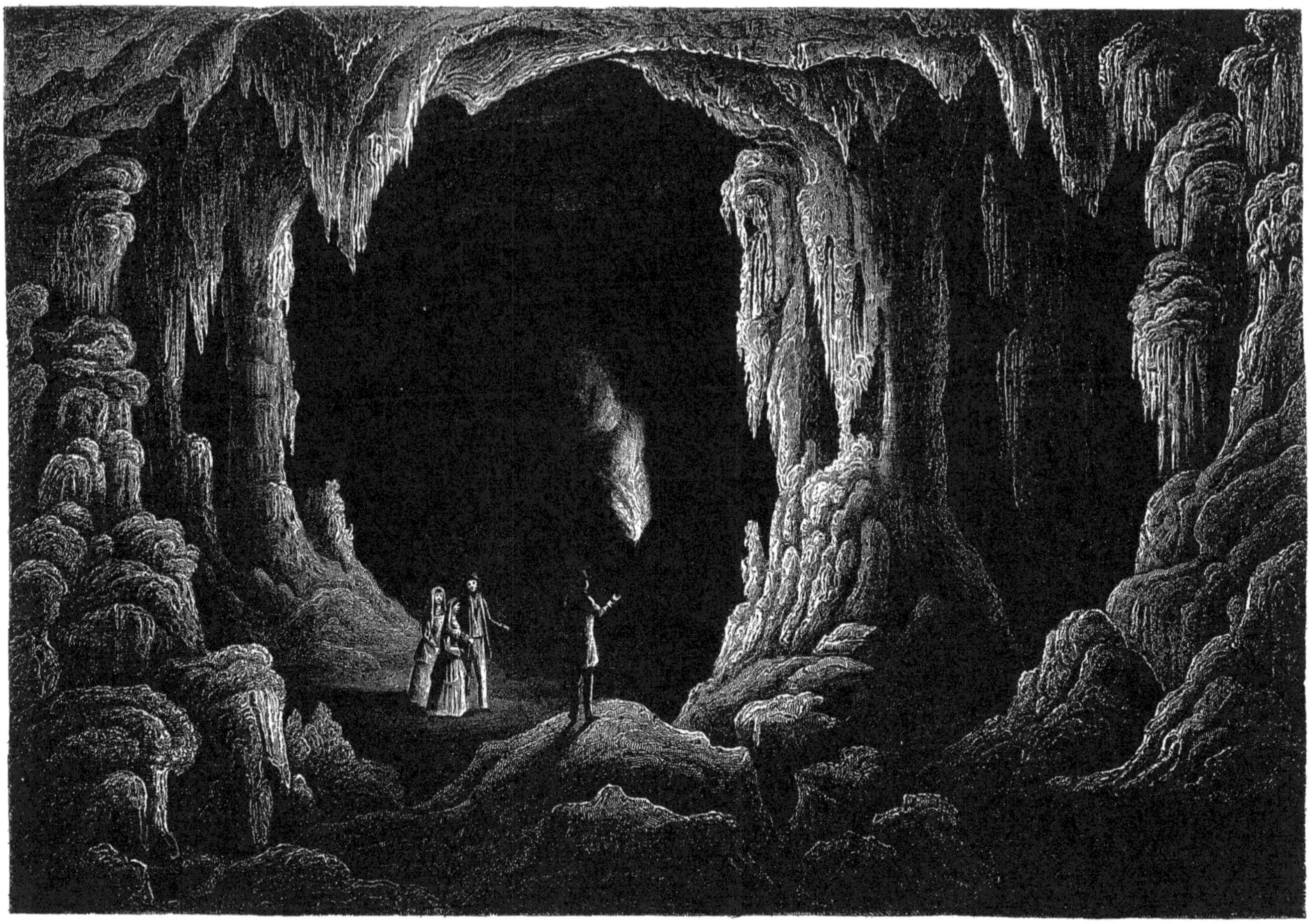

By 1854 Mammoth Cave was celebrated as a wonder of the world. Herrmann J. Meyer of Hildburghausen, Germany, published a series of books over a period of some years, all in the German language, in which he included very fine engravings of interesting places he visited in many countries. This illustration was called *Die Mammuths-Hohle.*

Metal plate engraving from *Meyer's Universum,* 1854.

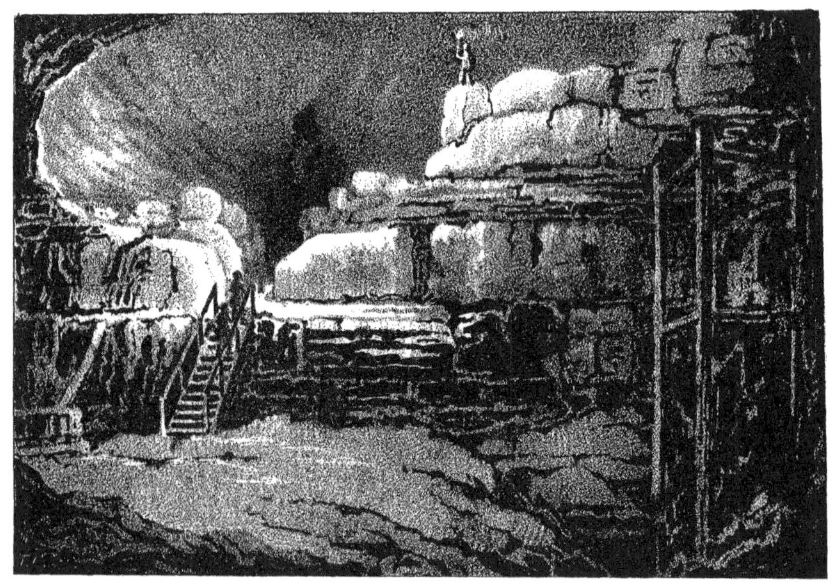

The Gothic Avenue of Mammoth Cave was so named for its arches and its medieval appearance. It is about forty feet wide, fifteen feet high, and two miles long.

Lithograph from anonymously published *Rambles in the Mammoth Cave During 1844,* 1845. Lithographed by Bauer and Teschemacher, Louisville, from a drawing by Thomas Campbell.

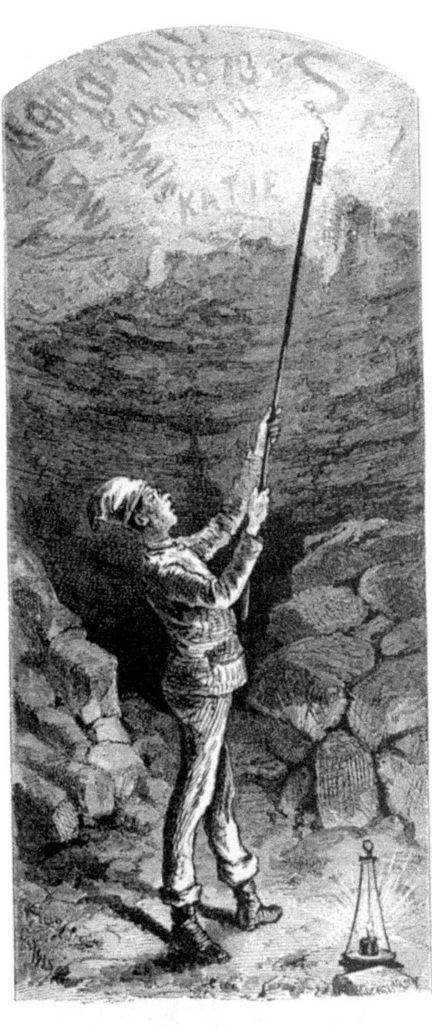

Graffiti inscriptions in the area of Mammoth Cave known as the "Subterranean Album" probably began with the saltpeter miners decades before the activity was illustrated.

Wood engraving from *Scribner's Monthly,* 1874, from a drawing by J. Wells Champney, Deerfield, Mass., and New York.

Dr. John Croghan of Louisville, owner of Mammoth Cave during the years 1839-1849, was one of several learned men who believed that the consistent temperature and humidity of the cave would prove healthful for consumptive patients. By 1843 the cave had become a well-known resort for invalids who wished to spend the winter season there, but use of the cave as a therapeutic center soon ended after the deaths of several of the patients, deaths that were probably neither delayed nor made more likely by the cave environment. A guidebook published in 1845 states that patients used two stone cabins and others of frame construction, well furnished, with good and comfortable accommodations.

Wood engraving from *Harper's Weekly,* February 10, 1877. Engraved by Henry Linton.

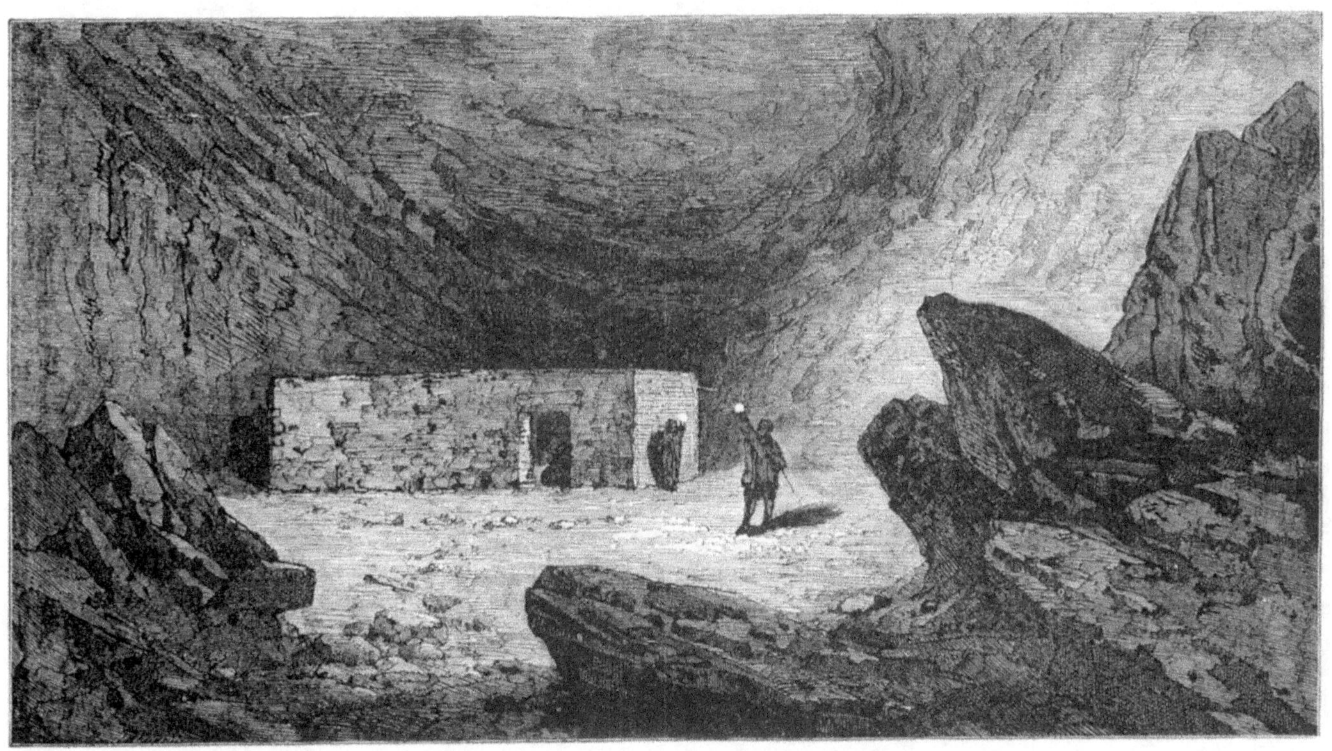

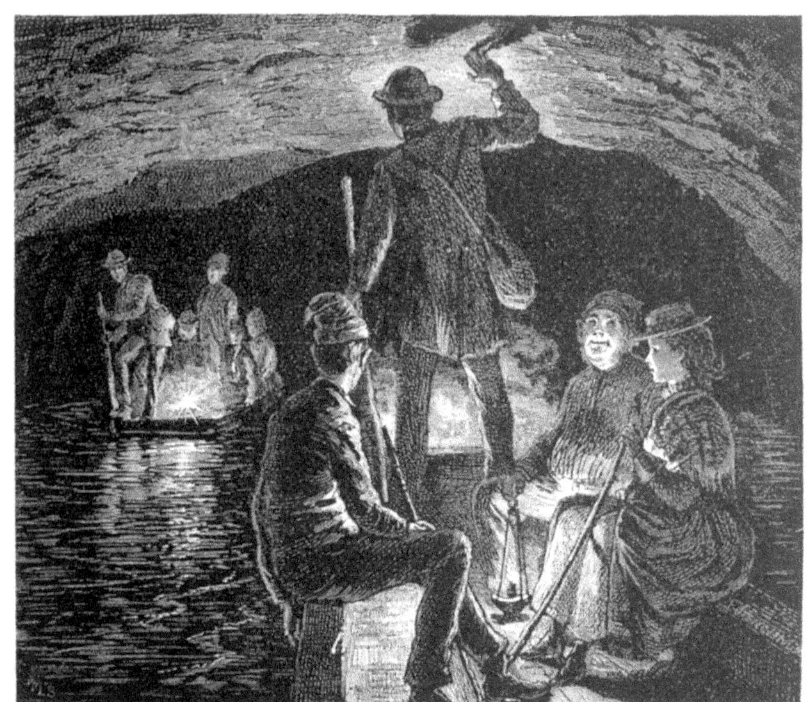

When the water in the cave is at its normal level, Echo River is three-quarters of a mile long, but a rise of only a few feet connects it with the Styx and the Lethe.

Wood engraving from *Scribner's Monthly,* 1874, from a drawing by J. Wells Champney, Deerfield, Mass., and New York.

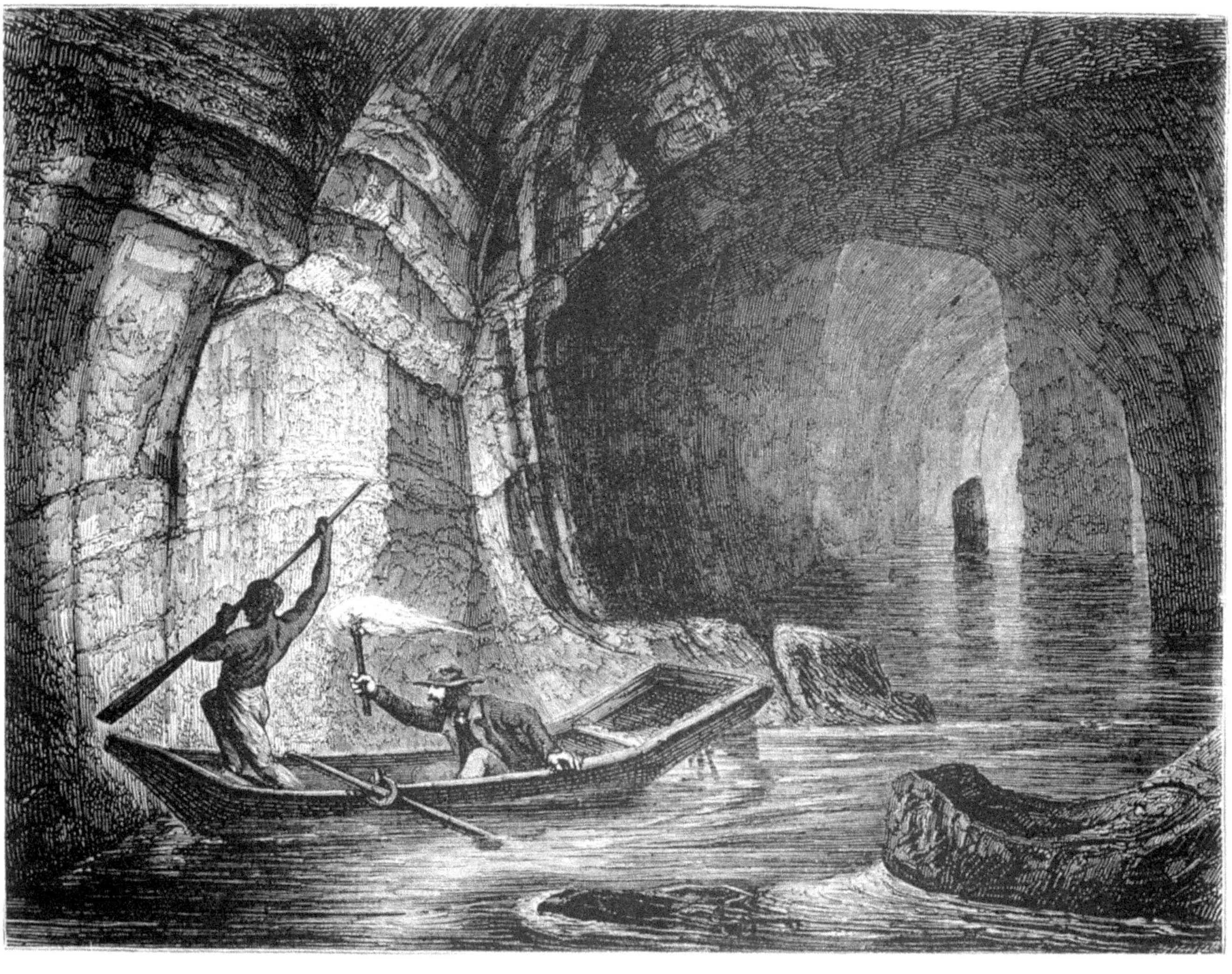

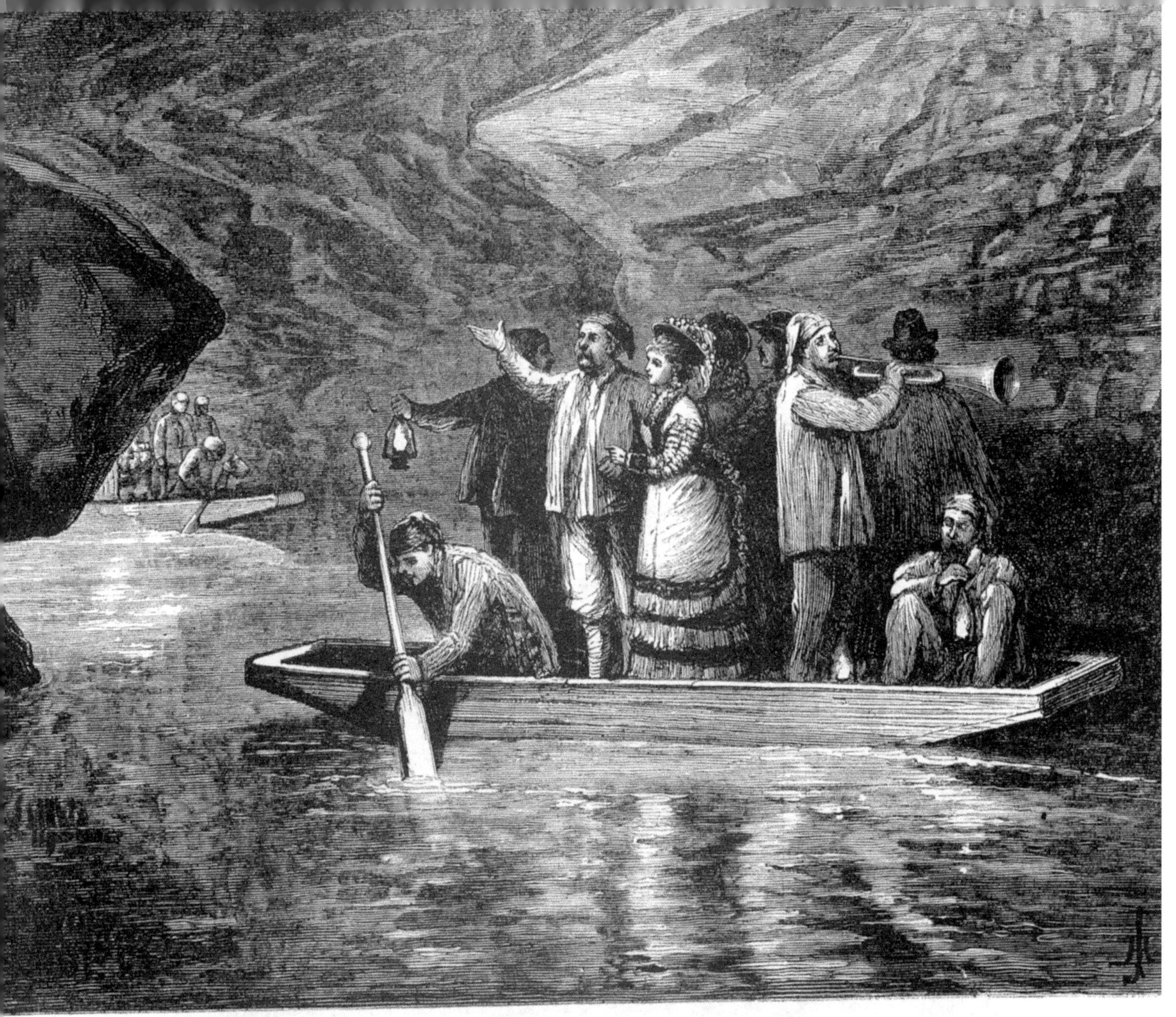

A visitor said that the first glimpse of the Styx River brought to mind the descent of Ulysses into hell. To those who viewed it from high upon an adjacent wall, the scene on the river was funereal and spectral.

Wood engraving from *Harper's Weekly,* February 10, 1877.

The cave guidebook by Horace Martin published in 1851 described the Styx River as "aptly named: people might well imagine it to be the famous stream whose name it bears." Small boats conveyed passengers over the river while the lamps of the guides reflected in the murky pool and visitors looking down from a stone bridge eighty feet above the river saw the shadowy figures of those in the boats as "the spirits of the departed being rowed over that profound flood to a place where final doom is to be awaited."

Wood engraving from *Le Tour du Monde,* 1859. Engraved by Trichon. Drawing by Gambard from a design by M. Deville.

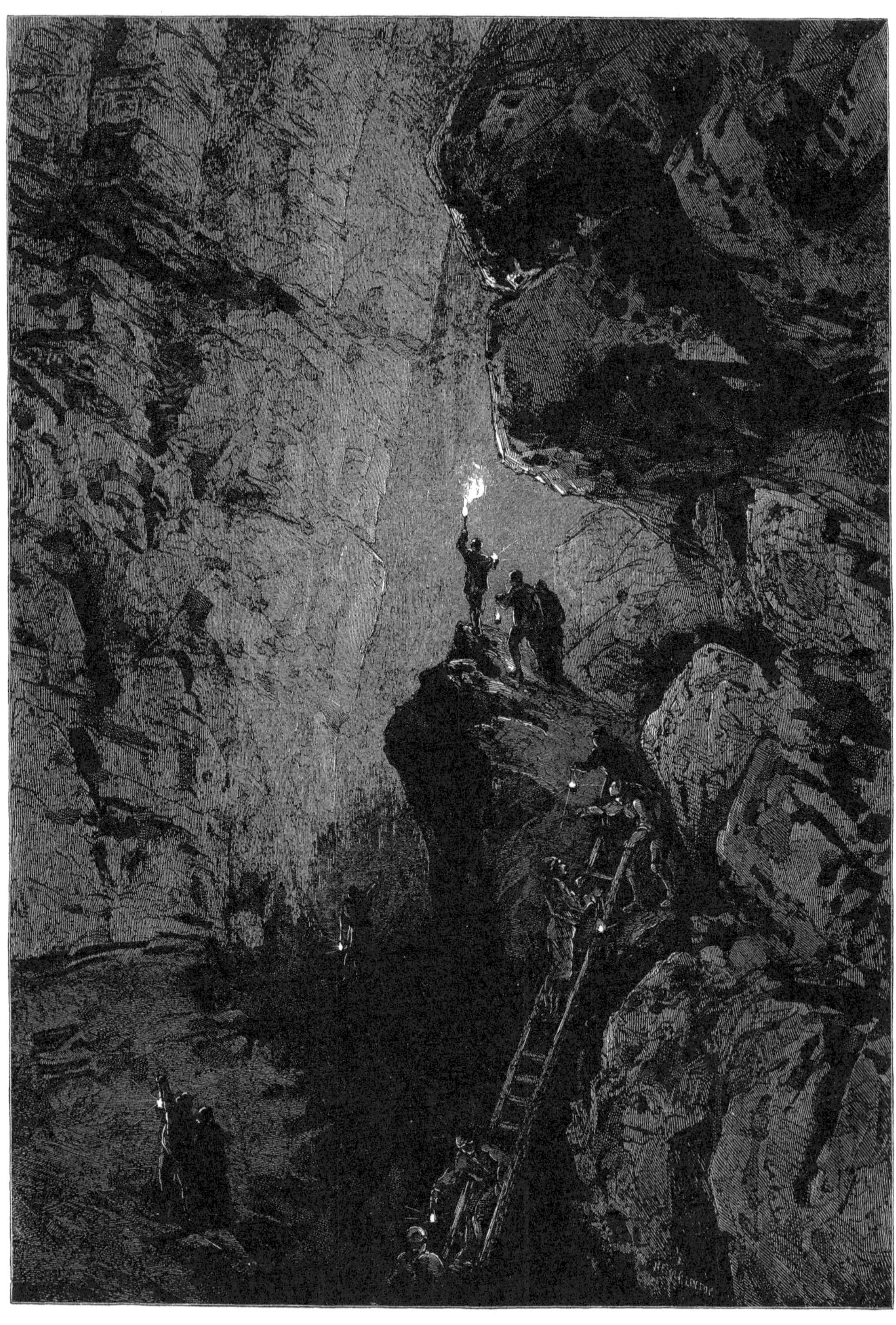

In the early guidebooks the Mammoth Dome was claimed to be nearly four hundred feet high with a waterfall entering the cave at its highest point.

Wood engraving from *Harper's Weekly*, October 28, 1876.

"Taking the waters" at mineral springs was a favorite pastime in nineteenth-century Kentucky. Esculapia Springs offered accommodations for two hundred visitors. It was located at a settlement also known as Marine in southwest Lewis County, fourteen miles from Vanceburg. Lewis Collins called the two springs, one of white sulphur, the other chalybeate, "equal, if not superior, to the waters of a similar kind in Virginia."

Wood engraving from Lewis Collins's *Historical Sketches of Kentucky,* 1847.

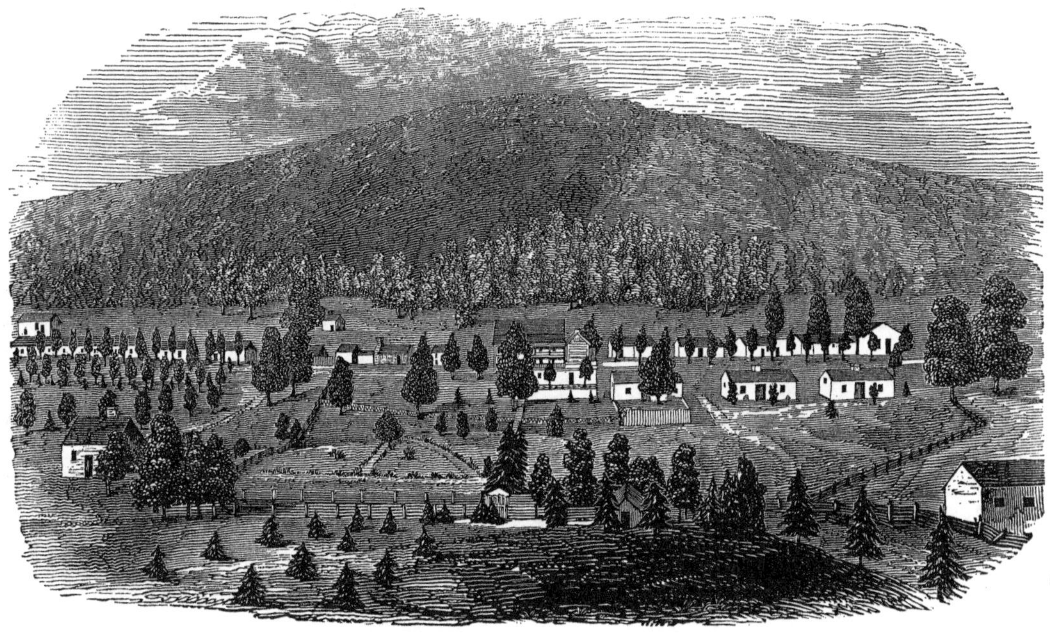

Two major springs flowed into the Licking River at Blue Licks about ten miles from Carlisle. The view below shows the resort at the lower springs, in 1847, after major improvements had been made. At that time it could accommodate as many as six hundred guests in a building 670 feet long and three stories high. Dr. Robert Peter, a prominent professor at Transylvania University and a chemist with the Kentucky Geological Survey from 1854 to the Civil War, estimated that the saline content of the water would provide fifty pounds of salt per hour, or 220 tons per year. The building shown in this engraving was destroyed by fire in 1862 and replaced by less extensive accommodations.

Wood engraving from Lewis Collins's *Historical Sketches of Kentucky,* 1847. Engraved by John or Horace Baker from a drawing probably by Harrison Eastman.

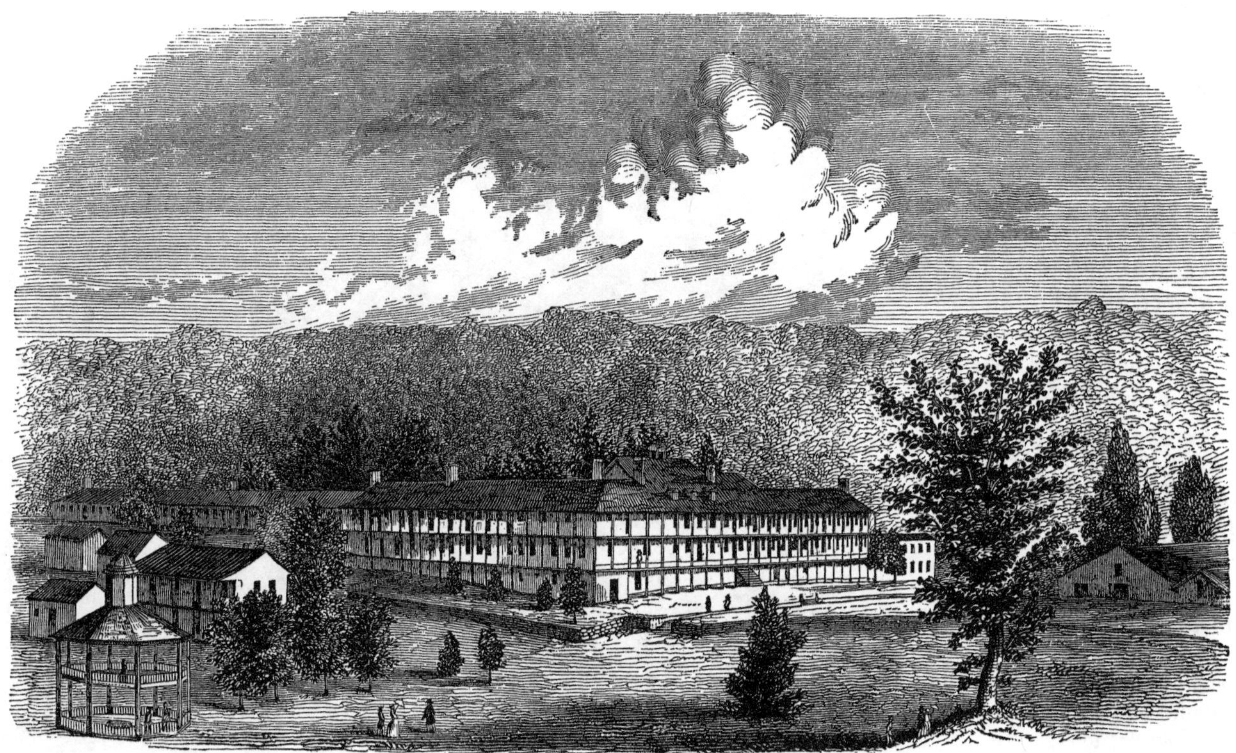

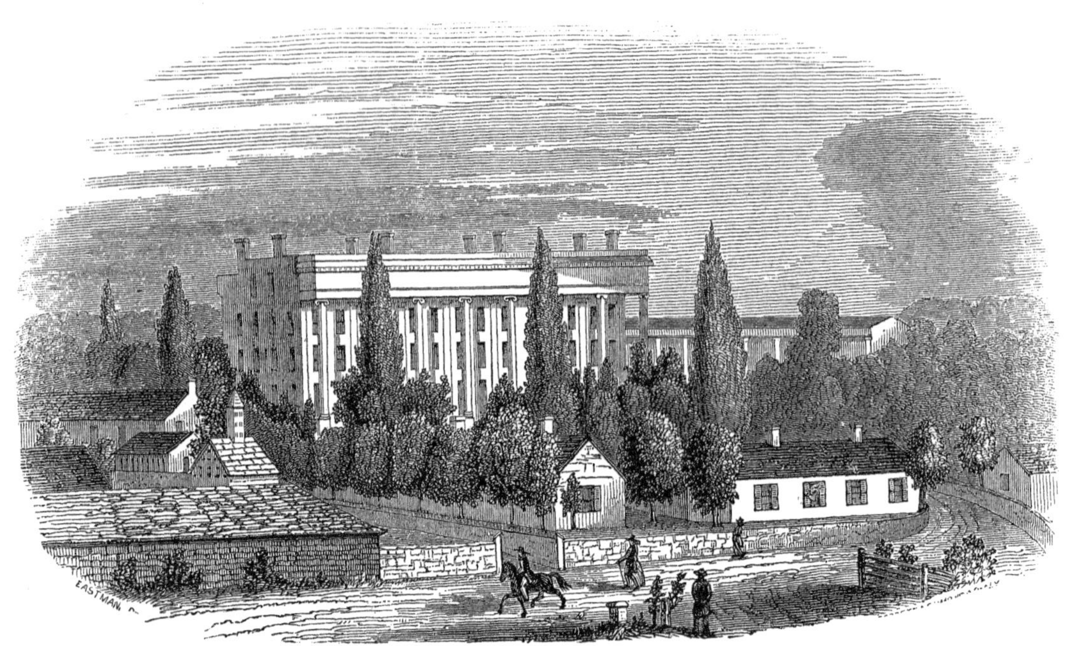

Lewis Collins describes Harrodsburg Springs as one of the most fashionable watering places in the state and says it was deservedly celebrated for the medicinal virtue of the water as well as for being a delightful summer resort. In 1827 Dr. Christopher Columbus Graham purchased the property—then called Sutton Springs—and spent large sums to provide the finest buildings in the west, with extensive and beautiful grounds, wide gravel walks, and a lake well-stocked with fish and enlivened by wild and tame water fowl. In its heyday, the establishment, which could accommodate five hundred visitors, was known as Graham Springs. An Appleton guidebook of 1867 still described it as "the grand field of tournament for western flirtation and the gathering point for politicians out of harness."

Wood engraving from Lewis Collins's *Historical Sketches of Kentucky,* 1847. Engraved by Benjamin or Cephas Childs from a drawing probably by Harrison Eastman.

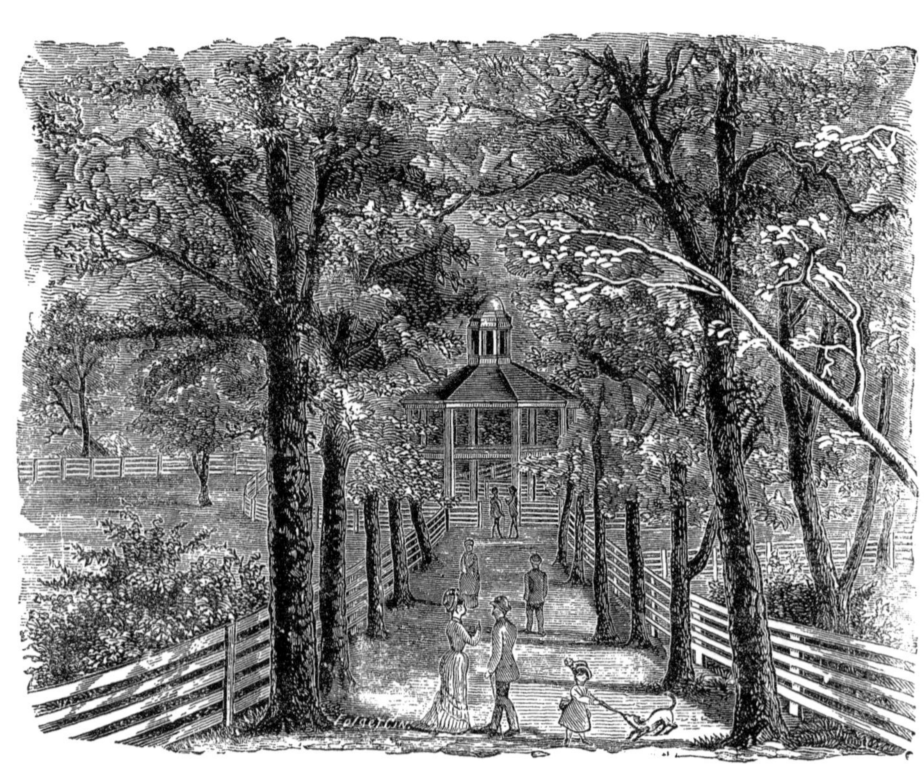

Transportation companies promoted springs to increase their own business. In 1889 the Kentucky Central Railway brochure noted that the water from Blue Lick Springs must be consumed at the site of the spring for it to have any effect. Those seeking a cure were required to drink the water fresh in order to derive the full benefit of odor and flavor as well as of its gaseous qualities, "which escape in great bubbles."

Wood engraving from the Kentucky Central Railway's *Guide to the Blue Grass Regions of Kentucky,* 1889.

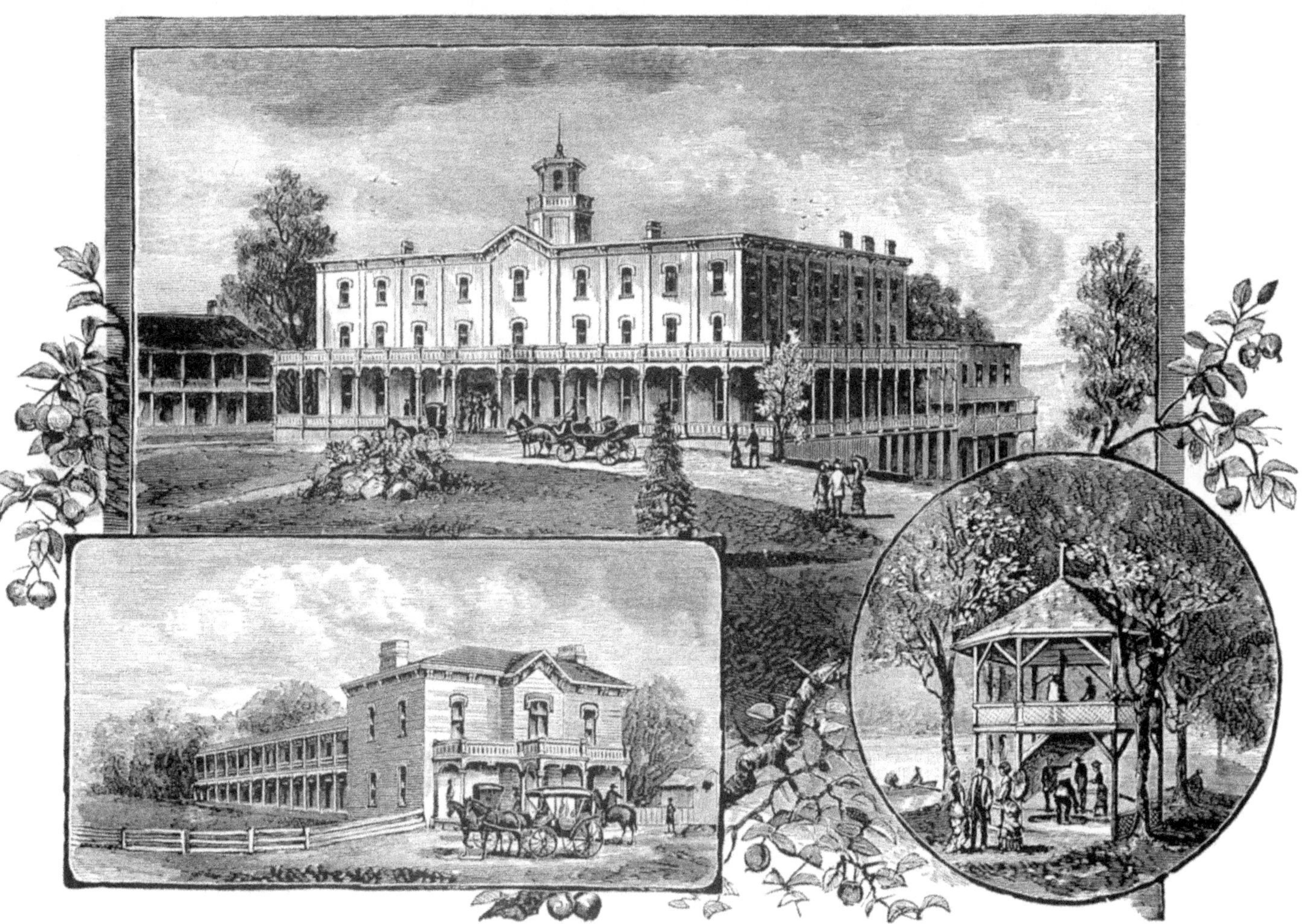

Richard Collins stated that Crab Orchard Springs had been one of the most popular watering places in the state for forty years. The hotel burned in 1871 but new owners rebuilt immediately and soon added a large and handsome brick building that provided 250 rooms heated by steam and lighted by gas. The building was used during the scholastic year as a boarding school for girls. The promotional comments published with this 1887 view stated that when the establishment was bought in 1882 by three men of Louisville, they "completely reformed it, making such changes as justify those acquainted with the resort in calling it the 'Saratoga of the south.'" It offered "good fare, numerous amusements, a fine orchestra, and courteous attention," as well as water from an American epsom spring that had "no counterpart in this country."

Wood engraving from the Louisville Board of Trade's *The City of Louisville and a Glimpse of Kentucky,* 1887.

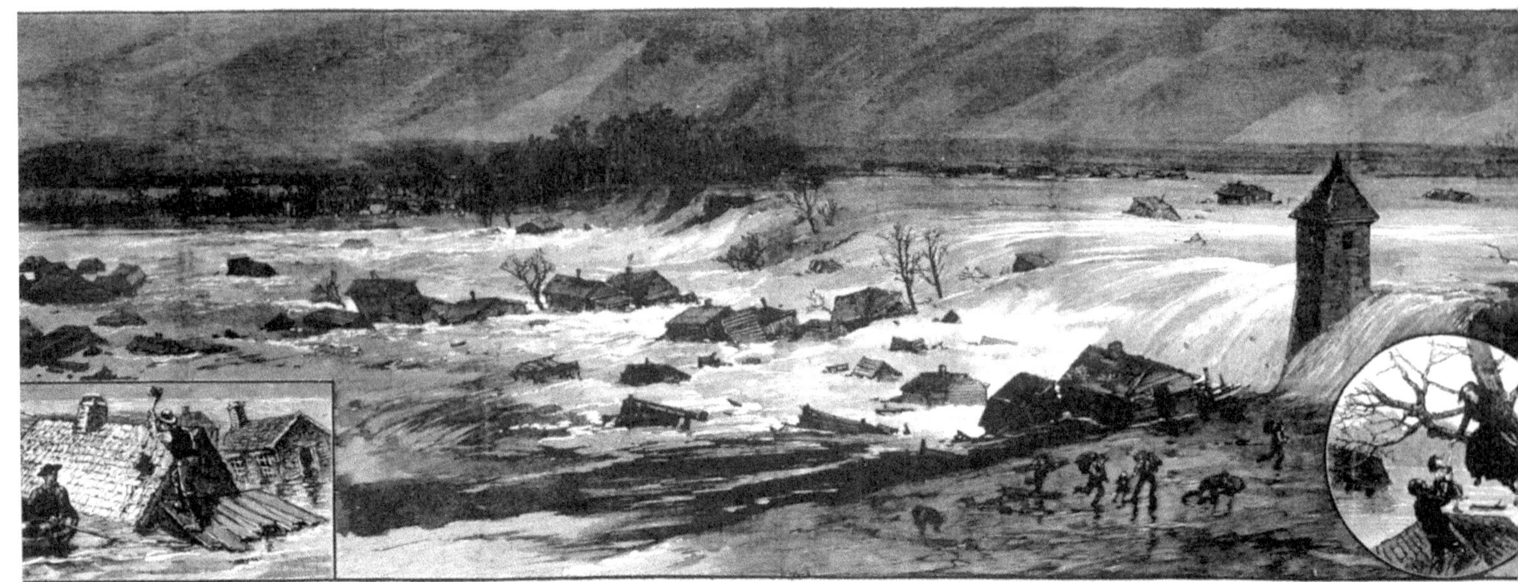

History records a number of Ohio River floods or freshets that did significant damage to settlements and properties along the river, such as this one in which the embankment at Louisville was broken. On February 16, 1883, the river reached the highest point ever recorded up to that time—44.5 feet above the low water mark. Just a year later this record was exceeded by more than two feet.

Wood engraving from *Harper's Weekly*, March 5, 1883, from a drawing by W.F. Clarke.

On March 27, 1890, about 8 P.M., heavy rain and high winds swept through the western district of Louisville in the company of a tornado that left death and ruin in its wake. It cut a swath about six blocks wide as far east as the Louisville Hotel on Main Street between Sixth and Seventh streets, crossed the river to Jeffersonville, then recrossed and blew down the water company's stand-pipe tower. Seventy-five people were killed and many were injured. Over five hundred dwellings and many major buildings were damaged or destroyed, including the Union Station and twenty-one passenger coaches, five churches, two public halls, three school buildings, thirty-two manufacturing establishments, and ten tobacco warehouses. Total damage was estimated at $2,500,000. (Additional views on next three pages.)

Wood engraving from *Frank Leslie's Illustrated Newspaper*, April 5, 1890.

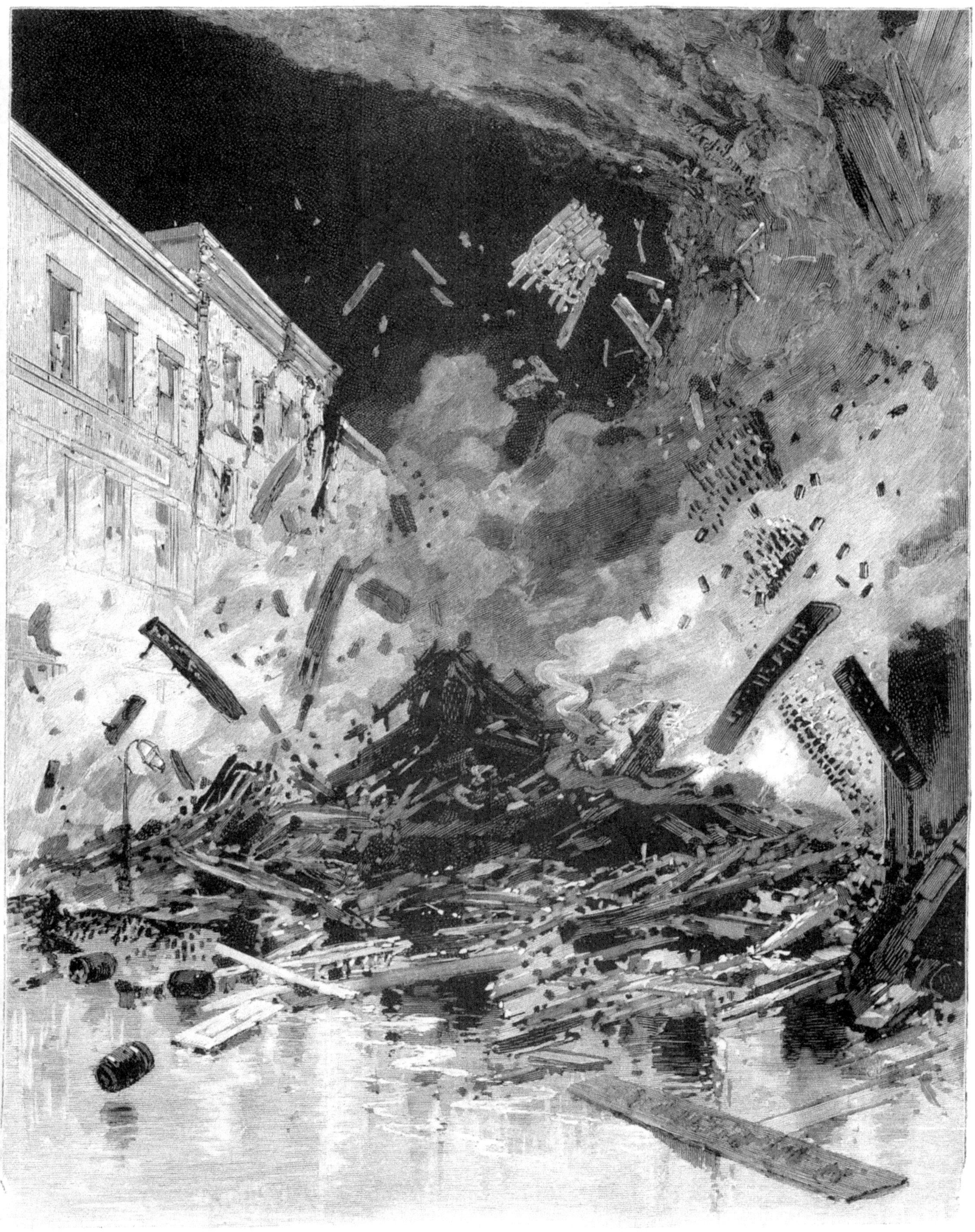

Wood engraving from *Harper's Weekly*, April 12, 1890.

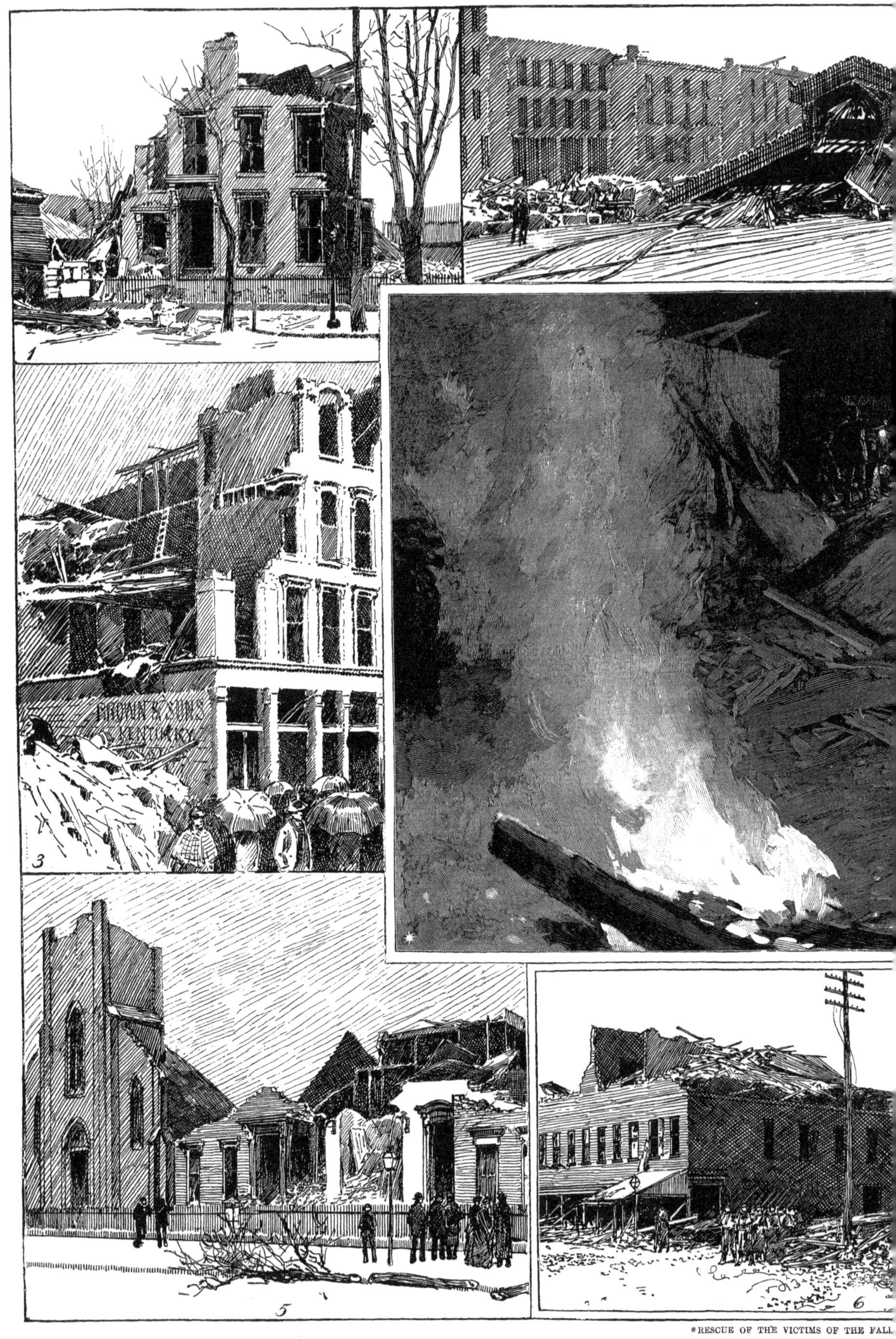

*RESCUE OF THE VICTIMS OF THE FALL

THE WORK OF THE TORNADO AT LOUIS

1. Residence of Dr. Griffith. 2. Wreck of the Union Depot. 3. Northeast Corner of Eight and Main Streets. 4. Ware

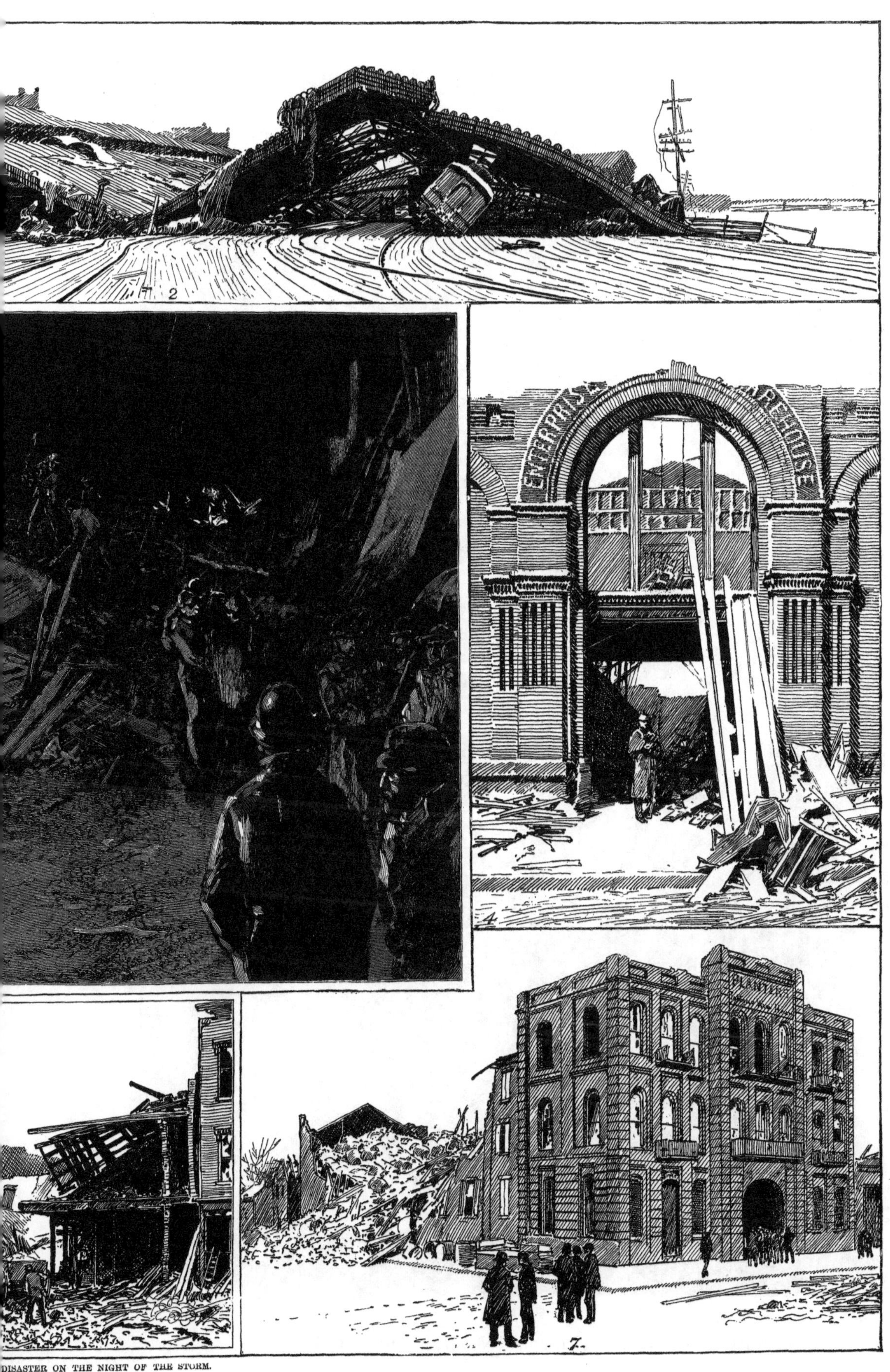

DISASTER ON THE NIGHT OF THE STORM.

ENTUCKY.—Drawn by H. F. Farny.—[See Page 289.]

Street. 5. St. John's Church and Parsonage. 6. Corner of Eleventh and Market Streets. 7. Warehouses on Main Street.

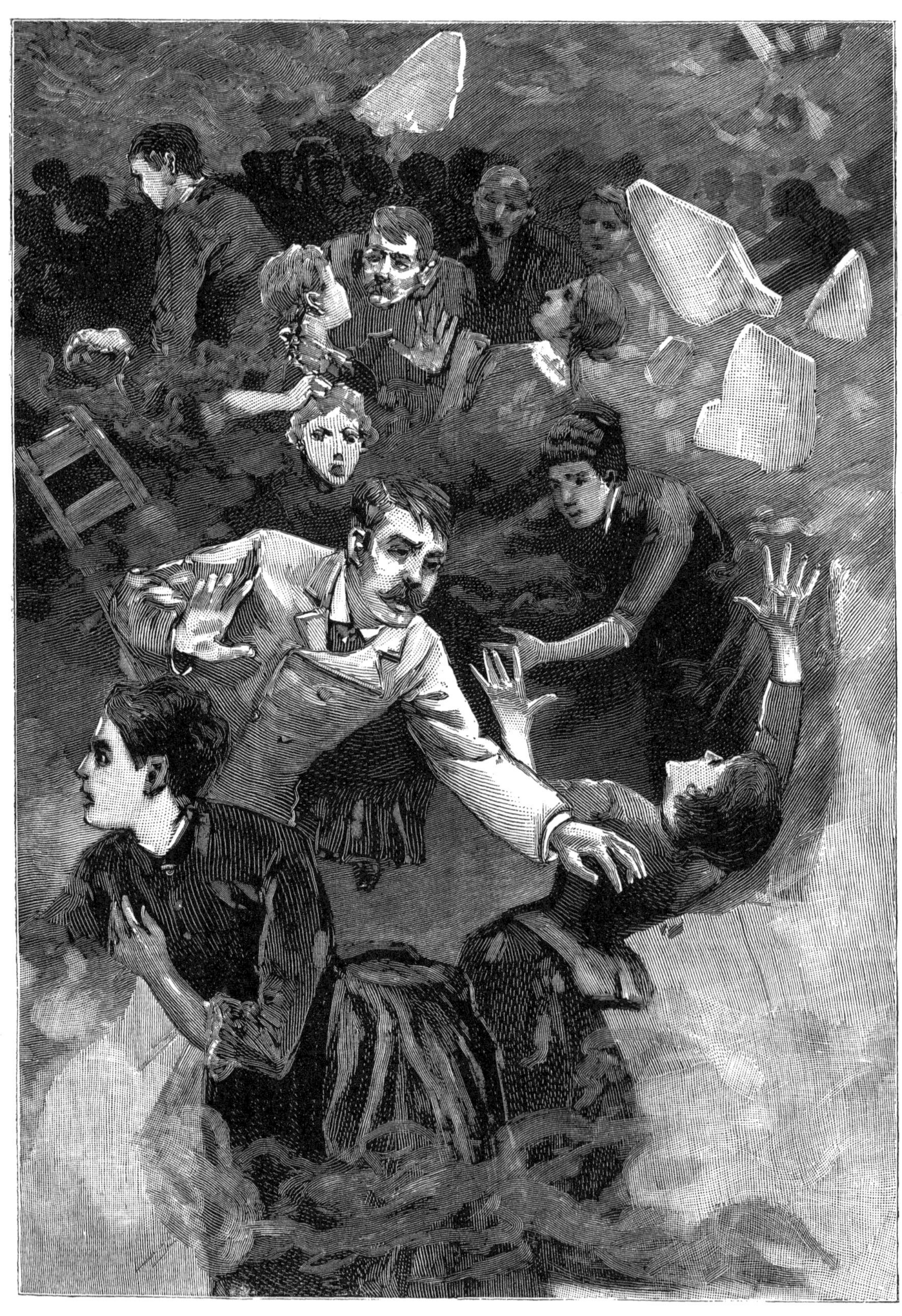

Wood engraving from *Frank Leslie's Illustrated Newspaper,* April 5, 1890.

THREE

Making a Living

From the very beginning of its settlement by colonists from beyond the mountains, Kentucky was viewed as a place of great promise. Accounts of this new region of virgin land praised its vast forests, huge animal herds, and extensive grasslands. A young George Rogers Clark proclaimed "a richer and more Beautiful cuntry than this I believe has never been seen in America yet." Driven by this vision, by the "Kentucky myth of plenty," people surged to the state. Within fifteen years of its first settlement, the region had over seventy thousand inhabitants. By 1830, it was seventh in population among all the states and had become an important part of the American system.

Not all those entering Kentucky found wealth and riches. But many did as the commonwealth became a major producer of agricultural goods. By 1840, Kentucky was the nation's chief provider of hemp, used in rope and cotton bagging. The state stood first in wheat production, second in tobacco, second in maize, third in flax, and fourth in rye. Its number of swine and mules placed it second nationally. Kentucky's reputation as a home for fine Thoroughbreds, as well as other purebred stock, was already firmly established. Kentucky's citizens, in short, were part of a prosperous agrarian world.

But as the United States became increasingly urbanized and industrialized, particularly after the Civil War, Kentucky struggled to maintain its prosperity and population. Even though the state's industrial production increased nearly 70 percent in the decade after 1880 and another 20 percent in the decade following that, such seemingly broad advances actually fell below the growing nation's figures for those years. Still, for Kentuckians working at new businesses and new enterprises across the commonwealth, the statistics meant little. They only knew that new services—drug stores, hotels, and the like—and more industry, such as iron furnaces, woolen mills, and distilleries, offered alternative and often more lucrative opportunities for making a living.

Even though these new hopes of eager entrepreneurs increasingly dotted the Kentucky countryside, overall the state remained predominantly agricultural. The introduction of the new burley tobacco after the Civil War brought farmers to rely more on that one crop and to become dependent on its vagaries of price. Major attempts to change the agrarian ethos of Kentucky did take place, and whole new towns—such as Middlesboro—planned as major industrial centers represented attempts in that direction. And in town after town, some major business did succeed and grow.

But only Louisville experienced the widespread and broad development envisioned by many of the state's urban areas. Growing prosperous during the Civil War, becoming a railroad center, developing a large trade to the devastated South in the postwar era, Louisville doubled in population in a thirty-year period, to two hundred thousand by 1900. With its chief manufacturing in metal and woodworking, it also boasted the largest plow factory in the world, the largest producer of jeans cloth, the largest dry goods store in the South, the textbook company that was "publisher to the lost cause," and much else. By the 1890s, the Falls City led nationally in the marketing of tobacco and was important in the distillery trade, bringing its famed editor Henry Watterson to proclaim, "A union of pork, tobacco, and whisky will make us all wealthy, healthy, and frisky."

To present that prosperity, if not that attitude, to the region and the nation, the city supported various expositions, including major ones in 1872 and 1880 and the massive Southern Exposition, begun in 1883 and continued for the next four years. Louisville's Board of Trade remained active as well, and illustrators caught much of the spirit of the burgeoning city. Yet seldom did artists notice the laboring class, who often struggled mightily to make ends meet. An occasional view of a farm laborer, a blacksmith, or a waiter only hinted at the lives of those who worked important but often forgotten jobs. They toiled in obscurity.

What the illustrations did suggest was the wealth of an important nineteenth-century state, one struggling to find its identity in a rapidly changing world, one torn between an agrarian and an industrial ethos. Yet the people who inhabited that state and that world worked to make a comfortable living so that future generations could build on their success. In a new century, their descendants would seek to do just that.

—J.C.K.

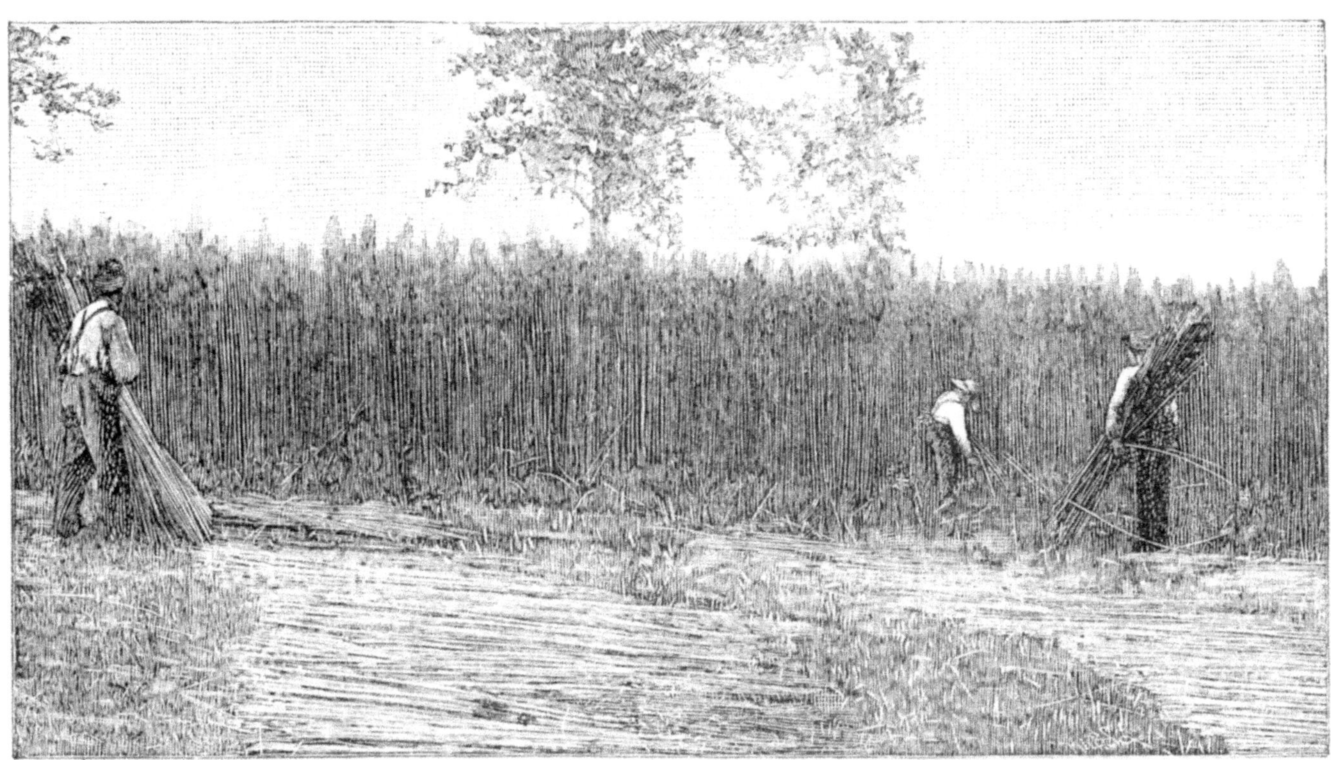

For years, hemp was the primary crop of many Kentucky farmers, and the state led the nation in production of hemp for much of the nineteenth century. Because of increased international competition and declining hemp markets, burley tobacco production eventually replaced hemp as Kentucky's most popular cash crop.

Wood engraving from Allen's *The Blue-Grass Region of Kentucky*, 1892.

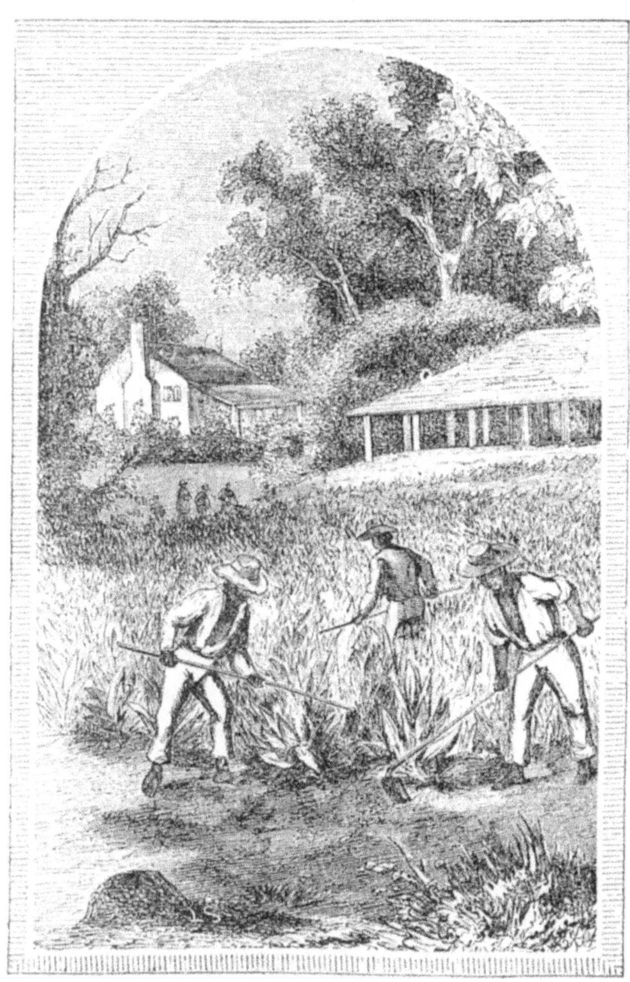

The location of this tobacco plantation is described as western Kentucky in the Green River country. In 1870, Daviess and Henderson counties were the leading producers of tobacco in the state. In that year Kentucky produced nearly half of all the tobacco in the United States, supplying more than Virginia, which had held first position in tobacco until upheavals associated with the Civil War brought about a great decline there. In the 1870s, other western Kentucky counties such as Christian, Caldwell, Hardin, Hopkins, Muhlenberg, and Ohio produced large amounts of tobacco.

Wood engraving from Howe's *Our Whole Country*, 1861.

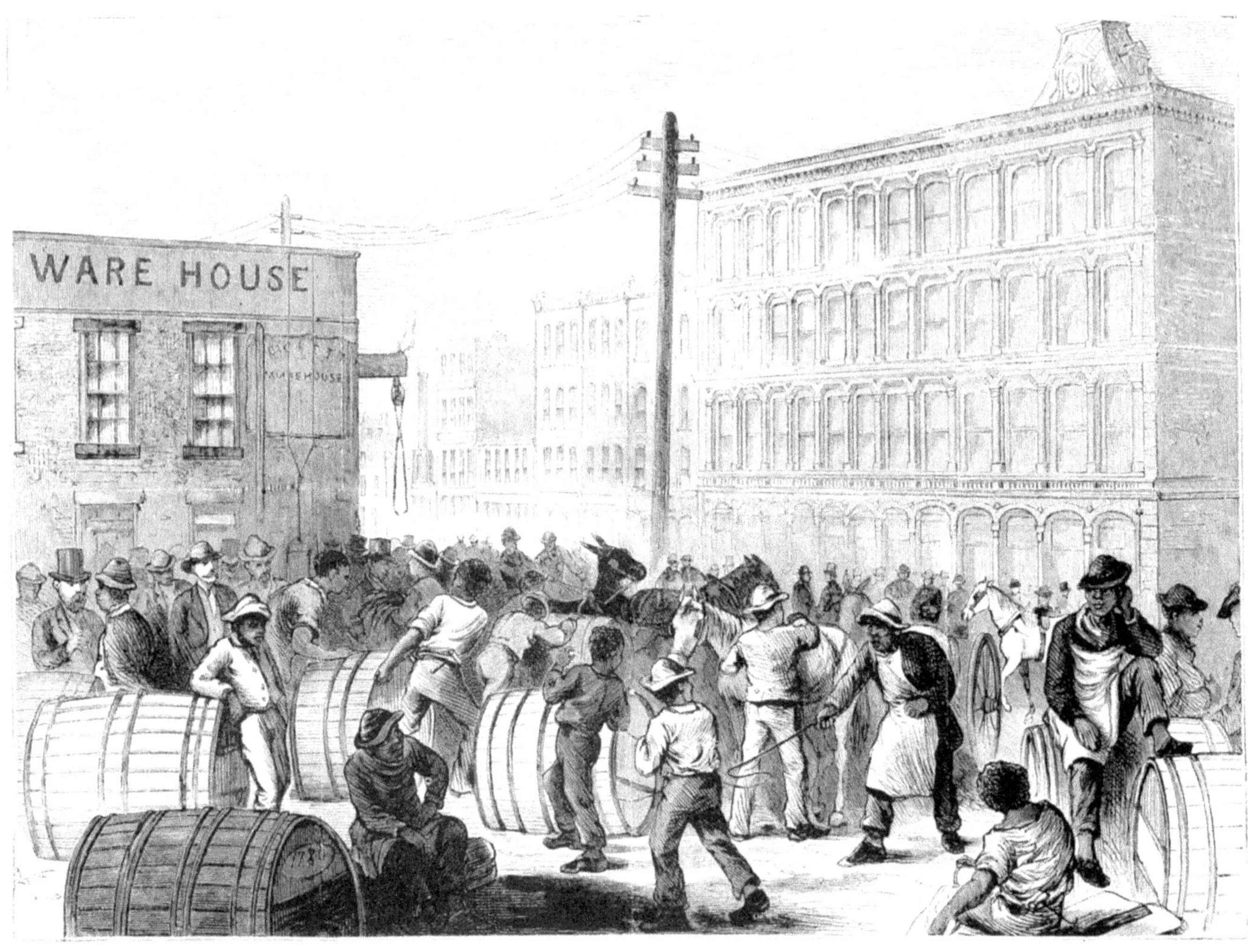

This view shows hogsheads (barrels) outside a tobacco warehouse in Louisville being loaded onto drays. In 1873, ten major tobacco warehouses operated in Louisville; seven of them were neighbors on Main Street between Eighth and Twelfth streets. In that year, fifty-three thousand hogsheads were sold through the Louisville warehouses, the highest sales total in the city up to that time. By 1885, this figure had doubled, and during the years 1865–1900 Kentucky was the leading state in tobacco production. The building at the left, identified as the Pickett warehouse, is still in use at Eighth and Main streets. The warehouse company was organized in 1852 and remained active into the twentieth century. In 1892, its sales of 24,048 hogsheads was the largest number of any warehouse in the world in one year.

Wood engraving from *Frank Leslie's Illustrated Newspaper,* May 10, 1873, from a drawing by George Kerr, Jr.

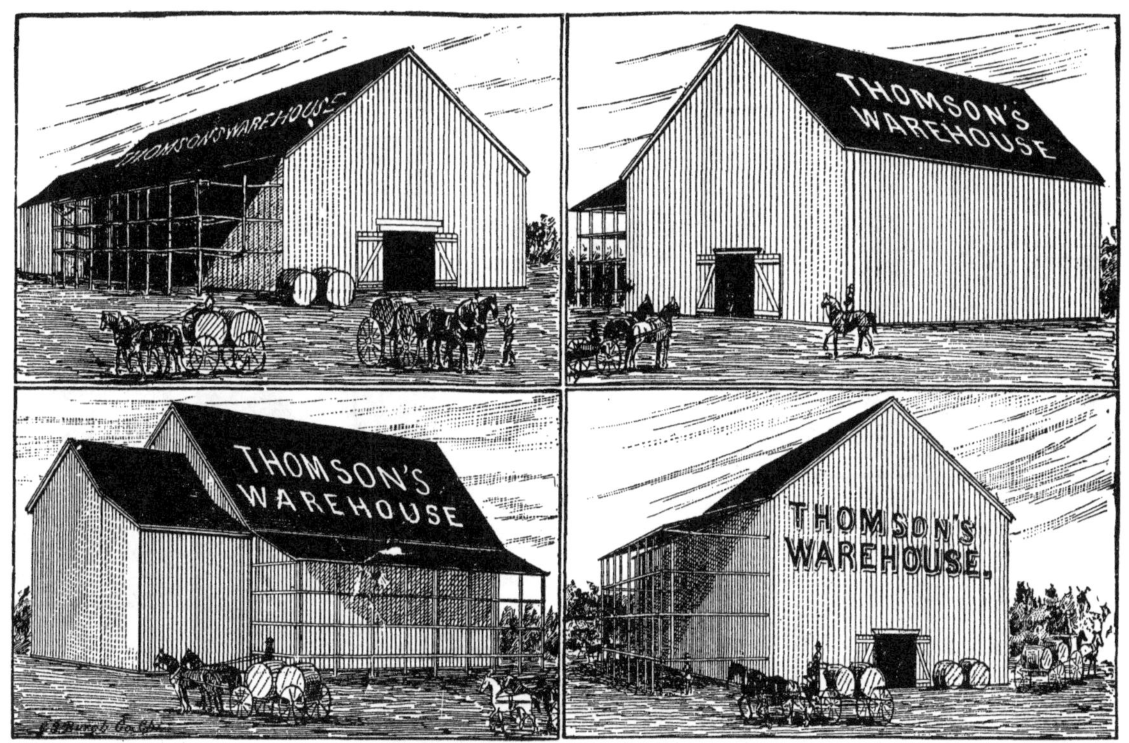

By 1880, H.P. Thomson grew white burley tobacco on sixty-five acres near Thomson Station in the eastern part of the county. He was said to be the largest single tobacco dealer in the state at that time.

Wood engravings from *Handbook of Clark County and the City of Winchester,* 1889.

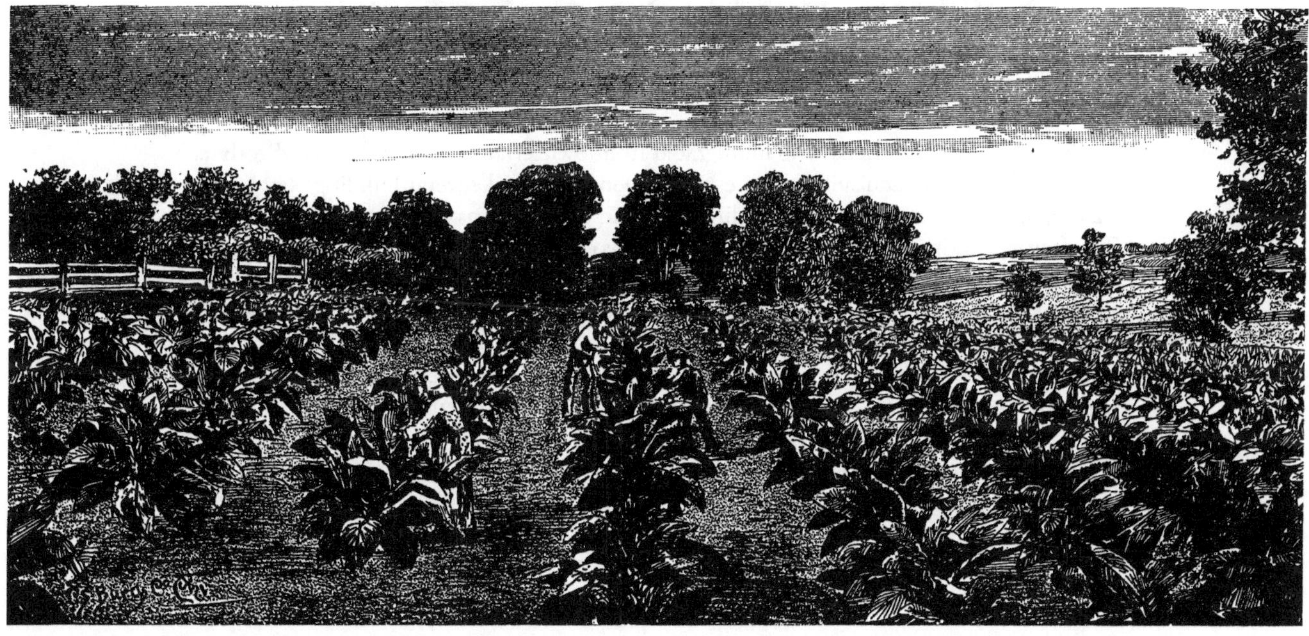

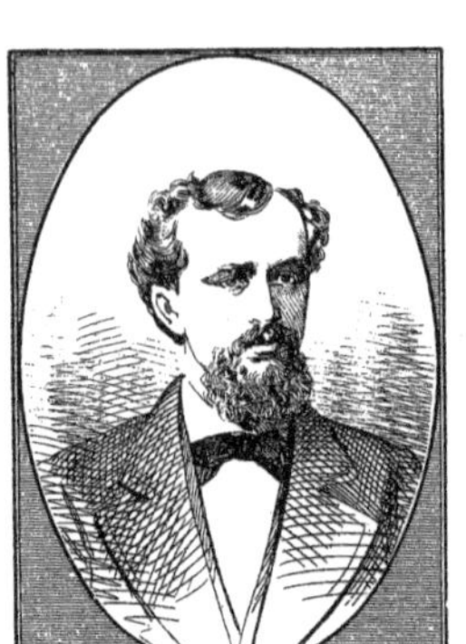

RUDOLPH FINZER.

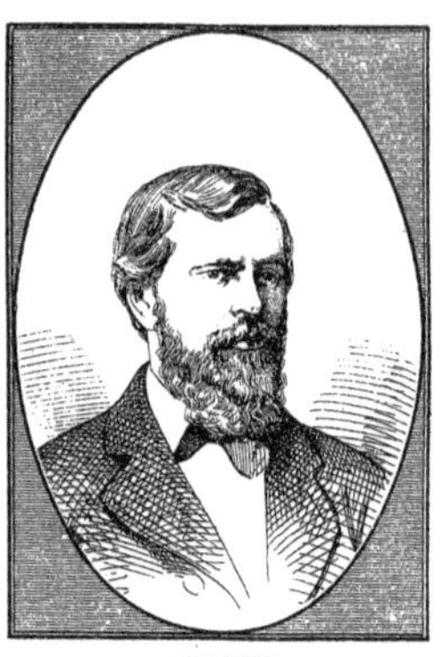

BEN FINZER.

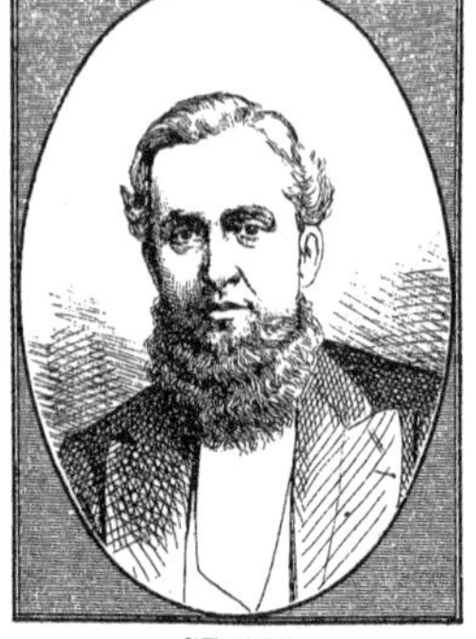

JOHN FINZER.

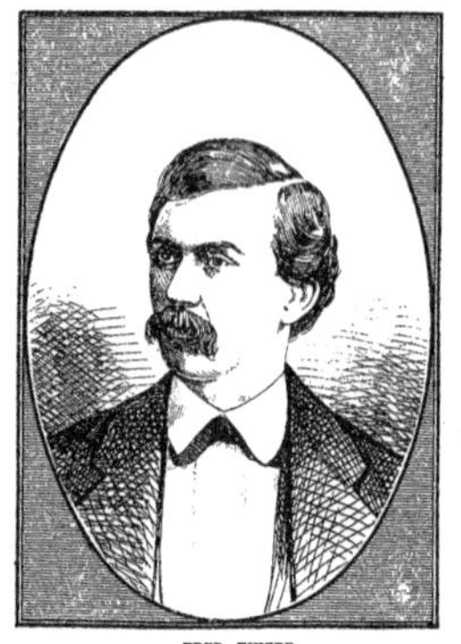

FRED. FINZER.

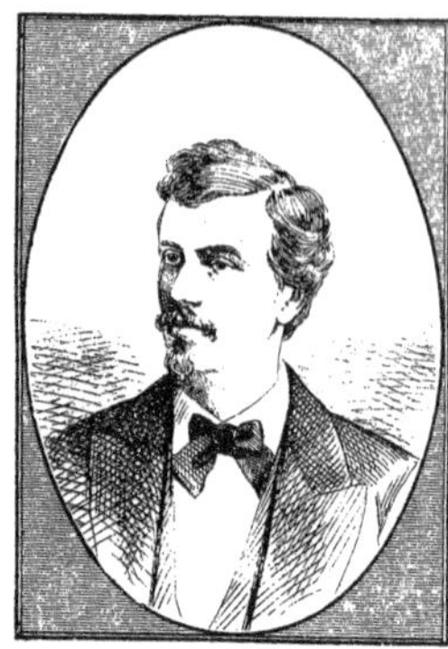

NICHOLAS FINZER.

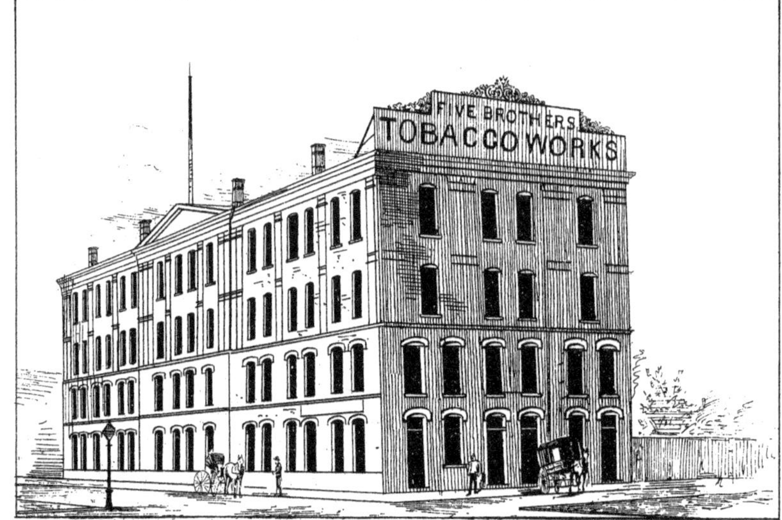

In 1866 the Finzer brothers, who immigrated from Switzerland, started the Five Brothers Tobacco Factory in Louisville. The establishment occupied several buildings on Jacob, Laurel, and Jackson streets. The building shown in this view was destroyed by fire in 1880. The factory continued in temporary quarters for two years while being rebuilt at the old site, and one of those later buildings is still in use as a furniture warehouse. A description of the business published in 1887 claims that by then it had reached a production of four million pounds of plug tobacco annually—in sixteen ounce plugs or blocks—and one million pounds of smoking tobacco; this made Five Brothers the leading tobacco manufacturer in the city. They employed six hundred "men, women, and children."

Wood engraving from *The Daily Graphic,* New York, April 18, 1875.

Kentuckians were proud of their fine livestock and sought to recognize superior husbandry. In 1841 Dr. Samuel D. Martin of Colbyville, a noted physician in Clark County for much of the nineteenth century, wrote to the editors of *The Cultivator* to describe Belmont, his nine-month-old Woburn pig. According to Martin, this breed was "gentle and docile in disposition, not disposed to be restless or to get out of enclosures."

Wood engraving from Gaylord and Tucker's *The Cultivator*, 1841.

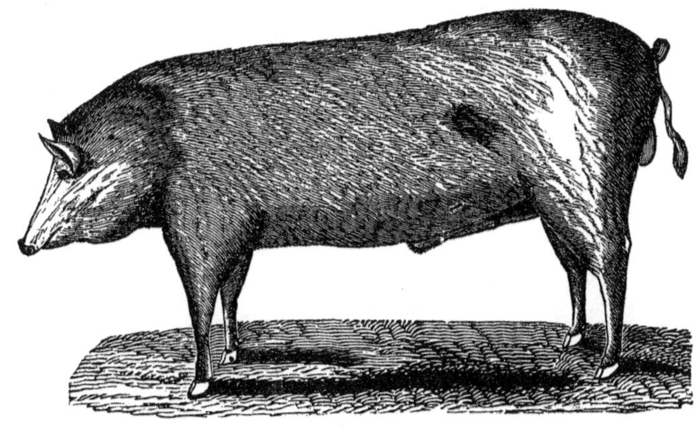

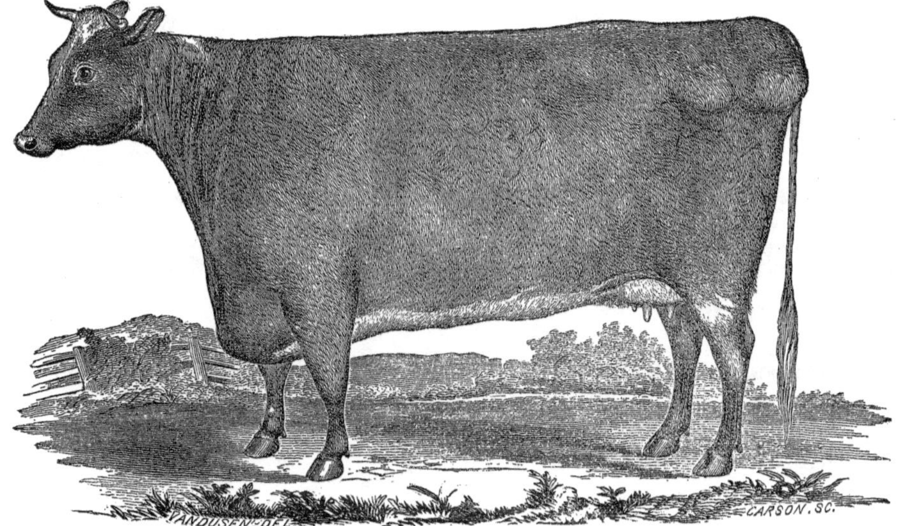

Lady Gage, a red and white cow imported by Searight and Wilson of Cincinnati, was owned by Robert and John Cunningham, Jr., of Bourbon County, sons of a county magistrate, state legislator, and noted turfman. John, Jr., was born in 1820 and gave his attention to farming and breeding shorthorn cattle.

Wood engraving from *Second Report of the Kentucky State Agricultural Society*, 1860. Engraved by Carson from a drawing by Robert Vandusen.

This yearling buck and two-year-old ewe were bred by Robert W. Scott of Locust Hill in Franklin County. Scott was one of the more progressive farmers and animal breeders of the Bluegrass. For the report of the U.S. commissioner of agriculture for 1866, he wrote of his many years of crossbreeding Southdown, Cotswold, Merino, and other sheep to enhance desired qualities and create the "Improved Kentucky" type.

Wood engraving from *Second Report of the Kentucky State Agricultural Society*, 1860. Engraved by J.W. Orr from a drawing by Robert Vandusen.

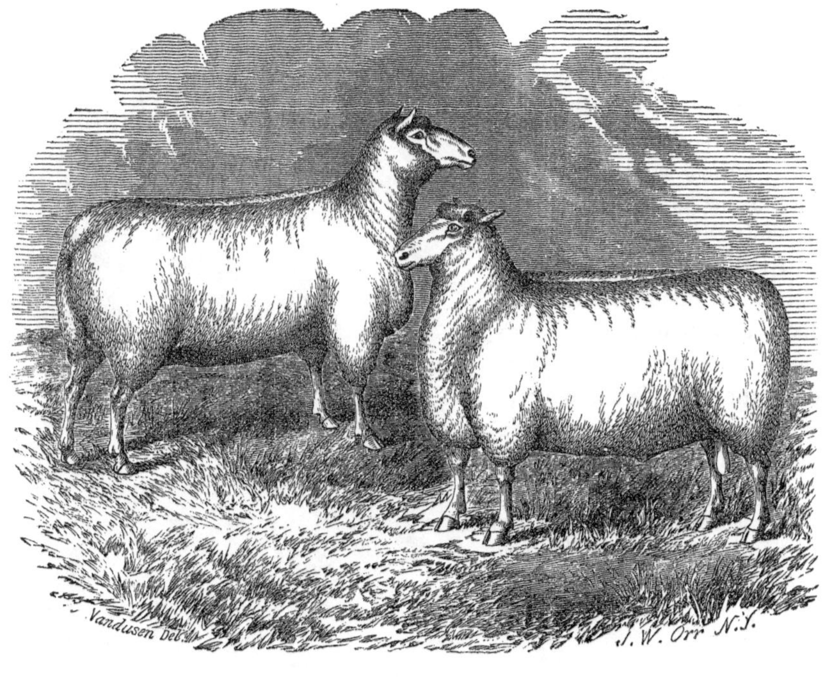

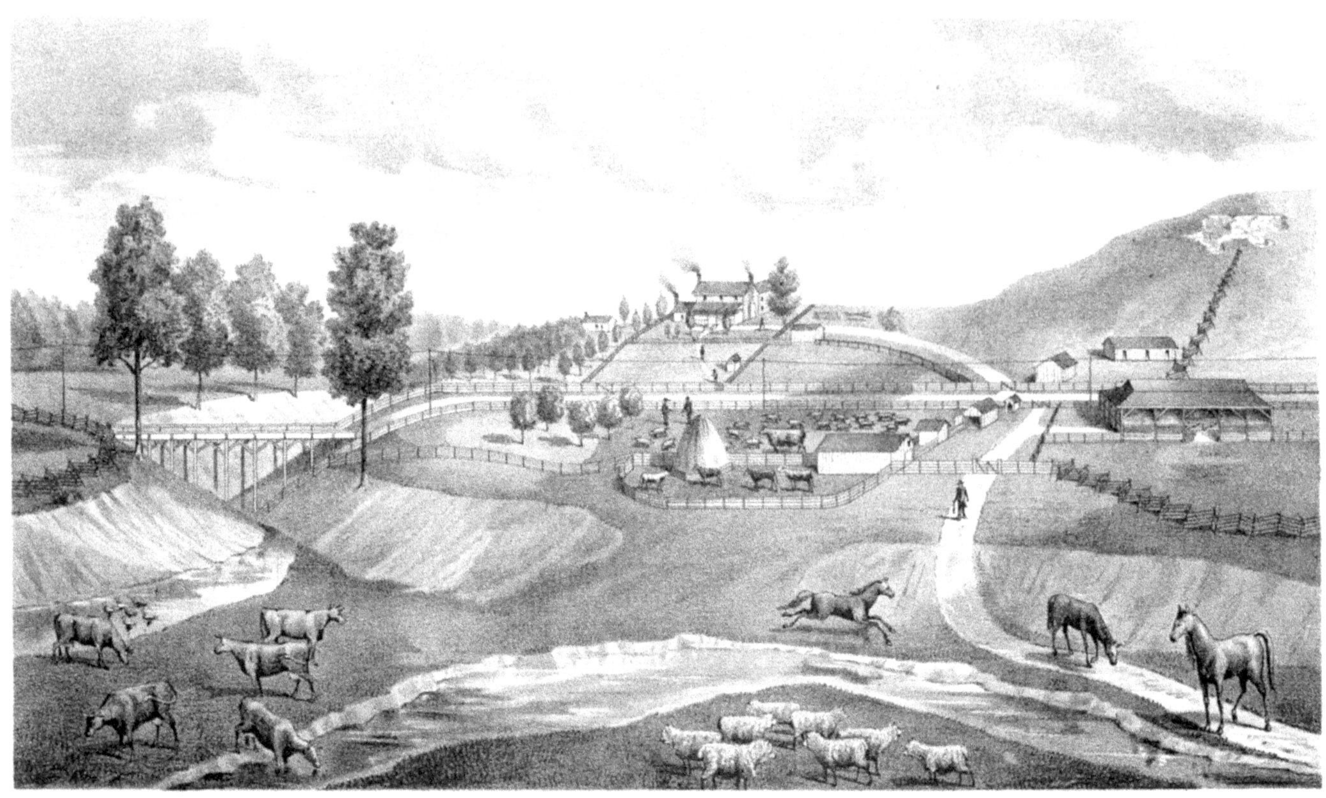

This view of the residence and stock farm of John P. Kinkead of Greenup County suggests the wealth and scope of such farms.

Lithograph from *Illustrated Atlas of the Upper Ohio River Valley,* 1877.

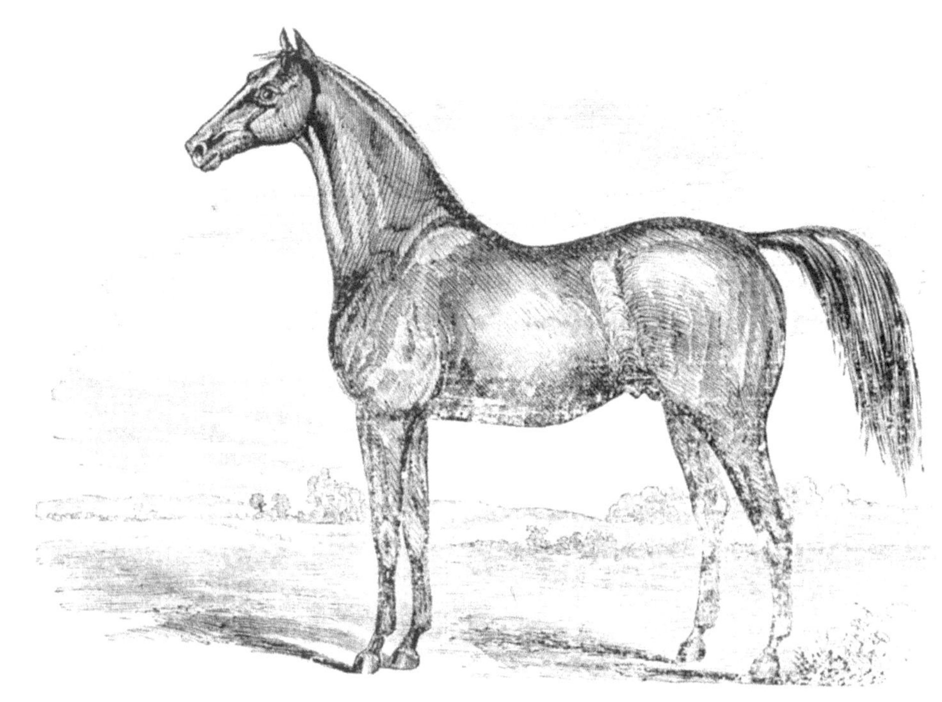

Revenue was awarded the first premium for Thoroughbred stallions four years and older at the fourth annual fair of the Agricultural Society at Lexington, September 1859. The horse was owned by Abraham Buford of Woodford County, a West Point graduate, a farmer, and a producer of race horses. Buford served the Confederacy as a brigadier general and was a state legislator in 1877–1888.

Wood engraving from *Second Report of the Kentucky State Agricultural Society,* 1860.

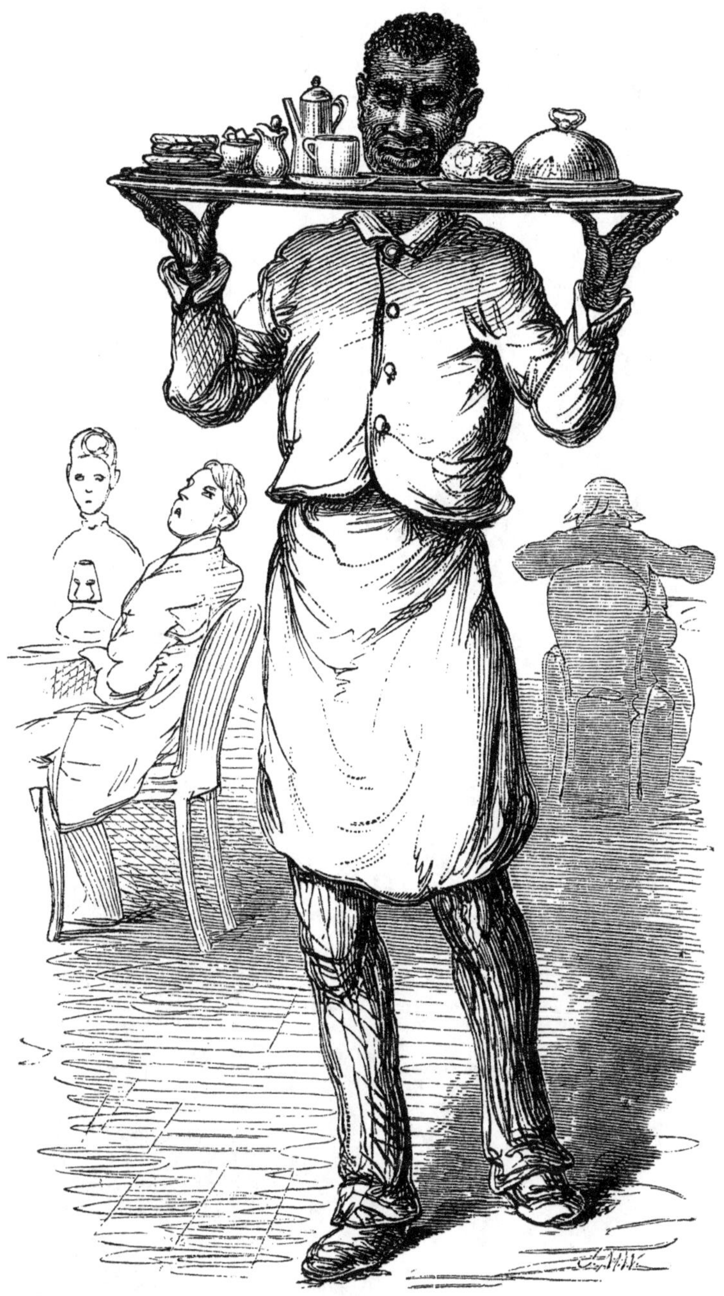

Blacks seldom captured the interest of artists of the time, and if they appeared in illustrations, they were usually secondary figures. This waiter at the Galt House was one of the "forgotten people" who were rarely depicted by artists as they went about their menial but important jobs. The Galt House—at its two locations on Main Street in Louisville—was the outstanding hostelry of Louisville between 1835 and 1921. Its earliest building at Second and Main streets was rebuilt before the Civil War and destroyed by fire in 1865. The second location was at First and Main streets.

Wood engraving from *Scribner's Monthly,* December 1874, from a drawing by J. Wells Champney, Deerfield, Mass., and New York.

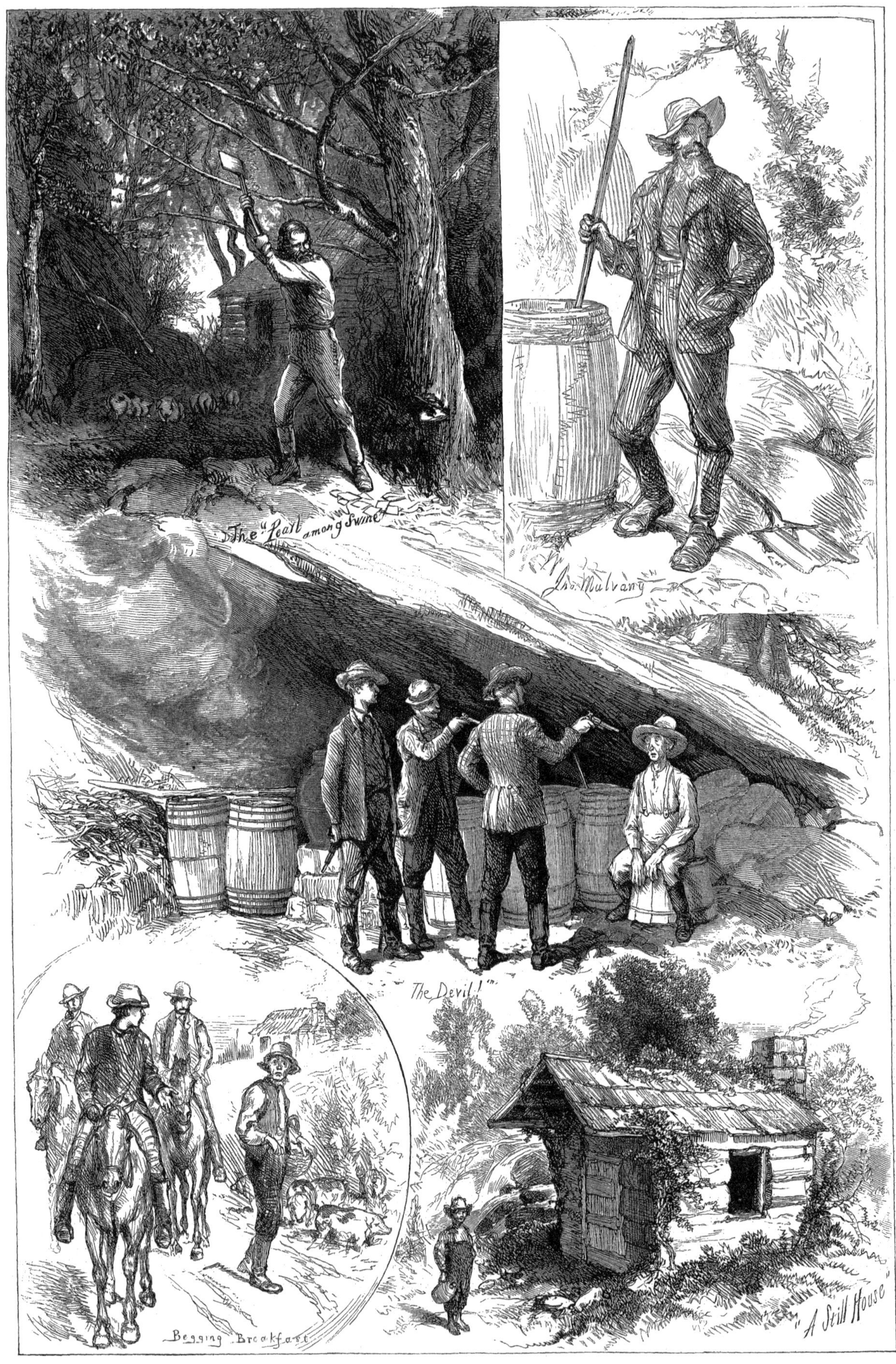
The "Pearl among Swine"
Jno. Mulvany
"The Devil!"
Begging Breakfast
"A Still House"

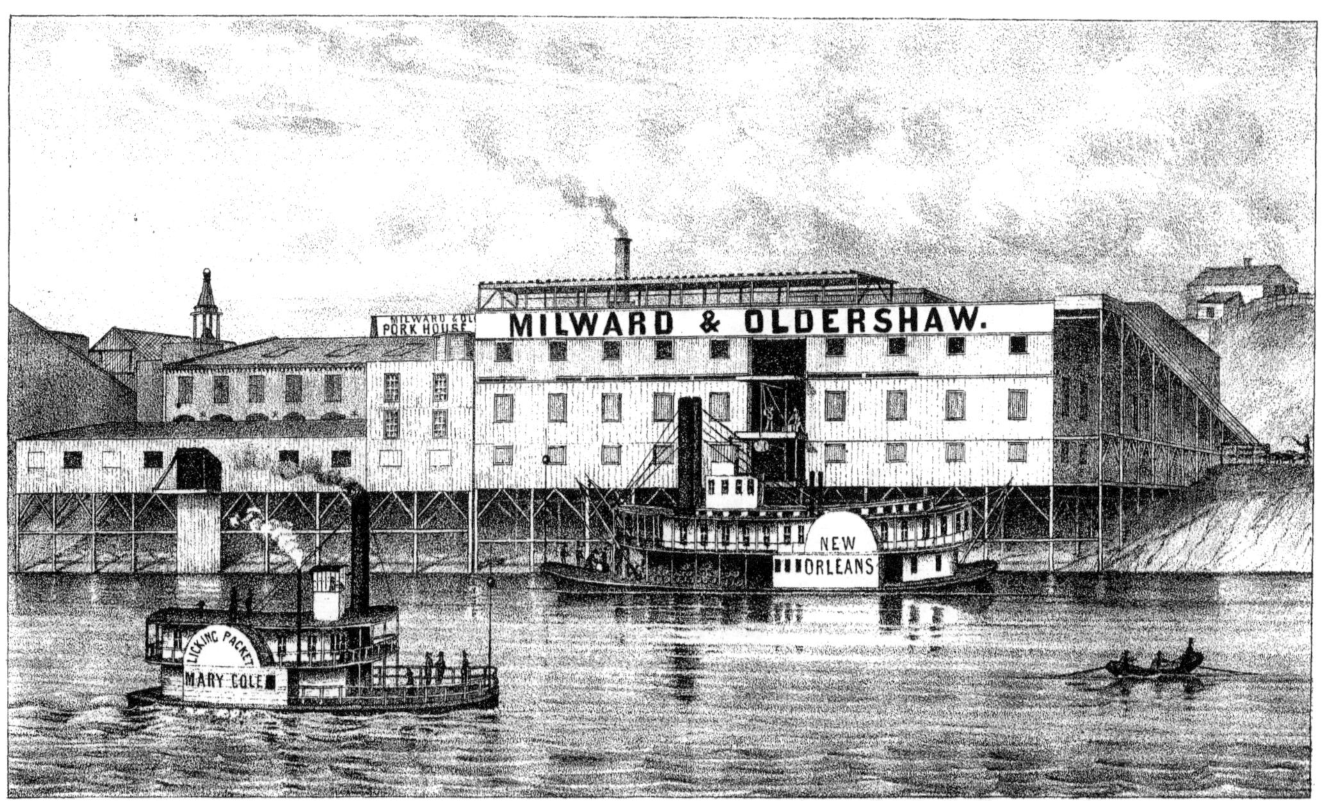

Kentucky's pioneers cured meat for commercial trade in the early years when buffalo was their raw material. Dried and salted pork became important exports in the early 1800s, and in the first half of the nineteenth century, Cincinnati and its vicinity became the principal source in the West for packed meat. The census reports of 1840 and 1850 place Kentucky second among all states in production of swine. The Milward and Oldershaw plant shown here was built in 1848 on the bank of the Licking River between Robbins and Eleventh streets in Covington. For the swine slaughtering season of 1849, which began in October, the firm's two hundred workers handled seven hundred to one thousand head of hogs per day. A laudatory article in the *Covington Journal* in October 1850 states that the hogs were driven up an inclined plane to the top of the building, where pens could hold up to seven thousand animals; the packing processes moved downward through the building from there. It was claimed to be the largest slaughtering and packing house in the nation but operated only a few years before being destroyed by fire.

Lithograph from Cist's *Sketches and Statistics of Cincinnati in 1851,* 1851. Lithograph by Otto Onken, Cincinnati.

Between 1877 and 1881 Internal Revenue agents seized almost five thousand stills and made eight thousand arrests in the moonshine states, but twenty-nine agents were killed and sixty-three were wounded in the effort. An illustrator for *Harper's* sketched these scenes from Hardin County and probably wrote the accompanying article. None of the names of the local residents the writer mentioned appear in the census records. He identified the man shown cutting down a tree with the pigs in the background as Jeems Pearl, therefore "a pearl among swine." The writer's identification of the marshal and the bailiff from Louisville who conducted the raid seems to be authentic. Failure to pay taxes, not the production of moonshine, was illegal in Kentucky. Except for a few years in the late 1700s and early 1800s, whiskey making in America was not taxed until 1862; that was the beginning of the moonshine game of wits that continues to the present.

Wood engraving from *Harper's Weekly,* October 20, 1877.

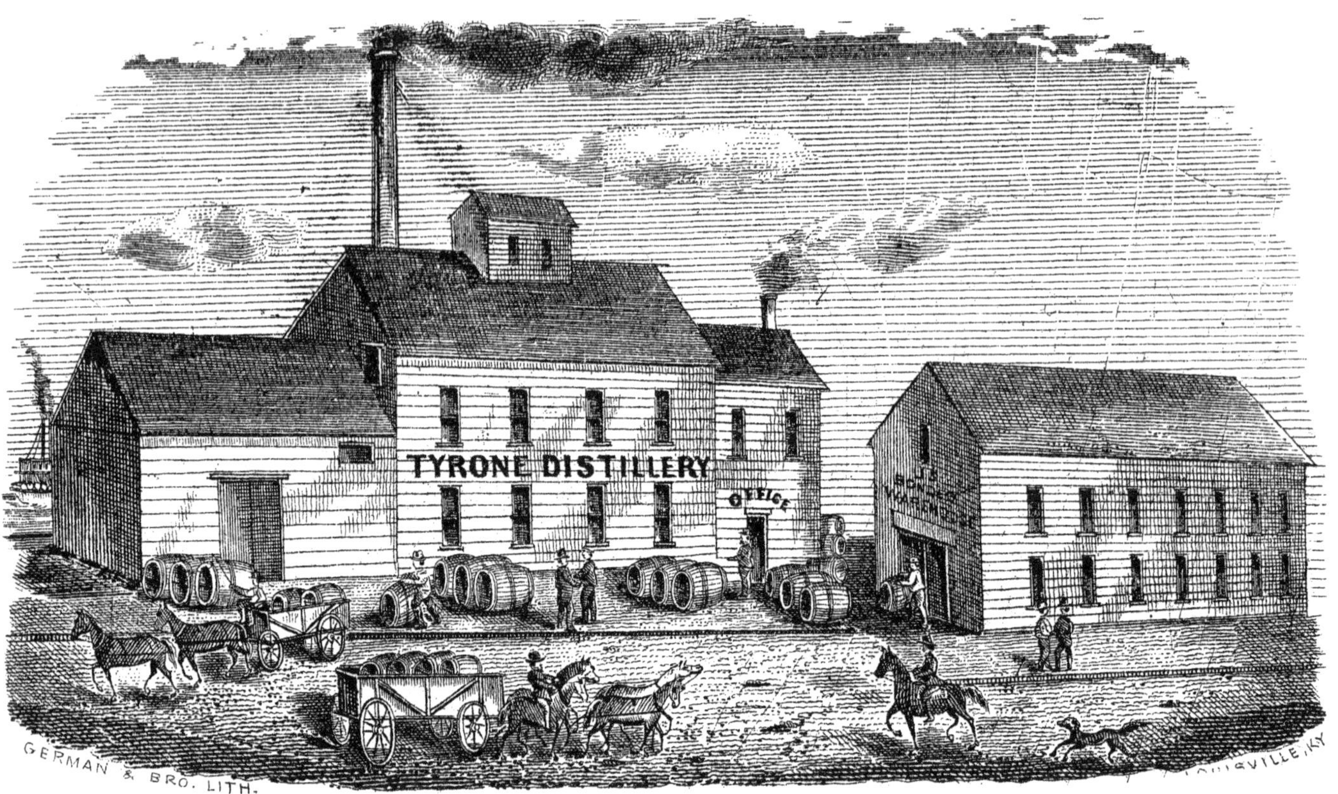

The Tyrone Distillery in Anderson County was established in 1868 by Ripy, Burrell and Company with offices in Louisville. In the late 1890s, according to a history of Anderson County, it was the largest independent sour mash distillery in the world. The distillery was dismantled after passage of the national prohibition act and rebuilt following repeal of that law.

Wood engraving from a letterhead printed by German & Bro. of Louisville, 1870. Engraved by Charles W. or Philip T. German.

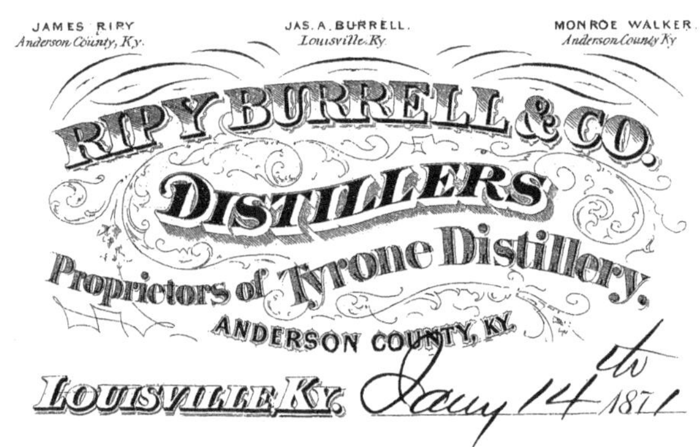

In the 1860s and 1870s Edmund H. Taylor, Jr., built three distilleries in Frankfort, including the Hermitage Distillery shown in this view. It stood on the Kentucky River between Second and Cross streets and included a manufacturing department, a cooperage, and seven warehouses. In the 1870s, the distillery was purchased by Gaines and Company, the makers of Old Crow whiskey. It was closed during the period of national prohibition and reopened thereafter only to make barrels.

Wood engraving from *The Daily Graphic,* New York, January 16, 1880.

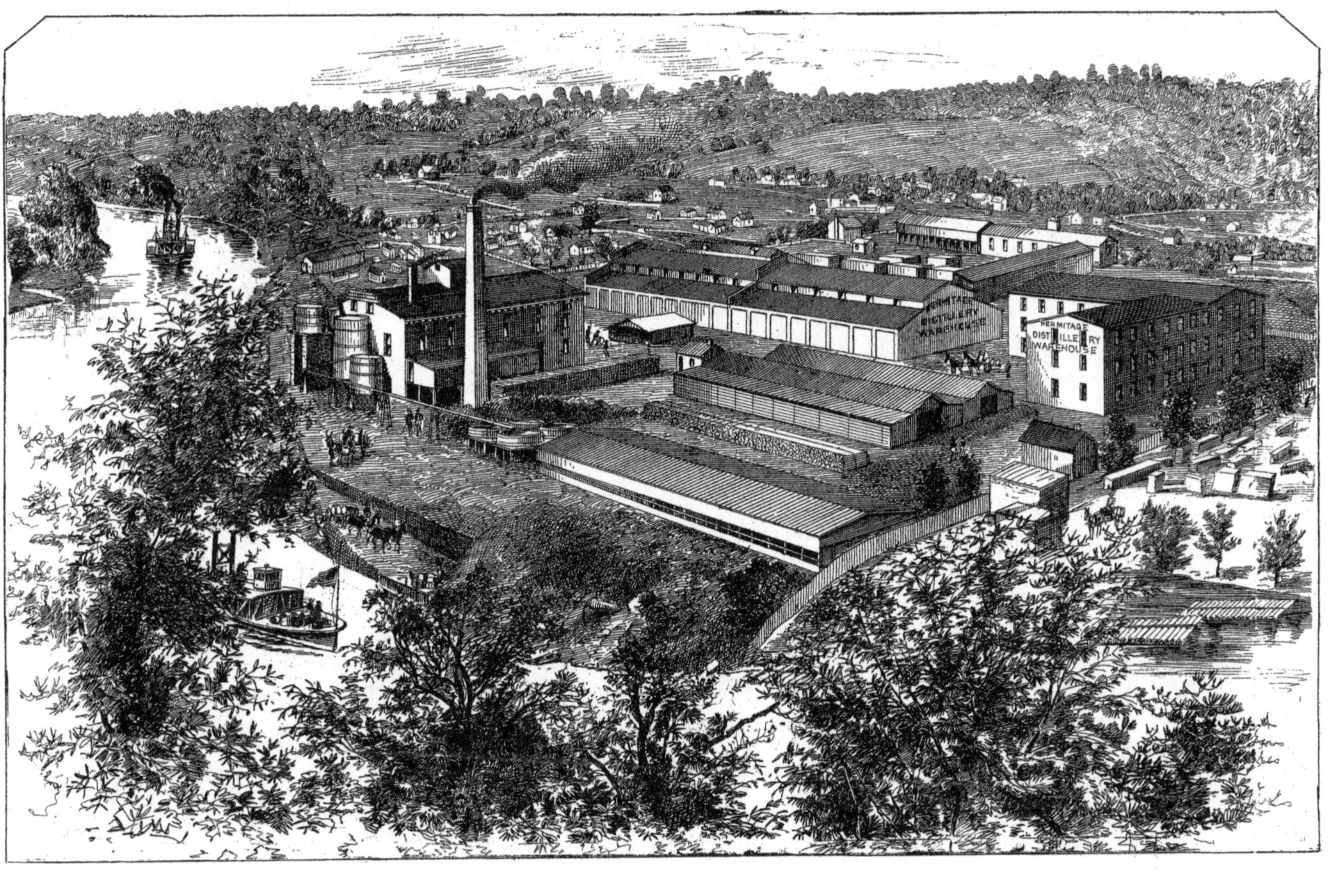

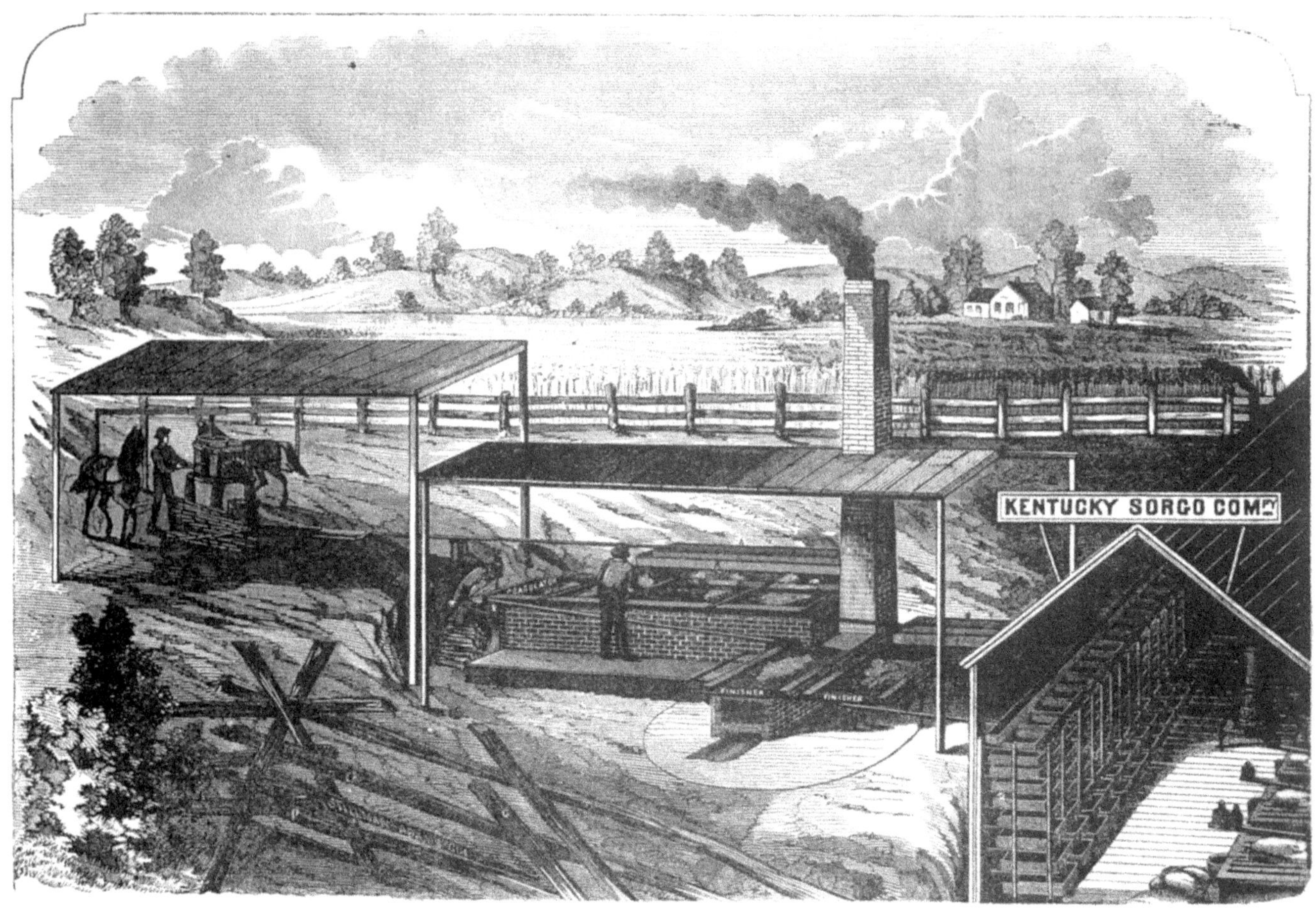

The Kentucky Sorgo Company in Dover in Mason County published literature describing the superiority of sugars and syrups made from sorghum cane and invited potential investors to research the profitability of the endeavor. The company patented a process for evaporation and centrifugal milling of the syrups so that crystalline sugar and palatable syrups were obtained without "that peculiar taste of sorghum." They were, according to a testimonial, "unlike the previous mean, sour, thick, nauseous sorghum molasses, full of impurities of various kinds." The company had a sugar house on the farm of John H. Seebolt in Jefferson County, nine miles from Louisville on what is now the Poplar Level Road. In the central part of the building illustrated, the equipment near the chimney is identified as "coagulator and finisher."

Wood engraving from an advertising pamphlet published for the Southern Sorgo Co. of Louisville, probably published in Louisville about 1869. Engraved by Stillman-Adams, Cincinnati.

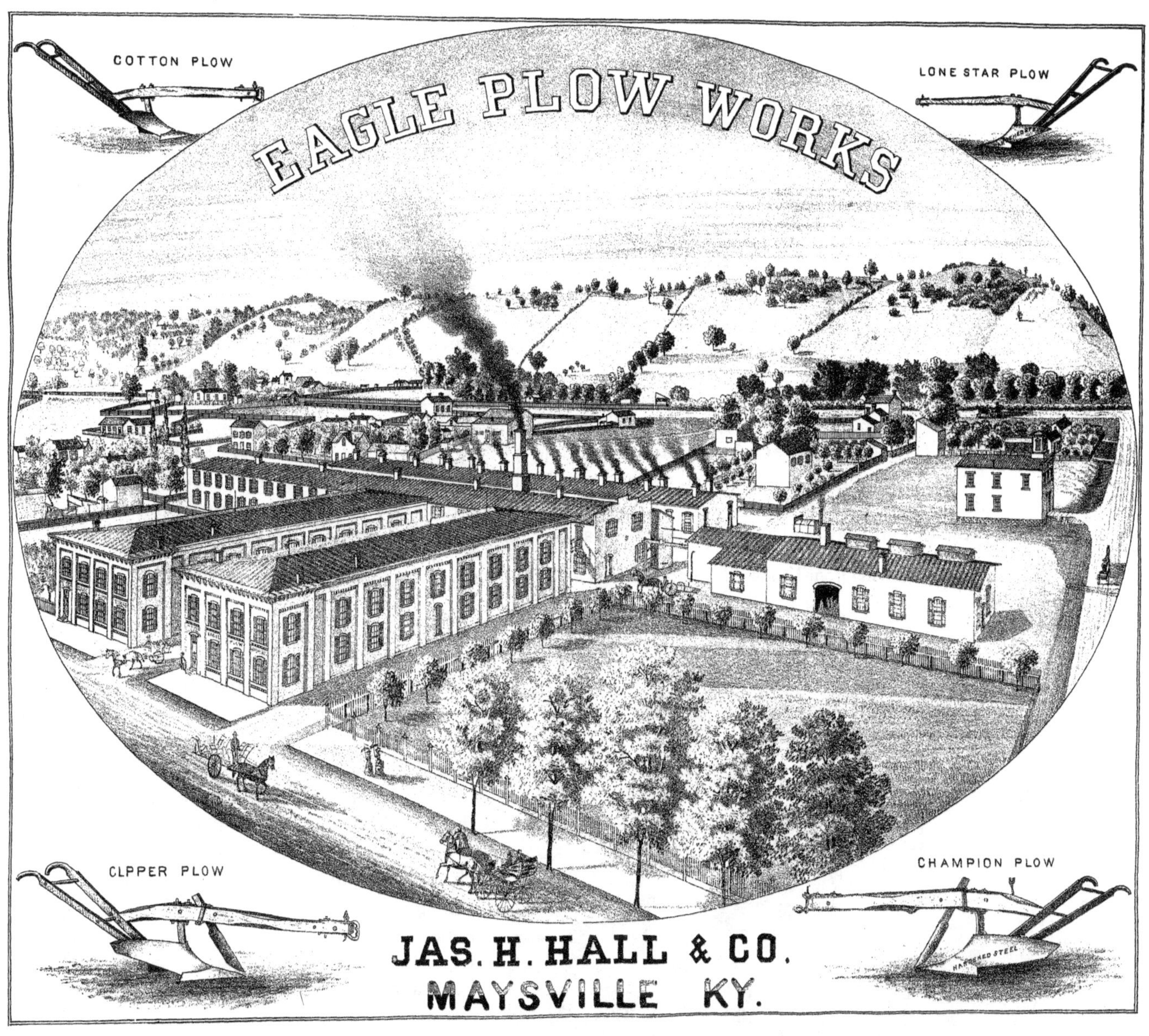

The James H. Hall Company Eagle Plow Works in Maysville in Mason County was incorporated in 1878 soon after this view was made. The factory was located on Second Street between Lexington and Walnut streets. In the 1876 atlas of Mason County, the firm's business notice offered "celebrated sugar and cotton plows, flukes, and sub-soils," suggesting that they had substantial trade in the southern states. Residences now occupy the factory site.

Lithograph from *An Illustrated Atlas of Mason County, Kentucky,* 1876.

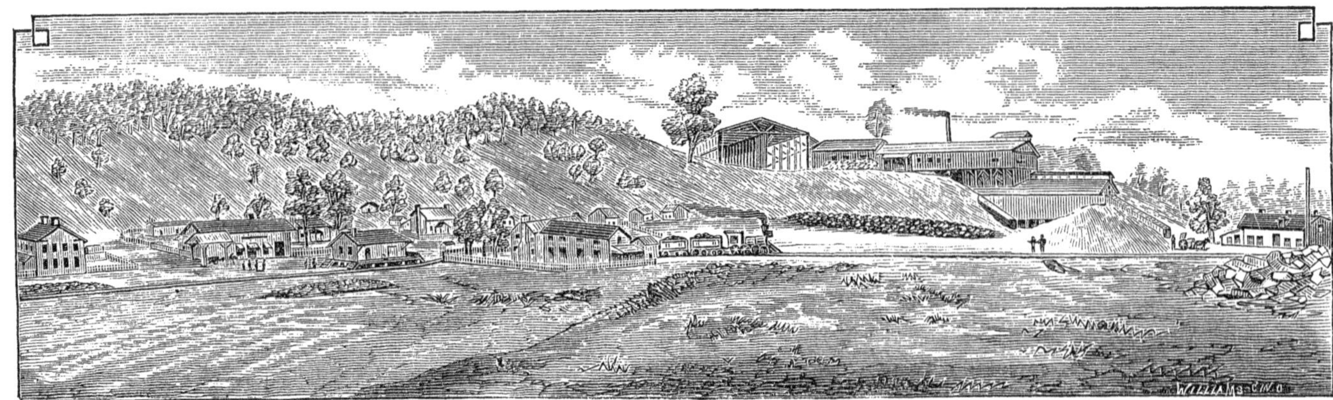

Small iron furnaces producing only for local needs were built very soon after the first settlers arrived in Kentucky in those areas where they discovered the necessary raw materials. The Hunnewell furnace, shown here, was built in Greenup County in 1844 and was taken over by the Eastern Kentucky Railway Company in 1870. Despite widespread and continuing efforts to take advantage of Kentucky's coal and iron resources, most of the state's furnaces were closed by 1885. Economic evolution and improved methods of smelting in industrial centers brought about the decline and eventual abandonment of less effective iron furnace operations in both eastern and western Kentucky, and what had long been a thriving industry became only a memory.

Wood engraving from Kenny's *Illustrated Cincinnati,* 1875. Engraved by Joseph A. Williams, Cincinnati.

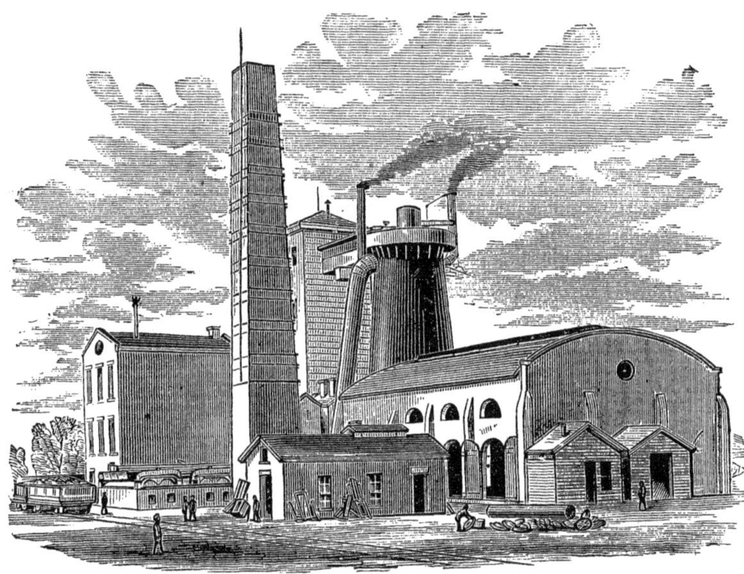

In 1854, an eastern railroad engineer employed by the Lexington and Big Sandy Railroad Company recommended Ashland as the site for a rail terminus and for manufacturing plants using pig iron from the surrounding area. He concluded there was sufficient room for manufacturing purposes, a fine location for a large town, and the best river landing for miles. The Ashland Coal and Iron Company was founded at the end of the Civil War to channel the wealth of northeast Kentucky's coal fields through Ashland, and the first steel blast furnace was built there in 1869. Ashland Coal and Iron was succeeded by Ashland Iron and Mining Company, which in turn became part of American Rolling Mill Company (Armco) in the 1920s.

Wood engraving from Kenny's *Illustrated Cincinnati,* 1875.

In 1876, Polk's *Kentucky State Gazetteer* praised the Carrollton Woolen Mills and described it thus: "This mammoth establishment covers over two acres of floor space, and is built for five sets of machinery, with a capacity of turning out 700,000 yards of cloth and 50,000 pounds of yarn per annum." The mill was also rated the principal manufacturing establishment in Carrollton. Another description noted that the mill employed eighty men, cost $78,000 to construct, and made jeans, linseys, and flannel materials for clothing makers in Chicago, St. Louis, New Orleans, and Louisville.

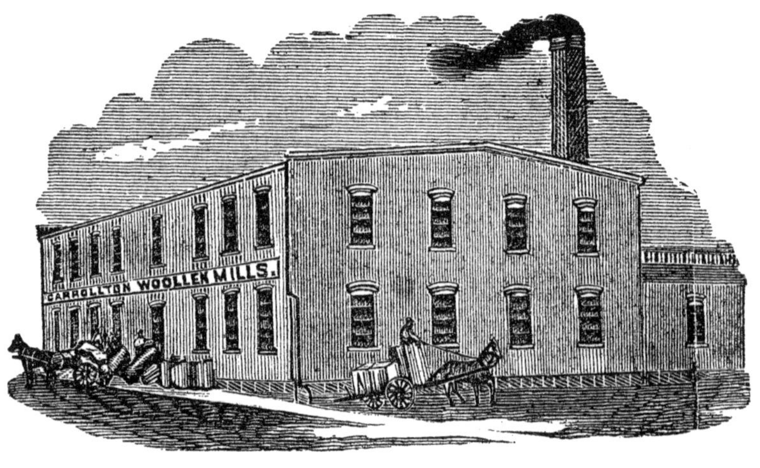

Wood engraving from Polk's *Kentucky State Gazetteer and Business Directory,* 1876.

At one time Mammoth Cave was an important source of saltpeter. Near the cave's Bottomless Well, shown at the right side of this view, is all that remained at mid-century of the three towers used for pumping saltpeter nitrate waters.

Wood engraving from *Ballou's Pictorial Drawing-Room Companion*, 1856.

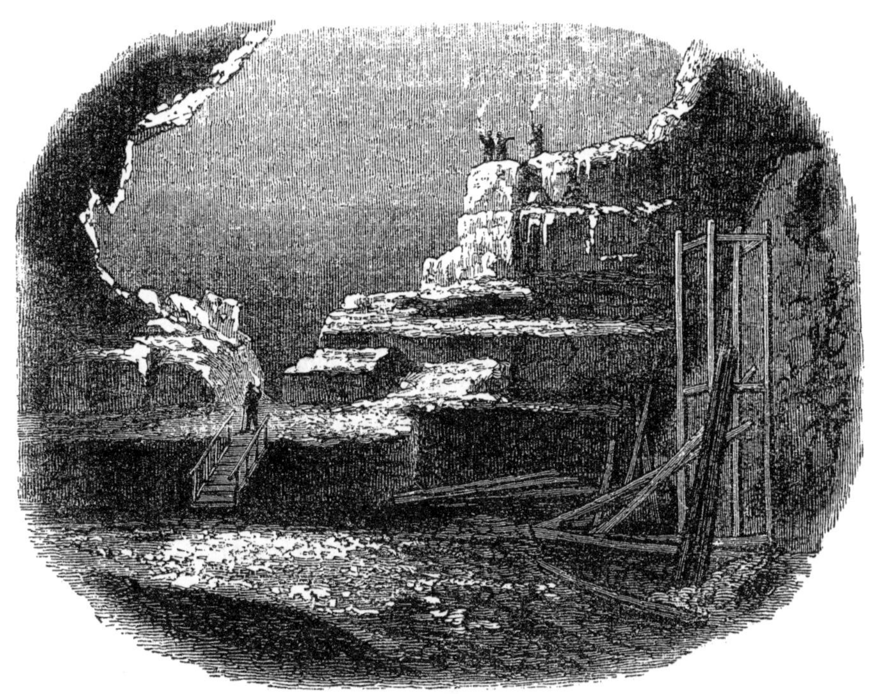

In the 1880s Kentucky state agencies and industrial interests joined forces in special efforts to promote and develop mineral resources across the state. The Kentucky Geological Survey reported excellent seams of variously constituted coals for domestic use, for gas enrichment, and for providing the coke needed for steel production in blast furnaces. Some of the coal seams were well situated near iron ore sources in Kentucky and neighboring states and close to abundant limestone supplies. Shown here is a coke oven in western Kentucky.

Wood engraving from the Louisville Board of Trade's *The City of Louisville and a Glimpse of Kentucky*, 1887. Engraved by Courier-Journal Job Printing Co.

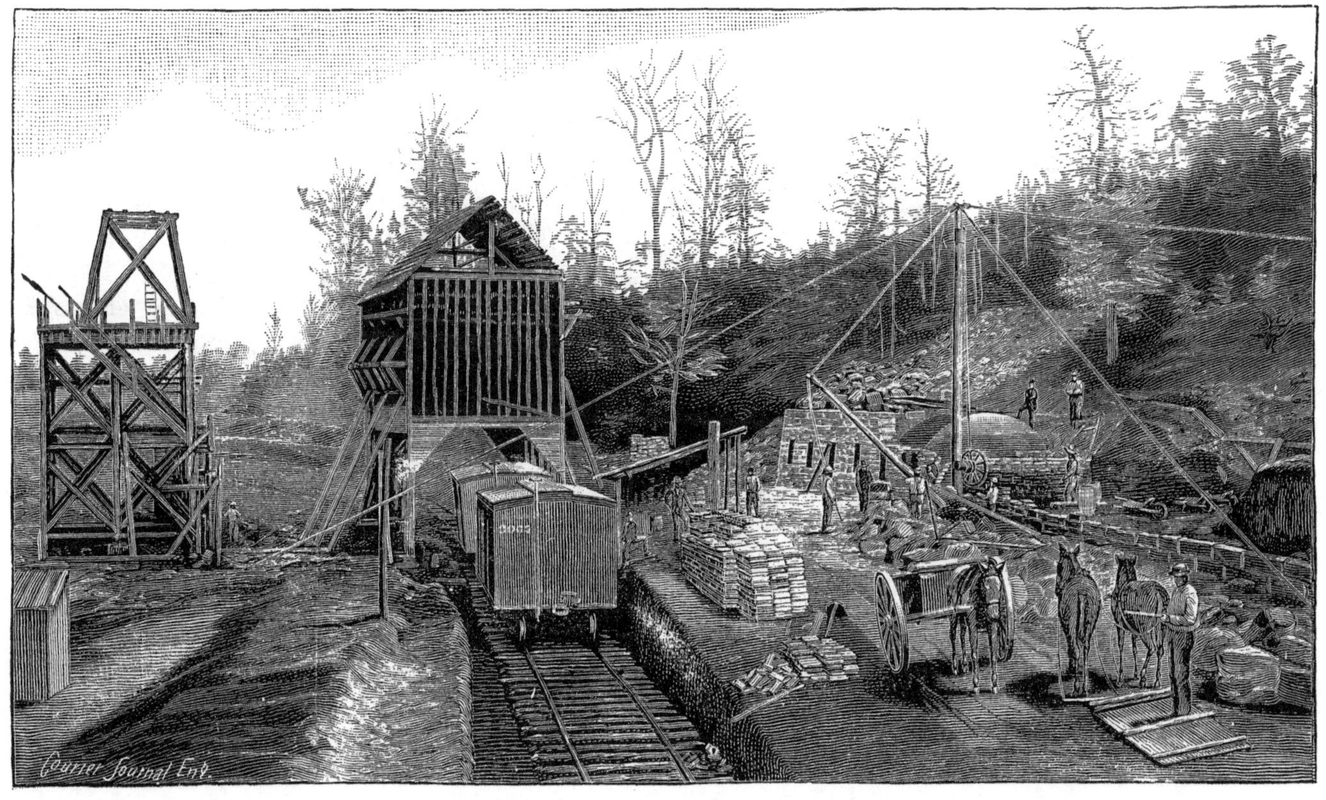

The Brinly Plough Factory in Louisville grew out of the Thomas E.C. Brinly blacksmith shop, established about 1840 at Simpsonville. The manufacturing department was moved to Louisville in 1858. By 1880 the claim could be made that Brinly plows—"the best and cheapest in use"—had won seven hundred premiums by participating in nearly all the plowing trials that had taken place in the country during the previous forty years. The Brinly Universal Plow could be connected in twelve configurations for different uses. The Brinly-Hardy Company remains at the same location on Main Street, producing attachments for riding mowers and garden tractors.

Wood engraving from *The Daily Graphic,* New York, April 29, 1875.

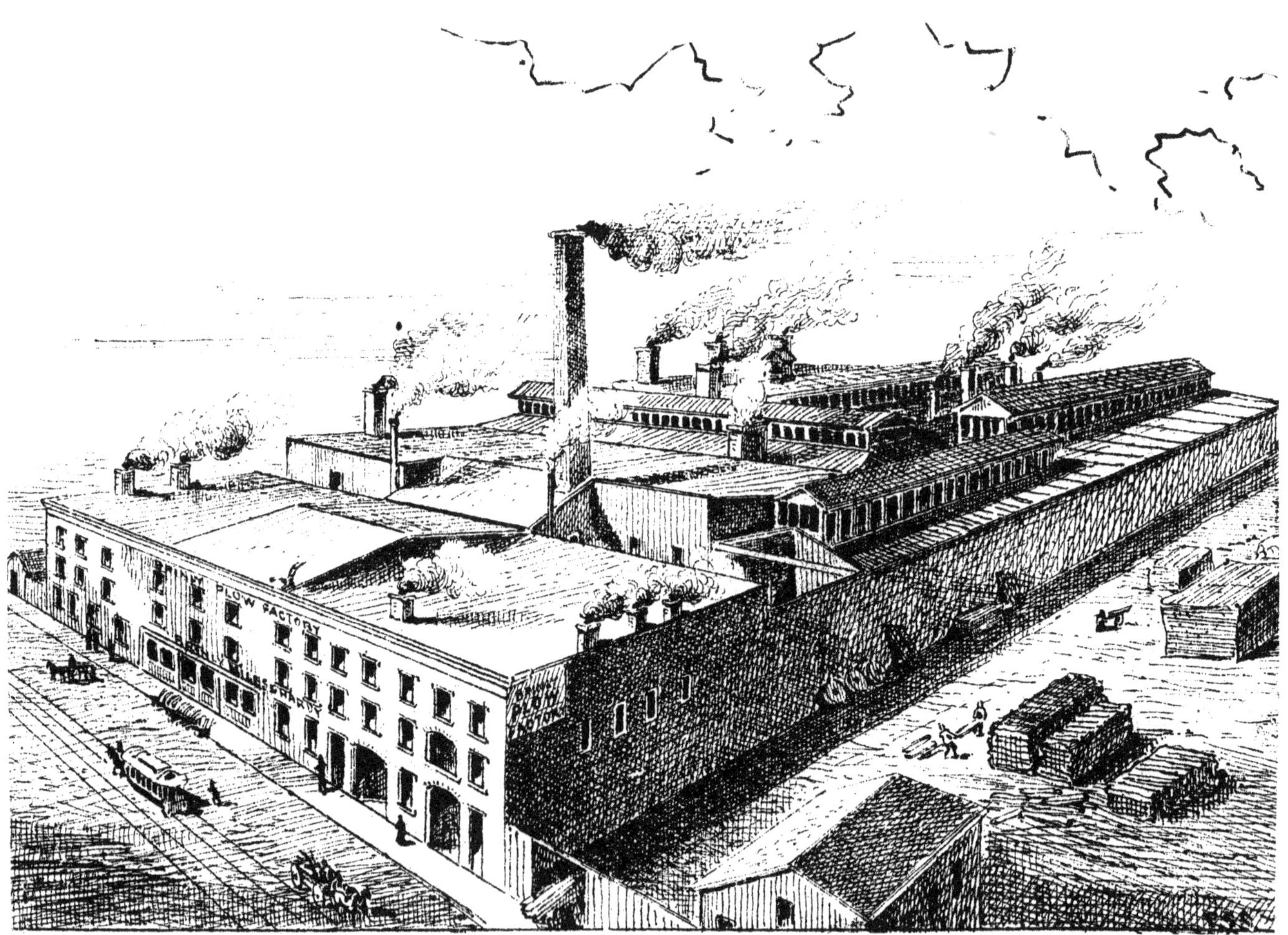

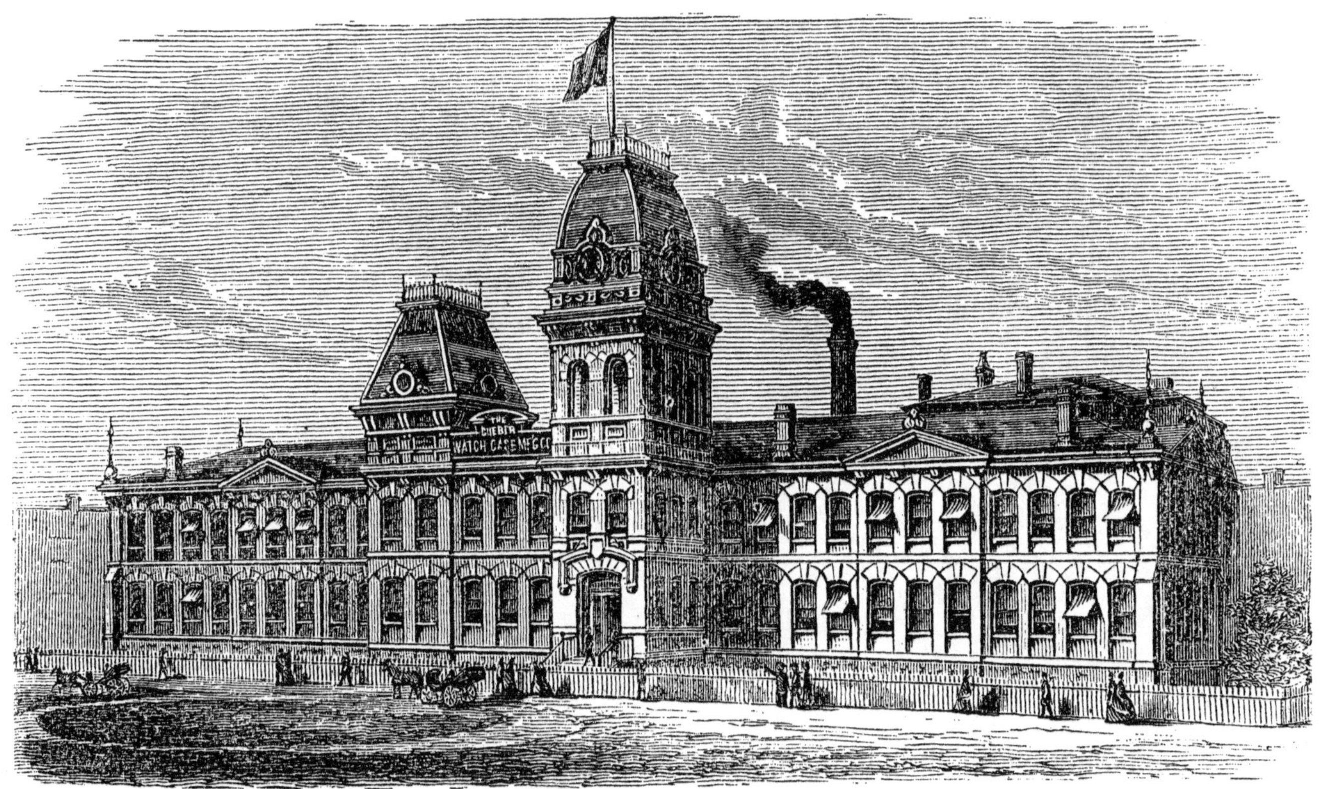

In December 1876 an advertisement for the Dueber Watch Case Factory in Newport included an illustration of this new facility, which had been completed in September of that year, at the corner of Washington Avenue and Jefferson (now Fifth Street). By 1880, the facility was the largest watch factory in the United States. The following year a new building was added, and employment reached four hundred; a third building was completed in 1883. Lacking room for additional expansion in Newport, in 1888 Dueber built a new factory in Canton, Ohio, and moved the company there the following year, closing the Newport factory. The building survived into the 1980s as a mill outlet clothing store.

Wood engraving from *Important Events of the Century,* 1877.

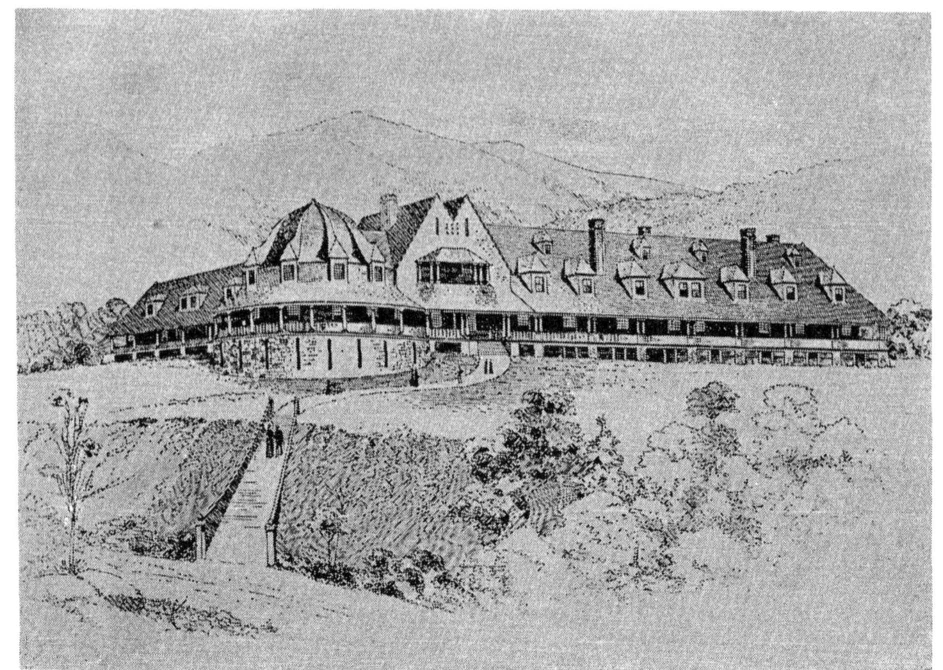

The Middlesborough Casino was destroyed by fire shortly before its completion and was not rebuilt.

Middlesborough—now known as Middlesboro—resulted from a very ambitious plan for community development, a plan designed to take advantage of the mineral wealth of the area. British investors committed millions of dollars, and the American Association Limited was organized in London to develop the project. The association was represented by agents in Boston and New York and, in Middlesboro, retained ownership of its mining properties, ran the area railroad, and sold lands for industrial and commercial activity and for private facilities. The town was named for the iron city in England, and most of its streets were named for British cities. Settlers began to arrive in 1889 and within a year Middlesborough had ten thousand inhabitants, who could enjoy, among other attractions, one of the first golf courses in the United States. In 1893 the collapse of a major banking house in London ended the prosperity and the promise. The following views, from an 1890 booklet published by developers, illustrated Middlesborough's remarkable progress to that time and described its great potential for future growth.

Photoengraved plates from architect's drawings published in a promotional booklet by the American Association or the Middlesborough Town Company, 1891.

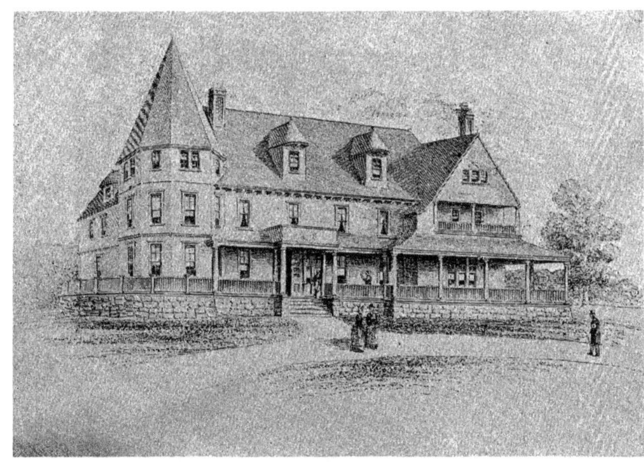

The Ocoonita Club (*left*) stood on the north side of Edgewood Road, adjoining the Middlesborough Hotel near the present-day Edgewood Court. After the collapse of the development plan, the hotel was renamed the Boonesway. Neither the Ocoonita nor the Middlesborough Hotel still exists.

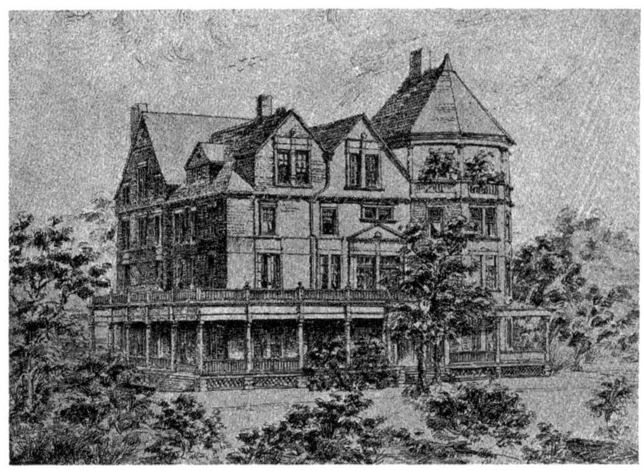

This "fashionable boarding house" on Arthur Heights (*right*) was known as the Belview Hotel and later became the University private school.

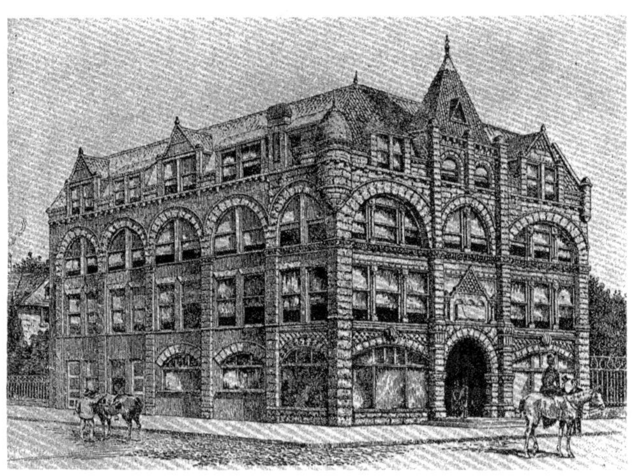

The Coal and Iron Bank at Cumberland Avenue and Twenty-second Street (*left*) became the Evans Hospital in the 1930s and was taken down in the 1960s.

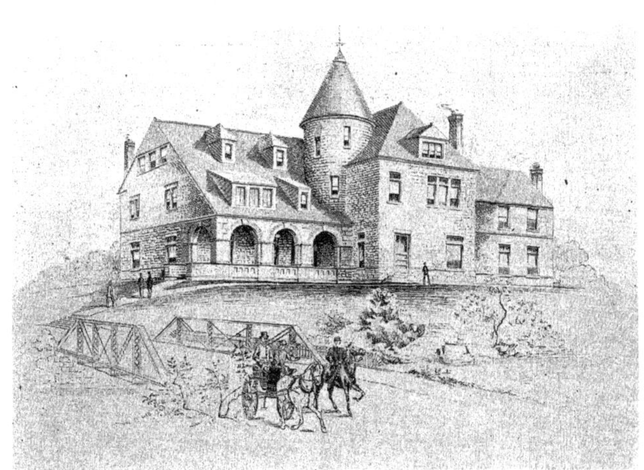

The offices of the American Association at Cumberland Avenue and Canal (*right*) are still in use as offices.

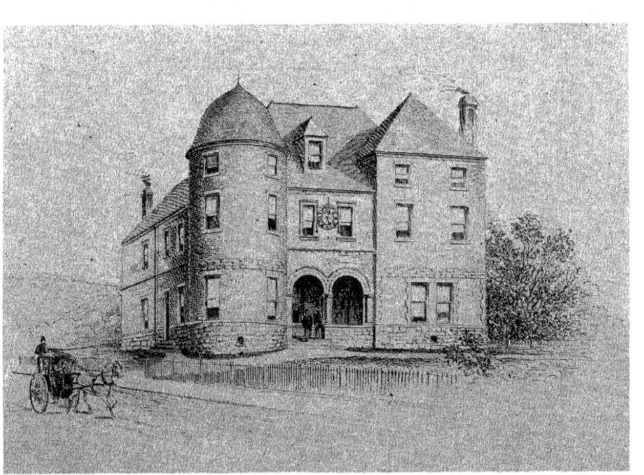

The education building of the First Baptist Church now stands on the original site of the offices of the Middlesborough Town Company (*left*), which was set up to sell the available real estate lots and parcels.

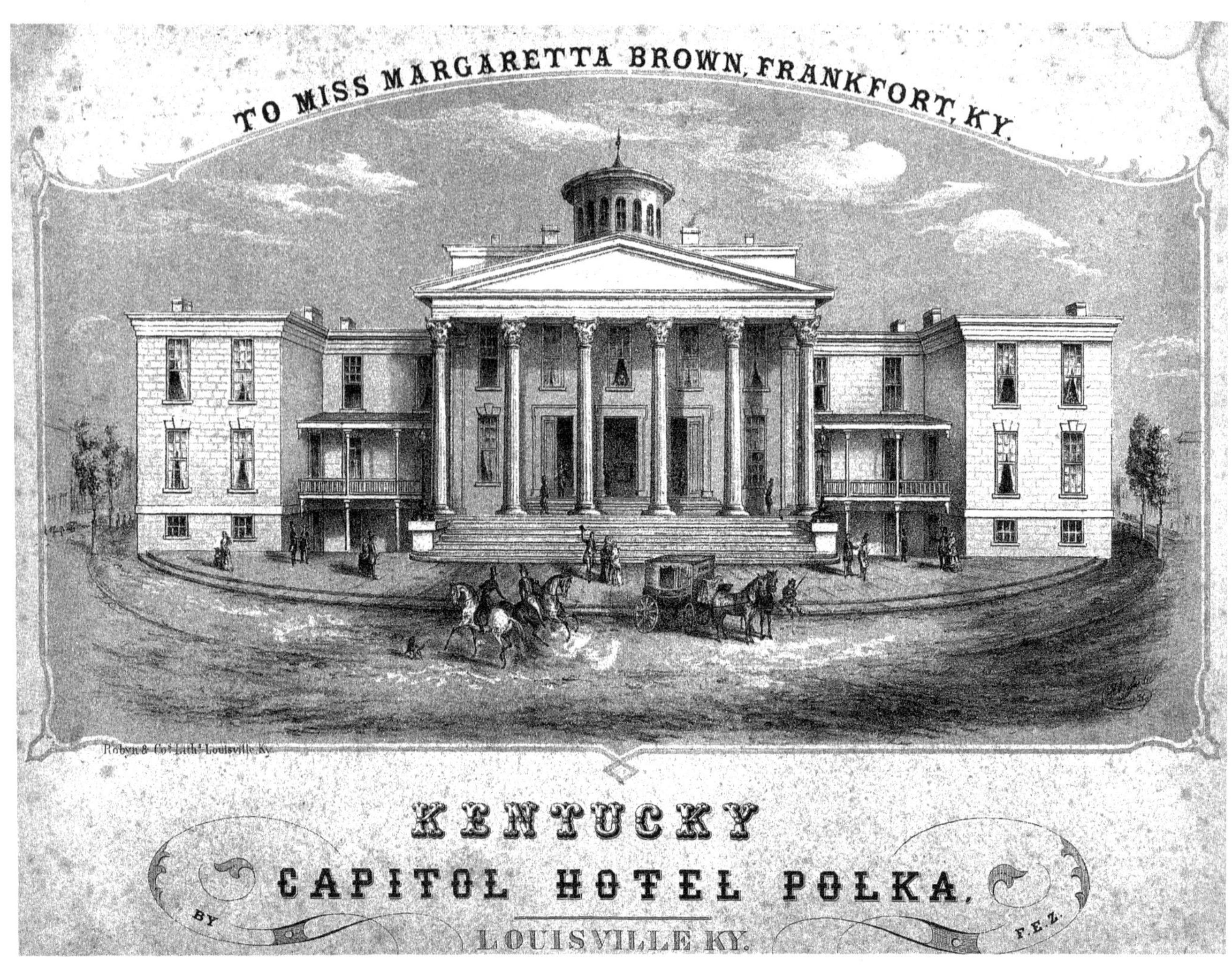

The "Capitol Hotel Polka" was written by "F.E.Z." and dedicated to Margaretta Brown, the granddaughter of John Brown, Kentucky's first U.S. senator. The Weisiger Tavern was opened in 1792 to accommodate some of the members of the first legislature. Its replacement, the building shown here, was designed in 1852 by Isaiah Rogers, who built hotels in many major cities. The principal part of the Capitol Hotel in Frankfort, on Main Street between Olive and Ann streets, was completed in December 1854 to accommodate 250 guests; a large wing was added later. For many years the hotel was the site of an annual masked ball to honor the members of the General Assembly. The building burned in 1917 and was reopened in 1923 in a new colonial-revival building. The hotel closed in 1962 and the building was renovated for a banking house and offices.

Lithographed sheet music cover, published by G.W. Brainard & Co., Louisville, 1854. Lithographed by Robyn & Co., Louisville, from a drawing by H. Bosse.

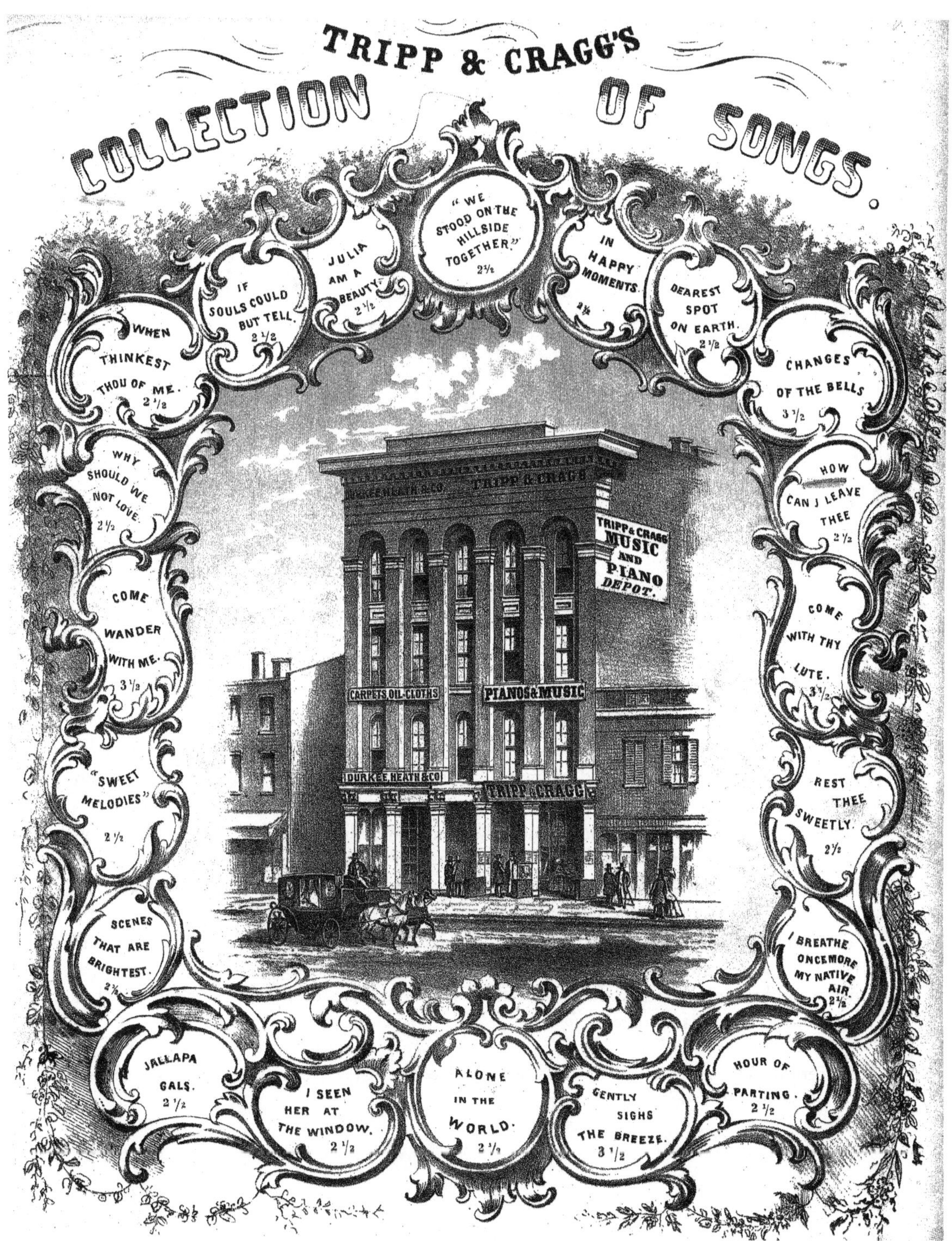

This collection of songs was sold in the Tripp and Cragg Music and Piano Depot in Louisville. The store was located on Fourth Street between Market and Jefferson streets, in the building known as "Love's Block." Louis Tripp published music and sold pianos in Louisville from 1858 to 1877, in partnership first with Thomas P. Cragg and later with G.W. Linton. The store's location was changed four times during that period, and from 1878 to 1887 Tripp's widow, Emily, ran the store.

Lithographed sheet music cover, published by Tripp & Cragg, 1858. Lithographed by Hart, Mapother & Co., Louisville.

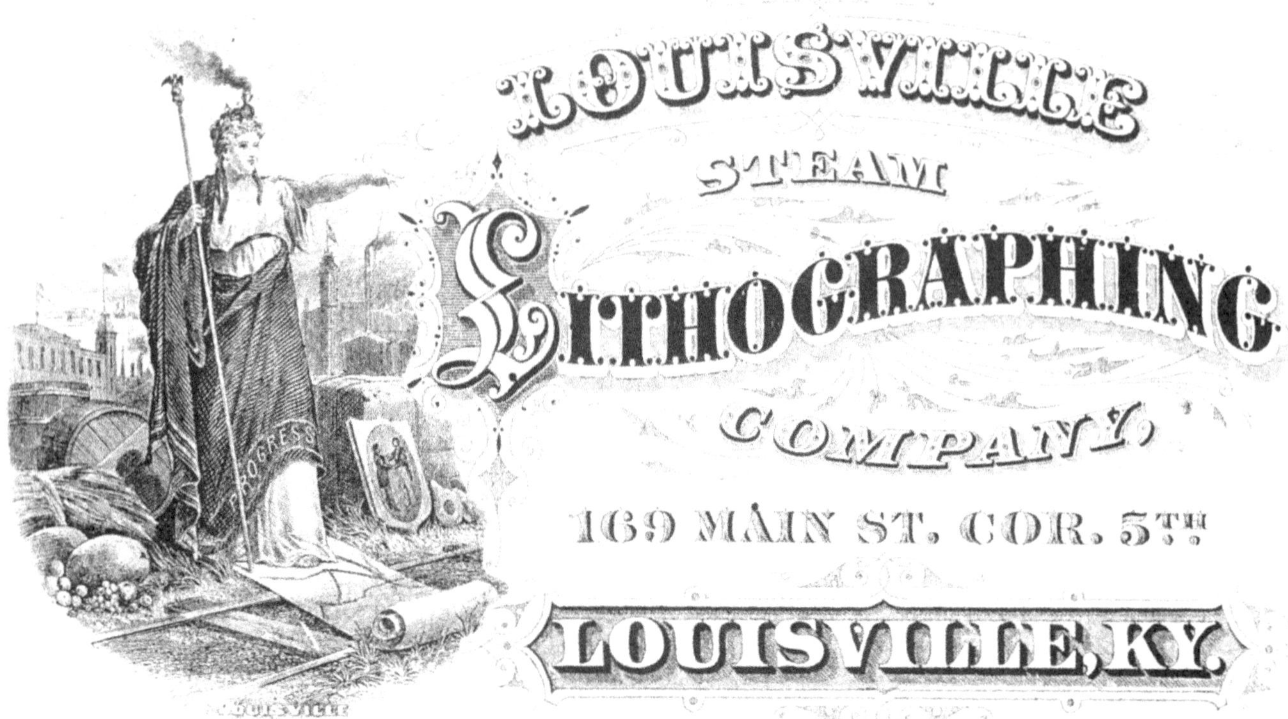

Southern cities competed strenuously to recover from the effects of the Civil War. Virtually untouched by the conflict and in many cases profiting from it, Louisville was in an especially good position. The allegorical figure of the city shown here was one artist's depiction of the spirit of the times and a symbolic embodiment of Louisville. The grand lady wrapped in her rich robes uses "Progress" as her keynote, wears a locomotive as her headpiece, and stands on a map of the railroad whose tracks travel away from her, presumably to distant points. Behind her stand the industrial exposition, the city hall, the water works pumping tower, and other significant structures new to Louisville at the time this view was made. Some of the rich products of the area—tobacco, grains, produce, meats, and manufactured products—lie at her feet. The state seal beside her symbolizes her devotion to statewide progress.

Copper or steel engraving from Caron's *Louisville Directory for 1876*. Engraved by Louisville Steam Lithographing Co.

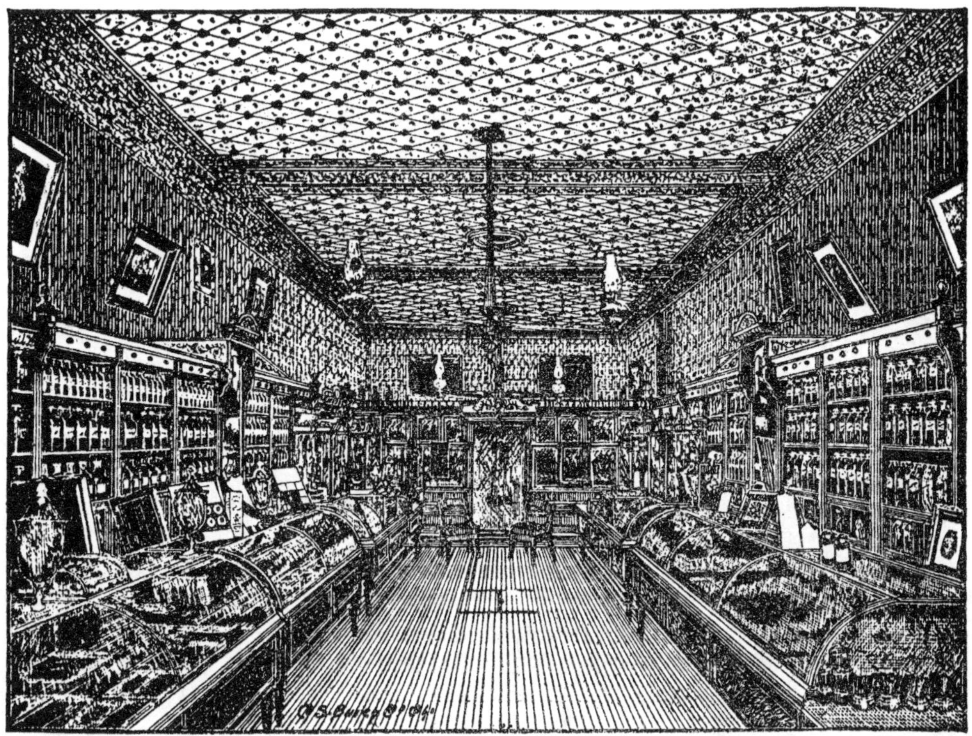

Typically, promotional brochures said only positive things about community businesses, and the *Handbook of Clark County and the City of Winchester* was no exception. The brochure called the drug stores of W.B. Logan (*above*) and T.L. Phillips (*below*) "perfect gems artistically." The city's buildings, the handbook states, "are almost without exception tasteful in design and substantial in construction."

Wood engravings from *Handbook of Clark County and the City of Winchester*, 1889.

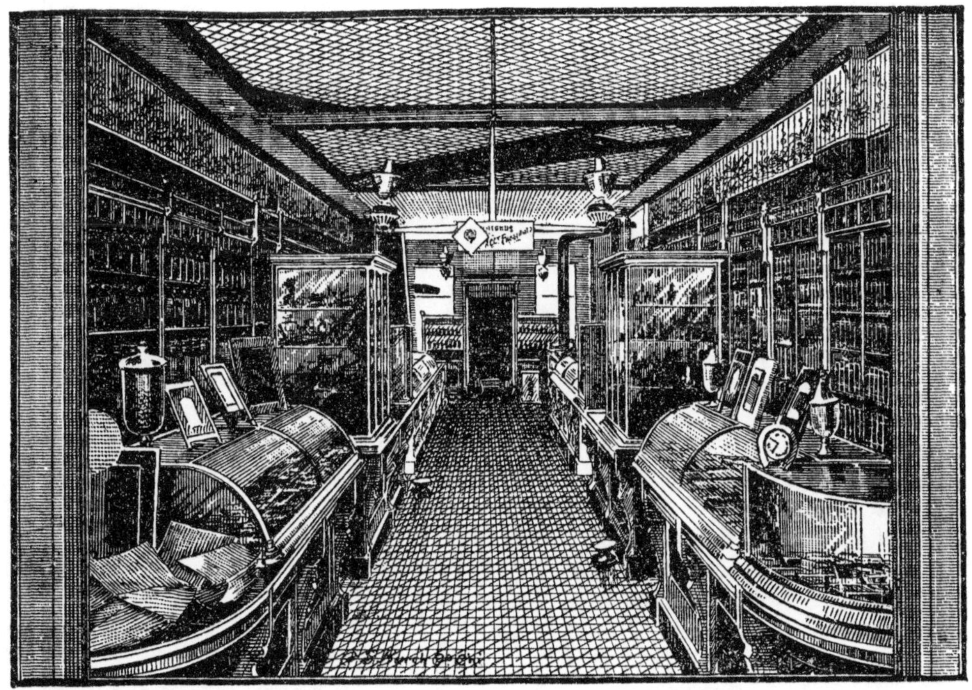

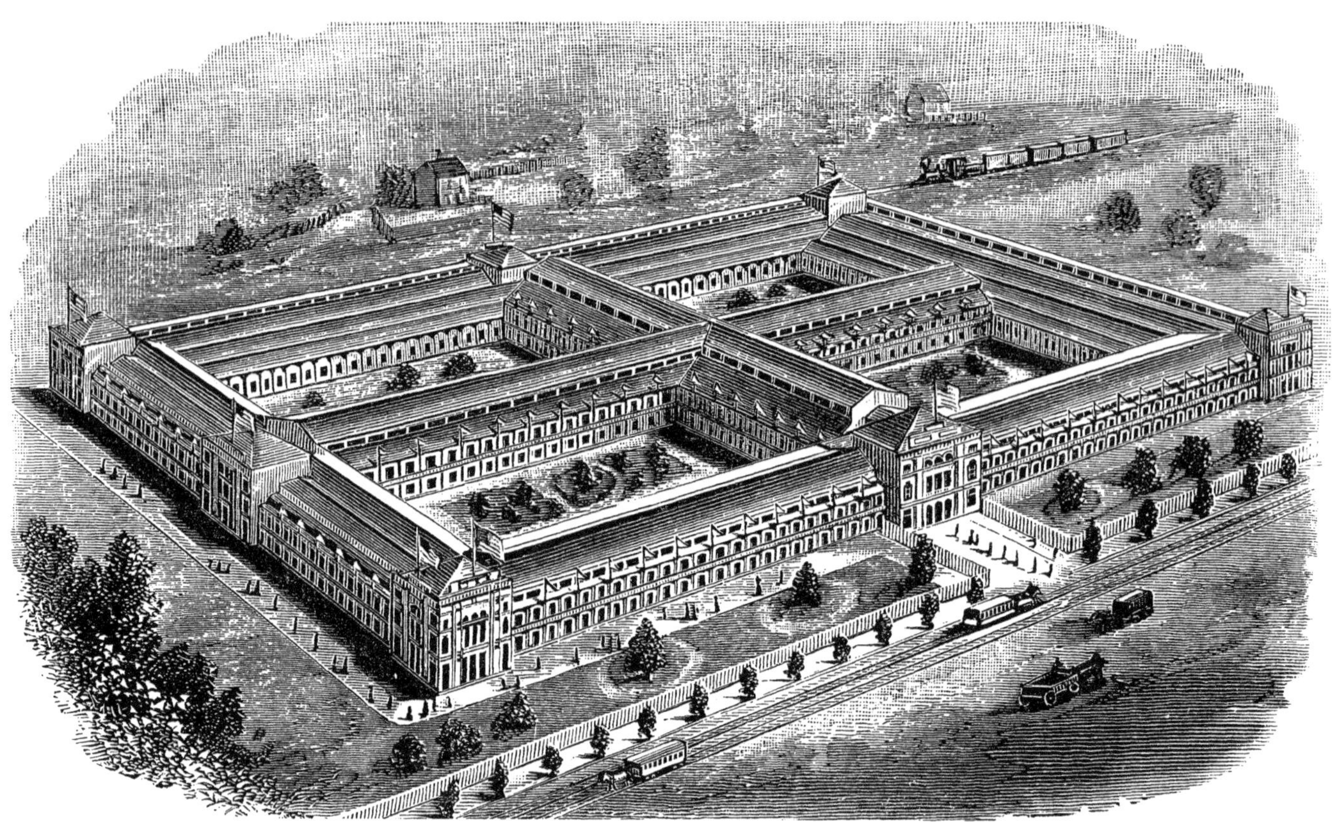

The Southern Exposition opened August 1, 1883, and continued for one hundred days. It ranks as Louisville's outstanding promotional effort, the result of the ambitious, progressive, and competitive spirit of the community. More than 1,500 industrial and commercial displays packed the building, which covered ten acres between Fourth and Sixth streets, the present site of St. James Court. The in-town estate of Antoine du Pont, known as du Pont Square, served as the midway and park, the site of the art gallery, and later Louisville's Central Park. The Edison Company installed 4,800 incandescent lights of sixteen candle power each under what was said to have been the largest contract ever made for lighting a building. Attendance totaled more than 770,000 people through the closing date in early November. It was so successful that the exposition was continued for each of the next four years.

Wood engraving from the Louisville Board of Trade's *The City of Louisville and a Glimpse of Kentucky,* 1887.

This interior view of the State Industrial Exposition at Louisville shows the elaborate fountains, indoor landscaping, and lighting that adorned the areas around the exhibits and restaurants. About 1870, the east side of Fourth Street from Guthrie to Chestnut was cleared for this hall, and the exposition was conducted there for several years. The brick building of 130,000 square feet was erected in only forty-five days in Renaissance style with Mansard towers at each corner and a dome twenty-five feet in diameter at the center. The first local exposition opened here in September 1872, but it was soon designated the National Industrial Exposition when response and interest developed from outside the area. Richard Collins's *History of Kentucky,* published only two years after the first season of the exhibition, reported that the 1872 display was "the grandest ever witnessed south of the Ohio River" and that it attracted as many as twenty thousand people daily.

Wood engraving from *Frank Leslie's Illustrated Newspaper,* 1880, from a drawing by James E. Taylor.

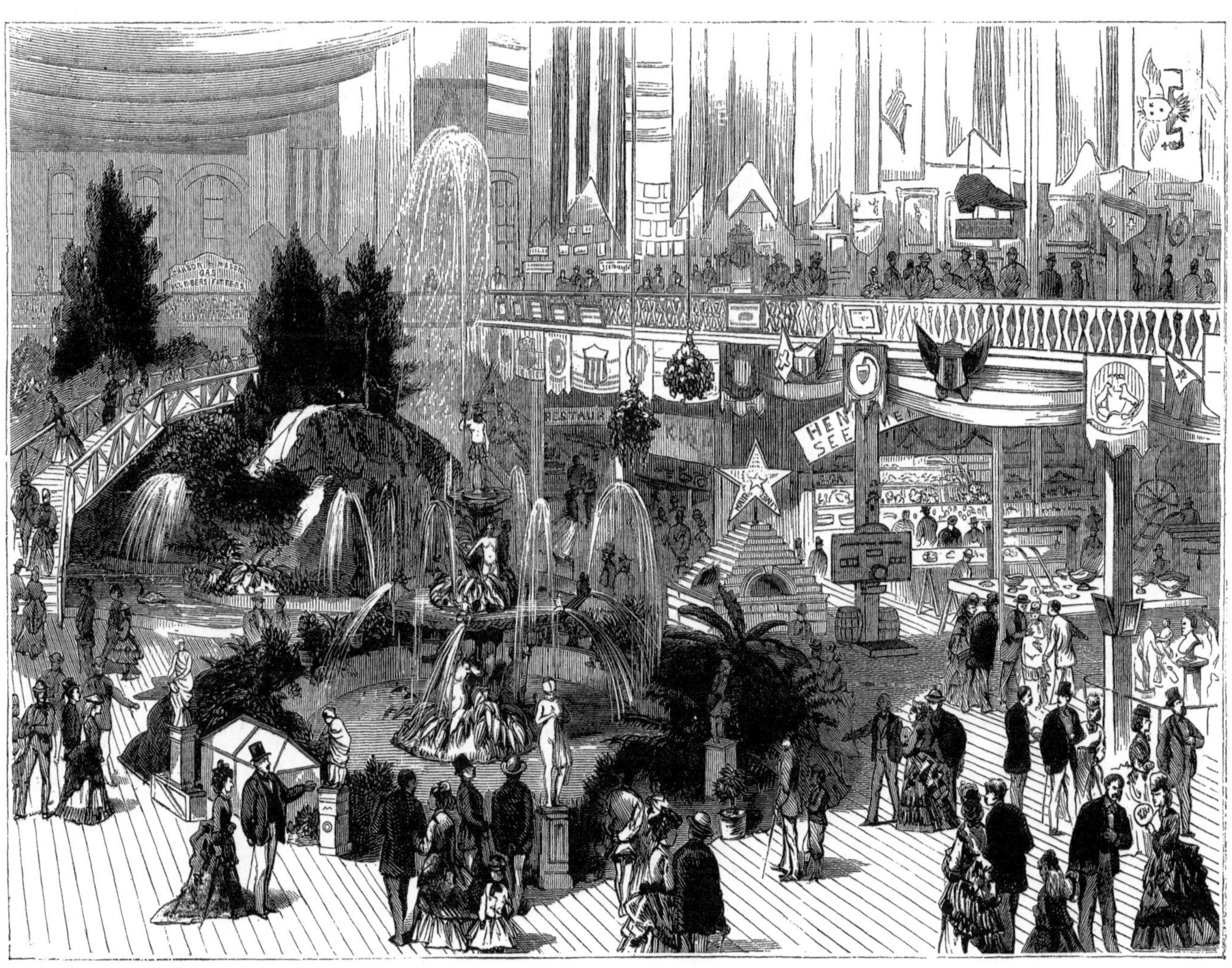

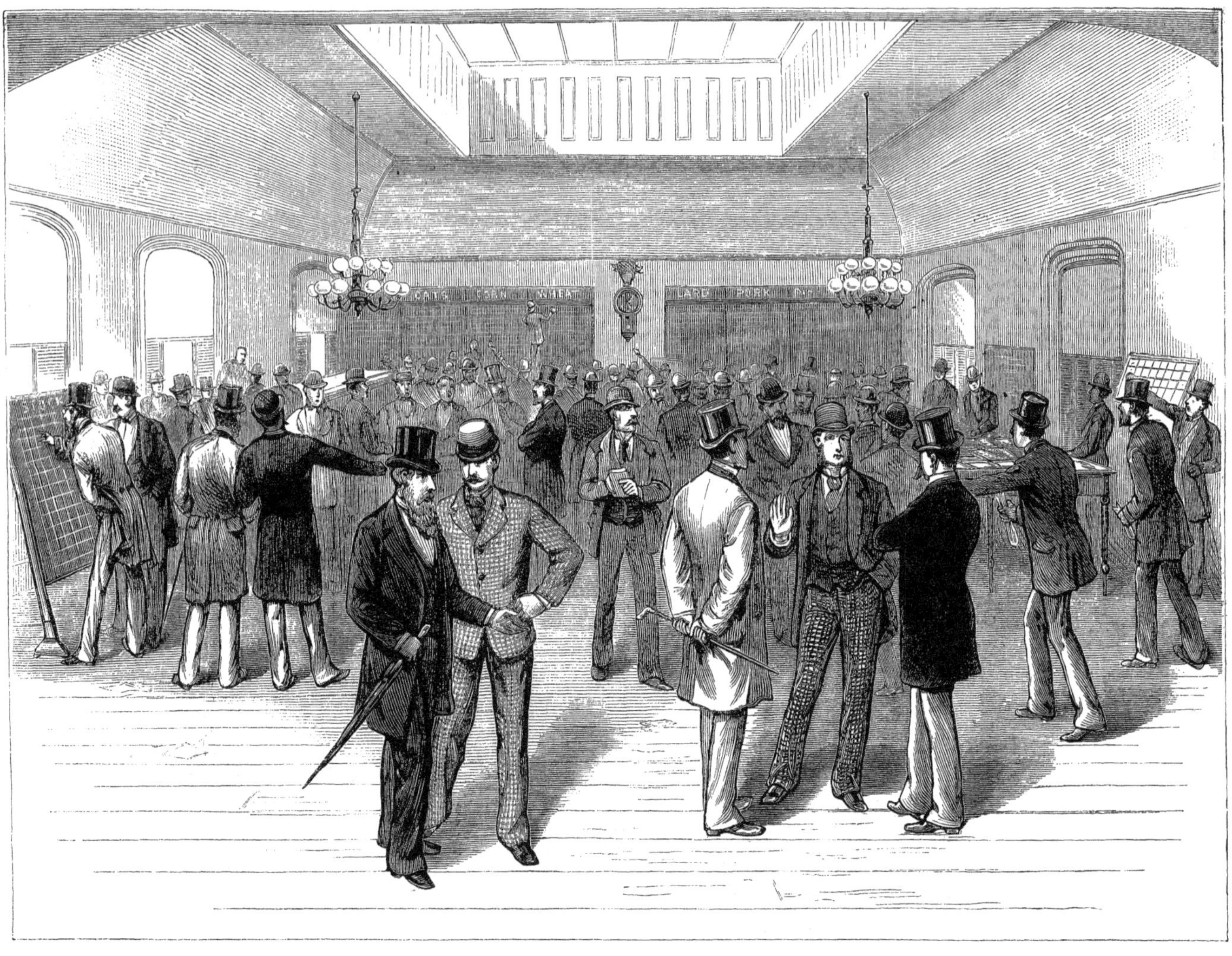

Trading was often brisk in the salesroom of the Louisville Board of Trade. The Board was organized in 1862 to counter suspicion that Louisville businessmen had Confederate sympathies. The organization bought the Lithgow Building at Third and Main streets in 1879 and added this "elegant exchange hall" in February 1880. The blackboards shown at the end of the hall indicate that the exchange dealt in oats, corn, wheat, lard, pork, and securities. The Board remained at this location until 1938, and the building itself survived until the urban renewal program of the 1960s.

Wood engraving from *Frank Leslie's Illustrated Newspaper,* June 3, 1880, from a drawing by Walter Goater.

The five-story *Courier-Journal* Building on the corner of Fourth and Green streets was described in 1887 as "one of the handsomest and most costly business houses in Louisville."

Both wood engravings from the Louisville Board of Trade's *The City of Louisville and a Glimpse of Kentucky,* 1887.

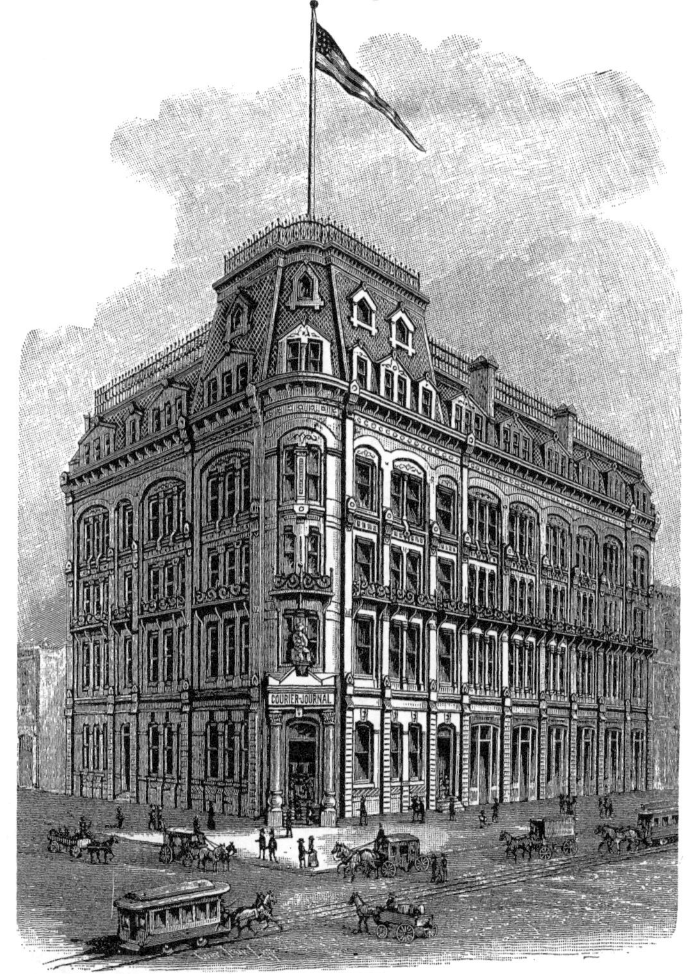

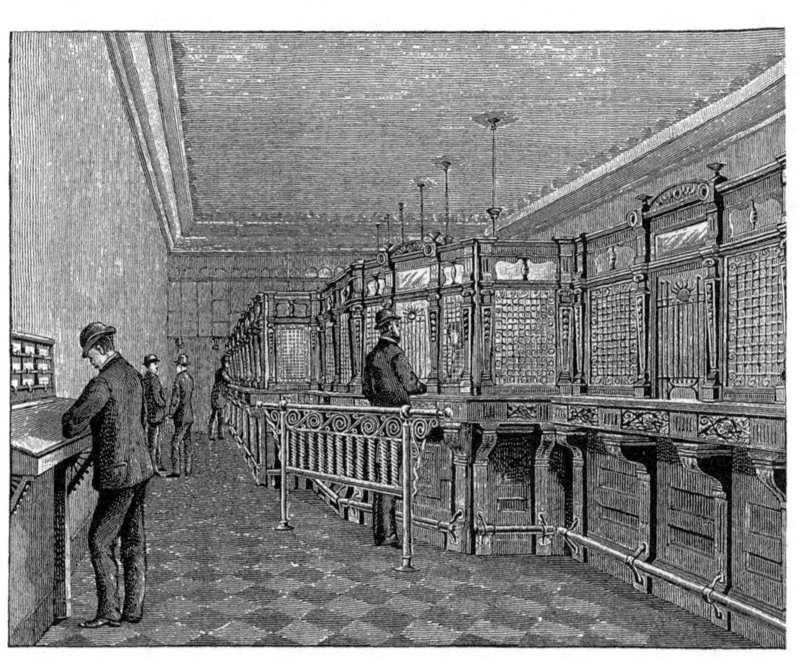

The Falls City Bank was called Falls City Tobacco Bank when it was chartered in 1865 during a countrywide depression. The bank survived the financial panic of 1873, even though it was robbed of more than $300,000 in cash and securities in that same year by thieves who cut into its steel vault from a rented room above it. In addition to "a general banking business in loans, deposits, discounts, foreign and domestic exchange," the bank was one of the depositories of the Sinking Fund of the City of Louisville and the Water Company's large account.

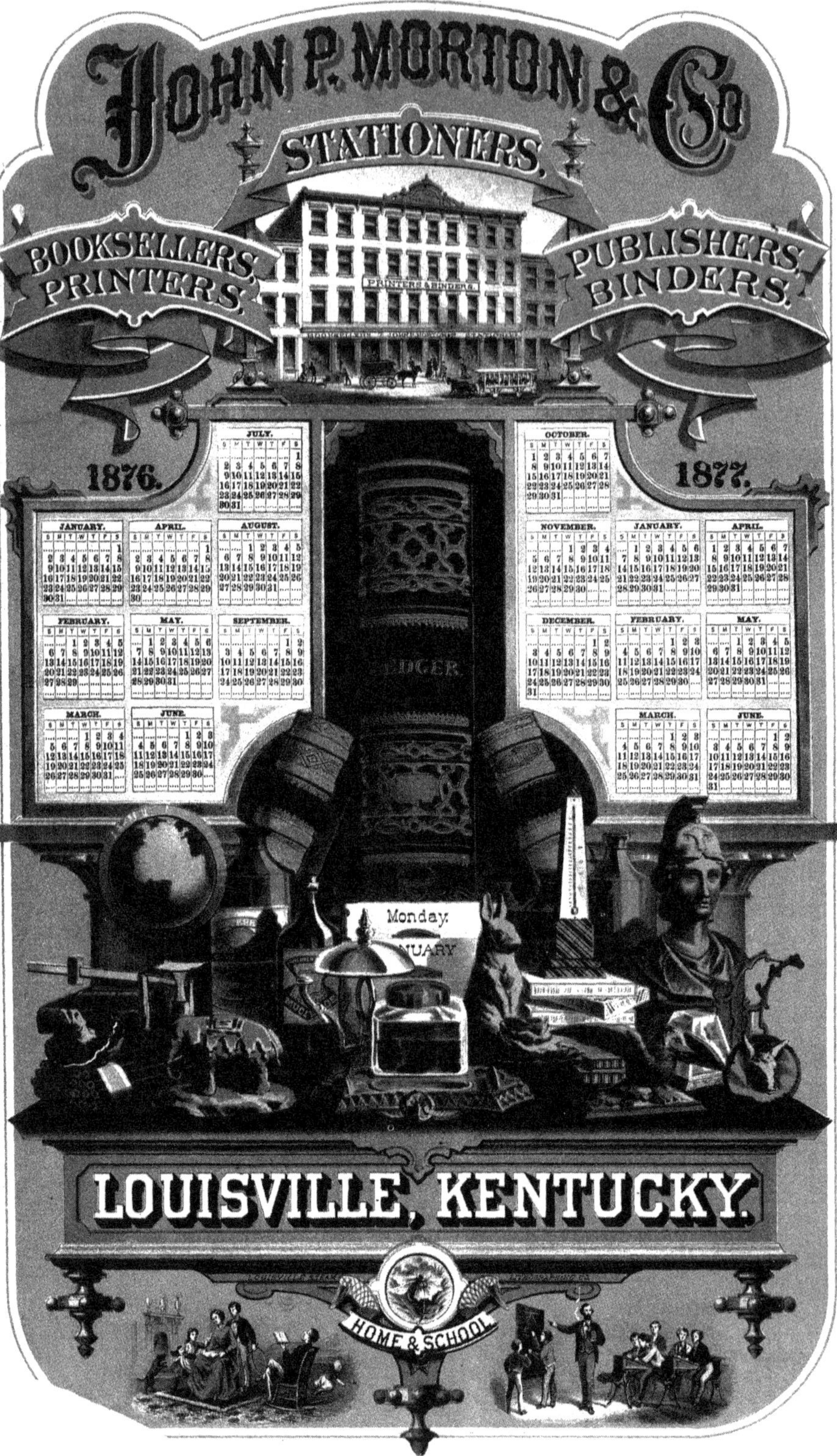

In 1824 John P. Morton began a long career in printing and publishing as a clerk for William Worsley, a book store proprietor and newspaper publisher. When Worsley withdrew from active participation, the firm became Morton and Company. After the newspaper was merged with another publication, the firm undertook job printing and book publishing, especially of schoolbooks. In 1861 the company became John P. Morton and Company, a name it retained when it became incorporated in 1888 and continued to use until the business ceased in the mid-twentieth century. The eighteen-month wall calendar shown here was lithographed in four colors. Most of the popular items carefully arranged on the display table below the calendar would have little use in today's office.

Chromolithograph wall poster, made by Louisville Steam Lithographing Co., 1875.

FOUR

Roads, Rivers, and Rails

Geographically, Kentucky has been both fortunate and unfortunate in its location. Its Ohio River border and numerous navigable streams have allowed easy water transportation in many locales. Locks and other manmade works have aided such endeavors. But the state's position behind the Allegheny Mountains slowed east-west transportation and made it difficult for railroads to link up in that direction. The presence of mountains in the eastern part of the state also long hindered proper development of roads and railways in that area. Only with the construction of major highways and the increasing availability of automobiles did rural Kentucky finally find a convenient window to the world beyond.

Historically, the first roads in the region were marked out by four-footed engineers. Animals left their paths across Kentucky, with the buffalo traces the largest and most visible. Kentucky's first chronicler, John Filson, was amazed at the bison and the "prodigious roads they have made from all quarters to a [salt lick], as if leading to some populous city." Another writer described buffalo traces "wide enough for a carriage or wagon . . . , in which the trees, shrubs, etc. are all trampled down and destroyed." The McAfees, early explorers and surveyors, located a buffalo trace over a hundred feet wide, with the ground worn down several feet by the thousands of hooves.

But other passages across the state also welcomed the first English-speaking explorers. Indians had supplemented the buffalo traces with their own system of smaller trails, the most famous being the Warrior's Path. Kentucky scout Simon Kenton described these "war roads" as having "marks and blazes upon trees, frequently the rough drawings of wild animals." Such routes, together with those of the great bison herds and natural watercourses, formed a network that allowed explorers and hunters, Indian and English, to move through the unsettled Kentucky land. These would form the genesis for Kentucky transportation routes for many years.

The famous first Wilderness Road, Boone's Trace, entered through a natural opening, followed the Warrior's Path in part, then included a section of a buffalo trace in its route. But even then it was little more than a trail for two decades. Not until the 1790s could a wagon travel that route; however, it was the passage for thousands on foot or on horseback, carrying their few belongings with them. It did not become a wagon trail until after statehood.

Few illustrators left visual records of those early roads. Occasionally a Cumberland Gap image appeared, but generally artists did not chose to record the buffalo traces, the Indian "war roads," even the Wilderness Road and others like it. The vehicles for later travel, the tollroads that grew up—they received attention. Yet those early basic land routes would simply be added to, not replaced, over the next century. Only with the coming of modern engineers, with new tools, including explosives, would the basic routes begin to change.

One enduring transportation route was the river. Locks and dams would change its face but the basic course remained the same. The early settlers of Kentucky, from the East, beyond the mountain, had followed that dangerous way to Kentucky. Indian attacks made the Ohio River route risky, but boats allowed easier transportation of goods and a more comfortable trip, barring attacks. After the first period of settlement had ended and stability and peace had come to Kentucky, the river continued to be vitally important as a means of transporting produce from the state, though that had always been basically a one-way, downstream trade.

When the first steamboat appeared in 1811, many things changed. As George Yater wrote of that steamboat's arrival in Louisville: "The *New Orleans* represented a technological revolution on the river that soon brought about a commercial revolution on shore." River towns grew in size and importance, and the western steamboats became not only commercial aids but social ones as well. The canal at Louisville made travel even easier. For the first time a comfortable, fast, two-way travel was possible between Kentucky and the rest of the nation. And for the first time illustrators turned their talents to a large-scale presentation of vehicles for transportation in the state. Especially attractive for news-oriented magazines were the all-too-frequent river disasters, which were vividly presented. But so too were the magnificent steamers themselves. For Americans, and for Kentuckians, it was the dawning of a new era of transportation.

The sound of trains and cars on railroad tracks soon would compete with and eventually drown out the echo of the steamboat whistle, for by the end of the nineteenth century the railroad replaced the river as the people's choice for transportation. In interior towns, away from navigable watercourses, people were at last mobile, and their goods could be sent quickly to far-distant markets. Little hampered by natural barriers, railroads linked forgotten parts of Kentucky. Small towns on the rail lines had access to the offerings of larger cities and could bring in more products for their stores. Tracks crisscrossed the state and opened up the eastern coalfields for widespread mining. With the trains came a variety of stations, some simple, some architecturally impressive, and bridges, including important ones at Covington and at High Bridge. In towns and cities on or near the railroad, the whole world changed.

Indeed, for Kentuckians of the nineteenth century, the technological revolution in transportation greatly expanded their lives. In 1800, a trip by horseback or carriage was the chief means of travel, supplemented occasionally by a one-way river journey. To cover long distances took much time and even more inconvenience. But by century's end, river steamers and railroads made most Kentuckians vastly more mobile. They stood poised for an even greater transportation revolution in the twentieth century.

—*J.C.K.*

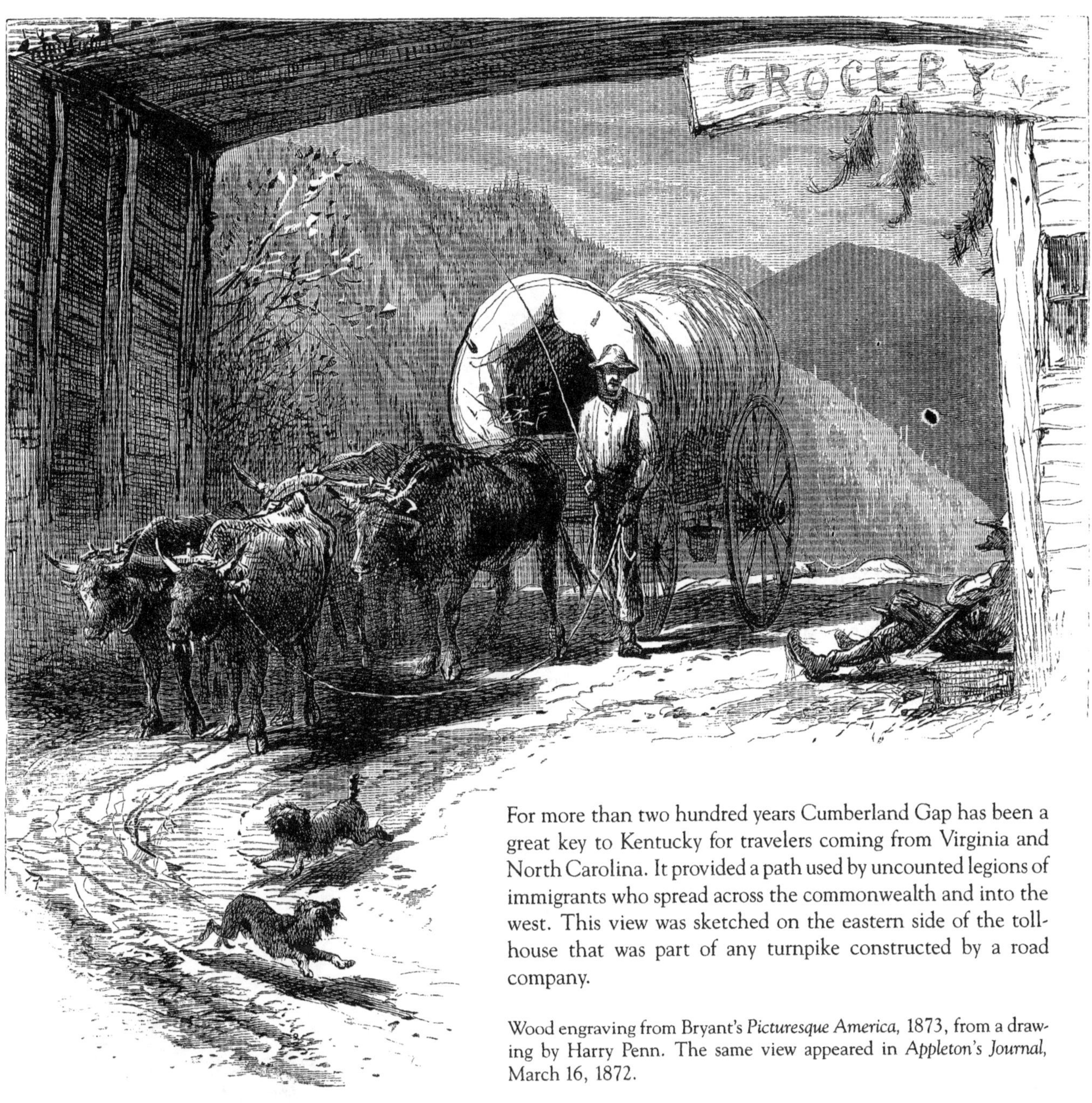

For more than two hundred years Cumberland Gap has been a great key to Kentucky for travelers coming from Virginia and North Carolina. It provided a path used by uncounted legions of immigrants who spread across the commonwealth and into the west. This view was sketched on the eastern side of the toll-house that was part of any turnpike constructed by a road company.

Wood engraving from Bryant's *Picturesque America,* 1873, from a drawing by Harry Penn. The same view appeared in *Appleton's Journal,* March 16, 1872.

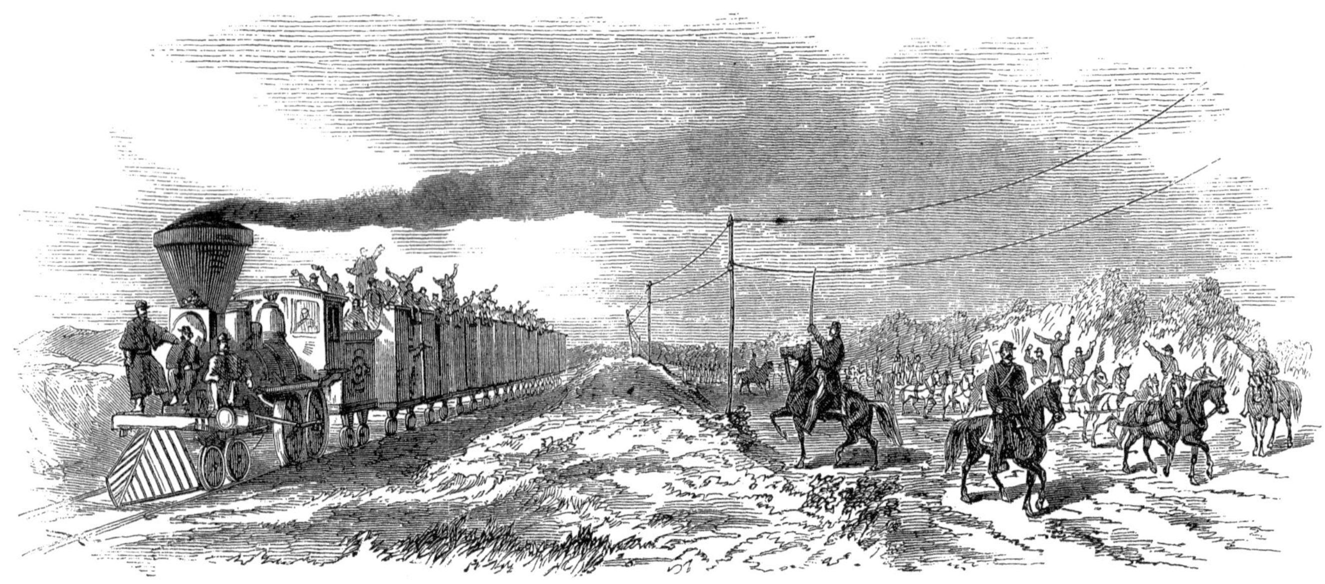

The turnpike road to Nashville was built by a private construction company chartered in 1833; the road is familiar to us now as U.S. 31W. This view shows federal troops under General Johnson advancing on Louisville by way of the Nashville turnpike and being overtaken by the equipage and baggage train on the Louisville and Nashville Railroad.

Wood engraving from *Frank Leslie's Illustrated Newspaper,* January 18, 1862, from a drawing by *Leslie's* "special artist with General Buell," probably William R. McComas, Cincinnati.

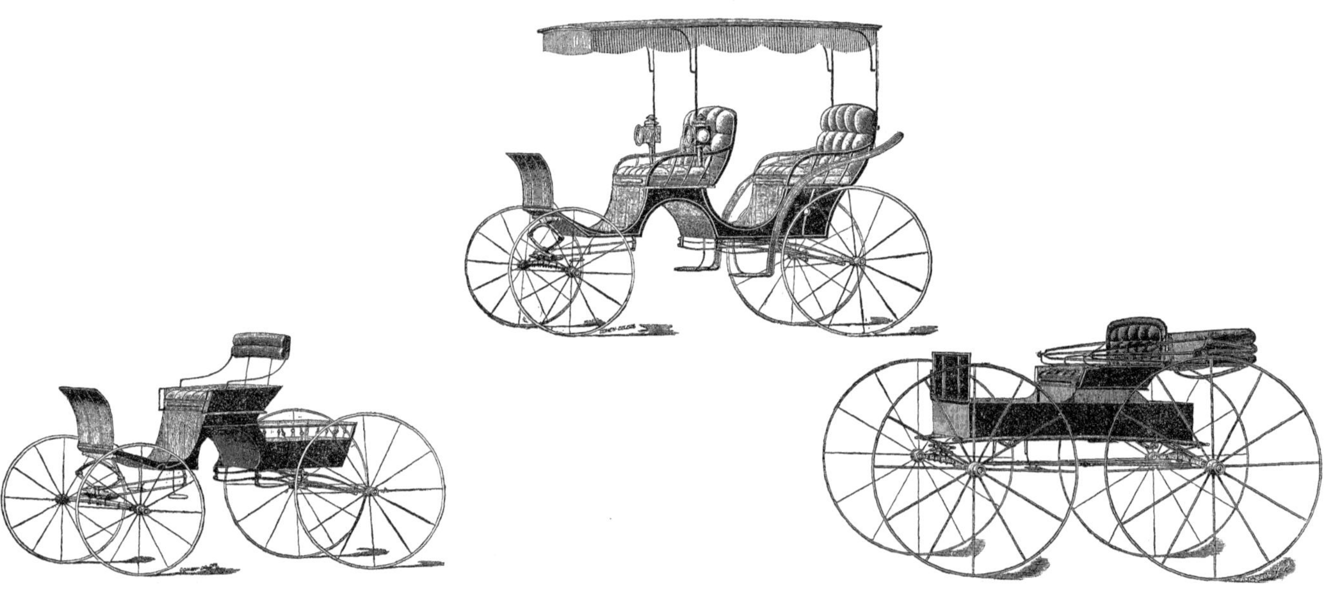

The Lippelmann Carriage Company in Cincinnati advertised in the 1889 *Guide to the Blue Grass Regions of Kentucky* to interest Kentuckians in one-passenger speeding carts, two-passenger road carts, surreys, and road wagons. At this time, selling points in personal transportation were already such things as comfort—"positively no horse motion"—and beauty—"extra strength [that] does not mar in the least the graceful lines of the exterior."

Wood engravings from Kentucky Central Railway's *Guide to the Blue Grass Regions of Kentucky,* 1889.

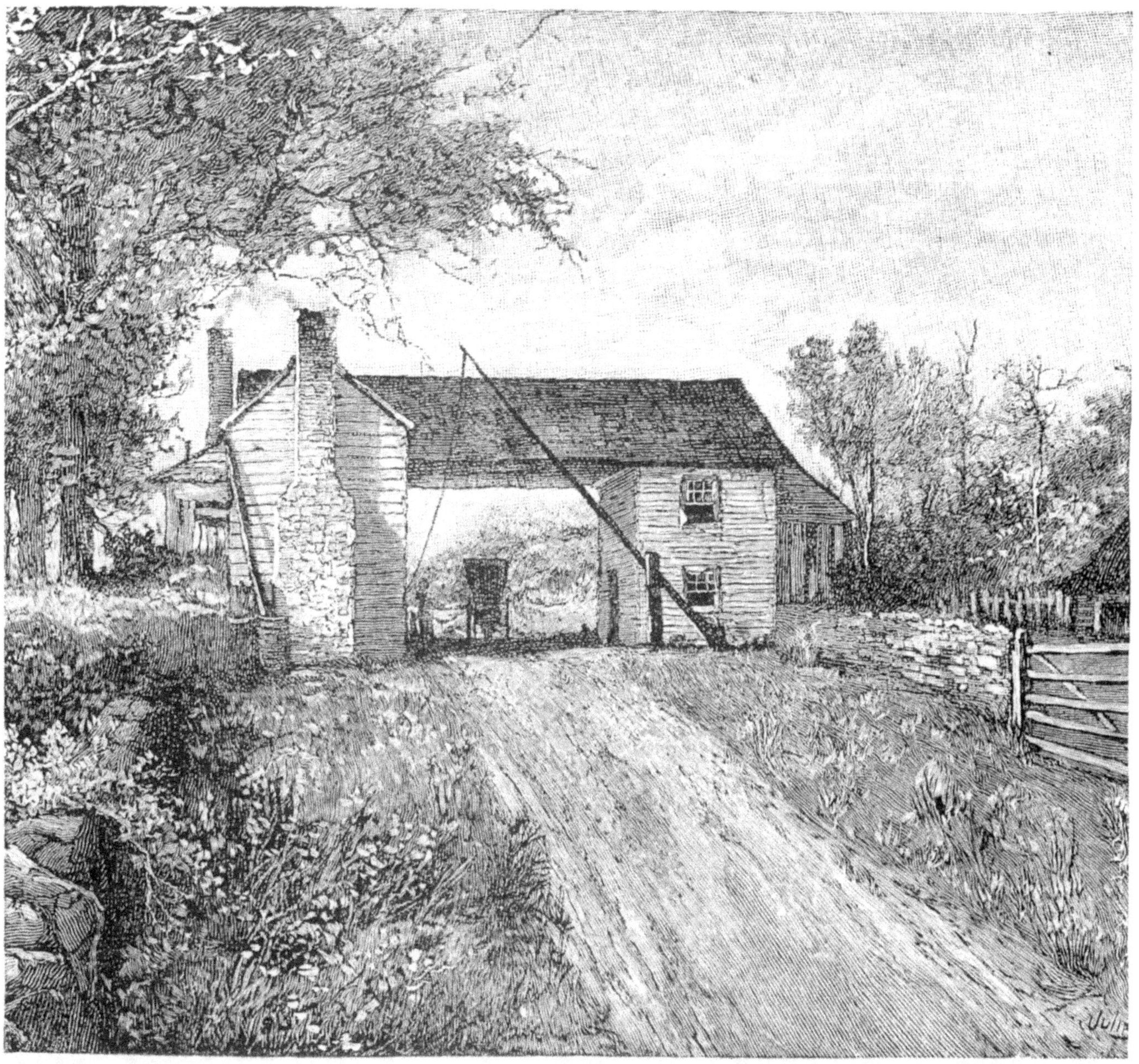

James Lane Allen, one of Kentucky's most widely read authors, toured Kentucky in the mid-1880s and provided a number of articles for *Harper's Monthly Magazine.* Julian Rix, a well-known artist, may have accompanied him. Allen did not describe this tollhouse on the Harrodsburg Pike, but he did write that they traveled over the "broad smooth level white glistening turnpikes of macadamized limestone. It is a luxury to drive, and also an expense, as one will discover before he has passed through many toll-gates. One could travel more cheaply on the finest railway. All limestone for these hundreds of miles is broken by a hammer in the hand." In the same article, "The Blue-Grass Region," he described how "the huge yellowish-red stage coach rolls over the marbled roads of the blue-grass country."

Wood engraving from *Harper's Monthly Magazine,* February 1886, from a drawing by Julian Rix, New York.

A visitor from France writing of his trip to Mammoth Cave included this view of a stopping point along the way. He did not specify the exact location but told of this caravansary, called a "forest house," somewhere in Kentucky. It was nothing more, he said, than a roof and a hard, soil-packed floor, with sleeping racks and animal stalls. Upon entering, he found a hundred men and animals sprawled over the floor, and was greeted with shouts, barking, neighing, bellowing, grunting, and snoring. Entrance to the building cost two cents; to occupy a sleeping rack cost twelve cents.

Wood engraving from *Le Tour du Monde,* 1859. Engraved by L. Dumont from a drawing by Janet-Lange from a sketch by M. Poussielgue.

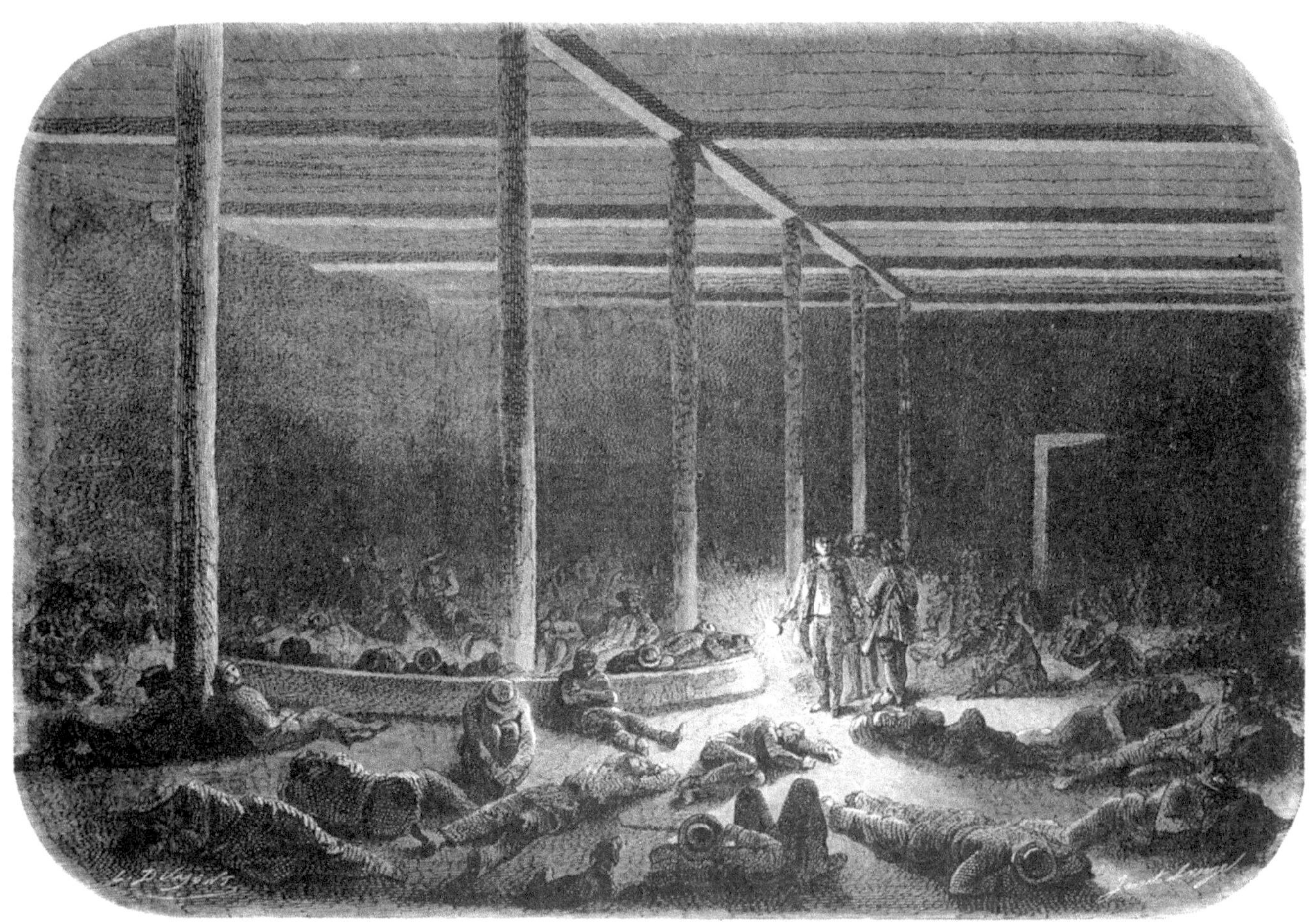

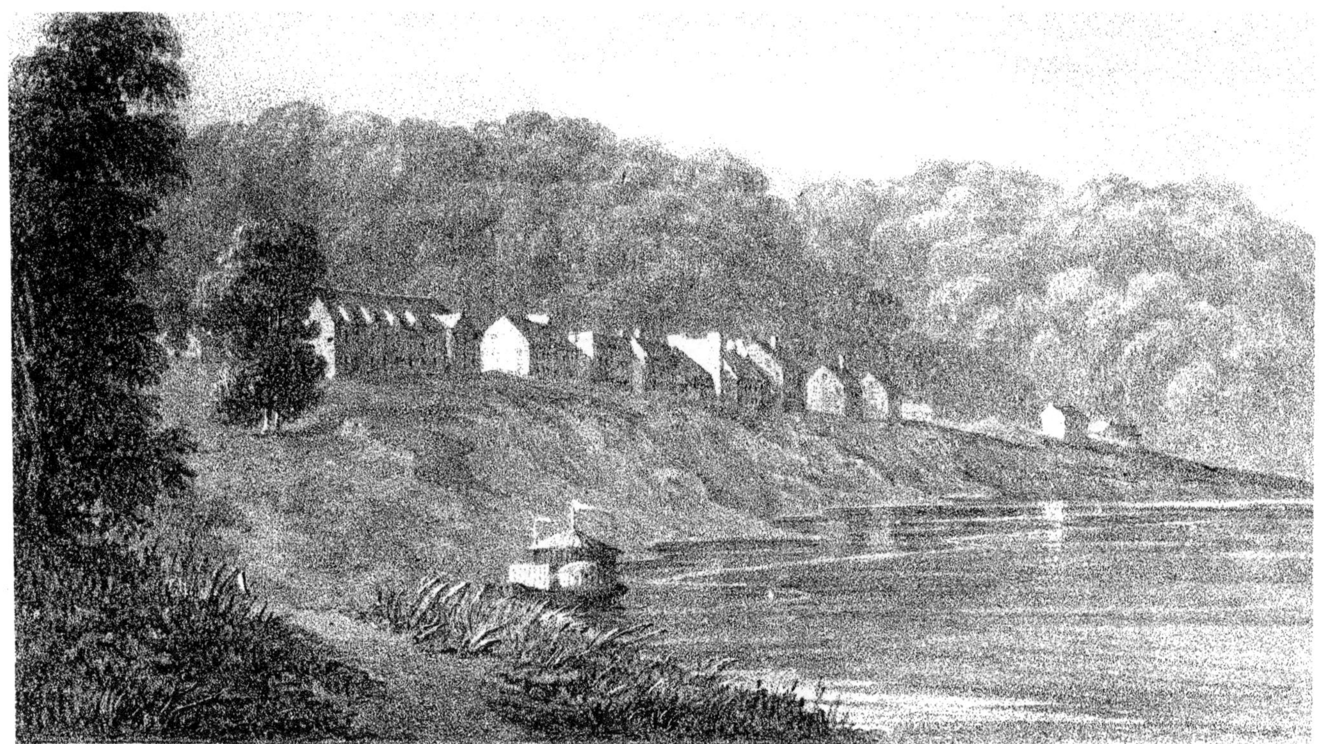

Maysville, first known as Limestone, was one of the chief ports of entry into frontier Kentucky. By the time of this view, its importance in that regard had declined. Adlard Welby makes only a brief reference to the ferry at Maysville, calling it a "team-boat" lately established. In a team-boat, the paddle-wheel is driven by one or more horses walking on a treadmill. Commercial operation of a ferry required a license granted by a county court after the need for the ferry had been adequately demonstrated.

Lithograph from Welby's *A Visit to North America,* 1821, from a drawing on stone by G. Harley from a sketch by Welby.

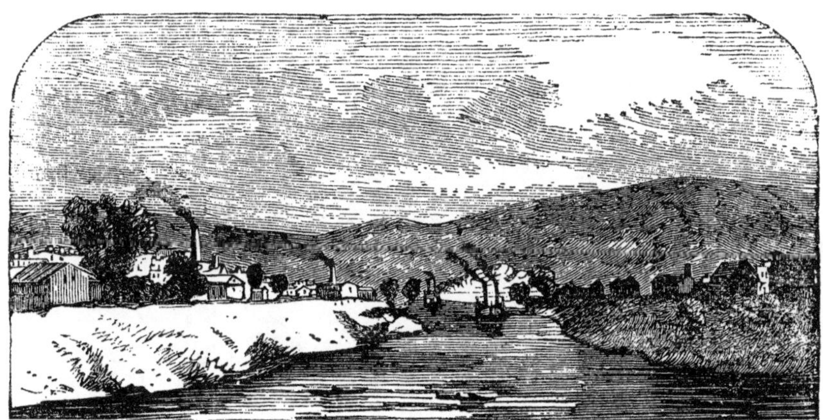

Ele Bowen wrote that Carrollton, located at the mouth of the Kentucky River, was settled in 1784 by a Mr. Elliott, was subsequently fortified by Gen. Charles Scott, and was finally laid off as a town in 1792. Its original name was Port William. From Carrollton, Bowen said, the Kentucky River was navigable for flatboats for about 150 miles and for steamboats as far as Frankfort.

Wood engraving from Bowen's *Rambles in the Path of the Steam-Horse,* 1855, from a drawing by Emile F. Beaulieu.

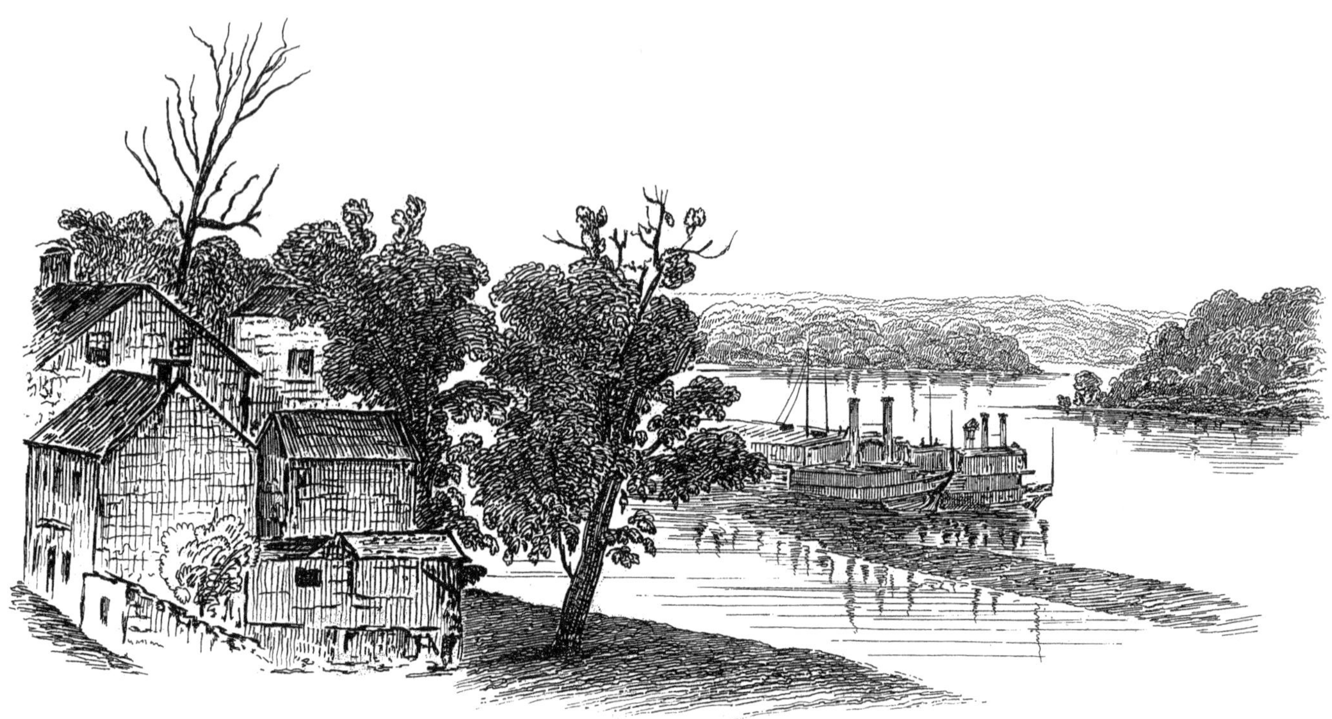

Shippingport was the natural harbor and landing place at the foot of the rapids near Louisville. With the coming of the steamboat it became a bustling metropolis, supplying the men and means for transporting freight and passengers around the falls. It is said that as many as forty boats arrived in a day. Basil Hall described Shippingport as "one of the great landing places from New Orleans or from St. Louis," and noted that a canal was being cut to allow boats to pass around the falls. The opening of the Louisville and Portland canal in 1830 began the decline of Shippingport and led to its disappearance in the twentieth century. This view was among those that appeared on Staffordshire wares produced by Enoch Wood of Burslem and Ralph Stevenson of Cobridge about 1830.

Copper plate etching from Basil Hall's *Forty Etchings Made with the Camera Lucida in North America in 1827 and 1828,* 1829. Etched by William H. Lizars from a drawing by Basil Hall.

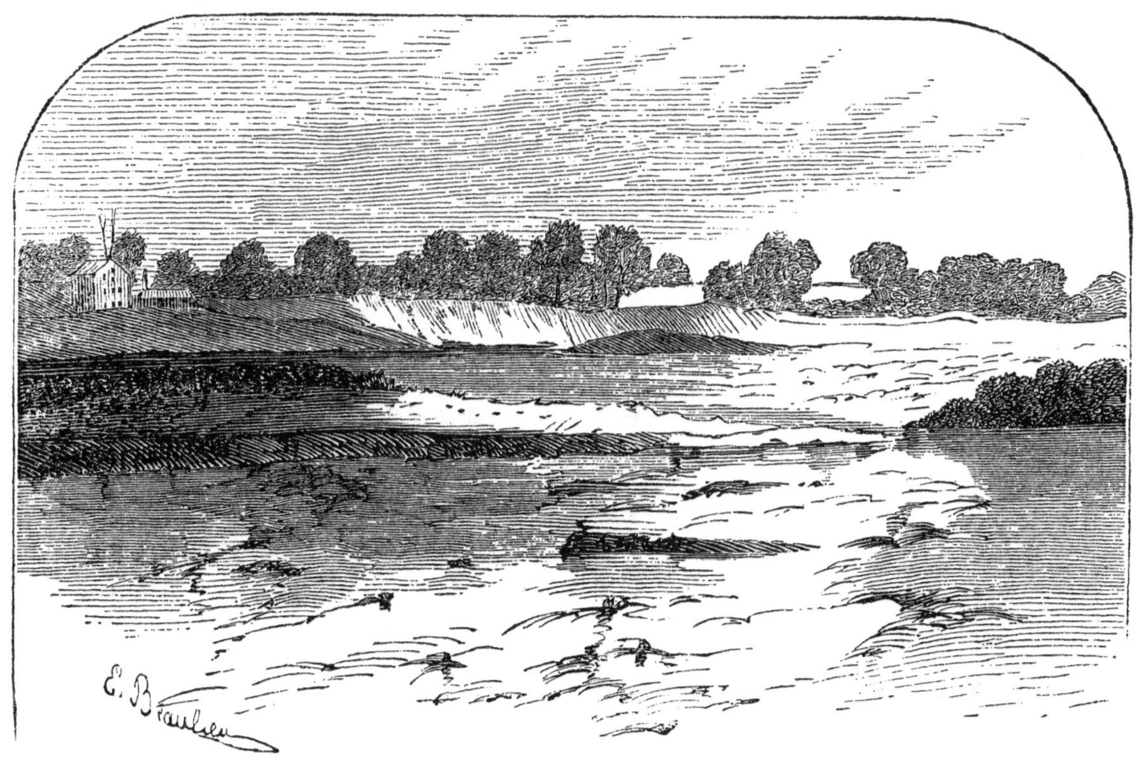

The interruption to navigation caused by the falls of the Ohio gave Louisville extraordinary advantages for trade and commerce. Ele Bowen wrote that "the falls are avoided by means of a canal, two and a half miles in length . . . cut out of a solid limestone rock." He considered the falls the principal reason for Louisville's present success as well as the grounds for its future promise.

The long-awaited canal bypassing the falls at Louisville was completed in 1832, but its limited width soon made it outdated; it was too small to allow passage of what Ele Bowen called "boats of the first class."

Both wood engravings from Bowen's *Rambles in the Path of the Steam-Horse,* 1855, from drawings by Emile F. Beaulieu.

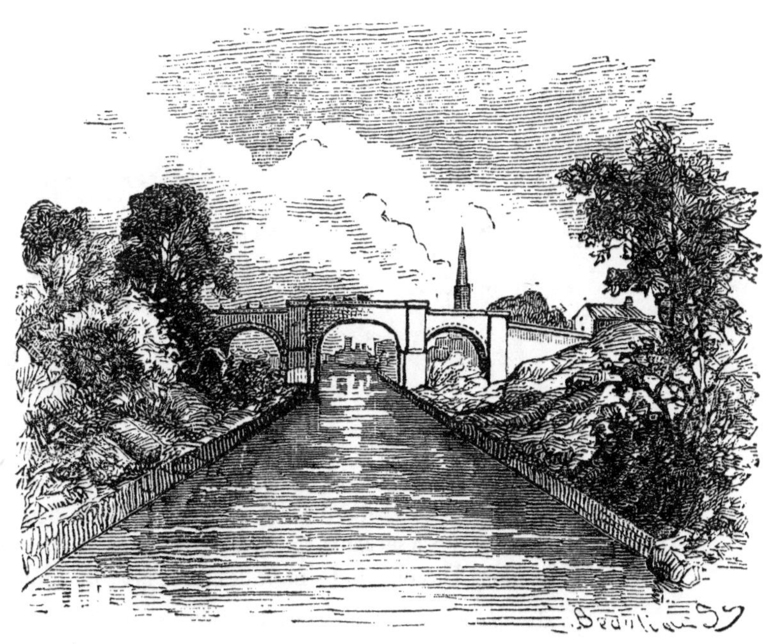

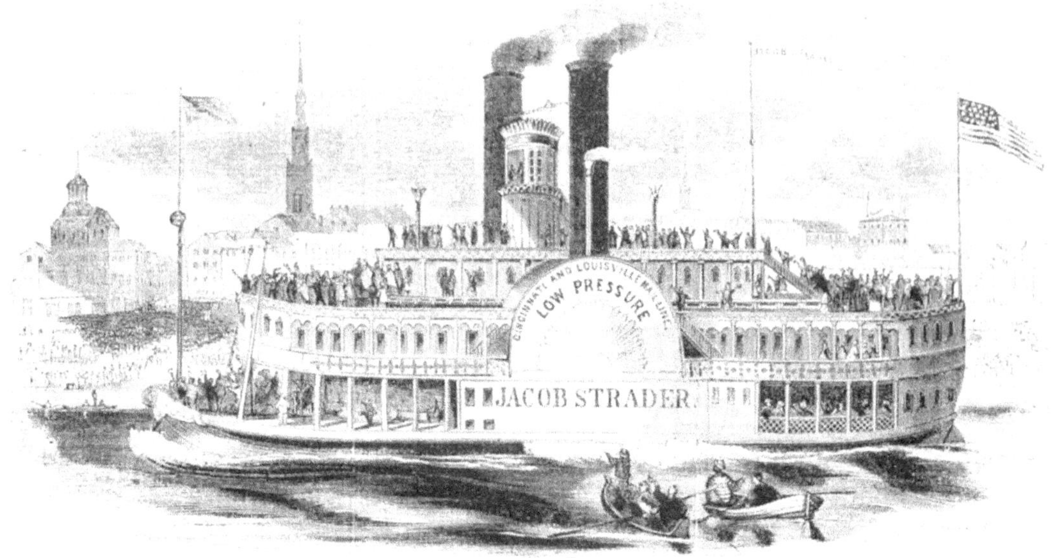

Carriage of mail by steamboats was started in the 1830s; a daily service between Cincinnati and Louisville began in 1837. The Louisville Mail Company steamboat *Jacob Strader* was said to be the largest boat on the Ohio when it was built in 1853. The main deck was 69 feet wide, built on a hull only 28 feet wide; this was an extreme example of the practice of extending the "guards" beyond the line of the hull. The boat had berths for 310 passengers and was named for a wealthy and prominent Cincinnatian and former steamboat captain.

Wood engraving from *Gleason's Pictorial Drawing-Room Companion,* October 14, 1854. Engraved by Samuel E. Brown.

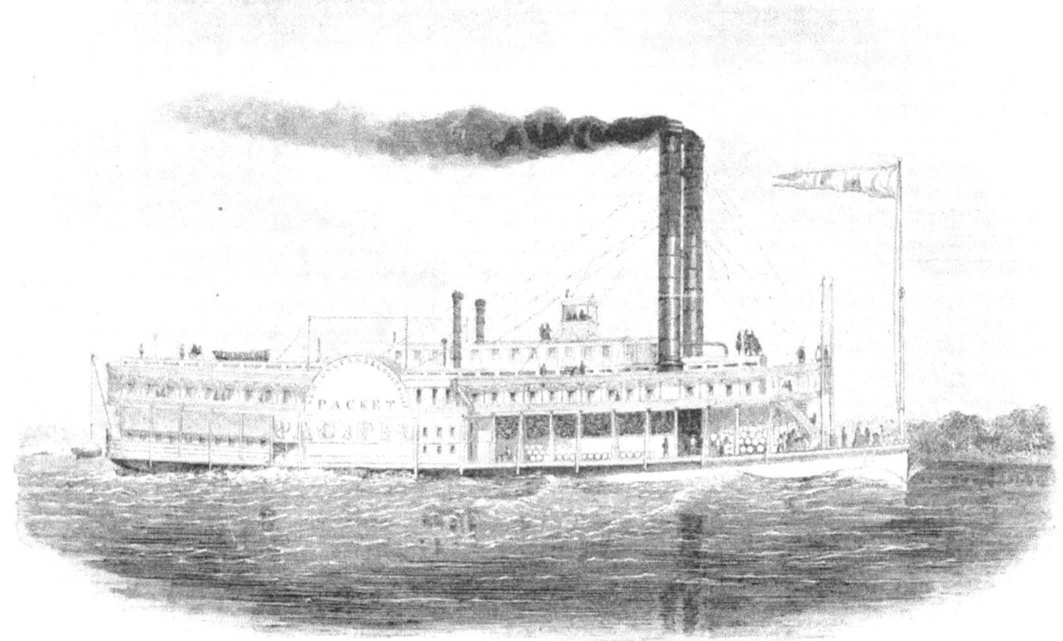

The steamer *Pacific* was one of ten built at a boatyard in New Albany, Indiana, in 1857. It was nearly three hundred feet long and could accommodate 120 passengers on trips between New Orleans and Louisville. The *Harper's Weekly* description stated that the boat contained a nursery, a servants' room, a bathroom, and a barber shop, "making her equal to the best arranged hotels" and a most desirable boat for southern travel.

Wood engraving from *Harper's Weekly,* February 25, 1860.

Steamboat disasters were frequent on Kentucky's rivers. Collisions, explosions, snags, and poor piloting all took their tolls. The steamboat *Moselle,* which ran between Pittsburgh and St. Louis, had made one round trip and was downbound on its second on April 25, 1838, when it exploded one mile above Cincinnati.

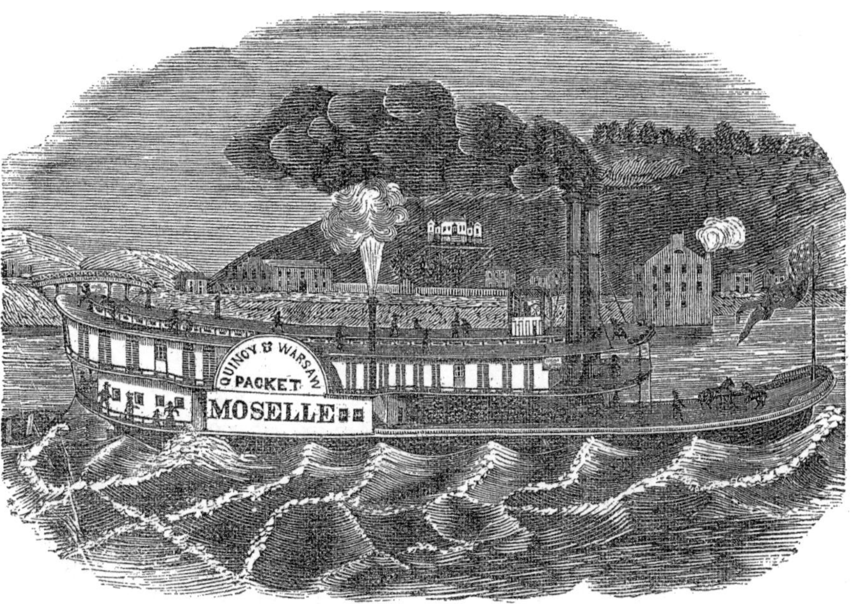

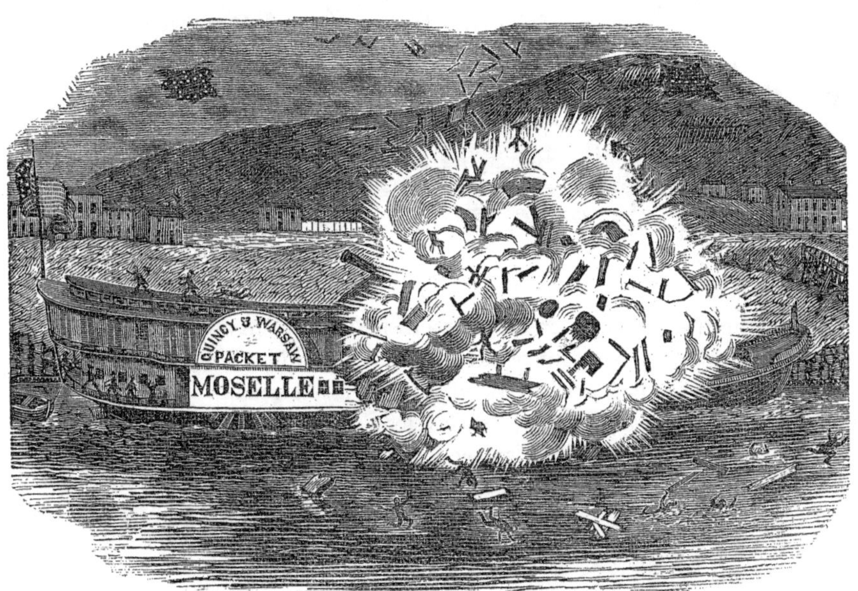

According to witnesses, the force of the explosion threw passengers, machinery, and other materials hundreds of yards in all directions. The explosion was attributed to the recklessness of the captain and the engineer, who had let the boiler build up an excessive amount of steam pressure. The U.S. Commission of Patents reported that the *Moselle* disaster resulted in the greatest loss of life in the nation for the period 1816 through 1848.

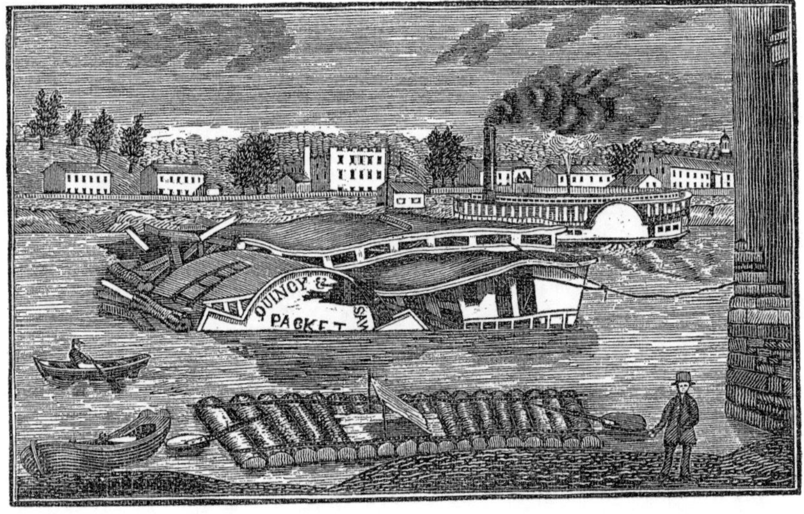

The known killed and missing totalled 136 persons, but because passenger records were incomplete, it was estimated that as many as 150 had died. This series of engravings, made from sketches by an unknown artist from Cincinnati, was unusual in that it provided not only a representation of the tragedy, but also "before" and "after" scenes.

Wood engravings from *Family Magazine,* 1841.

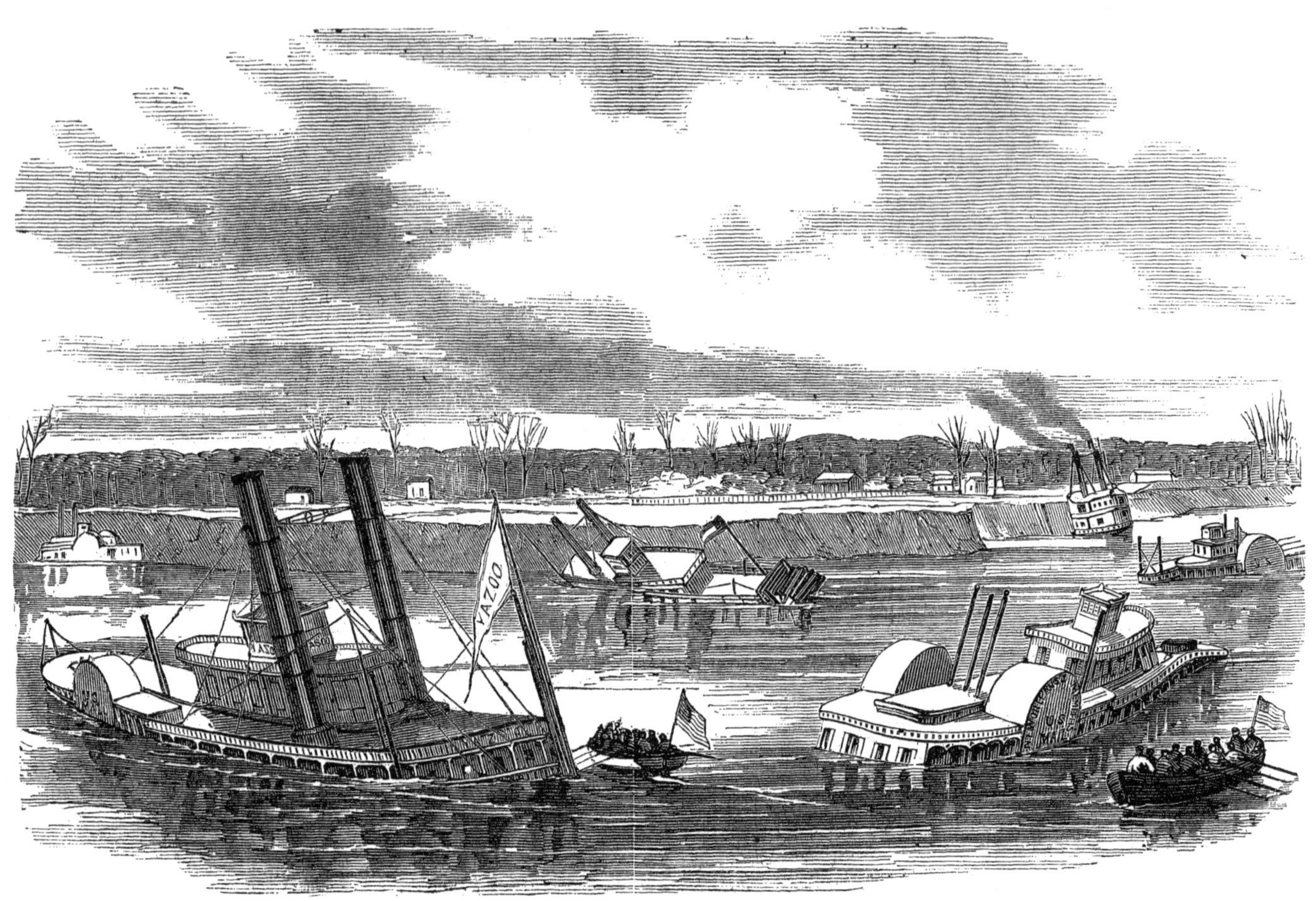

With the coming of the Civil War, the rivers became crucial to each side's cause. In an effort to stave off Union control of the Mississippi, Confederates fortified Island No. 10, located off the Tennessee shore just south of the Kentucky Bend, and it proved a major obstacle to opening the river for Union operations. This view shows steamers sunk by the rebels between Island No. 10 and New Madrid. Some damaged steamboats could be salvaged and returned to wartime service, but enemy action added greatly to the loss of steamers in strategic rivers. Because of changes in the channel, Island No. 10 has disappeared.

Wood engraving from *Harper's Weekly,* May 3, 1862, from a drawing by Alexander Simplot.

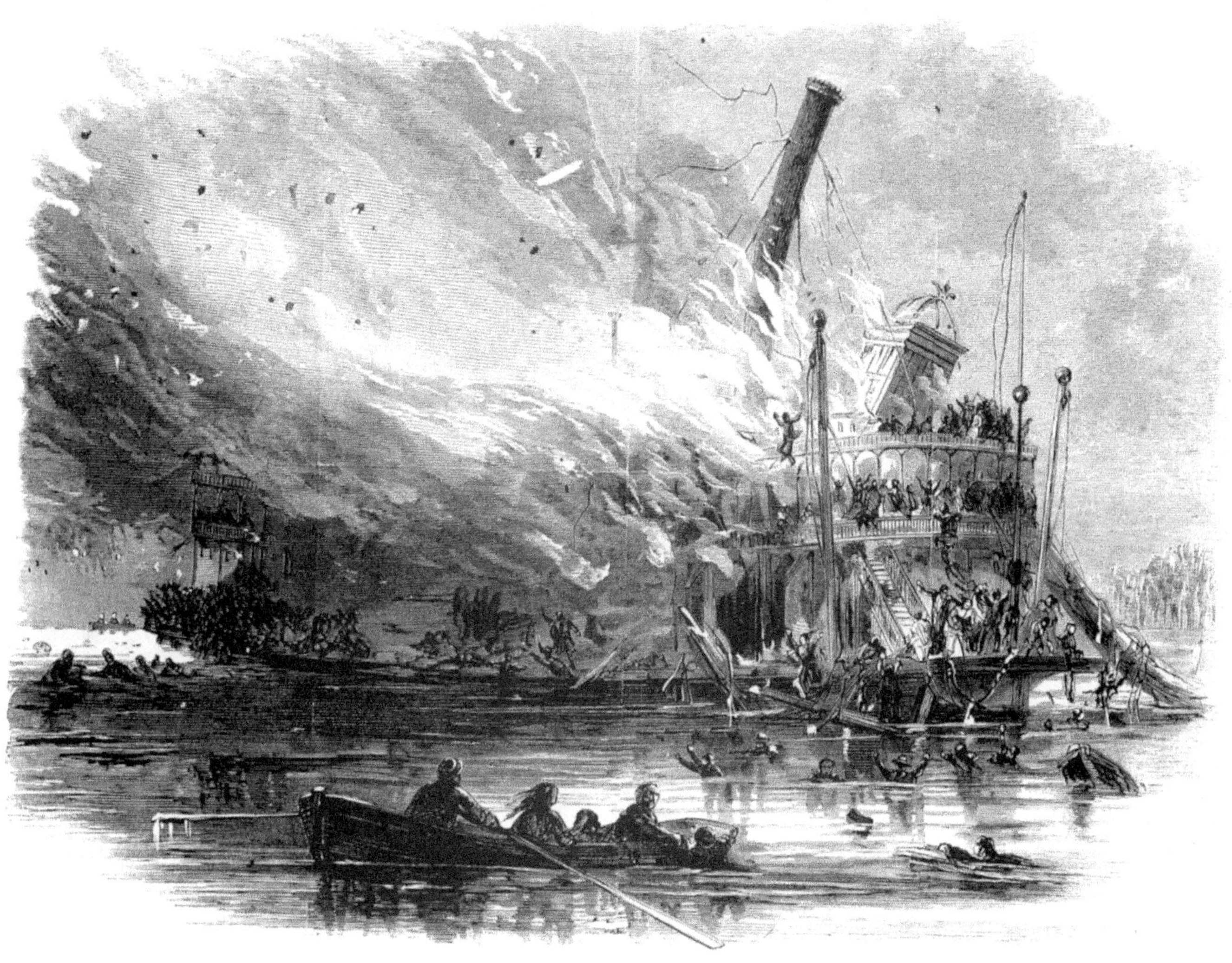

On March 18, 1868, twelve miles above Cincinnati, the steamer *Magnolia* exploded and burned. Nearly half of the 140 on board died in the explosion, in the subsequent fire, or by drowning. The people of the village of California, Kentucky, helped rescue the survivors. Because of steam engine and boiler explosions, collisions, fires, accidental sinkings, difficult operating conditions and bad weather, steamboats on the Ohio River had an average life span of no more than five years.

Wood engraving from *Harper's Weekly,* April 4, 1868.

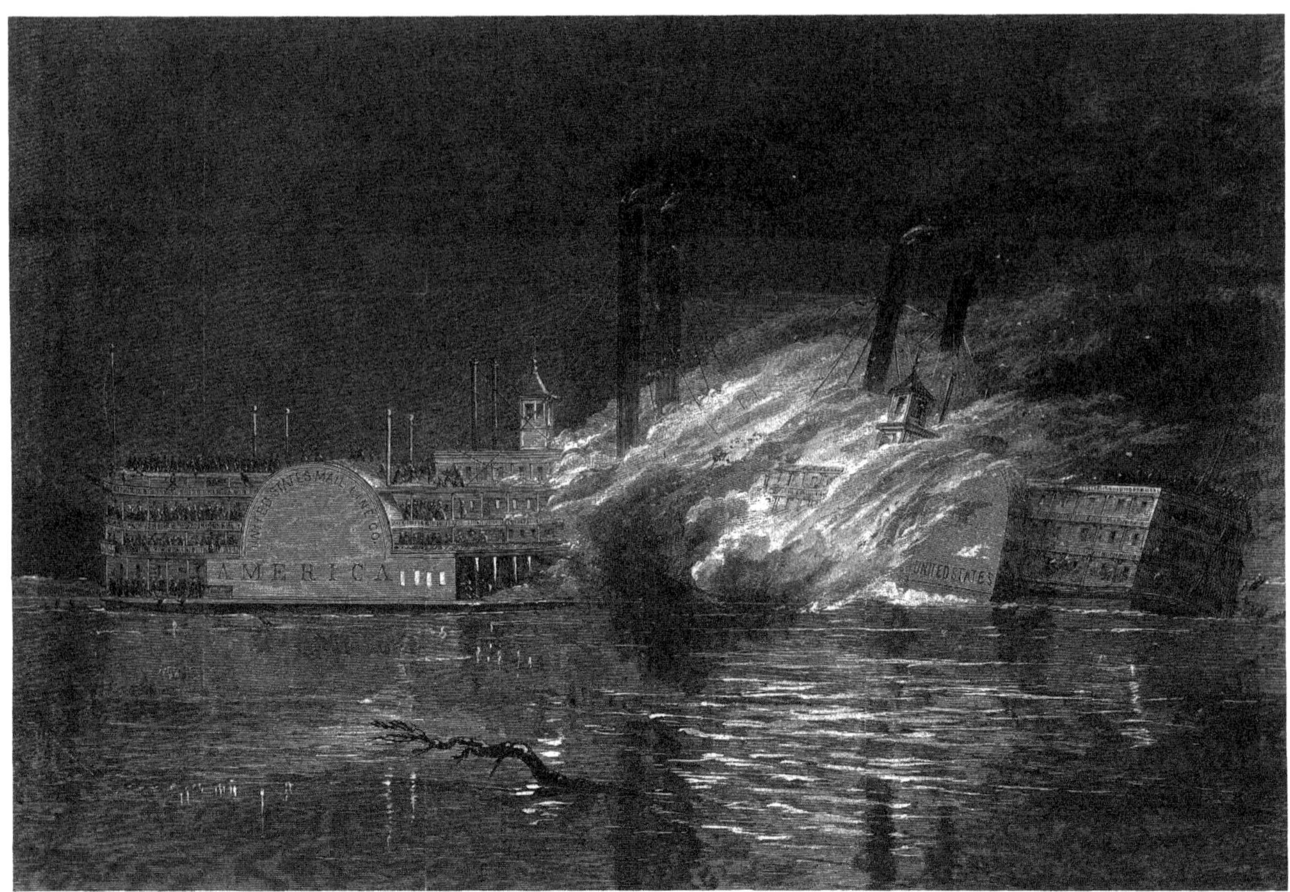

The steamers *United States,* en route to Louisville, and *America,* eastbound for Cincinnati, collided on the night of December 4, 1868, near Rahl's Landing, twenty-two miles above Madison. Both boats were owned by the Cincinnati and Louisville Mail Packet Company and provided daily service between the two cities, passing each other at about the same place on each trip. Weather and visibility were reported to be good, and the boats were apparently on proper courses shortly before the collision. A subsequent lawsuit charged that the pilot of the ascending *America* willfully neglected to follow pilot regulations and the signals given by the other boat. Seventy-four passengers and crew members lost their lives in the accident. The *Louisville Courier-Journal* described the boats as two of the largest and most luxurious on the river. They had double cabins—two decks of cabins for passengers—and were said to be worth $200,000 each.

Wood engraving from *Harper's Weekly,* December 26, 1868, from a drawing by Ephraim P. Frazer, Cincinnati.

The grand celebration of the completion of four new railway lines occurred in Louisville September 12, 1881. An estimated two hundred thousand citizens and visitors thronged the streets. A parade of civil and military organizations, with a trade procession representing every industry and business in the city, took three hours to pass. Animal balloons were liberated, and the day ended with a blaze of fireworks from floats and flatboats anchored in the river. The four railway lines celebrated were the Louisville, Evansville and St. Louis; the Chesapeake, Ohio and Southwestern; the Louisville and Nashville's Knoxville branch; and the Chesapeake and Ohio from Lexington to Frankfort, which completed an independent route from the Ohio River to the eastern seaboard.

Wood engravings from *Frank Leslie's Illustrated Newspaper,* September 23, 1882, from a drawing by C. Upham.

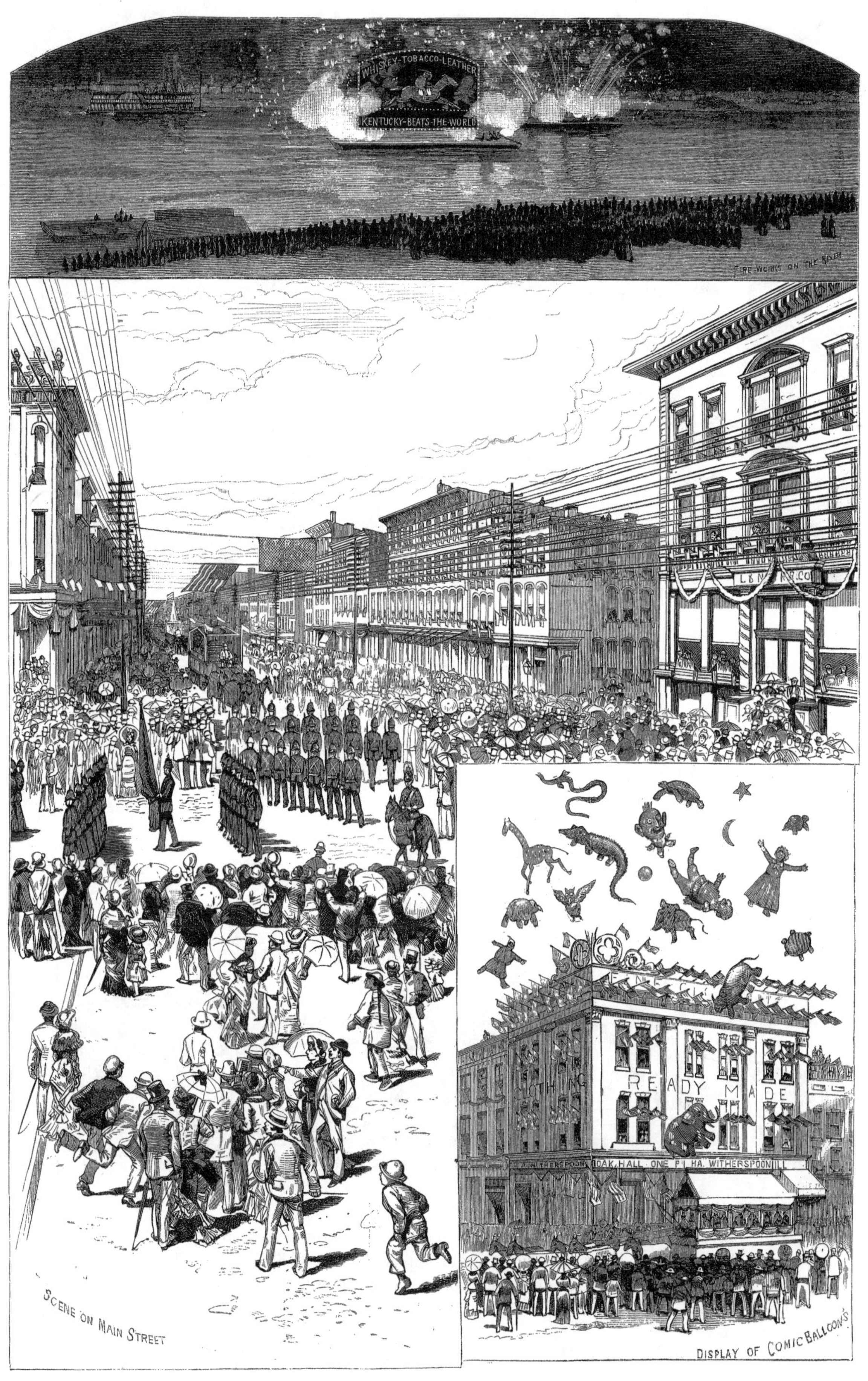
WHISKEY-TOBACCO-LEATHER
KENTUCKY-BEATS-THE-WORLD
FIRE-WORKS ON THE RIVER
L & N R.R. CO.
READY MADE
CLOTHING
OAK HALL
HA. WITHERSPOON
SCENE ON MAIN STREET
DISPLAY OF COMIC BALLOONS

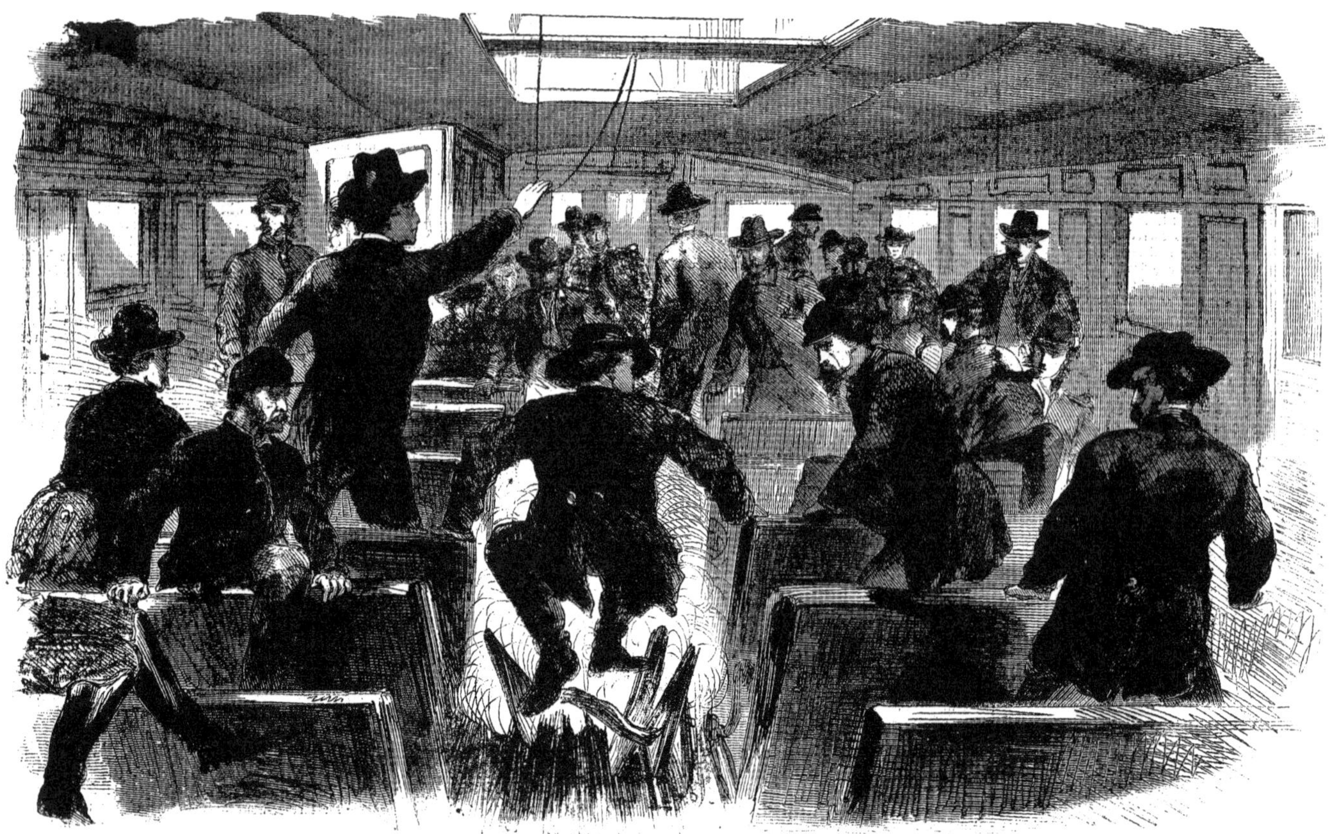

Like steamboat travel, railroad transportation could be dangerous. This accident occurred on the Louisville and Nashville Railroad near Lebanon Junction. The description accompanying this view stated that intensely cold weather made the iron rails brittle, which was a principal cause of accidents.

Wood engraving from *Harper's Weekly,* February 20, 1864, from a drawing by one of *Harper's* "special artists."

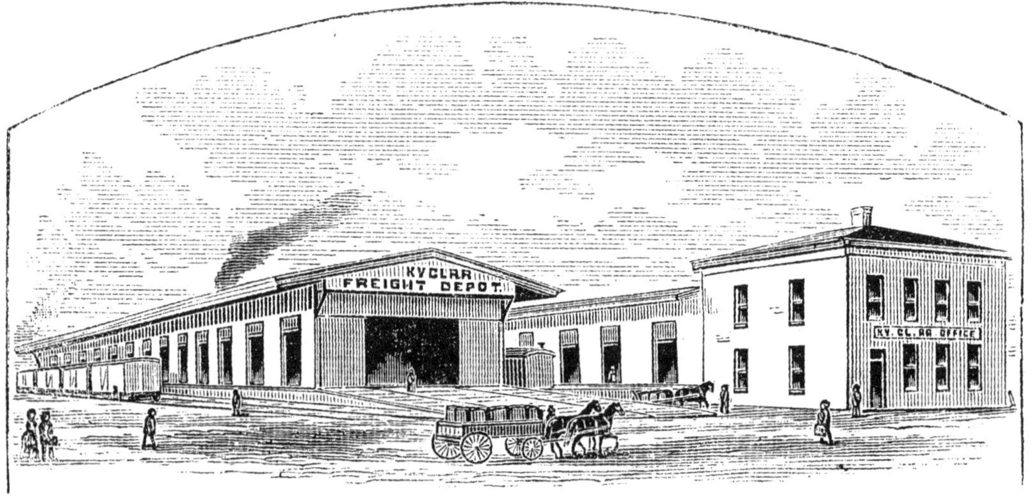

Train depots were an important part of any city, and locales often took great pride in their particular buildings. The Kentucky Central Railroad depot at Covington stood at Eighth and Washington streets. The railroad absorbed several smaller lines and was taken into the Louisville and Nashville in 1891.

Wood engraving from Kenny's *Illustrated Cincinnati,* 1875.

The Louisville and New Albany Daisy Line had 5.8 miles of track and crossed the Kentucky and Indiana bridges on a regular thirty-minute schedule. Its elevated station stood at Fourth and Water streets. In the year 1886 it carried 560,000 passengers at a fare of ten cents each. The railroad trestles shown here remained along the river at Louisville until the 1980s.

Wood engraving from the Louisville Board of Trade's *The City of Louisville and a Glimpse of Kentucky,* 1887.

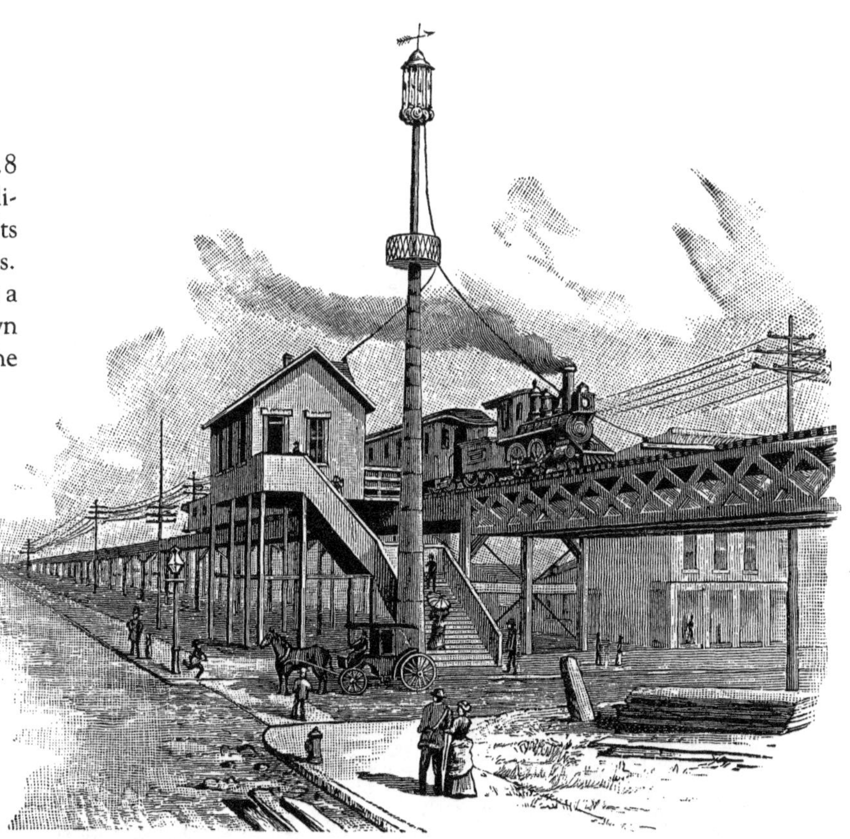

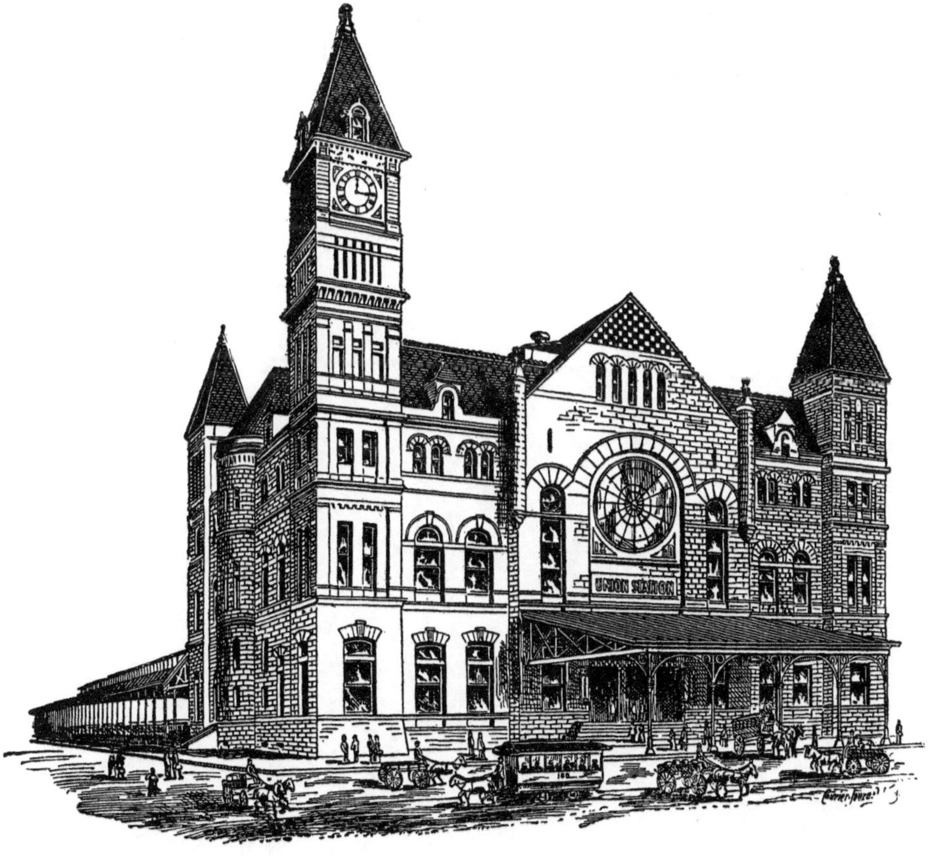

Union Station in Louisville was dedicated in 1891 and used principally by the Louisville and Nashville Railroad, along with several other companies. It superseded the Louisville and Nashville's first passenger station, which opened in 1858 at Ninth and Broadway, and its second passenger depot at Tenth and Maple streets.

Wood engraving from Elliott's *Illustrated Centennial Record of the State of Kentucky,* 1892.

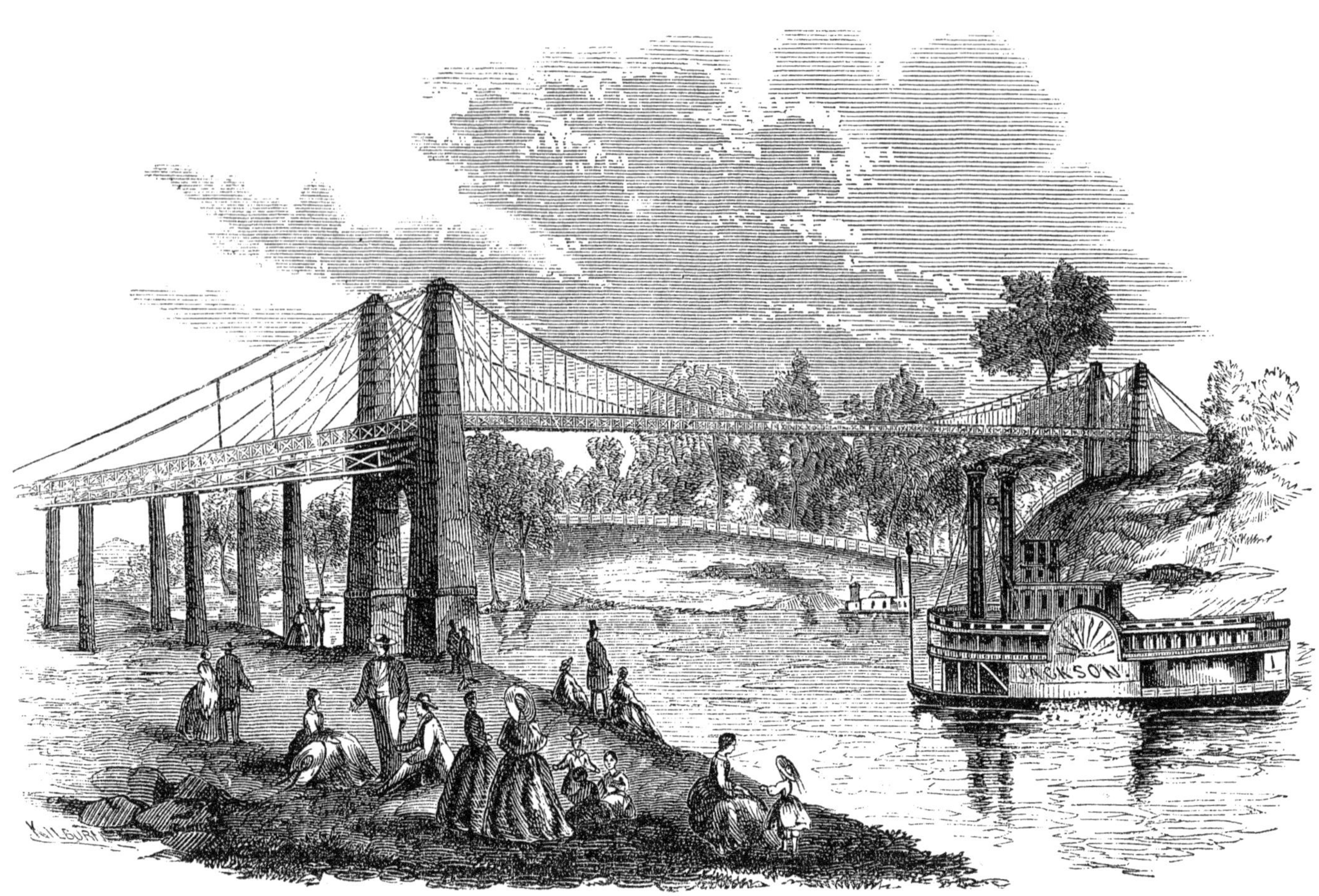

Early histories of Kentucky call attention to the fine suspension bridge over the Licking River between Covington and Newport. The bridge opened in December 1853, supported on cables that had been made in Newport. Less than a month later the cables and the roadway fell into the river when inadequate connections gave way. Repairs were made and the bridge served to join the adjacent cities for about eighty years before it was replaced.

Wood engraving from *Ballou's Pictorial Drawing-Room Companion,* December 20, 1856. Engraved and drawn by Samuel S. Kilburn, Boston.

The bridge over Green River on the Louisville and Nashville Railroad was designed by Albert Fink, the rail line's outstanding engineer, and built under his supervision. *Harper's Weekly* called it the second largest bridge on this continent—after the Victoria bridge at Montreal—with five spans that totaled a thousand feet in length. It stood 118 feet above low water level. This view appeared soon after the first through trip of 187 miles from Louisville to Nashville, which was made on October 27, 1859.

Wood engraving from *Harper's Weekly,* February 25, 1860.

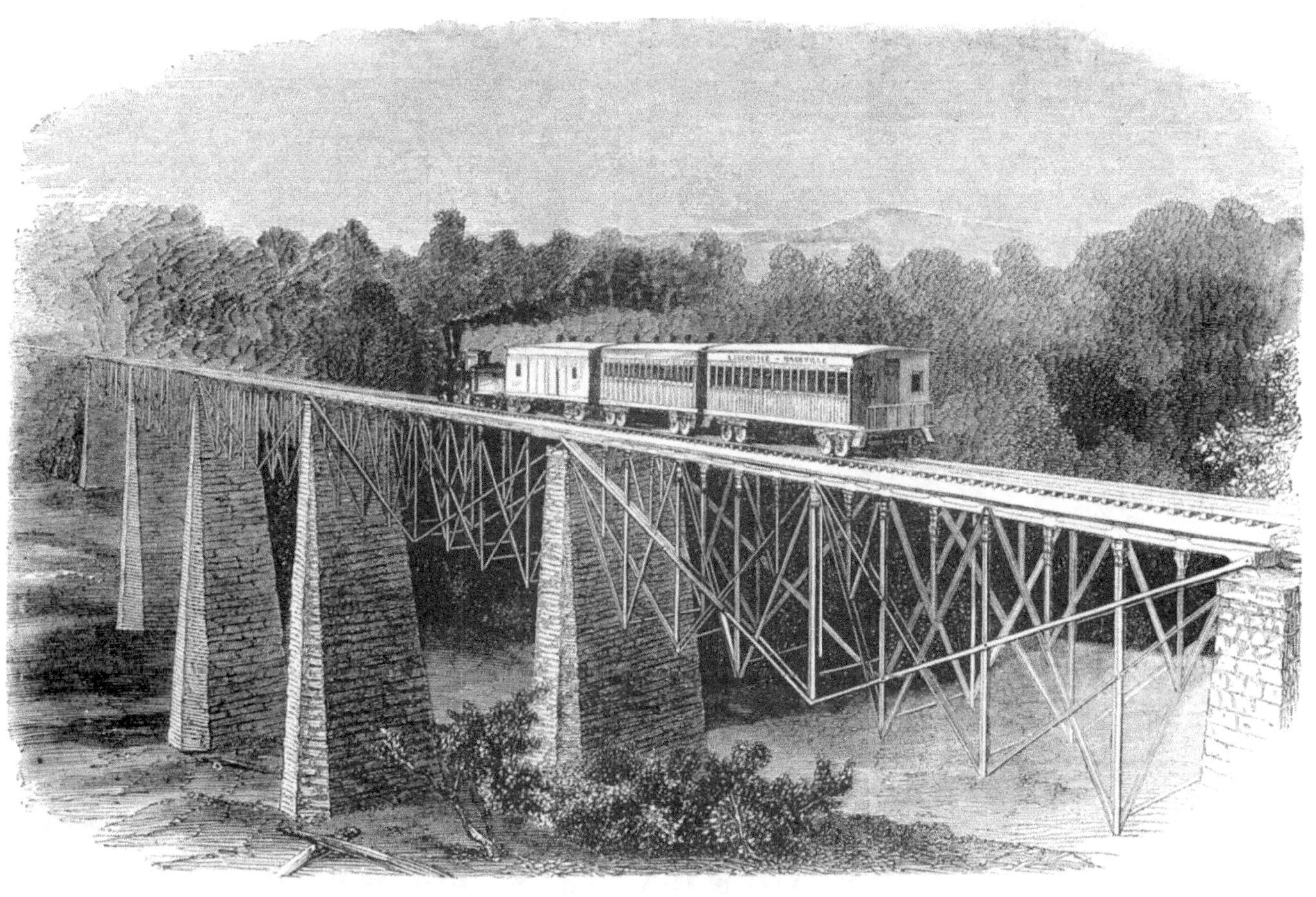

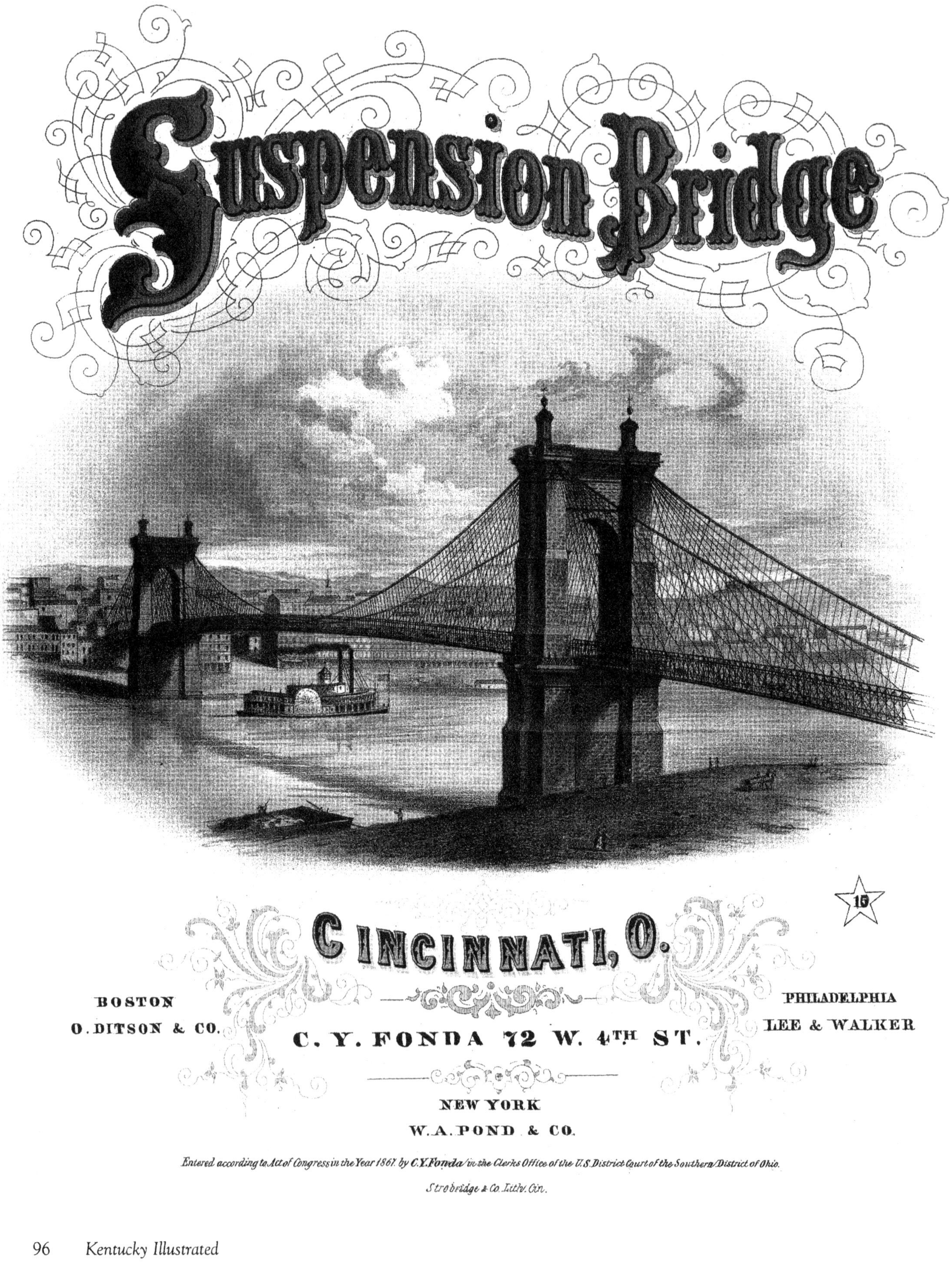

Suspension Bridge

15

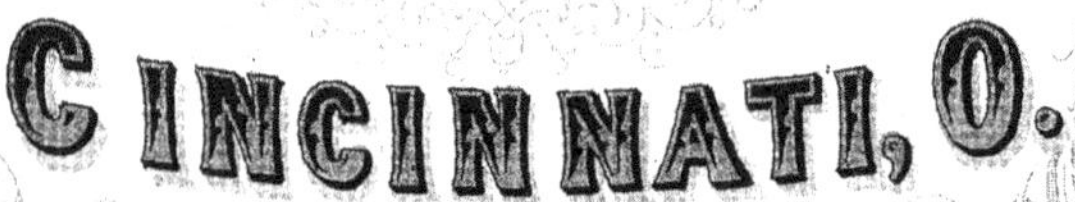

BOSTON
O. DITSON & CO.

C. Y. FONDA 72 W. 4TH ST.

PHILADELPHIA
LEE & WALKER

NEW YORK
W. A. POND & CO.

Entered according to Act of Congress in the Year 1867 by C.Y. Fonda in the Clerks Office of the U.S. District Court of the Southern District of Ohio.

Strobridge & Co. Lith. Cin.

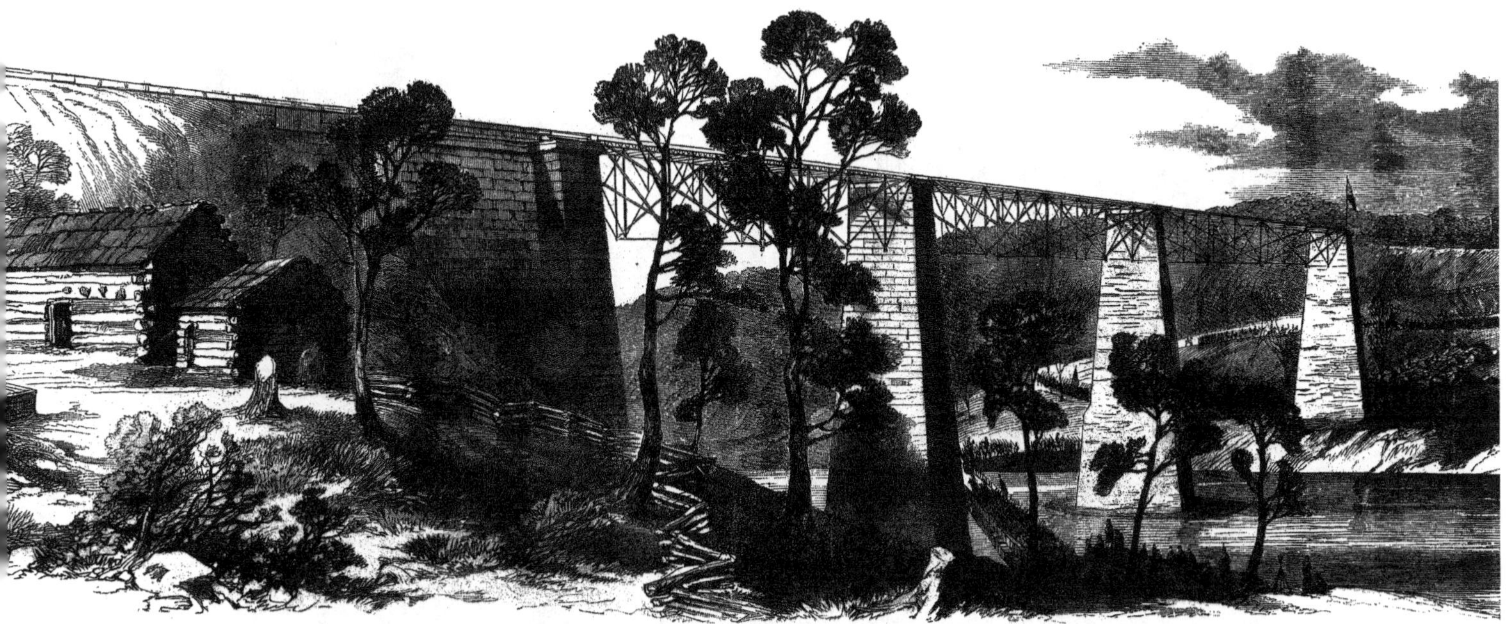

The great iron bridge over Green River on the Louisville and Nashville railroad was partially destroyed by the Confederates to obstruct the advance of the Union army under Gen. Don Carlos Buell. The iron bridge was a masterful achievement in its time, designed by Albert Fink, engineer and superintendent of the machinery and road department for the railroad. In wartime it became a vital link for the railroad. In October 1861 two spans and one pier were blown up by Confederate soldiers, and in December Fink and his repair crew began building a temporary trestle, which was in working condition a month later.

Wood engraving from *Frank Leslie's Illustrated Newspaper*, January 18, 1862, from a drawing by *Leslie's* special artist with Buell's army, probably William R. McComas, Cincinnati.

A bridge connecting Cincinnati and its sister cities of Covington and Newport had long been sought. First planned in 1846, the bridge was begun in 1856 but delayed by the financial crisis of 1857, by continuing funding problems, and by the uncertainties of the prewar period. It was finally completed between 1863 and 1866 at a total cost of $1,750,000. The magnificent bridge, still standing and in use, had a clear span of more than one thousand feet, the longest single span in the world at the time it was built. It was the work of architect and builder John A. Roebling, designer of many suspension bridges including the Brooklyn Bridge in New York, and was celebrated with the "Suspension Bridge Grand March," published in 1867.

Chromolithographed sheet music cover, published by C.Y. Fonda, Cincinnati, 1867. Lithographed by Strobridge & Co., Cincinnati. Music composed by Henry Mayer.

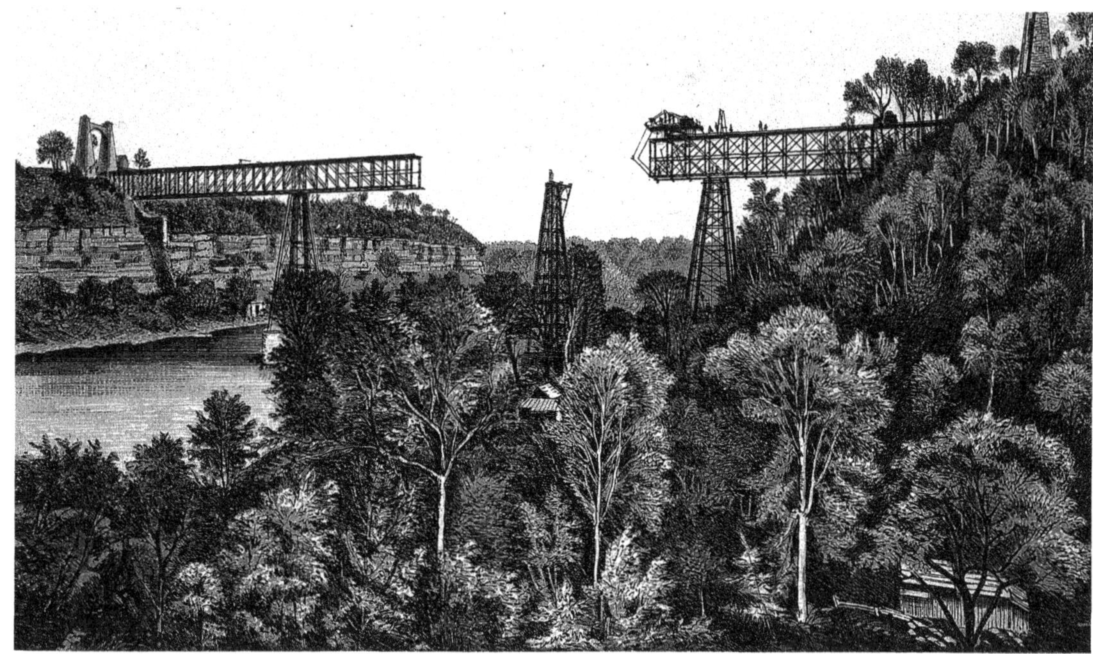

At the time it was built, High Bridge over the Kentucky River (*above*) was said to be the highest railway pier bridge in the world, the rails being 286 feet above the foundation of the piers. The Cincinnati Southern Railway souvenir booklet from 1880 called the bridge a marvel of engineering skill and a model of beauty. The area around the bridge soon became a favorite place to picnic and visit.

The Cumberland River Bridge (*below*) was seven miles south of Somerset, 1,258 feet long and 155 feet above the river. The souvenir booklet described the approach from the north, through a tunnel, noting that the sudden emergence from the tunnel's darkness onto the bridge made passengers feel that the train was "apparently suspended in mid-air."

Lithographs from *Views on the Cincinnati Southern Railway* souvenir view booklet, 1880. Photographed and published by James Mullen, Lexington.

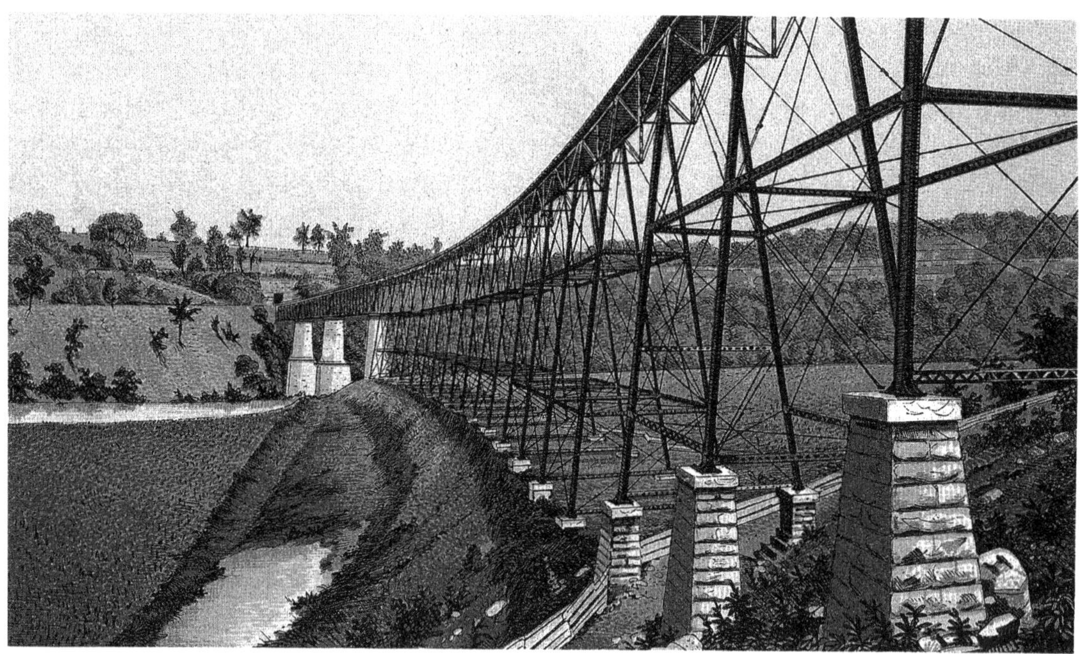

FIVE

Religion and Education

Born out of the frontier, Kentucky only slowly developed religious institutions. Although Episcopal church services were held as early as May 1775 at Boonesborough, few ministers made their way to the region before the 1780s. At times, whole denominations migrated, as was the case with the famous Traveling Church of the Baptists in 1781 and Catholic groups who moved to Nelson County a few years after that. The Presbyterian minister David Rice, together with nationally known clergymen who made the arduous trip here, such as Methodist Bishop Francis Asbury, tried to form churches among the far-flung populace. But those efforts had met with but limited success by century's end.

Then came events that focused national attention on Kentucky and partially transformed the religious face of America, particularly in the South. The Great Revival of 1799–1801 grew out of cultural and social conditions that left many, especially the young, seeking solace in a changing society. First in Logan County, then culminating in the massive Cane Ridge camp meeting of 1801, thousands upon thousands surged to revivals and revitalized religion in Kentucky.

The product of the Great Revival was religious diversity. Theological debates caused the birth in Kentucky of what became the Disciples of Christ Church, and split other denominations. Moreover, the atmosphere attracted other sects, among them the Shakers. In a communal atmosphere premised on work, simplicity, and sexual segregation, they operated efficient—albeit doomed—villages in two Kentucky locations.

Other already stable denominations grew rapidly in nineteenth-century Kentucky. Catholics saw Kentucky become the seat of the first see in the west, with Benedict Joseph Flaget as bishop. Groups such as the Sisters of Loretto, a sisterhood for female education, and Trappist monks at Gethsemane abbey added to the church's diversity. Large pre–Civil War immigration from Germany and Ireland provided a larger population base.

Protestant churches dominated the Kentucky landscape, however, and natural disasters, such as the 1811–1812 earthquakes, spurred membership growth. Despite debates over slavery, which split several churches, the congregations grew in number overall. The resulting large, handsomely designed buildings represented the religious strengths of the state. The frontier had been left behind.

Religion had a great deal to do with early education in Kentucky. In 1780, the Virginia General Assembly granted land to its territory beyond the mountains to establish a seminary of learning in Kentucky. Out of that, Transylvania Seminary opened in 1785 in the home of Presbyterian minister David Rice. Fourteen years later it consolidated with another school, and Transylvania University was born. Various colleges and universities proliferated after that, and many did not deserve the appellations given them. Some changed locations, virtually all faced financial difficulties, and several were damaged by the effects of the Civil War. But, despite that, certain schools, such as antebellum Transylvania, had a national reputation and educated numerous leaders.

Public education at a more elementary level, unfortunately, did not develop so well. Kentucky originally supported private academies, operated either by individuals or by religious groups. Funded by state donations of public land, these schools were often segregated by sex or by function (such as military schools) and might board students. Since they charged a tuition fee, education tended to bypass the poor. Not until the 1840s would a true system of free public schools develop, but even then Kentucky was one of the leaders in the South.

Yet, from that promise, no strong educational

legacy developed. After the Civil War, the commonwealth only belatedly recognized its responsibility to provide education for *all* its citizens, white and black alike. Segregated in a system certainly separate but usually not equal, African Americans would wait over a century for integrated schools, unrestricted to any citizens. But Kentucky, in that same era, did not adequately fund even its white schools. Public financial support, particularly at the local level, remained low, and the presence of excellent schools, such as Male High in Louisville, masked the real inequities and problems with the system.

Illustrators focused on the physical side of education—the bricks and mortar. Seldom did students appear in the images, and only occasionally did the predominant one-room school draw attention. Instead, the impressive college building, or the "unusual" education (such as the school for the blind), or the model public school edifice formed the dominant views. The reality of Kentucky education remained conveniently hidden away.

—*J.C.K.*

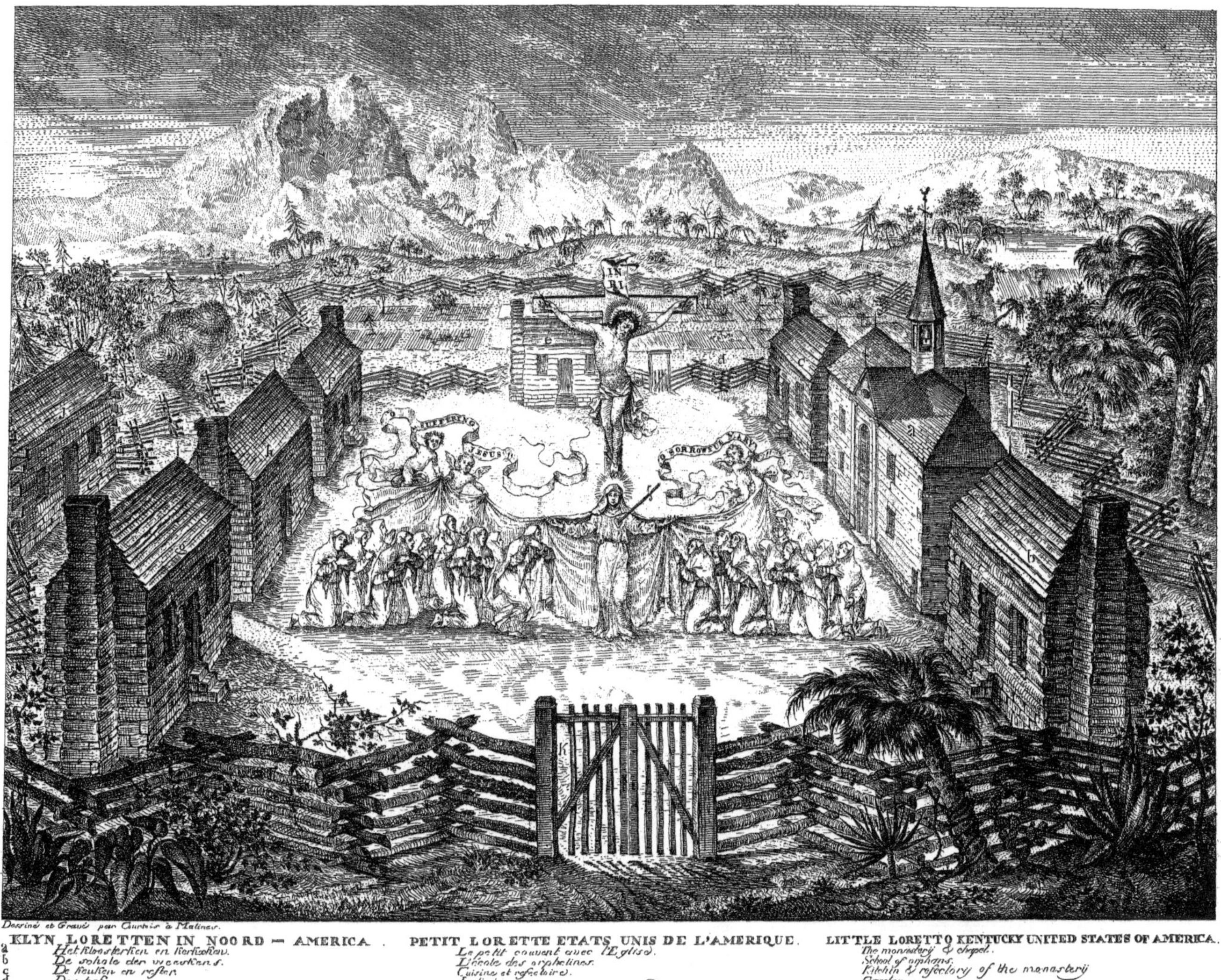

Reverend Charles Nerinckx founded the Sisterhood of Loretto in 1812 and established a motherhouse in Marion County, five branches in Kentucky, and three in Missouri. Accounts of the convent mention two log houses near Nerinckx's church of St. Charles, which provided the rude altar where the young Lorrettine novices worshiped. In 1808 Nerinckx wrote to his parents that a convent schoolhouse seventy feet long was under construction and would have a chapel about the same size with a turret and some outbuildings. The school burned soon after it was completed, and in 1812 another was started with three teachers in a cabin near Nerinckx's church. This view was apparently produced for distribution to potential donors, whom Nerinckx sought out by traveling the Low Countries of Europe. It was probably the European engraver who provided palm trees, rocky mountain peaks, and a sizable waterfall for Marion County, but each building is identified in the trilingual key at the bottom of the print, giving evidence of how the finished convent was envisioned.

Etching or copper plate engraving published at Mechlin, Belgium, about 1815. Drawn and engraved by Courtois of Malines, Flanders, possibly from a design by Father Charles Nerinckx.

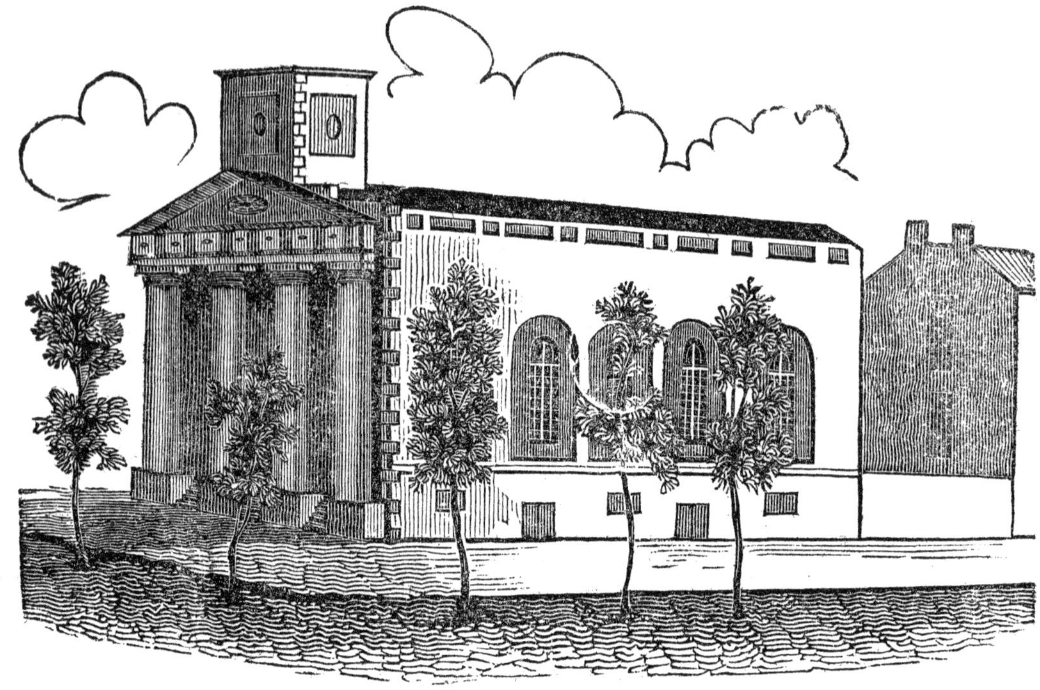

The Unitarian Church building in Louisville was begun in 1830, completed the following year, and dedicated in May 1832. Otis's Louisville directory called it "the neatest and most chaste specimen of architecture in the city." It stood at the southeast corner of Fifth and Walnut streets and was used until the Church of the Messiah was built in 1870 at Fourth and York streets, still the congregation's location. This is the earliest published view of a Louisville church. James Freeman Clarke, pastor of the church from 1833 to 1840, was editor of the monthly Christian periodical *Western Messenger,* where the view was published.

Wood engraving from *Western Messenger,* February 1839.

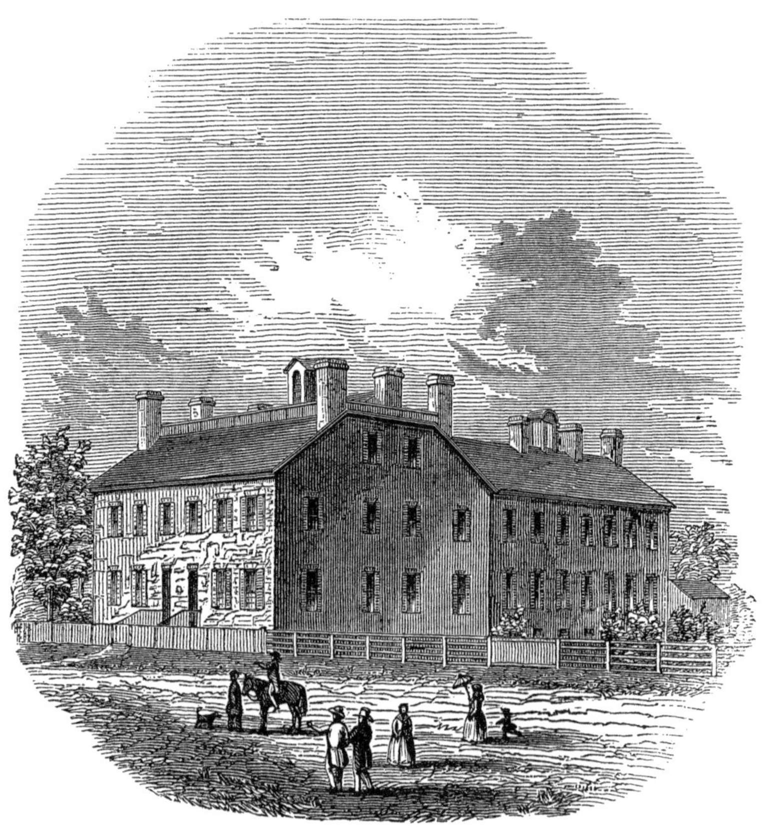

Lewis Collins described the settlement called Pleasant Hill or Union Village by noting that it "belongs exclusively to that orderly and industrious society called Shakers. It contains between three hundred and four hundred inhabitants, divided into families of from sixty to eighty each. Every important family arrangement moves with harmony and regularity of clockwork, in beautiful order." The main edifice was built of Kentucky marble and is known today as the Centre Family House. The Pleasant Hill colony was established at the home and farm of Elisha Thomas in Mercer County in 1806 and existed until the last Kentucky member died there in 1923. The United Society of Believers in Christ's Second Appearance were called "Shakers" by those outside the religion because of the violent physical motions associated with religious services.

Wood engraving from Lewis Collins's *Historical Sketches of Kentucky,* 1847.

The Second Presbyterian Church in Lexington was located on Market Street near Church Street, a short distance from Christ Episcopal Church. It was also known as the McChord Church, after its first pastor, James McChord, who served from 1815 to 1819. The building was constructed in 1847 and destroyed by fire in 1917. The architect, Thomas Lewinski, designed many public buildings and residences in and around Lexington, most during the 1840s.

Wood engraving from *The West,* 1854. Engraved by Horace C. Grosvenor, Cincinnati.

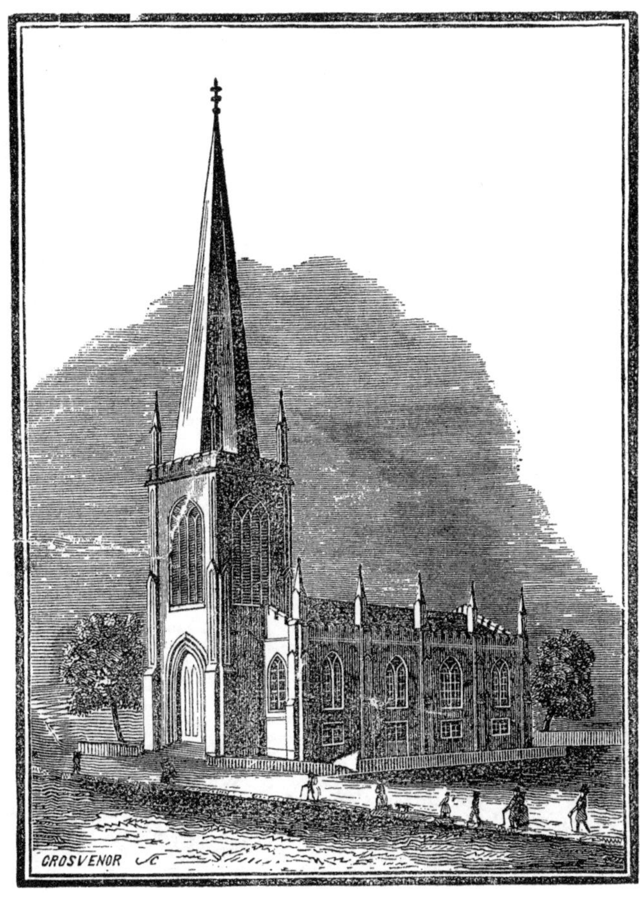

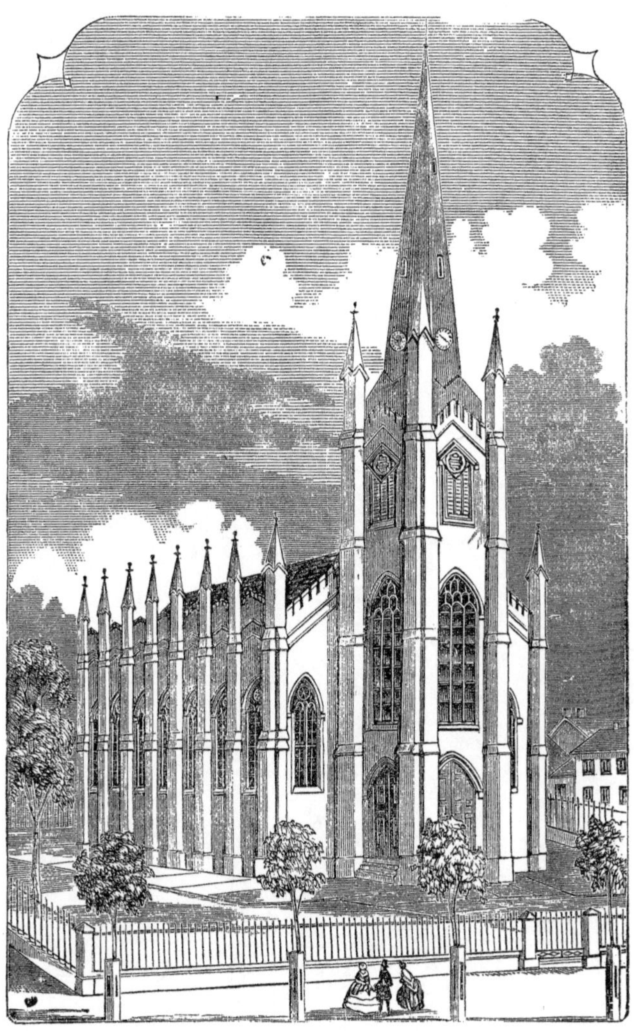

Baptists have been by far the most numerous Protestant denomination in Kentucky. One of the larger churches resulted when the First and Second Baptist churches in Louisville voted to unite into one congregation around 1850 and bought property on the northwest corner of Fourth and Walnut streets. They erected this building in 1853–1854 and called the new church Walnut Street Baptist Church. The congregation was particularly strong in establishing colonies in the city and was largely responsible for the establishment of the Southern Baptist Theological Seminary.

Wood engraving from *Religious Denominations of the U.S.,* 1855, from a drawing or engraving by J. Spittall.

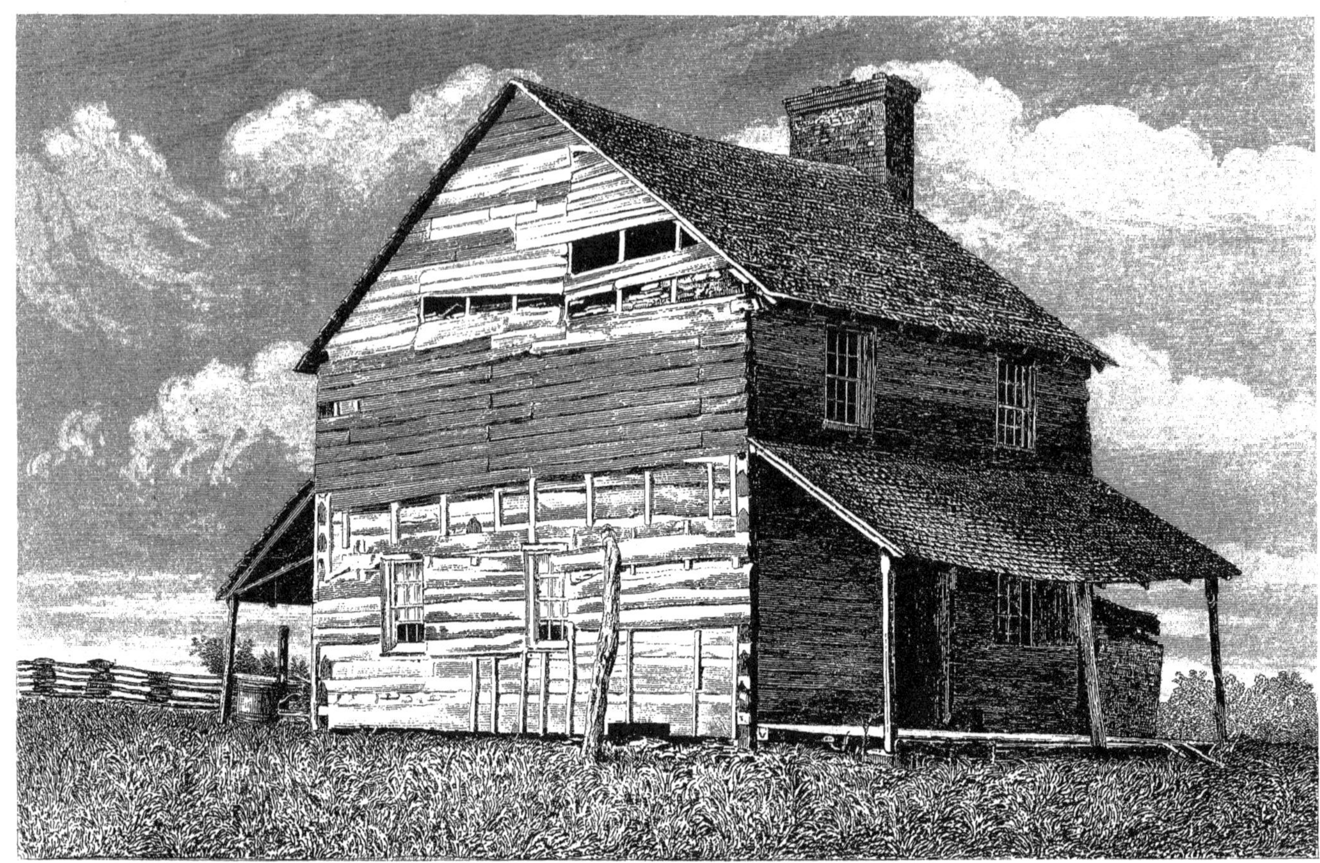

Methodist societies with circuit-riding preachers were first organized in Kentucky about 1784; meetings then were held in members' homes. This church was built at Richard Masterson's station about five miles northwest of Lexington. Masterson and his wife, Sarah, early leaders in Methodist church work, also had their home at the site, which is on Highway 421 in Fayette County. The building, which was the site of the first Methodist conference in 1790, no longer stands.

Copper or steel engraving from Redford's *History of Methodism in Kentucky,* 1868. Engraved by John Sartain, Philadelphia, from a photograph by James Mullen, Lexington.

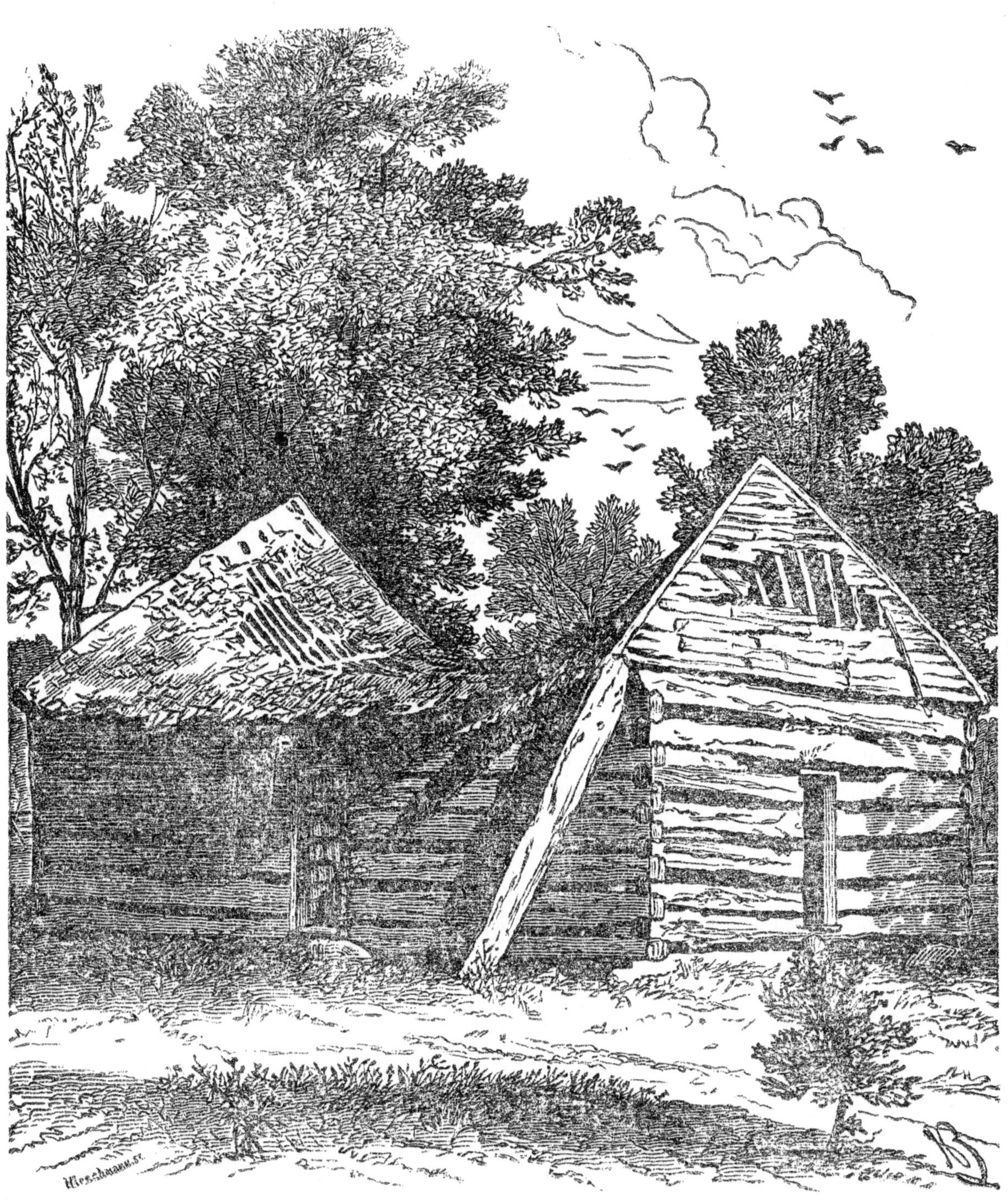

Some Kentucky churches in the antebellum era tacitly supported slavery, while others openly attacked it. One of the antislavery groups centered around Old Glade Church near Berea. John G. Fee, one of the founders of Berea College, first preached there in 1853. Fee had been invited to preach in Madison County through the influence of Cassius M. Clay, who favored Fee's antislavery activities. A marker stone now identifies the location.

Wood engraving from *Berea College, Ky.*, 1875. Engraved by Hirschmann from a drawing by H. Bishop.

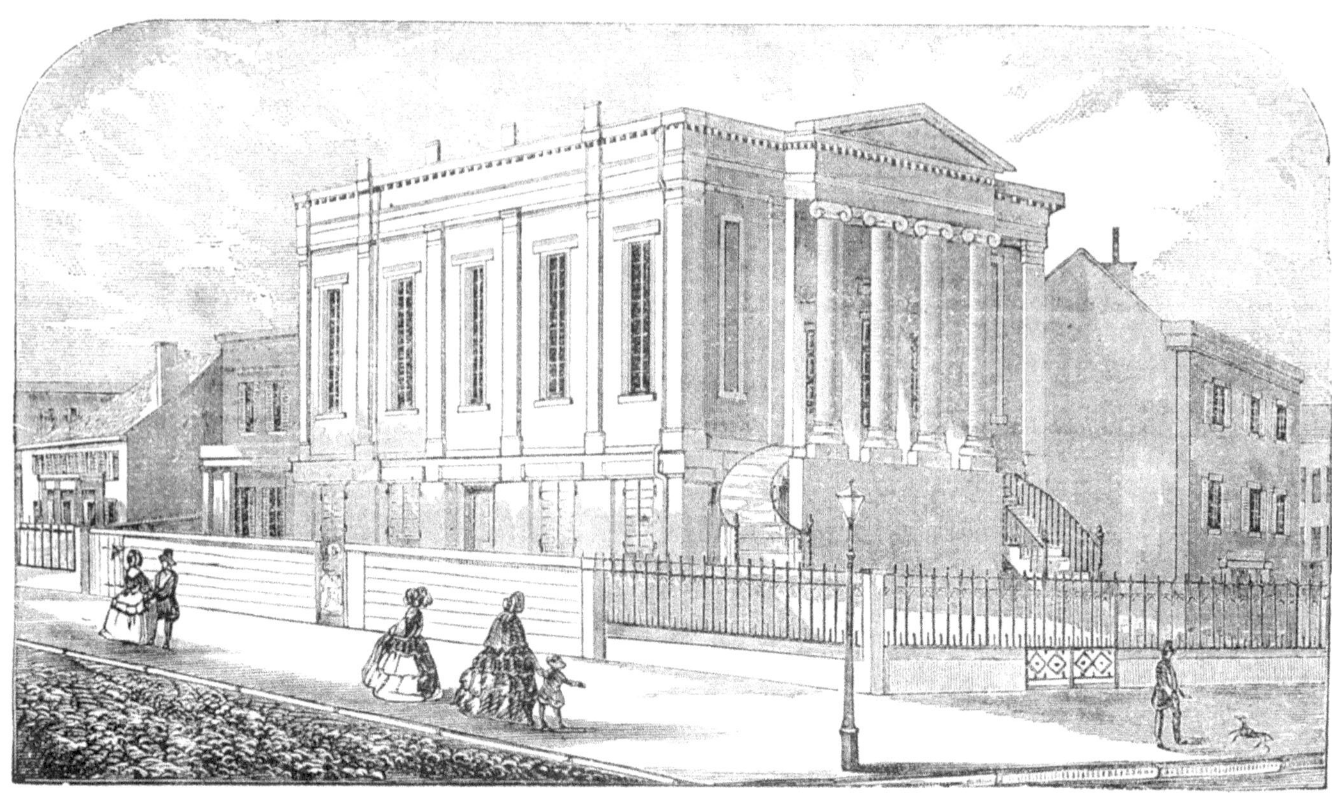

In the early 1850s a location on Fourth Street in Louisville was given up by the Methodist congregation; services were held for some time thereafter in the building of Louisville's first public school at the southwest corner of Fifth and Walnut streets. The congregation purchased that property and replaced the school with this building, the Walnut Street Methodist Church, in 1853. A theater replaced the church on this site about 1910.

Wood engraving from *Edwards' Official Directory of Louisville,* 1868.

The Second Presbyterian Church in Louisville was first established in 1830 on Third Street between Green and Walnut streets. In the post–Civil War division of the church into northern and southern elements, that property was sold at auction to the Louisville Water Company, and a temporary building was erected in 1870 on Broadway at Second Street. Four years later the building, illustrated here, was dedicated. With its furniture and organ it had cost $90,000. It was destroyed by fire in 1956 and the congregation relocated in the eastern suburbs of Louisville.

Wood engraving from *The Daily Graphic*, New York, 1875. Engraved by C. Hartt, New York.

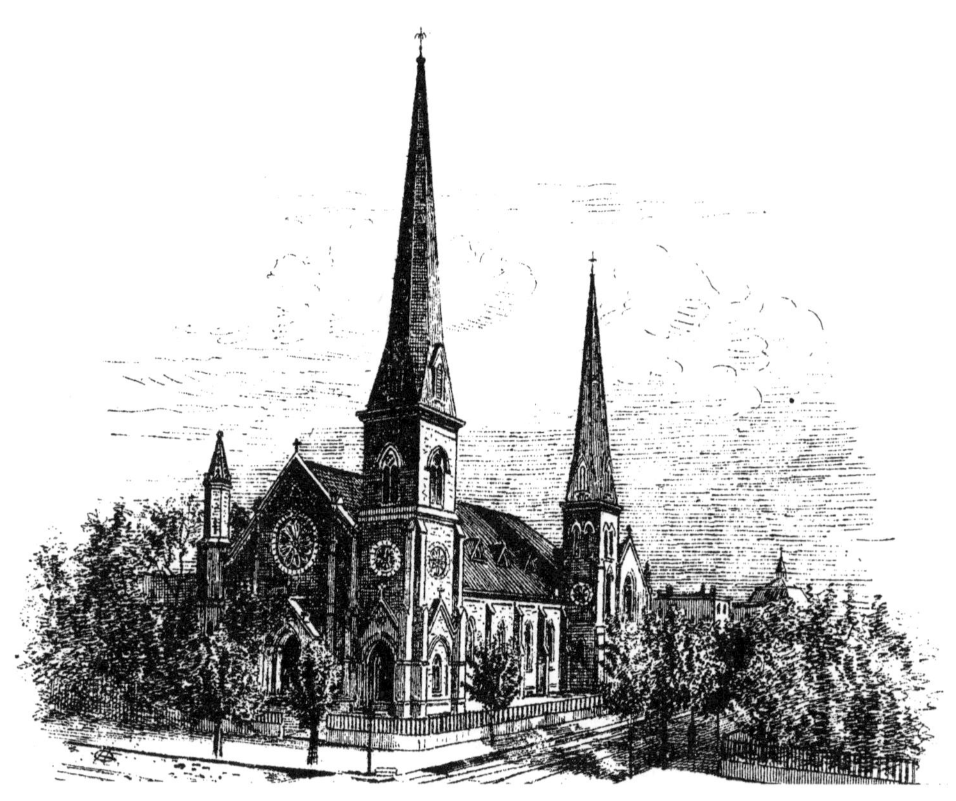

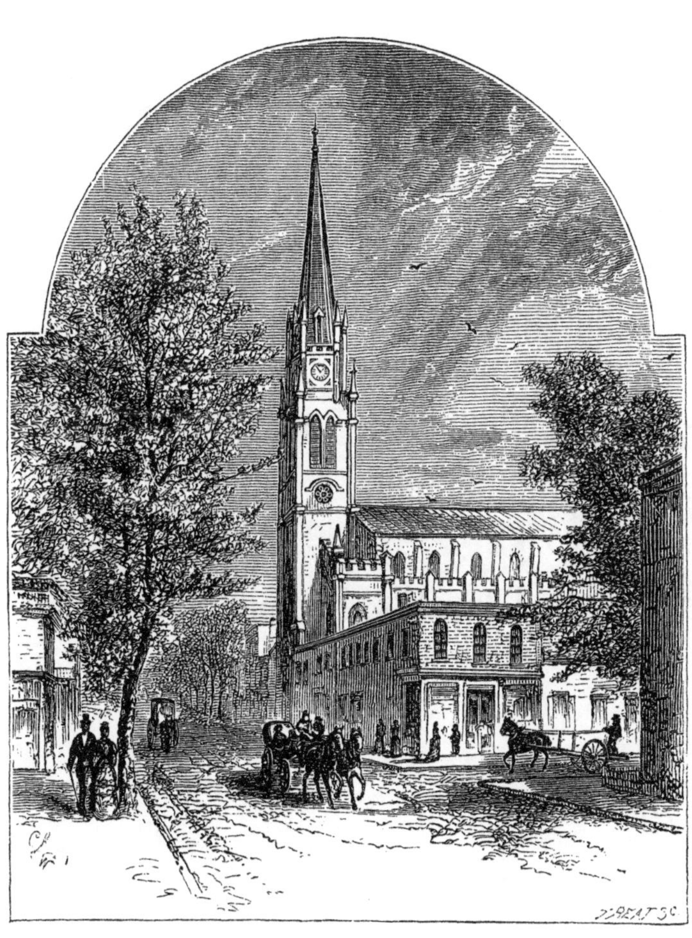

While Bardstown, and St. Joseph's Cathedral there, had been the early center of Kentucky Catholicism, the growth of Louisville's population soon made it the core. Bishop Flaget's see was transferred to Louisville from Bardstown in 1841, and the Church of Saint Louis was soon replaced by St. Mary's Cathedral of the Assumption, designed and built by William Kelly of Baltimore. Construction was started in 1849 and completed three years later. The cathedral became a memorial to Bishop Flaget, who died in 1850.

Wood engraving from *Scribner's Monthly*, December 1874, from a drawing by J. Wells Champney, Deerfield, Mass., and New York.

The earliest penitentiary building in Kentucky was completed in 1800 near the center of Frankfort and was the first of its kind west of the Alleghenies. The twin towers marking the entrance to the compound at Holmes and High streets remained until 1950, several years after the prison was relocated to Oldham County. Very early in the institution's history, religious instruction was provided, though Dr. Sneed, in his record of the prison, suggests that the keeper of the penitentiary often did little to support such activities. The education level of inmates was also very low. The prison keeper's report for 1855 lists only one prisoner who had "received a classical and scientific education," eighteen who had "a general English education," sixty-five who could "read, write, and cypher," eighty-seven who could "only spell and read," and sixty-six who were "entirely destitute of education."

Lithograph from William C. Sneed's *A Report on the History and Mode of Management of the Kentucky Penitentiary from its Origin in 1798 to March 1, 1860*, 1860. Lithograph by Henry Hart and Dillon M. Mapother, Louisville, from a photograph by C.A. Clarke, Frankfort.

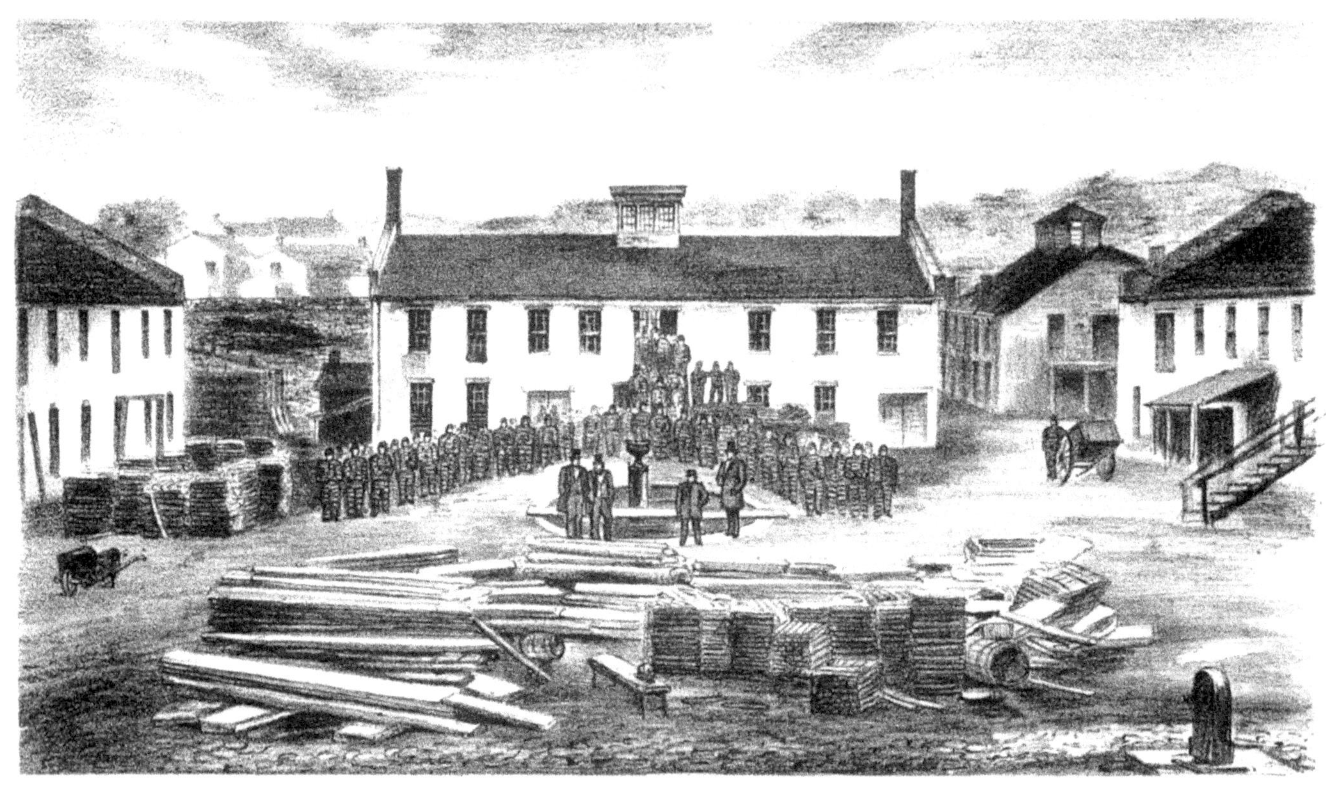

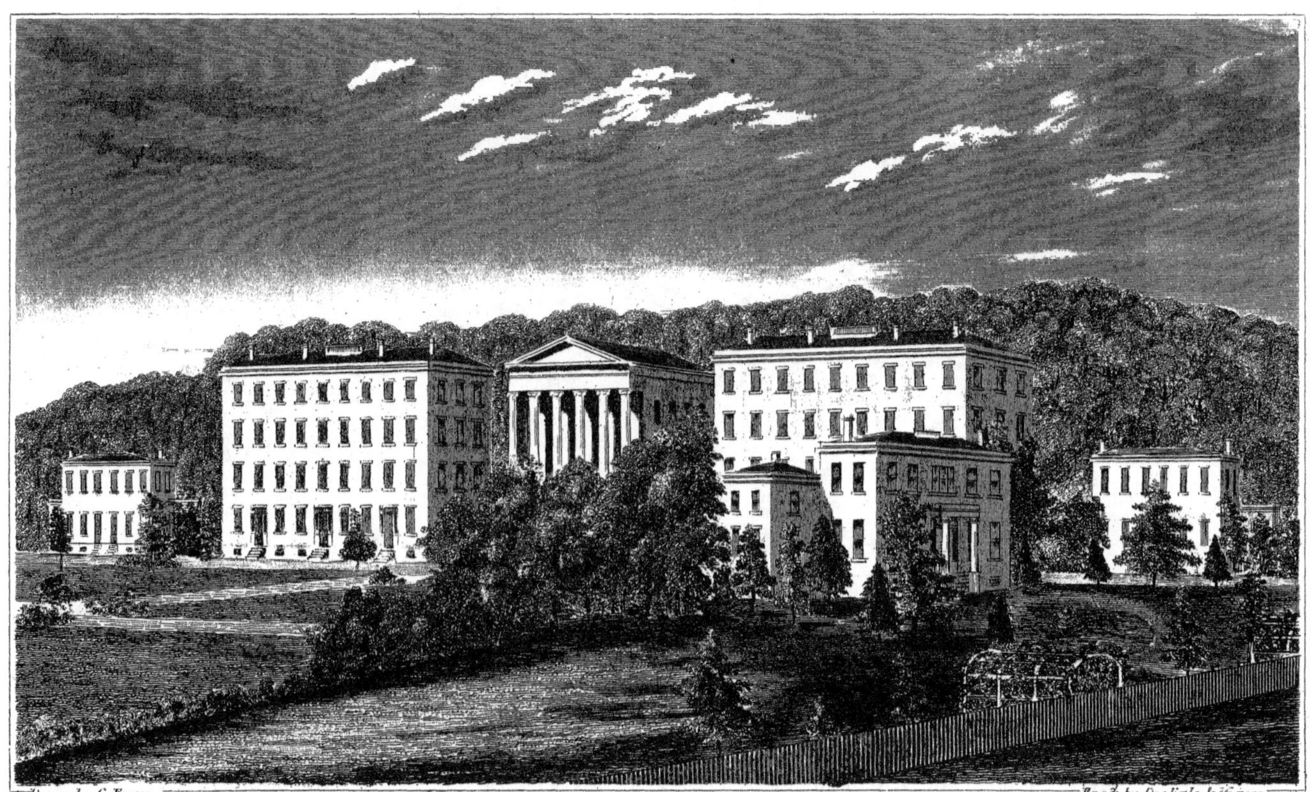

The Western Baptist Theological Institute was formed in Cincinnati in 1834 and built soon after south of Covington. Lewis Collins describes the college as a richly endowed institution in a flourishing condition. The building was used as a Union hospital during the Civil War and later became St. Elizabeth's Hospital.

Copper plate engraving from Cist's *Cincinnati, Its Early Annals and Future Prospects*, 1841. Engraved by Curtis M. Doolittle and Samuel B. Munson from a drawing by Charles Foster.

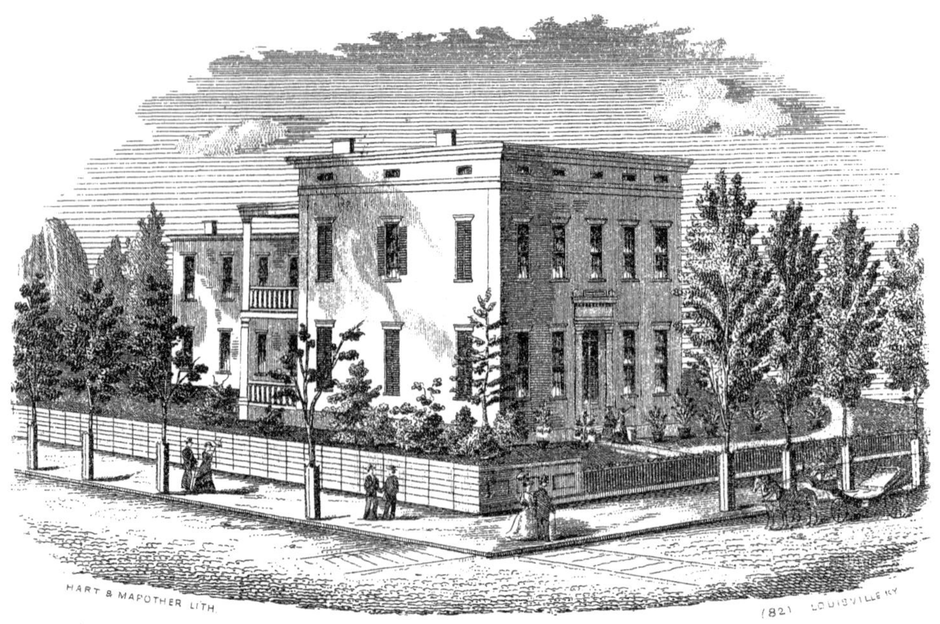

The Louisville Female Seminary was located on the southwest corner of First and Chestnut streets. Its full page advertisement in Edwards's directory of 1868–1869 offered accommodations for both boarding and day students, and the study of English, French, and vocal and instrumental music. The seminary rated a favorable notice in the *Louisville Monthly Magazine* in June 1879, which informed readers that the school had graduated one hundred seventy young ladies to date, including its largest class of twenty-one in 1870. According to the article, the object of the principal, Mrs. W. B. Nold, was to educate young ladies under home influences.

Lithograph from *Edwards' Official Directory of Louisville,* 1868. Lithograph by Henry Hart and Dillon M. Mapother, Louisville.

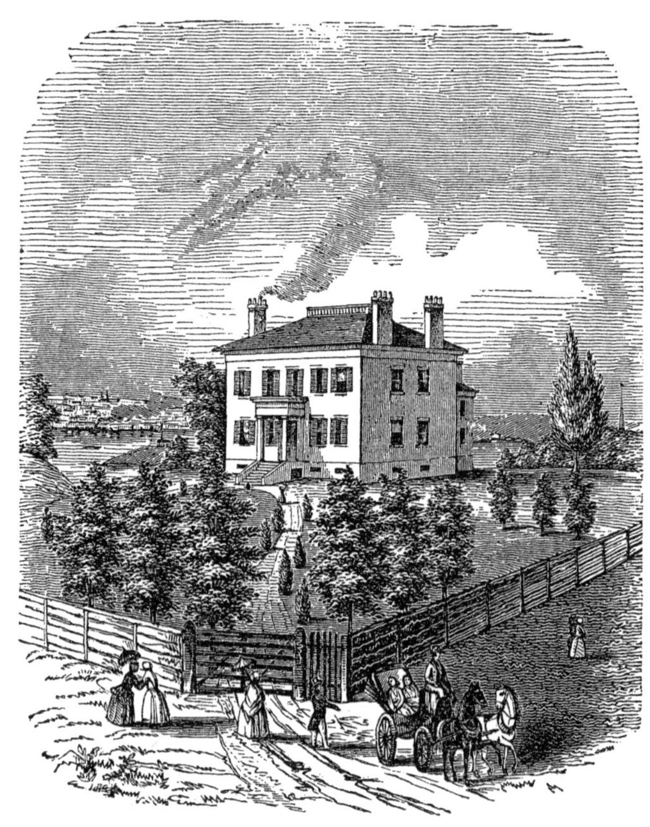

Private academies educated many of the state's citizens at a time when public education efforts were only beginning. Instruction for young women often focused on activities then considered most fitting for females—music, needlecraft, manners, penmanship, and sometimes foreign languages and literature. Orr's Female Academy in Covington, founded by Rev. William Orr, was described by Lewis Collins as "one of the best literary institutions of its kind in the state."

Wood engraving from Lewis Collins's *Historical Sketches Of Kentucky,* 1847.

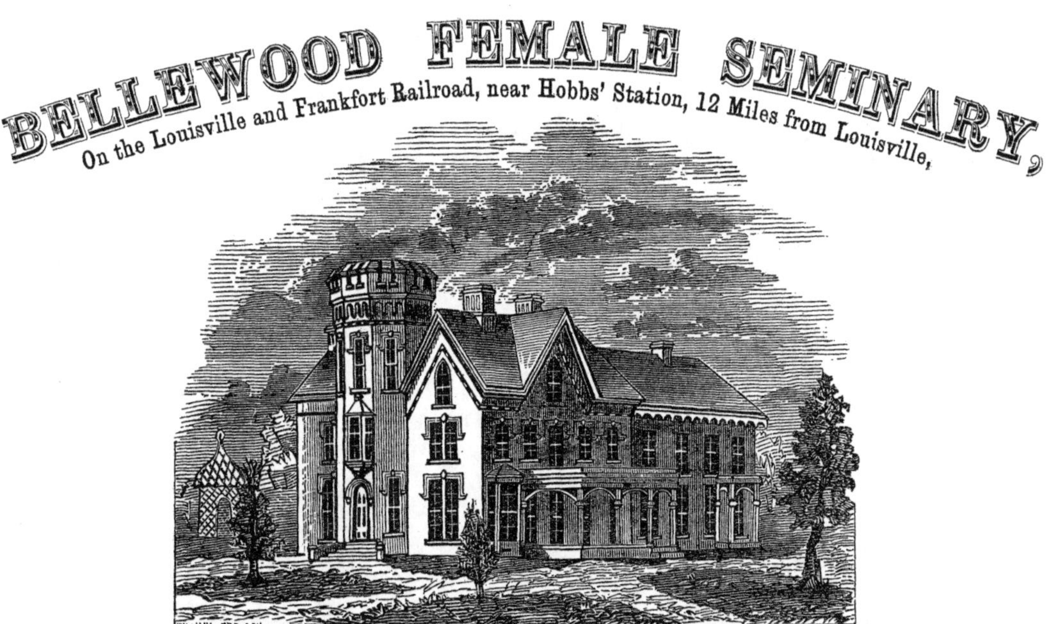

REV. W. W. HILL, D. D., PRINCIPAL,

TEACHER OF MENTAL & MORAL SCIENCE, GEOLOGY, RHETORIC, LOGIC, ASTRONOMY, &C.

MISS NANNIE SHERRARD,

ASSISTANT PRINCIPAL, & TEACHER OF TRIGONOMETRY, GEOMETRY, ALGEBRA, ARITHMETIC, ENGLISH GRAMMAR, NATURAL HISTORY, GEOGRAPHY, &C.

REV. R. C. McGEE, A. M.

TEACHER OF CHEMISTRY, NATURAL PHILOSOPHY, NATURAL THEOLOGY, HISTORY, &G.

MISS MOLLIE L. BELKNAP, MISS MARY S. HOGAN,

TEACHERS OF MUSIC ON THE PIANO, ORGAN, GUITAR AND VOCALIZATION.

MISS E. M. LEWIS,

Teacher of Painting and Drawing, Embroidery, Needle-Work, Calisthenics, &c.

The Bellewood Female Seminary in Hobbs Station was established about 1860 in what is now Anchorage, near Louisville, by Dr. William W. Hill, then the pastor of the Middletown Presbyterian Church. Its curriculum varied from the average women's school in the wide range of classes and subjects offered. The school chapel served Dr. Hill's congregation and the community as a neighborhood church until the congregation erected a new building in 1869. The school was said to have been known throughout the South during the Civil War nd remained in operation under several headmasters. The building illustrated here served in later years as the Presbyterian Orphanage as well as the public school for Anchorage and survived until 1929.

Wood engraving from a Bellewood Female Seminary promotional leaflet, 1866. Engraved by Williams, Louisville.

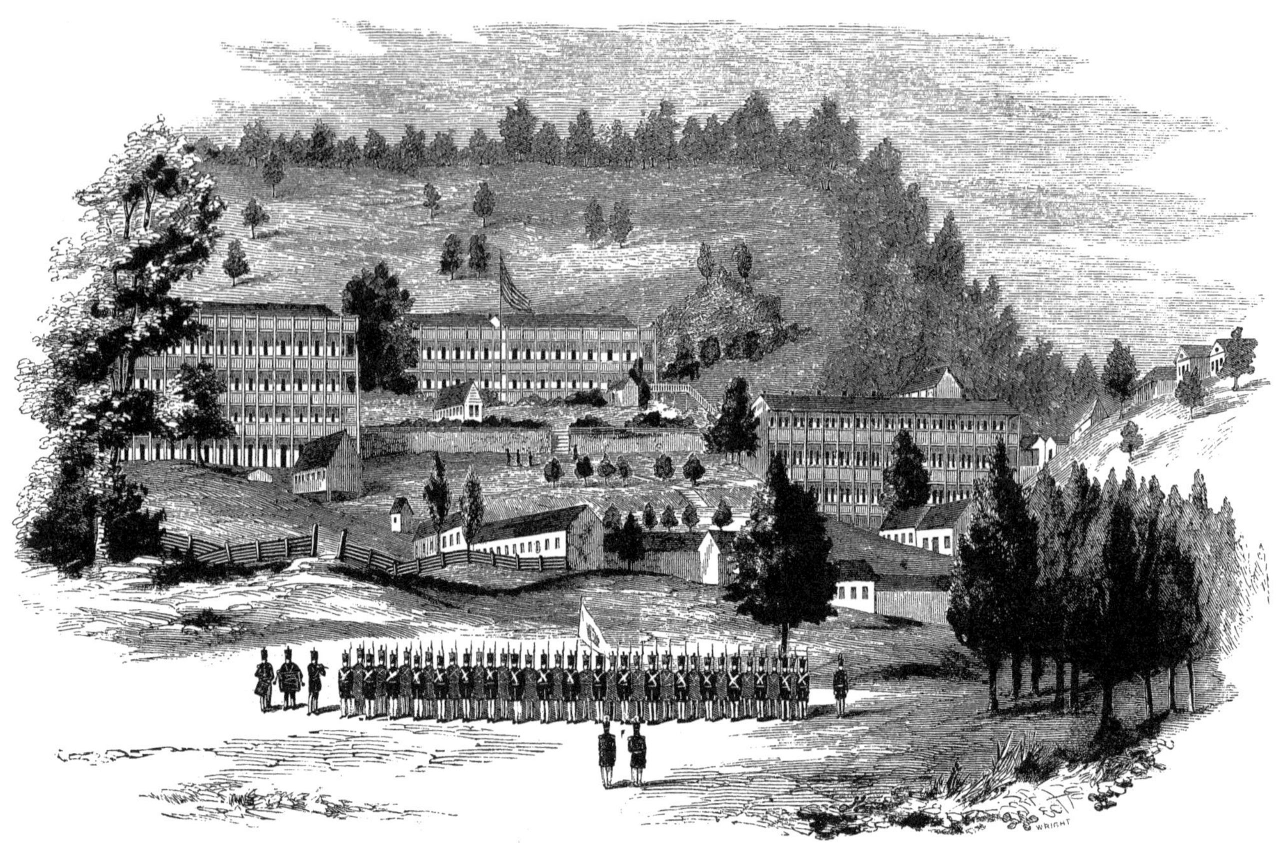

Although America's peacetime army was small, the martial spirit was strong, particularly in the South. Several Kentucky schools provided instruction under military guidelines. One, the Western Military Institute, was opened about 1846 at College and Military streets in Georgetown by Col. Thornton F. Johnson, a graduate of West Point. In 1829, Johnson was the first faculty member elected by the board of trustees of Georgetown College, and in 1836 he founded Bacon College at Harrodsburg. The military school was moved in 1850 to Blue Lick Springs in Nicholas County and was relocated again in February 1851 to Drennon Springs in Henry County, where it remained until the institute was closed about 1860.

Wood engraving from *Gleason's Pictorial Drawing-Room Companion,* January 1, 1853. Drawn or engraved by Wright, possibly Neziah Wright, Cincinnati, or G. Wright, New York, from an earlier engraving provided by the commandant of the school.

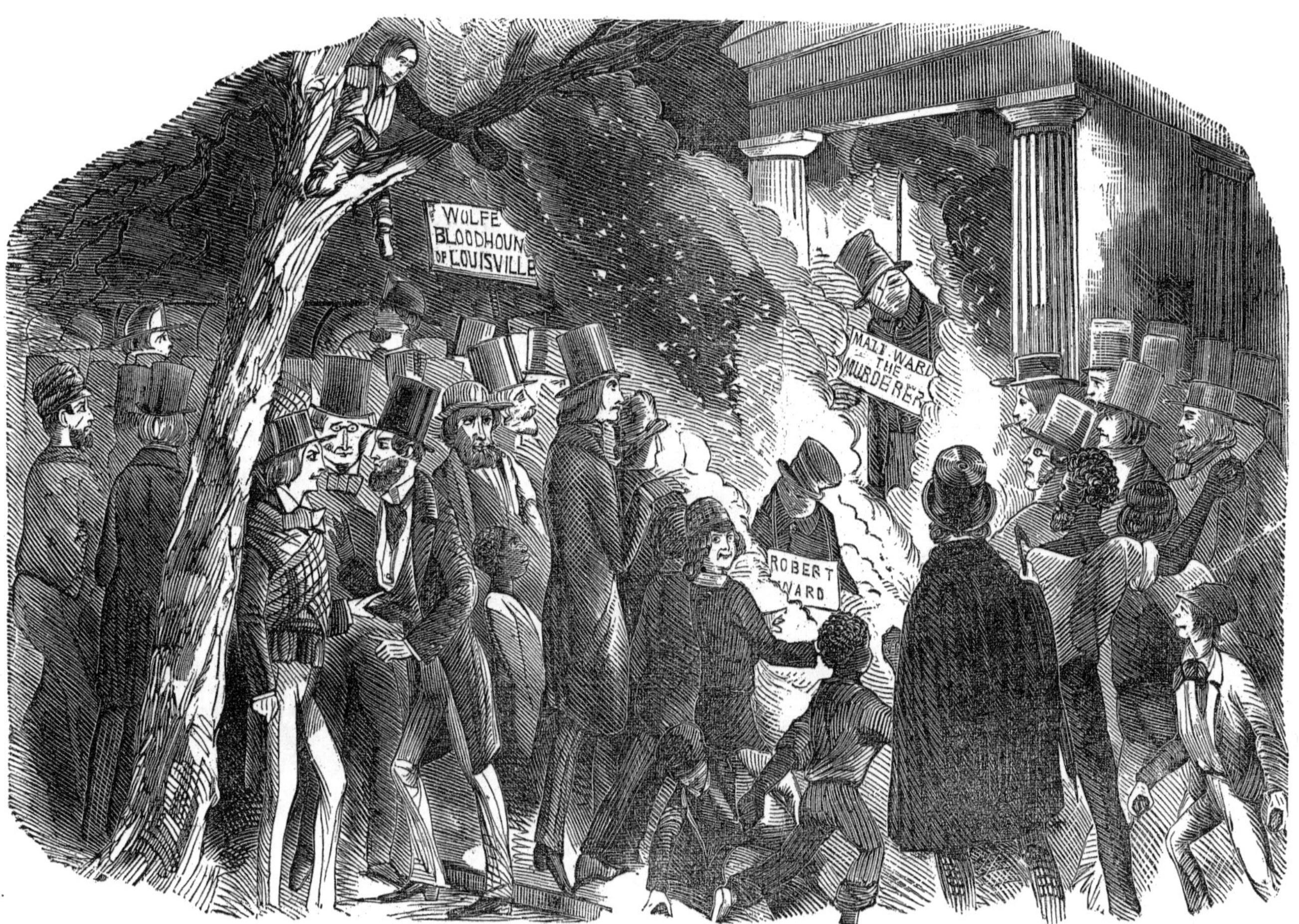

Current events began to be illustrated in the East in the late 1830s by such publishers as Nathaniel Currier. This illustration is one of the earliest of the kind published in the West, and we know nothing of the publication in which it appeared. Shown here is a depiction of the citizens of Louisville burning Matt and Robert Ward in effigy. Some Kentuckians took education and honor very seriously, among them Matthew F. Ward, who shot and killed Professor William H. Butler, a teacher in the public school and formerly a tutor to the Ward children, after Butler disciplined Ward's younger brother. Public feeling ran so high that the trial, involving scores of witnesses, had to be held in Elizabethtown. When the jury gave a verdict of "not guilty," Louisvillians were incensed. A mob of eight thousand people burned in effigy the principals, the jury members, the defense lawyers, and a character witness. They also damaged and set fire to the home of Robert Ward, the boy's father, at Second and Walnut streets, which is the incident illustrated here.

Wood engraving from *The Whole World*, c. May 1854.

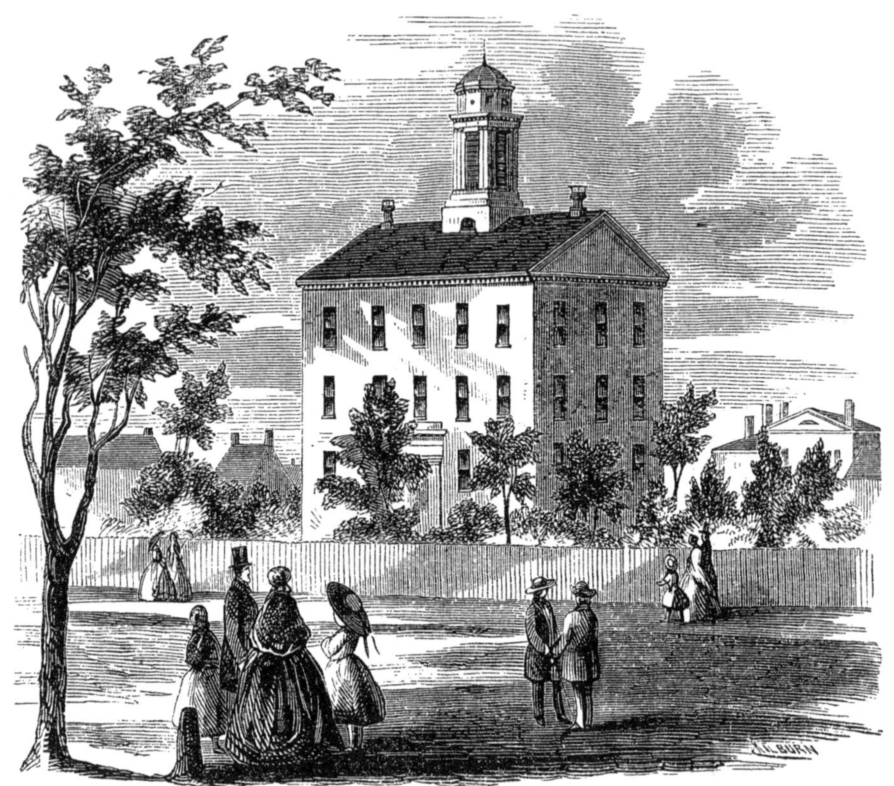

Ballou's described the Free School in Newport as a substantial brick building well adapted to its purposes and noted that pupils received an excellent education under competent teachers who were liberally paid. Lewis Collins's 1847 *Historical Sketches of Kentucky* stated that Newport had "an admirably managed free high school and district schools."

Wood engraving from *Ballou's Pictorial Drawing-Room Companion,* December 1856, from a drawing by Samuel S. Kilburn, Boston, during his tour of the West in 1856.

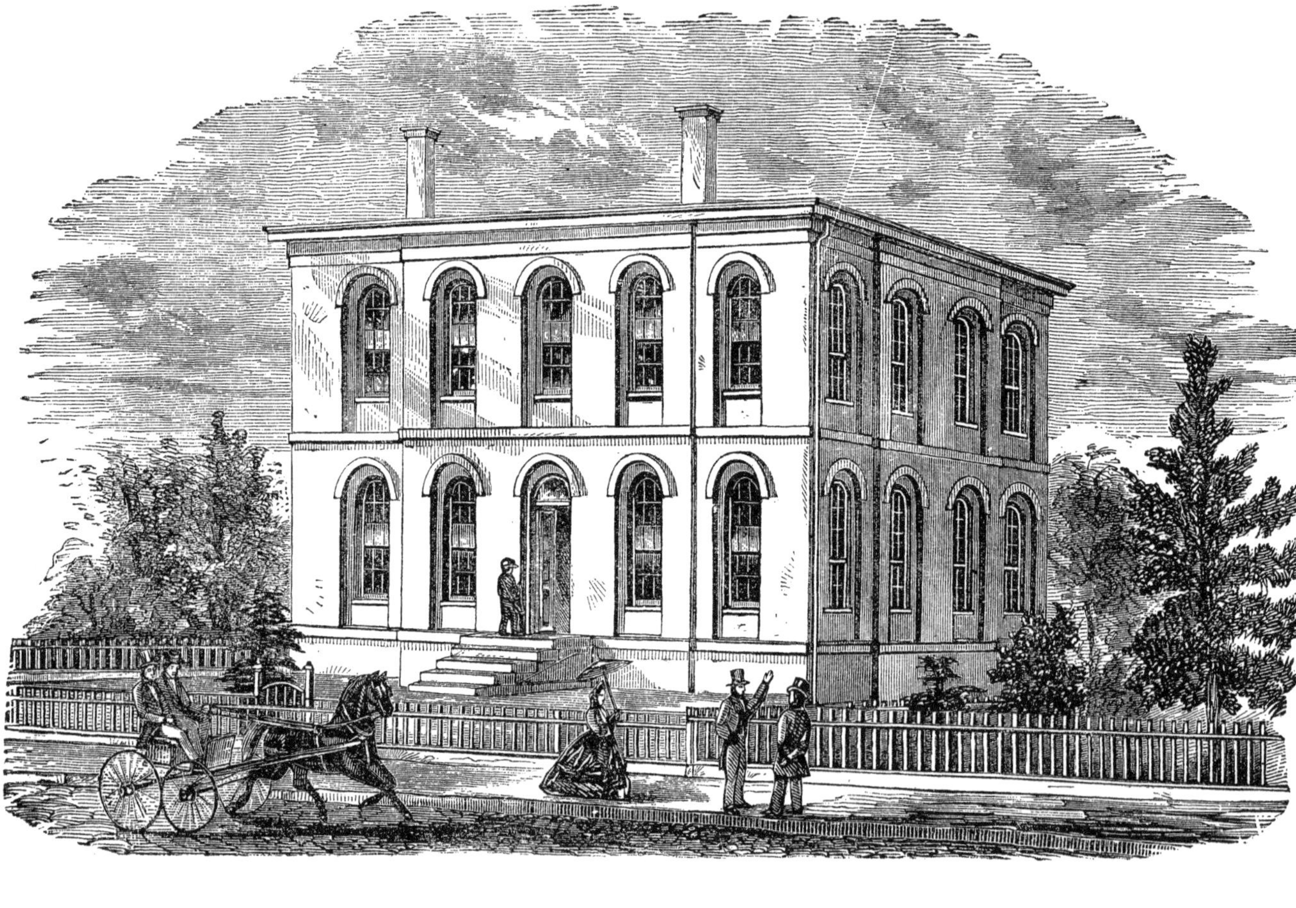

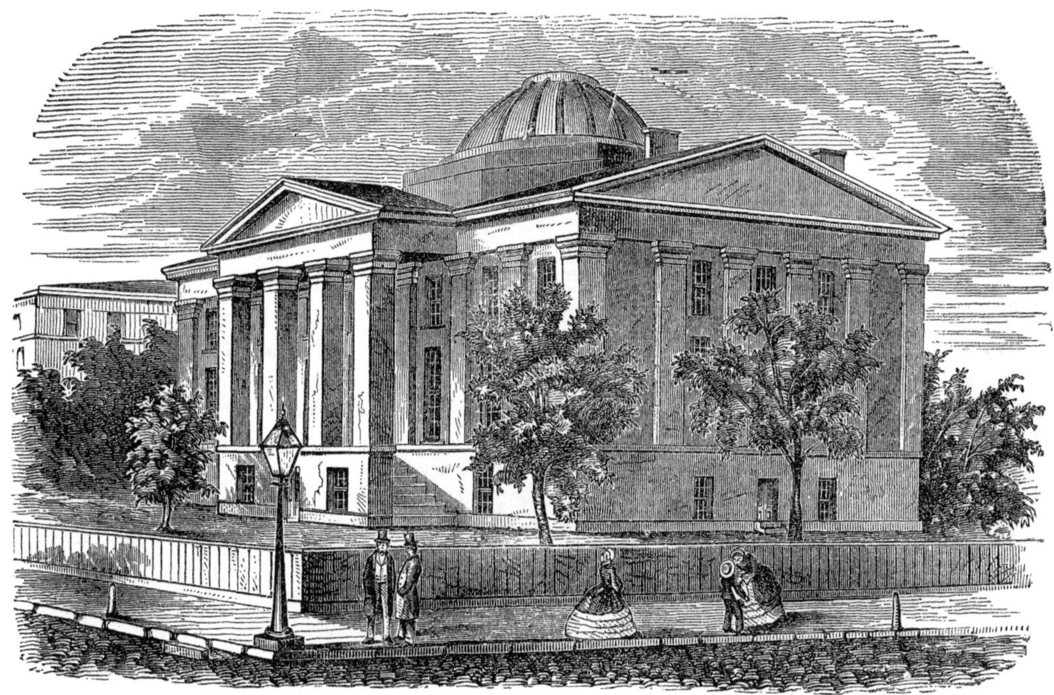

Male High School opened in 1856 in a building at Ninth and Chestnut streets that was formerly part of the University of Louisville. The board of trustees for public schools for 1869–1870 reported the average daily attendance at the Male High School as 134 students and seven teachers. Pupils from the district and private schools made application to be admitted. The Female High School was completely rebuilt at the site of the former residence of Haiden T. Curd and occupied in 1873; Male High School eventually moved to this "new" girls' building in 1898—when that school once again received a newer facility—and to Brook and Breckinridge streets in 1915. Some years after the Civil War, the dome shown in this view was removed.

Wood engraving from *City of Louisville Municipal Reports for 1870,* 1871.

This 1852 building of the Montgomery Street School in Louisville (*left*) still stands, with later additions, at the southwest corner of Twenty-fifth and Montgomery streets. The school was one of the city's smaller institutions; it began the 1869–1870 school year with 290 pupils and ended the year with 261. Of the seventeen school buildings that existed in Louisville in 1870, only two survive. The Montgomery Street School was known as the Emma Dolfinger School into the 1960s, and it stood vacant for some years before its purchase and renovation in 1978 as the Portland Christian School.

Wood engraving from the *Annual Report of the Board of Trustees of Public Schools of Louisville,* 1871. Engraved probably by Henry Hart or Dillon M. Mapother, Louisville.

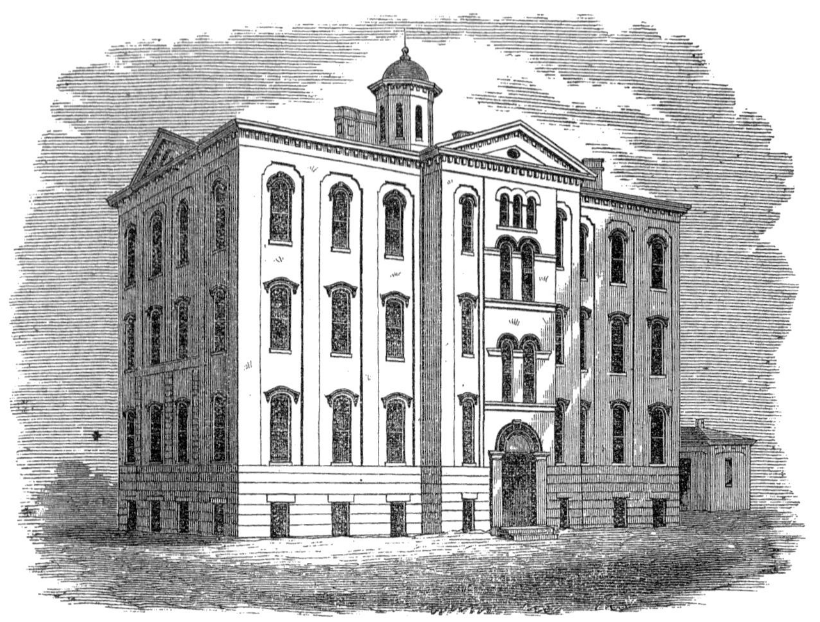

The City School building of Henderson was new at the time of the superintendent's report of 1874, having been completed at the corner of Green and Center streets in 1870. A history of Henderson in 1887 describes the school as "handsome and commodious," with fourteen large rooms, fifteen excellent teachers, the latest furniture, and slate blackboards. In 1873, the average daily school attendance in Henderson was 646 students, and $12,500 was appropriated for school purposes, of which $10,700 was distributed in salaries to the superintendent, the principals of the high school, grammar and primary departments, and to eleven assistants. The average cost per child for salaries—$15.22, according to the report—was less than half the cost in Louisville. At this time Henderson had a population of about 4,200.

Wood engraving from the *Annual Report of the Superintendent of Public Instruction,* 1874.

The Colored Normal School in Louisville, also known as the Central Colored School, was constructed in 1873 at the southeast corner of Sixth and Kentucky streets and is still standing after being used for many purposes. The Central High School, Louisville's principal secondary school for black students before the schools were racially integrated, began at this location in 1882. In his annual report for 1874, Howard A.M. Henderson, superintendent of public instruction of Kentucky, called the building a "fine house for a colored school . . . . being equal if not superior to any other schoolhouse in the city, except the Female High School." He reported also that there were 10,944 pupils in Louisville's public schools; of these, 1,093 were in the colored schools, which were receiving "strongly manifested interest" and largely increasing attendance. Louisville's charter of 1870 first provided for the organization of schools for black children, in accordance with a state act of 1866, which authorized school districts to open separate schools.

Wood engraving from *Scribner's Monthly,* December 1874, from a drawing by J. Wells Champney, Deerfield, Mass., and New York City.

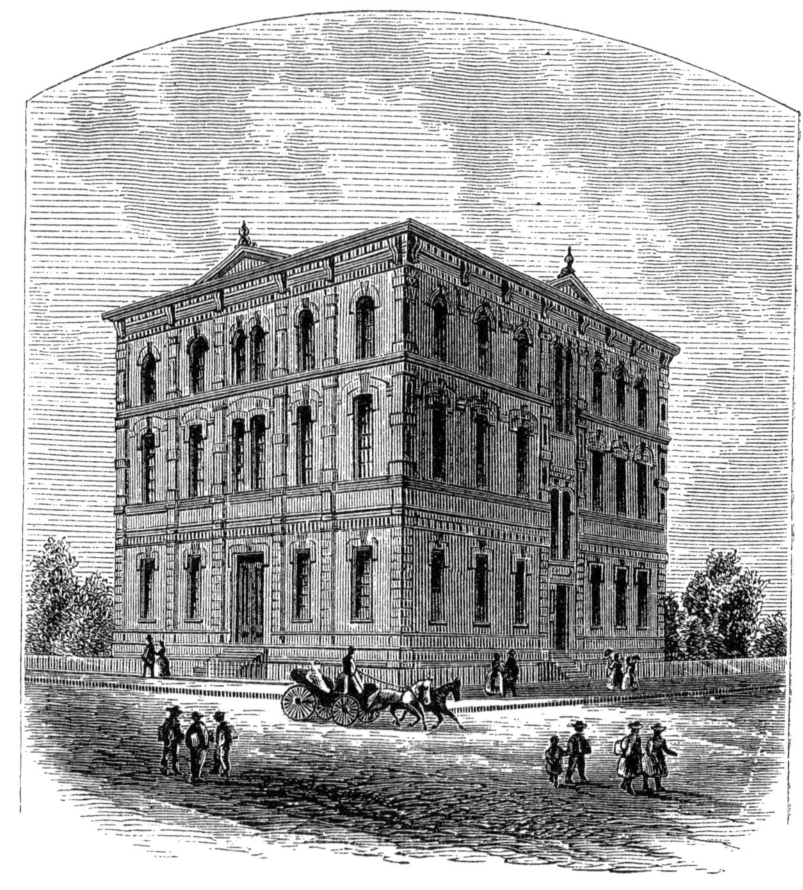

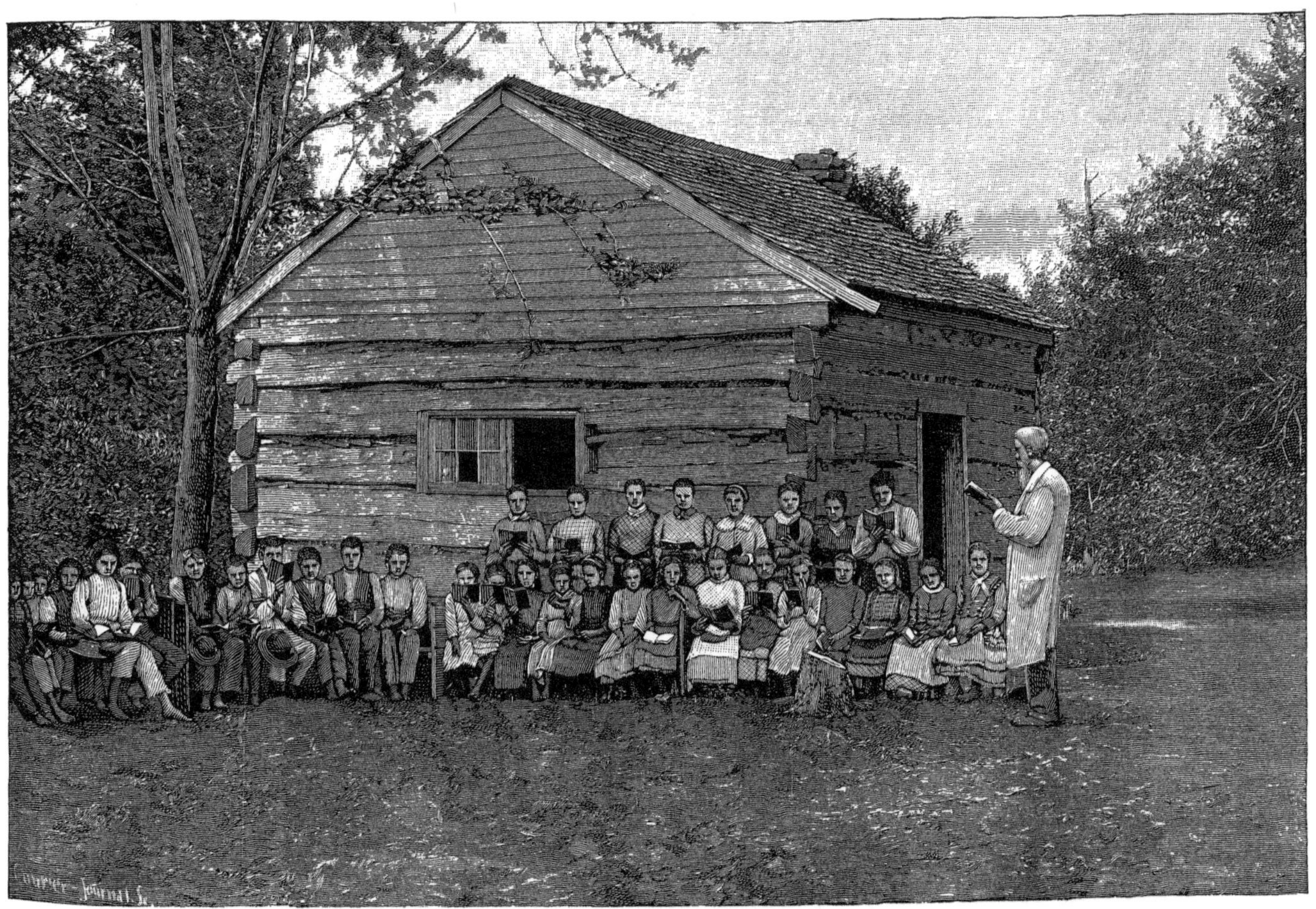

This illustration of a mountain school on a warm day was probably engraved from a photograph from the state superintendent of public education's file. In 1857 settlers on Kingdom Come Creek took advantage of district tax legislation that enabled the community to tax itself to build and operate a neighborhood school. The building was a simple log structure on land donated by John Ison, likely the same school that appears in this illustration. The early mountain schoolhouses had no electricity or running water, were lit by kerosene lanterns, and were warmed by potbellied stoves; children brought their food from home. School was held the few months of the year when there was little work on the farms, and the teachers were frequently preachers of the region. Log schools were still being built as late as 1940, and one- and two-room schoolhouses survived in mountain counties into the 1960s.

Wood engraving from the Louisville Board of Trade's *The City of Louisville and a Glimpse of Kentucky*, 1887. Engraved by Courier-Journal Job Printing Co., Louisville.

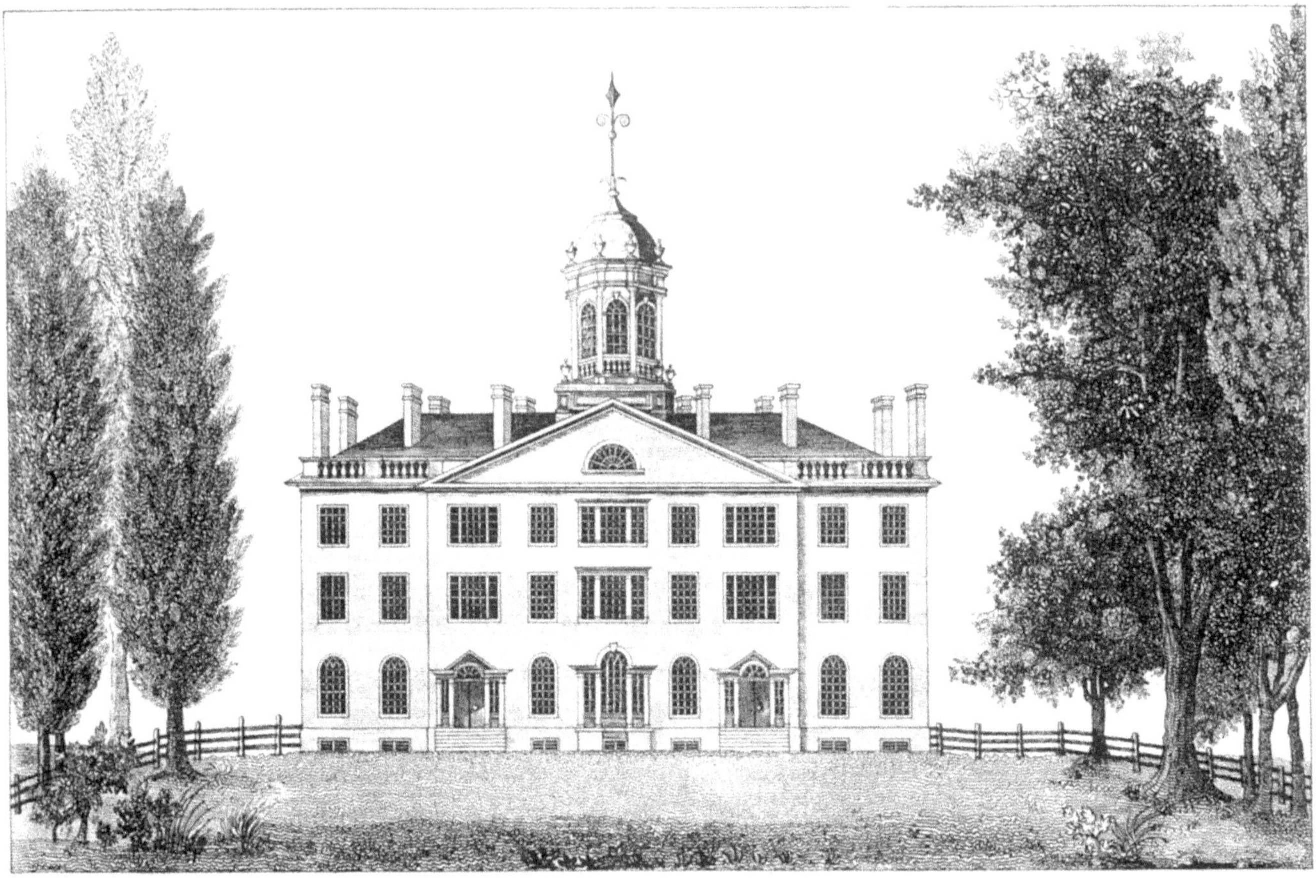

Copper plate engraving (*above*) from Caldwell's *Discourse on the Genius and Character of the Rev. Horace Holley, L.L.D.*, 1828. Engraved by Enoch G. Gridley, Cincinnati, from a drawing by Matthew H. Jouett.

Higher education in Kentucky fared well early in the state's history as Transylvania University had a national reputation and large enrollment, especially under the administration of Dr. Horace Holley. The principal building of the university, shown above, was erected from plans designed by Matthew Kennedy, a Lexington builder and architect. Until it was destroyed by fire in 1828, it stood in what is now Gratz Park, at approximately the location a bandstand was later erected. After the fire, the Morrison building and other structures on the present campus were constructed. This view was used in a series of United States scenes on plates, bowls, and pitchers made by Enoch Wood and Sons of Staffordshire, England. Matthew Jouett, Kentucky's foremost artist, widely known for the excellence of his portraits, produced only a few scenic works. This is his only drawing of Transylvania and was probably made shortly before his death in 1827.

Transylvania University had an excellent medical school, although defections to Louisville later damaged its reputation. The school was founded in 1818; Medical Hall, shown here (*right*), was not opened until 1840. By 1847, the medical college had eight professors and 175 students. The building in this engraving was destroyed by fire in 1863.

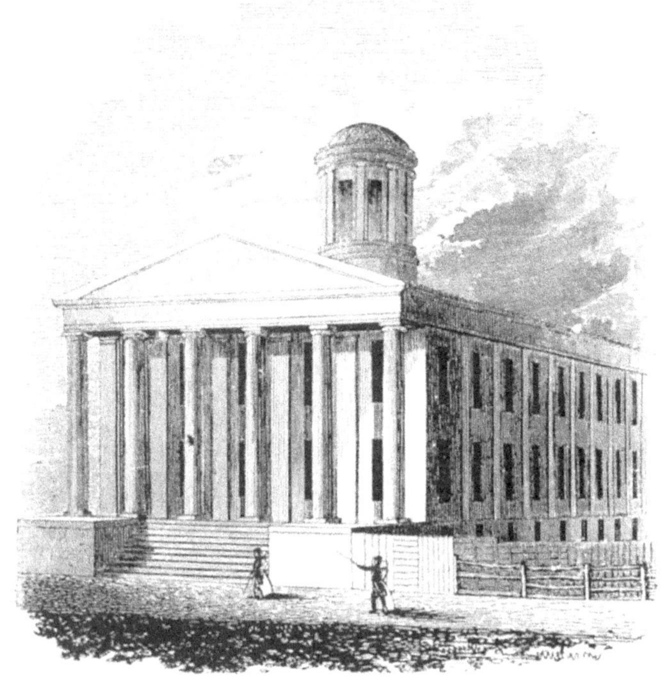

Wood engraving from Lewis Collins's *Historical Sketches of Kentucky*, 1847.

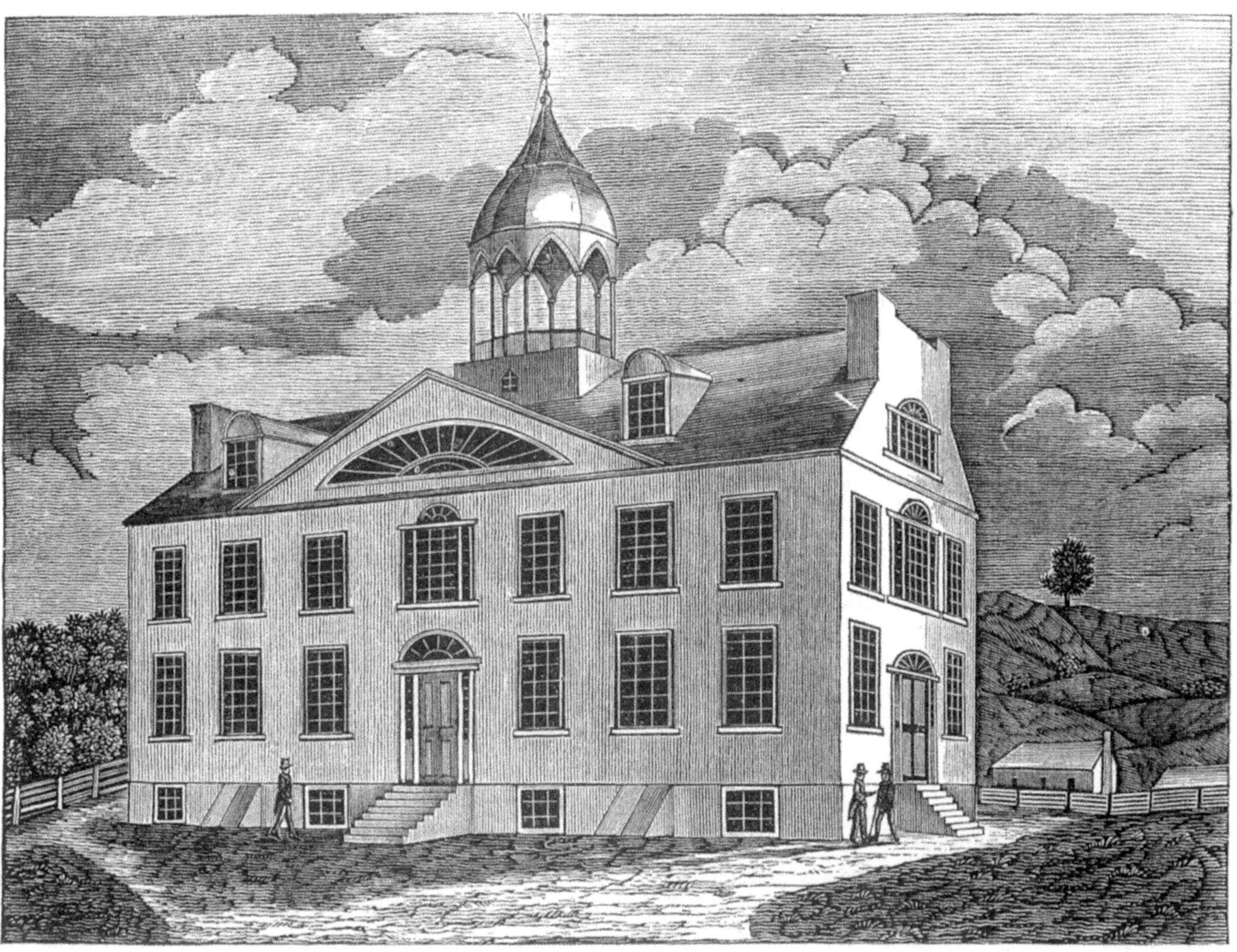

Augusta College was founded in 1822 under the patronage of the Methodist Episcopal Church as a successor to Bethel Academy, an unsuccessful Methodist school first located on the Kentucky River in Jessamine County in the 1790s. A writer for the *Family Magazine*, probably J.S. Tomlinson, Augusta College president, stated that the village of Augusta presented but few inducements to indulge in vice or extravagance and that moral and religious influence was decided and pervasive. The tuition for each twenty-one-week session was $16.00; room, board, laundry, tuition, lights, and fuel cost $2.50 per week. The building illustrated here was destroyed by fire in 1852, rebuilt in a plainer style, and was lost to fire again in 1856. Perrin's 1887 *History of Kentucky* states that the college closed a few years after being rebuilt a second time and had since been in use as a high school. The 1884 atlas of Bracken and Pendleton counties shows a square block near the center of the town still identified as Augusta College, with one large building indicated on the property.

Wood engraving from *Family Magazine*, 1838.

Centre College in Danville was founded as a result of the legislature's appointment of a new board of control at Transylvania University, an event not satisfactory to the Presbyterians who were involved there. The school's name was derived from its location in the central part of the state. Presbyterian influence predominated in its activities, and it came under close control of the church about 1825. When this view was published in 1847, Centre had about 175 students, and by 1886 it could claim to have educated fourteen representatives in Congress, four U.S. senators, five state governors, one U.S. vice-president, and one U.S. Supreme Court justice.

Wood engraving from Lewis Collins's *Historical Sketches of Kentucky,* 1847. Drawing by Harrison Eastman.

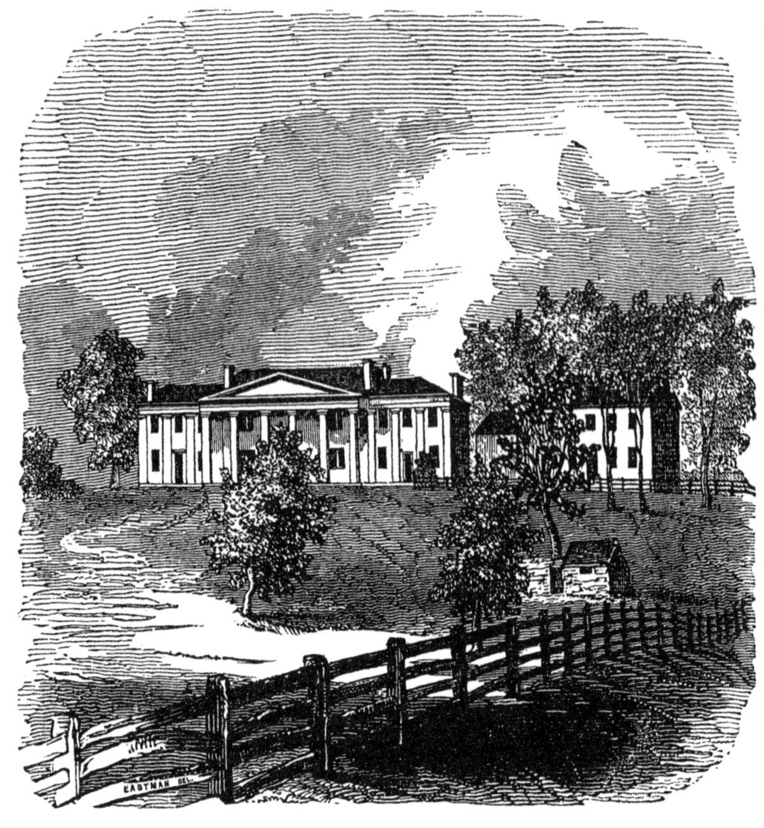

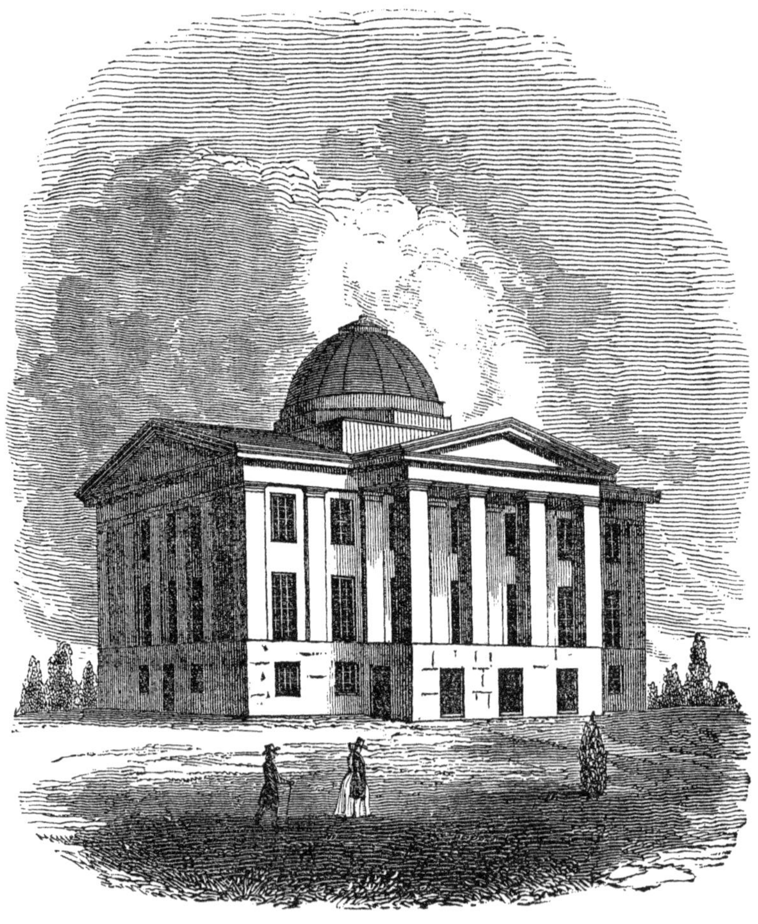

The University of Louisville was founded in 1846 by combining the Louisville Medical Institute with a newly established law department. This view was taken shortly after. Lewis Collins notes that the first course of lectures in law was delivered that year to about thirty students. The medical college was chartered by the legislature in 1833 but was not organized until 1837 by an ordinance of the city council, which appropriated funds for a library, chemical apparatus, and suitable buildings. The building was designed by Gideon Shryock. Dr. Charles Caldwell, a former Transylvania medical school professor who had been dismissed there for advocating that Transylvania move to Louisville, was instrumental in the founding of the Medical Institute. In 1834 Caldwell published an article about the controversy surrounding the opening of another medical school; he had information, he said, from a young medical student in Louisville, that seduction, dissipation, and the general distracting character of the place were injurious to those who wished to acquire knowledge. That information did not deter Caldwell from moving to Louisville soon afterward.

Wood engraving from Lewis Collins's *Historical Sketches of Kentucky,* 1847.

Bacon College, founded by the Disciples of Christ Church at Georgetown, was chartered by the legislature in 1836 and moved in 1839 to Harrodsburg. Lewis Collins mentions "courses of study equal to those of the best regulated American colleges, with long and successful experience on the part of the college officers." The building illustrated here was erected in 1842–1843 during Kentucky's Greek revival period and was used by the college until 1850. For several years after that it served as a high school building and after 1857 was again the home of the college, reorganized at that time with the name Kentucky University. The building burned in 1864, and the college then moved to Lexington to merge with Transylvania.

Wood engraving from Lewis Collins's *Historical Sketches of Kentucky,* 1847.

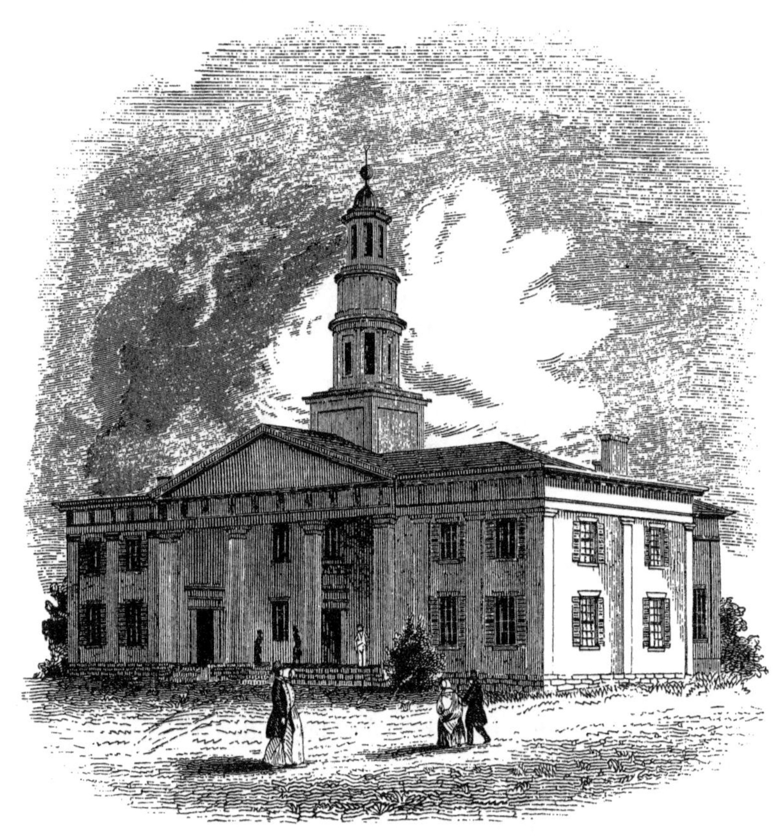

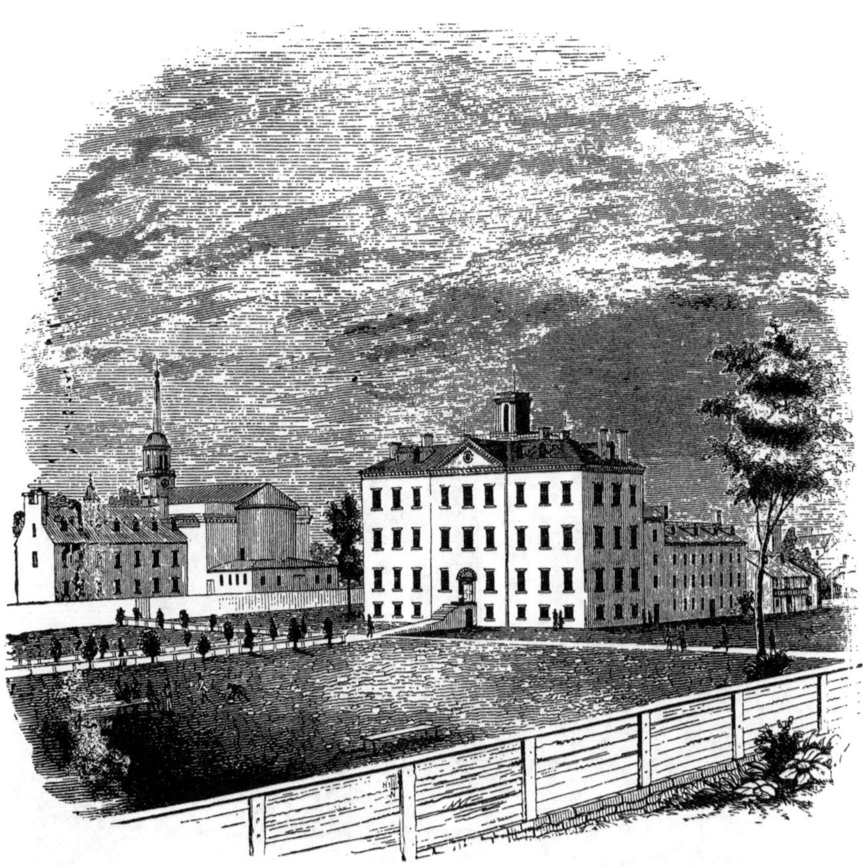

St. Joseph's College in Bardstown was founded in 1819 by Bishop Benedict J. Flaget in the Roman Catholic community in Nelson County. It was chartered in 1825 by the legislature and soon became Kentucky's leading Catholic school as well as a celebrated institution for young men. The building shown here was erected after a fire in 1838 had destroyed the original 1820 structure. The college was patronized chiefly by Kentuckians and was closed during the Civil War. It reopened as a seminary and later had a dual role as seminary and college; still later it was used as an orphanage. The Xavierian brothers revived the structure for use as a high school in 1911, and it ended its long career in education in 1968. It is currently occupied by government offices and other tenants.

Wood engraving from Lewis Collins's *Historical Sketches of Kentucky,* 1847.

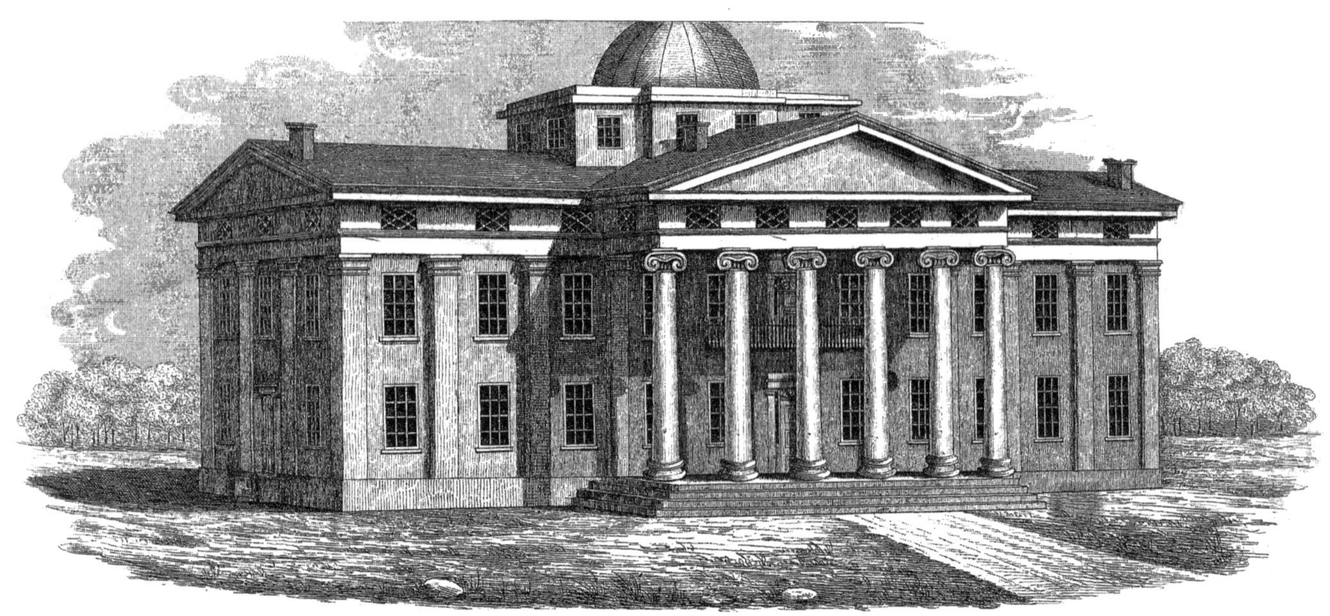

Shelby College and Observatory in Shelbyville was organized in 1836 and came under control of the Episcopal Church in 1841. The edifice was described in the catalogue as a handsome brick building with a president's house on the grounds, which included about eighteen acres. In 1848 additional construction was begun and astronomical instruments were ordered from Europe. Lewis Collins noted that the locality was healthy and the population intelligent, refined, and remarkably moral. Rev. William I. Waller, M.D., was president and the leading member of the five-man faculty. The college roster shows a large majority of students from Shelbyville and Shelby County but included many from other parts of the state and a few from Louisiana, North Carolina, and Missouri. The general course of instruction had major components of mathematics, Greek, and Latin throughout the four year program, and cost forty dollars per year. Additional fees were charged for modern language, drawing, and music, taught by "fully competent gentlemen residing in Shelbyville."

Lithograph from the *Catalogue of the Officers and Students of Shelby College, 1848–1849*. Lithograph by Emil Teschemacher and Philip Kling, Louisville.

A new Board of Education of the Kentucky Conference of the Methodist Episcopal Church South was chartered by the legislature in 1860, but its institution, the Kentucky Wesleyan College, did not begin to function until 1866 at Millersburg. To seek larger enrollment, the school moved in 1890 to Winchester and in 1951 to Owensboro.

Wood engraving from Richard Collins's *History of Kentucky*, 1874.

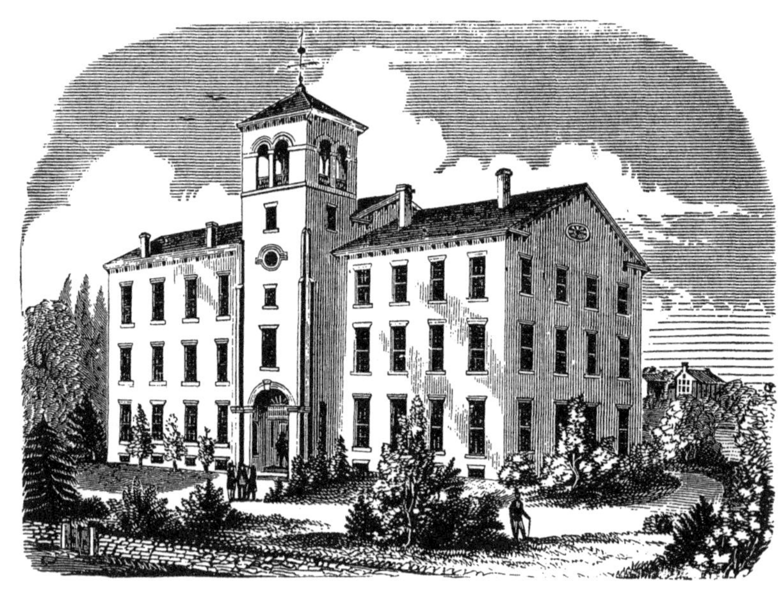

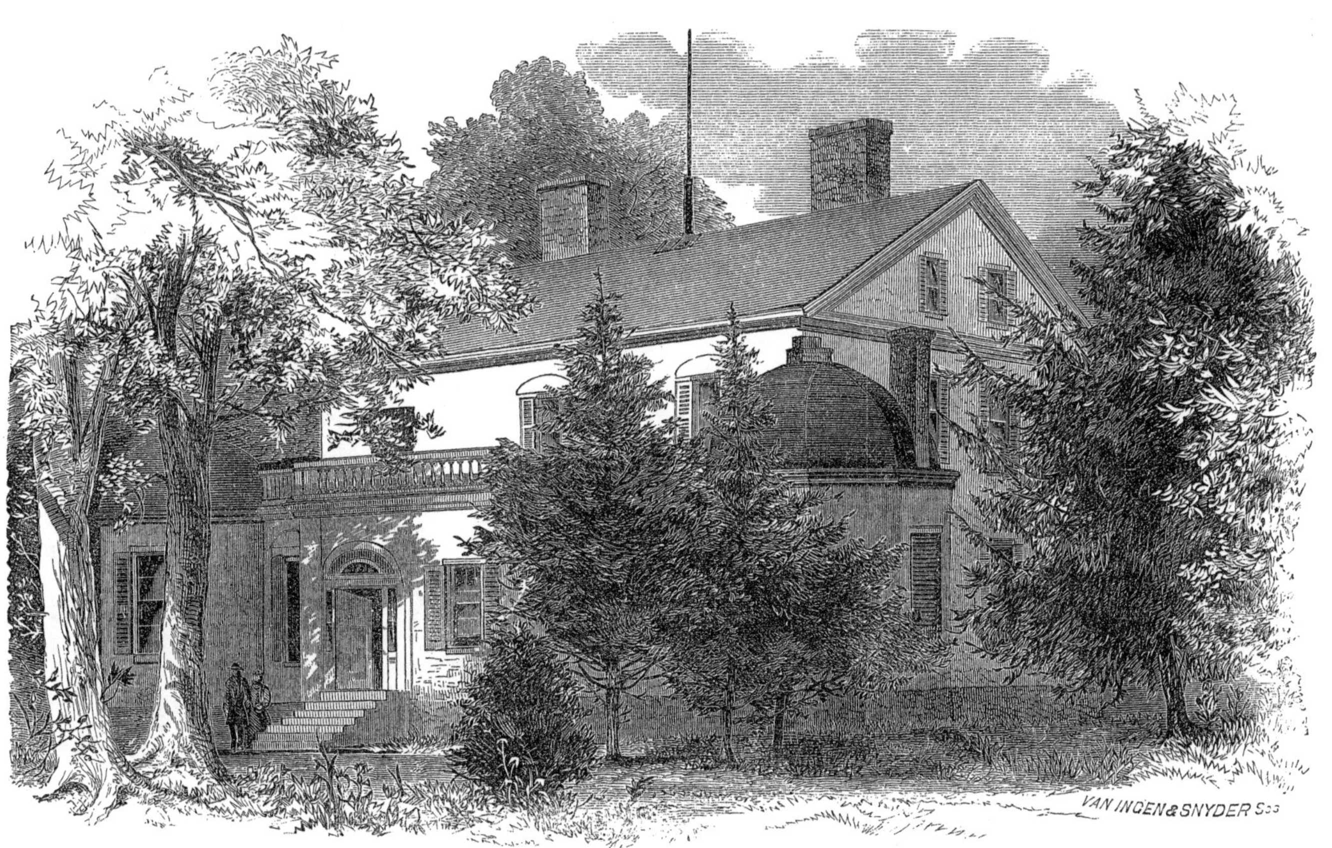

Kentucky University was an outgrowth of Bacon College, which had been given an extended charter and a new name in 1858. In 1865 the school moved to Lexington, taking over the property of—and merging with—Transylvania University. The departments included a college of liberal arts, a college of the Bible, and a college of law. At the same time, the state agricultural and mechanical college became affiliated with the university. In 1866 an alumnus of Bacon College bought for the school the homestead of Henry Clay and the adjoining estate, called Woodlands. An atlas of Fayette County published in 1877 shows a square block near the center of Lexington as part of the Kentucky University campus as well as a tract of land southeast of Clay Avenue. The atlas shows only one large building on the eastern campus, probably the old Clay residence. The horticultural department is said to have stood on the tract known as Woodlands, which adjoined Ashland.

Wood engraving from the *Report of the Commissioner of Agriculture for 1870,* 1871. Engraved by Van Ingen & Snyder.

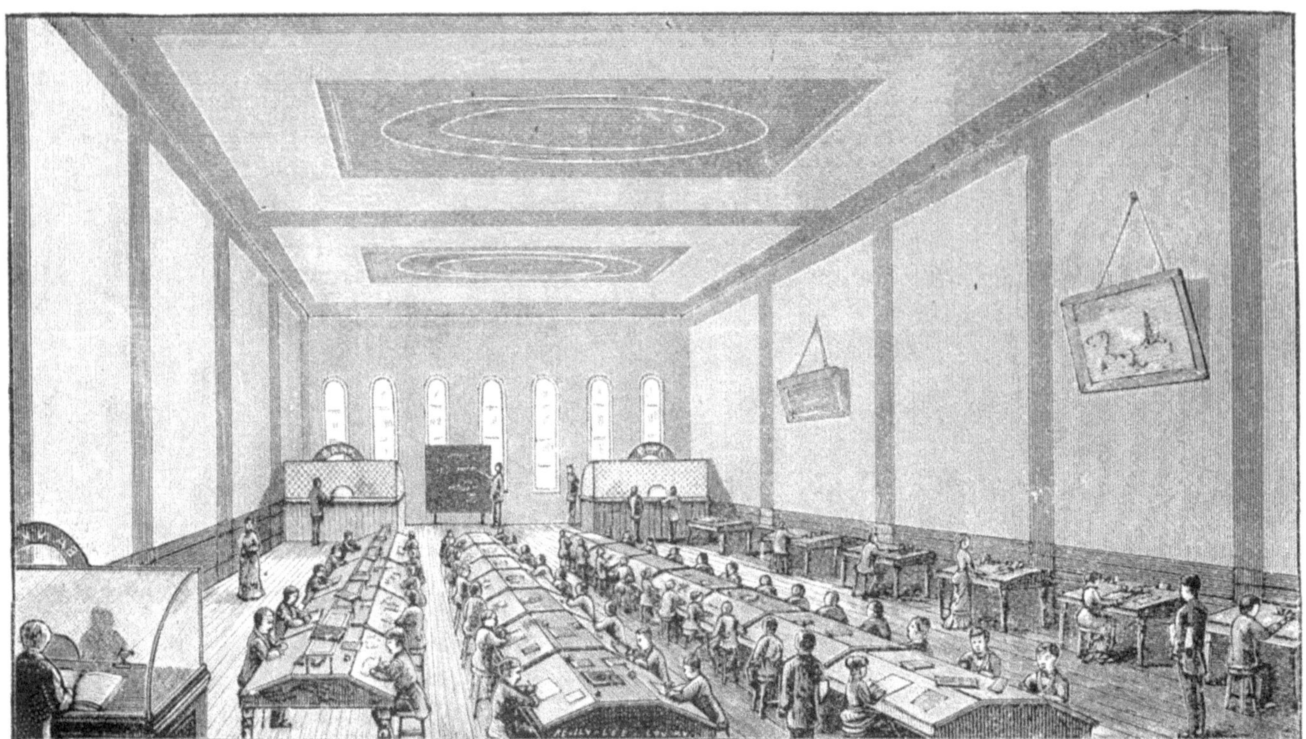

In the latter half of the nineteenth century efforts to promote immigration and land development were sponsored by states, regions, cities, railroads, and land agents. In 1885 the Bowling Green and Warren County Immigration Society published a booklet citing many reasons why Bowling Green was a desirable place for those seeking "an intelligent, moral, and social community." It noted that the Normal School and Business College was the largest and most flourishing of its class in the south. The school, established in 1875 by A.W. Mell, claimed an enrollment of five hundred students in 1885, including representatives from all the southern states and some from the north. This view shows the interior of the business department.

Wood engraving from a booklet of the Bowling Green and Warren County Immigration Society, 1885. Engraving by the firm of Charles F. Reilly and George D. Lee, Louisville.

The Kentucky Institution for the Education of the Blind in Louisville (*right*) was chartered by the legislature in 1842 and was the sixth of its kind in the United States. It was at first maintained by the city and had five students in its first class. Views of the principal building erected on Frankfort Avenue in 1855 appeared in a number of publications, but this is the only representation we have of its interior. The students are shown learning the Braille alphabet, sewing and knitting, upholstering, making brooms, and caning chairs.

Wood engraving from *Frank Leslie's Illustrated Newspaper,* June 19, 1880, from a drawing by Walter Goater for a series of Leslie's articles entitled "The South in 1880."

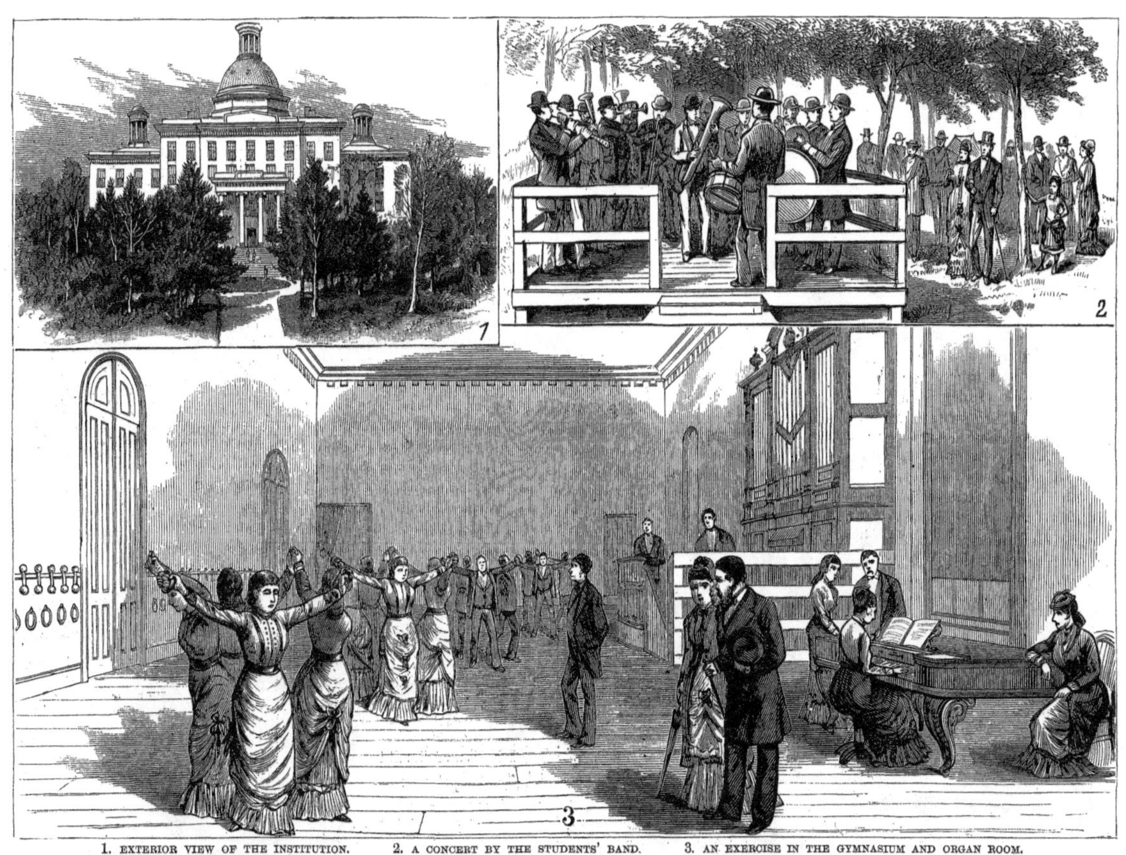

1. EXTERIOR VIEW OF THE INSTITUTION. 2. A CONCERT BY THE STUDENTS' BAND. 3. AN EXERCISE IN THE GYMNASIUM AND ORGAN ROOM.

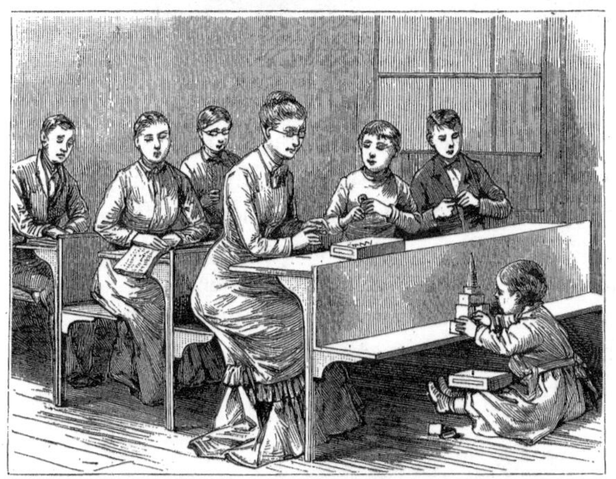

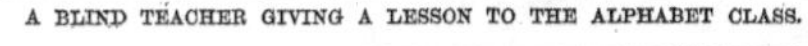

A BLIND TEACHER GIVING A LESSON TO THE ALPHABET CLASS.

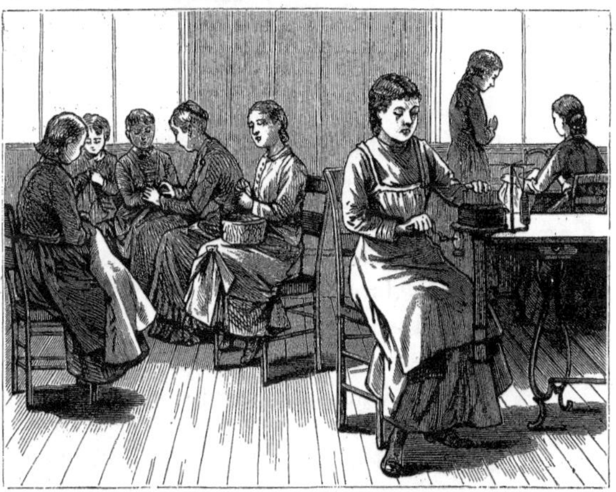

THE CLASS IN SEWING AND KNITTING.

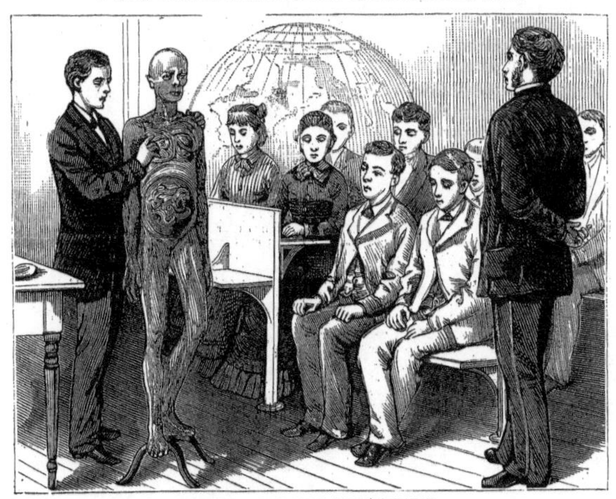

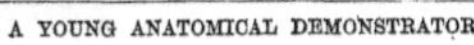

A YOUNG ANATOMICAL DEMONSTRATOR.

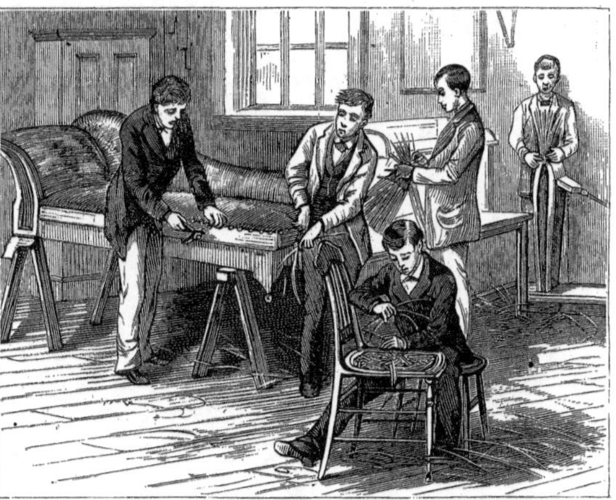

UPHOLSTERY, BROOM-MAKING AND CHAIR-CANING IN THE WORKSHOP.

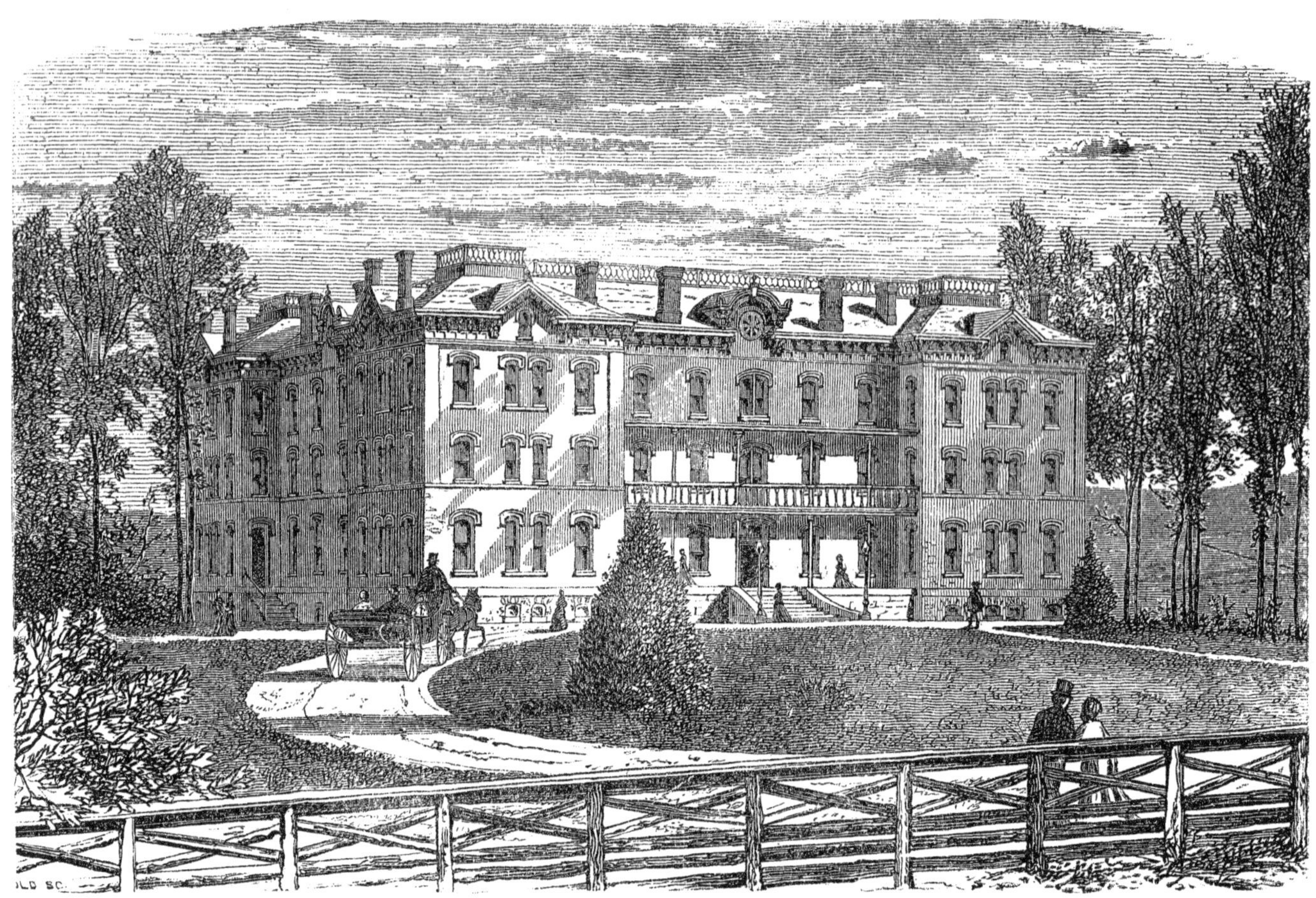

Ladies' Hall, built around 1872 to accommodate young women at Berea College, was modeled after Ladies' Hall at Oberlin College in Ohio. It stands today as Fairchild Hall, named in 1937 for E. Henry Fairchild, first president of the college. The basement and first floor provided the work, administration, and common rooms. The two upper floors contained rooms, each with a closet, for ninety women, with water tanks, water closets, and bathrooms on both floors. The garret was one large room, "an excellent place for exercise or for drying clothes in stormy weather." On one side a grove of trees provided a place "in which, by permission, young gentlemen may meet the ladies for croquet."

Wood engraving from *Berea College, Ky.*, 1875. Engraved by Old, Cincinnati.

SIX

The Civil War

Of all the names given the conflict of 1861–1865—the Civil War, the War Between the States, the War of the Rebellion, or the War for Southern Independence—in Kentucky one name in particular described the fighting. It was the Brother's War.

Kentuckians on the eve of war were a confused, uncertain people. They still had a semblance of a strong two-party system, and their history told them that time often defeated a political enemy. For some, the South's fears following Lincoln's election seemed an overreaction. Furthermore, this was the state of "the Great Compromiser," Henry Clay, who had tried to keep his America united through the art of political give-and-take. His successor in spirit, John J. Crittenden, was trying to do the same thing once more, while keeping Kentucky true to its motto, "United We Stand, Divided We Fall."

Adding to the political complexities was the question of slavery. Of all the slaveholding states in 1850, Kentucky ranked third highest in the number of slaveowners. On the average those citizens held few slaves but nonetheless large numbers of Kentuckians were part of the slave system. At the outset of war, the abolition of slavery was not the stated goal of native Kentuckian Lincoln and his administration. But many of his supporters had such an aim. Would the Civil War, asked Kentuckians, be a war for the Union or against slavery, or both? If it was the first, then slaveholders could fight for the North. If it was the second, problems arose. Overall, Kentucky wanted both Union and slavery in 1861. Such conflicts created a divided mind within the commonwealth.

Yet, Kentucky had to do something, as state after state left the Union to join the Confederacy (led by another native Kentuckian, Jefferson Davis). Kentucky's fighting-age men soon had to make choices, and recruiting stations were set up to attract them to one cause or another. At first, the mostly northern illustrators showed army life as regular, orderly, and clean. Soon reality appeared, and then, as fighting started, the illustrations changed. But while the struggle for men's hearts took place at the recruiting camps, a larger struggle was seeking to win the minds of Kentuckians. The supposedly pro-Confederate state guard, led by Simon B. Buckner, worried unionists in the legislature, and a force more favorable to them, the home guards, was created. The legislature proclaimed Kentucky a neutral state. There seemed to be three nations—the United States, the Confederate States, and Kentucky.

But such a course of action could not endure. Buckner and many of his supporters went South to fight. At places like Camp Dick Robinson, federal troops were raised. Finally, in 1861, Confederate soldiers took Columbus in western Kentucky. Federal troops, led by U.S. Grant, soon responded, and Kentucky's neutrality ended. While officially the state remained in the Union, a group of southern sympathizers formed a government, with its capital at Bowling Green, and Kentucky became a star in both flags.

Novelist John Fox, Jr., later wrote of that time: "When the great news [of war] came, it came like a sword that, with one stroke, slashed the state in twain, shearing through the strongest bonds that link one man to another." Nowhere was that truer than in the commonwealth, from which perhaps one hundred thousand men, black and white, eventually fought for the Union and some forty thousand for the Confederacy. A defense line stretched from Columbus, Kentucky, and Island No. 10 on the Mississippi, through Bowling Green and across to where the first major action took place, at Mill Spring, in eastern Kentucky. A Confederate defeat there, coupled with actions around forts Henry and Donelson, brought a general withdrawal by southern forces. Only one major campaign affected Kentucky, when Braxton Bragg's 1862 Confederate invasion caused hurried defensive actions, especially in northern Kentucky. Battles at Munfordville and Richmond preceded the bloody day at Perryville. Confederate retreat ended large-scale fighting in the state.

Death and destruction did not end that October day in 1862, however. Cavalry-style raids by legitimate Confederate soldiers like John Hunt Morgan and Nathan Bedford Forrest periodically created problems for Union forces in Kentucky. Outlaw groups and guerrilla bands, like Quantrill's, raided, burned, and killed across the commonwealth. Since the major fighting had passed by the state, few artists remained behind to show that aspect of war. Yet in some ways it left more bitterness and hardship than did the fighting of regular armies. Nor did the illustrations show the reaction of Kentuckians to the introduction of the abolition of slavery as a war aim, to the presence of black troops in the state, or to the unwise actions undertaken by some Union commanders in the commonwealth. For all those reasons Kentucky turned more and more against the administration in Washington and eventually became more comfortable with the southern viewpoint. The Confederacy won its important Kentucky victories after the war ended.

—*J.C.K.*

The period following the war with Mexico saw the formation of independent military companies in many parts of the nation. These units were often very popular and were, on occasion, the subject of musical compositions, as in the sheet music shown here. The Louisville Citizen Guards was formed in 1858, captained by Simon B. Buckner. Buckner subsequently served as a general in the Confederate army, was later a Louisville newspaper editor, and finally served as governor of Kentucky. With the coming of preparations for war, the Louisville Citizen Guards became part of the Second Regiment of the Kentucky State Guard.

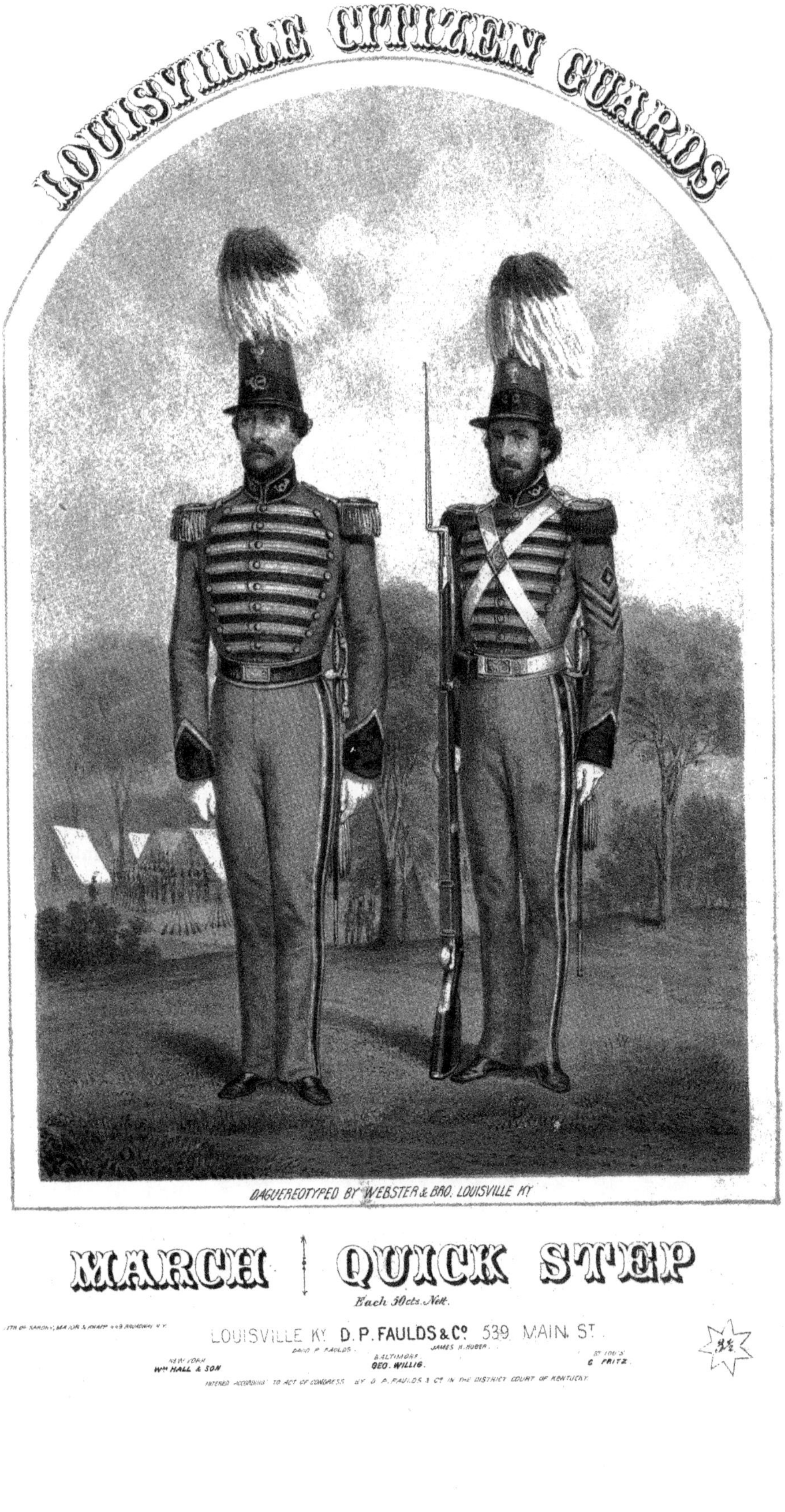

Lithographed sheet music cover, published by D.P. Faulds & Co., Louisville, 1858. Lithographed by Sarony, Major & Knapp, New York. Drawn from a daguerreotype by Webster & Bro., Louisville.

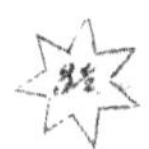

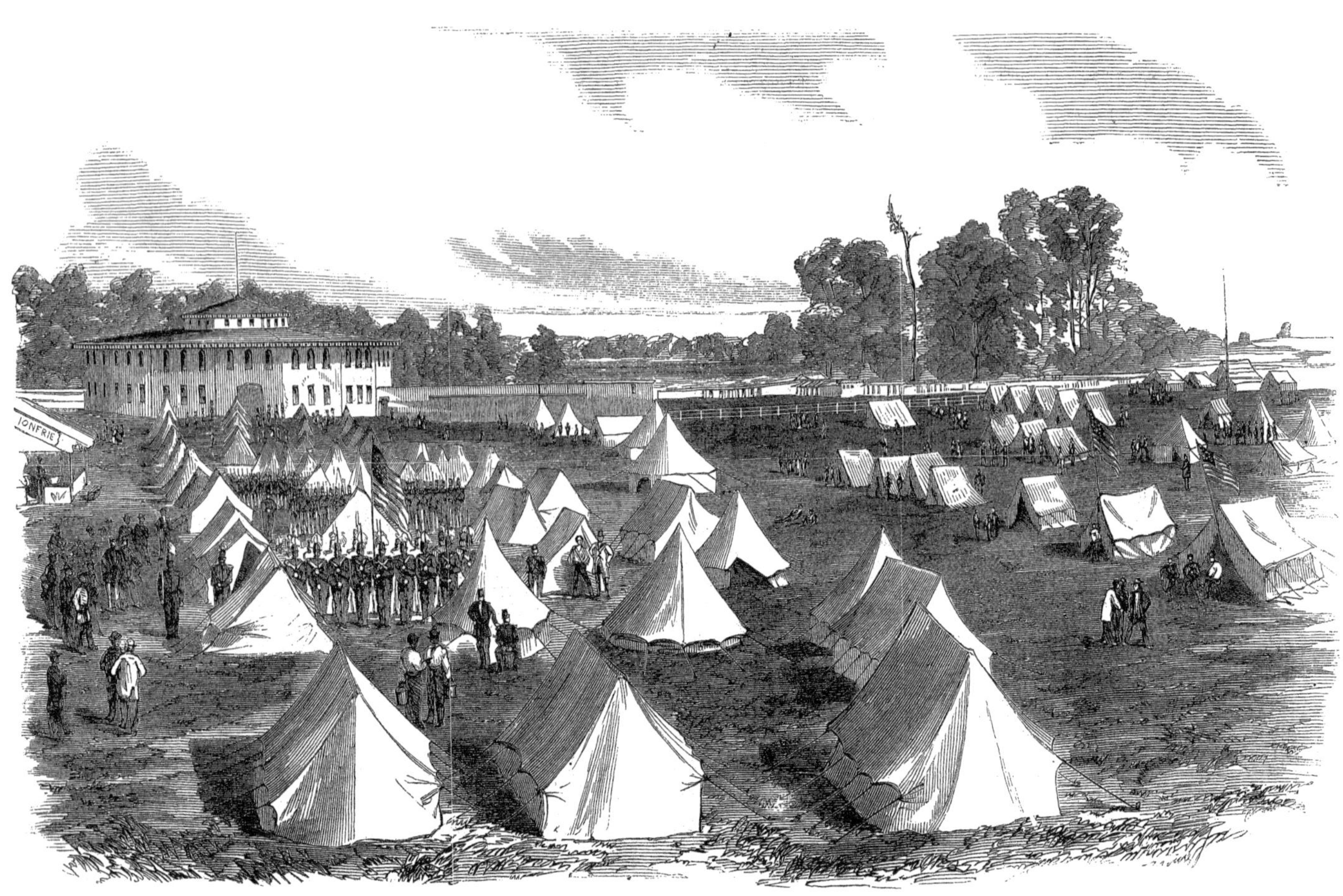

With armed civil conflict on the horizon people turned to militia companies for preparedness. The Kentucky legislature provided for their organization into one body under Maj. Gen. Simon B. Buckner in March 1860. Camp Boone, shown in this view, was the Kentucky State Guard's first encampment, held in August 1860 for training purposes. It was located on the thirty-eight-acre fair grounds on Frankfort Avenue in Louisville. During the early years of the war, the fair grounds were heavily used for troop encampment, and extensive damage was done to the facility.

Wood engraving from *Frank Leslie's Illustrated Newspaper,* October 6, 1860. Engraved from a photograph by Shaw, Nickerson and Garrett, Louisville.

Numerous camps sprang up across Kentucky as Union forces organized. Cynthiana was occupied by federal troops in late September 1861. The city was captured twice by John Hunt Morgan's men during their July 1862 and January 1864 raids. In the latter raid, much of the business section was destroyed by fire. Shown here is the presentation of a flag to Kentucky volunteers at Camp Bruce near Cynthiana.

Wood engraving from *Harper's Weekly,* October 5, 1861, from a drawing by Captain Finch.

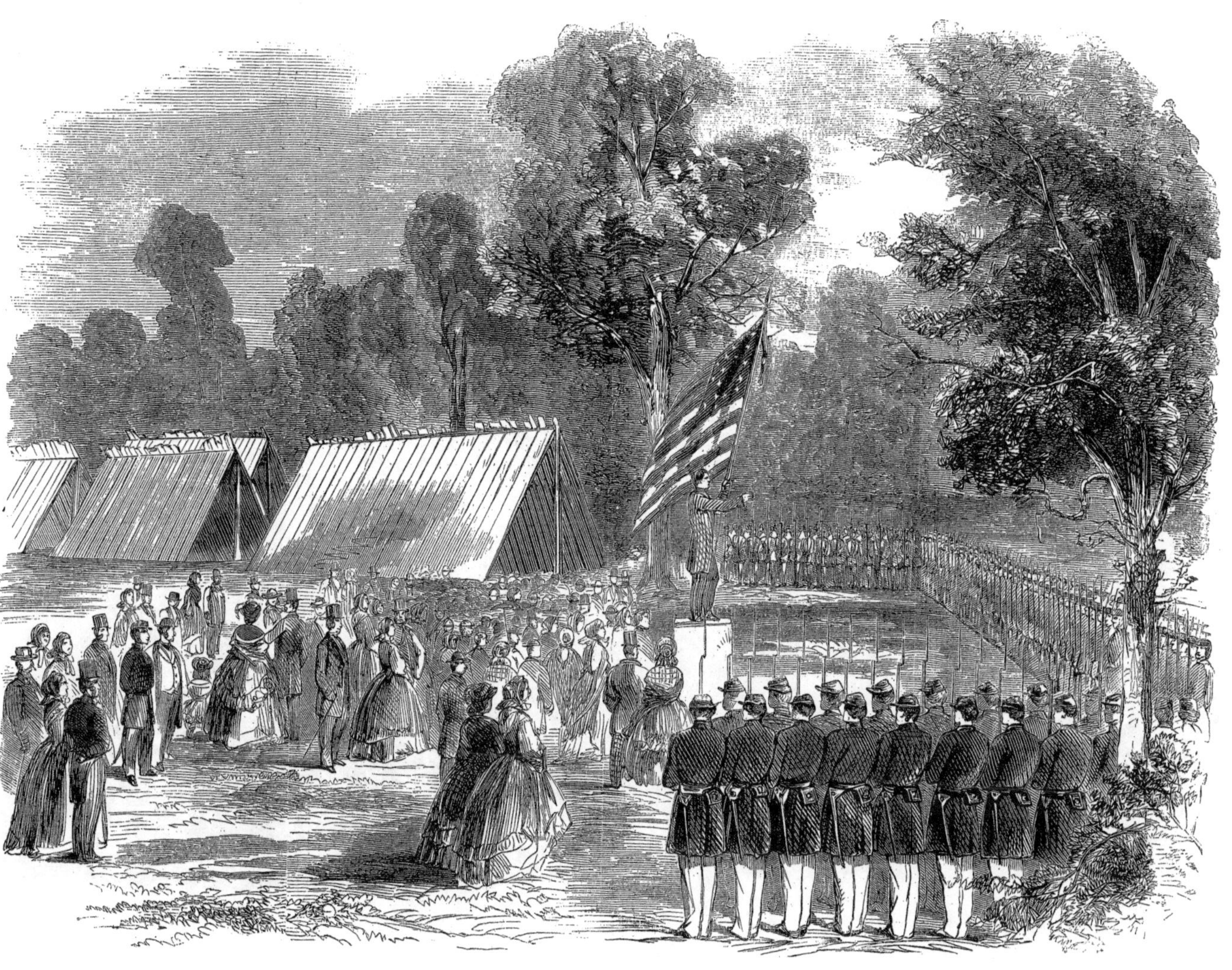

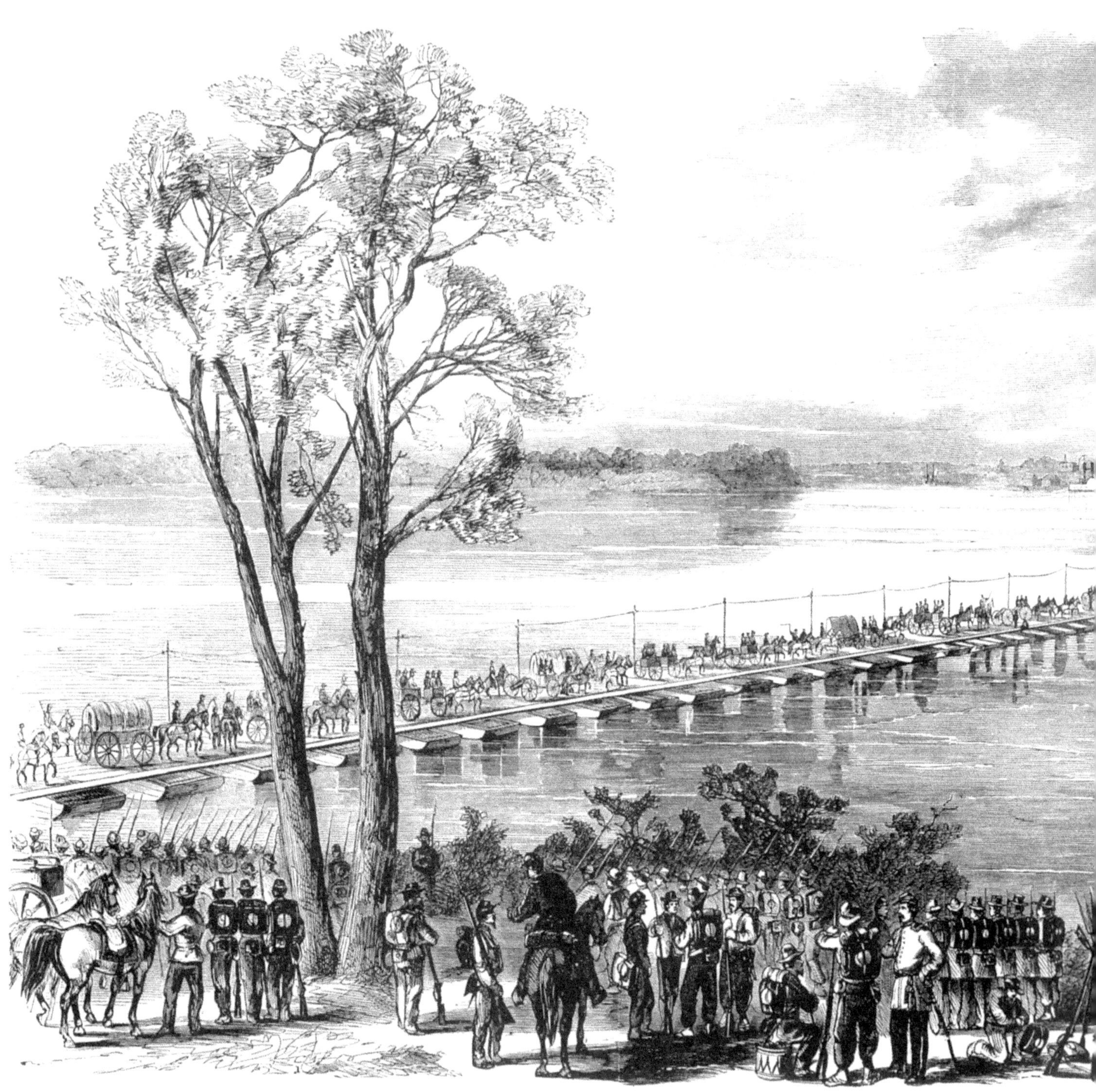

A great bridge of boats a mile in length was built by the national forces at Paducah. Shown here is the passage of the First Division of Illinois Artillery and Infantry. The bridge was built on coal barges anchored to the riverbed and included two draw sections for passage of vessels. A twenty-foot-wide trestle was built on each barge, covered with planks, and held together by pegs. The bridge was put into place soon after Paducah was occupied but

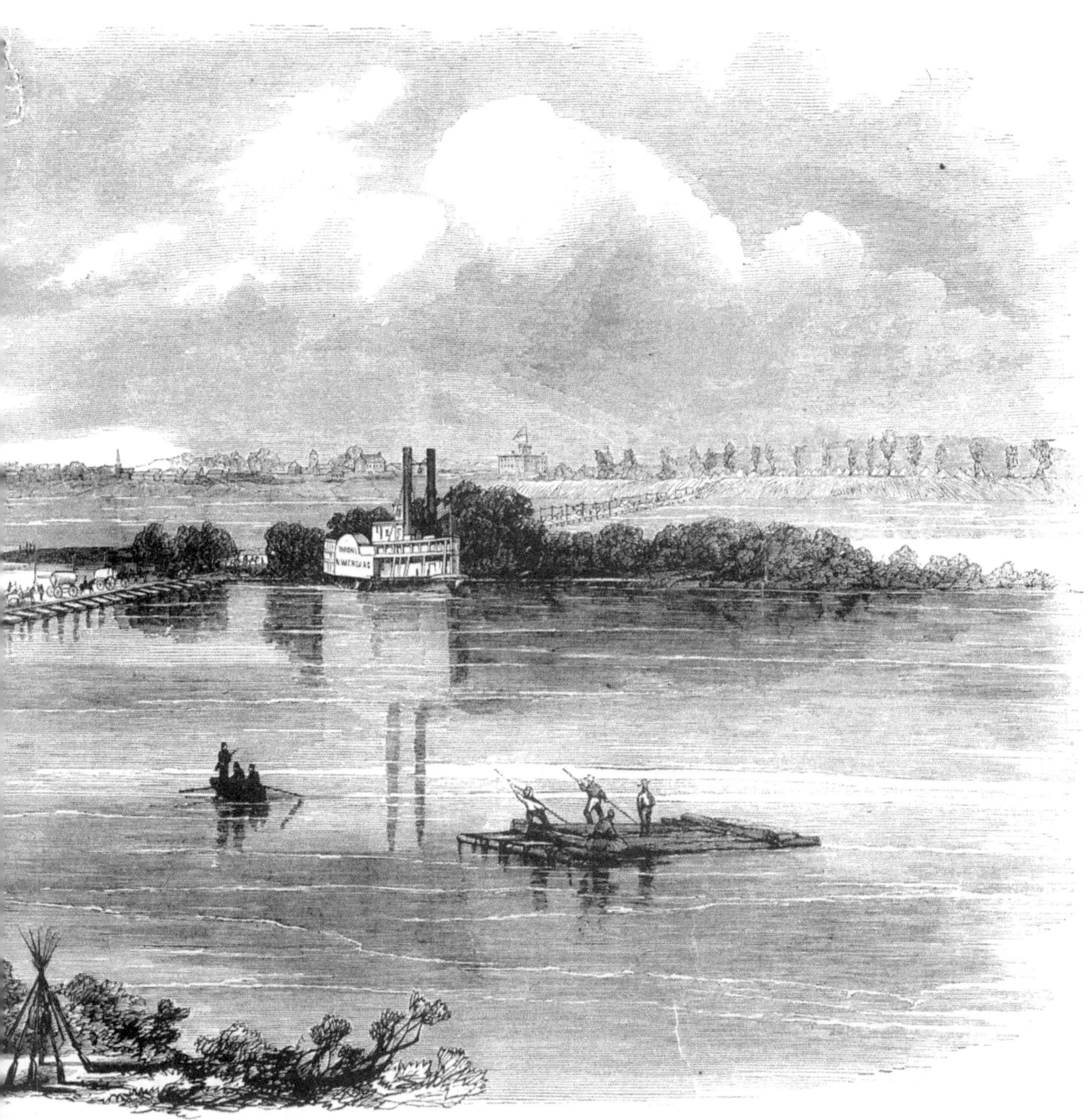

remained only a short time before being swept away by high water. The bridge was said to have been built in four days and was at that time an example of military engineering unprecedented in our history. This view from the Illinois shore shows Low Island in the foreground and Fort Anderson, formerly the Paducah Marine Hospital, in the distance.

Wood engraving from *Frank Leslie's Illustrated Newspaper,* October 12, 1861.

Federal troops are shown in this view landing on the shore of the Kentucky side of the Ohio River opposite Cairo for the purpose of constructing Fort Holt. The fort was intended to defend the southern approach to Cairo, an important base for Union military operations. The fort was named for Kentuckian Joseph Holt, postmaster general in 1859 and secretary of war in 1860–1861.

Wood engraving from *Frank Leslie's Illustrated Newspaper,* October 12, 1861, from a drawing by William R. McComas, Cincinnati.

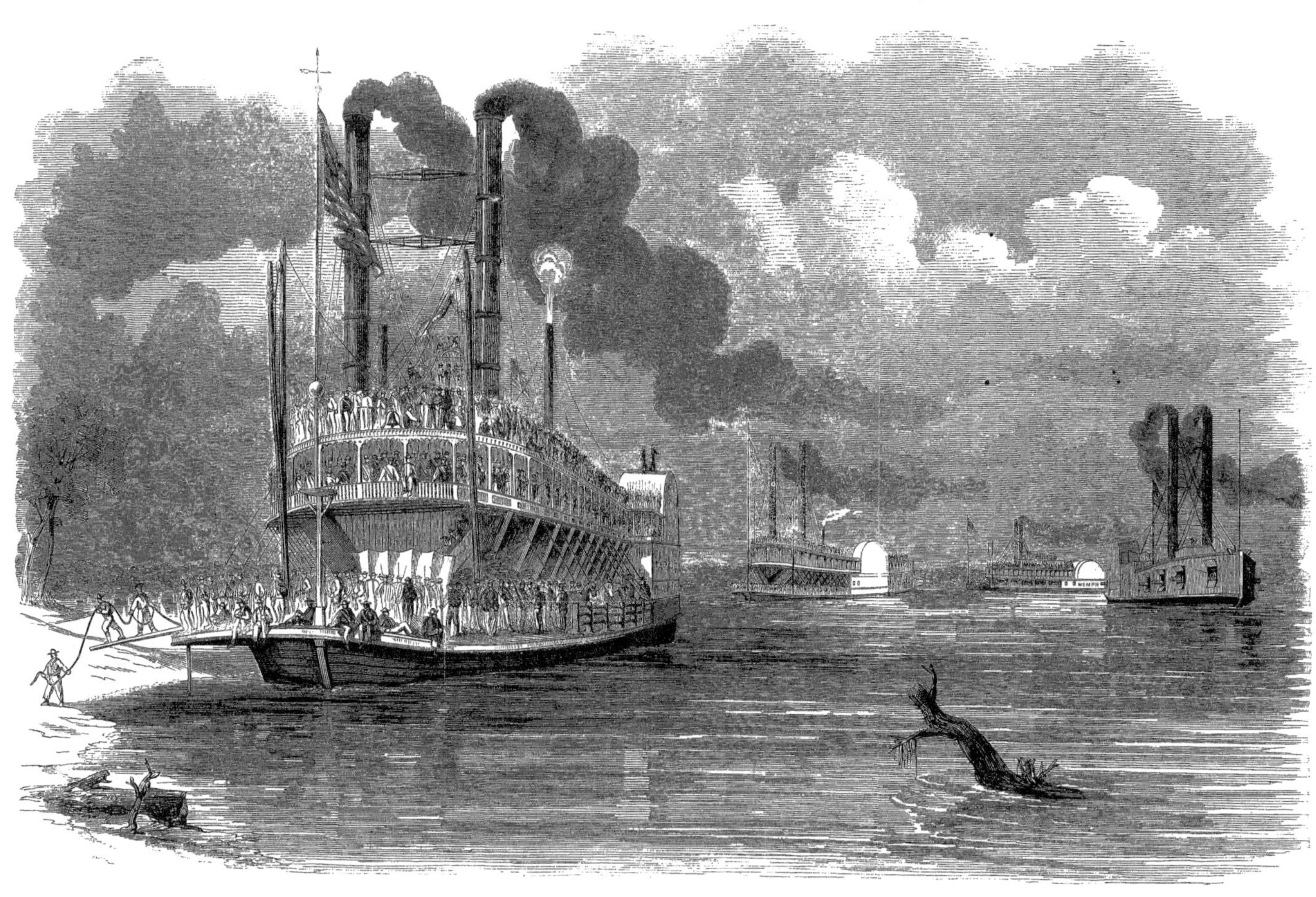

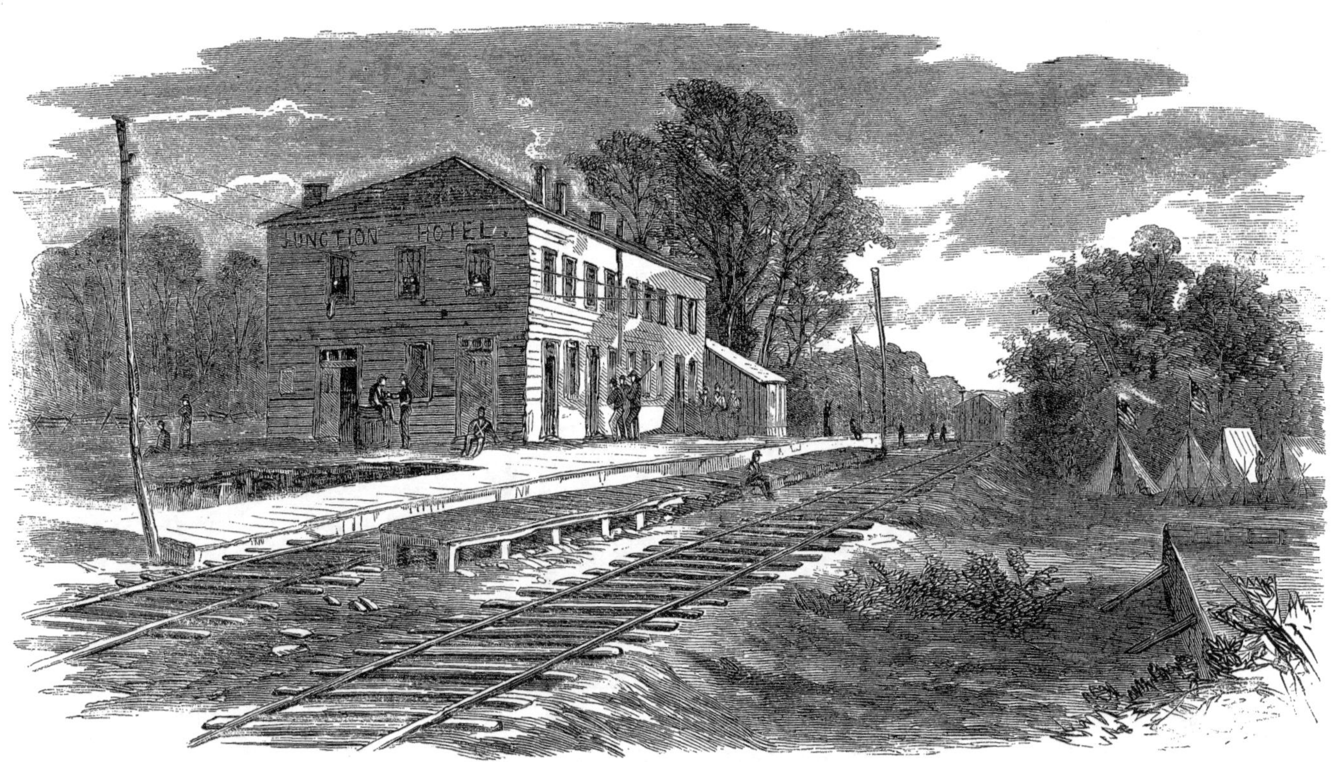

Strategically located on the railroad lines, Lebanon Junction was used for a time by Union General William T. Sherman as his headquarters when he briefly commanded the Kentucky military theater. As this view indicates, the presence of rail transportation was often a more important consideration to the troops than was village size.

Wood engraving from *Harper's Weekly*, October 19, 1861, from a drawing by Henry Mosler, Cincinnati.

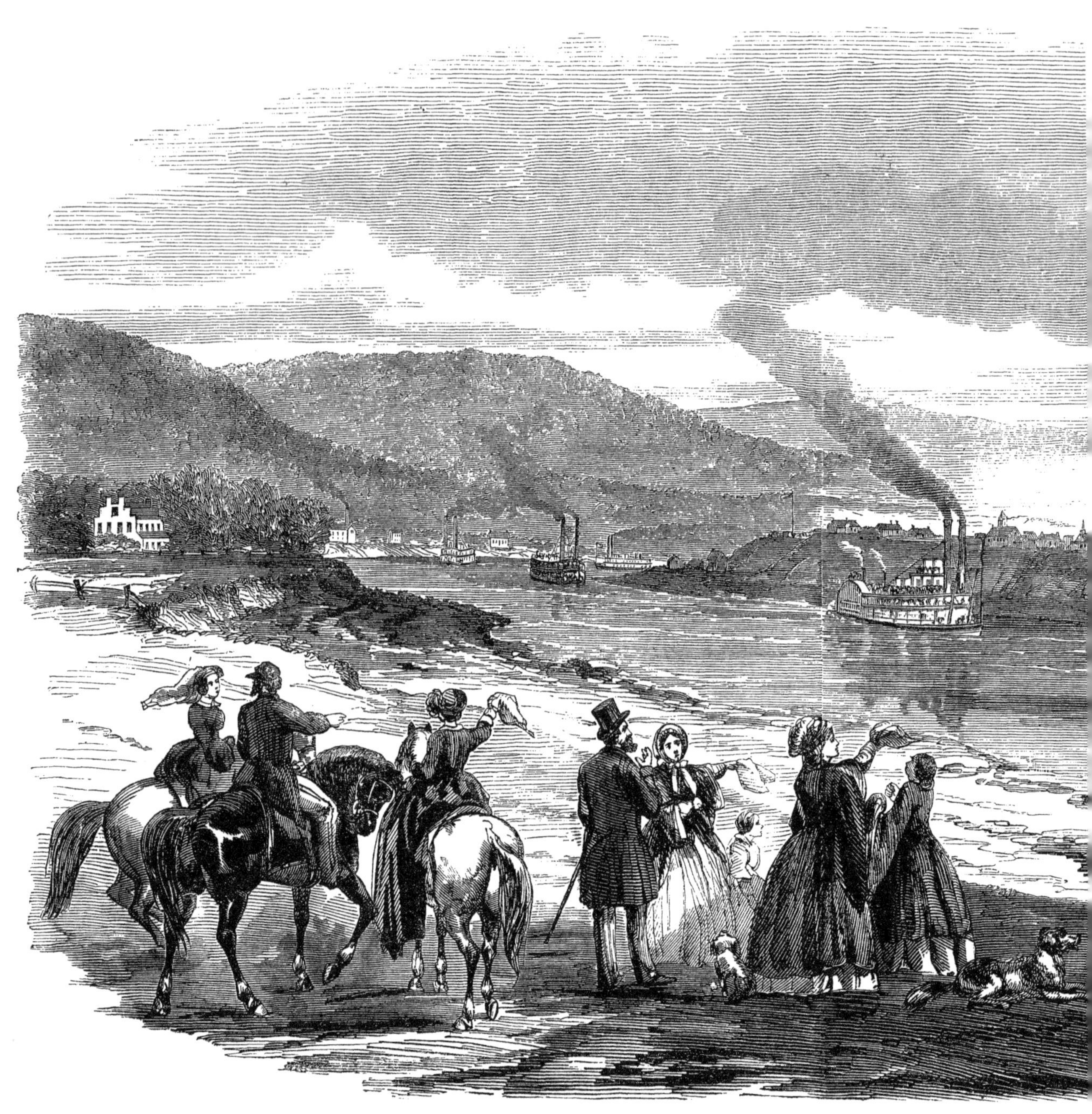

Federal control of the waterways was very important to military successes in the West. This portion of the Cumberland River passed through Livingston, Lyon, and Trigg counties. This scene, depicting U.S. troops steaming up the river, was sketched in late 1861 or January 1862 when preparations were being made for anticipated heavy fighting at Fort

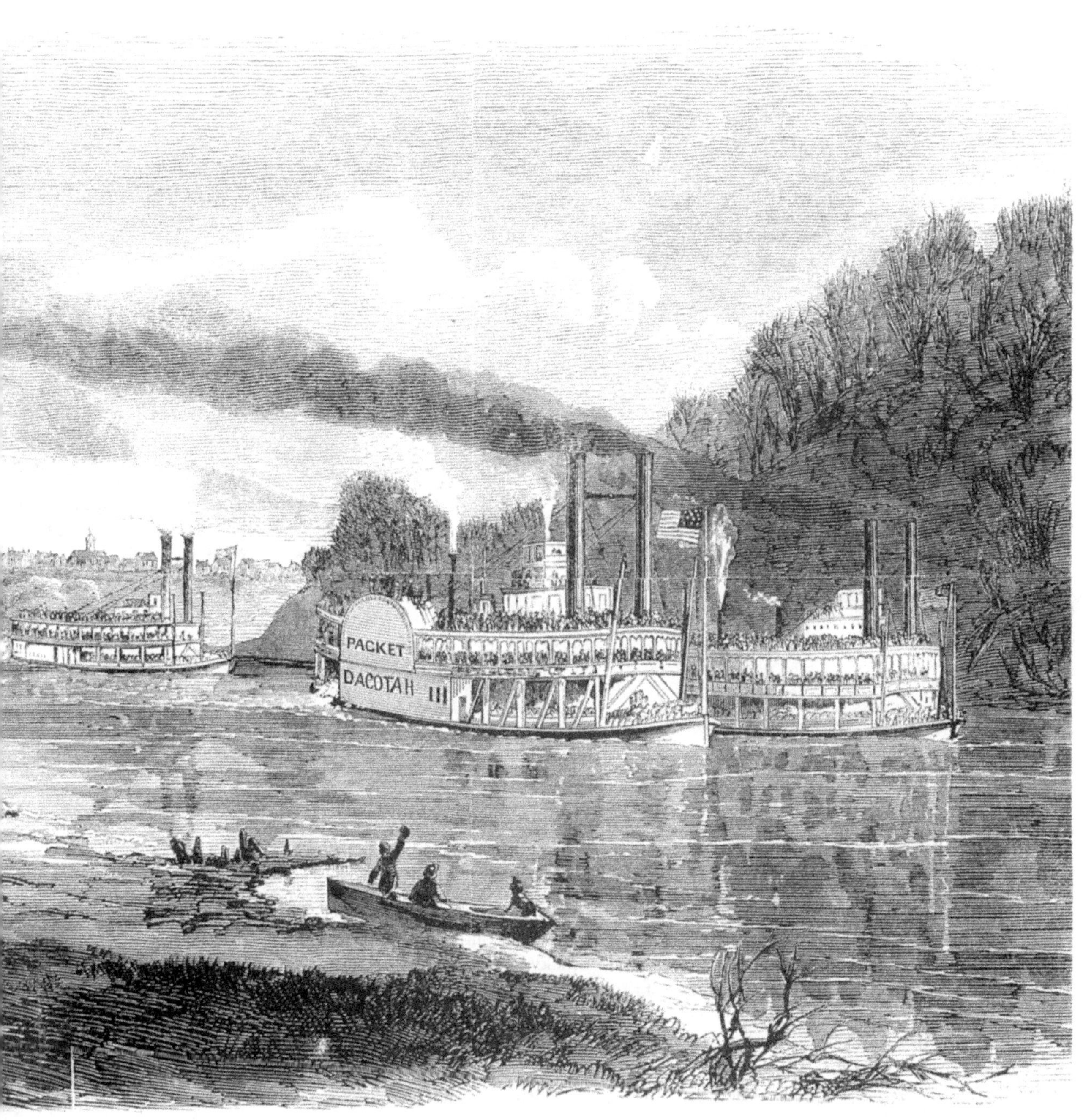

Henry and Fort Donelson. The steamer *Dacotah* had been in the Pittsburgh-Cincinnati trade before the war and was burned in March 1864.

Wood engraving from *Frank Leslie's Illustrated Newspaper,* February 1, 1862, from a drawing by Allison, possibly Joseph B. Allison.

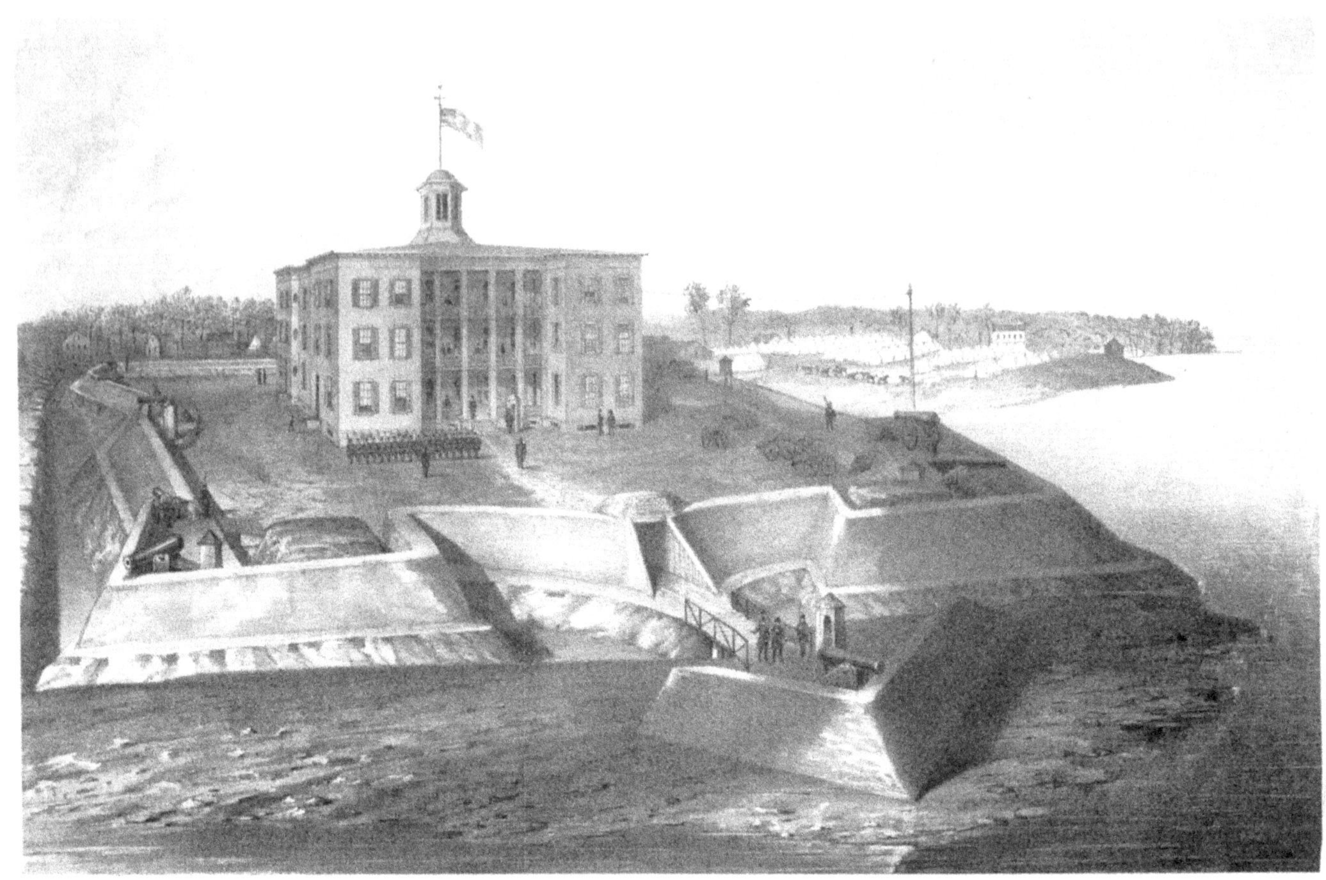

After Confederates seized portions of western Kentucky, Gen. U.S. Grant's forces took Paducah. The troops occupied the telegraph office, the railroad depot, and the Marine Hospital, shown here. Grant directed that a portion of his one thousand men be quartered in the hospital, one of seven hospitals for seamen and mariners authorized by Congress in the 1840s in the Mississippi and Ohio River valleys. Fort Anderson, as it was called, was named for Kentucky-born Robert Anderson, the former commander at Fort Sumter in South Carolina and the Union commander in Kentucky for a short period in 1861. The fort stood at what was then the western edge of the city, which is just out of sight to the left, or eastward, in this view. The fort proved its worth in March 1864 when a portion of Nathan Bedford Forrest's Confederate forces attacked Paducah. They advanced through the streets under fire from the fort but could not cross the deep ditch around it. The Confederates held the city for ten hours and burned the railroad depot, the steamer *Dacotah,* and military stores and buildings before departing.

Lithograph in two colors published as a patriotic print by Middleton, Strobridge & Co., Cincinnati, 1862, from a drawing by Alfred E. Matthews, Cincinnati, a member of the Thirty-first Regiment of the Ohio Volunteer Infantry.

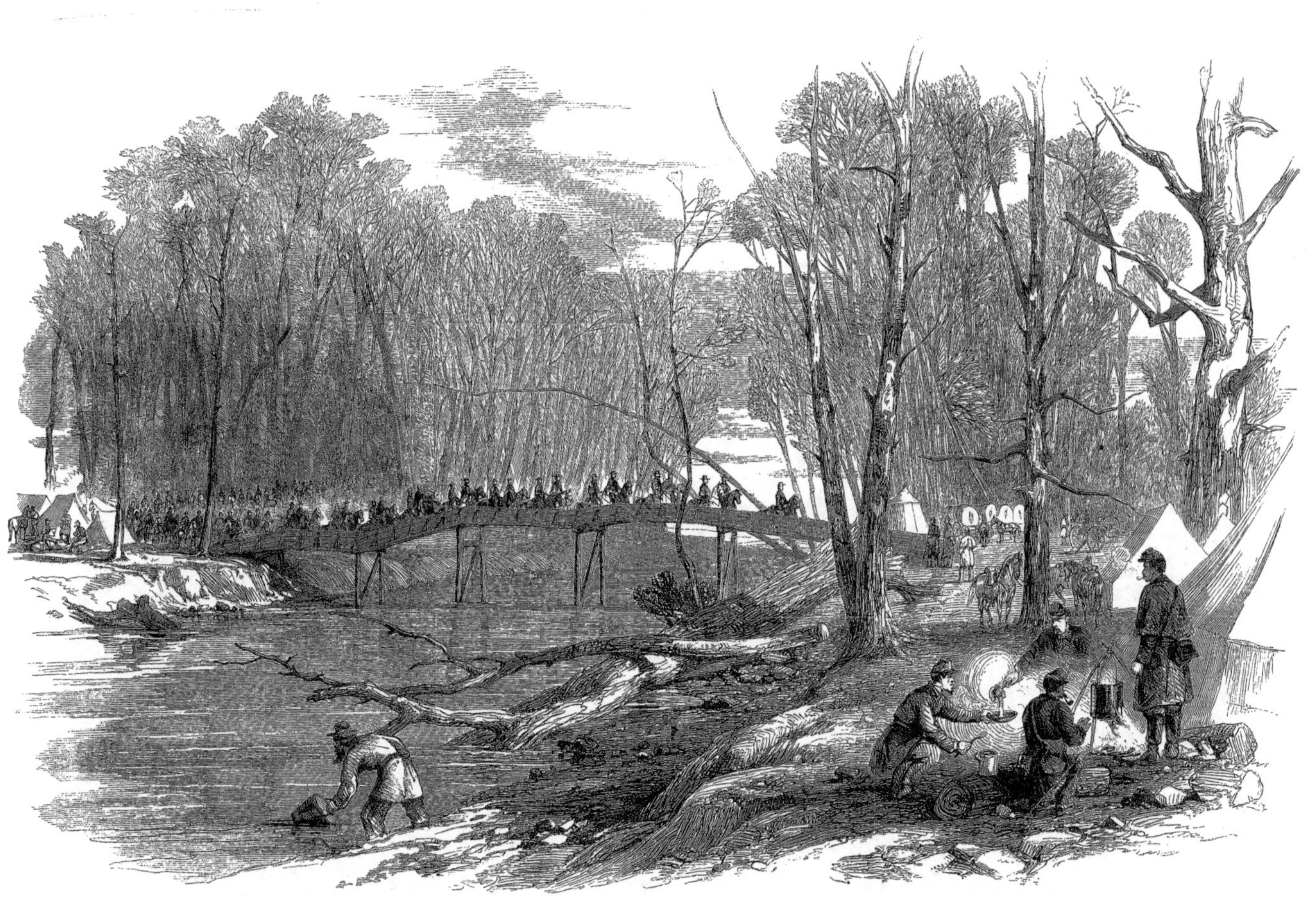

Confederate occupation of Columbus in early September 1861 was a major threat to federal use of the Mississippi River. A combined effort by Union forces in October 1861 resulted in the battle of Belmont, Missouri, opposite Columbus, and an approach overland from Paducah, but the Confederates were able to maintain their position. This well-composed view was sketched at the Blandsville bridge in an area occupied by Grant's troops in mid-January 1862 and shows Grant's bodyguard passing over Mayfield Creek bridge.

Wood engraving from *Frank Leslie's Illustrated Newspaper,* February 15, 1862, from a drawing by *Leslie's* special artist accompanying the patrol.

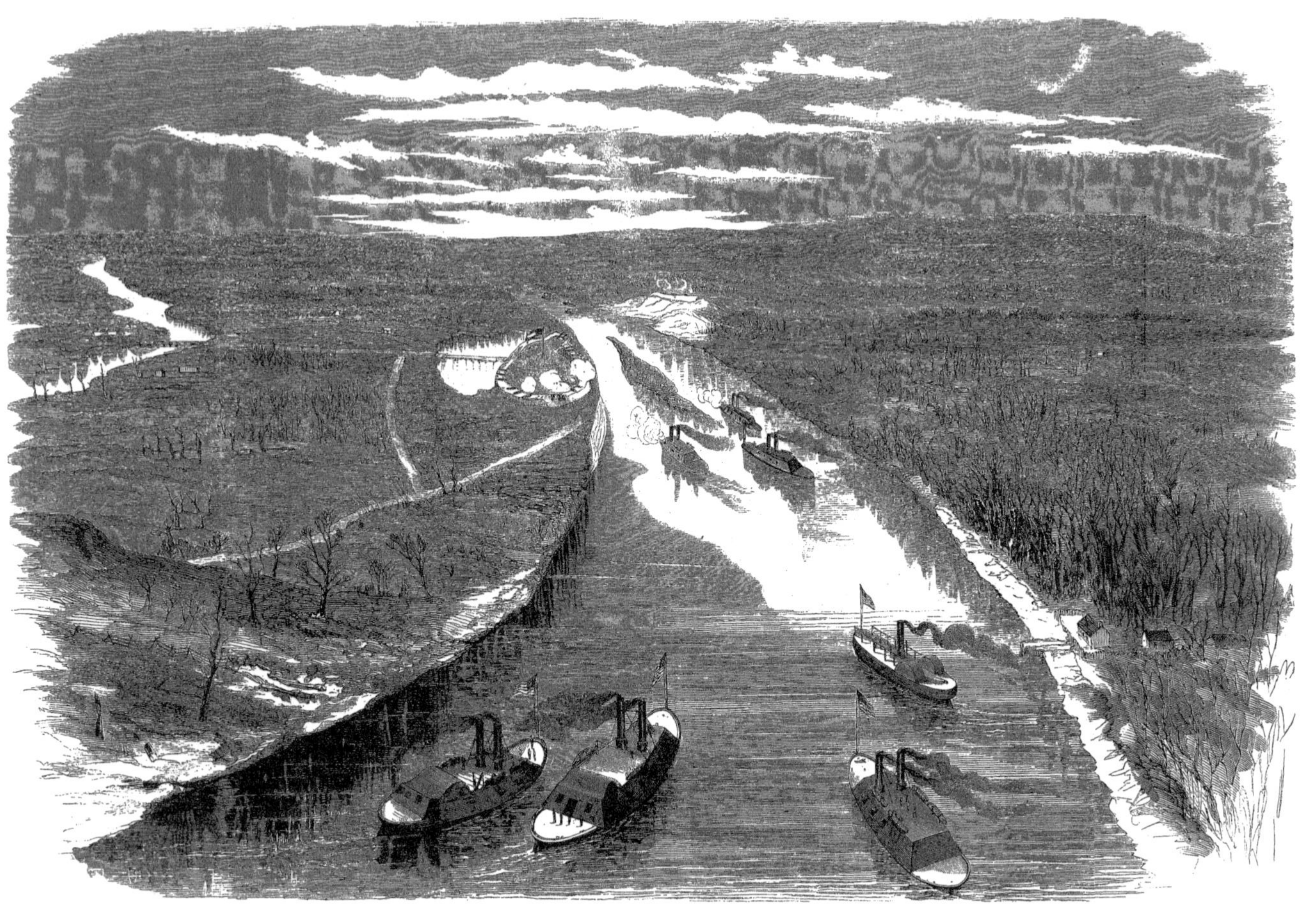

This view of Union gunboats advancing up the Tennessee River was made by an artist on the Kentucky side looking upriver toward Fort Henry, which was located just south of the state line. After a terrific bombardment by the seven Union gunboats illustrated, Gen. Lloyd Tilghman surrendered Fort Henry with a garrison of a few men. Over two thousand infantrymen had been sent away earlier when it became clear that they could not repulse the Union strength. The Confederate Fort Donelson, a few miles away on the Cumberland River, surrendered on February 16. In combination, the two surrenders forced the Confederates to abandon their Kentucky defense line.

Wood engraving from *Harper's Weekly,* February 22, 1862, from a drawing probably by Alexander Simplot, who also shortly after sketched the capture of the fort.

In early September 1861, when it was expected that Gen. U.S. Grant would try to occupy Columbus, Confederate Gen. Leonidas Polk ordered Confederate troops to move into Columbus and Hickman, where their position would put them in control of Mississippi River traffic. Polk's actions violated Kentucky's position of neutrality. The Confederates held the Columbus area until February 1862 when the surrender of Fort Henry and Fort Donelson led them to give up most of their Kentucky positions. This view of the "iron bluffs" at Columbus shows Polk's headquarters, sandbag battery, fortifications on the bluffs, a railway for reaching them from the landing, and torpedoes after they were abandoned. *Harper's Weekly* published the report of a correspondent for the *Chicago Times*; he described mines anchored in the riverbed so as to float just below the surface and devices called "infernal machines," which were huge land mines containing grape shot and canister and as much as two bushels of coarse explosive, buried and wired to electric battery stations in caves under the bluffs.

Wood engraving from *Frank Leslie's Illustrated Newspaper*, 1862.

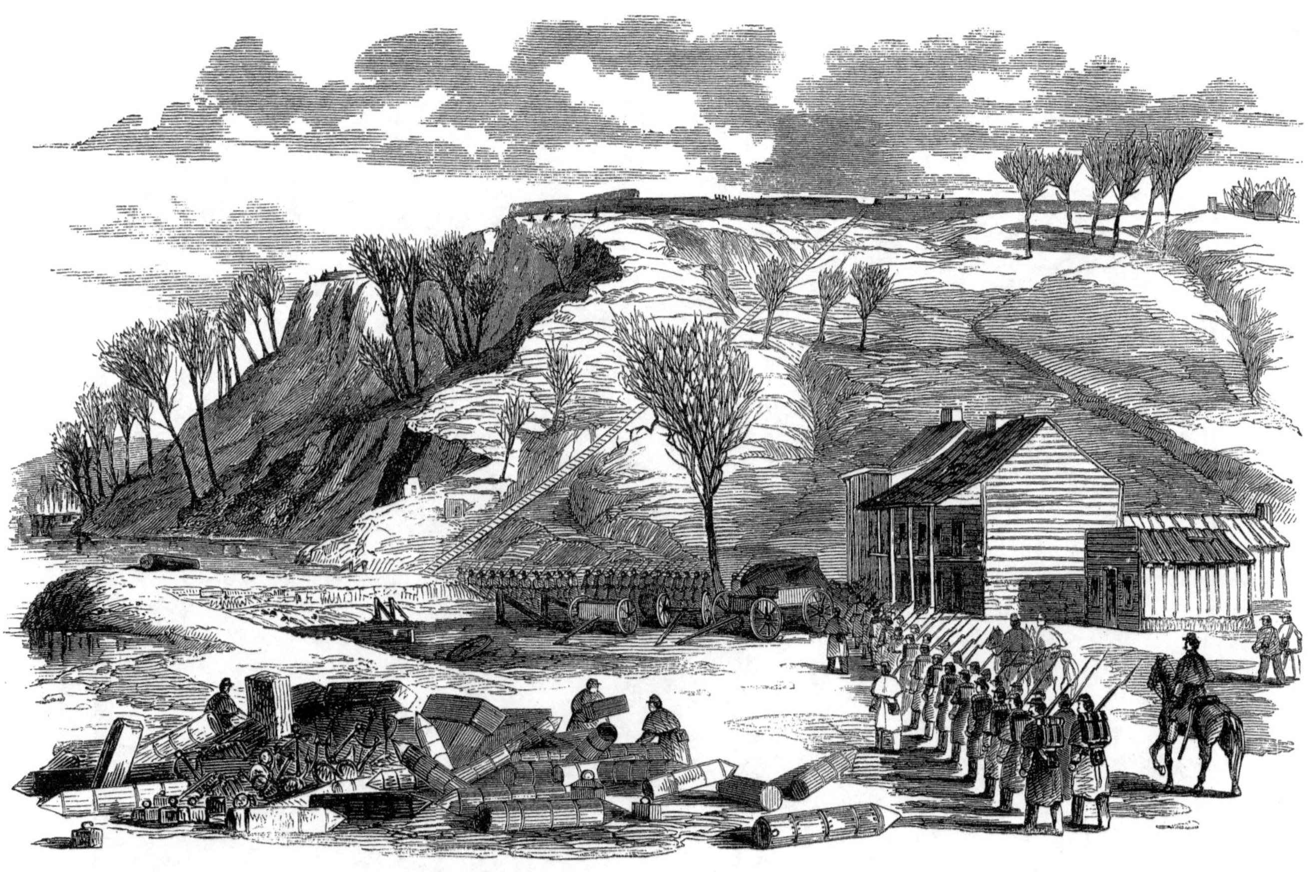

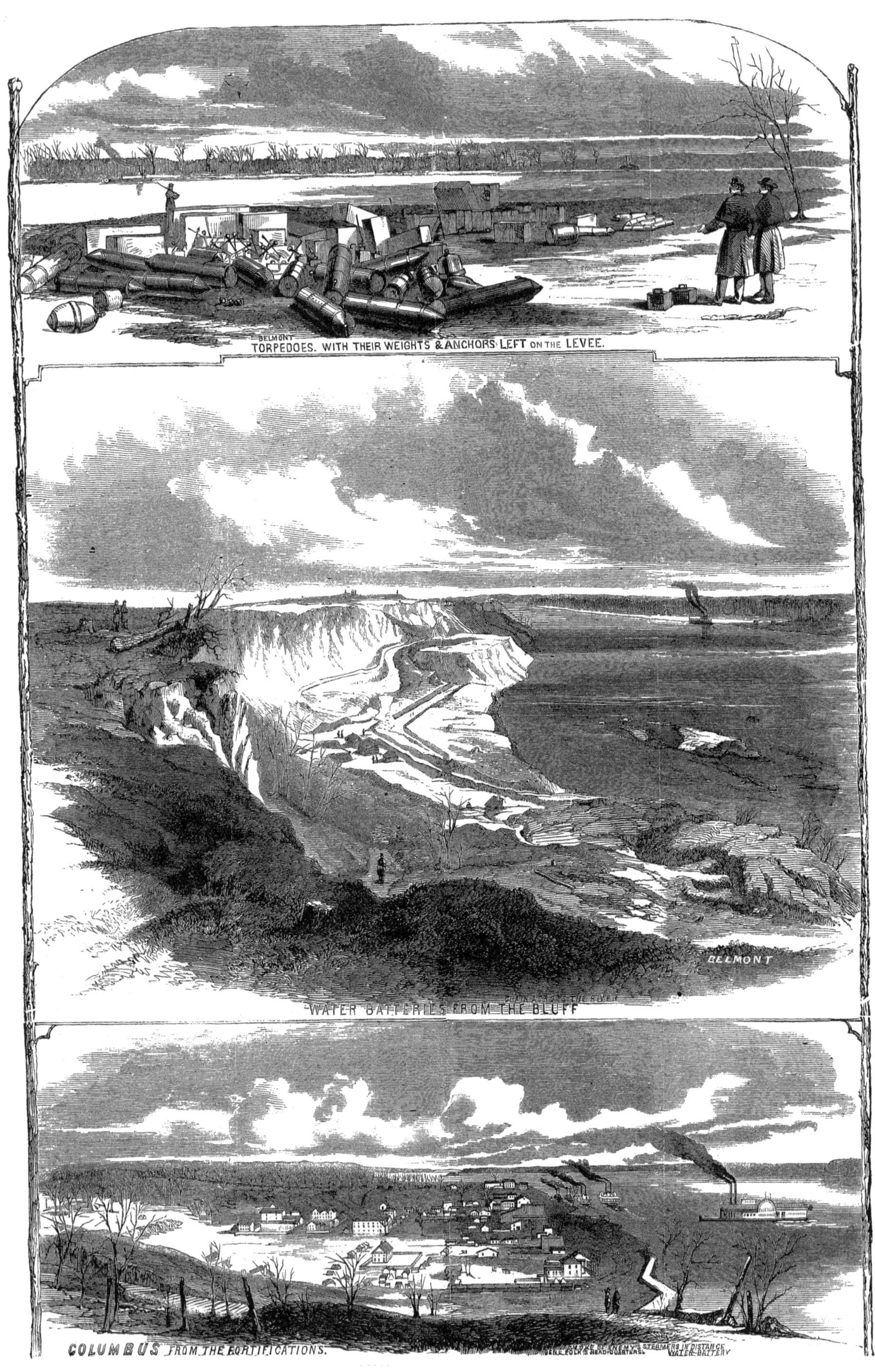
BELMONT
TORPEDOES. WITH THEIR WEIGHTS & ANCHORS LEFT ON THE LEVEE.
BELMONT
CHAIN ACROSS THE RIVER
WATER BATTERIES FROM THE BLUFF
COLUMBUS FROM THE FORTIFICATIONS.
SMOKE OF ENEMY'S STEAMERS IN DISTANCE
GEN. POLK'S HEAD-QUARTERS.
WATER-BATTERY

After forts Henry and Donelson fell, Confederate troops withdrew from Columbus in February 1862. Some moved south to New Madrid, Missouri, and others occupied Island No. 10 near Kentucky Bend where they were again in position to maintain effective control of river traffic. After Union troops occupied Columbus, its citizens tried to mend the wear and tear caused by its previous occupants. The city was the staging point later in 1862 for a gunboat expedition against Vicksburg and, in April 1864, was asked to surrender—but refused to do so—when Col. Abraham Buford's cavalry was harassing the area.

Wood engraving from *Harper's Weekly,* March 29, 1862, from a drawing by Alexander Simplot.

While the Confederates controlled river traffic, steamers, ferry boats, and various other river craft were destroyed between Island No. 10 and New Madrid. The intense bombardment of Island No. 10 and the fortifications opposite on the Kentucky shore (*below*) reduced the effectiveness of the Confederate defenses, and the attacking federal mortar fleet and gunboats were able to gain the surrender of the fortifications. With the loss of Island No. 10, the Confederate west defensive line in Kentucky was completely broken. Union reports claimed that they took 233 officers, 5,500 soldiers, 125 cannon, 10,000 firearms, 2,000 horses and mules, and 1,000 wagons, plus uncounted provisions and ammunition. Before this was accomplished, the Union army attempted to bypass the Confederate stronghold by excavating a canal across the neck of the Missouri peninsula that forms the Kentucky Bend.

Wood engraving from *Frank Leslie's Illustrated Newspaper,* April 5, 1862, from a drawing by Henri Lovie, Cincinnati.

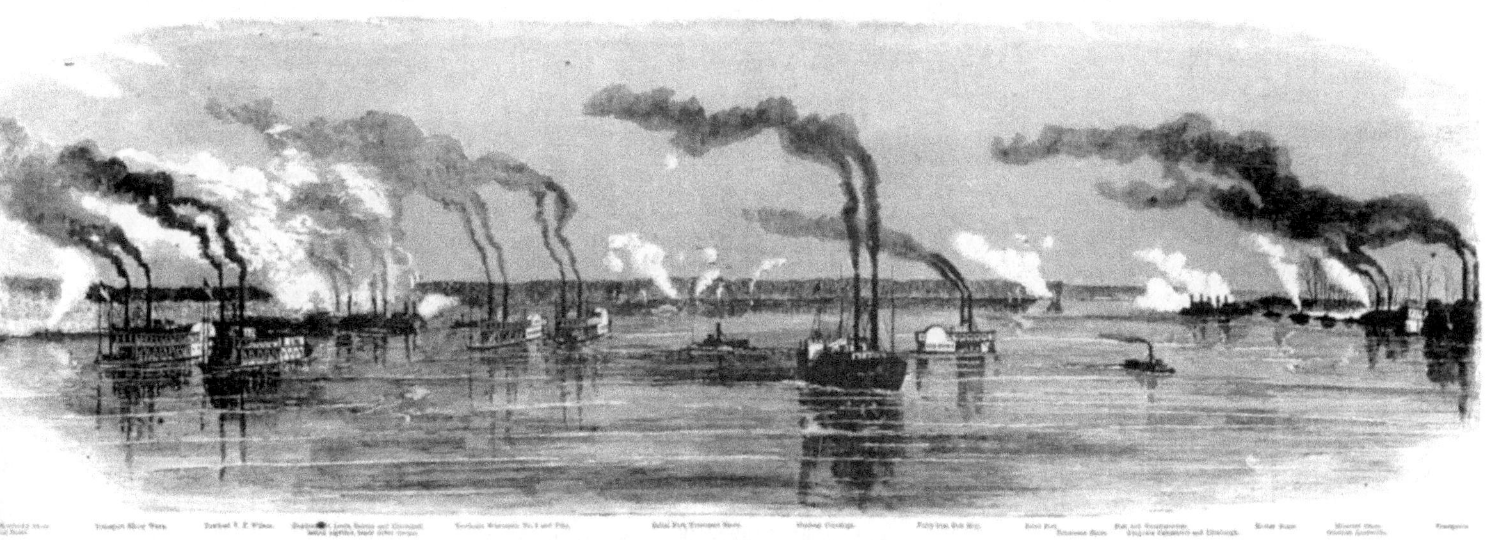

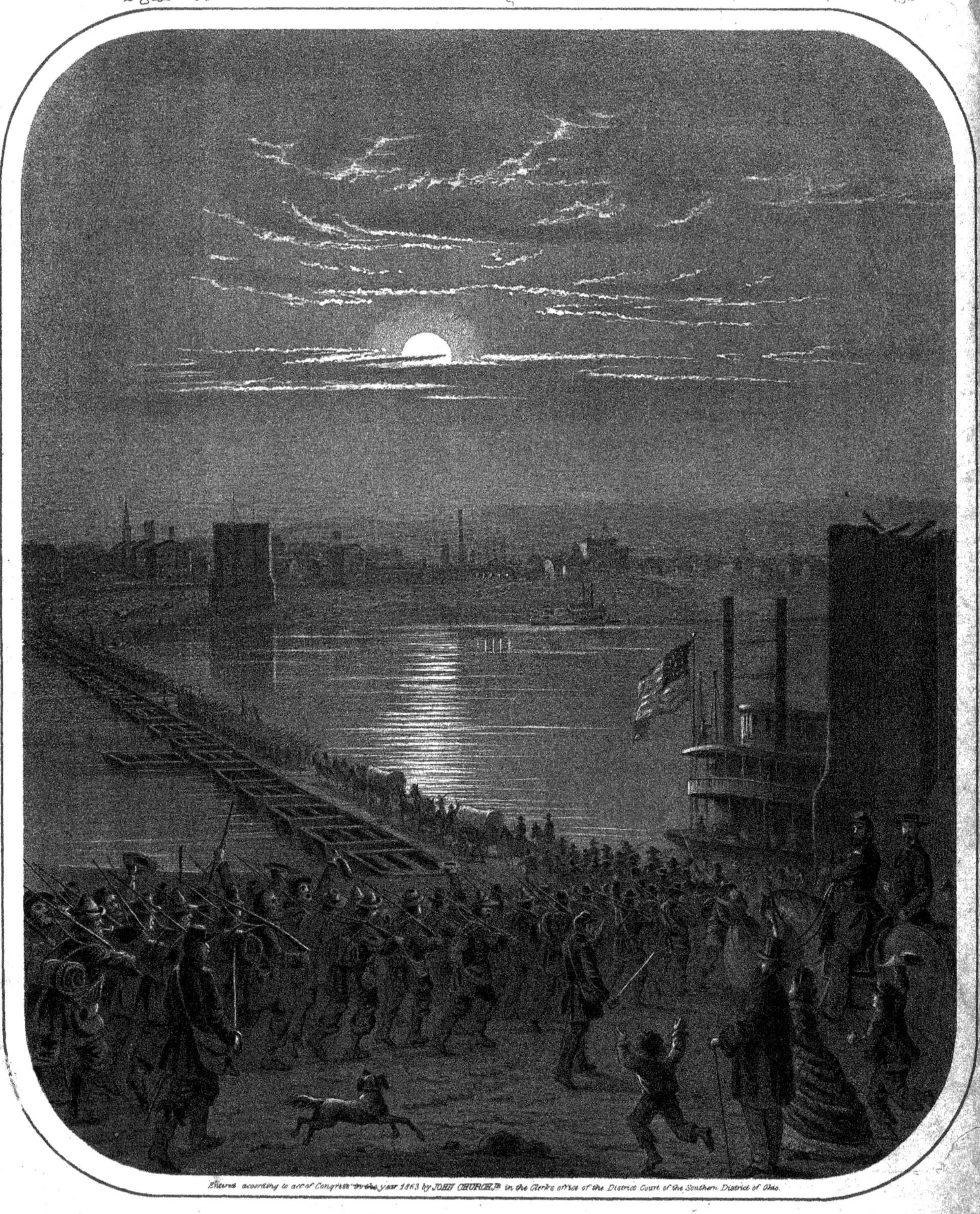
"Dedicated to those brave and loyal men who hastened to the defence of Cincinnati in her hour of danger."
SQUIRREL HUNTER'S MARCH.
Entered according to act of Congress in the year 1863 by JOHN CHURCH JR. in the Clerk's office of the District Court of the Southern District of Ohio.
CINCINNATI,
Published by JOHN CHURCH JR. 66 West Fourth Str.
PHILADELPHIA,
BOSTON,
NEW-YORK,
4

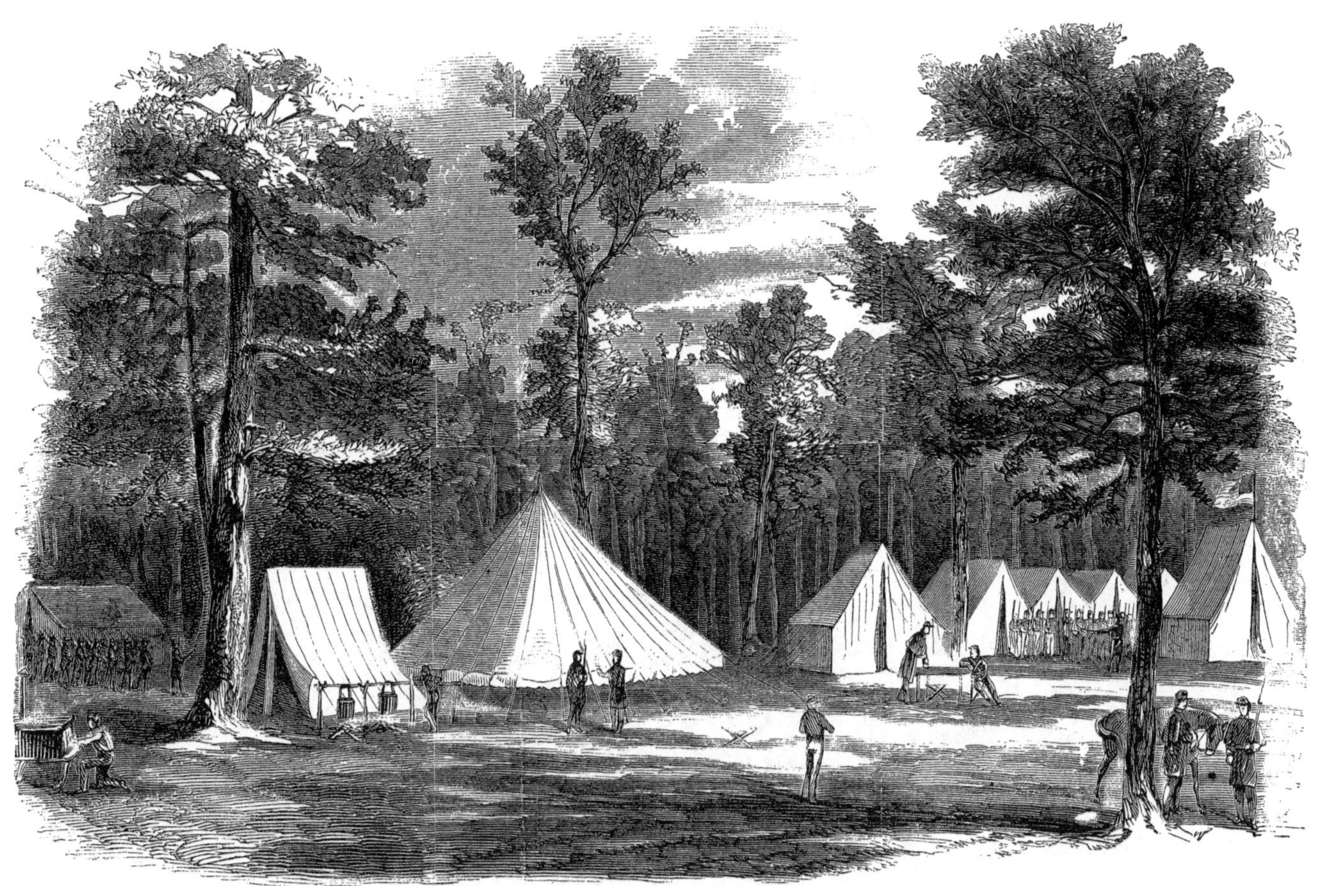

In the central part of the state, Confederates had a large force as well. In 1861 they held portions of southern Kentucky, notably Columbus and Hickman in the west, Cumberland Gap and nearby areas in the east, and Bowling Green in the central position. Gen. Lovell H. Rousseau's brigade was part of Gen. William T. Sherman's forces confronting the main Confederate army under Gen. Albert Sidney Johnston. Rousseau's camp, near Muldraugh's Hill, shown here, was about thirty miles south of Louisville by railroad.

Wood engraving from *Harper's Weekly,* October 12, 1861, from a drawing by Henry Mosler, Cincinnati.

"Squirrel Hunter's March" was "dedicated to those brave and loyal men who hastened to the defense of Cincinnati in her hour of danger." In August and September 1862, Confederate Gen. Edmund Kirby Smith captured Richmond, Lexington, Frankfort, Shelbyville, Paris, Cynthiana, and Maysville; Covington, Newport, and Cincinnati seemed within his reach. More than twenty-five thousand U.S. troops, volunteer militia, and civilians, who were called "squirrel hunters," crossed the bridge of coal barges ready to repulse the Confederates.

Two-color lithographed sheet music cover, published by John Church, Jr., Cincinnati, 1863. Lithographed by Ergott, Forbriger & Co., Cincinnati.

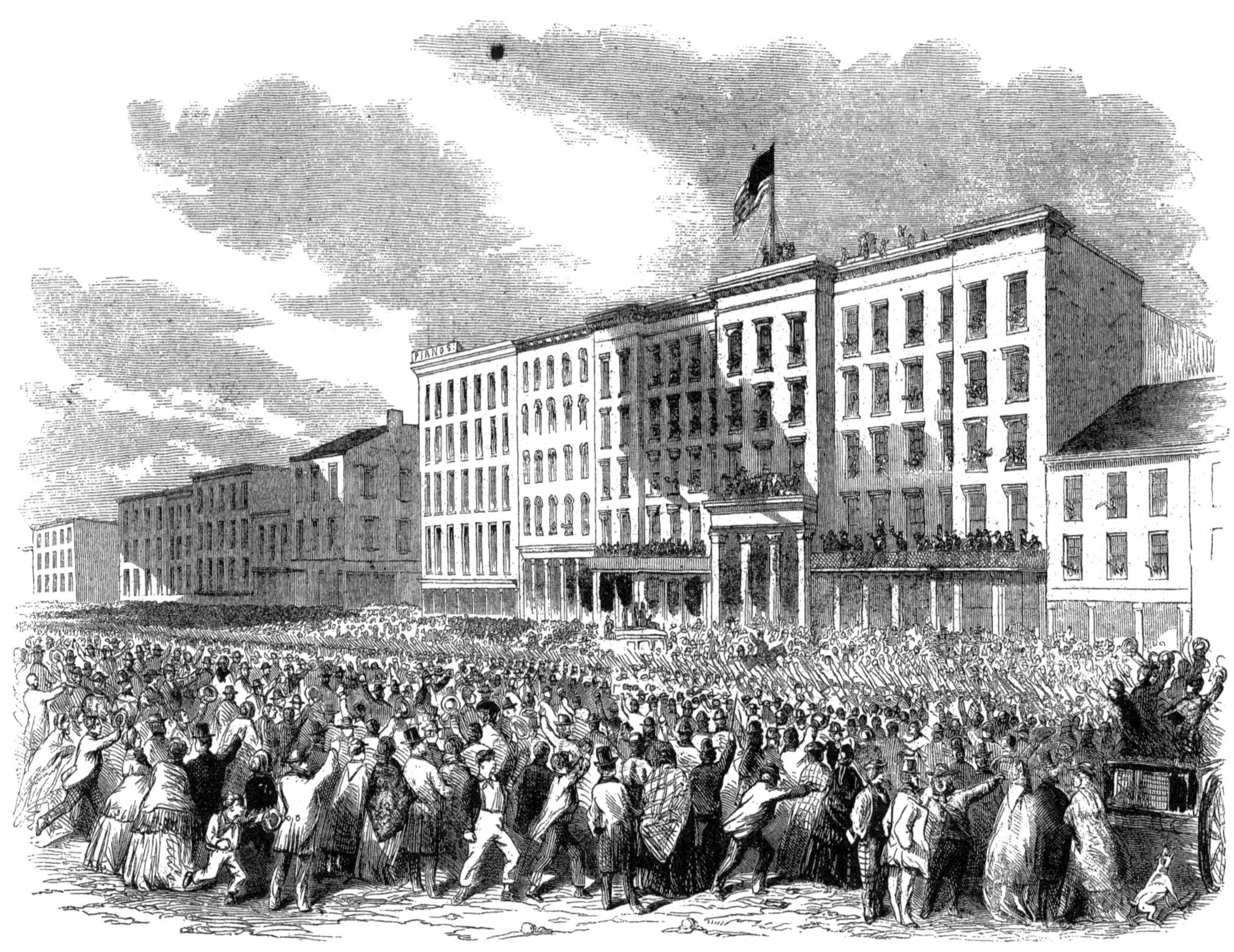

Union troops from Illinois, Indiana, and Ohio poured into Kentucky to challenge Confederate positions then being taken. The Forty-ninth Ohio regiment, led by Col. W.H. Gibson, arrived in Louisville September 21, 1861, and became part of Gen. William T. Sherman's expedition south from Louisville to meet the anticipated rebel advance from Bowling Green. A news story in the *Louisville Journal* said that the regiment "paraded our streets, and were warmly greeted by Union men and women. They paid their compliments to General Anderson at the Louisville Hotel." The hotel is prominent in this view as the building from which the flag is flying. The regiment occupied Muldraugh's Hill promptly, then proceeded to the large encampment gathering at Nolin in Hardin County near the Rolling Fork bridge of the Louisville and Nashville railroad. Henry Mosler, the artist of this scene, was one of *Harper's* wartime artists. He provided thirty-four drawings for the illustrated periodical, and a majority of them were Kentucky war scenes.

Wood engraving from *Harper's Weekly,* October 12, 1861, from a drawing by Henry Mosler, Cincinnati.

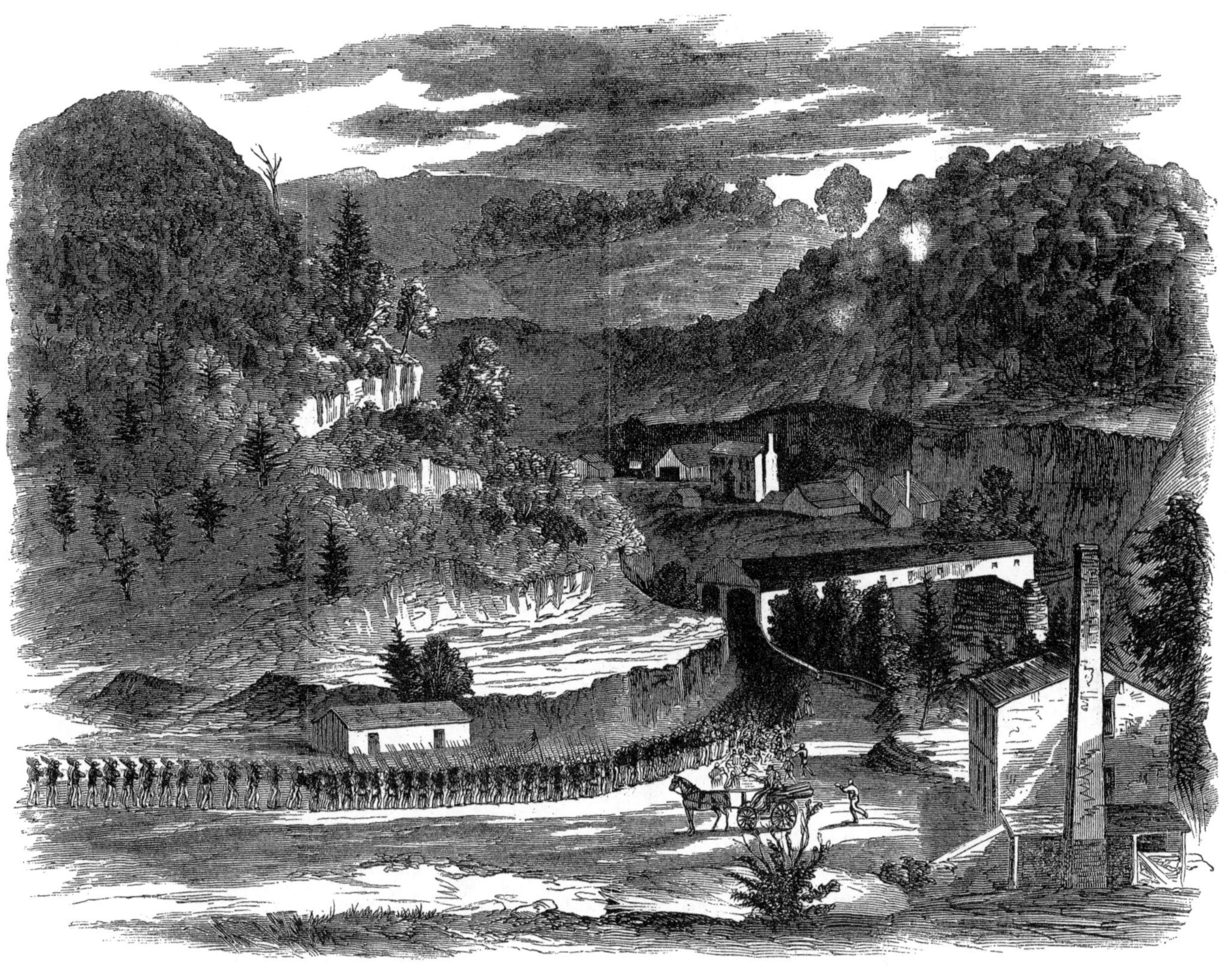

The Thirty-first Regiment Ohio Volunteers under Col. James Walker was one of the units assigned to hold the Union line across the central part of Kentucky. This sketch was made October 2, 1861, the day before the regiment arrived at the growing encampment at Camp Dick Robinson near Bryantsville, a few miles northwest of Lancaster. The river crossing was made at what we now call Camp Nelson; Boone's Knob appears at the left side of the view. The story was told that Daniel Boone, fleeing in his canoe from pursuing Indians, was able to hide behind this knob by canoeing around it in a time of very high water levels.

Wood engraving from *Harper's Weekly,* November 23, 1861, from a drawing by Alfred E. Matthews, Cincinnati, an artist and member of the regiment, who drew war scenes for several publishers.

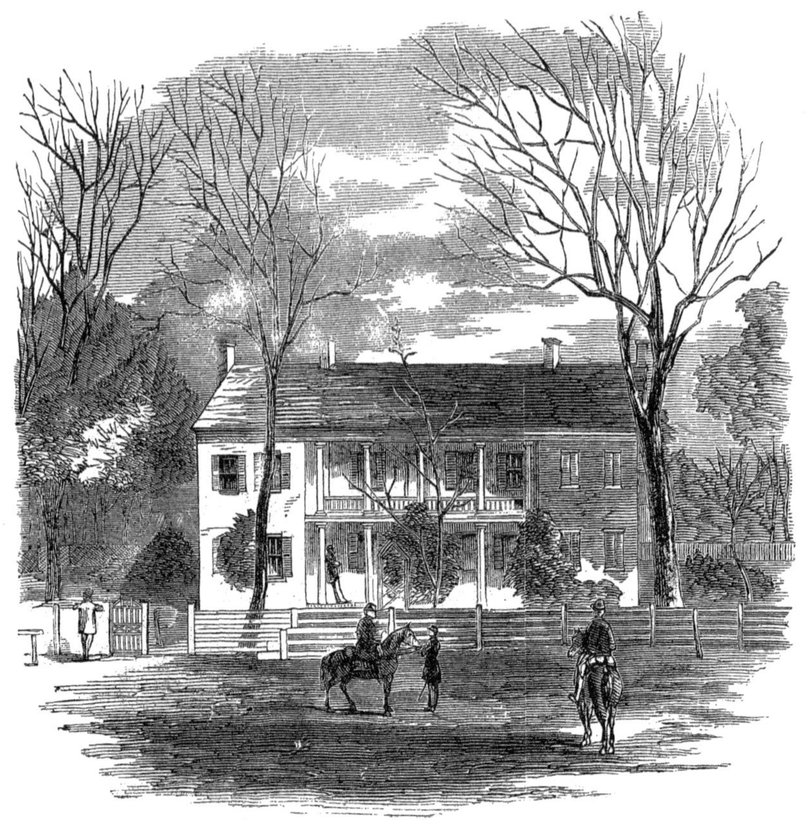

Camp Dick Robinson near Bryantsville, named for the owner of the house and property, had begun as a small unit assembled to protect military stores in the building at a county road junction. In August 1861 Union Gen. William Nelson established a camp there for expediting recruiting in eastern Kentucky and Tennessee, for training enlistees, and for combining military companies into regiments. It was the first Union recruiting station south of the Ohio, and Confederates called it a violation of the position of neutrality taken by Kentucky authorities.

Wood engraving from *Harper's Weekly*, November 23, 1861, from a drawing by Alfred E. Matthews, Cincinnati.

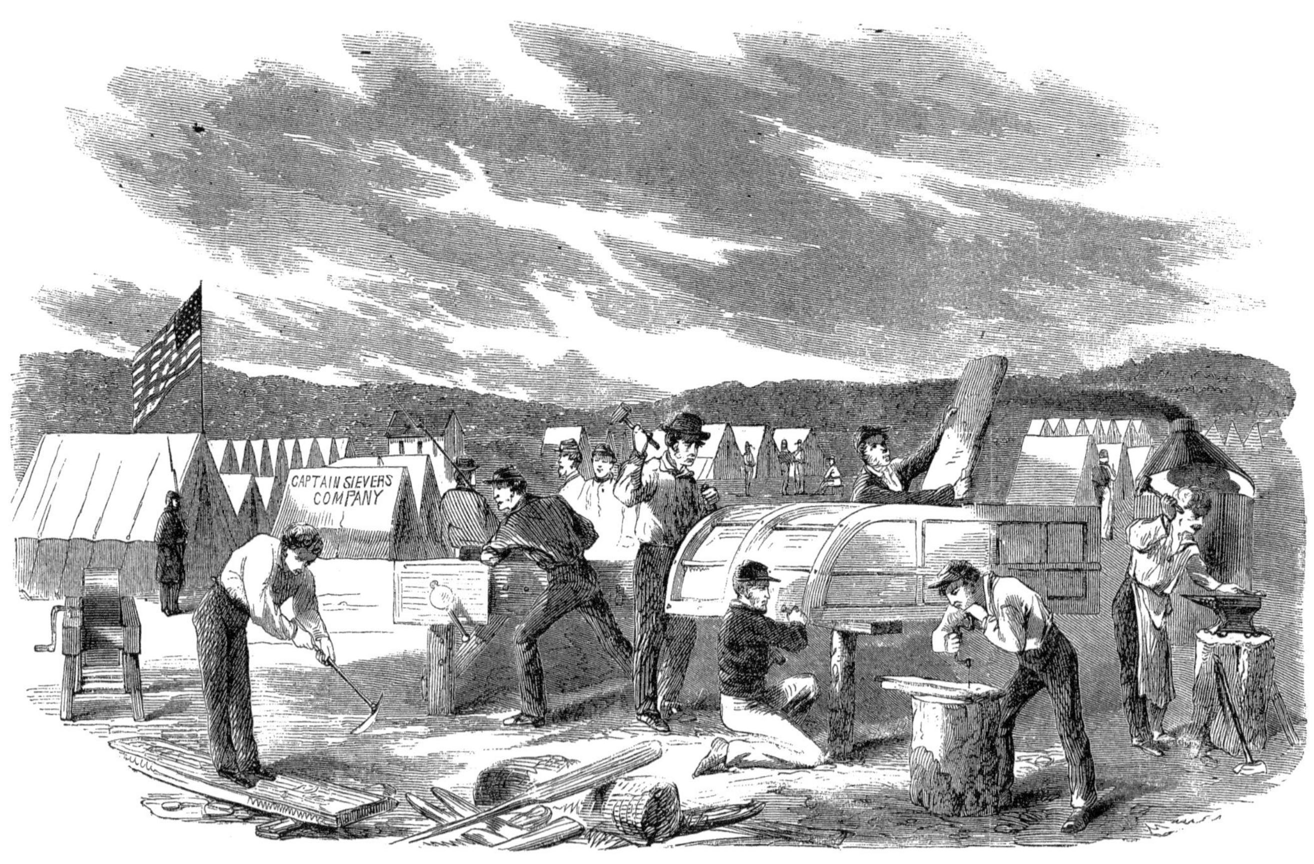

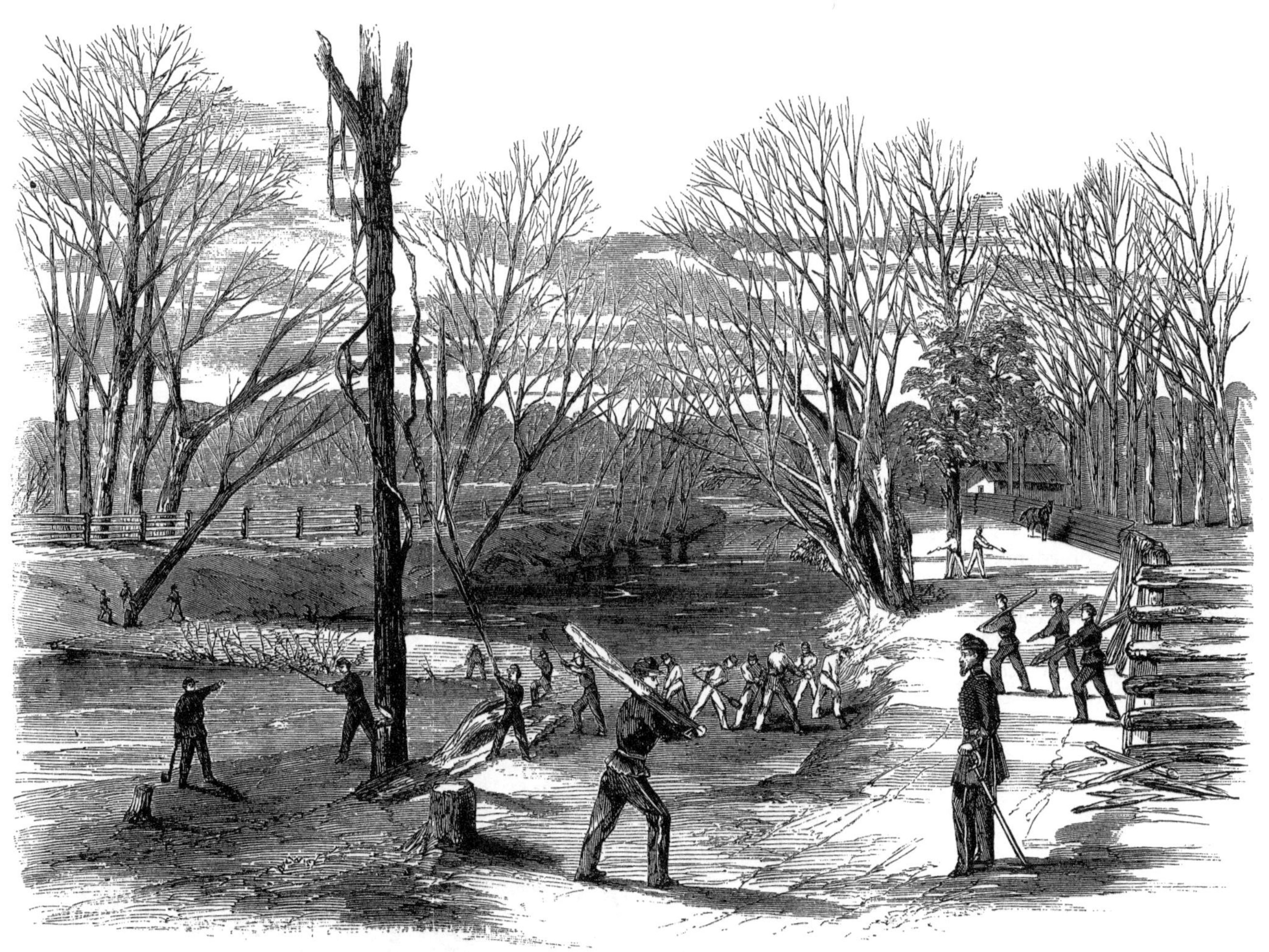

Muller's Battery Company, Seventy-seventh Pennsylvania Regiment, commanded by Col. Henry A. Hambright, was among those at Nolin in late 1861. Engineers, pontoniers, mechanics, and foot soldiers all had to become competent in turning local raw materials to their military and personal needs. The company is shown here building a bridge over the Nolin River.

Wood engraving from *Frank Leslie's Illustrated Newspaper,* January 4, 1862.

In November 1861, the Thirty-second Indiana Regiment, commanded by Col. August Willich, was stationed at Woodsonville—or Rowlett's Station—near Green River as part of Gen. Don Carlos Buell's southern advance line. It was attacked there in mid-December by troops under Gen. Thomas C. Hindman. In some of Buell's reports, he called this regiment the "German" troops. *Harper's* correspondent, or perhaps the artist himself, wrote that the regiment was one of the best drilled in the service and composed almost exclusively of Germans. Serving under Colonel Willich were men with names such as VanTrebra, Welschbillig, Schmitt, Krauth, Schutz, Giegolodt, Frenck, Kimmel, and Pietzuch. The pontoons being built by the regiment (*left*) were to be used as wagon beds.

Wood engraving from *Harper's Weekly,* December 14, 1861, from a drawing by Henry Mosler, Cincinnati.

Sometimes called the Battle of Rowlett's Station, the engagement of December 17, 1861, took place near the southern end of the Louisville and Nashville bridge. It involved relatively small numbers of troops—probably about 1,500—and was not strategically important in the war effort. As shown here, General Buell arrived on the north side of Green River, and Colonel Willich's Indiana regiment repulsed the Confederates.

Wood engraving from *Frank Leslie's Illustrated Newspaper,* January 18, 1862, from a drawing by *Leslie's* artist accompanying Buell, probably William R. McComas, Cincinnati.

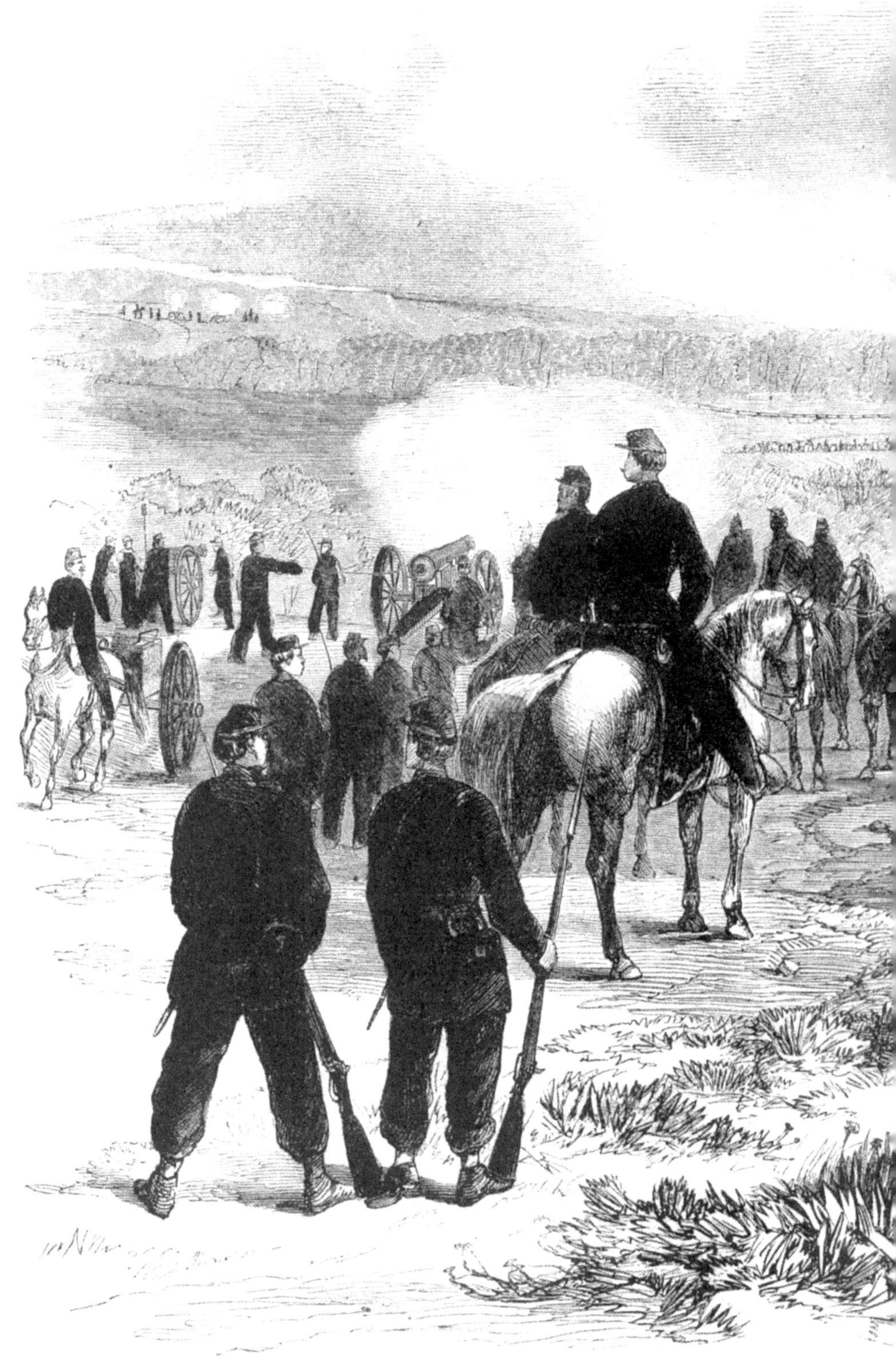

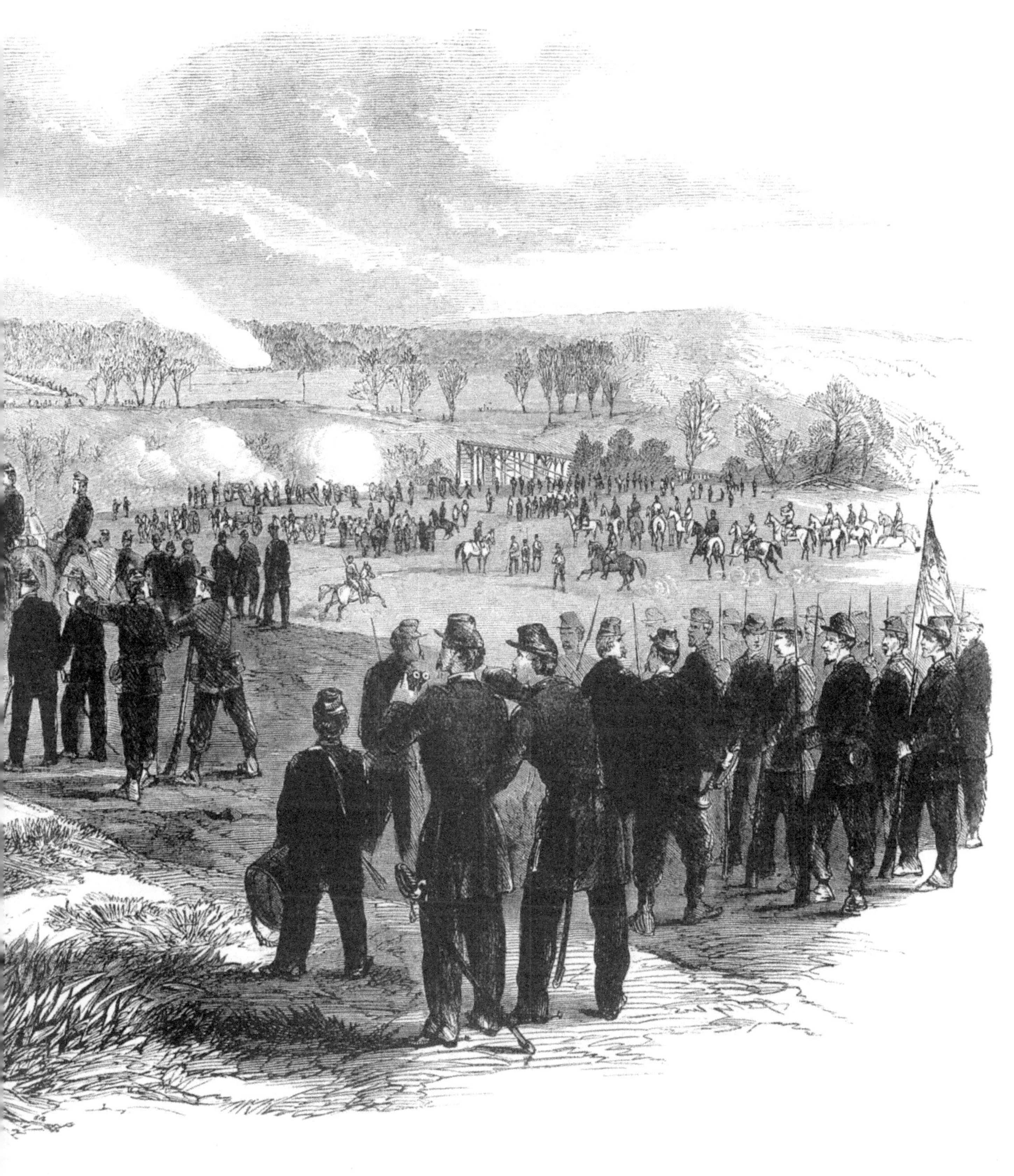

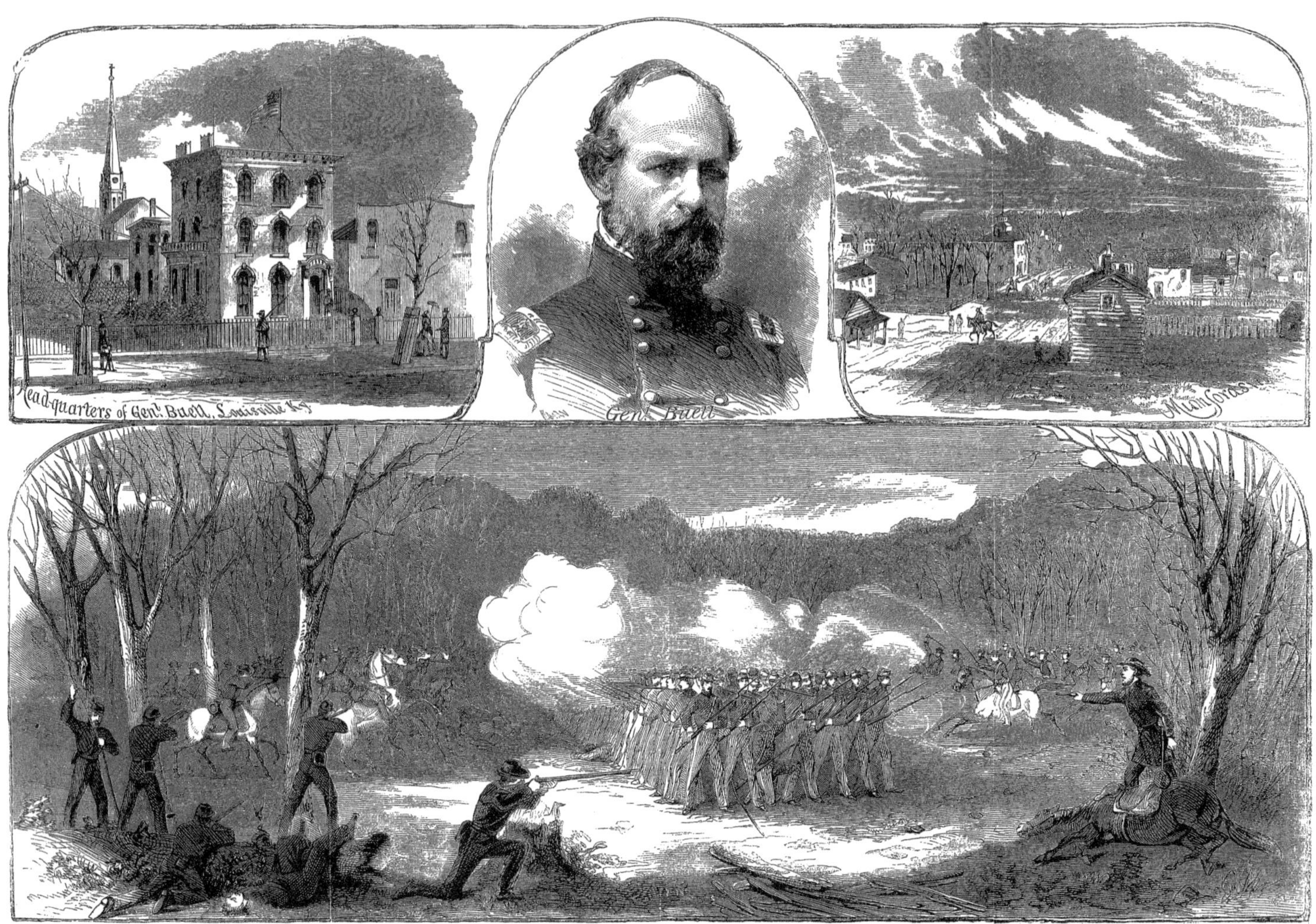

This illustration shows the battle at Rowlett's Station on Green River when Colonel Willich's Thirty-second Indiana Infantry, guarding the southern end of the railroad bridge, was attacked by Colonel Terry's Texas Rangers. Above the scene of the battle is a portrait of General Buell, commander of the Department of the Ohio, flanked by a view of the general's headquarters and a depiction of Munfordville, a village of about three hundred people and the county seat of Hart County.

Wood engraving from *Harper's Weekly,* January 11, 1862, from a drawing by Henry Mosler, Cincinnati.

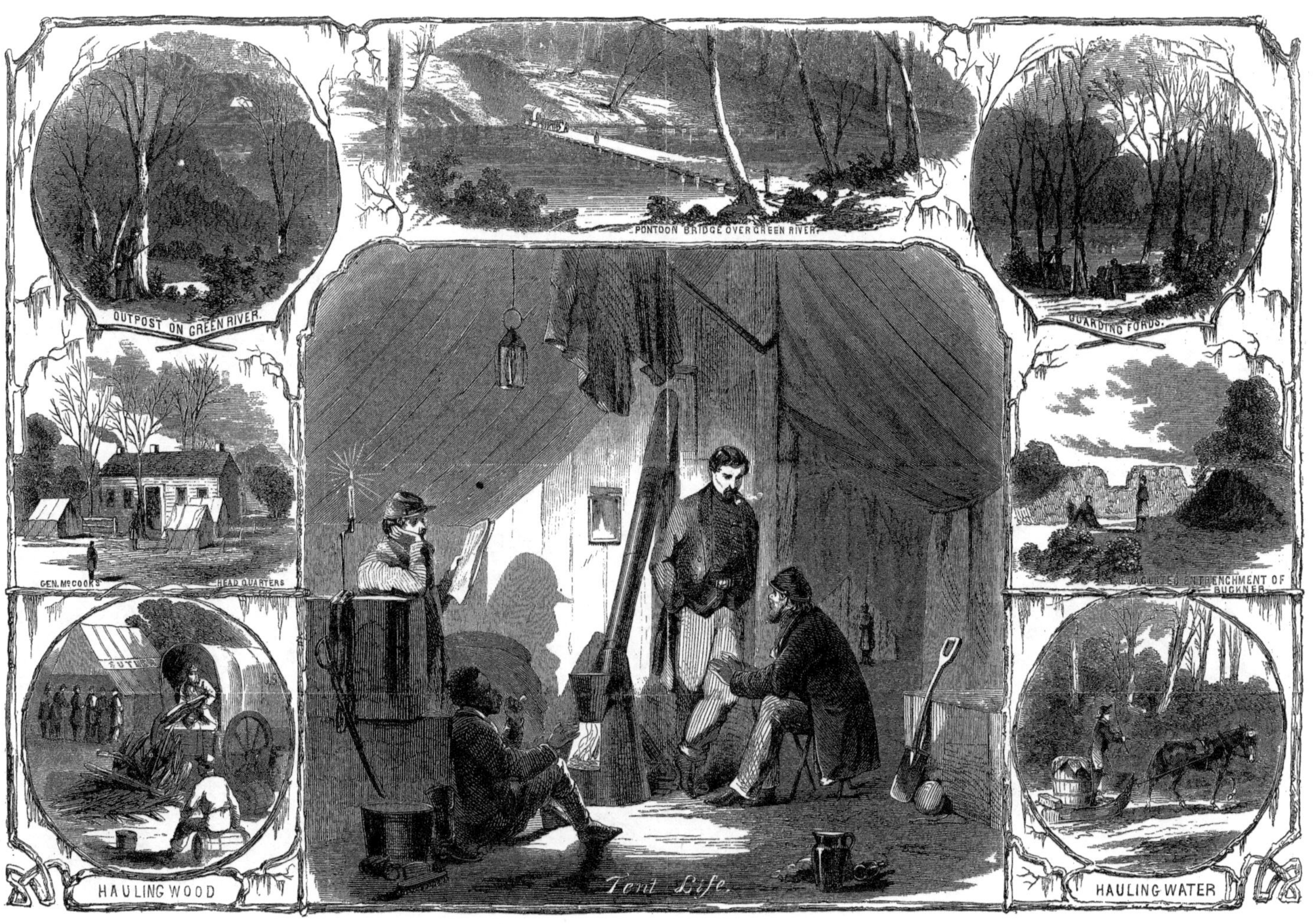

Scenes such as these helped readers of *Harper's* realize the difficult conditions facing the troops even when they were not engaged in battle. In the view of troops hauling wood, the artist included the tent of the sutler, the merchant who was authorized to follow the army and sell provisions, liquors, and personal items to the soldiers. In the larger view of tent life, we see the socket of a bayonet being used for a candlestick and the presence of a black servant. Accompanying this illustration, *Harper's* quotes a letter from a soldier in Munfordville to the *New York Tribune.* In the letter, dated January 16, 1862, the correspondent notes that the almost uninterrupted rain of the last few days had softened the ground to the depth of several feet and that roads and camps were "almost fathomless. Unavoidable confinement for days within the narrow walls of a tent," he wrote, "is one of the sorriest features of military life, and your correspondent is most heartily tired of it."

Wood engraving from *Harper's Weekly,* February 1, 1862, from a drawing by Henry Mosler, Cincinnati.

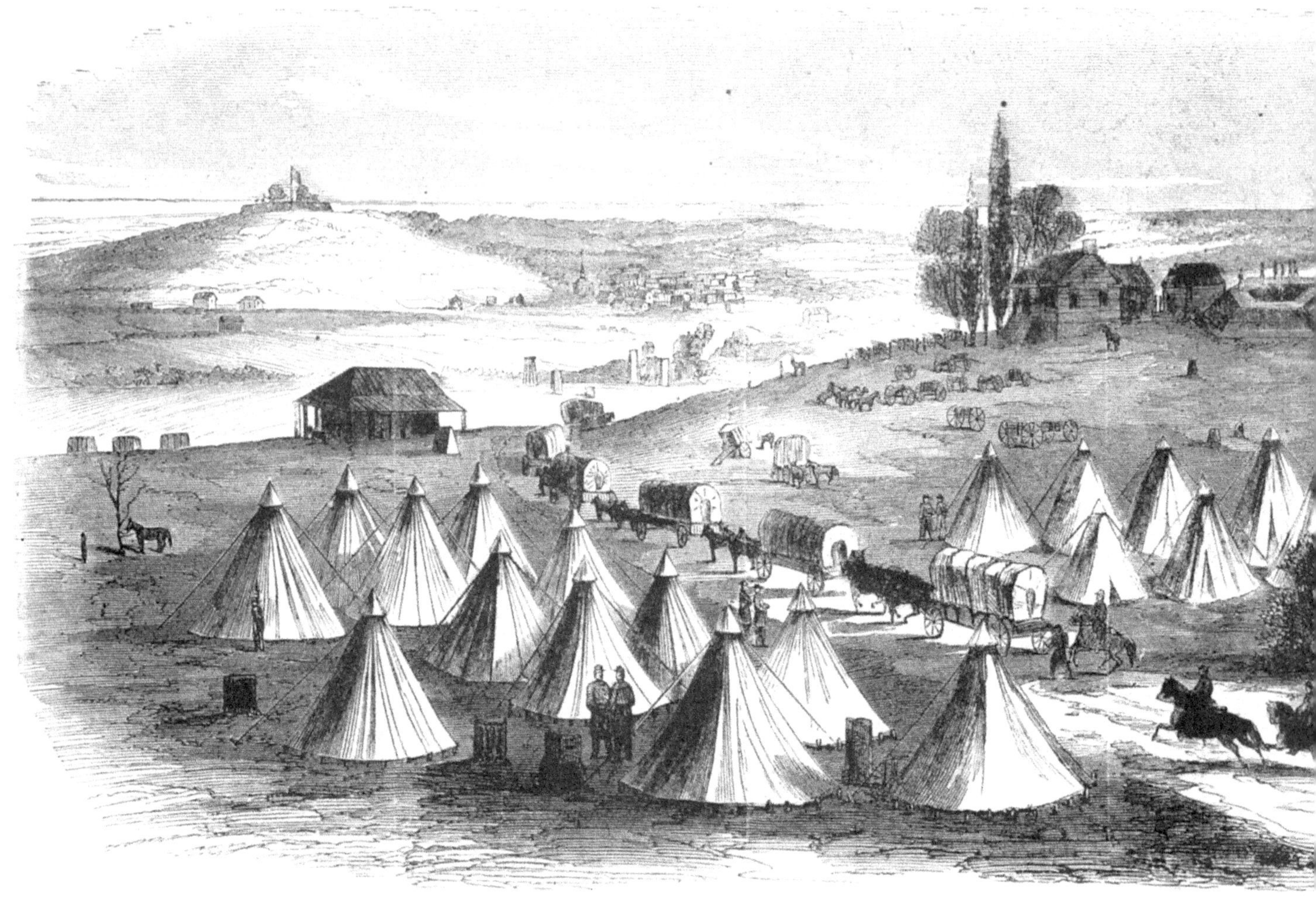

Bowling Green was occupied by Confederate troops under Gen. Simon B. Buckner in mid-September 1861 and was held until mid-February 1862. This view shows the Union camp and Confederate fortifications after evacuation by Confederate Gen. Albert S. Johnston and occupation by U.S. troops under the command of Gen. Ormsby McKnight Mitchell. When Buckner's men moved into Bowling Green he notified James Guthrie, president of the Louisville and Nashville railroad, that he intended to reopen the rail line south of Bowling Green and pay the railroad for transporting his troops. Before they left Bowling Green, the Confederate troops destroyed as much useful property as they could, and General Mitchell's troops took over the city on February 16, just a week before Fort Donelson in Tennessee was surrendered. Mitchell reported to Union headquarters that he found at Bowling Green significant stores of corn, flour, beef, shoes, sugar, coffee, nails, tents, and saddles—all highly desirable supplies for regimental quartermasters—despite the Confederate efforts to leave nothing of use behind.

Both wood engravings from *Frank Leslie's Illustrated Newspaper*, March 18, 1862, from drawings by William R. McComas, Cincinnati.

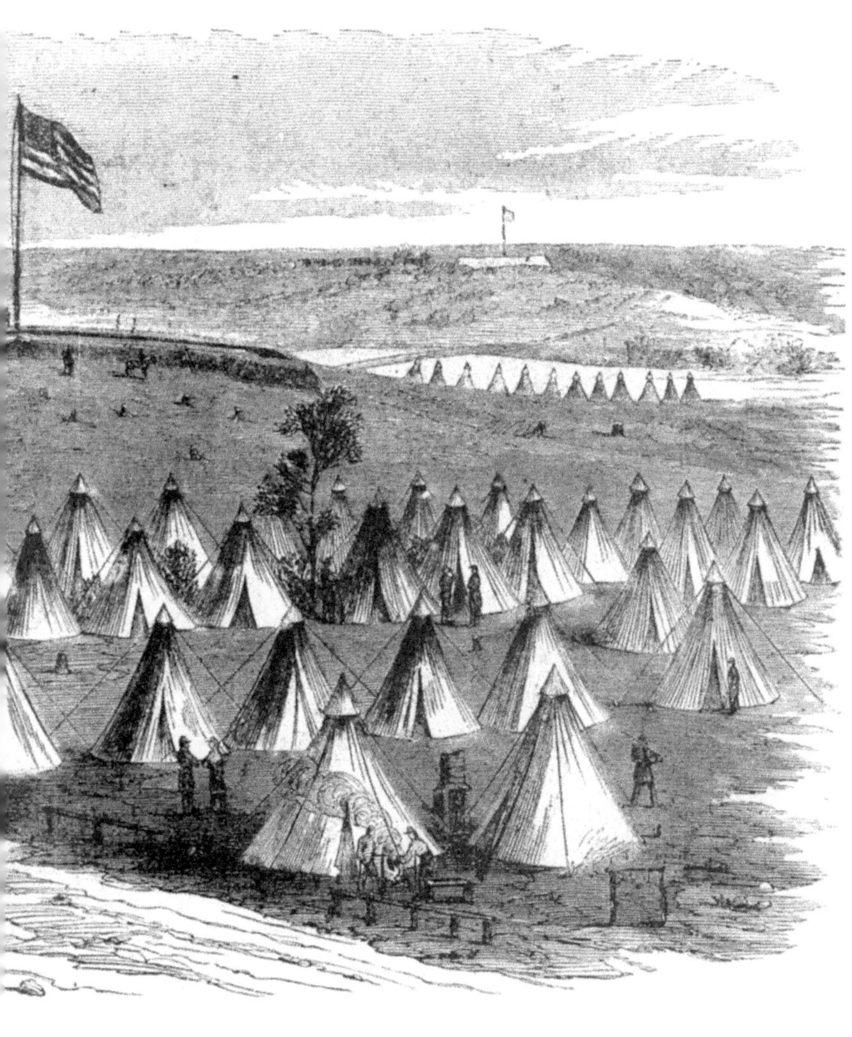

Before their withdrawal from the city in February 1862, Confederate forces burned the railway depot and the roundhouse, Judge William Payne's flour mill, D.B. Campbell's sawmill, the Washington Hotel, and a number of stores and warehouses filled with clothing, provisions, medicines, and other supplies they felt could be used by the Union troops. Both the railroad bridge and the turnpike bridge over Barren River were destroyed. The view below shows the public square with the courthouse and market in Bowling Green and a portion of the town burnt by the southern forces.

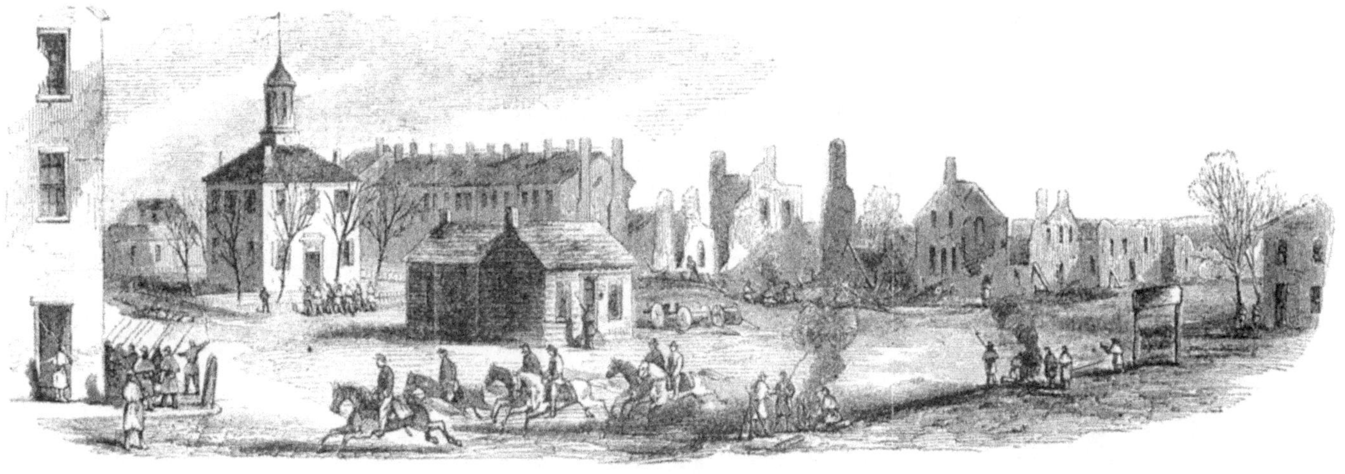

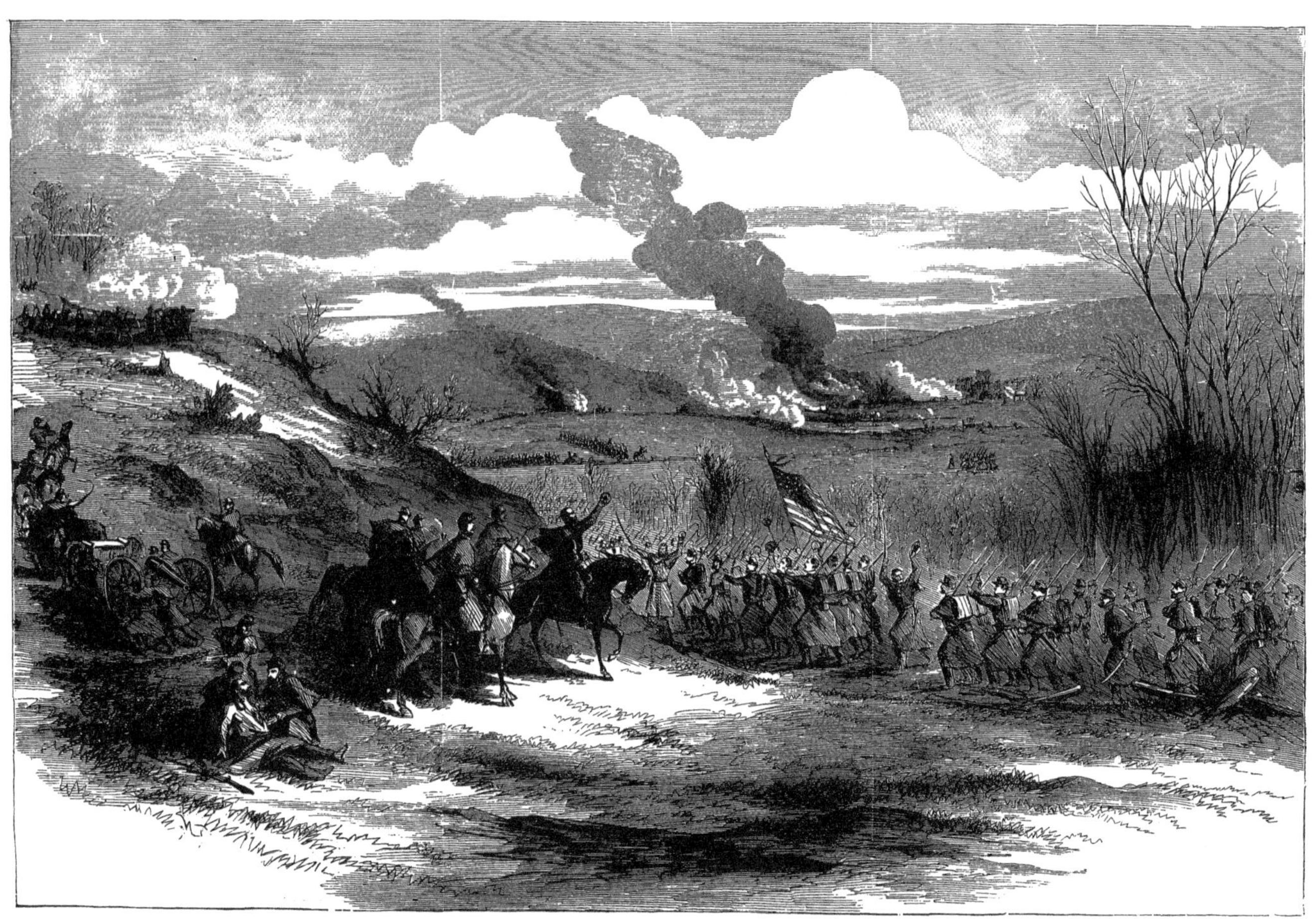

The eastern part of the Confederate defense line saw its own share of battles. This conflict, the battle between Gen. Humphrey Marshall's and Col. James A. Garfield's troops, destroyed military stores and camp equipages in Floyd County on January 10, 1862, at Forks of Middle Creek near Prestonsburg. Marshall's Confederate troops were defeated with considerable loss of lives, supplies, and equipment. A correspondent for the pro-Union *Louisville Journal* wrote that Garfield's forces were "too much for the fat General," noting that Marshall was "too bulky to run fast" and that Garfield did not "allow him time to blow." The conflict illustrates the connection between politics and generalship at that stage in the war. Humphrey Marshall was a graduate of West Point, an attorney in Louisville and the District of Columbia, an officer in the Mexican War in 1846, and a member of both the U.S. Congress and the Confederate Congress. Garfield was the young Ohio college president who became, in turn, the youngest Union brigadier general, then legislator, congressman, and finally president.

Wood engraving from *Harper's Weekly,* February 1862, from a drawing by Thomas Nast.

The Battle of Mill Spring caused the collapse of the Confederate defenses in the eastern half of the state. In this view Col. Robert L. McCook's Ninth Ohio drives back Confederate soldiers. Colonel McCook later described how he was shot through the right leg by one bullet while another went through his overcoat. His horse was killed, and he went on foot for part of the day before receiving medical attention. Lithographed battle scenes such as this—usually colored by hand in "assembly line" fashion—first became popular at the time of the Mexican War, when publishers took advantage of the public interest in current affairs to put the rather new and relatively simple lithographic process to use for depictions of dramatic events. This type of work continued through the Civil War and beyond, but many of the views were inaccurate, providing imaginative and stylized versions of scenes such as this one, which shows soldiers in orderly ranks and files rather than under actual battle conditions. Publishers distorted perspective, depicted inappropriate or fanciful uniforms, and paid limited attention to actual terrain. In many instances the resulting picture showed little more than imaginative scenes titled as actual events, but heroic images fit the popular perception of the excitement and the methods of war. Nathaniel Currier was one of the most prolific lithographers catering to the mass market.

Lithograph by Currier and Ives, New York, 1862.

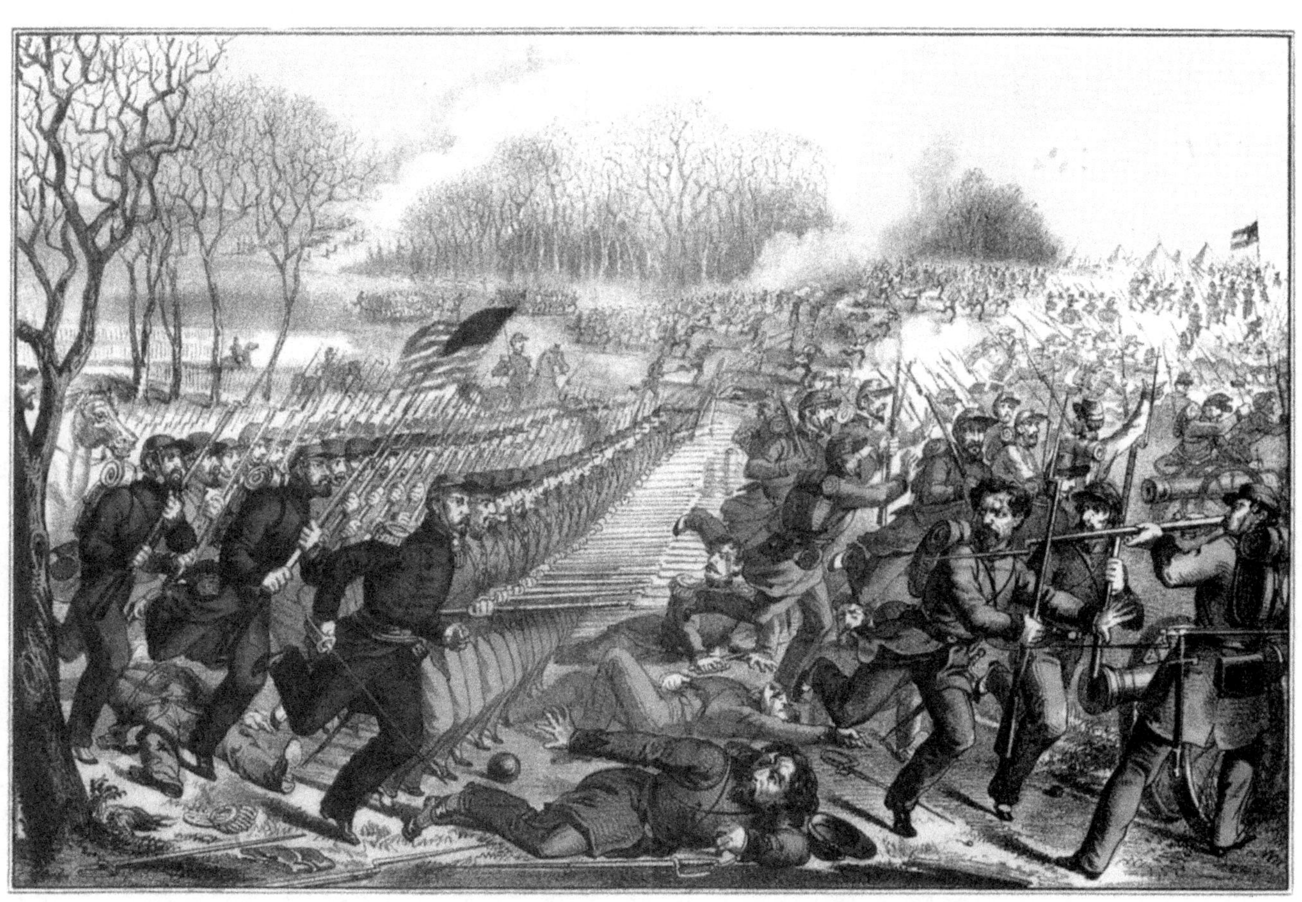

Confederate Gen. George B. Crittenden led about four thousand soldiers from the fortified camp at Beech Grove to meet Maj. Gen. George H. Thomas's Union forces near Logan's Cross Roads about ten miles north of Mill Spring on January 19, 1862. After several hours of intense fighting, Union reinforcements prevailed and forced the Confederates to retreat to their camp on the north bank of the river. During the night after the battle they quietly crossed the river and retreated further south into Tennessee. Though there has always been some disagreement about the circumstances of his death, Confederate Gen. Felix K. Zollicoffer was killed in the battle.

Wood engraving from *Frank Leslie's Illustrated Newspaper,* February 8, 1862, from a drawing by an officer engaged in the battle, or by Henri Lovie, Cincinnati, one of *Leslie's* war artists.

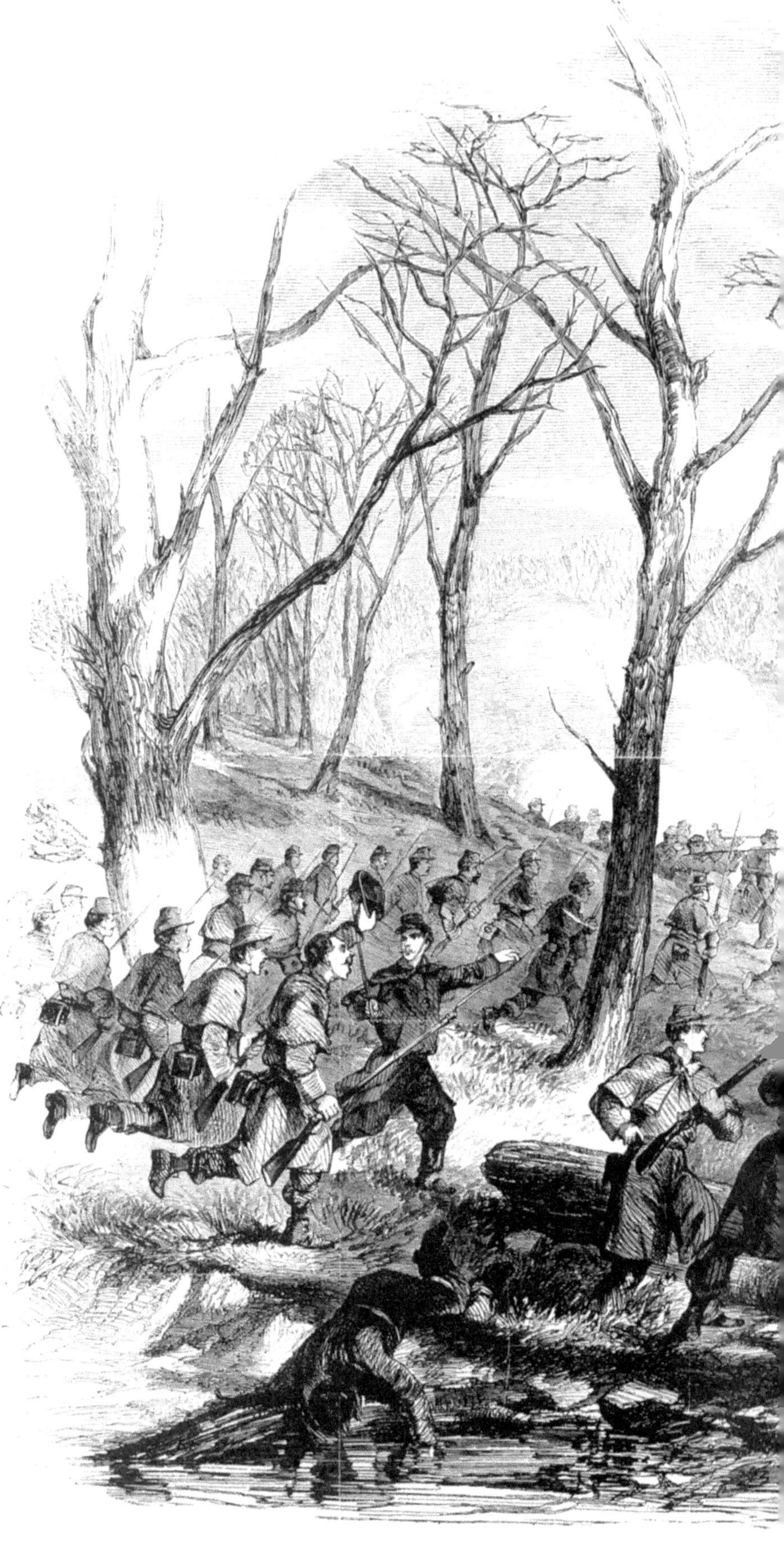

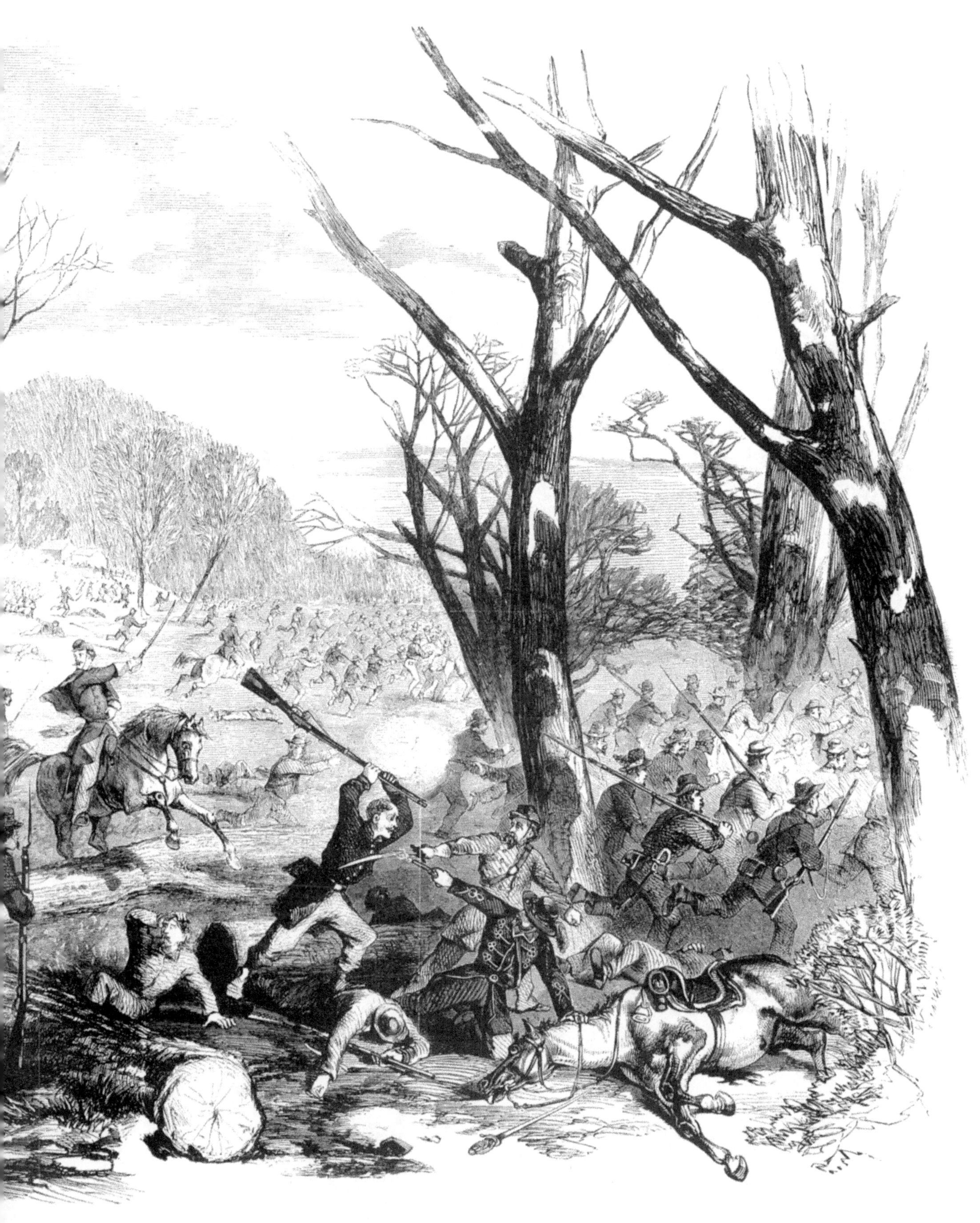

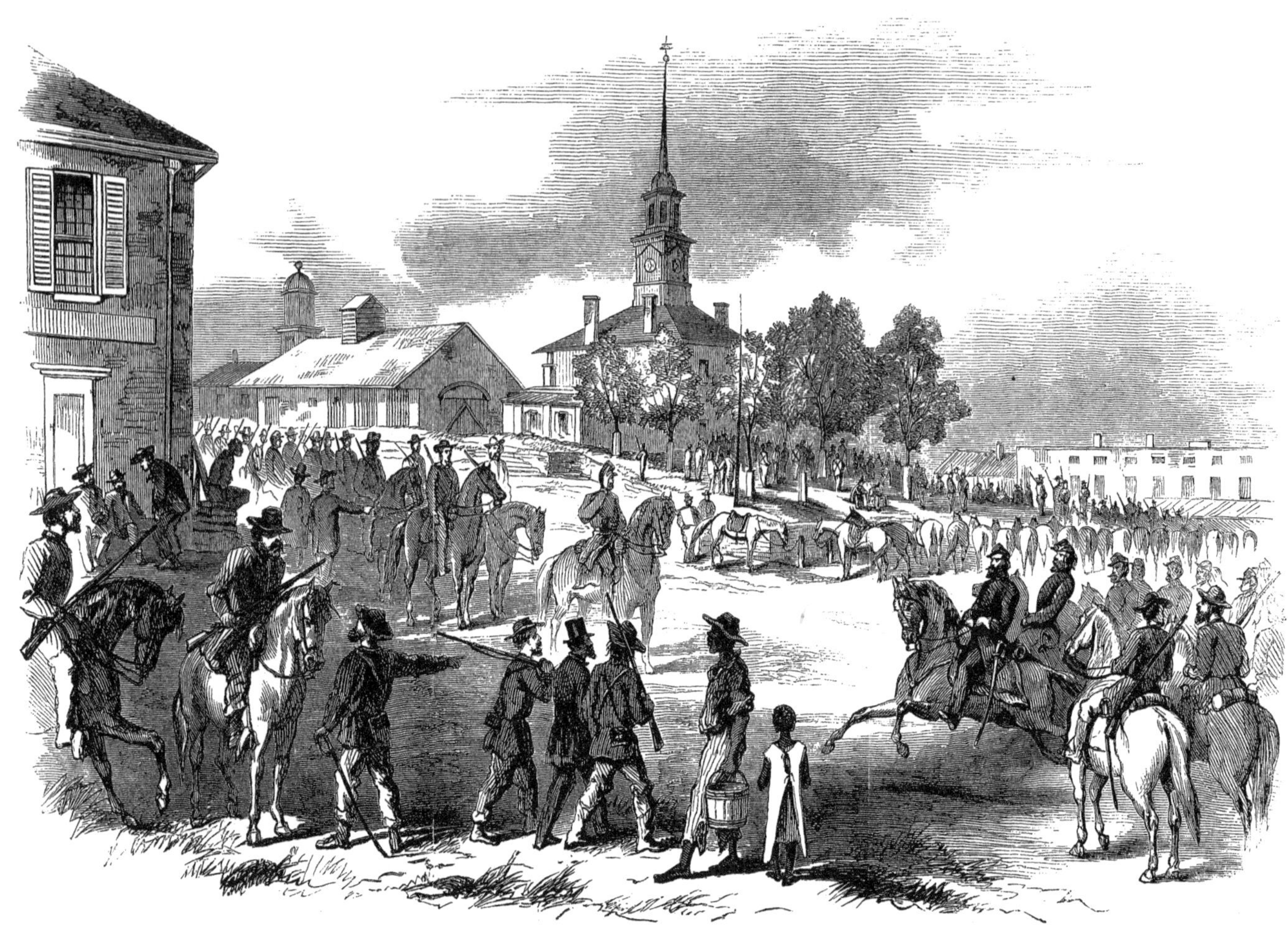

Confederate raider John Hunt Morgan left Knoxville July 4, 1862, with more than eight hundred men and officers, for his first raid into Kentucky. He and his soldiers bivouacked in the courthouse square in Paris on July 18. His skillful and deceptive tactics and extreme mobility created fear and confusion throughout the Bluegrass region, in which he captured—and promptly abandoned—seventeen towns as well as hundreds of Union troops and home guards, who were quickly paroled. He destroyed military supplies wherever he found them and gathered three hundred recruits for the Confederate army who rode back into Tennessee with him. In twenty-four days the raiders rode more than a thousand miles. Morgan began almost immediately his second major raid into Kentucky, which continued through August and September. In July 1863 he led his men through Kentucky into Indiana and Ohio. Out of such raids grew the Morgan legend, and he became a hero to the Confederacy.

Wood engraving from *Frank Leslie's Illustrated Newspaper,* August 16, 1862, from a drawing by Henri Lovie, Cincinnati.

After the retreat of the main Confederate forces from Kentucky in early 1862, the chief military conflicts for the next months came about as a result of raids by small groups of Confederates. A fight between the federal troops and the Morgan Confederate forces took place July 17, 1862, at the Licking bridge in Cynthiana. Morgan's men defeated a Union force of about five hundred men composed of home guards, a Newport militia company, and Cincinnati firemen. Thirty soldiers were killed and about eighty wounded in two hours of fighting. Federal forces retreated to Lexington, and after the town was captured the railroad depot was burned and government supplies destroyed. This is the best existing view of an antebellum Kentucky covered bridge. It continued to carry U.S. highways 27 and 62 until replaced in 1950.

Wood engraving from *Frank Leslie's Illustrated Newspaper,* August 16, 1862, from a drawing by Henri Lovie, Cincinnati.

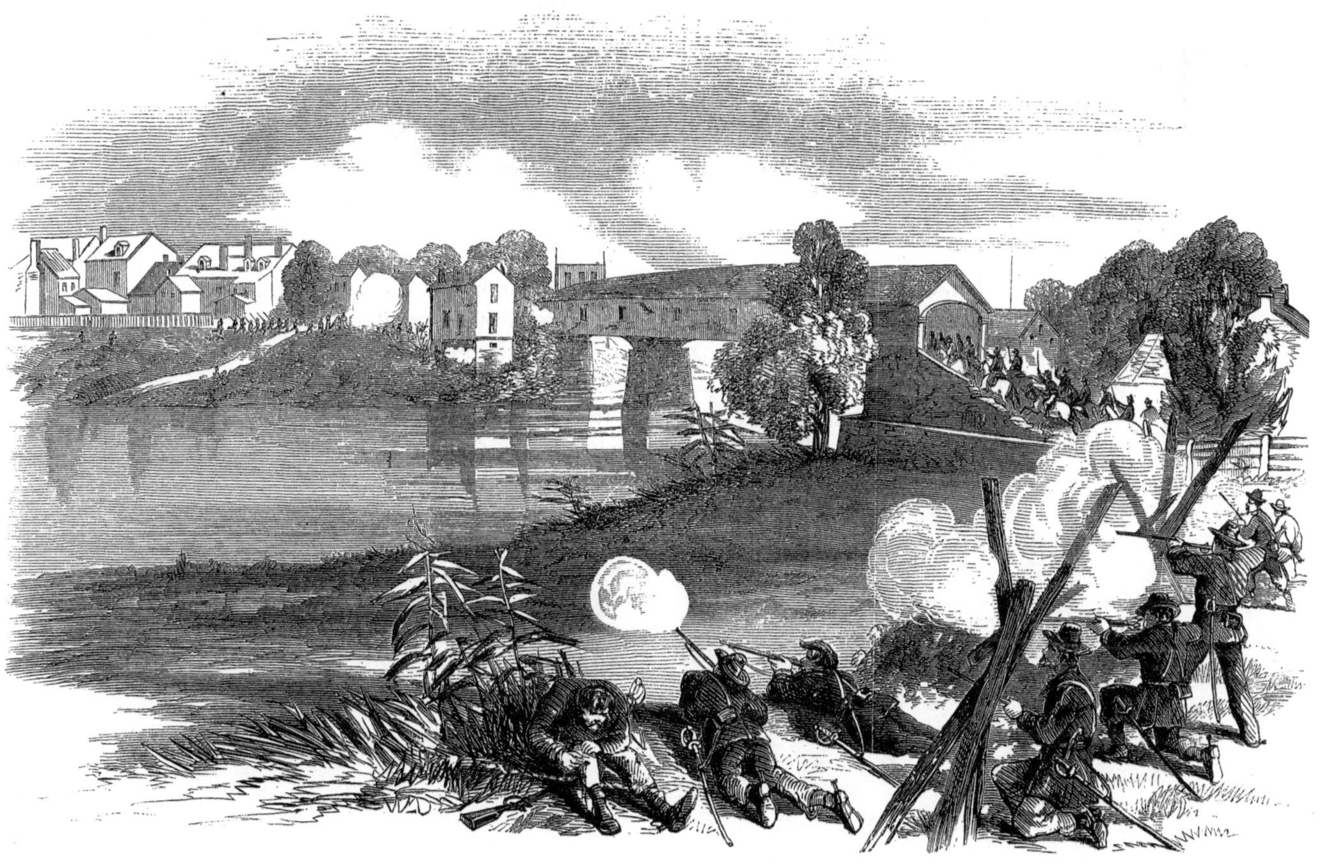

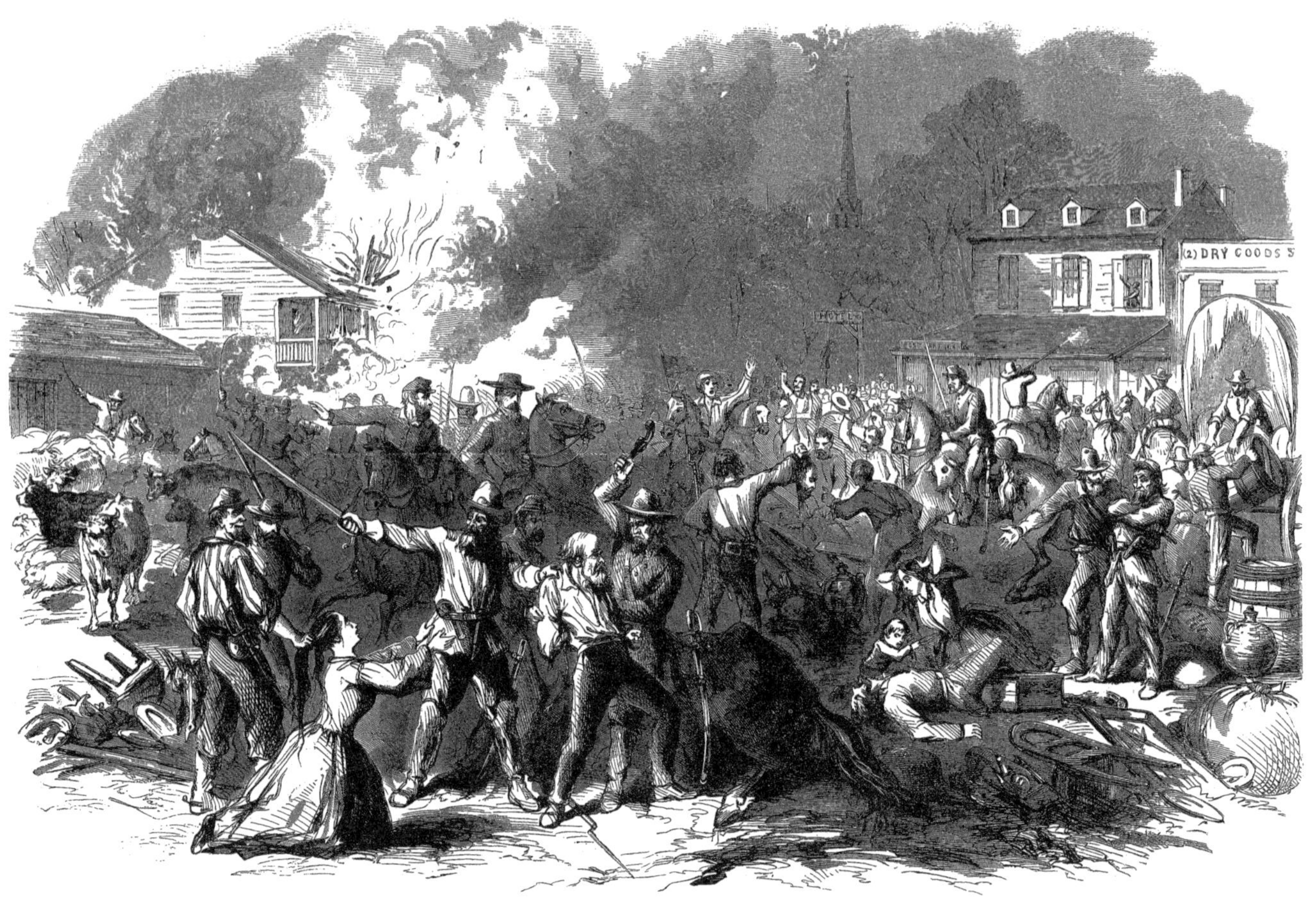

Harper's Weekly had no artists traveling with Confederate troops. The scene presented as John Hunt Morgan's men sacking a peaceful village in the West is a fanciful conception by Thomas Nast, who would later be recognized as one of the outstanding political and satirical cartoonists of the nation. As part of the propaganda war, Nast portrayed the Confederates as unkempt ruffians and brought all their real or rumored activities into one grand scene of brutal deeds, misdemeanors, and felonies. Nast's anti-Morgan propaganda cartoons appeared about three weeks or a month after the events depicted.

Wood engraving from *Harper's Weekly,* August 30, 1862, from a drawing by Thomas Nast.

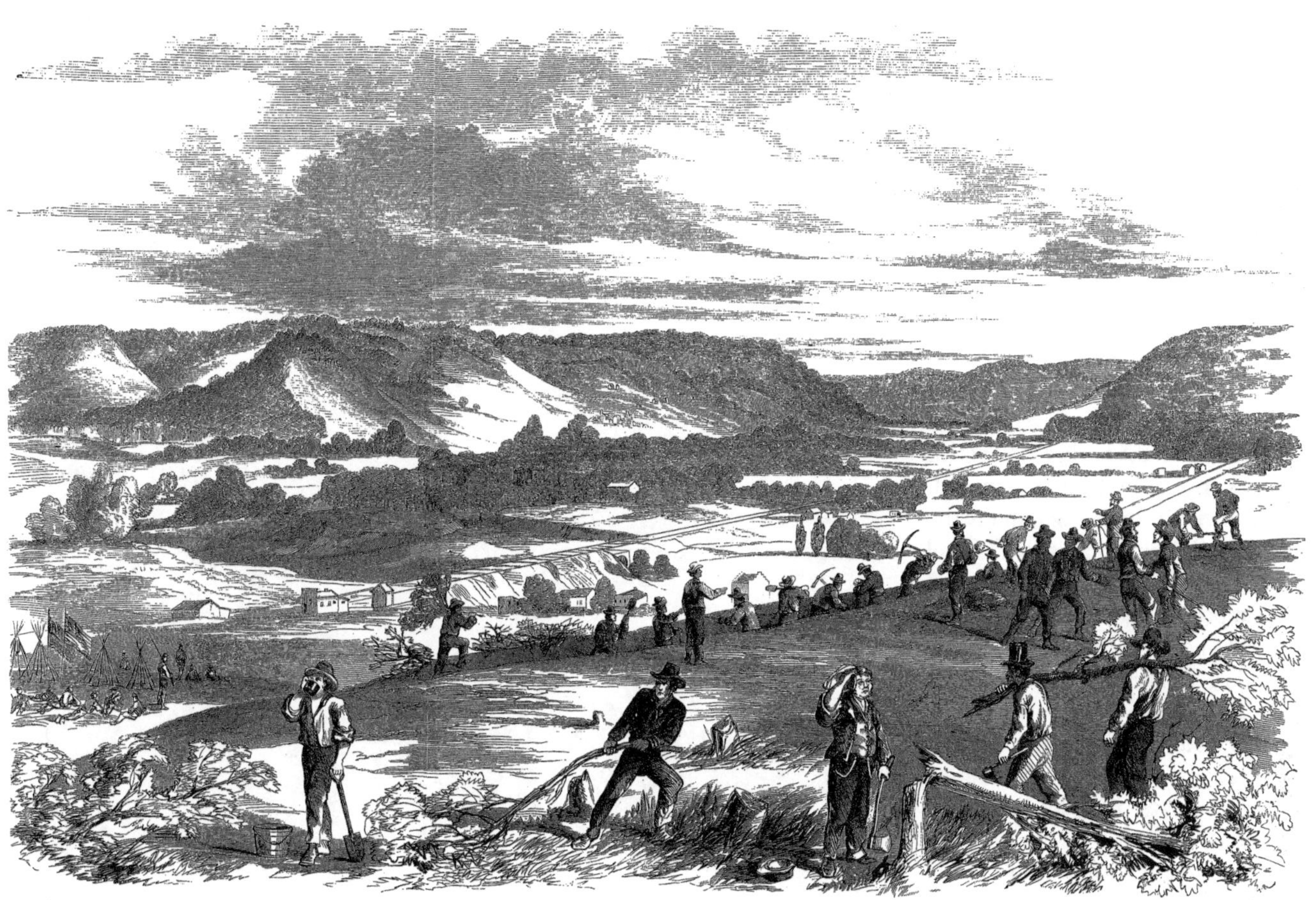

Union citizens dug rifle pits and felled trees on Tunnel Hill near Covington to resist the approach of Confederate troops. At the northernmost part of the Confederate approach to Cincinnati, Confederate Gen. Henry Heth and five thousand soldiers of Gen. Edmund Kirby Smith's corps were camped a few miles south of Covington. Great agitation was created in Covington, Newport, and Cincinnati; males were not permitted to leave except to go southward to the defense lines. Clergymen and older men were pressed into military service, forced to drill or man the trenches. But in the end, actions elsewhere caused the Confederates to fall back before a battle took place.

Wood engraving from *Frank Leslie's Illustrated Newspaper,* October 4, 1862, from a drawing by Henri Lovie, Cincinnati.

The Battle of Munfordville on September 14, 1862, resulted in a Confederate defeat, but two days later, after the arrival of reinforcements, the federal troops were surrounded and captured. The great Green River railroad bridge, shown in the background of this view, was once again heavily damaged. The regiment in the foreground is the Seventh Mississippi, under Colonel Bishop. Today, just south of the bridge is an imposing monolith erected in 1884 to honor another Mississippi officer, Col. Robert A. Smith of the Tenth Regiment, who was mortally wounded leading his men into the battle. Although Colonel Smith is buried in his home state, the plot beside the monument contains six graves, in which rest one unknown soldier from each of the six Mississippi regiments in Gen. James Chalmers's advance force, which fought at the bridge.

Wood engraving from *Frank Leslie's Illustrated Newspaper,* October 25, 1862, from a drawing by Henri Lovie, Cincinnati.

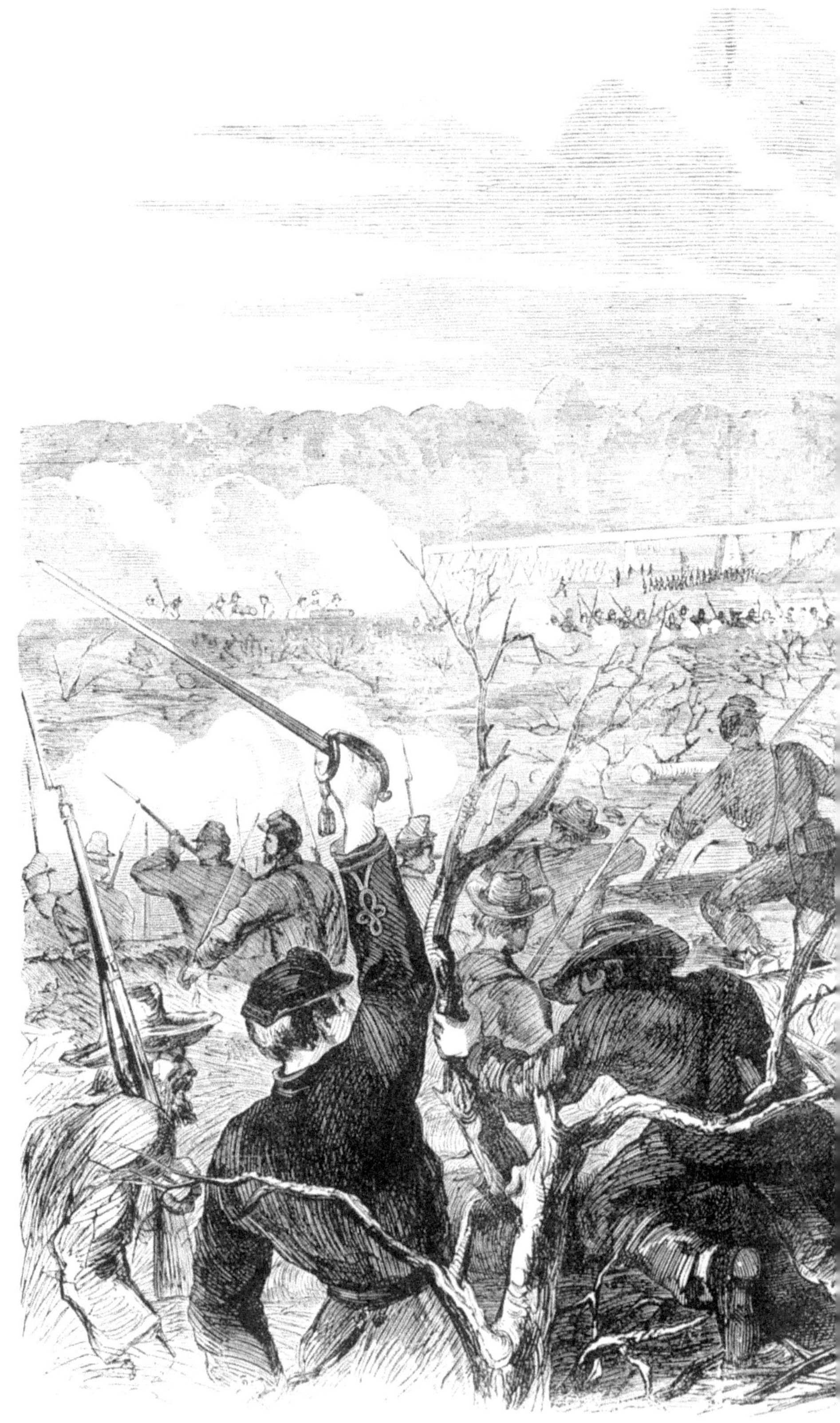

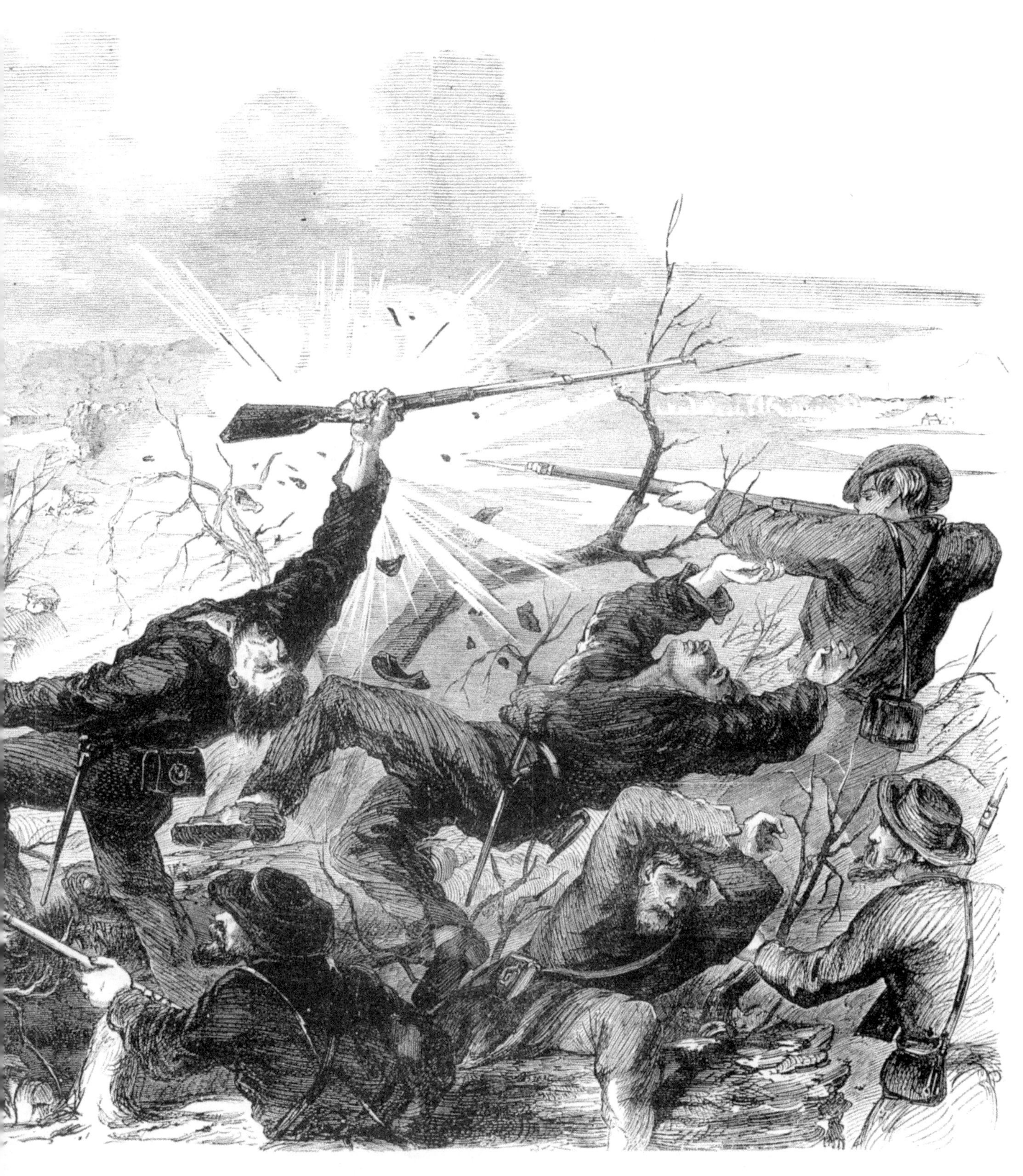

The Confederacy's northern thrust by the armies of Braxton Bragg and Edmund Kirby Smith in August and September 1862 was answered by the arrival of Don Carlos Buell's Union forces in Louisville and his subsequent pursuit of Bragg. In early October the Confederates occupied Frankfort and inaugurated there a provisional Kentucky Confederate government, but actions that later culminated in the bloody battle of Perryville signaled a retreat southward. The bridge pier in the background of this view indicates that the location is on Rolling Fork of Salt River south of Lebanon Junction in Bullitt County. The long gray line of marching men are fording the river at a low stage of water. The body of soldiers in the foreground appears to be marching twenty-five abreast on a narrow country road. The engraver would have added many of these details to the original sketch by the artist.

Wood engraving from *Harper's Weekly*, October 25, 1862, from a drawing by Henry Mosler, Cincinnati.

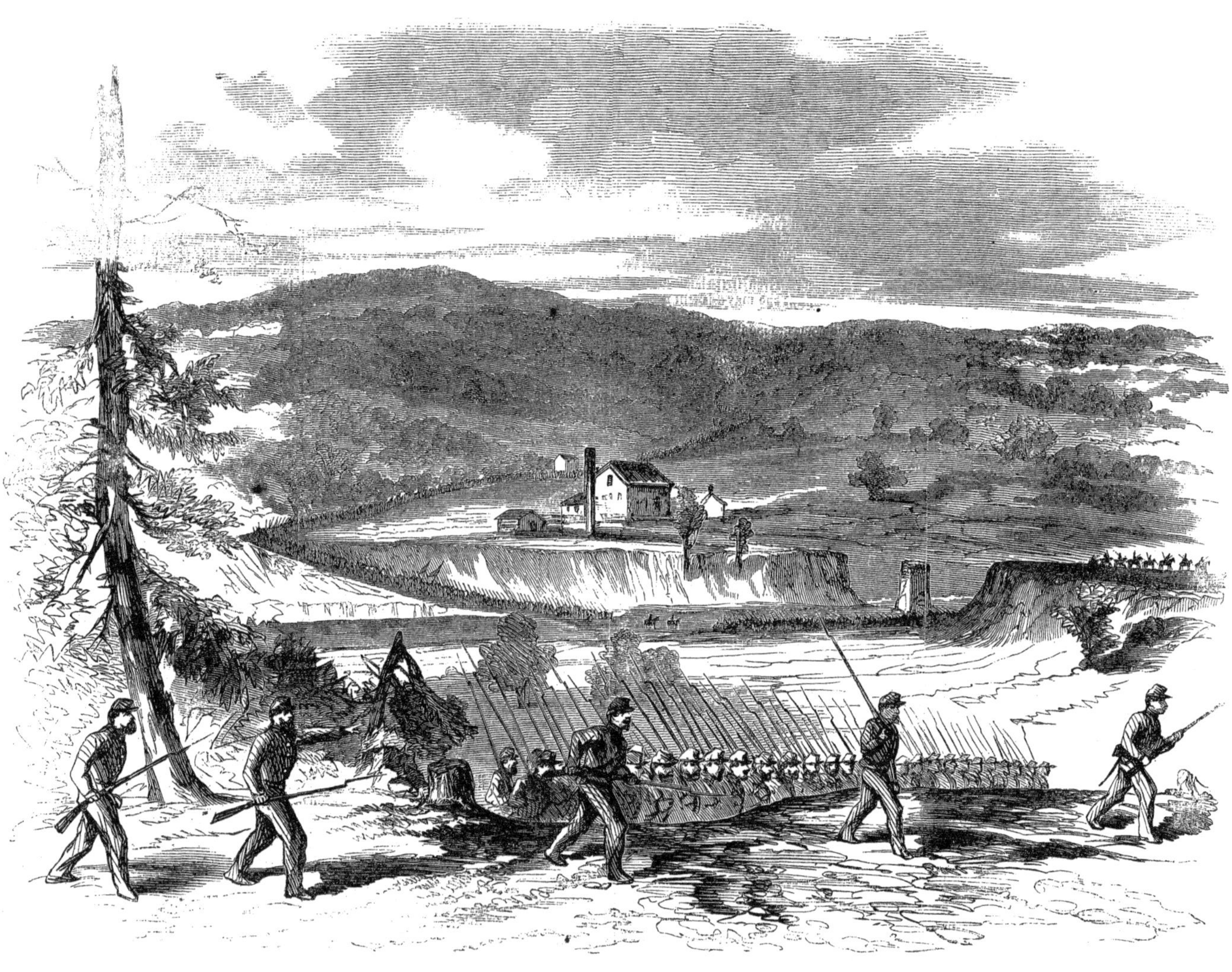

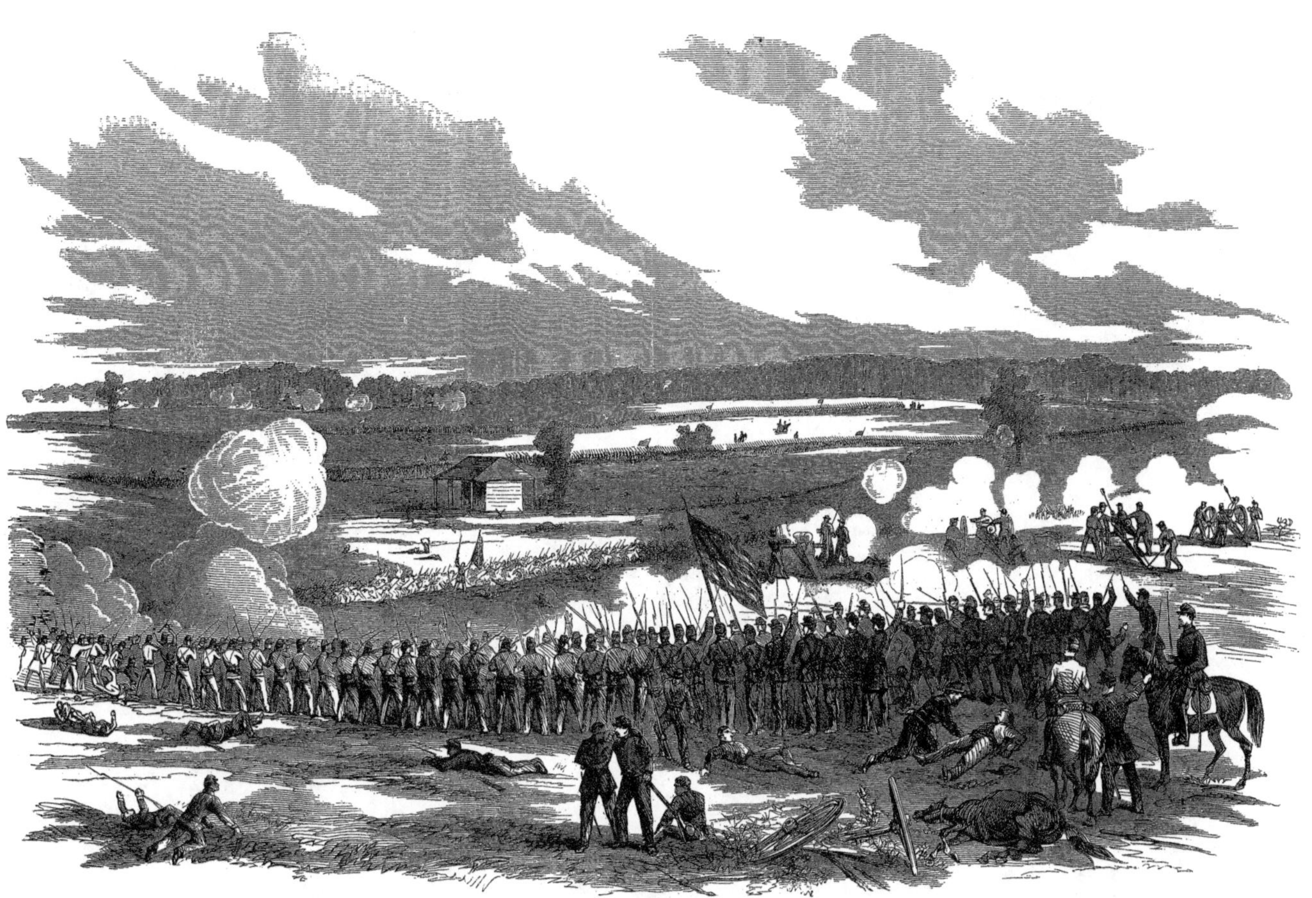

In September 1862, the Confederate armies of generals Bragg and Kirby Smith turned back from their positions not far from Louisville and Covington in an effort to consolidate against Union forces. In an unplanned meeting, about sixteen thousand of Bragg's men confronted Buell's army of about twenty-five thousand at Perryville. The battle of Perryville on October 8, 1862, was soon being called "the bloodiest battle of modern times." An estimated 7,800 were killed, wounded, and missing. Reporting on the battle, a correspondent for the *New York Times* said, "Never, perhaps was there a battle fought at so short a range, and never were fires so murderous and destructive. The thunder of cannon and the crash of musketry can be compared to nothing I have ever heard. The simultaneous falling and splitting of a thousand forest trees might perhaps be *something* like it." The fighting there from midday until dark ended with no clear victor, but the arrival of federal reinforcements persuaded Bragg to withdraw.

Wood engraving from *Harper's Weekly,* November 1, 1862, from a drawing by Henry Mosler, Cincinnati.

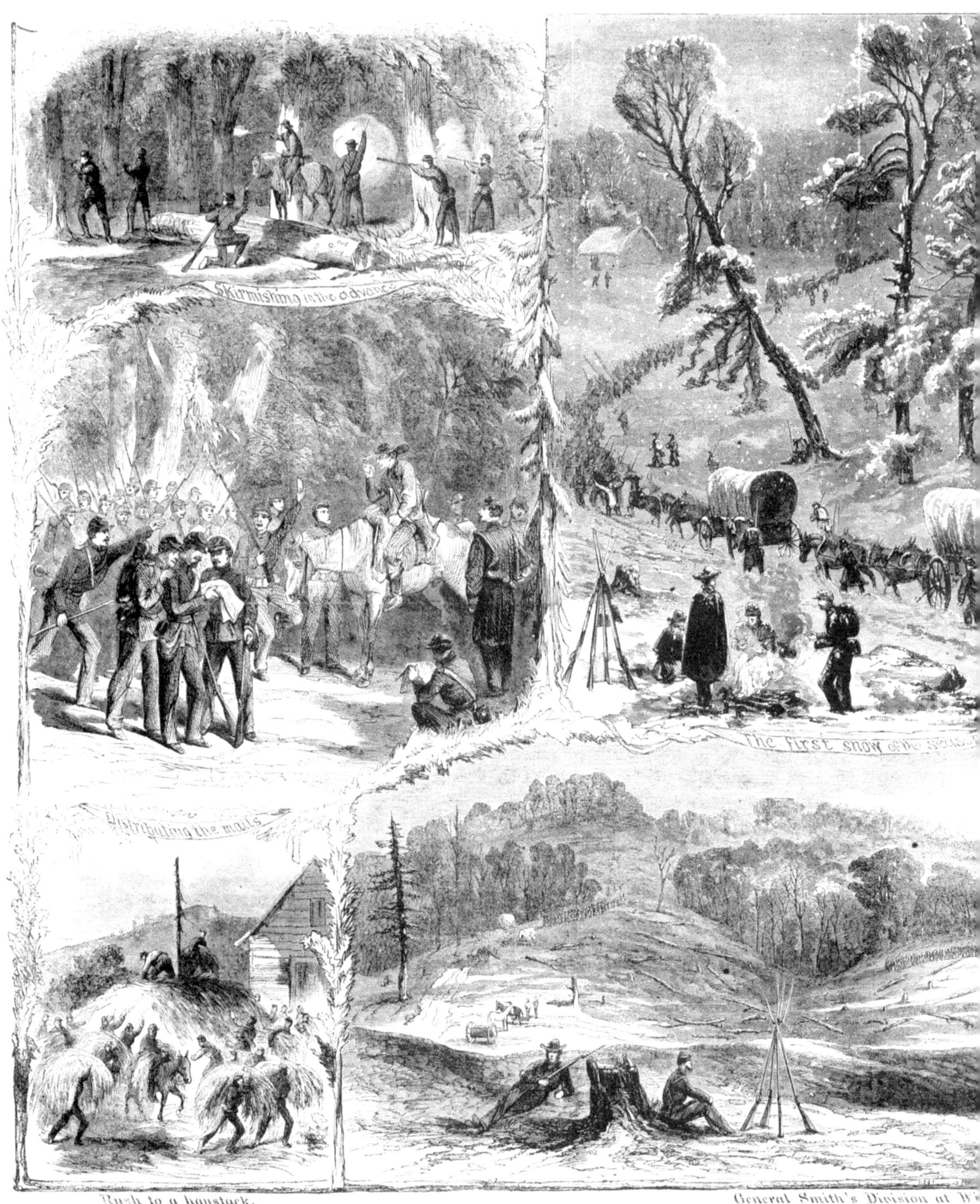

Rush to a haystack.

General Smith's Division at W

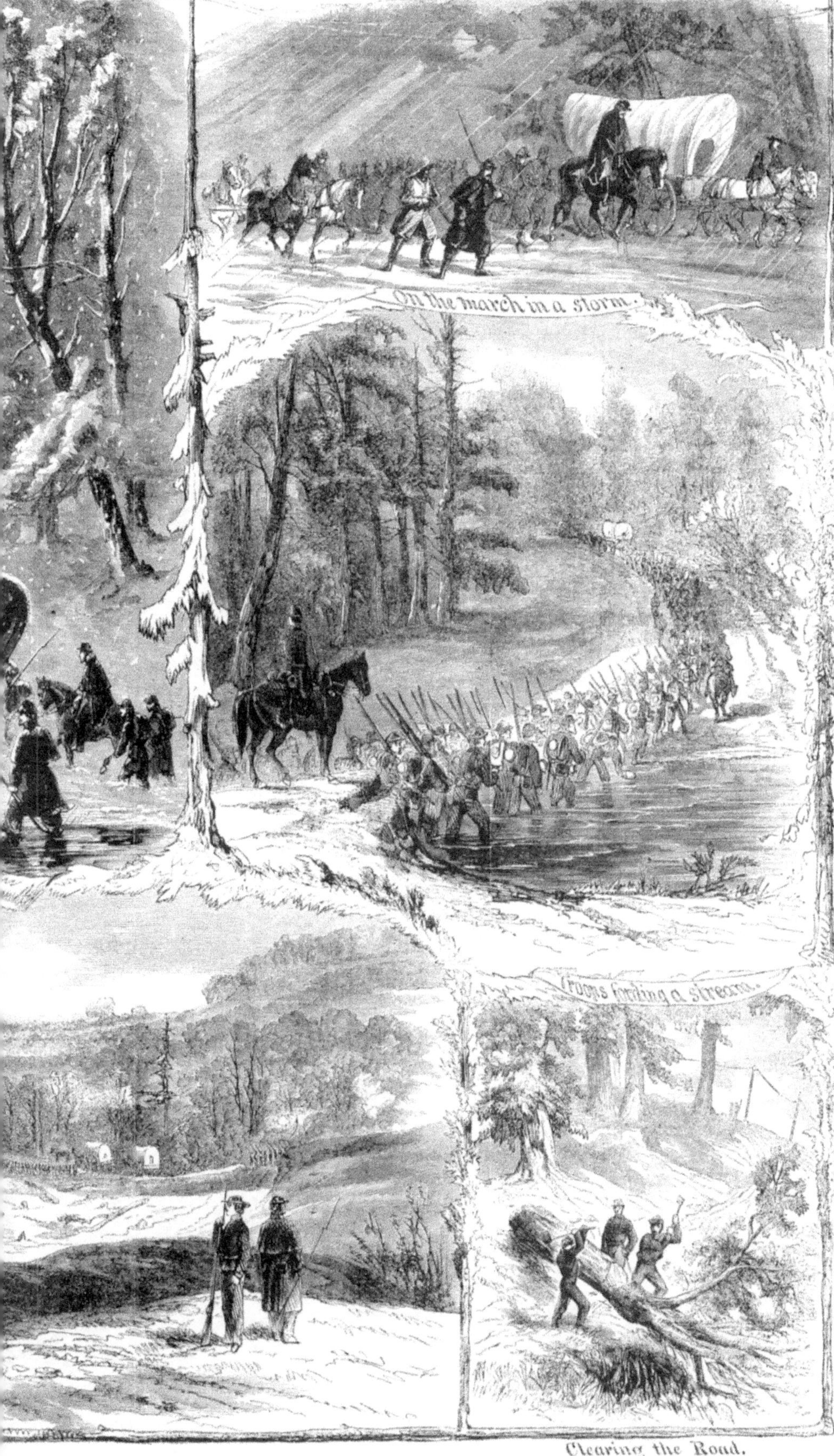

These sketches of the Army of the Ohio on the march were made as portions of McCook's First Army Corps and Gilbert's Third Army Corps headed southward after the battle at Perryville, through Rockcastle County near Mt. Vernon. Winter travel was extremely difficult on war-torn country roads. To accompany his sketches, the artist Henry Mosler wrote, "on October 26 we started for Mt. Vernon toward Somerset on our way to Bowling Green. It had snowed all the day before and the mountain road had become one mass of mud, in some places knee-deep. After a weary march of fifteen miles the troops encamped at Somerset without tents. You may fancy how they enjoyed the cold night, in their chilled, wet condition, sleeping in the open air. The rear of Bragg's retreating army felled every tree that stood near enough to the road to fall across it, and our advance column had to clear them away. We were often so close in pursuit that we could hear the crash of the falling trees." This scene, which Mosler made at Wild Cat, includes some of the earthworks thrown up for earlier battles.

Wood engraving from *Harper's Weekly*, November 22, 1862, from a drawing by Henry Mosler, Cincinnati.

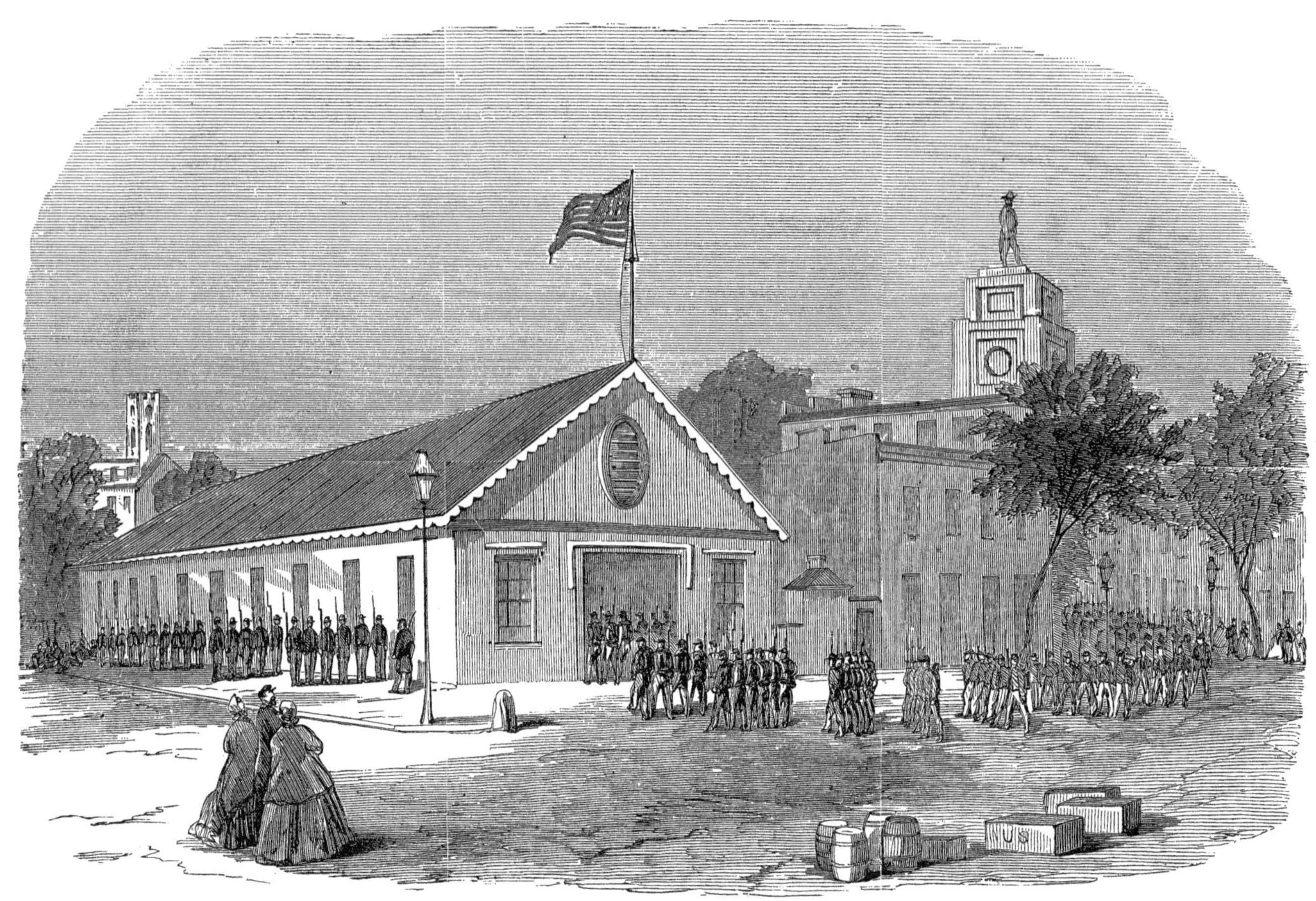

As the Confederate armies moved out of Kentucky late in 1862, Union troops followed them through innumerable cities, towns, and communities, which could then return to their former antagonisms and wartime disruptions without the presence of an occupying army. Shown here are the 105th Ohio Volunteers passing through Lexington.

Wood engraving from *Harper's Weekly,* 1862.

Cumberland Gap was considered to be a strategic point of great value, but no important fighting took place there, and its possession was determined principally by the movements of superior forces on both sides. Confederate forces occupied the gap in August 1862 during their advance into Kentucky. On September 9, 1863, federal troops captured two thousand Confederates there, and it remained in Union control thereafter.

Wood engraving from *Harper's Weekly,* October 10, 1863.

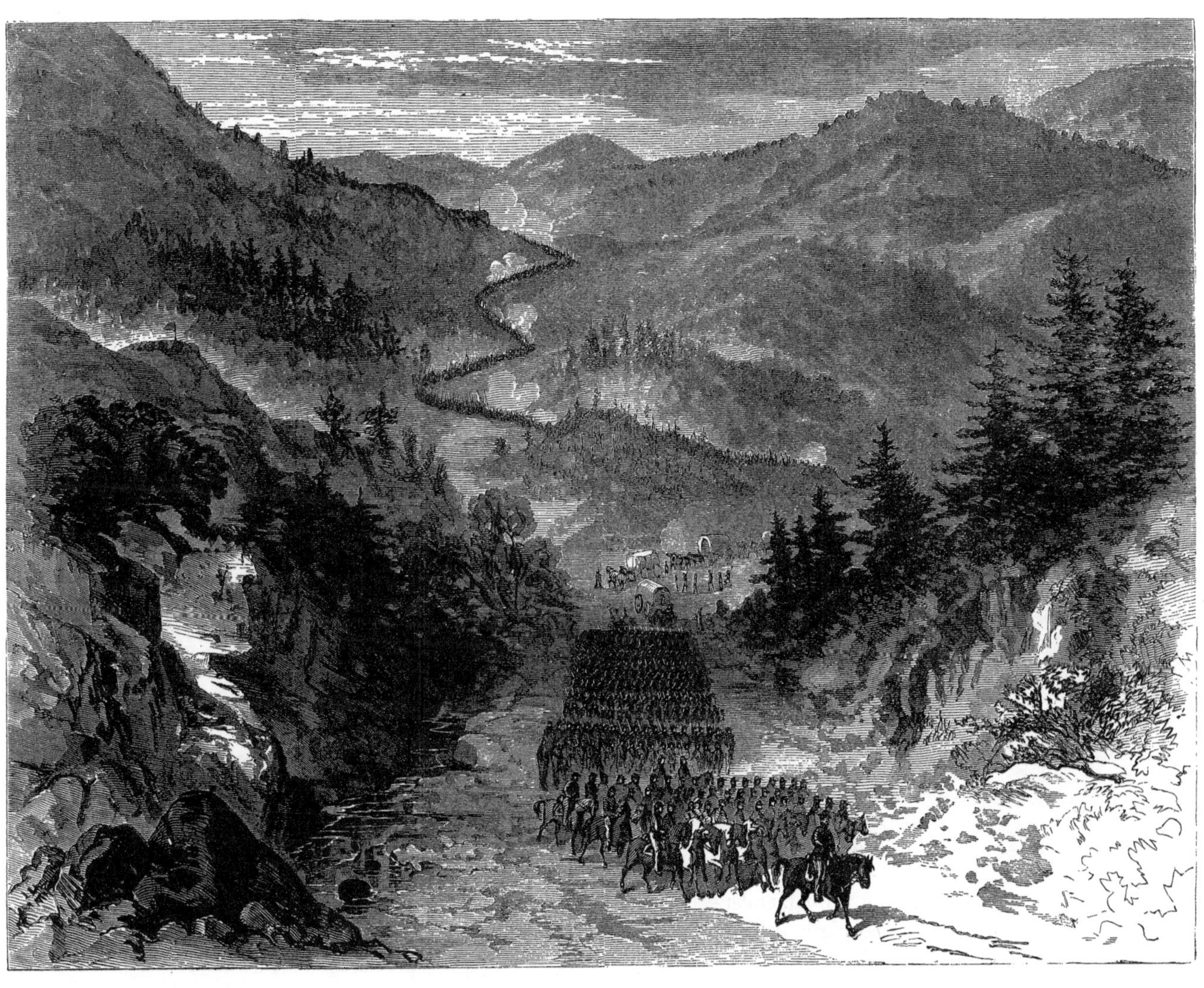

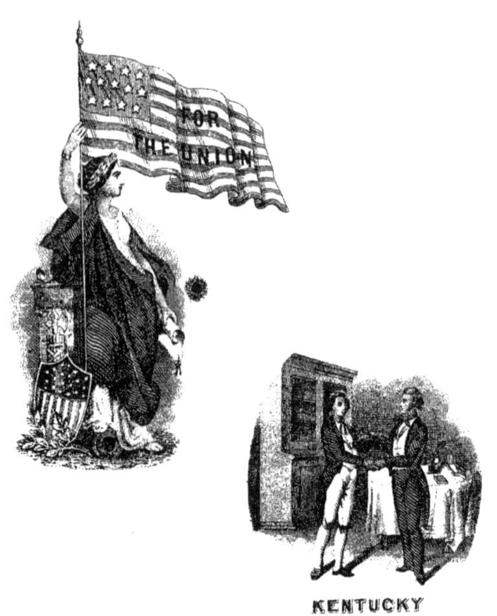

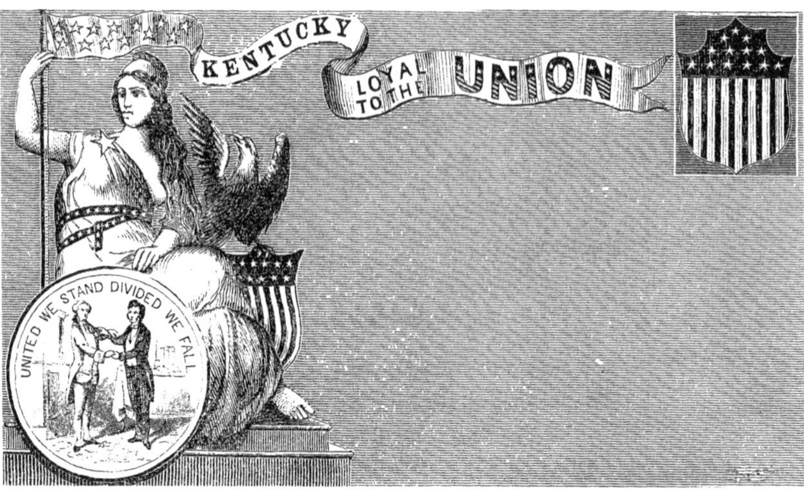

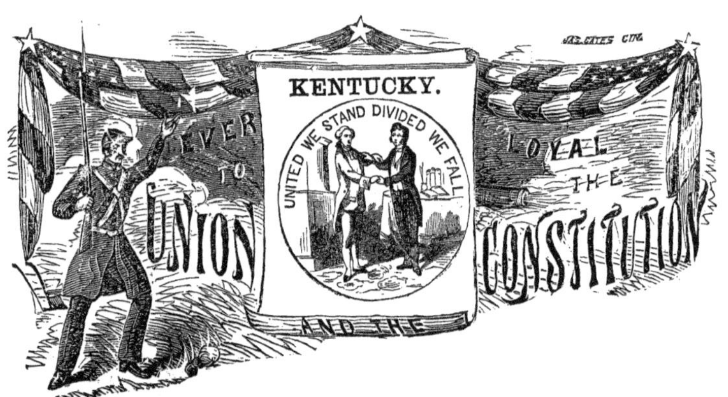

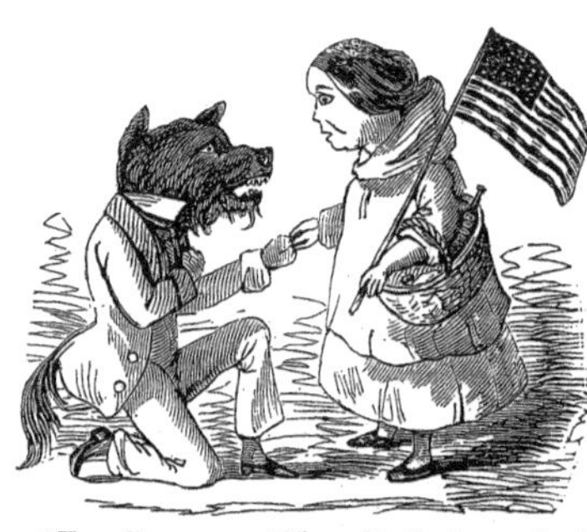

" THE SECESSION WOLF" offering to lead Kentucky, " Or any other State," out of the Union. " That's what's the matter."

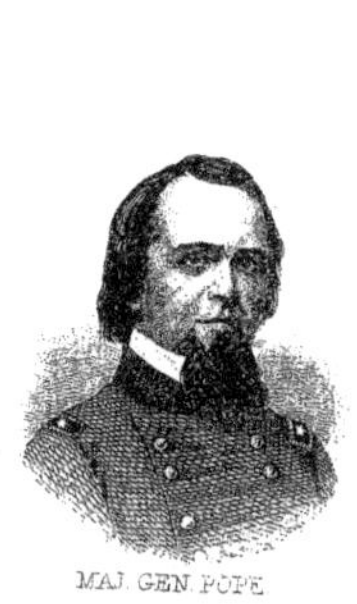

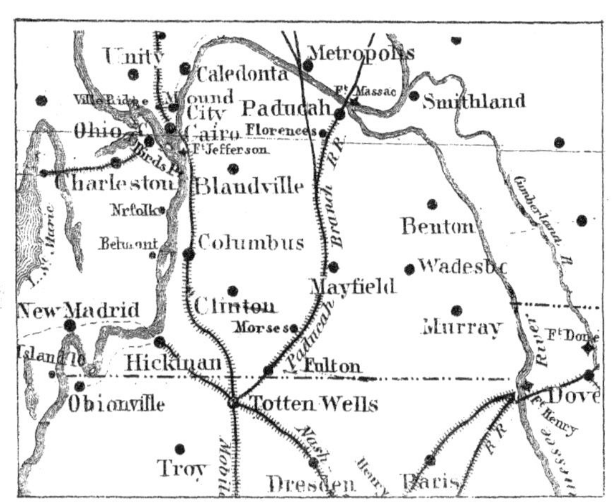

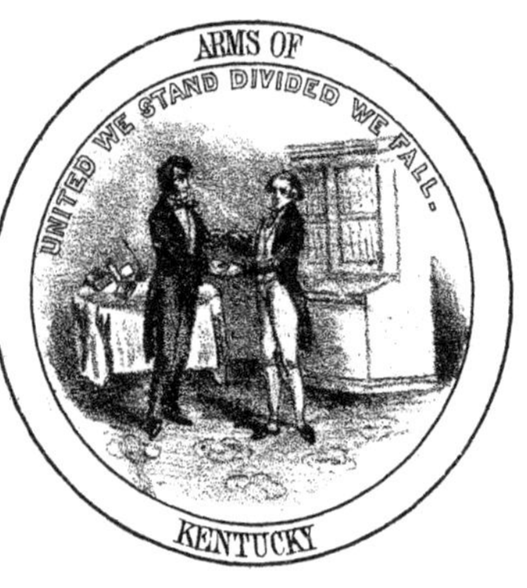

KENTUCKIANS!

Beware of Traitors.

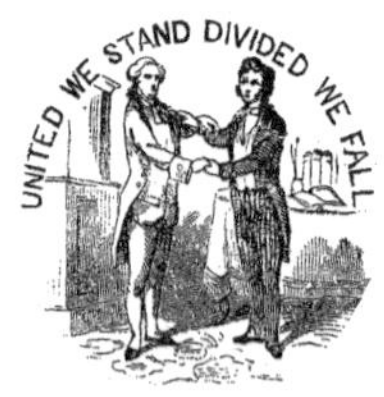

"If Kentucky to-morrow unfurls the banner of resistance, I never will fight under that banner. I owe a PARAMOUNT allegiance to the whole UNION—a SUBORDINATE one to my own State."
Henry Clay.

"Patriotic covers," or envelopes, allowed Americans to send mail with more than the usual message. Some commemorated people and regions, while others bore overtly political mottos, especially during the Civil War.

SEVEN

The Rural and Urban Landscape

Kentucky's population remained more rural than urban until 1970, a half-century after America's population made that statistical switch. Throughout its history, the state has maintained an agrarian ethos, even as it voiced the words of urbanism. Yet, for illustrators, it was the city and the town that appealed throughout. A few images of stock farms or homes of the prominent or even selected scenic vistas did appear, but they were dwarfed by those of urban places.

Louisville was by far the commonwealth's largest city for most of the nineteenth century and attracted the most interest as a result. A place where important leaders (such as Zachary Taylor) lived, where national figures (such as President Rutherford B. Hayes) visited, and where major conventions (such as the American party's) met, the Falls City grew in size and significance as the century progressed. Hospitals, alms houses, and orphan homes represented the commitment to caring for the less fortunate; mob rule and labor violence showed the other side of the city.

Frankfort, the capital city, also attracted the illustrators. They focused chiefly on the seat of government, the capitols, on various monuments in the Frankfort Cemetery, and on the state penitentiary. Occasionally grand plans that never materialized were even presented, as in the case of a projected new capitol to be built in the 1870s, a project that was not realized for more than three decades.

In Lexington, a similar instance took place as an illustrator pictured a monument to Henry Clay. It too was never built, replaced instead by a simpler, less expensive version. As the one-time "Athens of the West" and the home of Henry Clay, Lexington received some attention, sometimes unwanted (as in the case of a hanging). But as the century wore on, it fell in size—to fourth among Kentucky's cities by 1900 (behind Louisville, Covington, and Newport). Surprisingly, the two northern Kentucky cities larger than Lexington attracted little interest from illustrators, perhaps because of their proximity to Cincinnati.

Other parts of Kentucky were the subject of illustrations in varying degrees. Central and south central locales occasionally drew attention, often in connection with a specific event (a battle) or place (a resort spring). Generally the same was true of river towns, ranging from Maysville to Paducah. Eastern Kentucky locales, however, remained almost ignored, and western Kentucky ones stood underrepresented. The rural world was nearly forgotten in engravings and lithographs, even though the majority of Kentucky citizens lived and worked there.

—J. C. K.

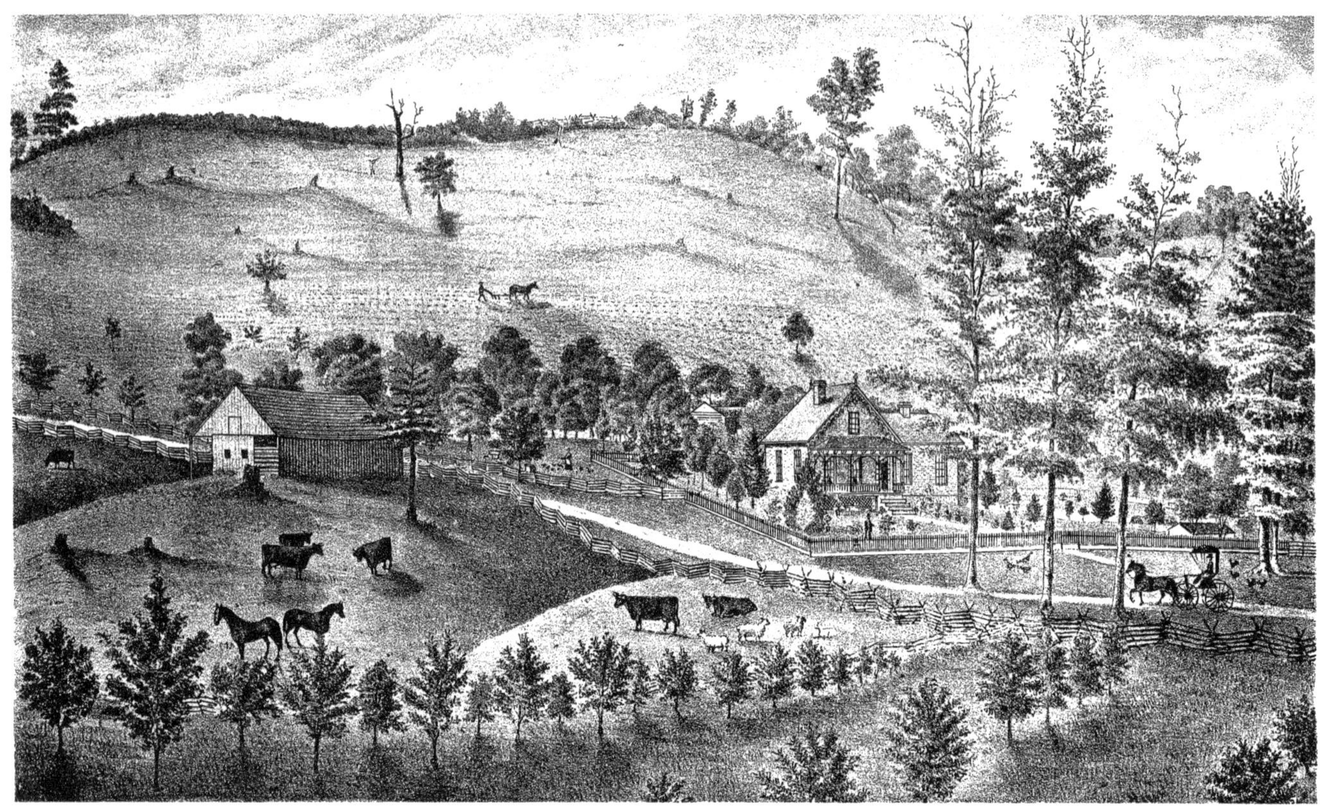

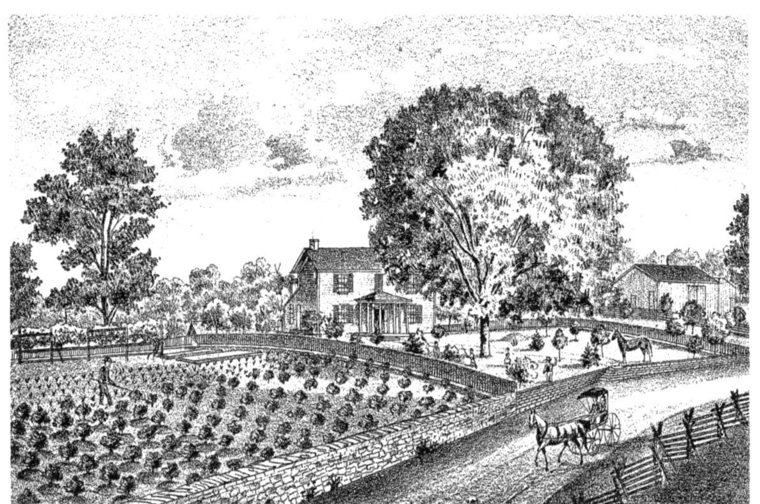

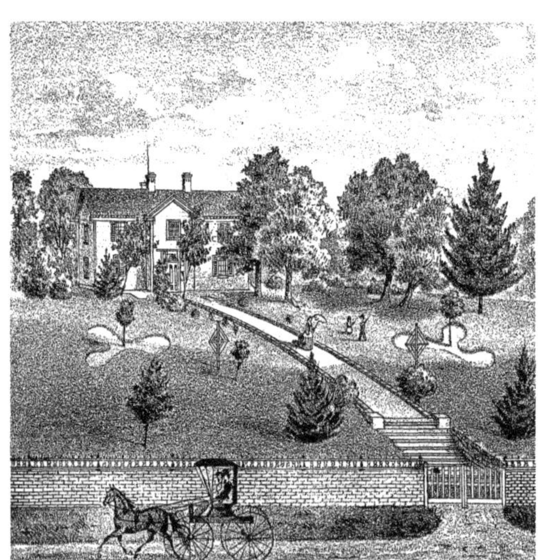

Kentucky presented contrasting faces, in both urban and rural settings. In the city, rundown shacks existed as did grand mansions. Similarly, in agrarian Kentucky, small, tenant-operated places often attracted descriptive attention, but there too existed stately homes and fine farms. The land around Maysville and Mason County had been settled early in the commonwealth's history and the rural residences showed that development.

Lithographs from *An Illustrated Atlas of Mason County, Kentucky,* 1876.

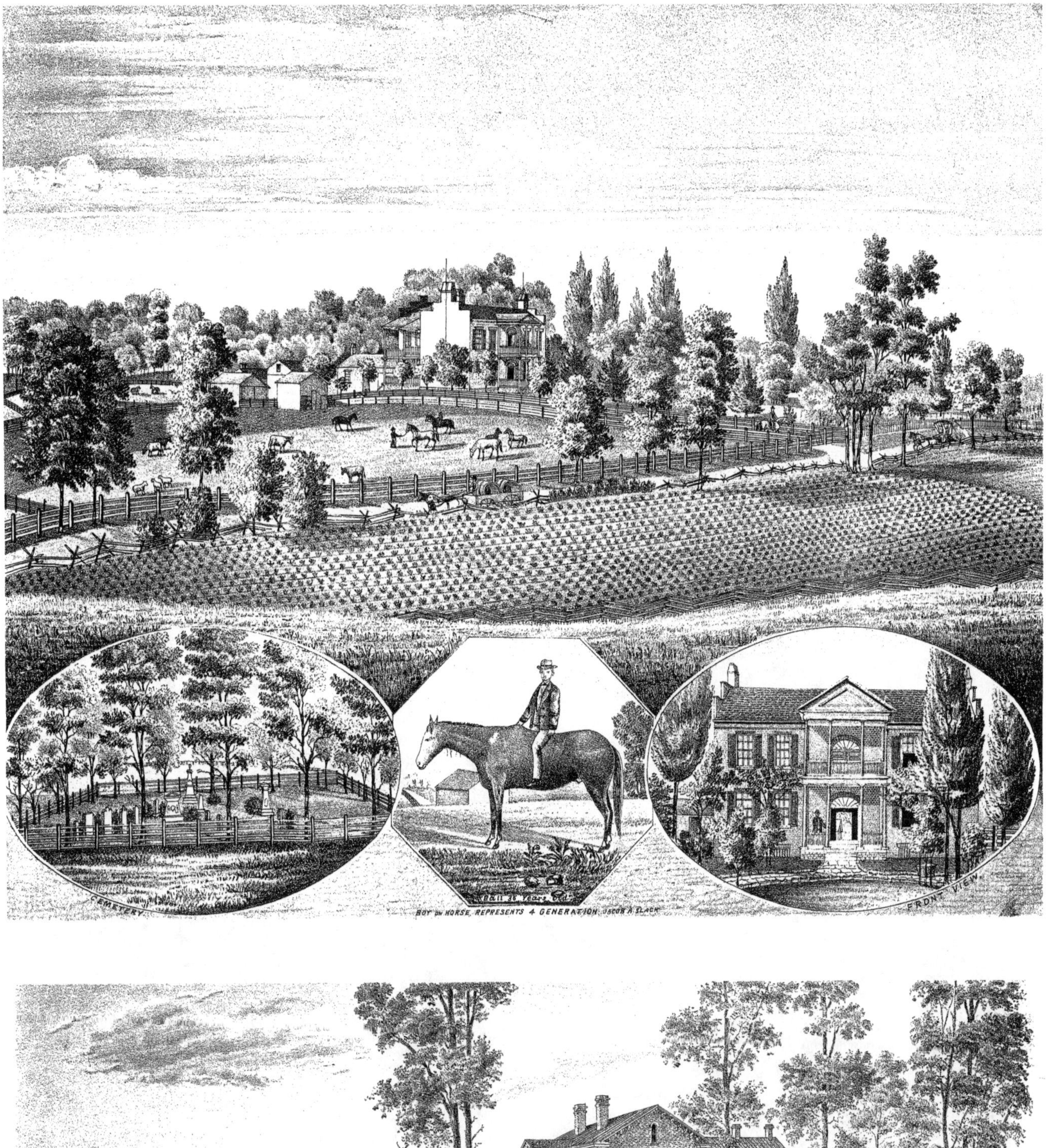

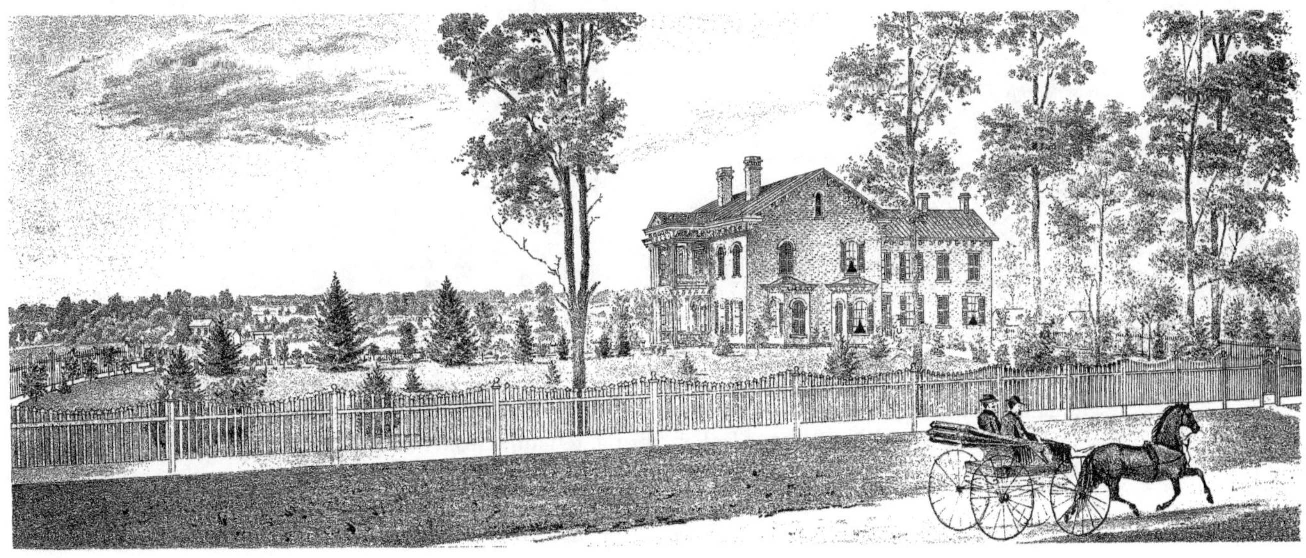

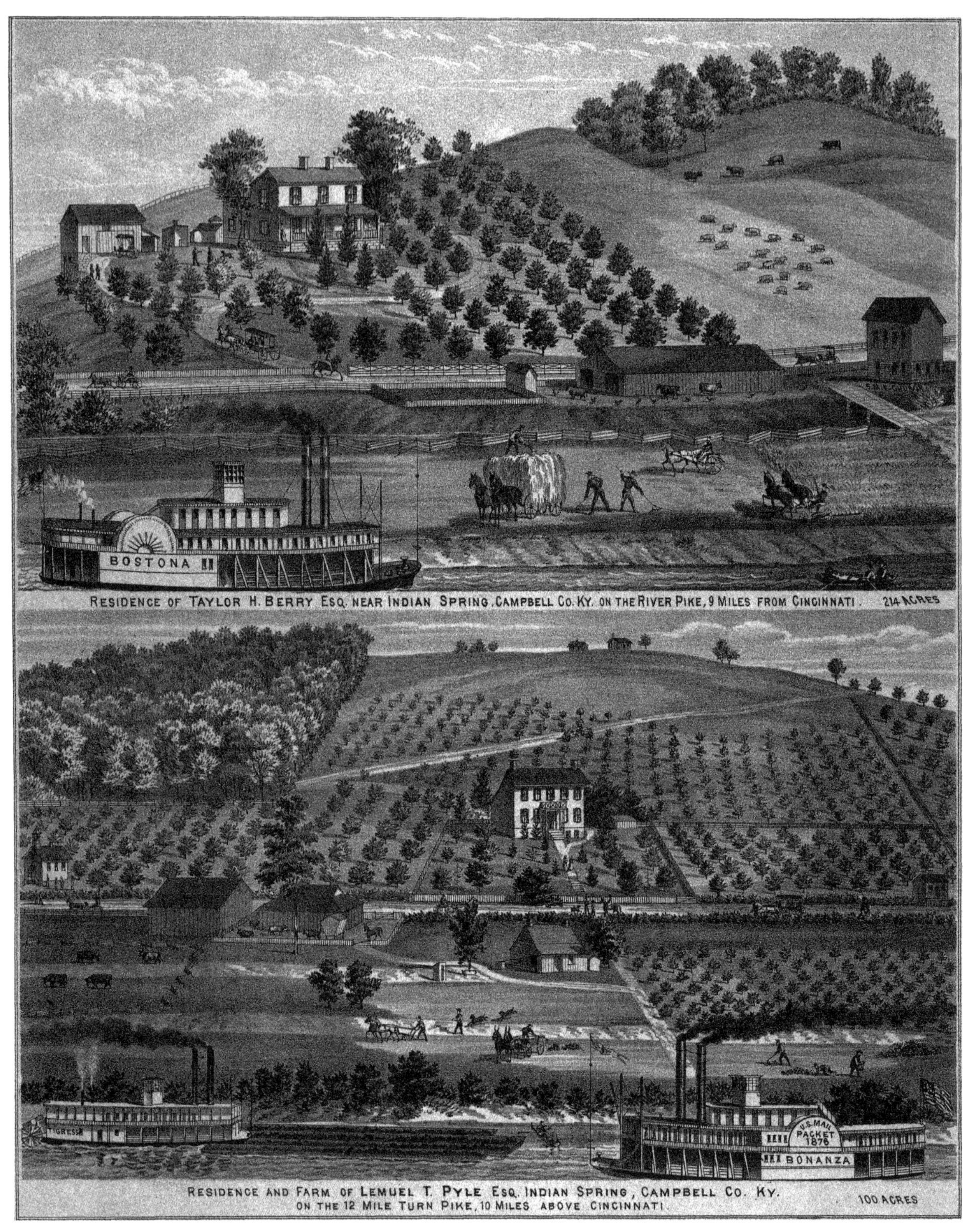

Campbell County was also known for large and beautiful farms. The residence and farm of Lemuel T. Pyle, a fruit grower, was in Indian Spring, ten miles from Newport. And nearby, Taylor H. Berry, farmer and livestock dealer, established his 214 acre farm.

Lithograph from *Illustrated Atlas of the Upper Ohio River Valley*, 1877.

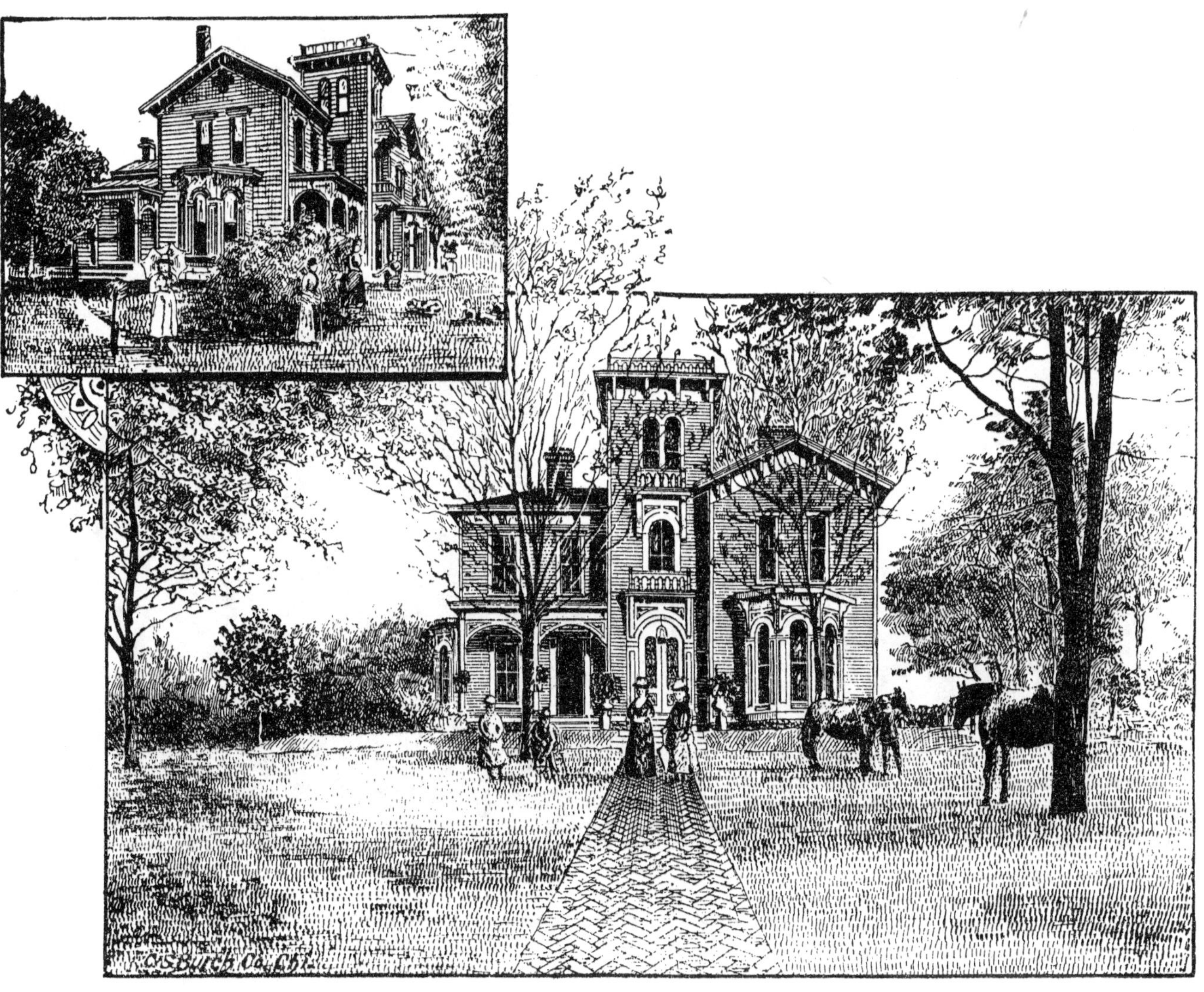

The artist depicted not only two views of the residence of Dr. Washington Miller in Winchester, but also livestock, a groom, family and visitors, and the brick walk leading away from the house.

Wood engraving from Beckner's *Handbook of Clark County and the City of Winchester,* 1889.

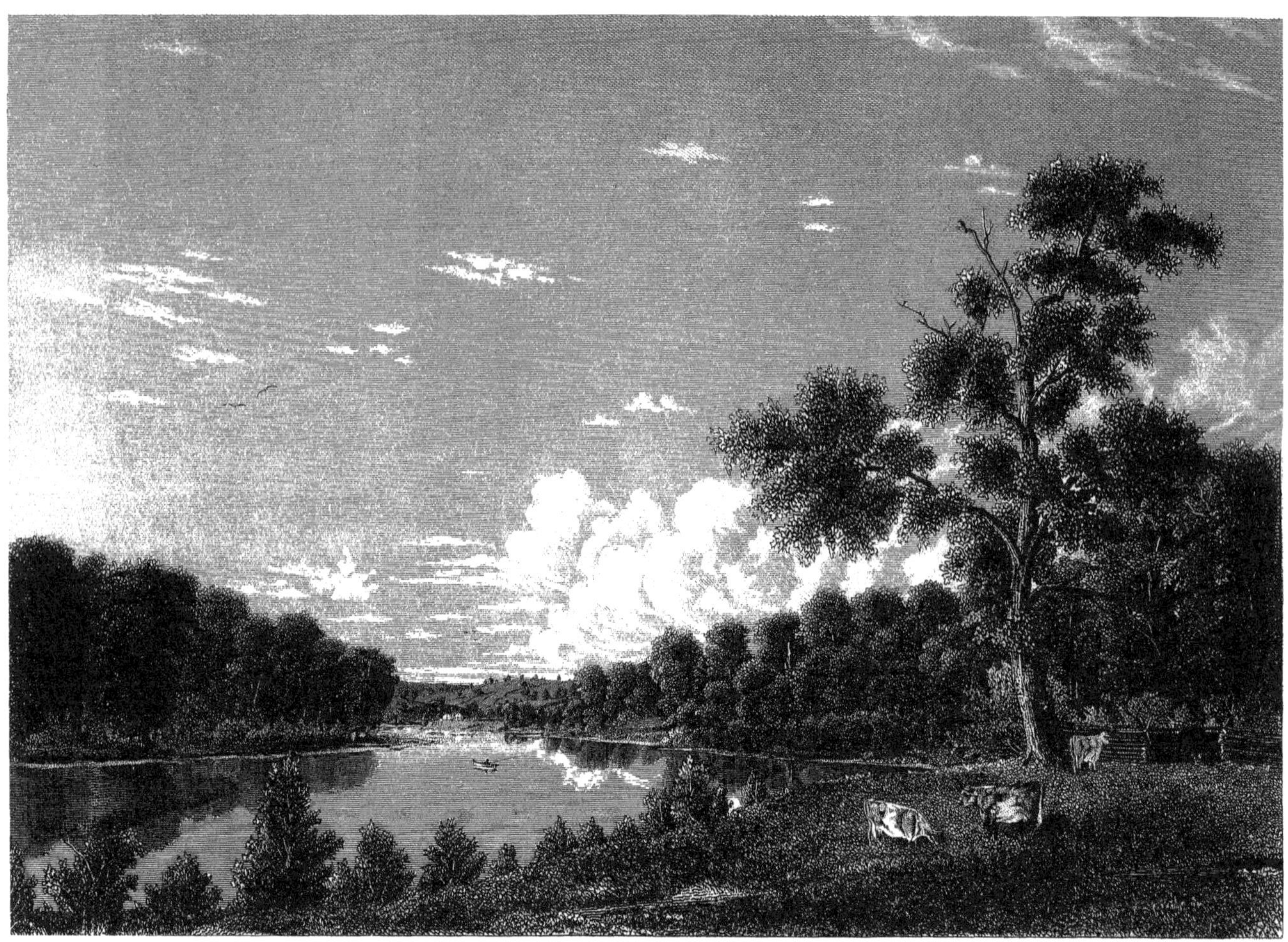

The John Hinkson and John Miller companies ascended the Licking River in canoes up to the Lower Blue Licks in March and April 1775. Col. John Todd and his Kentucky volunteers suffered a bloody defeat on the banks of the river in August 1782. A system of twenty-one locks and dams was planned to open the river to northeastern Kentucky. Though work began in 1837, no part of it was ever completed. This view, called "Twenty Miles up the Licking," illustrates a portion of the river in the southeastern part of Kenton County, probably between Visalia and Kenton.

Copper engraving from *The Ladies Repository,* 1846. Engraved by William Wellstood from a painting by J.H. Hine.

Christopher Gist, an agent for the Ohio Land Company, landed at the mouth of the Licking River in 1751. From 1779 to 1782 the mouth of the river was the rendezvous point for expeditions against the tribes north of the Ohio River who were conducting raids on the new settlements in Kentucky. Newport was established on the east bank, with Covington on the west bank. From the earliest explorations, the Licking was an important access route to the central parts of the state.

Copper engraving from *The Ladies Repository*, 1856. Engraved by F.E. Jones from a drawing by Charles Bauerlie.

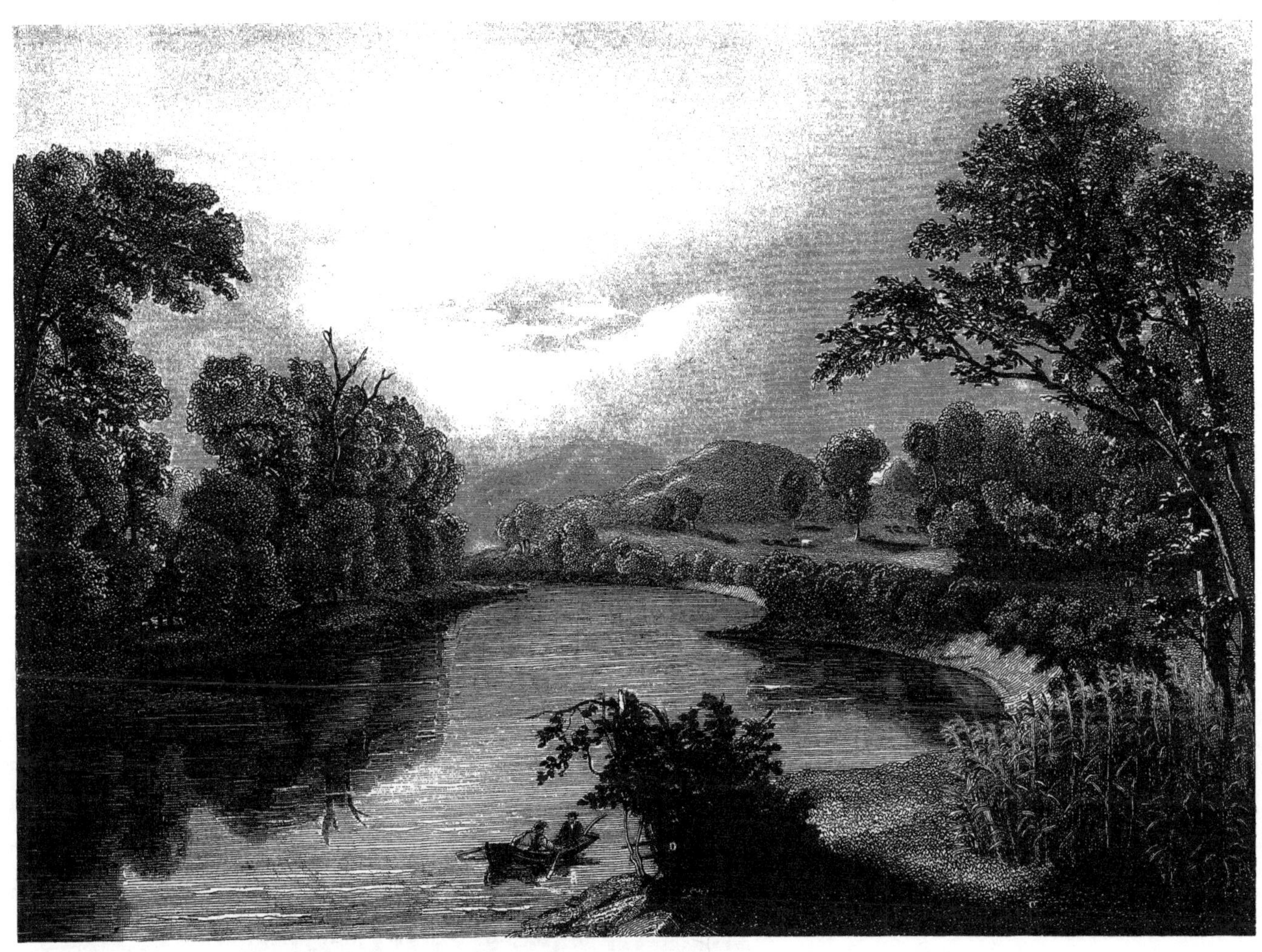

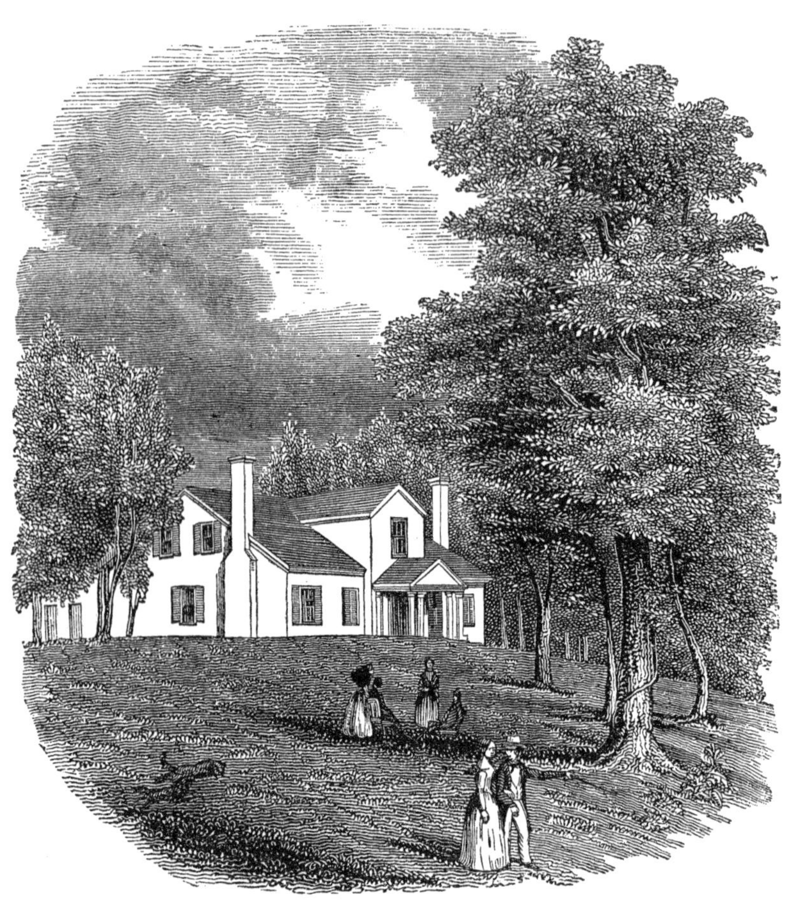

Forest Retreat in Nicholas County was the home of Thomas Metcalfe, governor of Kentucky from 1828 to 1832. Metcalfe was a stonemason, nicknamed "Old Stonehammer," and is believed to have been his own architect for Forest Retreat, completed in 1820. The home is still a private residence, located on U.S. 68 four miles northwest of Carlisle.

Wood engraving from Lewis Collins's *Historical Sketches of Kentucky,* 1847.

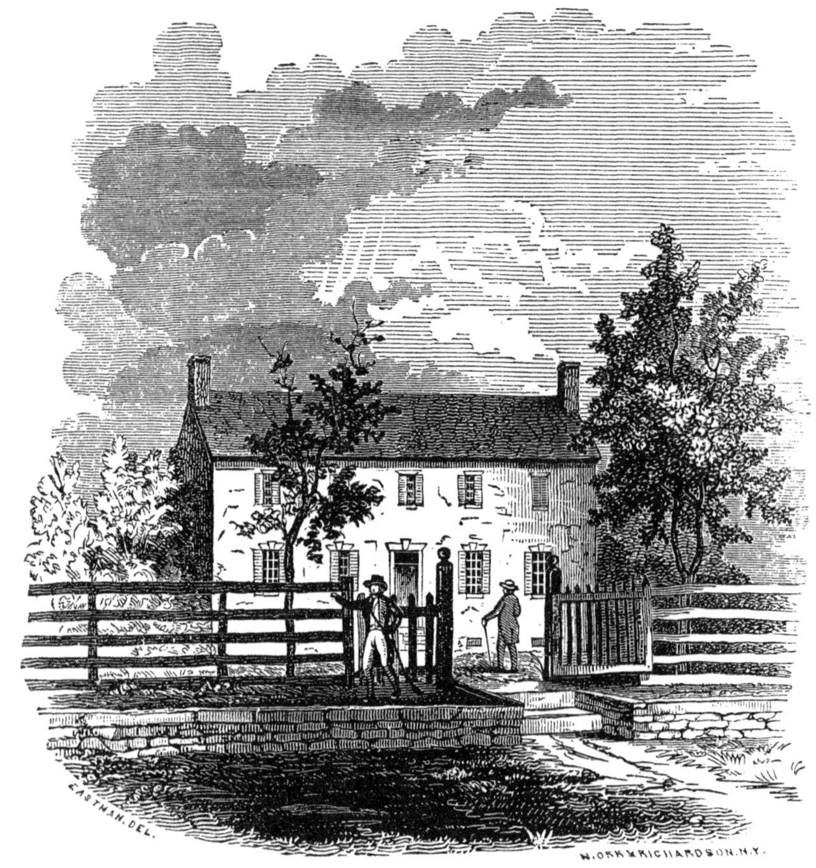

James Garrard's early stone house was built in 1786 at Talbot Station in Bourbon County. Garrard, a revolutionary war soldier, Baptist minister, state legislator, and the second governor of the commonwealth, served consecutive terms in that office, from 1796 to 1804. This residence is said to have been damaged by the earthquake of 1811, but it survives as a private residence at Mt. Lebanon, near Paris.

Wood engraving from Lewis Collins's *Historical Sketches of Kentucky,* 1847. Engraved by N. Orr & Richardson, New York, from a drawing by Harrison Eastman.

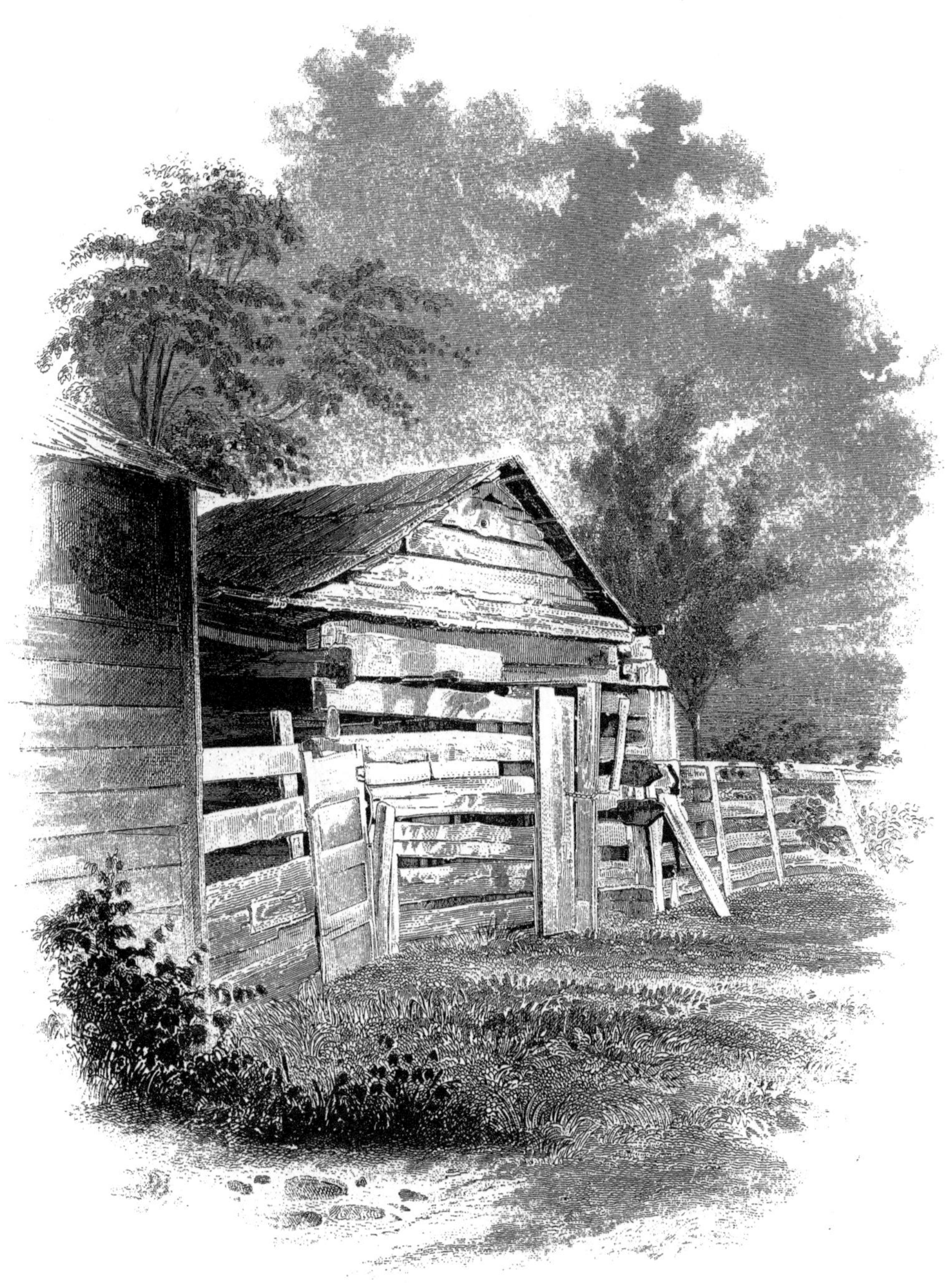

Lincoln was born in 1809 in Hardin County, in that portion later included in Larue County. We are familiar with the Abraham Lincoln Birthplace National Historic Site at Hodgenville, where what is said to be the early cabin is preserved. Richard Collins's *History of Kentucky* records that in February 1872 a log house in Elizabethtown that was once the home of the future president and his mother was torn down. That cabin may be the same one shown here, which recent research indicates may have been built by Thomas Lincoln and lived in thereafter by Thomas and Nancy Hanks Lincoln, with their first child Sarah, before they moved to the Hodgenville site. It was the residence some years later of Mrs. Johnson, the widow of the Elizabethtown jailer, but young Abraham would not have lived there.

Steel engraving from Raymond's *Life and Public Service of Abraham Lincoln,* 1865. Possibly engraved by A.H. Ritchie.

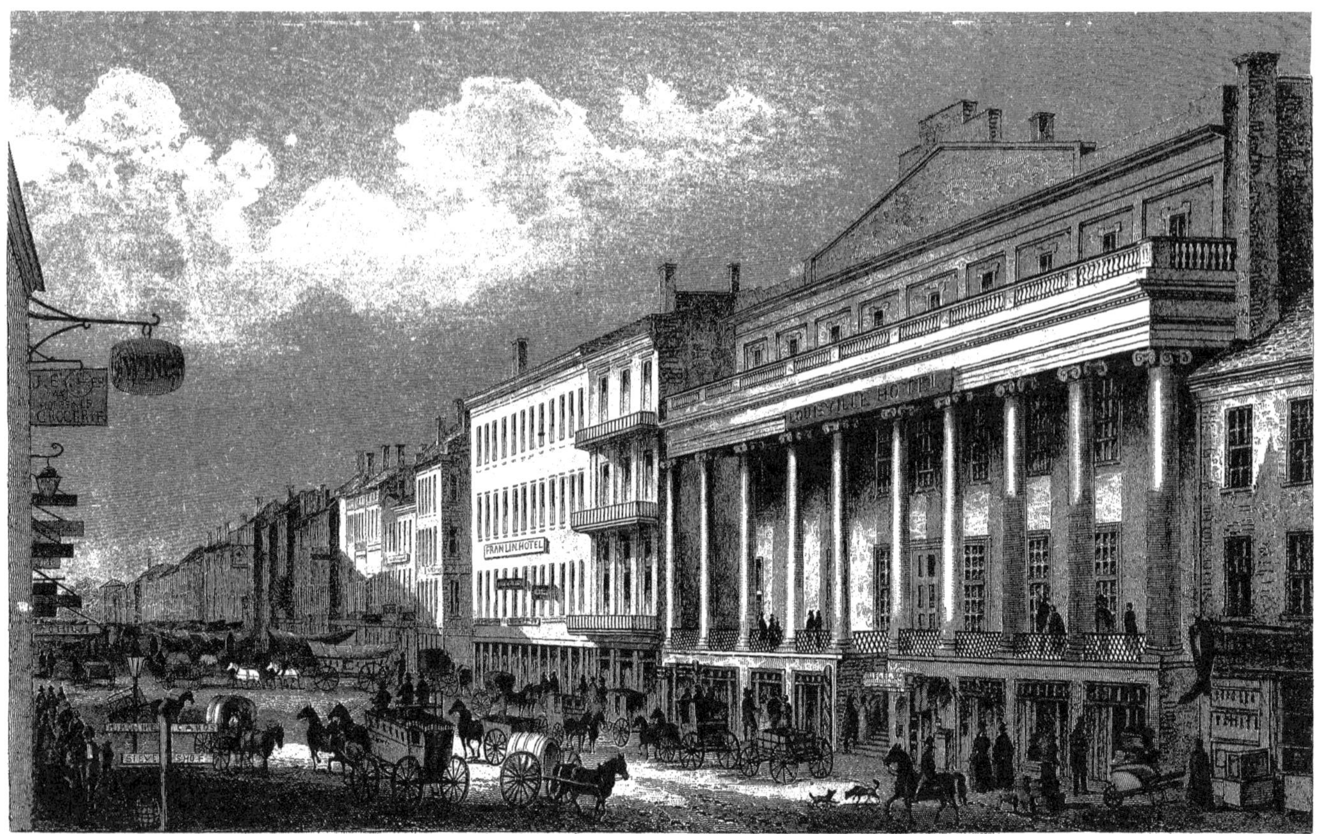

The urban landscape attracted the attention of engravers, and no place in Kentucky attracted them more than Louisville, which was by far the commonwealth's largest city. One of its attractions was the Louisville Hotel, built in 1832 on the south side of Main Street between Sixth and Seventh streets. It was replaced in 1855 with an entirely new building, which stood until 1950. The hotel was once known as "the showplace of the West" because of its cut-glass chandeliers, walnut paneling, art-glass windows, statuary, paintings, and mirrors. Louisville's first city directory of 1832 predicted that the hotel, then under construction, would "surpass in elegance and arrangement any in our western country, and in extent will exceed most in the United States." The hotel's advertisement in the *Louisville Journal* in November 1833 announced its opening and boasted that it would offer nearly two hundred apartments and seventy single lodging rooms, as well as "wines and liquors selected from the most celebrated vaults of New York and Boston."

Copper engraving from *Meyer's Universum*, Hildburghausen, Germany, 1854.

Louisville became Kentucky's largest commercial center, and the first Louisville markethouse, the Speed Market, was erected soon after 1804 on Market Street between Fourth and Fifth streets. There were five public markets, all on Market Street, at the time this view was sketched, and four of the city blocks on Market Street still retain the extra width provided for the market houses. Market masters, city officers appointed to oversee the operation of the houses, operated under city council ordinances, which regulated market masters' duties, hours of business, size and operation of stalls, rents, weights and measures, permissible vehicles, and the care and treatment of the "beasts" used for produce wagons, as well as disposal of trash, wholesomeness of produce and meats, size of rolls of butter (except in the four summer months), "spiritous" liquors, and smoking areas. Two of the original sites on Market Street were turned into tiny parks—between Shelby and Campbell streets, and between Sixteenth and Seventeenth streets—but these were paved over about 1900 for improvements in the Market Street car line.

Wood engraving from *Ballou's Pictorial Drawing-Room Companion,* October 1856. Engraved by Charles F. Damoreau, New York, from a drawing by Samuel S. Kilburn, Boston.

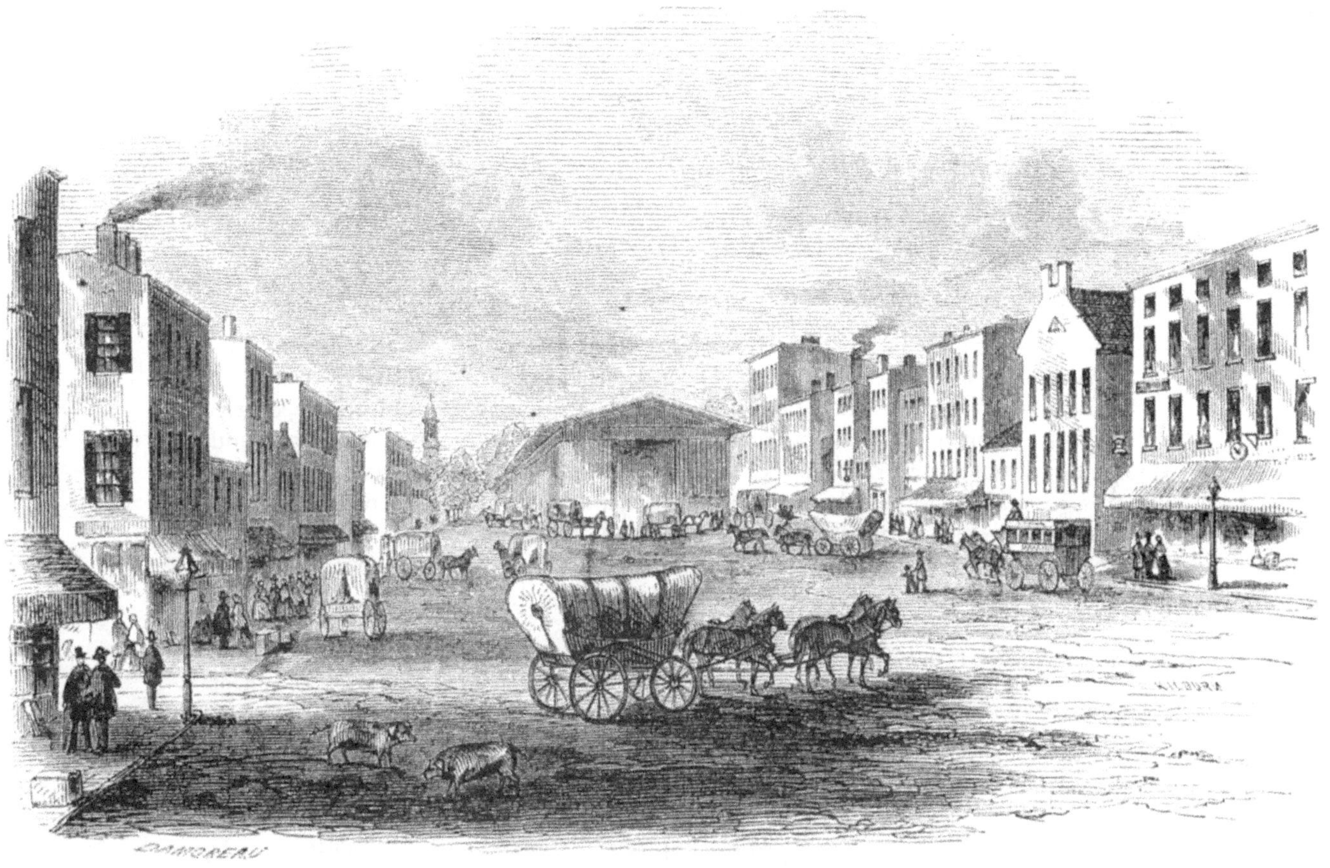

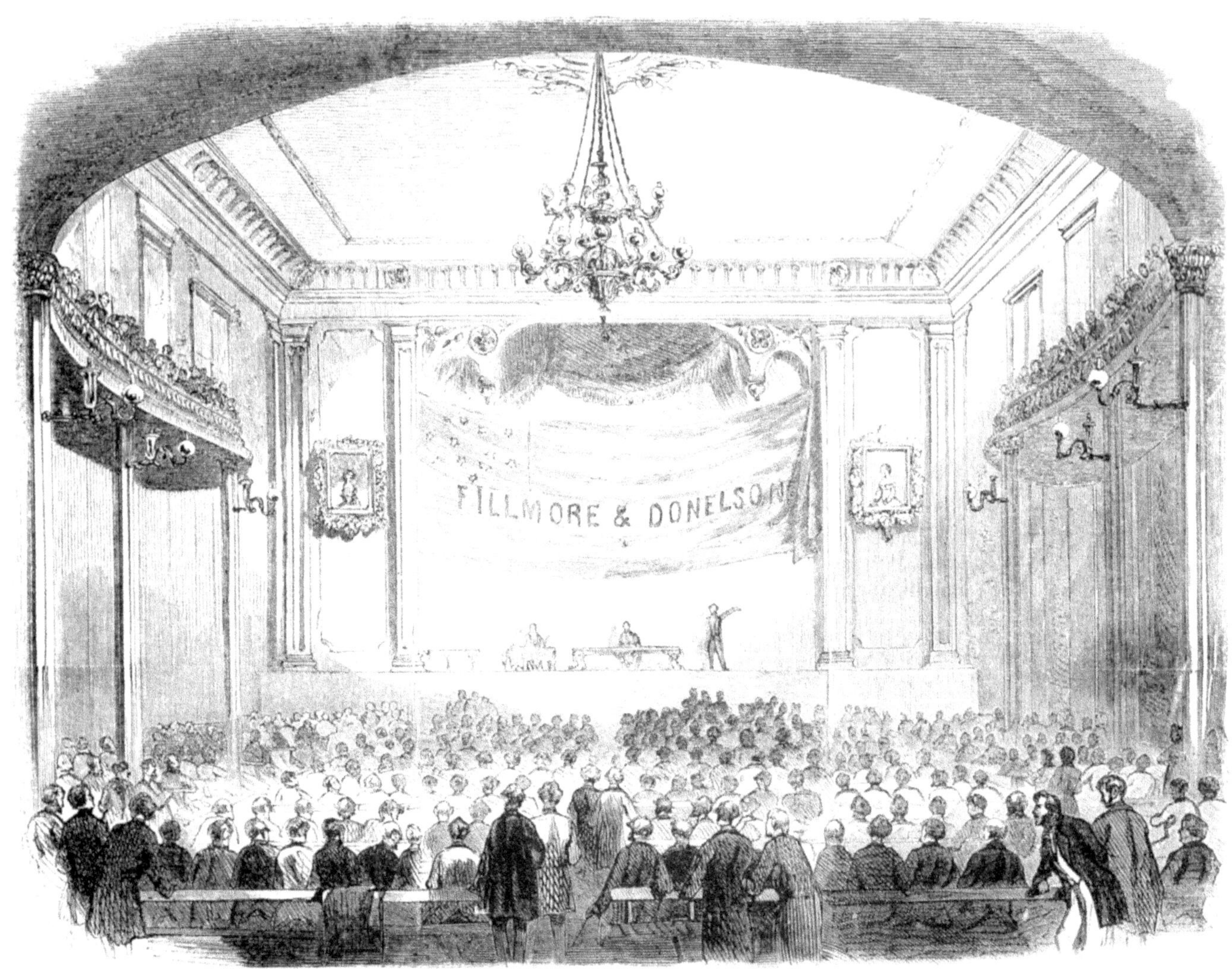

The American party's national convention was held at Louisville's Mozart Hall June 2 and June 3, 1857. The American party had been formed after the Whig party's decline and death. Often known as the Know-Nothing party because of its members' response to questions about it—"I know nothing"—it was identified with anti-Catholic and anti-immigrant stands. In 1855 Kentucky elected the party's nominee as its governor in a race that included a riot in Louisville that left over twenty dead. The party's national convention of 1856, held in Philadelphia, nominated Millard Fillmore for president and Andrew Jackson Donelson of Tennessee for vice-president. In the Louisville session depicted here, most states were represented, although it turned out to be the final meeting of the council.

Wood engraving from *Harper's Weekly*, June 1857.

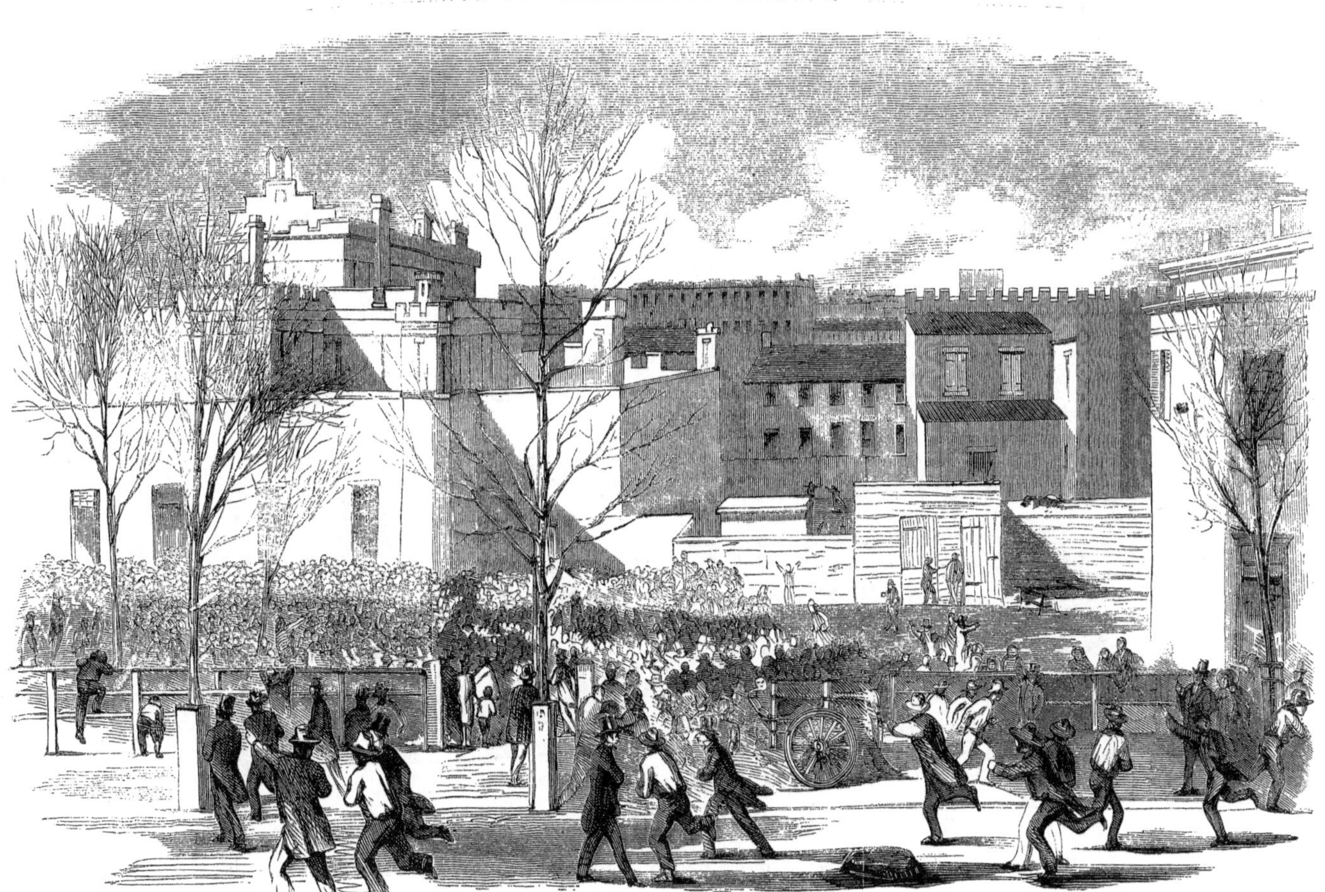

Many Kentuckians held slaves, although the average number they owned was small; not many instances of violence occurred, but fear of uprisings was widespread. Four slaves were charged with murdering four members of the Joyce family at their home on Brier Creek in a remote part of southwestern Jefferson County in December 1856. One of the slaves was found in possession of a watch and coat that had belonged to one of the victims, and his statement implicated the other three slaves. Though all four were acquitted on May 13, 1857, a mob led by a Joyce family member made several attempts to get into the jail, as illustrated here, finally using a cannon from the artillery room to force the defenders to retire. Louisville Mayor William S. Pilcher, attempting to calm the mob, received a severe wound in the face from an object thrown from the crowd. A newspaper reporter wrote that "the rioters who wreaked their vengeance upon the victims appeared to be more awe-stricken than exultant." One of the incarcerated slaves, Jack, who was the property of Hiram Samuels of Bullitt County, was given a razor; he cut his own throat and died instantly. The other Samuels slave was hanged from a tree in the courthouse square, and the remaining two were marched through the square and hung near Fifth Street.

Wood engraving from *Frank Leslie's Illustrated Newspaper,* June 13, 1857. Engraved from a photograph by Webster & Brother, daguerrean photographers of Louisville.

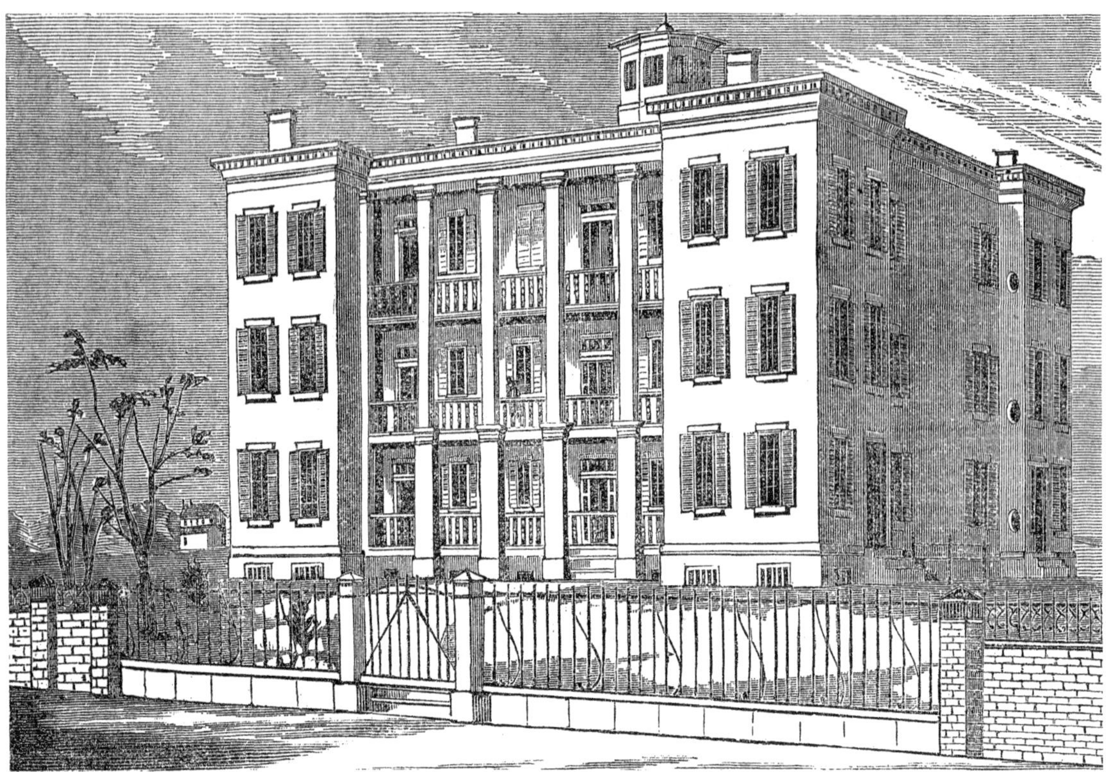

In 1845 the U.S. Treasury Department began a program of building "marine" hospitals on the western rivers to care for ailing rivermen. Maj. Stephen Long of the Corps of Topographical Engineers, formerly an engineer for the B & O Railroad, purchased the building site, prepared the drawings, and obtained the bricks and stone for the U.S. Marine Hospital in Louisville. The location was on the south side of High Street between Ninth and Tenth cross streets (now Twenty-second and Twenty-third streets) in Portland. Work was started late in 1845 but, because of Long's other responsibilities, the hospital did not admit its first patients until January 1852. During the Civil War the building was used as a base supply hospital for the Union army, and it was operated for many years after the war by the Sisters of Mercy. The building still survives as storage for a newer hospital built adjacent to it in 1933.

Wood engraving from *Edwards' Annual Directory,* 1864.

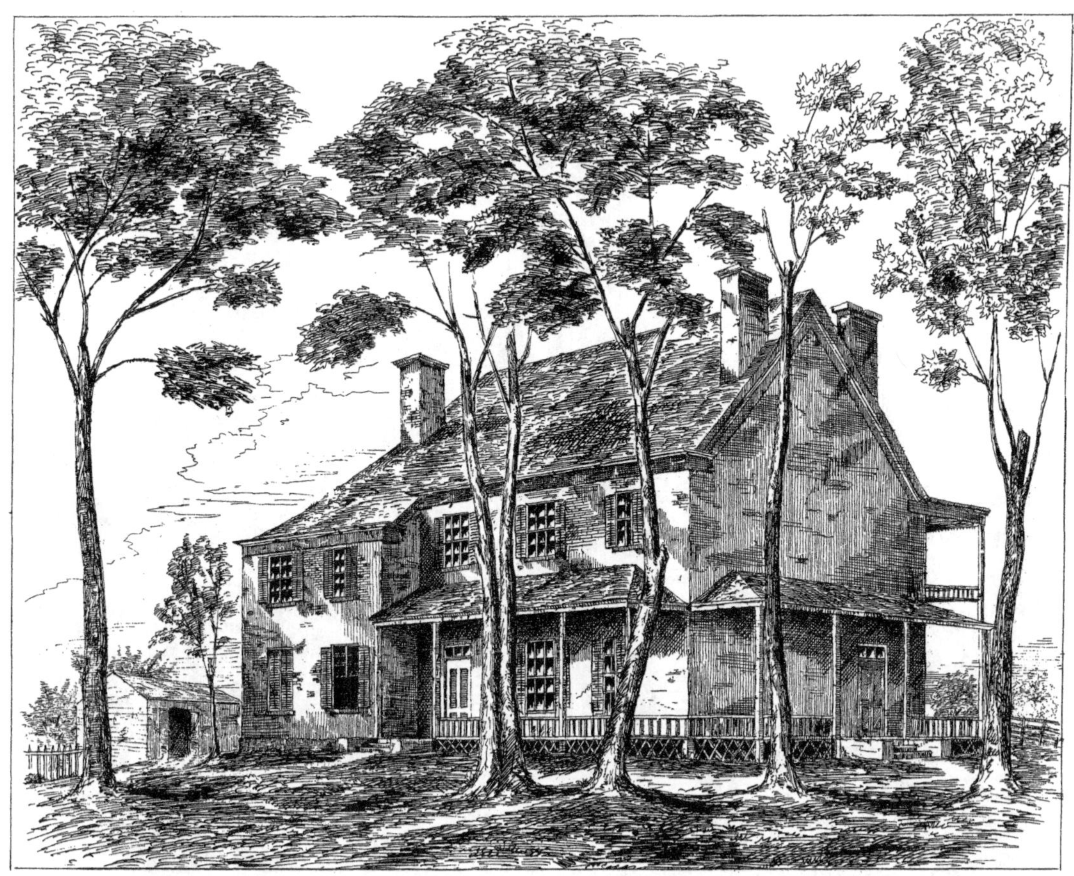

The original house of the Taylor farm, built in eastern Jefferson County by Richard Taylor, father of President Zachary Taylor, was altered and enlarged several times; this engraving presents its "Victorian" appearance. In 1785 Richard Taylor brought three sons, including Zachary, to Kentucky, and six more children were born in the commonwealth. The property passed out of Taylor family ownership in 1867. Substantially damaged in Louisville's 1974 tornado, the house has been maintained in excellent condition and remains a private residence.

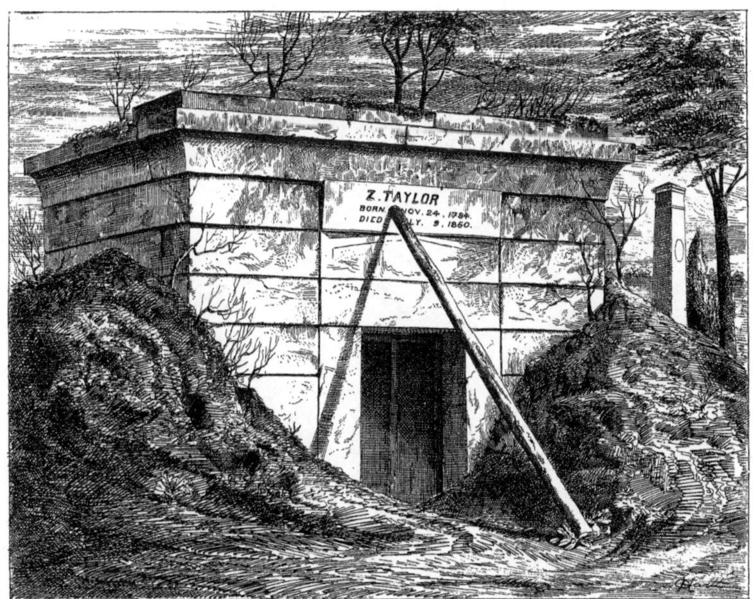

The Taylor family vault and cemetery on the Richard Taylor farm became the centerpiece of Zachary Taylor National Cemetery, just east of Louisville. Sixty Taylor descendants and relatives rest in the original plot, and burials continue to be made there. The vault shown in this view is no longer in use. Zachary and Margaret Smith Taylor now rest in a small tomb built in 1931 a few yards from the early structure and the fine monument erected in memory of the president.

Wood engravings from *The Daily Graphic*, January 19, 1875, engraved by C. Hartt, from a sketch by J.T. Hopkins, Louisville.

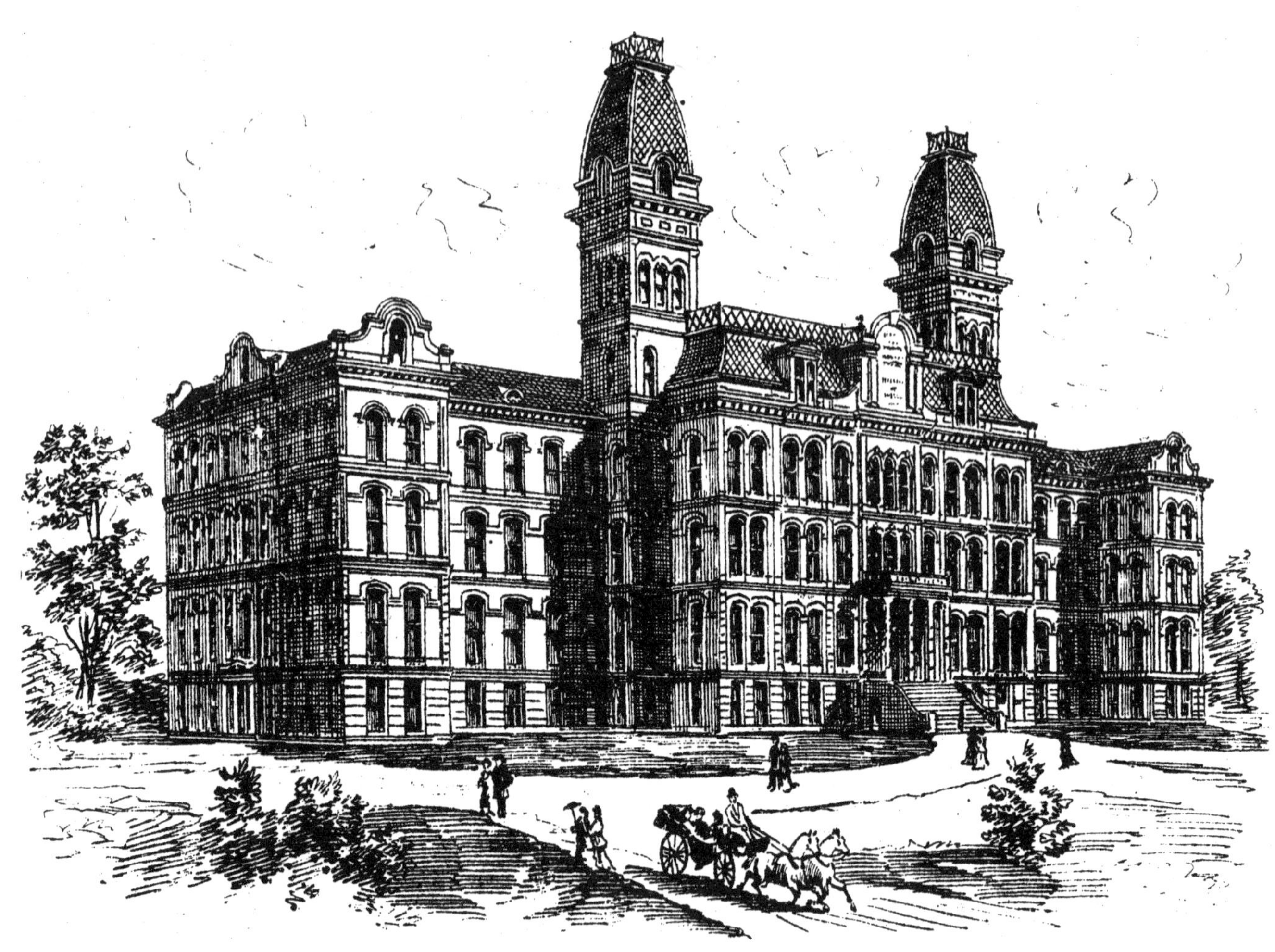

The Masonic Widows' and Orphans' Home in Louisville was incorporated in 1867 and the cornerstone laid October 1869. The north wing was completed a year later. Richard H. Collins took note in his 1874 history that the portion of the building shown here was the home of one hundred children. The unfinished sections were contracted for in early 1874—a main building and the south wing—to cost $48,000, and these were completed in 1875 with room for five hundred. Built of brick and stone, it was the largest and most imposing charitable institution in Louisville. The central part of the building was destroyed soon after completion by the windstorm of June 1875 but was immediately rebuilt and dedicated in October 1876. The building stood on the east side of Second Street between Bloom and Shipp streets; this was later the site of the relocated Louisville Girls High School.

Wood engraving from *The Daily Graphic,* April 29, 1875.

A widespread railroad strike throughout the eastern states caused violence to erupt in many places in 1877. Louisville experienced a mild disturbance that year when men employed on the sewer and reservoir construction projects struck for higher wages. They demanded an increase of twenty-seven cents per day. They advanced through the streets, shouted down the mayor's address to them at the courthouse, and marched in procession to the Nashville and the Short line depots, breaking home and store windows and streetlamps as they went. The *Courier-Journal* of July 25 describes the "disorderly proceedings of last evening" in which the mayor was "hooted" at the courthouse, and the windows of his home and others "were stoned and smashed by thieves, beats, bummers, and thugs and irresponsible outlaws who need to be met with powder and bullets."

Wood engraving from Pinkerton's *Strikers, Communists, Tramps and Detectives*, 1878. Engraved by Earlie from a drawing by J. Beale.

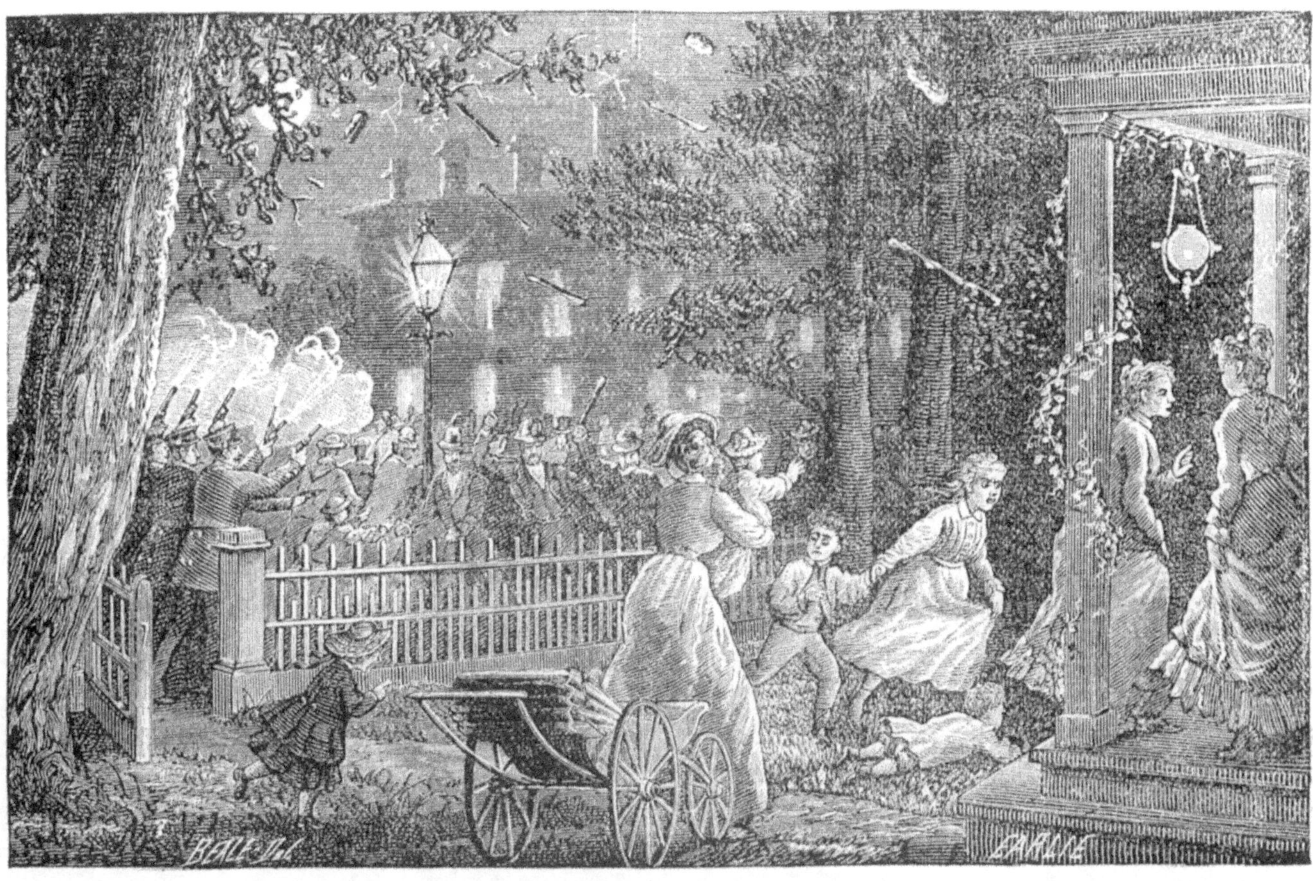

President Rutherford B. Hayes spoke on September 17, 1877, from a platform in front of the Galt House hotel, where a grand evening reception was held for him. The group shown in the illustration to the right includes Mrs. Hayes, Secretary of State Evans, Secretary of the Interior Schurz, Secretary of War McCrary, Postmaster General Key, Governor Van Zandt of Rhode Island, and Governor Matthews of West Virginia. The Louisville Industrial Exposition had opened September 4 for its sixth season, and Hayes's program included both an afternoon and an early evening visit to the show, with opportunities for personal contact with the citizenry of Louisville. The formal reception in the parlors of the Galt House was called "the great social event of the year." Some observers took the president's visit as a sign that the strife of the Civil War could be forgotten and party differences ignored. Confederate veterans were among those various groups that marched in the welcoming procession.

Wood engraving from *Harper's Weekly*, October 1877, from a drawing by I.P. Pranishnikoff.

This panoramic scene of Louisville was sketched from the Kentucky Institution for the Education of the Blind, a building erected in 1855, that overlooked the city from the east and was itself visible for miles in Jefferson County and southern Indiana. It was razed in 1967 after modern facilities were provided on the school campus. The Fink railroad bridge completed in 1870 is prominent in the view.

Wood engraving from *Frank Leslie's Illustrated Newspaper*, June 5, 1880, from a drawing by Walter Goater.

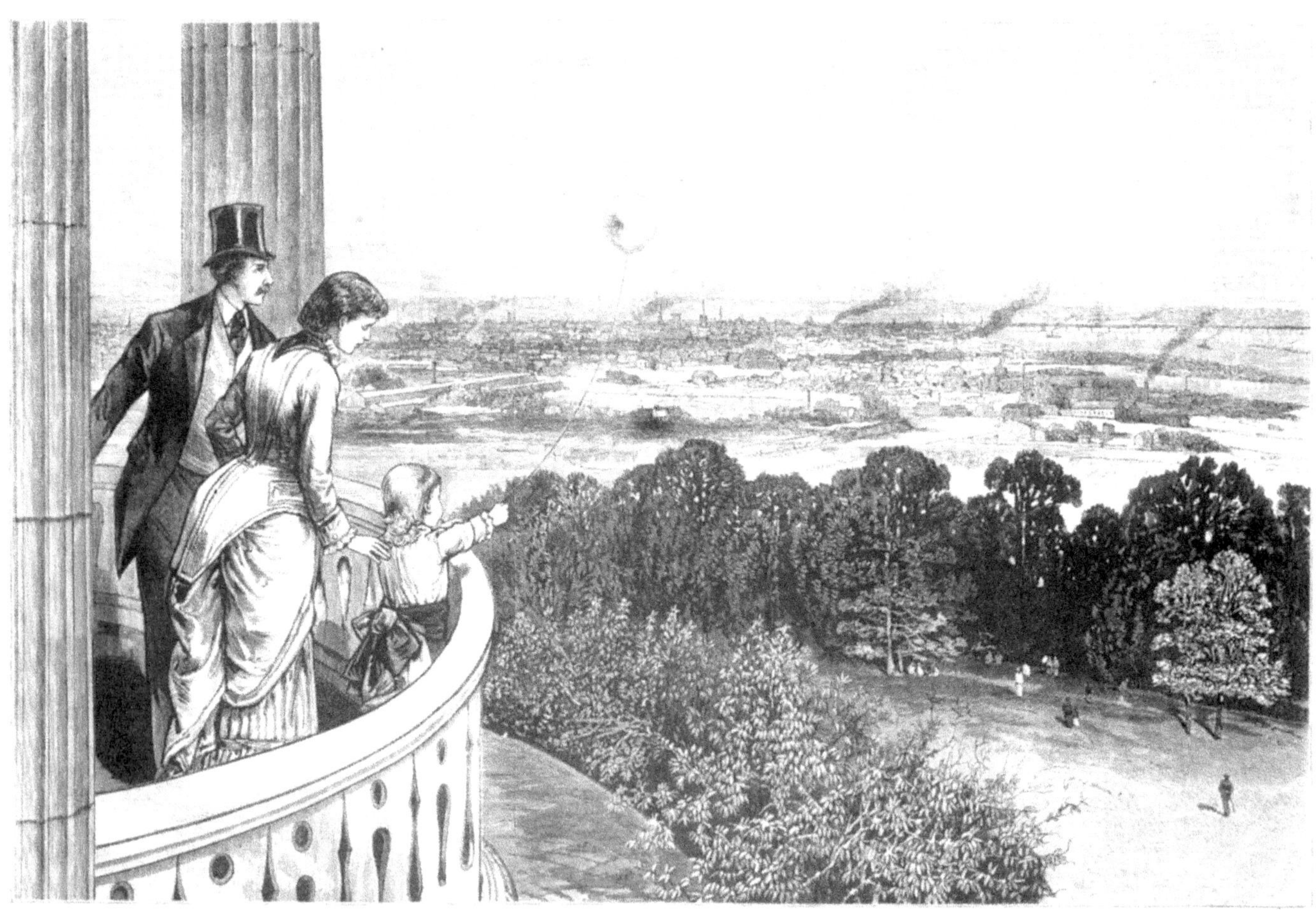

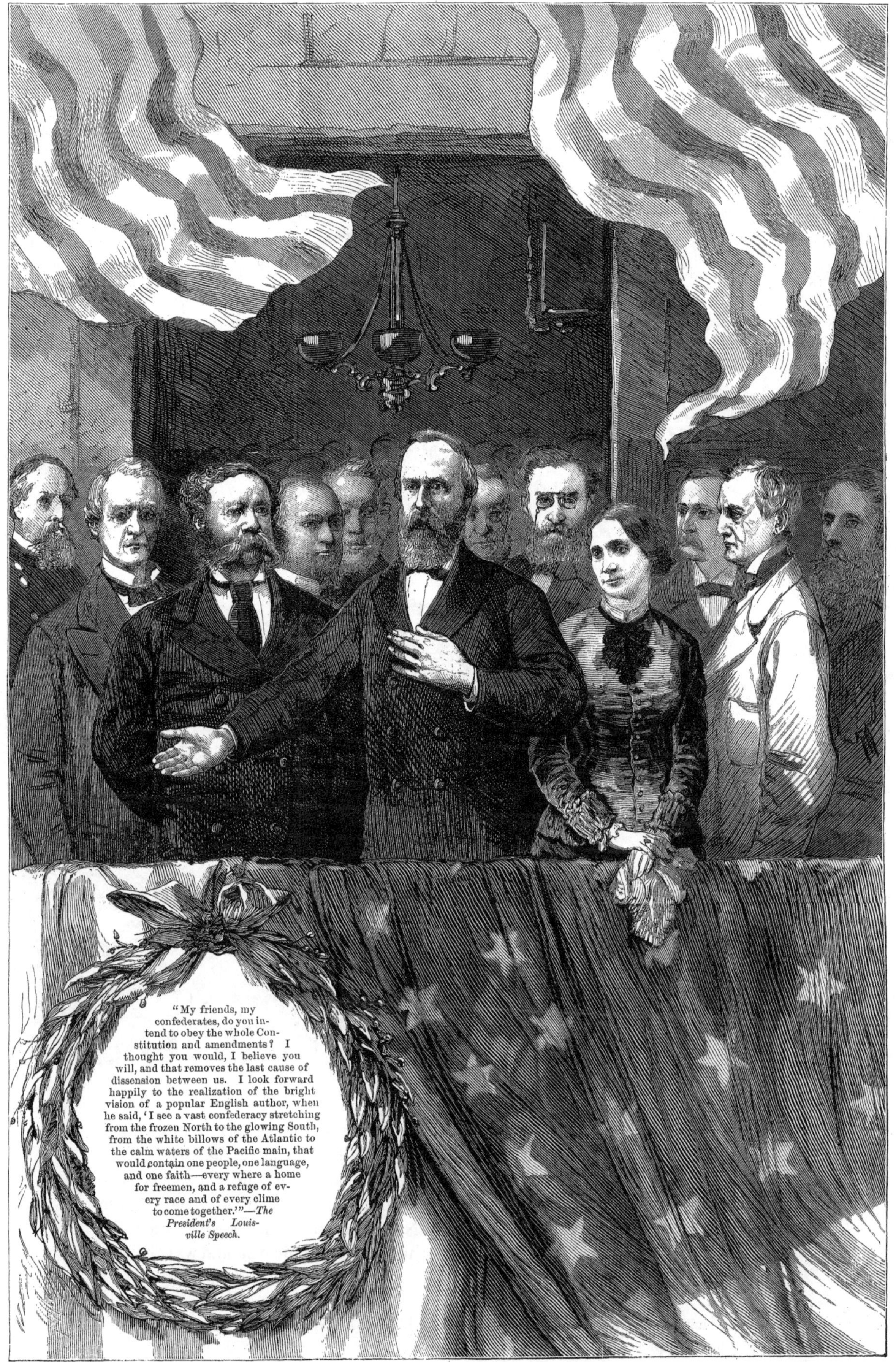
"My friends, my
confederates, do you in-
tend to obey the whole Constitution and amendments? I
thought you would, I believe you
will, and that removes the last cause of
dissension between us. I look forward
happily to the realization of the bright
vision of a popular English author, when
he said, 'I see a vast confederacy stretching
from the frozen North to the glowing South,
from the white billows of the Atlantic to
the calm waters of the Pacific main, that
would contain one people, one language,
and one faith—every where a home
for freemen, and a refuge of every race and of every clime
to come together.'"—*The
President's Louis-
ville Speech.*

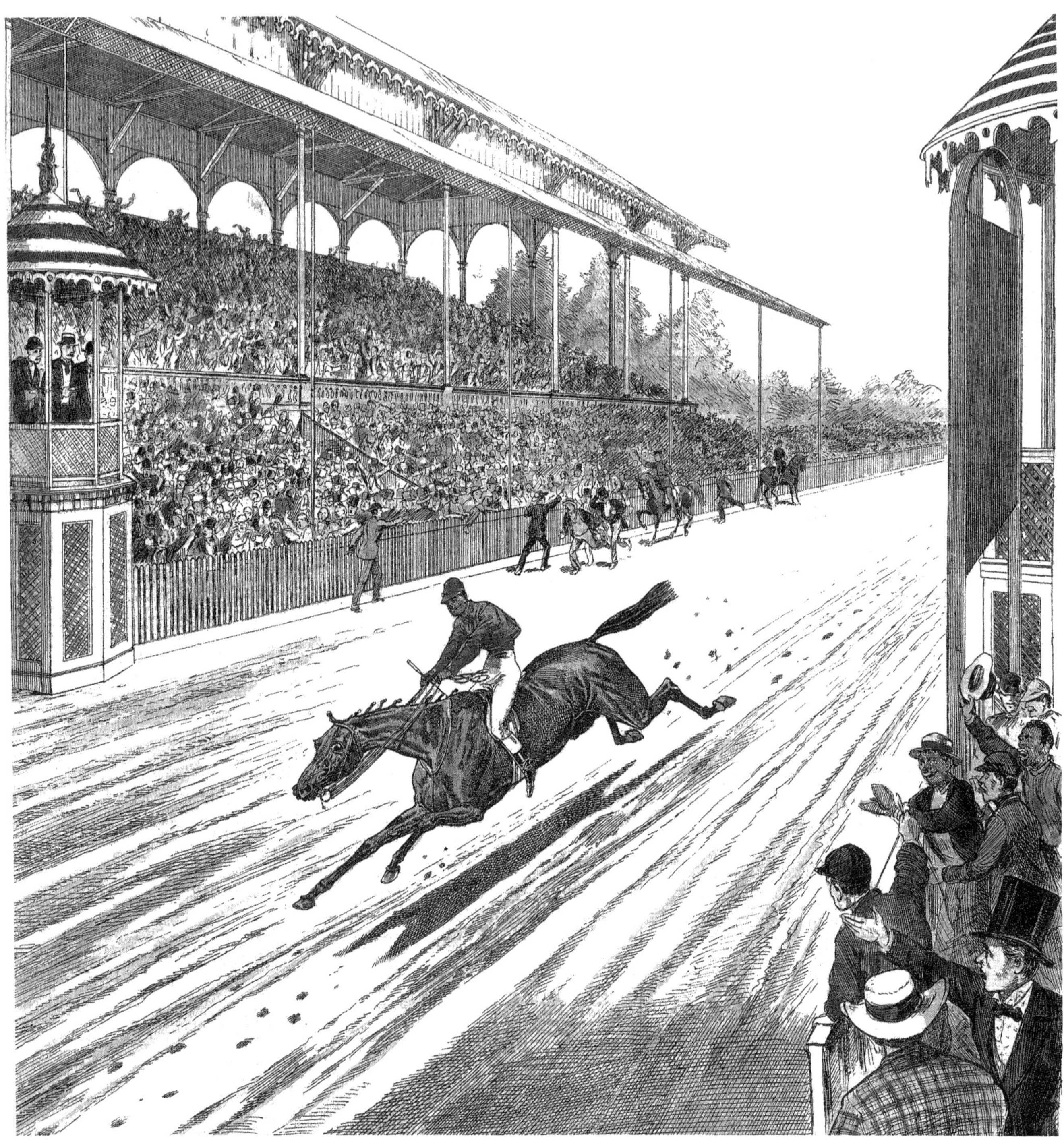

Racing became more intimately associated with Louisville as the century went on. The well-publicized match race between Ten Broeck and Mollie McCarthy on July 4, 1878, drew a crowd of thirty-five thousand local citizens and visitors to the Louisville Jockey Club track—known later as Churchill Downs. Reporters from at least twenty-five out-of-town newspapers as far distant as San Francisco and New York attended. Bluegrass-bred Ten Broeck distanced the Californian Mollie McCarthy in the four-mile heat and was declared the winner.

Hand-tinted wood engraving from *The Daily Graphic,* July 1878, from a drawing by Edward C. Boyd, a Louisville artist employed by the publisher.

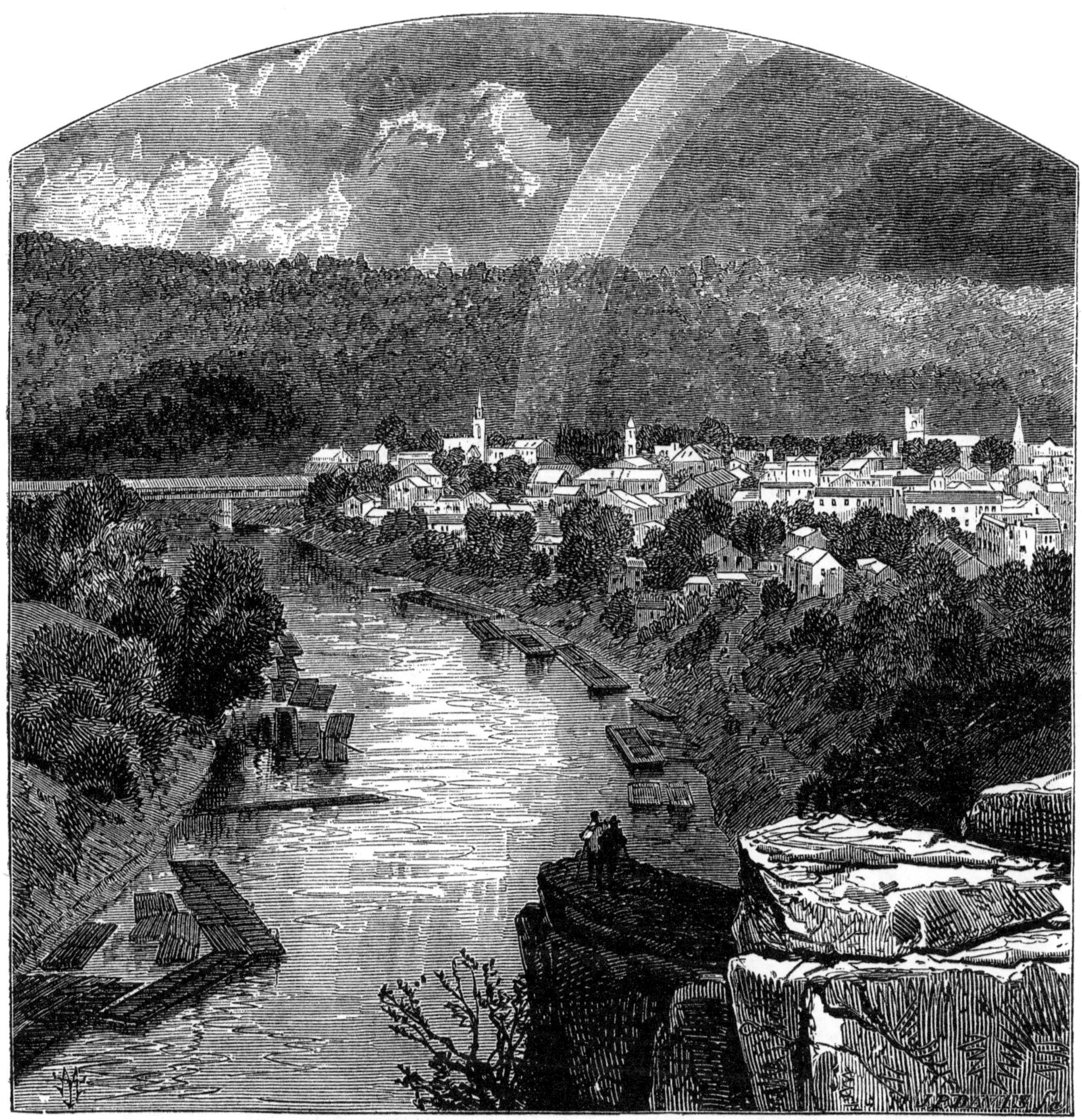

It is said that Frankfort's name perpetuates the memory of Stephen Frank, who was killed in 1780 in a skirmish between a group of hunters and a band of Indians and whose camping site was thereafter called "Frank's Ford." The city was founded by General James Wilkinson and chartered by the Virginia legislature in October 1786. It was selected as the state capital by a group of commissioners appointed in 1792 by the new officers of the commonwealth.

Wood engraving from *Scribner's Monthly,* December 1974. Engraved by J.P. Davis.

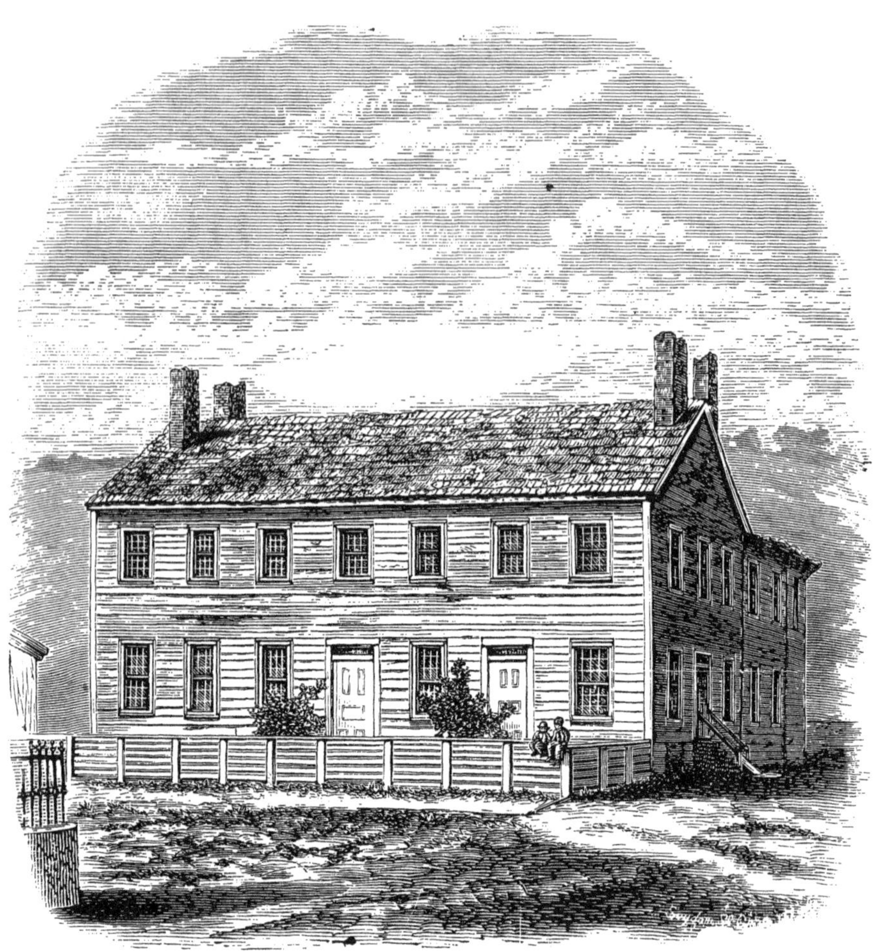

The first location of Kentucky's government house in Frankfort was a temporary one, a two-story log building on the east side of Main Street. Sessions of the legislature were held there in June and November 1792. When those charged with selecting a location for the capital decided upon Frankfort—in consideration of several inducements offered by Andrew Holmes and other citizens of the town—the Holmes house, shown here, at Wapping and Wilkinson streets, became in 1793 the next temporary statehouse. After the completion of the first permanent statehouse, the Holmes house was bought by Maj. Thomas Love and was a popular inn for many years. The building was used until 1870.

Wood engraving from Lewis Collins's *History of Kentucky,* 1847.

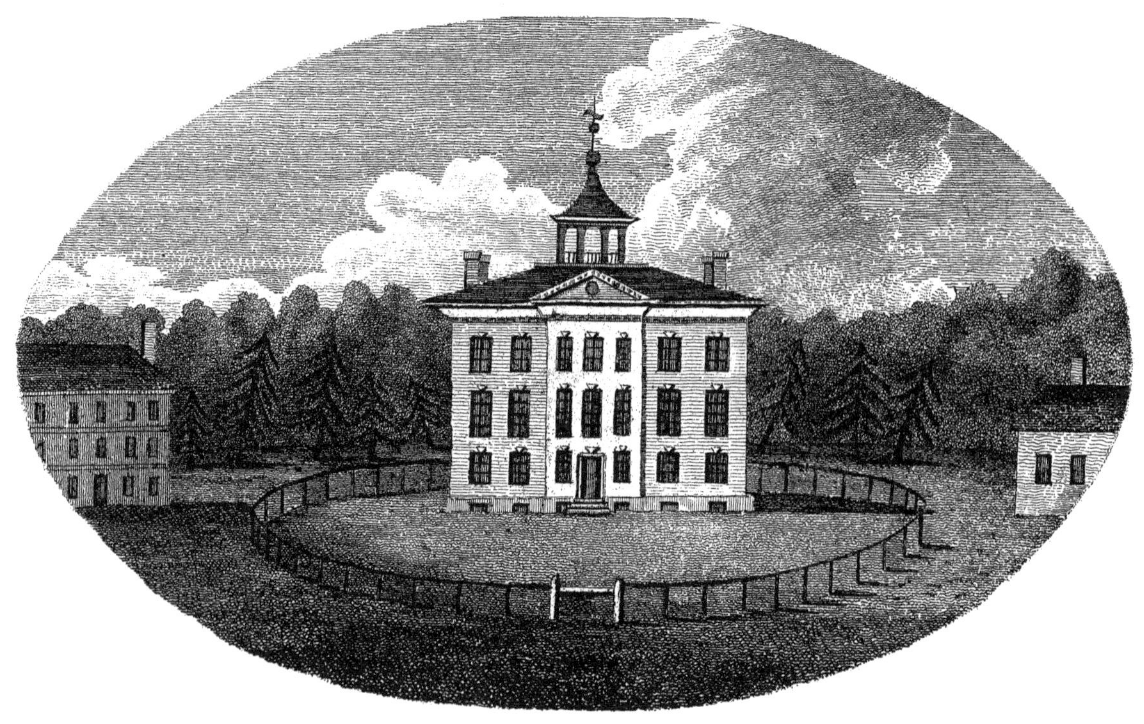

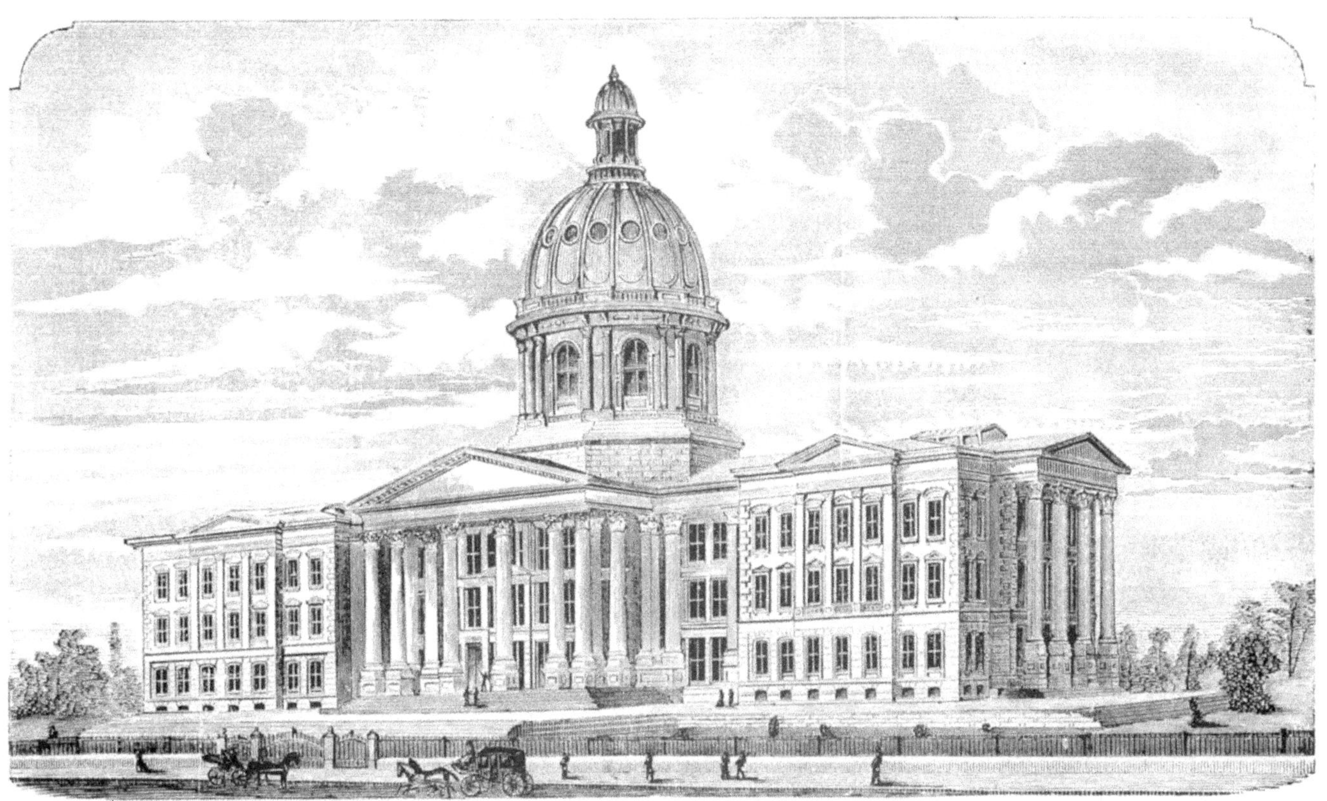

After the end of the Civil War, a new capitol building was proposed to replace the Gideon Shryock building, which had served as a statehouse since 1830. As the first phase of construction, only the east wing of the proposed building was erected, during the period from 1869 to 1872, and the earlier building was saved because the state did not have funds for further work. When money was finally available—in the twentieth century—space needs had grown, and a larger building was designed to be built on the other side of the river. The new building was referred to as the "fire-proof public offices" in early discussions and legislation. It is currently used by the Kentucky Historical Society for its museum, library, offices, and workrooms.

Wood engraving from Richard Collins's *History of Kentucky,* 1874.

Between Louisville and Lexington, Frankfort often found itself dominated by one or the other of these cities, but as the capital of Kentucky it began to grow in its own right. The statehouse in Frankfort was the first permanent capitol in Kentucky, built of local limestone. It was occupied by the third General Assembly in November 1794 and was destroyed by fire in November 1813. The second and the third buildings designed as permanent capitols were erected on the original site facing Broadway between Lewis and Madison streets. This rare contemporary view (*left*) of the first capitol varies considerably from the engraving in Richard Collins's 1874 history.

Copper engraving from *New York Magazine,* July 1796. Engraved by John Scoles, New York, from a sketch made by a correspondent for the magazine.

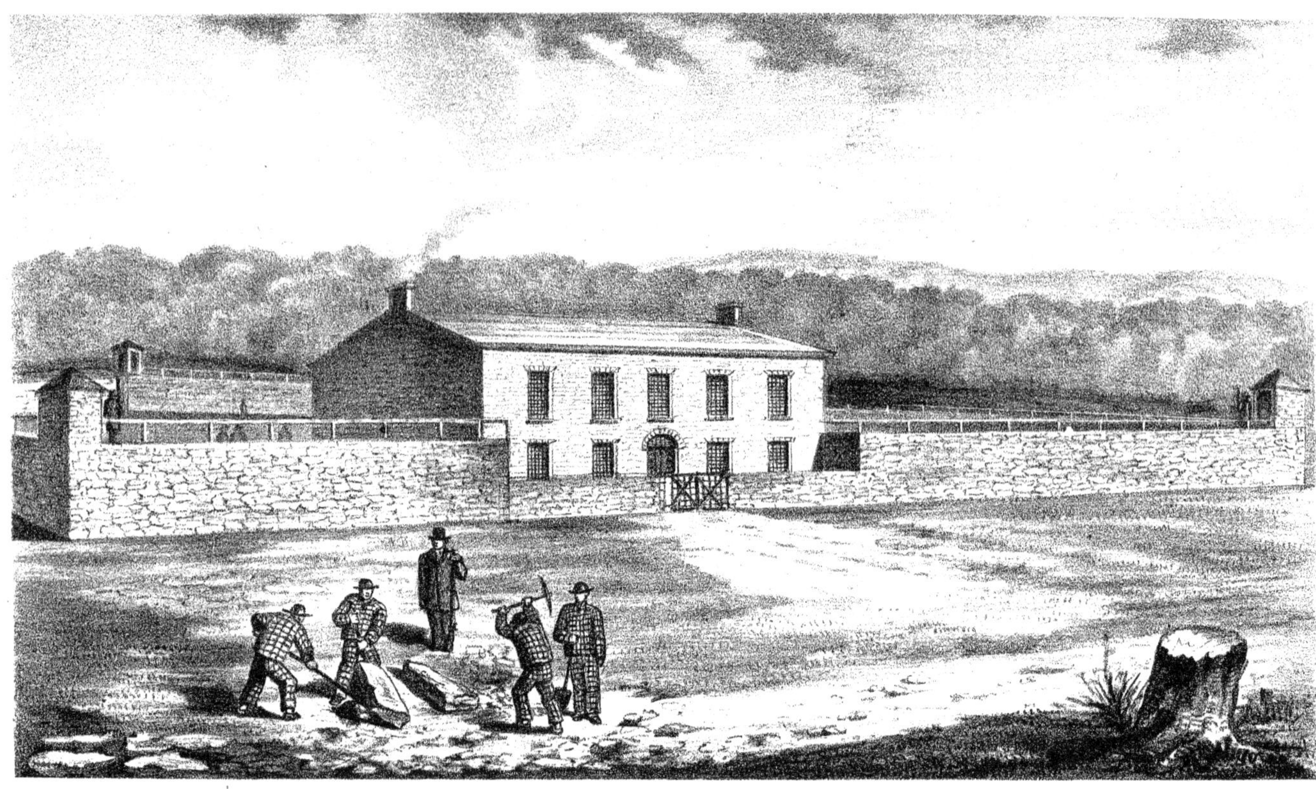

This view of the first penitentiary in Kentucky shows the appearance of the prison before major alterations in 1823. As early as 1801, one year after the prison opened, the board of inspectors noted that the walls were not sufficiently protected and ordered them to be capped with brick, wood, or stone. In the period from 1816 to 1825, 319 prisoners were received and there were thirty-one escapes, these principally over or through the walls. During that period the longest term given to any prisoner was seventeen years, but only a few sentences were for more than four years; the average was about three. With 114 gubernatorial pardons and the escapes, the prison population remained well below one hundred, but, even then, crowded quarters were a problem. Governor Slaughter's message to the legislature in 1818 stated that "the building is not sufficient to accommodate the number confined." The keeper's report in September 1818 showed fifty-seven convicts in the prison, in seventeen cells, each six feet by eight feet.

Lithograph from Sneed's *History and Mode of Management of the Kentucky Penitentiary,* 1860. Lithograph by Henry Hart & Dillon M. Mapother, Louisville.

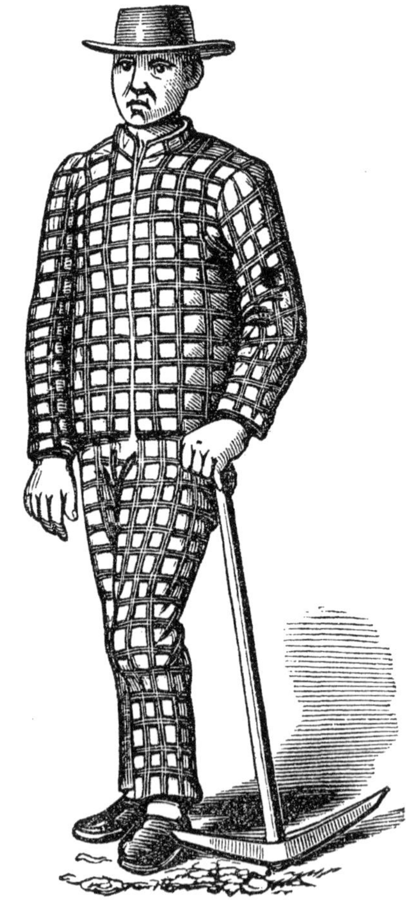

Before the first prisoner was received at the new Kentucky Penitentiary in 1800, the prison inspectors appointed by the Franklin County Court adopted as the required prison wearing apparel "in the summer season, country linen for shirts, overalls and hunting shirts; the linen to be checked with deep yellow, the diamonds one inch square; the hunting shirts to reach below the hips. In the winter, suits of country linsey, same make and figure, with an under jackcoat, shoes and socks, a hat made of leather, with a flat crown, and a brim about three inches wide." In 1826, prison keeper Joel Scott reported that his prisoners were clothed in summer with a tow linen shirt and pantaloons and in winter, a denim hunting shirt, vest, hat, shoes, and socks of variegated colors.

Wood engraving from Sneed's *History and Mode of Management of the Kentucky Penitentiary,* 1860.

William Sneed's history of the penitentiary, in which this birds-eye view from Blanton's Hill appeared, recorded the history of the prison to 1860. Up to that time, about three thousand convicts had been received at the prison and the number in confinement in December 1859 was 290. Jeremiah W. South had just finished his first year as keeper; he reported his prisoners to be in good health, but their living and working conditions needed much improvement. In addition, he said, the increased rent imposed upon him by the legislature, the new allowance of coffee for the convicts, and the doubling of time for rest at dinner justified his call for an investigation by a committee of the legislature.

Lithograph from Sneed's *History and Mode of Management of the Kentucky Penitentiary,* 1860. Lithograph by Henry Hart & Dillon M. Mapother, Louisville, from a photograph by C.A. Clarke, Frankfort.

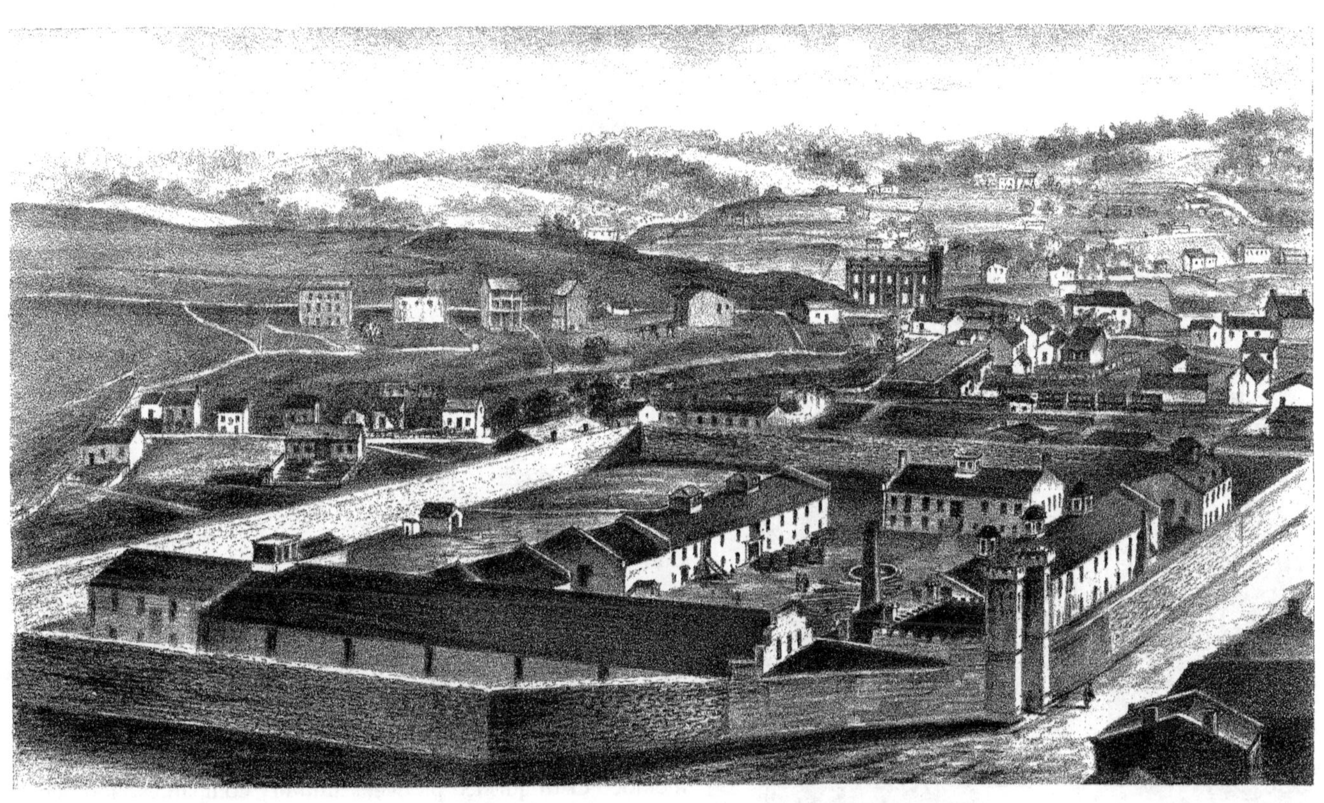

John Mason Brown of Frankfort is given credit for introducing the idea of a corporation to own and operate a public cemetery in Frankfort, following the example of the Mt. Auburn, a garden cemetery started by the Massachusetts Horticultural Society. The Frankfort Cemetery was incorporated in 1845 by the General Assembly and began with a thirty-two-acre tract then known as Hunter's Green. The cemetery now contains one hundred acres. The winding lanes, beautiful trees, and great variety of monuments contribute to the cemetery's charm. It has been called "Kentucky's Westminster Abbey," for among those buried there are hundreds of Kentucky's leading military men, statesmen, political figures, authors, and artists.

Wood engraving from *Scribner's Monthly,* New York, December 1874. Engraved by Treat.

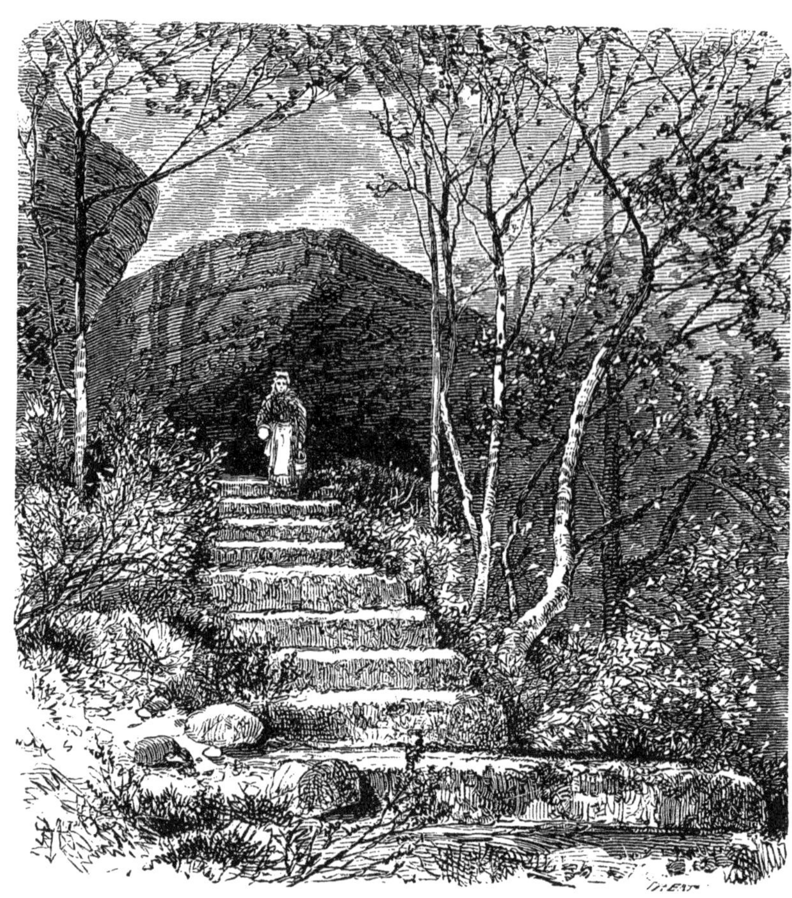

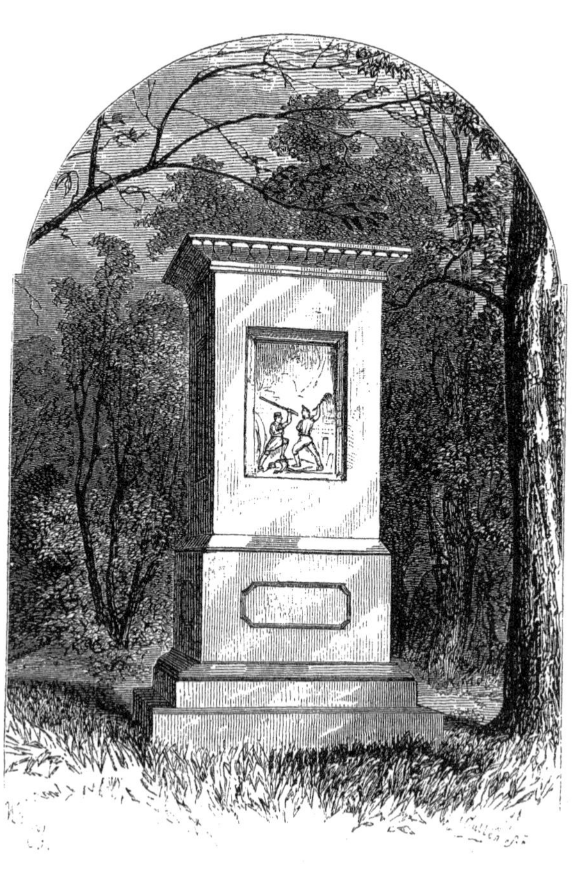

Daniel Boone died in September 1820 at the home of his son-in-law in Charette Village, Missouri, and was buried near there on the banks of the Missouri River. In accordance with measures adopted by the Kentucky legislature, the remains of Boone and his wife Rebecca were removed from Missouri and reinterred in the public cemetery at Frankfort on September 13, 1845. A procession more than a mile in length accompanied the coffins to the graves. It included distinguished pioneers, military companies, and benevolent and fraternal groups. Boone's monument was built by the state in 1862, was damaged by federal soldiers during the Civil War, repaired in 1868 by order of the legislature, and subsequently damaged over the years by souvenir hunters. It was completely rebuilt in 1910.

Wood engraving from *Scribner's Monthly,* December 1874. Engraved by Cullen from a drawing by J. Wells Champney, Deerfield, Mass., and New York.

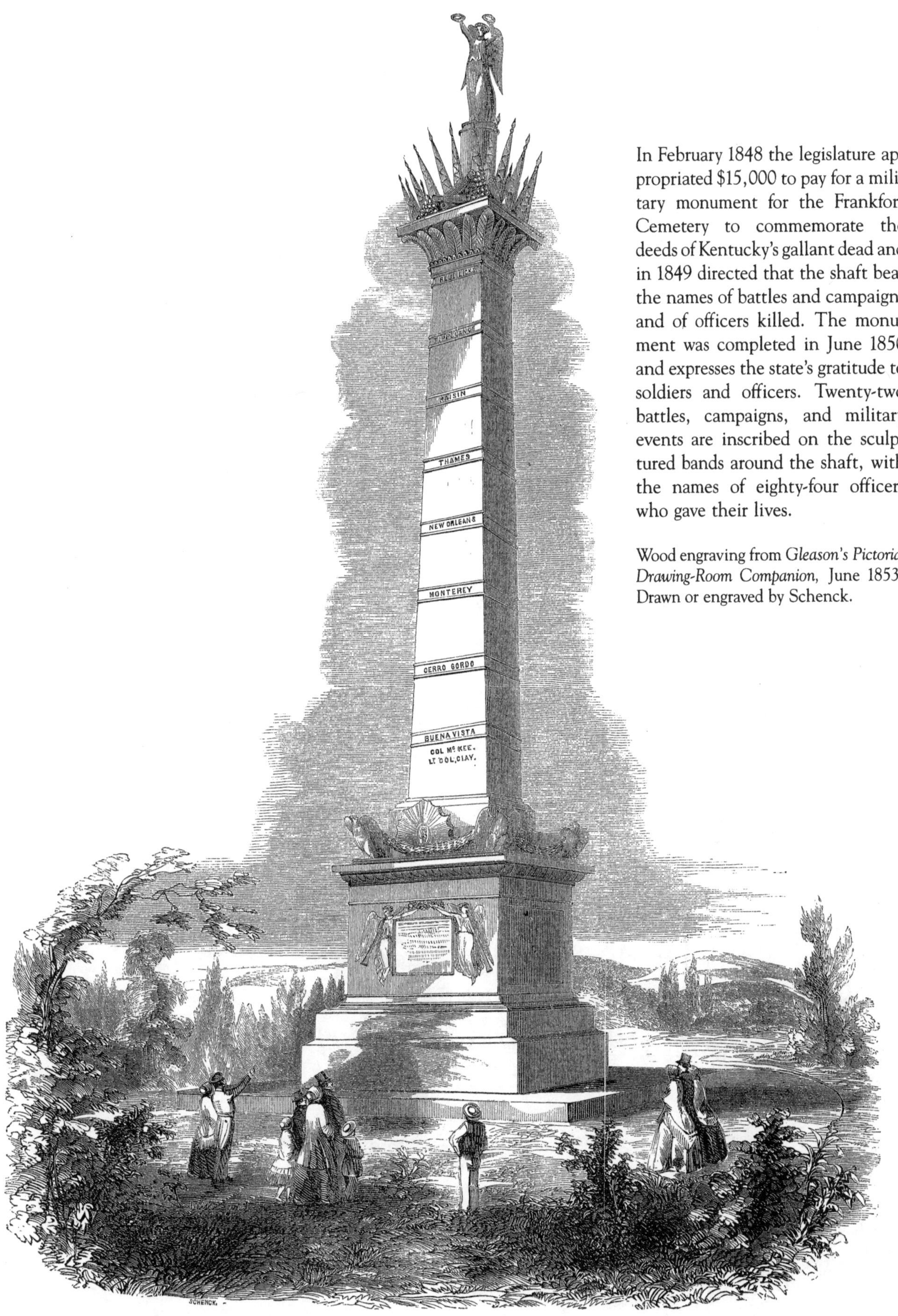

In February 1848 the legislature appropriated $15,000 to pay for a military monument for the Frankfort Cemetery to commemorate the deeds of Kentucky's gallant dead and in 1849 directed that the shaft bear the names of battles and campaigns and of officers killed. The monument was completed in June 1850 and expresses the state's gratitude to soldiers and officers. Twenty-two battles, campaigns, and military events are inscribed on the sculptured bands around the shaft, with the names of eighty-four officers who gave their lives.

Wood engraving from *Gleason's Pictorial Drawing-Room Companion,* June 1853. Drawn or engraved by Schenck.

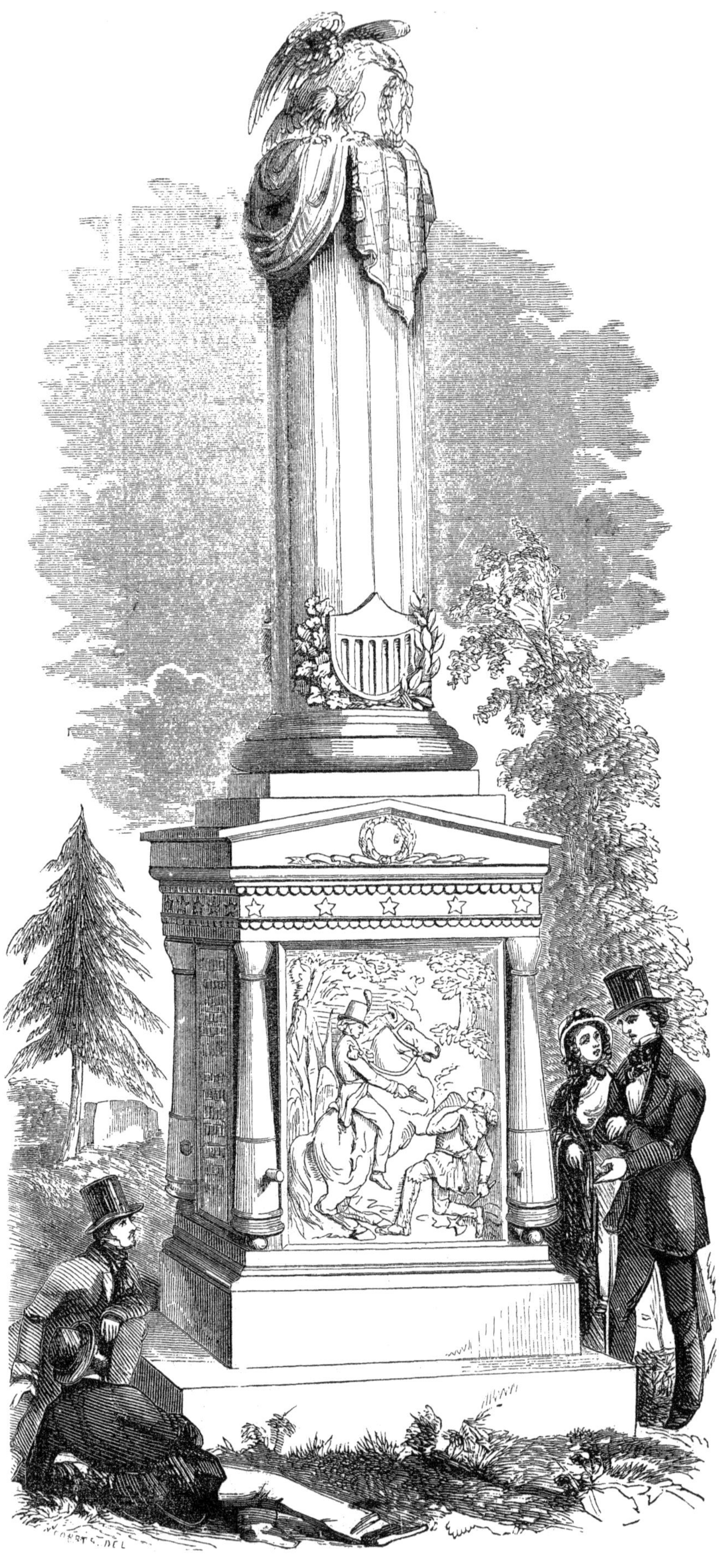

This monument in Frankfort was erected in memory of Richard M. Johnson, who was born in Jefferson County in 1780 and made Scott County his home for much of his life. He went to a country school and to Transylvania University, then studied the law under two reputable jurists. At age nineteen he entered that profession, served in the Kentucky legislature from 1802 to 1804, and was a U.S. congressman from 1807 to 1819 and from 1829 to 1837. Between those years in the House of Representatives, he served as U.S. senator from 1819 to 1829. He ran for vice-president in 1836 on the slate with Martin Van Buren and was elected to that office by the Senate when no candidate could claim a majority of the electoral votes. In 1840 he stood again with Van Buren against Harrison and Tyler and was defeated. Much of Johnson's fame came from the fact that he was credited with killing the Indian chief Tecumseh during the Battle of the Thames River, near Detroit, in October 1813. A controversy raged for a number of years after the battle concerning the correct version of that incident, but the bas-relief on the Frankfort monument portrays Johnson killing the chief. Johnson died in November 1850 in Frankfort while serving in the General Assembly.

Wood engraving from *Ballou's Pictorial Drawing-Room Companion,* 1863, from a drawing by a correspondent.

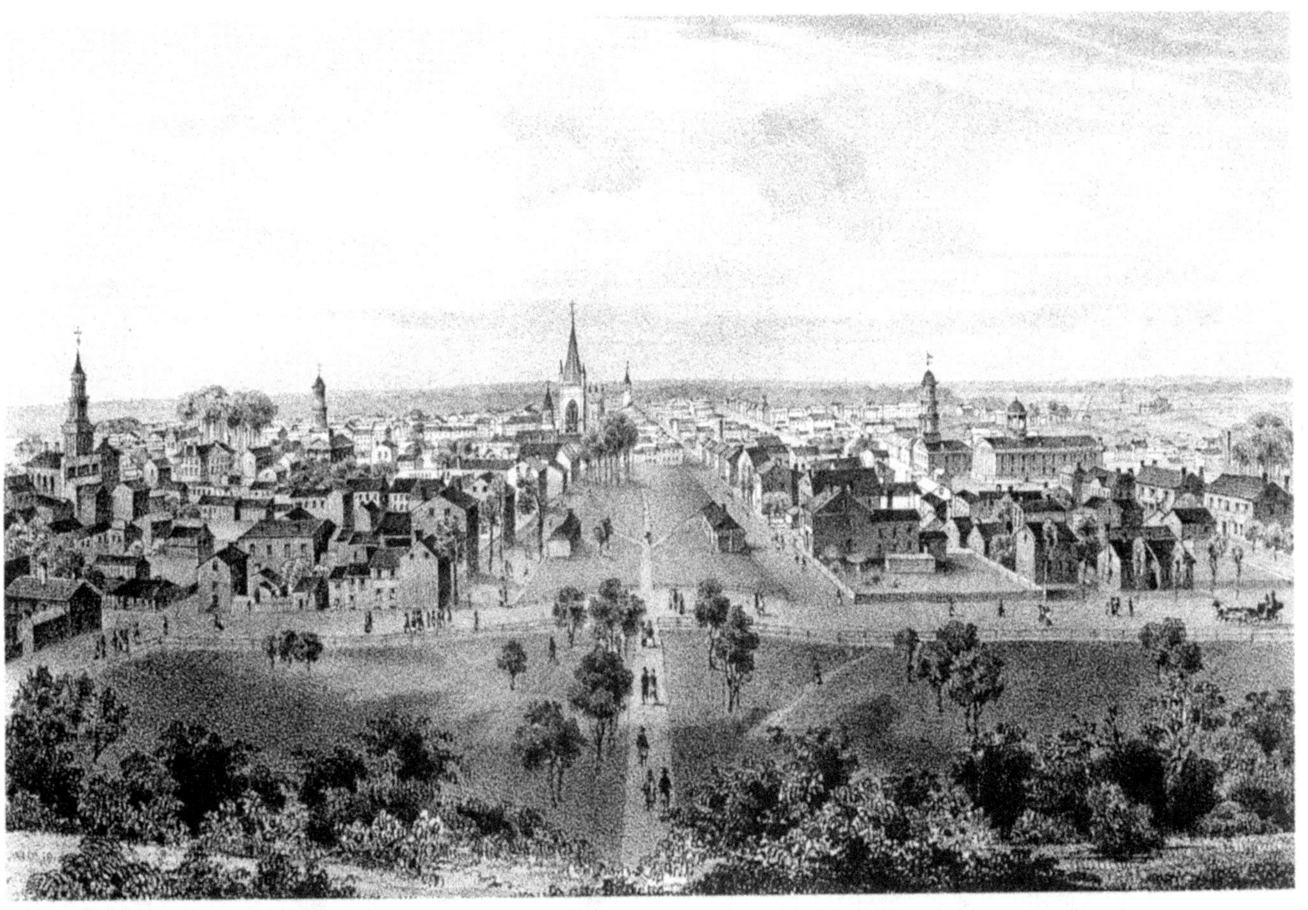

Lexington in the first third of the nineteenth century was the state's cultural center, its "Athens of the West." The view of Lexington shown here is seen from the dome of Morrison Chapel at Transylvania University. Gratz Park appears in the center foreground. The large spire at the center of the view was that of the Second Presbyterian Church, destroyed later by fire. The taller steeple in the right half of the view was that of the Christian Church, and the tall steeple at the extreme left belonged to St. Catharine's Academy.

Lithograph from Onken's *Western Scenery*, 1851, from a drawing by Ferdinand von Laer, Cincinnati.

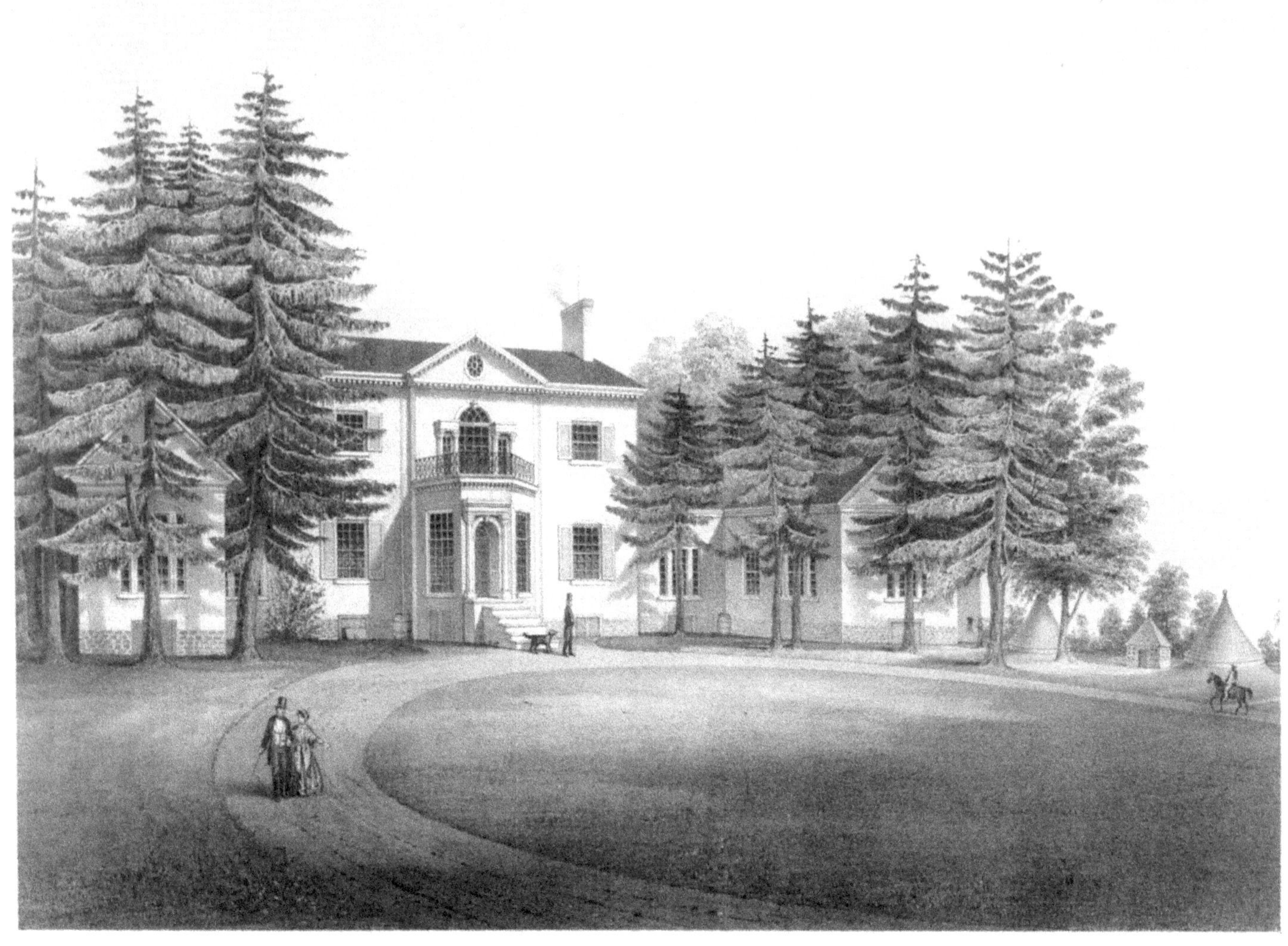

This illustration of Ashland, home of Henry Clay, was published in the year of his death. Lewis Collins included a view of Ashland in his history book of 1847 and described it as a spacious brick mansion, without architectural pretension, surrounded by lawns and groves planted with every variety of American shrubbery and forest tree. The estate consisted of "500 or 600 acres of the best land of Kentucky" a mile and a half southeast of the Lexington courthouse. Clay occupied the house until his death in June 1852. His son James bought the property at a public auction held in 1853 as part of the settlement of the estate. The house was taken down about 1857 to remedy alleged structural defects and rebuilt on the same plan. Thomas Lewinski, a Lexington architect, was employed for the project, and though some of the old building material was reused, the appearance was obviously changed.

Chromolithograph published by Bascom Cooper, 1852. Lithographed by Thomas Sinclair, Philadelphia.

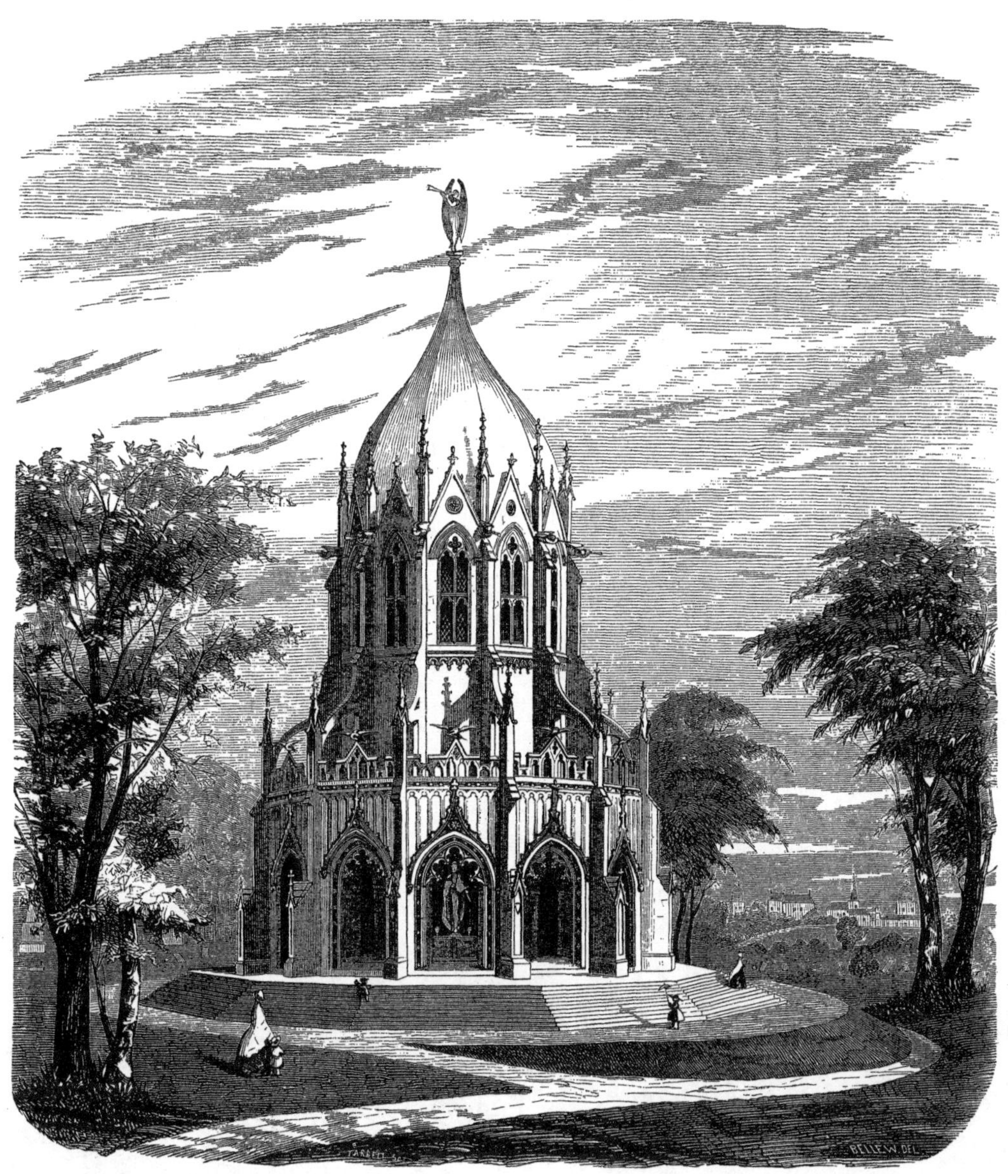

Henry Clay died in Washington June 29, 1852, and was buried in Lexington on July 10. The funeral ceremonies were grand and impressive; thirty thousand people joined the funeral procession. An association was formed to provide a suitable monument for Clay, and after sufficient funds had been raised or pledged, including an appropriation of $10,000 made by the legislature, an invitation for the submission of suitable designs garnered one hundred proposals. The Gothic design shown here was declared the winner, but construction estimates proved too costly, and a very different design by Julius Adams, a Lexington civil engineer and architect, was accepted. The cornerstone was laid July 4, 1857 with Masonic ceremonies. The forty thousand people present included many distinguished guests and many groups of citizen soldiers, fraternal groups, and fire companies. Delays in construction and in the collection of funds plagued the monument association. In 1860 the legislature found it necessary to augment the monument funds, and the completed monument was inaugurated on July 4, 1861. The bodies of Henry and his wife Lucretia Hart Clay were placed in sarcophagi and finally moved into the vault of the monument in April 1864.

Wood engraving from *Ballou's Pictorial Drawing-Room Companion,* August 1855. Engraved by Edmund N. Tarbell from a drawing by Frank H. Bellew.

Lewis Collins called the lunatic asylum at Lexington, now known as Eastern State Hospital, one of the noblest institutions of the state, reflecting honor upon the city and the commonwealth. The buildings were "extensive and commodious" while the grounds were "handsomely improved and ornamented." It was established in December 1822 and opened in 1824, the second such institution in the United States. In 1847, Superintendent Dr. John R. Allen began a reign based on moral treatment rather than close confinement and physical restriction. A surviving portion of the original building, much changed by substantial alterations, is located east of the present columned main entrance.

Wood engraving from Lewis Collins's *Historical Sketches of Kentucky*, 1847. Engraved by N. Orr & Richardson, New York.

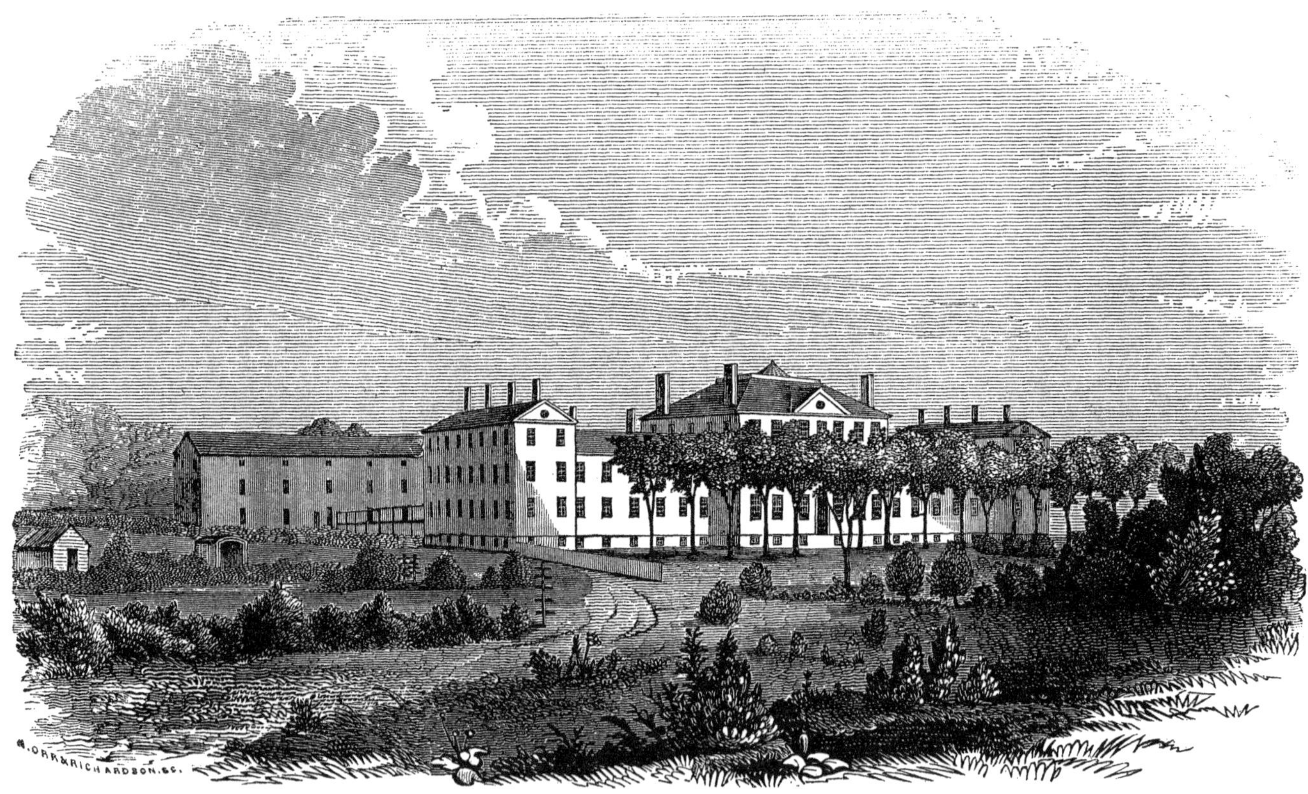

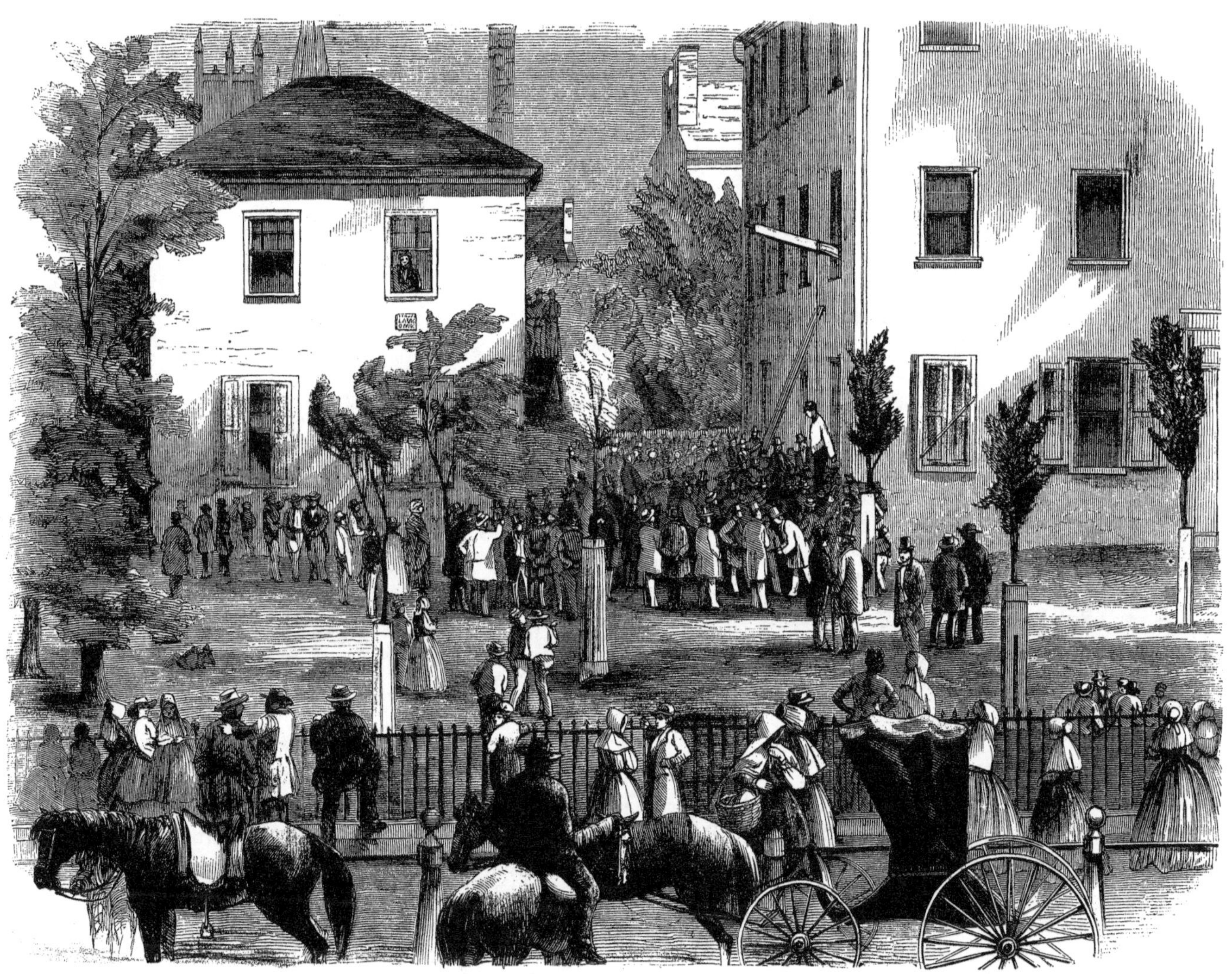

Though mob violence was relatively rare in Lexington, citizens took the law into their own hands in the case of William Barker, a known criminal. Barker killed the city marshal, Capt. Joseph Beard, after Beard broke up an early morning altercation in which Barker was engaged. He fled, but was caught and jailed. Citizens gathered in response to the ringing of the fire and courthouse bells, forced the jailer to surrender his keys, and took Barker to the courthouse where he was hanged from a beam thrust out of a second story window.

Wood engraving from *Harper's Weekly,* July 31, 1858. From a melainotype by J.C. Elrod, Lexington.

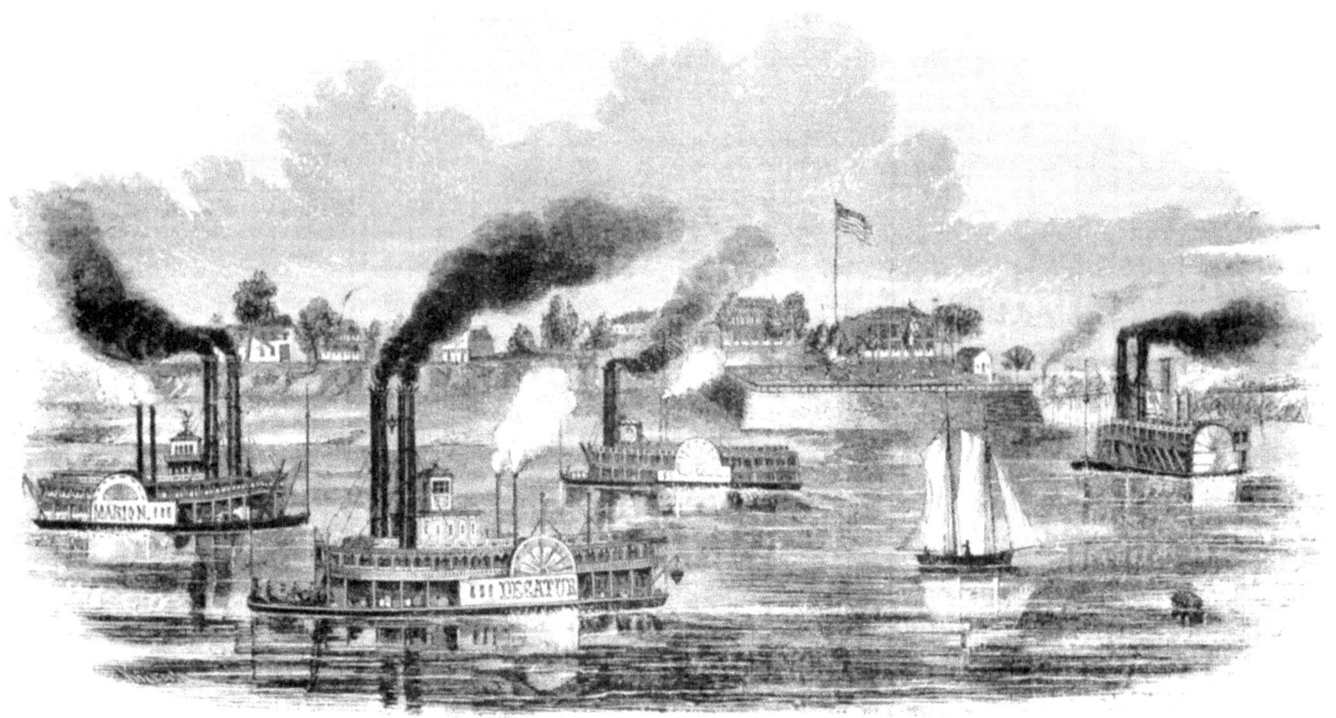

In northern Kentucky, the cities of Newport and Covington began to grow in their own right as the century progressed. After Fort Washington on the north side of the Ohio River, opposite the mouth of the Licking River, was destroyed in 1808, the barracks at Newport were built as an army post. They were subsequently used during the War of 1812 as both an assembly point for Kentucky troops and a military prison. The post later became a training station for Mexican War volunteers, and in 1851, according to the short-lived Cincinnati periodical *Illuminated Western World,* about 150 soldiers were in training there at any one time. The barracks became a Union recruiting depot during the Civil War and temporary quarters for holding "secessionist" citizens. The post was turned over to the city in 1895 to be made into a park. Most of the buildings at the site were sold for relocation or demolition.

Wood engraving from *Ballou's Pictorial Drawing-Room Companion,* December 1856, from a drawing by Samuel S. Kilburn, Boston.

The city hall and courthouse in Covington (*right*) was built in 1843 on Greenup Street at Third Street. Its statue is of George Washington. The position of Covington at the mouth of the Licking River led to its rapid growth, and it acquired nearly all the advantages of a county seat, including the official recording of real estate deeds and conveyances. The official county seat is at Independence in the central part of Kenton County. Extensive remodeling of the Covington courthouse in 1872 gave it an entirely new appearance. The building was taken down in 1899, and Covington's second city hall and courthouse was opened in 1902 on the same site.

Wood engraving from *Ballou's Pictorial Drawing-Room Companion,* December 20, 1856, from a drawing by Samuel S. Kilburn, Boston.

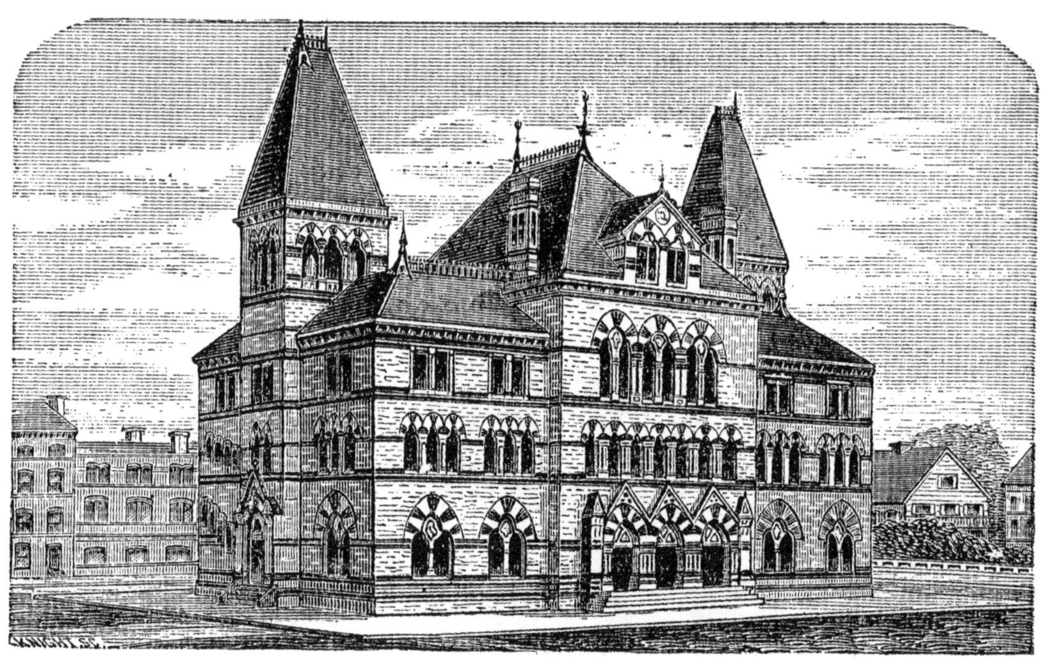

A site selected in 1873 for the new government building in Covington was on Scott Street between Lower Market and Third streets. The new post office and U.S. courts building was to cost $130,000 and was completed in 1876. The basement was constructed of concrete to cover the entire plot of land at the site before the specifications for the building itself were received. A newspaper article gave credit for the project to Covington's spokesmen in the U.S. Congress, especially Representative William E. Arthur. The building was turned over to the city of Covington about 1966 and was demolished soon after. Covington's third city hall and courthouse was erected on the site in 1970.

Wood engraving from *Important Events of the Century,* 1877. Engraved by Knight.

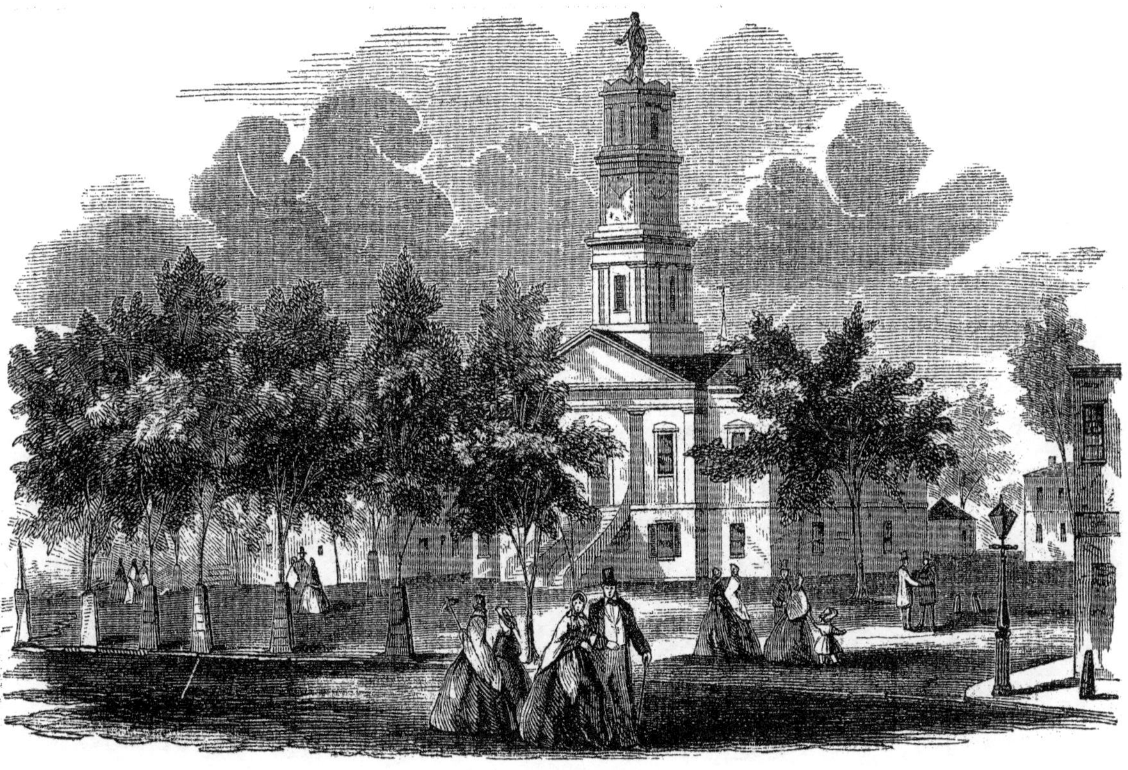

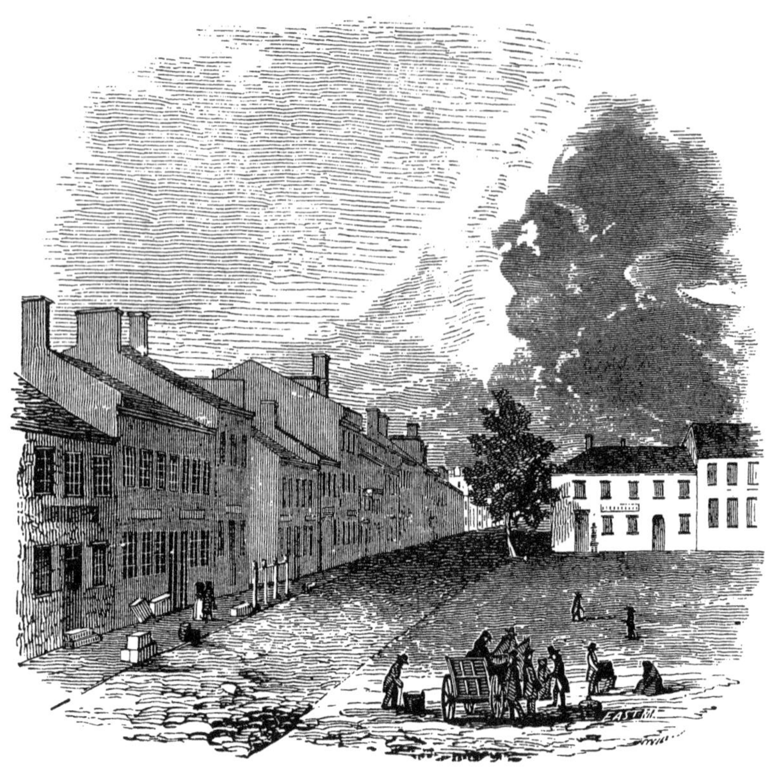

Late in the 1780s, early settler Lawrence Protzman laid off his land in town lots and provided the village with the name of Hopewell. Later called Bourbonton, it took the name Paris about 1789 in gratitude to America's French ally. The year this illustration was made, about 1,200 people lived in Paris.

Wood engraving from Lewis Collins's *Historical Sketches of Kentucky,* 1847, from a drawing by Harrison Eastman.

Perryville (*below*) was a typical small Kentucky town when war came to it in 1862. Confederate forces about sixteen thousand strong were retreating southward under Gen. Braxton Bragg, but met part of Gen. Don Carlos Buell's Union army of about twenty-five thousand troops. Total casualties in killed, wounded, and missing from both sides were estimated to be 7,800. From the mood of this view it seems that Perryville returned quickly to its quiet small-town existence.

Wood engraving from *Harper's Weekly,* November 1, 1862, from a drawing by Henry Mosler, Cincinnati.

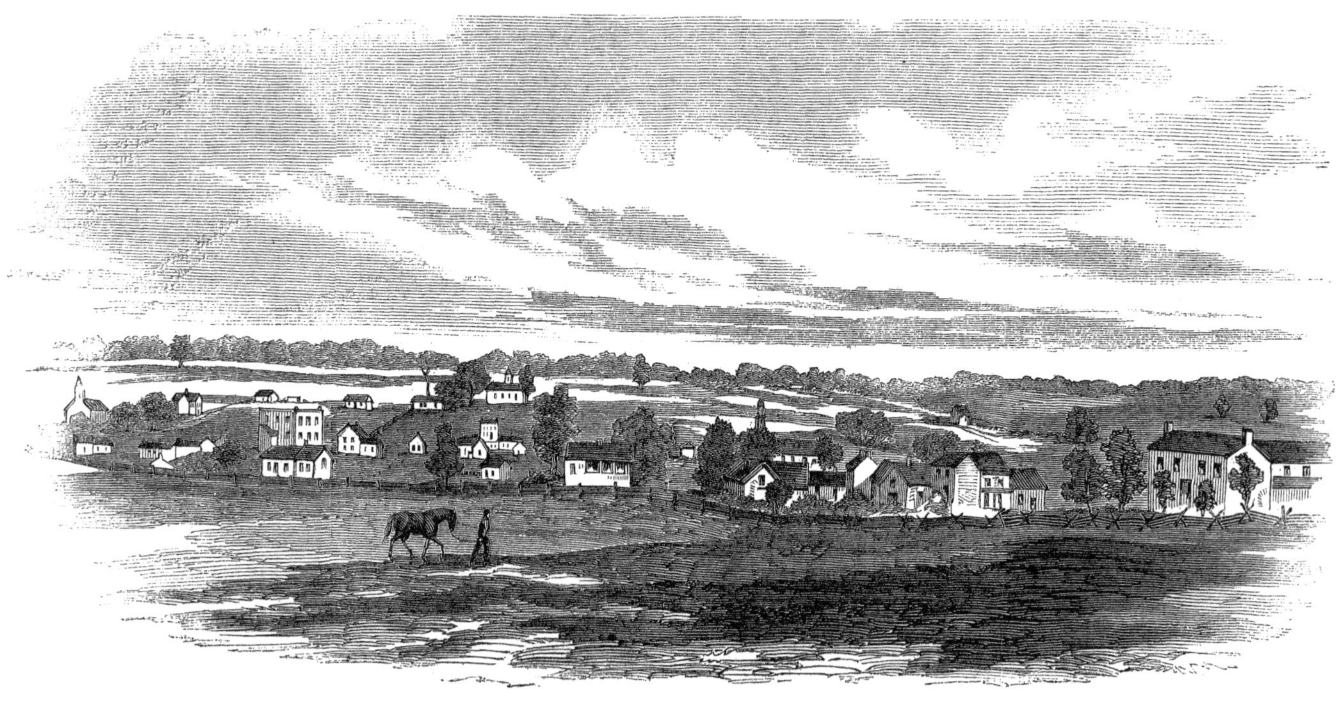

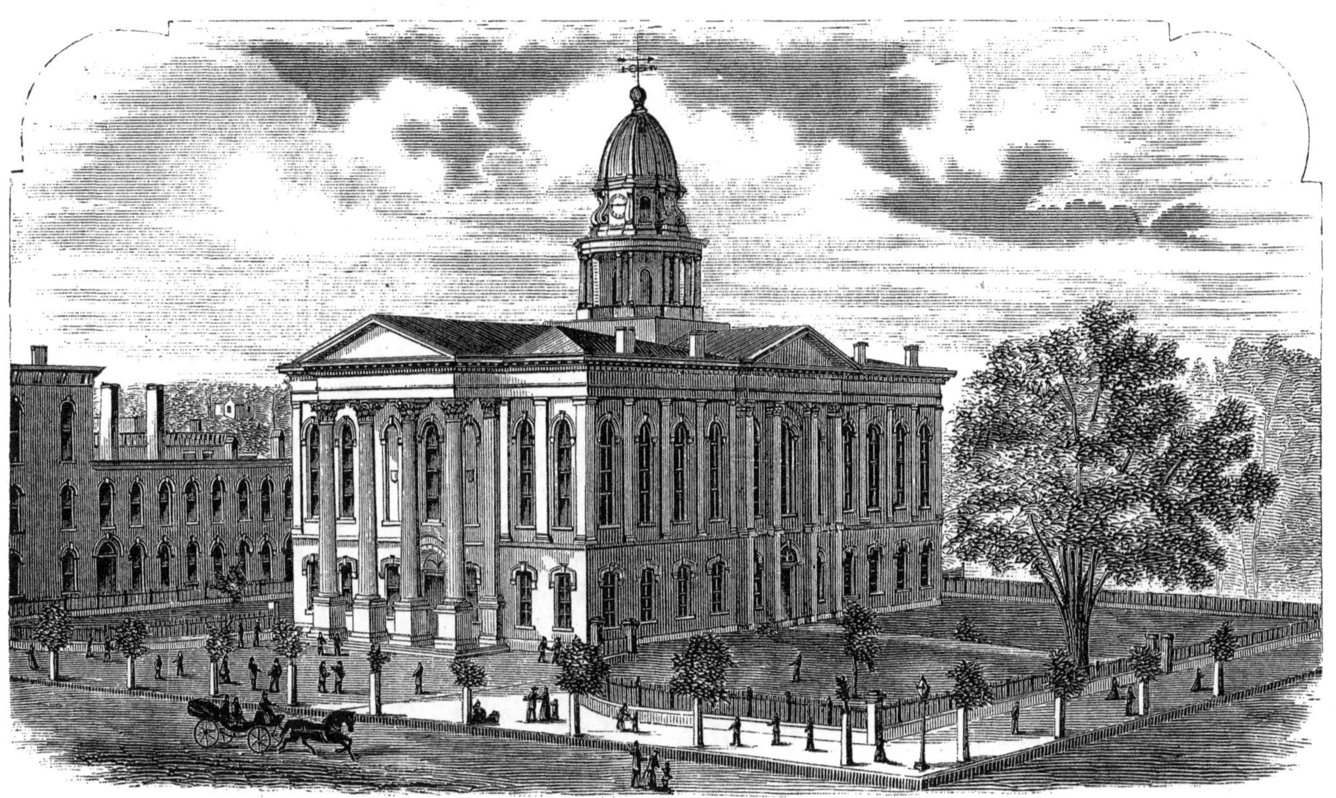

The Warren County Courthouse in Bowling Green was built in 1868 on what is now Tenth Street near the public square—later Fountain Park. The building is of red brick in the Greek Revival style with solid stone Corinthian columns cut from the quarries on Barren River a few miles below the city. George Hodgman's Kentucky state directory of 1870 states that "among the most important public buildings [is] the court house, recently completed at a cost of $130,000, and considered the most beautiful and complete building of its kind in the state."

Wood engraving from Richard Collins's *History of Kentucky,* 1874.

Smithland, on the Ohio River at the mouth of the Cumberland, had a population of about one thousand in 1847 and the most extensive leather tannery in the West. William Croghan of Jefferson County in an October 1805 letter indicated that he planned to apply to the Livingston County Court for permission to found the town of Smithland. The town was established by the county court a month later. The early settlement is said to be named for Col. James S. Smith, Indian fighter and Kentucky legislator, who gave a tract of land at the Smithland location to a building contractor as payment for his services. The town is identified in Jedediah Morse's *American Gazetteer* of 1804 and was looked upon as a coming metropolis. Immigrants and travelers using the Ohio, the Cumberland, the Tradewater River, and the Tennessee—which empties into the Ohio just a few miles away—provided a bustling trade for a time. The town faded and dwindled when the railroads took both passenger and freight traffic from the steamboats.

Wood engraving from Lewis Collins's *Historical Sketches of Kentucky*, 1847.

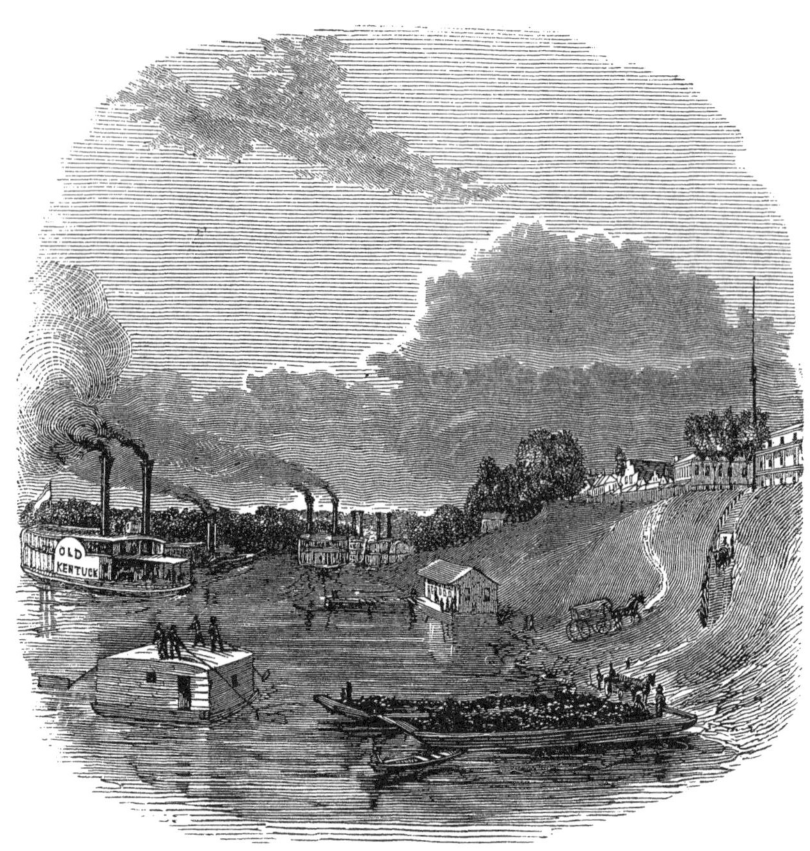

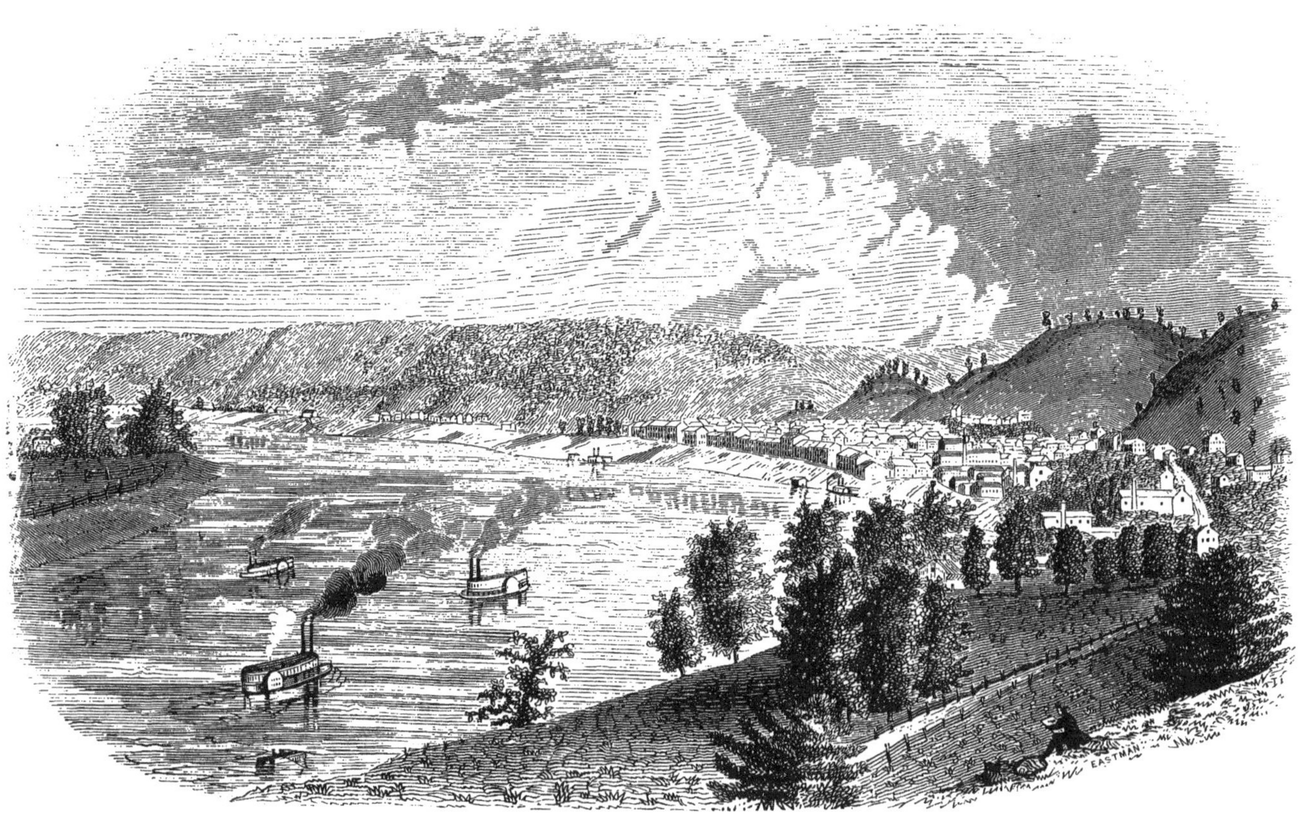

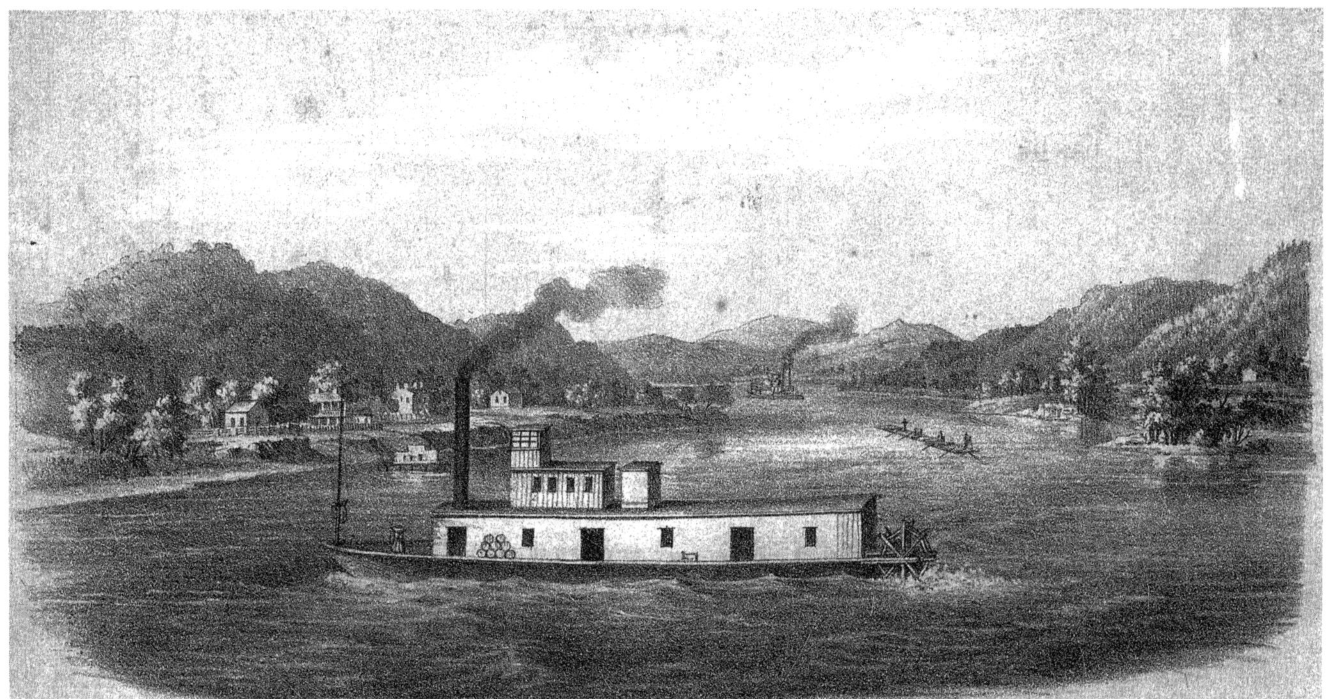

Chester, a small river town in Mason County, was incorporated in 1878. In his history of 1874, Richard Collins calls it a growing suburb of Maysville. In the 1870s Chester was the location of the Maysville Trotting Park race course, the extensive greenhouses of Diedrick and Company, the Maysville Cemetery, and the Mason County infirmary. Woodville, a suburb just east of Maysville, and Chester, its eastern neighbor, were both absorbed into Maysville in that city's later expansion.

Lithograph, about 1875, source and publisher unknown.

At the time this view of Maysville (*left*) was published, the city had just become the new county seat of Mason County after intense opposition from the citizens of Washington, which had been the seat of government since the county was formed in 1788. In 1847 Maysville had a population of about five thousand and numerous commercial and industrial firms. The settlement had first been called Limestone, for the adjacent creek of that name. Maysville was the northern terminus of the earliest macadamized road west of the Alleghenies. The Maysville and Washington Turnpike Company was incorporated in January 1829, and the first four-mile stretch was completed in November 1830. By 1835 the road had been extended to Lexington and had thirteen tollhouses and six covered bridges. Maysville was important as a trading place and distribution point for the northeastern part of the state.

Wood engraving from Lewis Collins's *Historical Sketches of Kentucky*, 1847.

Sources

Allen, James Lane. *The Blue-Grass Region of Kentucky, and Other Kentucky Articles.* New York: Harper and Brothers, 1892.

Allen, James Lane. "The Bluegrass Region." *Harper's Monthly Magazine,* June 1886.

Annual Report of the Board of Trustees of Public Schools of Louisville, 1871.

Annual Report of the Superintendent of Public Instruction of Kentucky, for the School Year Ending June 30, 1874. Frankfort: J.A. Hodges, Public Printer, 1874.

Atlas of Bourbon, Clark, Fayette, Jessamine and Woodford Counties, Ky., from Actual Surveys and Official Records. Philadelphia: D.G. Beers, 1877. Reprint. Evansville, Ind.: Unigraphic, 1974.

Ballou's Pictorial Drawing-Room Companion, 1855-1863.

Berea College, Ky.: An Interesting History Approved by the Prudential Committee. Cincinnati: Elm Street Printing, 1875.

Bogart, W.H. *Daniel Boone and the Hunters of Kentucky.* New York: C.M. Saxton, 1859.

Bowen, Ele. *Rambles in the Path of the Steam-Horse: An Off-Hand Olla Podrida.* Philadelphia: William Bromwell and William White Smith, 1855.

Bowling Green and Warren County Immigration Society booklet, 1885.

Bryant, William Cullen, ed. *Picturesque America.* 2 vols. New York: D. Appleton & Co., 1873.

Caldwell, Charles. *Discourse on the Genius and Character of the Rev. Horace Holley, L.L.D.* Boston: Hilliard, Gray, Little, & Wilkins, 1828.

Caron, C.K. *Louisville Directory for 1876.* Louisville: Louisville Steam Lithographing Co., 1876.

Catalogue of the Officers and Students of Shelby College, Shelbyville, Kentucky, 1848-1849. Shelbyville, Ky.: Henri F. Middleton, 1849.

Cist, Charles. *Cincinnati: Its Early Annals and Future Prospects.* Cincinnati: Charles Cist, 1841.

Cist, Charles. *Sketches and Statistics of Cincinnati in 1851.* Cincinnati: William H. Moore & Co., 1851.

City of Louisville Municipal Reports for 1870, 1871.

Collins, Lewis. *Historical Sketches of Kentucky.* Maysville and Cincinnati: J.A. and U.P. James, 1847.

Collins, Lewis. *History of Kentucky.* Revised, enlarged, and updated by Richard H. Collins. Covington, Ky.: Richard H. Collins, 1874. Reprint. Berea, Ky.: Kentucke Imprints, 1976.

Edwards, Richard. *Edwards' Annual Directory* (1864), and *Edwards' Official Directory of Louisville* (1868). Louisville: Southern Publishing Co.

Elliott, Sam Carpenter, editor and compiler. *The Illustrated Centennial Record of the State of Kentucky, 1792 to 1892.* Louisville: George G. Fetter Printing Co., 1892.

Family Magazine. 1838-1841.

Flint, Timothy. *First White Man of the West: Or the Life and Exploits of Col. Dan'l Boone, the First Settler of Kentucky, Interspersed with Incidents in the Early Annals of the Country.* Cincinnati: George Conclin, 1849.

Frank Leslie's Illustrated Newspaper, 1857-1890.

Gleason's Pictorial Drawing-Room Companion, 1853-1854.

Handbook of Clark County and the City of Winchester. Chicago: W.M. Beckner, 1889.

Harper's Monthly Magazine, 1859-1886.

Harper's Weekly, 1857-1890.

Howe, Henry. *Our Whole Country.* Cincinnati: E. Morgan and Sons, 1861.

Illustrated Atlas of Mason County, Kentucky, An. Philadelphia: Lake, Griffing, & Stevenson, 1876. Reprint. Maysville, Ky.: Mason County Historical Society, 1970.

Illustrated Atlas of the Upper Ohio River Valley. Philadelphia: Titus, Simmons & Titus, 1877.

Imlay, Gilbert. *Topographical Description of the Western Territory of North America.* London: John Debrett, 1793.

Important Events of the Century, 1776-1876. New York: United States Central Publishing Co., 1877.

Kenny, D.J. *Illustrated Cincinnati: A Pictorial Hand-Book of the Queen City.* Cincinnati: George E. Stevens & Co., 1875.

Kentucky Central Railway. *Guide to the Blue Grass Regions of Kentucky.* Cincinnati: Henderson-Achert Lithography Co., 1889.

Ladies Repository, 1846-1856.

Louisville Board of Trade. *The City of Louisville and a Glimpse of Kentucky.* Louisville: Courier-Journal Job Printing Co., 1887.

Louisville Municipal Reports for the Fiscal Year Ending December 31st, 1870. Louisville: Thomas Bradley, 1871.

Martin, Horace. *Pictorial Guide to the Mammoth Cave.* New York: Stringer & Townsend, 1851.

McClung, John A. *Sketches of Western Adventure: Containing an Account of the Most Interesting Incidents Connected with the Settlement of the West from 1755 to 1794.* Dayton, Ohio: Ells, Claflin & Co., 1847.

Meyer, Herrmann J. *Meyer's Universum.* Hildburghausen, Germany: Herrmann J. Meyer, 1854.

Middlesborough, Kentucky. Louisville: Courier-Journal Job Printing Co., 1891.

Narrative of the Massacre by the Savages of the Wife and Children of Thomas Baldwin. New York: Martin and Wood, 1835.

Onken, Otto. *Western Scenery: Or Land and River, Hill and Dale, In the Mississippi Valley.* 1851.

Owen, David Dale. *Report of the Geological Survey in Kentucky, Made During the Years 1854 and 1855.* Frankfort: A.G. Hodges, State Printer, 1856.

Pinkerton, Allan. *Strikers, Communists, Tramps and Detectives.* New York: G.W. Carleton & Co., 1878.

Polk, R.L.and A.C. Danser. *Kentucky State Gazetteer and Business Directory.* Louisville: R.L. Polk and Co., 1876.

Poussielgue, M. "Visite aux Grottes de Mammouth, Dans le Kentucky (États-Unis)." In *LeTour du Monde.* Paris: Hachette, 1859.

Rambles in the Mammoth Cave During 1844. Louisville: Morton & Griswold, 1845.

Raymond, Henry J. *Life and Public Service of Abraham Lincoln.* New York: Derby and Miller, 1865.

Redford, A.H. *History of Methodism in Kentucky,* 1868.

Religious Denominations of the U.S., 1855.

Report of the Commissioner of Agriculture for 1870, 1871.

Rochelle, Roux de. *États-Unis d'Amerique.* Paris: Firmin Didot Freres, 1837.

Scribner's Monthly, December 1874.

Second Report of the Kentucky State Agricultural Society to the Kentucky Legislature, for the Years 1858 and 1859. Frankfort: J.B. Major, State Printer, 1860.

Smith, J. Calvin. *The Illustrated Hand-Book, a New Guide for Travelers Through the United States of America.* New York: Sherman and Smith, 1846.

Smith, Z.F. *History of Kentucky.* Louisville: Courier-Journal Job Printing Co., 1886.

Sneed, William C. *A Report on the History and Mode of Management of the Kentucky Penitentiary: From Its Origin, in 1798, to March 1, 1860.* Frankfort: J.B. Major, State Printer, 1860.

Views on the Cincinnati Southern Railway. Lexington: James Mullen, 1880.

Welby, Adlard. *A Visit to North America and the English Settlements in Illinois, with a Winter Residence at Philadelphia.* London: J. Drury, 1821.

Winterbotham, William. *Historical, Geographical, Commercial and Philosophical View of the American United States.* London: J. Ridgway, 1795.

www.ingramcontent.com/pod-product-compliance
Lightning Source LLC
LaVergne TN
LVHW082004060826
844660LV00031B/1274
* 9 7 8 0 8 1 3 1 5 5 8 9 0 *